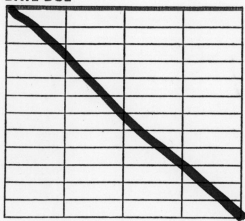

by Franz Schurmann and Orville Schell

THE CHINA READER

⋆ IMPERIAL CHINA: *The Decline of
the Last Dynasty and the Origins
of Modern China   The 18th and 19th Centuries*

⋆⋆ REPUBLICAN CHINA: *Nationalism, War,
and the Rise of Communism   1911–1949*

⋆⋆⋆ COMMUNIST CHINA: *Revolutionary
Reconstruction and International Confrontation
1949 to the Present*

by Franz Schurmann

IDEOLOGY AND ORGANIZATION IN COMMUNIST CHINA

Communist China:
Revolutionary Reconstruction
and International Confrontation
 *1949 to the Present*

3 *The China Reader*

*Edited, annotated,
and with introductions
by FRANZ SCHURMANN
and ORVILLE SCHELL*

Communist China
Revolutionary Reconstruction and International Confrontation
 1949 to the Present

RANDOM HOUSE, New York

Library of Congress Catalog Card Number: 66-21489

Manufactured in the United States of America, by The Colonial Press
Inc., Clinton, Massachusetts

The authors wish to thank the following for permission to reprint:
Abelard-Schuman Ltd. for *Peking Diary: A Year of Revolution* by Derk
Bodde. Copyright, 1950, by Henry Schuman, Inc.

The American Academy of Political and Social Science for *United States
Foreign Policy* by Ralph N. Clough.

Asian Survey for "Communist China: A Quiet Revolution" by Michel Oksen-
burg (January 1966); "Economic Aftermath of the Great Leap in Communist China" by Kang Chao (May 1964); "Vietnam and Politics in Taiwan"
by Joyce Kallgren (January 1966).

Atlas Magazine for "Confession of Hua Lo-keng" from *Remolding of Intellectuals* (April 1966), translated from Renmin Ribao, Peking.

Maximilian Becker for *Red Star Over China* by Edgar Snow (1961).

The Council on Foreign Relations for *Communist China and Asia* by A. Doak
Barnett, © Copyright, 1960, by The Council on Foreign Relations.

Thomas Y. Crowell and Faber and Faber Ltd. for *China in Crisis* by Sven
Lindqvist, Copyright ©, 1963, by Sven and Cecilia Lindqvist.

Harvard University Press for *The United States and China* by John K. Fairbank, © Copyright, 1959, by the President and Fellows of Harvard College.

The McGraw-Hill Book Company for *Communist China's Economic Growth
and Foreign Trade* by Alexander Eckstein, Copyright ©, 1966, by the Council
on Foreign Relations, Inc., used by permission of the McGraw-Hill Book
Company, Inc.

The New York Times for "Washington, The Two Concepts of China" by
James Reston, © Copyright, 1962–1966, by The New York Times Company.

Pantheon Books, a Division of Random House, Inc., for "Science and Educa-
tion in China" by C. H. G. Oldham, in *Contemporary China*, edited by Ruth
Adams, © Copyright, 1966, by the Educational Foundation for Nuclear
Science.

Frederick A. Praeger, Inc., for "The Military Potential of China" by Samuel
B. Griffith, in *China and the Peace of Asia*, edited by Alastair Buchan, ©
Copyright, 1965, by Frederick A. Praeger, Inc.; Frederick A. Praeger, Inc.,
and Asia Publishing House for *China and the World: An Analysis of Com-
munist China's Foreign Policy* by Vidya Prakash Dutt, © Copyright, 1964, by
Vidya Prakash Dutt.

Random House, Inc., for *The Other Side of the River* by Edgar Snow, ©
Copyright, 1961, 1962, by Edgar Snow, reprinted by permission of Random
House, Inc.

University of California Press for *Ideology and Organization in Communist
China,* © Copyright, 1966, by the Regents of the University of California.

To the Faculty Peace Committee

F.S.

To my parents

O.S.

"It is of great importance that we try to learn something more about the strange and fascinating Chinese nation, about its past and its present, about the aims of its leaders and the aspirations of its people. Before we can make wise political—and perhaps military—decisions pertaining to China, there are many questions to be asked and, hopefully, answered: What kind of people are the Chinese? To what extent are they motivated by national feeling? To what extent by ideology? Why are the Chinese Communist leaders so hostile to the United States and why do they advocate violent revolution against most of the world's governments? To what extent is their view of the world distorted by isolation and the memory of ancient grievances? And to what extent, and with what effect on their government, do the Chinese people share with us and with all other peoples what Aldous Huxley has called the 'simple human preference for life and peace'? We need to ask these questions because China and America may be heading toward war with each other and it is essential that we do all that can be done to prevent that calamity, starting with a concerted effort to understand the Chinese people and their leaders."

—J. William Fulbright

Preface

When Random House approached us early in 1966 to do a reader on China for fall publication, our first thoughts were that it could not be done, and in any case there were already many books on China available. But the worsening situation in Eastern Asia made us feel that a well-thought-out reader could help answer some of the serious questions concerning China. The great quantity of literature on China is, ironically, one of the main obstacles to understanding. At John J. Simon's urging we decided that a reader which distilled down some of these materials and provided some commentary would be a contribution.

Our reader's three volumes cover China's past and present. Nevertheless they form a whole: the first two volumes are not the chronological predecessors of the third but, rather, provide material elucidating China's present state of mind. History is more than background or ultimate cause: it is the framework of the present.

We have taken material from scholars, journalists, literary men, and political leaders. Our criteria for selection have been relevance and readability. We have abridged some selections, while trying not to change the sense of the original. Generally we have used existing translations, but have made our own in a few cases. Footnotes have been removed, since most of them are of interest only to the specialist. We wish to express our gratitude to all who have given permission to include their writings.

Each selection or set of selections has an introduction which guides the reader into the material and analyzes the problems dealt with. Some of our selections reflect points of view and approaches with which we do not fully agree, but we have felt it important to present a broad spectrum of thinking on a subject so complex as China. People may disagree with some of our analysis, but at least we hope to have provided some ideas with which one can disagree. There is a wealth of descriptive material on China; what is lacking is interpretation. We welcome all dialogues that may ensue from the ideas we present.

Each section has an introduction which sketches out the main trends and characteristics of the period in question. Here we go beyond analysis and make judgments and evaluations. We hope that this will help the reader get a sense of the period as a whole.

Each volume has a general introduction which states our convictions about China. The tragic events of the last few years have made us realize that the scholar has a duty to do more than analyze material and act as a technical expert for those who make decisions. He must take a rational and moral position on issues. As Sinologists we are involved with the country and people of China. As citizens we are members of a country which one day may be at war with China. Such a war would be a tragedy for the American and the Chinese peoples. In our general introductions we express our personal opinions on the meaning of China's past and present. We fear that America's and China's role in the world is leading to ever more hostile confrontation. We do not believe that earnest words about better relations between the two countries are going to eradicate the dangers. Our readers will see numerous instances where the Chinese have talked one way and acted another. We are now beginning to realize that our government does the same.

China is a strange and fascinating nation, but it is understandable. Understanding may not have much effect on political action, but it will help reason and moral judgment, to which we hope this reader will contribute.

Franz Schurmann
Orville Schell
Berkeley, California, 1966

Contents

Introduction

With the triumph of Communism in 1949, the face of China changed rapidly. Communist organization immediately started putting China's broken pieces together again: a new administration was created, inflation was controlled, businesses were nationalized, the poor were mobilized. Along with Soviet-type order which replaced the chaos of Nationalist rule, a curtain of bleakness and impersonality fell over China. Foreigners resident in China admired the Communists' discipline and determination, but also lamented the growing gulf between them and the Chinese. One by one they began to leave. China entered a new world.

Today China's leaders reiterate that the Chinese Revolution has not yet ended: vestiges remain to be swept away, foreign enemies still threaten, new institutions must be strengthened, new men must be trained. But 1949 marked a transition from struggle to construction. The new leaders were finally able to begin rebuilding the country. For over a decade and a half they have been building, and despite failures and setbacks, they have scored great successes: the country is united and organized; a powerful but flexible political system governs the remotest parts of the country and the smallest units of society. The Communists have created the foundations of a modern industry, science, and technology, and China is becoming one of the world's great industrial nations. They acknowledge Soviet help in earlier years, but now pride themselves on having done it on their own, through "self-reliance." Life is not easy for the ordinary Chinese, but it is much better than it was before.

In economic terms China still ranks among the world's

poorest nations, a condition readily admitted by her leaders, who know that though China's hundred million city-dwellers may be moving fast into the modern world, her economic revolution will not have been completed until her six hundred million peasants have been made into modern producers, and that will take a long time. Nevertheless, no matter how long it may take them, China's leaders and those trained to succeed them are determined to make her into a great power, the equal of the United States and the Soviet Union.

The Chinese Communists won their revolutionary struggle and carried out their programs of socioeconomic construction through ideology and organization. Ideology is a systematic set of beliefs about the world and how men act in it. The Chinese Communists' ideology is in part a theory of history, a vision of the past and of the future, and in part a set of principles for building organization, creating a new society, and changing men spiritually. Their theory of history contains the legacy of the past, interpreted through the ideas of Marxism. No matter how stereotyped their Marxist writings on history may be, the words "feudal" and "semicolonial" conjure up memories of real things: gentry clutching their landed holdings, officials seeking personal gain, social and economic stagnation, unchanging poverty—and the whole image of foreigners lording over China for more than a hundred years. But their theory of history also contains a certainty that China will develop into a great country, and that the poor will inherit the world's riches. Their principles of organization teach them how to build and maintain a party, how to keep government effective, how to train men for the new society. The Chinese Communists have an extraordinary genius for organization, something they learned when they realized that ideology can and must be more than a pure vision of past and future, that it must serve as a practical tool for meeting the problems of the present.

Organization is a systematic structure of bodies of men mobilized to achieve goals. In the advanced Western countries structures of organization are characterized by a highly defined technical division of labor—men need only learn their tasks, and the organization works and achieves its goals. But how can organization work in a country as poor and technically deficient as China was before 1949 and to some extent is still today?

The Nationalists and their warlord allies held their armies and bureaucracies together by webs of personal relationships, but the failure of that approach to organization is well attested in the previous volume. The Chinese Communists learned that in the absence of technical means and instead of webs of personal relationships, ideology could function to hold organization together and make it work. Party, government, and army—all organized according to new principles—are the instruments of rule in China today. In cities and villages men live their lives in and through organization. China is a totally organized society.

In the West the economic revolution preceded the organizational revolution. In China the process has worked in reverse. Through ideology and organization the Chinese leaders are creating the foundations of a modern economic and technical order.

As one reads accounts of China's domestic and foreign policies, alternations will be noted between visionary and practical approaches. Ideological visions about Chinese society gave rise to the Great Leap Forward. Mao Tse-tung's global conception on the revolutionary wave of the third world gave rise to a vigorous Chinese foreign policy to create a bloc of Asian, African, and Latin American nations in opposition to both the United States and the Soviet Union. But at other times the Chinese have been eminently practical in their approaches to domestic and foreign problems. The Chinese distinguish between theory and practice, something they learned during their long years of struggle. Theory—the vision of past and future— was crucial for unifying the movement, but everyday exigencies had to be dealt with in concrete terms. This does not mean that the Chinese Communists relegate theory to the spiritual realm, regarding it as something that inspires men but has no practical use. On the contrary, theory can sometimes be invoked to mobilize millions of men to implement great programs in a way that practical directives can never do. The Chinese Communists invoked visionary theory in the land reform of 1946–1949, during the collectivization of 1955–1956, and during the Great Leap Forward of 1958–1960. At other times, as practice becomes more important, theory turns into a leitmotif, sometimes stronger, sometimes weaker.

Visionary ideology is frightening to Americans, who see it

as grandiose dreams so unrelated to the immediate needs of the present that it can lead men to do horrible things; they think of Hitler and Stalin. The periods in which the Chinese Communists invoked visionary ideology for practical purpose were violent. During the revolutionary terror (1946–1949) thousands of landlords were killed by the peasants to avenge ancient wrongs and to clear the way for a new society. The Great Leap Forward was implemented by totally and fanatically mobilizing society. In the early 1960s Mao Tse-tung envisioned a wave of revolution erupting in the third world and engulfing the advanced nations. Americans were horrified by the revolutionary terror of the "agrarian reformers," terrified by the armies of "blue ants" which made the Great Leap Forward, and saw in Mao's vision of the revolutionary third world confirmation of their deepest fears of expansionist Communism.

Where the Chinese Communists have invoked visionary ideology, it has almost always been to mobilize the poor. In 1946 they unleashed revolutionary land reform to build up their armed forces in the face of Nationalist military superiority. In 1955 and 1958 they mobilized millions of peasants and workers for socioeconomic breakthrough. Though lacking the means, in the early 1960s, the Chinese Communists believed that the third world of poor nations would mobilize itself in opposition to the rich nations. The notion that the poor are particularly receptive to visionary ideologies may be seen as another of Mao Tse-tung's generalizations from Chinese historical experience: almost every peasant rebellion was motivated by Buddhist or Taoist millenarian beliefs, or in the case of the Taipings, Christian.

The history of Chinese Communism has been marked by long periods of careful, practical development interspersed with short periods of intense ideological mobilization. Since China sees herself as part of the world and not as a universe apart from it, her vision of the forces of world revolutionary processes has conjured up fears of Chinese expansionism, particularly in America. Americans see the Chinese patiently organizing "national liberation movements" in different parts of the globe and preparing them for the moment they can strike to seize state power. The war in Vietnam is seen as a "test case."

Expansionism can only mean the extension of one nation's

control over another, by military, political, or economic means. When the Chinese Communists invoked visionary ideology at home for mobilizational purposes, they already had control over the people they wanted to mobilize. For example, two years before implementing collectivization, the Chinese Communists launched a program of rural Party organization designed to put cadres in every village. When the organizational buildup was completed, they began collectivization. If we look at the countries and movements which have been objects of Chinese ideological or practical foreign policy, it is hard to find one which the Chinese control. China has signed border agreements with Outer Mongolia, Afghanistan, Pakistan, Nepal, and Burma. She may have influence over them, but no control. Outer Mongolia is firmly in the Soviet camp: Pakistan remains a member of CENTO and SEATO; Nepal is neutral; Burma, with three Communist insurgent movements, rests assured that the Chinese are helping none of them. China had troops in North Korea until March 1958; today North Korea has veered back toward the Soviet camp. And in the case of North Vietnam, the persistence of strong pro-Soviet tendencies in Hanoi makes it hard to argue that it is a Chinese puppet. In fact, China's most faithful ally is the socialist country most distant from its borders—Albania.

Several years ago the Chinese launched intensive efforts to cultivate pro-Peking parties or splinter movements within the Communist world. Today, even so faithful a political ally as the Japanese Communist Party has moved away from Peking, and the picture of Chinese "control" elsewhere is similar. This inability to create a new China-centered international is remarkable when compared with Stalin's power to decide the life and death of Communist Parties throughout the world. It could be argued that the Chinese ultimately have no way of controlling an organization like the Jeunesse of the Brazzaville Congo Republic, but surely if they had wanted to, they could have transformed North Korea and North Vietnam into obedient satellites.

A reading of Chinese documents on the trends of world revolution, notably the article on people's war by Lin Piao, reveals that the Chinese believe that these movements must and will arise by themselves and that they must struggle with their own resources. More significant, however, is the apocalyptic belief of the Chinese that a violent clash between nascent revolutionary movements and the forces of world imperialism, notably the United States, is inevitable. They see the "national liberation movements" in the context of their own experiences with the Nationalists and the Japanese. During the years of their long struggles against both foes, they received no help from abroad (the equipment captured in Manchuria in 1945–1946, whether or not turned over to them by the Soviets, was Japanese). In simple terms they see a process of world revolution marked by "national liberation movements" breaking out here and there, everywhere opposed by the United States, leading finally to a worldwide crisis.

The Chinese leaders are pessimistic about world peace, for they have lived their entire lives in war, and thus have no reason to believe that mankind can avoid another global catastrophe. But they also remember their history of defeats: time and again the enemy attacked them only to see their movement get bigger and stronger. They believe the same will happen in the third world.

The Chinese leaders think in terms of decades and even centuries, and they speak of decades of economic development. They have said that the Sino-Soviet dispute and the confrontation with America would go on for a very long time, during which they want above all to preserve their national security, as did Stalin in his day. They regard the American military threat as a permanent fact of life. They have lost faith in the Soviet Union's promise to defend them. They see world détente as a situation which makes the Communist countries and the poor nations slacken their vigilance, while the United States continues to arm. Hence they see any conflict or movement that weakens the United States as strengthening their own national security.

It would be pleasant to end this introduction on a note of Confucian optimism: No matter how bad things are, things will work out in the end. Such is not possible. Whatever the correctness of the Chinese image of the world, one cannot deny that they have every reason to see it as dangerous and menacing. The gulf between America and China was created not by the paranoiac visions of the Chinese, but by a long history of relations between China and foreign powers. Verbal changes in America's China policy will not convince the Chinese, as long as nothing changes in regard to Taiwan and Vietnam or the balance of forces remains as it is. War and military power reinforce ideology and so make it more difficult for nations to interact practically with each other. This applies to China, but it also applies to America. The Vietnam war has already produced a flowering of global thinking in America, which in turn has strengthened China's (and Russia's) ideologies. The more ideological the world becomes, the greater the danger of war, and vice-versa. The Chinese see this trend as inevitable. Many in Washington agree.

We in America would do well to realize that Sino-American amity will not come about merely because a more moderate "second generation" will come to power in China. Both sides will have to make some drastic changes in their ideological views of each other and their practical relations with each other before hostility can be succeeded by coexistence.

I. The People's Republic of China—The Basic Framework

On October 1, 1949, the Chinese People's Political Consultative Conference, a national assembly made up of a coalition of diverse political forces dominated by the Communists, formally proclaimed the Chinese People's Republic. Despite Mao Tse-tung's reference to "new democracy" as a stage before socialism, what appeared to come into being with extraordinary rapidity was an Asian Soviet Union: government, economy, army, law, education, mass media were all closely modeled on those of the Soviet Union. Within a few years new Soviet-style buildings made parts of Peking resemble Moscow. Everywhere the Soviet Union was proclaimed the fatherland of socialism, the example for China to follow, the Chinese people's best friend.

Many old China-hands refused to believe that China could change so fundamentally. Talk about China shaking off the Russian yoke began only weeks after the "Liberation." China's Western friends saw Russification as only a transient phase—sooner or later the "real China" would re-emerge.

But China had been undergoing her Revolution for years. Exactly one century earlier the Taipings began the revolutionary process, and it had gone through many stages, involving peasants, intellectuals, and workers, and had finally culminated in the Civil War and "Liberation." When the Communists came to power, they remained true to their principles: they carried the Revolution to its irrevocable conclusion by sweeping away the entire institutional structure of the *ancien régime* and with it those classes which had maintained it—officials, gentry, big bourgeois, and foreigners. Unless one understands the totality of the Chinese Revolution, one cannot understand the transformation China experienced nor the history of the People's Republic of China.

The Communist leaders knew the destructiveness of revolution: it tears down what has to be torn down but guarantees nothing to replace it. The Chinese Communists had organization—a disciplined Party and army—and they had experience

3

in governing. But ruling over remote peasant regions is not preparation for the complexities of governing a country the size of China. They despised Nationalist China with its amalgam of Western-style government and Chinese-style "personal relationships," and they saw Western parliamentary democracy as a sham behind which power elites ruled in the interests of capitalism and imperialism. Whatever feelings they may have had about the Soviet Union, they saw it as the fatherland of socialism, a powerful revolutionary country which had survived history's most terrible war and was emerging as the second greatest power in the world. They resolved to become a second Soviet Union, using the power of their organization to implant the alien institutions in Chinese soil.

For two thousand years the state had been an intimate part of Chinese society. Every poor boy aspired to become a scholar so that he could ultimately become an official. So ingrained was the idea of "official" in Chinese minds that even the name for the supreme deity was "heavenly bureaucrat" (*t'ien-kuan*). Now the state, with its bureaucracies, armies, laws, education, and official doctrine, became Soviet.

Today, over a decade and a half later, Chinese nationalism has reasserted itself. With bitter determination the Chinese have expunged Russian influence and culture from their country, and they point proudly to Chinese-designed products. Yet Soviet institutions and influence from the early 1950s still remain. China is a Communist country, and the Soviet impact is part of its legacy.

We have called this period one of unity and development. The two great tasks facing the new Communist government were the political and social unification of the country and the launching of basic economic development. From the previous volumes we know the legacy old China left to the new rulers: a country torn apart by a half century of war and political dissent and a century and a half of decline that left it one of the most backward nations in the world. "Wealth and power" (*fukuo ch'iang-ping*) had been the dream of all Chinese reformers and revolutionaries. The Communist leaders shared that dream.

Unity was not created at one stroke with the founding of the People's Republic. Dissidents still fought in many parts of the country. The victorious cadres began to settle down in the cities. In Manchuria a new threat developed from Kao Kang, the Party boss of that vital industrial region. The new administrative system was terribly short of trained personnel. Though the outside world may see the Chinese Communists as arrogantly confident, they are actually worriers, with a deep streak of pessimism. They were concerned about unity during that first year of power, but became less so when the Korean War allowed them to mobilize the country for patriotic defense. Within four years the goal of unity had been achieved. By 1954 Party organization had been solidly built up in the cities and spread over the far-flung countryside. Illiterate Party cadres had been replaced to a large extent by men who had some education. Kao Kang had been defeated in 1954 and Manchuria was brought back into the Chinese polity. The economy had been stabilized and new development programs launched. In September 1954 the provisional government was made permanent with the proclamation of a new constitution. The Communists unified the country not by force but by organization, for which years of experience had given them a special genius.

The strength of unity can be measured only by the challenge of crisis. Between 1960 and 1962 China underwent a crisis of food shortage, of declining morale, and of political dissent which would have destroyed most other nations. Unity not only survived, but Peking hardly resorted to coercion to maintain its authority. Organization had proven itself.

Economic development began from the moment of final victory. First what was left of the economy had to be reconstructed. The disastrous inflation of previous years was ended once and for all. The Communists set up a Soviet-type banking system which took effective control of all money and credit. In 1953 the First Five Year Plan was launched with major stress on building a heavy-industry base. There was new construction, particularly of Soviet-supplied complete industrial plants. The rate of growth was high. But society had to pay for the industrialization. Agriculture supplied the bulk of the savings, leaving the peasants in continuing poverty. Consumer-goods production rose much more slowly than that of production goods. Living conditions in both cities and villages were not good.

Yet with any available means the Communists improved

the people's lot. Industrial workers became a new elite, with relatively high pay and fringe benefits. Above all, the Communists used their organizational skills and power to create an infrastructure for future development. China became a clean country, children were given special care and education, people were made literate. But all this occurred within a context of strictest "Communist discipline." The easygoing Chinese of an earlier day was taught that suffering, hard work, self-control, constant study, and unswerving compliance with the commands of state and Party were needed for the great cause of building a new country.

The period from 1950 to the early 1960s falls into two distinct parts. Until the mid-1950s the Chinese closely followed the Soviet model of development. Once they had assimilated what the Soviets could teach them, however, they embarked on their own path, symbolized by the Great Leap Forward of 1958 (see pp. 180–192, 206–212, 407–416). The Great Leap Forward arose from a vision on the part of the leaders that all of China, her people, society, economy, and political system, could be mobilized for final "take-off" into great power status. Not only a few areas like Manchuria would grow, as during the previous period, but all of China, in particular her most backward areas, would leap forward from the primitive to the modern. The Chinese people had learned Soviet methods well, Mao felt, but they also had their own talents and wisdom, "latent forces" the Communists called them, with which to speed up the developmental process. Though in our selections the Great Leap Forward appears as a grandiose program and a terrible failure, in future years it may be regarded as one of the most significant periods of Chinese history. The Great Leap Forward in many ways completed the Revolution by tearing the peasant out of his traditional ways. Its failure, like earlier ones on the battlefield, taught China's leaders some elemental lessons about the nature of their society.

The following selections deal with basic problems faced by the Chinese Communists during the first decade of the People's Republic. The situation in China after 1949 takes on a radically different appearance. Gone are the colorful personalities, dramatic battles, wide-open cities, intrigues, free reporting by Chinese and Westerners. As the curtain of impersonality came down over the old China, the life of the nation and its people took on an abstract character. We in the West have an extraordinary wealth of material from post-1949 China, but it is all written in a new clinical political language. Difficult and painful as it is for the Westerner, we must nevertheless try to understand it by reading between the lines if we wish to understand the new China. It is the language of an ideology and an organization which became the principal instruments of China's new rulers for change and development.

A reader is not a history, and so we have not attempted to trace events from one point in time to another. China is a complex country. The world is not entirely unaware of much that has happened in China and of many of her main characteristics. But few understand it as a whole or see its parts fitting together in a larger unity. We trust that these selections will help fill out the picture and arrange its parts into a more meaningful pattern.

1. CHINA'S DOMESTIC POLICY: UNITY AND DEVELOPMENT

✿ "Liberation": The Communists Rapidly Introduce a New System

IN JANUARY 1949 the People's Liberation Army accepted the surrender of Fu Tso-yi, one of Nationalist China's finest generals, and "liberated" Peking. Derk Bodde, Professor of Chinese at the University of Pennsylvania, was in Peking and describes his impressions of the first months of Communist rule. Since the occupation was peaceful and orderly, Bodde's impressions do not reflect that sense of dramatic change felt by much of the world when China's ancient capital fell into Communist hands. Despite the orderly transfer of power, one can already see a Communist system in operation.

The People's Liberation Army was powerful and disciplined. Bodde describes its victory parade in Peking "as probably the greatest demonstration of Chinese military might in history," but it is notable that "it was primarily a display of *American* military equipment, virtually all of it captured or obtained by bribe from Kuomintang forces in the short space of two and one half years."

Characteristic of Communist rule was the close attention paid to press and propaganda: newspapers were quickly converted into organs of the new government, posters appeared everywhere, indoctrination began immediately. In contrast to the Kuomintang the Communists were acutely concerned with the people's attitudes, and despite general support for the new system, were determined to refashion people ideologically. Equally characteristic was the immediate attention given the chaotic economic situation, particularly through the establishment of state-controlled trading corporations.

Even in the first days of the "Liberation" the new government's pro-Russian policies were evident: "Decadent U.S. films are to be ousted by healthy Russian films"; Western news correspondents were placed under severe restrictions. Whatever the nature of the relations between the Soviet and the Chinese Communist Parties at the top, at the level of visible urban life the "lean to one side" policy was clearly in evidence.

What emerges from these early impressions of Communist rule in China is the sense of purpose the Communists displayed. They came into the cities with a program, and despite monumental difficulties, were determined to carry it out.

DERK BODDE *
From *Peking Diary*

January 26 (Wednesday), 1949

LIBERATION!

This is now the great slogan of the day. Everyone talks and writes happily of the "liberation" of Peking by the great "People's Army." So far as the physical appearance of the city is concerned, little has happened as yet. Fu Tso-yi's soldiers are still much in evidence, though said to be gradually moving out, and I have yet to catch my first glimpse of the Communist "Eighth Route Army." During the last two days, however, walls and telephone poles have been plastered with multigraphed posters, exhorting the population to conduct itself peacefully and work for the building of a new China. Most spectacular of all has been the arrival of the long-promised "great illumination." Tonight as I write these words, street lights are burning all over the city for the first time in six weeks.

The absence of greater change, of course, is due to the

* Derk Bodde, *Peking Diary* (New York: Henry Schumann, 1950), pp. 98–99, 102–104, 114–121, 135–136.

peacefulness of the turnover and the fact that the old guard still remains in power—an old guard, however, using a vocabulary amazingly different from what it was mouthing only a few days ago. The formerly reactionary *World Daily News* is a typical example. A fair part of today's issue consists of transcripts from the Communist radio, put out, however, under the date line of the Kuomintang Central News Agency's Peking office.

Much of the new talk, of course, stems from deliberate opportunism or plain ignorance of the significance of what is taking place. Take our Shansi students, for example. During the past two or three days they have covered the walls of the compound with a rash of handwritten posters congratulating themselves and the city on its liberation. On one of these they had the audacity to write: "Protection of the people's property is our first duty." This after special workers employed by our landlord had spent the greater part of a day nailing metal sheets over a locked door which the students had broken open the night before. Another large wooden gate, leading into the rear garden, has now been completely demolished. The same students also took the opportunity to daub our gate with the slogan DOWN WITH AMERICAN IMPERIALISM!

Yet despite the opportunism, hypocrisy, and lack of comprehension from many sides, there is no doubt in my mind that the Communists come here with the bulk of the people on their side. As one walks the streets, the new feeling of relief and relaxation can definitely be sensed, even though it is hard to describe it in tangible terms. . . .

February 3 (Thursday)

THE CHANGES BEGIN

Events follow each other so rapidly these days that it is hard to remember what has happened even three days ago. The People's Liberation Army is in complete control, and only occasional groups of "enemy" soldiers are still to be seen.

The entire Peking Hotel is in process of being taken over by Communist functionaries. When I went there for a haircut two days ago, a young soldier, fully equipped, walked idly up and down the room the whole time I was in the barber's chair.

The seven-man "coalition" interim committee began functioning yesterday, headed by Communist General Yeh Chienying, chairman and city mayor. It is subject, however, to the orders of the Peking-Tientsin Headquarters of the People's Liberation Army.

Yesterday Chin reported that he had seen long lines of carts bringing food into the city. Prices have dropped slightly, but it is obvious that few serious steps in this direction can be taken before the process of converting gold yuan into the new regime's "people's notes" has been completed. This will be done during the next twenty days at places designated by the People's Bank (into which the former Nationalist government's Central Bank has already been converted). The exchange is set at GY$10:PN$1 for all persons save laborers, students, teachers, and "poor people." These, having secured certificates indicative of their status, will be permitted to exchange up to GY$500 apiece at the favored rate of GY$3:PN$1.

All has gone smoothly so far save for one unpleasant incident: a demonstration for increased wages by several thousand municipal employees in which they wrecked the house of the former mayor, attacked and wounded the chief secretary of the municipality, pilfered a supply of ration flour, and broke into the municipal building, looting and scattering official papers. Though a hundred were arrested, they were later released after being lectured to and forced to restore what had been taken.

Today's big event has been the grand victory parade signalizing the formal takeover of the city. It unfortunately coincided with the first real dust storm of the winter. A fierce wind moaned through the scaffolding still enveloping the partially dismantled tiled archway at the south end of Morrison Street. It raised such dust from the nearby glacis that during the biggest gusts it was literally impossible to see across the field. My face was black with grime by the time I returned home.

Prominent in the parade were thousands of students and workers from schools and organizations throughout the city. Many of their colored paper banners and Mao Tse-tung portraits were torn to tatters by the wind. Among the students also marched some well-known university professors. Some groups danced to the rhythmic drum-and-gong beat of the *yang ko* or "planting song"—a simple traditional peasant dance performed in unison by large groups, which is already becoming enormously popular here as the result of the general Communist emphasis upon folk art. More familiar to me was a band of stilt walkers, cavorting merrily in colorful costumes above the heads of the crowd. Other groups, directed by "cheerleaders," chanted, as they marched, the famous "eight points" of Mao Tse-tung.

Of chief interest was, of course, the Liberation Army itself. I missed the first contingents of infantry and cavalry, as well as part of the motorized units. But in what I did see, lasting about an hour, I counted over 250 heavy motor vehicles of all kinds—tanks, armored cars, truckloads of soldiers, trucks mounted with machine guns, trucks towing heavy artillery. Behind them followed innumerable ambulances, jeeps, and other smaller vehicles. As probably the greatest demonstration of Chinese military might in history, the spectacle was enormously impressive. But what made it especially memorable to Americans was the fact that it was primarily a display of *American* military equipment, virtually all of it captured or obtained by bribe from Kuomintang forces in the short space of two and one half years.

And what about the reactions of the civilian participants and spectators? Granted that some of the former paraded only because they had been told to do so, and that many were schoolchildren too young to realize the full significance of what was happening, the fact remains that the enthusiasm of most was too obvious to have been feigned, and this notwithstanding that many had been exposed to wind and dust for some four hours before I saw them. I have no doubt that not a few on this day felt a keen sense of personal participation in an event symbolizing the beginning of a new era in Chinese history. The reaction of the spectators, on the other hand, was, like that of most Chinese crowds, less outspoken. Nevertheless they seemed in general quite favorably disposed and obviously deeply impressed by the display of power. As the stream of trucks continued, I heard several exclaim with wonder: "Still more! Still more!" . . .

March 4 (Friday)

THE FIRST MONTH

It is now thirty-two days since the People's Army marched into Peking. Following the spate of meetings, parades, and congratulatory messages of the first two weeks, changes of a more concrete nature are beginning to make themselves felt. The honeymoon seems over.

Physically, conditions continue to return to normal. The enormous piles of unsightly refuse which had accumulated in the streets during the siege are gradually being carted away. The reopening of the Palace Museum, and probably of many other parks and museums, is promised within a week. Already the city wall is open as a promenade to those who wish to use it. From its top the evidences of destruction wrought by Peking's former defenders are clearly apparent: on the wall itself, in the tunnels and piles of brick and earth remaining from hundreds of dugouts and gun emplacements; beyond the wall, in the gray waste of razed buildings which circle the city in a belt several hundred yards wide. Of these, only heaps of rubble now remain, from which boys are gradually carrying away the bricks on their backs. At one or two places a start has been made at rebuilding, but for the most part the scene is one of bleak desolation.

On the production front the papers are filled these days, quite à la Russe, with enthusiastic accounts of how the workers are rehabilitating industry to a point equal to, or even higher than, its presiege level. Improving communications are making it possible for thousands of refugees to return to their homes, helped by free transportation and grain allotments from the government. It was inspiring to revisit the Temple of Confucius a few days ago and compare its present stately calm with the former scene of refugee squalor, misery, and confusion. Almost the last evidences of that unhappy time are the piles of refuse now being carted away in preparation for its formal reopening a few days hence. Voids remain, however, where doors, windows, and furniture used to be—all burned as firewood during the siege.

As for the economic picture, incomplete figures show that during the period of monetary reconversion ending February 23, over 817,000 workers, students, teachers, and "poor people," or not far below half of the city's population, made use of the favorable three-to-one exchange rate. Developments since that date include a census-taking of the city's poor and the distribution of 150,000 catties (Chinese pounds) of millet to an unspecified number; also a registration of the unemployed, especially those possessing technical skills.

Of more lasting importance is the activation of a new monolithic governmental organ, the North China Trading Corporation. About a week ago this organization began to sell grains, coal, and certain kinds of cloth at prices slightly below those on the open market. For this purpose it uses shops of its own as well as privately owned subsidiaries scattered throughout the city. The latter are permitted to continue selling their own commodities at unfixed prices, the theory being that in the course of time these will be forced by competition to approximate the government levels. At present it is far too early to judge of the success of this device. Prices, after continuing to rise since I last wrote, have dropped slightly during the past three or four days, but not enough to be significant. Chief defect in the system so far, according to a Chinese friend, is the inferiority in quality of government commodities to those on the open market, as well as the fact that they are sometimes mixed with the latter by certain unscrupulous private dealers and then sold at the higher open-market rates.

Coincident with these steps, the authorities have banned further transactions in the Chinese silver dollar, which must be turned in to the People's Bank for people's notes. So far, however, the ban has been only lightly applied. The hawkers who formerly blocked traffic with their numbers at certain street corners and dinned the air with their clinking, now walk singly along the streets, muttering: "Buy one! Buy one!" to passers-by.

Salaries of all workers in public institutions, including professors in the government universities, are now computed in terms of catties of millet. The immediate aim is to restore them to their late-1948 levels, which, though better than those of the siege, are still far from adequate. A professor, for example, now receives the equivalent of about twenty silver dollars monthly, compared with a prewar (pre-1937) salary of four hundred silver dollars. For laborers the discrepancy is considerably less.

Shortages of imported goods are making themselves felt, particularly in gasoline, causing fewer cars than before to be seen on the streets.

In the political sphere, the last week of February saw the transfer of the North China People's Government, headed by Tung Pi-wu, from Shihchiachuang to Peking.

Far more publicized has been the arrival here of several hundred persons representing over twenty anti-Kuomintang political groups. Included are the Kuomintang Revolutionary Committee and the Democratic League, as well as overseas Chinese representatives and unaffiliated figures. These, no doubt, will become the non-Communist nucleus for the "coalition" government eventually to be created for all China. Another event has been the arrival, cordial reception, and departure after ten days, of an "unofficial" five-man peace delegation from the South.

A final item is the announcement, a couple of days ago, that the "reorganization"—in other words, indoctrination—of Fu Tso-yi's surrendered troops is now completed. Those who wish will be allowed to join the Liberation Army; others will be given three months' terminal pay and free transportation to their homes. Certainly a generous treatment and speedy metamorphosis! Fu himself apparently remains in the western suburbs, but is never mentioned.

In the educational sphere, the past weeks have seen the reopening of lower and middle schools. In that to which our amah sends her children, each pupil was asked to supply one table and chair—any kind would do—to replace those destroyed by Fu's soldiers during their siegetime occupation. There was nothing compulsory in the request, however, and our amah begged out of it on grounds of financial disability. Kuomintang textbooks, though eventually to be revised or replaced, remain in use for the time being. Peita and other government universities have at last been "taken over" by the People's Government in the sense that one or more members of that regime have been formally attached to each institution. No curricular or other changes, however, are contemplated at the present time.

Just how short the Communists are in trained personnel is shown by their efforts to recruit ten thousand men and women graduates of middle schools or higher institutions to serve in the "Southern expedition." Their problem is that of finding persons who possess the requisite technical ability combined with enthusiasm for the cause and willingness to undergo great personal hardship. Many students have the latter qualities in abundance; only a few possess the former. Their eager response to the recruiting campaign is exemplified in the case of Tsinghua, which reopened classes yesterday with an attendance of only 1,804 out of its former enrollment of 2,482. Most of the 678 absent students have apparently decided to forego further studies in order to work for the revolutionary cause in the South.

With an eye to the future, the Communists are also establishing three "universities"—really gigantic indoctrination and training institutes—to be known respectively as North China University, the North China People's Revolutionary University, and North China Military Administration University. All three are now preparing to hold entrance examinations.

The notice of the Military University appearing in the *People's Daily* is no doubt typical. It announces that training in military administration is to be given to six thousand students. A preliminary half-year term will, in the case of selected groups, be followed by a further curriculum lasting from one to one and a half years. Subjects will include Marxism, ideology of Mao Tse-tung, sociology, fundamental problems in the Chinese Revolution, contemporary political policy, fundamental knowledge about the People's Liberation Army, and military science and technology. Anyone can apply who is of good physique and habits, has graduated from a lower middle school (tenth grade by American standards), and is between the ages of eighteen and twenty-eight.

It is in the realm of what may be called indoctrination, or, less charitably, thought control, that we reach the most questionable aspect of the new program. The authorities are trying, with considerable success, to see that only their point of view reaches the people. Slogans and posters carrying their message now adorn all public places. Many, printed in bright colors, are very effective, for example the one depicting a galloping cavalry-man holding aloft a red banner, beneath which appears the caption: "Plant the victorious banner throughout China!"; or that of an army officer pointing to the way ahead, with huge tanks looming in the background.

A reading room and adjoining sales room for New Democracy literature have been opened at a strategic location on Morrison Street, where they attract such crowds that one can enter only with difficulty. What I was able to examine on one brief visit proved unimpressive: piles of tiny pamphlets containing crude black-and-white pictures arranged in comic-strip fashion to illustrate the evils of landlordism, the benefits of peasant cooperation with the People's Army, and similar themes.

Movies are now said to be subject to censorship. In the words of the March 2 *Peiping Digest*: "Decadent U.S. films are to be ousted by healthy Russian films. Fifty Russian movies are already in circulation in North China and thirteen are to be shown in Peiping."

Newspapers have suffered a high mortality, at least seven having been closed in Peking, including that to which I had subscribed, the *World Daily News*. This leaves the city with only two dailies, the official *People's Daily,* and a tabloid, the *Hsin-min Pao* (*New Citizen*), which is the only paper surviving from the old regime under its own name. Others will probably be started before long, judging from what occurred in Tientsin, where the official *Tientsin Daily* has already been joined, or is about to be joined, by three revamped papers. Among these, the most important is the *Chin-pu Jih-pao* or *Progressive Daily,* a reincarnation of the famous *Ta Kung Pao.*

I have begun to subscribe to it again and notice that, like every other paper, it faithfully follows the Communist line, using the New China News Agency as its only source of information about the outside world. Within liberated China itself, however, it maintains something of its former wide coverage by the use of news letters from local correspondents. These give it a piquancy and individuality lacking in the more standardized official organs.

How many dailies are published in Communist China today? According to the editorial reply to a letter to the editor in the March 2 *People's Daily,* the total is sixty-three, distributed as follows: Manchuria (including part of Inner Mongolia), twenty-two; North China, sixteen; Northwest, six; Central Plains, seven; East China, twelve. Only four cities have more than one paper: Harbin, two; Mukden, four; Shihchiachuang, three; Chengchow, two. These figures are obviously incomplete inasmuch as they list only one paper apiece for Peking and Tientsin.

During the past few weeks, however, I have concluded that the integrity of the press depends on more than simply the number of its papers, important though this may be. It does not greatly matter, after all, if a city possesses one, two, or five papers, provided they all print essentially the same news derived from the same source. As a matter of fact, what can be said of the press here in China can also be made to apply, in some respects, to the American press: too many American cities maintain only one paper, too many papers depend for news solely on a single news agency, too many Americans read the same feature columns syndicated throughout the country. The real difference between America and Communist China, however, can be summed up in a sentence: a speech by Mao Tse-tung has a fair chance of being at least partially reported in America; a Truman speech has no chance at all of being printed in Communist China, unless it suits the purpose of the authorities to permit it.

Most disturbing act of thought control is the February 27 order halting all further news activities of Peking's foreign correspondents. Though only seventeen persons are affected (Australian, Swiss, Swedish, and Dutch, as well as American), the order in effect means the complete cessation of news (other than over the Communist radio) from Communist China to the outside world, since Peking is the only city in North China in which foreign correspondents are stationed. The same order bans the further circulation here of the U.S. Information Service news bulletins, both Chinese and English, thus leaving the short-wave radio (for those who have one) as the only "free" organ of information from the outside world.

It is difficult to see the justification for a step which, in its sweeping inclusiveness, transcends anything attempted even in Soviet Russia. The official explanation is that of "conditions during the present state of military activity." The *Progressive*

Daily goes a good bit further by beginning its February 28 editorial with the words: "Though among foreign correspondents in China good ones are certainly not wholly lacking, in the final analysis most of them are stupid and are rotten eggs." As illustration it cites the unfortunate AP and UP dispatches describing the Communist entry of Peking.

If these are the real causes for the present step, the Communists could have attained their objectives equally well either by expelling the two correspondents directly involved or by imposing general censorship. Though either step would have undoubtedly aroused criticism abroad, neither could have been as disastrous as the present move, the only practical effect of which is to close the mouths of the new regime's potential friends abroad, strengthen its enemies, and make more difficult the reestablishment of those diplomatic and commercial ties from which the Chinese Communists themselves stand to benefit.

But probably it is too much to expect the Communists to pay much attention to long-range consideration such as these in a matter in which the question of prestige with their own people is involved. Nor is it surprising that their decision should be approved by the students, always inclined to be hot-headed, or that it should be ignored by the bulk of China's toiling masses, for whom the problem of filling next day's rice bowl is far more important than the academic question of press freedom. But what about those many non-Communist intellectuals and liberals who have repeatedly in the past risked personal safety by protesting against Kuomintang violations of the press? It is disappointing that on this occasion not one has raised his voice in public criticism. . . .

SPIRIT OF THE NEW CHINA

Last Sunday, a lovely spring day, the three of us took a walk through the Pei Hai. As we passed one of the old temples that line the lake's northern shore, we noticed that two of the three large bronze incense burners before its gates had been toppled from their marble pedestals. "More of the work of Kuomintang soldiers," we commented.

A few minutes later, repassing the temple, we met eight or

ten young People's Army soldiers, out for a stroll like ourselves. The next moment one of them—obviously a natural leader, though a private like the rest—noticed the overturned incense burners as we had done and ran toward them, waving to his comrades as he did so. In a matter of seconds he and three or four of the others, despite their loads of rifles and blanket rolls, were struggling to lift one of the tripods back to its pedestal. The task was terribly difficult, for the tripod was about three feet high and enormously thick and heavy, besides being so round and smooth that only two or three men could get a real grip on it. All efforts seemed doomed to failure. The burners simply could not be lifted from the ground without ropes and poles.

But then the leader had an inspiration. He called his comrades again to the task, and together they rolled the burner over the ground until it touched the foot of the pedestal. Then, pressing it with all their strength against the side of the stone, they slowly rolled it up the stone's vertical face and thus onto its upper surface. After that it was comparatively simple to pull the burner back upon its legs and slide it until they slipped once more into their original sockets, whereupon the soldier who had conceived the operation leaped happily inside the incense burner, waved his arm, and shouted in triumph. Then, jumping down again, he and his comrades ran to the other prostrate burner and within a few minutes had restored this, too, to its original position. And we three foreigners, together with a small group of Chinese children which had by now assembled, applauded and shouted: *"Hao! Hao!"* ("Good! Good!") As we did so I thought to myself: This is probably the first time in decades— perhaps in centuries—that a group of Chinese soldiers, undirected from above and with no expectation of gain or praise for themselves, have spontaneously performed an act requiring initiative, effort, ingenuity, and cooperation, simply in order to put to rights a monument belonging to the public.

☯ Theory and Methods of Chinese Communism

THE WORD ideology is disquieting to American minds. It is something "they" have and "we" do not. Americans are aware of religious dogmatism, but they do not associate the word ideology with it. Ideology is something totalitarian movements have, in particular Communist movements. It appears to be a doctrinaire way of thinking expressed in a unique jargonistic language to which the individual subordinates his free rational mind. Ideology is perceived to be antithetical to the way in which the free world works. Here we have a free market place of ideas to which each individual and group bring their own ideas. In the back-and-forth of argumentation some ideas will prevail and become instruments of power, but the market place remains; thus as circumstances change, new ideas will arise and triumph. But "they" have replaced the market place of ideas with ideology, a fixed set of categories and language of thought, which appears to exist and develop independently of individual human intervention or is mysteriously manipulated by those who control the instruments of power.

American visitors who cross over the Iron Curtain are not disabused of their beliefs that ideology reigns supreme in the Communist countries. True, in Eastern Europe one often finds intellectuals who speak ideas and language familiar to the West. Yet as one reads newspapers, one sees the ideas and language of Marxism-Leninism, and, quite often, as arguments with intellectuals move into the political realm, the way they talk becomes Marxist-Leninist, though more autonomously and individually expressed.

As one goes farther east the differences between official and private expression narrow. In China, as even the most sympathetic tourists report, the individual usually talks in the same way as his government, even when voicing criticisms and dissatisfaction.

There are many things in Communist countries Westerners can understand immediately. Everyday life is not so different that good reportage cannot communicate how the citizen of Moscow or Peking lives, works, and enjoys himself. Economists generally can analyze the economic situation of the Eastern countries in the same terms as they do those of the Western countries. Ideology, however, is another matter. Since ideology is of such paramount importance in China, we shall try to sketch out what it is and what part it plays in the political system of Chinese Communism.

Karl Mannheim, the German sociologist of knowledge, saw the rise of modern man's ideological thinking in men's growing distrust in each other's words and in the imputation to one's adversary of a *real* mode of thought which went deeper than his words and was not even accessible to his consciousness. No matter how changing and varied the "other's" words and actions might be, "I" was convinced that, *in reality,* they derived from a unified, unconscious mind over which the "other" had no control. Thus what mattered was not so much what the "other" said, but rather that deep, inside core from which his thoughts and words sprang. The next step in the development of ideological thinking came when men came to regard the "other's" inner mind, his individual ideology, as but a particular manifestation of a broader collective mind shared by many men rooted in the same social circumstances. The "other" was no longer simply an individual, but a particular human instance of "they." What men said or did was an expression not merely of an individual unconscious mind but of a broader ideological unity: the "other" reflected "their" ideology. The third step came when men regarded this collective ideology not as a fixed thing but something which changed in response to changing world conditions. Mannheim places the development of ideological thinking in the nineteenth century, when, particularly after the Industrial Revolution in England and the social revolution in France, the world began to see itself caught in a process of continuing revolutionary change.

If Martin Buber speaks of the "I-Thou" relationship, ideological thinking speaks of "We-They." Mao Tse-tung speaks of "We-Enemy."

Let us remember that Marxism arose on the basis of a systematic analysis of its enemy, capitalism. Marx drew a picture of how the world, societies, classes, and individuals acted. That picture formed a whole where the same categories and language could analyze and contribute to the understanding of any of its parts. Marxism started as a conception of the enemy.

Marxism became the ideology of revolutionary movements, notably in Russia and China. As these movements grew, the leaders began to use systematic analysis of "the enemy" as a basis for systematic analysis of "us." Thus Lenin analyzed not only the world and Russia, but the Russian Social Democratic Party. From this self-analysis grew an ideology of organization, and action which since has been called Leninism. A similar process was repeated in China from which Chinese Communist ideology of organization and action grew, namely "the Thought of Mao Tse-tung," popularly known in the West as "Maoism." Thus the Russian, the Chinese, and all other Communist parties developed "they-we" ideologies, which permitted them to see all particular actions and events as part of a systematic whole. The growth of Communist ideology was far from an exercise in abstract philosophy. It gave these movements powerful weapons for carrying out protracted struggle against their enemies and maintaining solidarity within the organization, even in periods of defeat and failure.

The Chinese Communist Party arose in the wake of the October Revolution, that is, in a period in which ideological thinking already was projected onto both "they" and "we." Throughout the works of Mao Tse-tung and other Chinese Communist leaders one finds global analyses, discussions of the class situation in China, as well as self-analysis of Party organization and action. The categories and language used are systematic since they allow for macroscopic and microscopic analysis with the same ideological instruments.

Despite their deep commitment to the Marxist-Leninist world view (the theory), the Chinese Communists realized eventually that all things could not be explained or all action based on purely ideological thinking. Thus the disaster of 1927 (see Volume II) resulted largely from the blind faith the Com-

munists placed in Comintern directives. During the Kiangsi Soviet Period (see Volume II) they went to the opposite extreme: while voicing continuing loyalty to theory, they proceeded to make revolution as they felt the situation dictated,
which was not so different from what the Taipings had done
eighty years earlier. By the time of the Yenan Period, when
Mao began to write on philosophy and theory and Liu Shao-
ch'i on principles of organization, they realized that universal
theory and concrete practice, while crucial to the movement,
also had to be linked, not dogmatically but flexibly. If practice
failed, one could always retreat to theory, and when the latter
was unusable (as was strongly implied in the Seventh Party
Congress of 1945) then practice could be stressed. In any case,
periodic pendulum-swings from one to the other fundamentally
harmed neither.

From this realization grew the philosophical distinctions
between theory and practice and their linkage. Theory was the
world view, the conception of "they"; practice was, in effect,
the principles and methods of "our" organization and action,
adapted to concrete circumstances. Both were equally systematic, though the latter, as something particular and not universal,
could change frequently. Linking the two, however, was something which in time would come to be called the Thought of
Mao Tse-tung. The Chinese Communists have consistently
spoken of Mao's contributions to Marxism-Leninism as the
application of universal laws (theory) to concrete circum-
stance (practice). We must think of Mao Tse-tung's Thought
as a set of interconnected visions, large, structured conceptions
of how man acts in society and politics, at home and abroad.
These visions are all based on a fundamental philosophical belief taken from Marxist theory: the law of contradiction, but
they all relate to concrete situations. In our introduction to the
selections on Mao Tse-tung (see pp. 79–80), we point out
that his three great visions have related to the nature of revolution and society in China, to the global conflict between socialism and capitalism and the proper role of the socialist
world, and to the historical significance of the revolutionary rise
of the "third world."

.   .   .

Let us now turn to Mao Tse-tung's selection on contradiction. Chinese have traditionally thought in terms of complementary opposites: every phenomenon can be divided into its yin and yang, two parts which fit together harmoniously to form a perfect circle. But for Mao, raised in a period of intellectual revolution, the juxtaposition of opposites led not to harmony but to mortal struggle: one must triumph over the other. Mao sees every human phenomenon as riven into struggling opposites: the individual fights the cleavage in his soul between old and new, the class is marked by struggle between poor and rich, city and village are juxtaposed in struggle, and finally, on a global level, socialism and capitalism cannot coexist eternally.

The distinctions between different kinds of contradiction and struggle reflect the practical bent in Mao's thinking. The universality of contradiction means that ideological theory can never assert any conception that implies harmony rather than struggle as a basic principle. Thus, for example, peaceful coexistence as a concrete policy is all right, but as theory is wrong and must be fought uncompromisingly. Since theory and practice are not dogmatically linked, however, specific contradictions emerge at different times and places and in different forms. Thus to assert the theoretical universality of contradiction does not force you to go out and act on each of them. Similarly, in the case of struggle and antagonism, as long as there are juxtaposed opposites, there is struggle, but that does not imply an immediate fight to the death; that is antagonism.

In *On Contradiction,* Mao speaks abstractly about the different kinds of contradictions, reducing them to two basic kinds: antagonistic and non-antagonistic contradictions. Neither the terms, which derive from Lenin and Stalin, nor the idea is new. The philosophical distinction can be simply stated: antagonistic contradictions are those between "We and the Enemy" and must ultimately lead to mortal struggle between the two; non-antagonistic contradictions are those existing among the "We" and can be peacefully resolved.

Since it is always best to understand Mao's writings in concrete terms, even when written in the most abstract language, let us cite one practical application of this principle of contradiction. For years the Communists have operated simultaneously with two general policy conceptions: class struggle and the united front. Class struggle means that the juxtaposition of opposites in the individual and in the world is absolute and has to be fought out with all means. For example, class struggle requires building up a disciplined proletarian Communist Party held together by the tightest ideological unity. United front policy, on the other hand, proposes a coalition including class enemies, without regard to ideological uniformity. Class struggle and united front are in obvious contradiction. What is antagonistic contradiction for the former is non-antagonistic contradiction for the latter. To him who asks for constancy, Mao would respond: what the particular quality of a universal contradiction is depends on time, place, and the concrete problems of world history.

Is this hypocrisy or pedantic verbiage to fool the opposition? It would seem so in many instances, particularly after the Hundred Flowers period (see pp. 151–156). But we would do well to remember that even in moments of visionary extremism, Mao never believed that he could fully do away with the contradictions in Chinese society: the intellectuals who are not fully committed to socialism remain as do the rich peasants and the urban bourgeoisie. Mao is a Marxist and believes that until the material foundation of Chinese society has been transformed, hostile class elements will remain. Antagonism has no purpose unless you can be victorious, as Mao's guerrilla tactics tell us. Thus, as long as the opposition does not disappear from Chinese society—and from the world—an approach which, on occasion, ignores antagonistic contradictions and advocates a united front has its purposes. The united front permits "non-antagonistic struggle" to take place, notably through persuasion and thought reform.

In the second selection, from Mao Tse-tung's celebrated speech "On the Correct Handling of Contradictions Among the People," delivered in February 1957, Mao outlines the great political, social, economic, and ideological contradictions he sees in Chinese society. Here, during the Hundred Flowers period, he advocated "non-antagonistic struggle" as a means of resolving those contradictions. Some months later, however, that speech became the basis of a grand vision out of which the Great Leap Forward developed. Far more than an economic drive, the Great Leap Forward was a vast campaign to bring about, in the space of a few years, a total transformation of Chinese society. Suddenly these same problems and contradictions became "antagonistic."

The third selection, on the general line the Chinese Communist Party proposed for the international Communist movement, outlines Mao's vision of the historical trends in the contemporary world. It is an analysis of "They," the imperialist camp, and "We," the socialist camp. It lists twenty-five basic points, about which we shall briefly comment. There must be no tampering with basic ideological theory, that is, no deviation from the principle of fundamental antagonism between imperialism and socialism. On the other hand, the rather indiscriminate lumping together of slogans implies flexibility as far as practical policies are concerned. However, there is no deviation from the fundamental principle that the United States is the socialist camp's chief enemy. Given this, there are now four great fighting fronts: the Soviet Union and the United States, Communist Parties in the industrialized countries and their governments, the poor and the rich nations, and the rich capitalist nations themselves. It is the historical role of all socialist forces at each of these fighting fronts to maintain rigorous hostility to capitalism and imperialism, but they must also realize that the main fighting front today (what Mao would call the principal contradiction) is in the third world. Thus the other revolutionary forces must support the national liberation struggles with all their power, and avoid any tendency to settle into non-revolutionary routinization. On war and peace, the Chinese appear to accept the Soviet idea that total war is not inevitable, but they propose toughness and willingness to fight as the best road toward eventual peace. Moreover, they concede that peaceful coexistence has its purpose as a specific policy in certain times and places. Turning to internal matters, the Chinese propound the position that no socialist state can regard the Revolution as other than unfinished: the internal struggle must always go on. Therefore it is crucial that the Communist Party remain a disciplined revolutionary instrument. The document ends with a commitment to continue the polemic between true Marxism-Leninism and modern revisionism until, in effect, the contradiction has been resolved.

Aside from the specific issues in the Sino-Soviet dispute

(*e.g.,* nuclear sharing and Vietnam), there has also been a clash between two different world views, each obviously influenced by the national interests and perspectives of the parties involved. If a single unified theory is so important to the organization and action of Communist Parties and to their ideological thinking, a dispute over world view then becomes an extremely serious matter. The dispute essentially revolves around differing Soviet and Chinese assessments of "they," principally the United States. As the Chinese put it, "the strategic objectives of U.S. imperialism have been to grab and dominate the intermediate zone lying between the United States and the socialist camp, put down the revolutions of the oppressed peoples and nations, proceed to destroy the socialist countries, and thus to subject all the peoples and countries of the world, including its allies, to domination and enslavement by U.S. monopoly capital." The Soviets agree that "the contradiction between capitalism and socialism is the chief contradiction of our epoch." But "the correlation of forces in the world arena is changing all the time in favor of socialism." And thus there is no need to promote potentially expansive and dangerous wars of liberation in most countries of the underdeveloped world.

Let us move now from global theory to the important area of ideological practice. To Liu Shao-ch'i the ideal Party member is one whose entire life centers on the Party. He must subordinate his personal interests and private life to the Party. His reward is the knowledge that he is part of the revolutionary vanguard, a leader of his people. Life in the Party is not easy, however. If the traditional Chinese scholar-official lived his life at a secure distance from the people, the Party member must constantly work and live among the masses. It is only through action among the masses that his ideological convictions become tempered. Self-cultivation and indoctrination are endless processes. No one ever achieves ideological perfection. Those who believe otherwise fall victim to complacency, corruption, and the arrogance of victory and power.

In a later selection on thought reform (see pp. 135–147) we shall point out that the Chinese Communists have always been deeply concerned with individual identity and its transformation. Since individual thought reform has been so uniquely Chinese Communist and absent in the Soviet tradition, one may ask why it should have assumed such importance in the Chinese Communists' practical ideology. The aim of thought reform is to substitute ideological for individual thinking, to make a man fully conscious of his own mode of thought, break it down through group action, and then, through group "help," reconstitute a new unity based on the categories and language of the ideology. Mannheim, in tracing the beginning of total ideological conceptions, stated that "henceforth the world as 'world' exists only with reference to the knowing mind, and the mental activity of the subject determines the form in which the world appears." More simply, an individual's ideological conception of the world is real if it is truly reflected in his thought. Thus, concretely, the thought of Mao Tse-tung is true only if every individual in Mao's society, China, emerges with a microscopic version of that same thought.

Politics, as the Chinese have known for centuries, is a matter of human relations in a context of power. Political relations, to be effective, must be based on moral, rational, and emotional bonds between leaders and followers, and not on naked command and constraint. The Chinese Revolution destroyed the traditional Confucian political relationships, leaving only ties of personal relationships on which the Kuomintang and the warlords based their power. But personal relations are often fragile and are not enough to hold a large-scale organization together. The Communists were determined to create new and strong bonds of political relations. This, in substance, is the aim of thought reform and Communist self-cultivation. During the Yenan Period, the Communists were not afraid to recruit young men of leadership ability first and subject them to indoctrination afterwards.

We can see in all of these documents the notion of contradiction and of struggle; even more, we see a systematic conception of the world through whose categories and language everything can be understood and policies for action proposed. Theory, vision, and practice were in closer conformity in 1958 than at any other time during the history of the Chinese People's Republic. As the great crisis in the domestic economy and in Sino-Soviet relations set in, the unity of theory and practice began to crumble. Soviets and Chinese began a dispute over theory. Mao projected his vision away from China to the great international world. And in China herself practice became pragmatism, with decisions and solutions made for problems as they arose and generally in a common-sense manner.

The unified conceptions of ideology have suffered in the past years, yet the Chinese Communists are making strenuous efforts to convince people that unity still exists. For years a vast socialist education movement has been under way in China, giving people, particularly peasants, ideological and practical education. Today every mass medium each day and in almost every article propagates the Thought of Mao Tse-tung. China's leaders are clearly afraid that once Chairman Mao departs from the scene, the ideology may wither. After all, people normally tend to think of the world in pluralistic fashion, and the huge strides China has made in modern education tend to move people even further away from ideological and toward pragmatic thinking. In the "red and expert" controversy, the pure "expert" is usually accused of being ideologically lax and reluctant to see everything in its ideological dimensions.

Daniel Bell, in discussing the exhaustion of Marxist ideologies in the West, notes that "ideologists are 'terrible simplifiers.' Ideology makes it unnecessary for people to confront individual issues on their individual merits" (*The End of Ideology,* p. 405). Today we find a new kind of "contradiction" in China. In area after area the Chinese are acting pragmatically on individual issues, often without worrying whether they fit into a larger scheme. They trade with almost any nation, save the United States. They allow a range of different economic practices at home, as long as results are guaranteed. But there are other areas in which ideological thinking, the "terrible simplifications," hold sway. If economic action is pragmatic, in politics and education it remains ideological. If relations with West Germany and Japan are practical, relations with the United States and the Soviet Union are ideology-dominated. In Mao's words, the contradiction between these two different modes of behavior could be termed struggle but not antagonism.

Events are threatening to turn struggle into antagonism, however, and are forcing theory and practice closer together. If escalation of the war in Vietnam should result in Chinese intervention, then the Chinese will face a conflict with the United States which they had hitherto talked about only in the realm

of theory. It will no longer be possible for them to continue to
maintain that delicate division between ideological and practical
actions.

As we have observed earlier in this introduction, one of the
sources of ideological thinking is the systematic conception of
what "they" are and do in reality. If the areas of the Communist
world other than China should become convinced that the traditional Marxist and the present Chinese image of the capitalist
world was true after all, then we may find that ideology has
not yet reached its end.

China today is at a crossroads. Her ideology points in one
direction, her actions in another. It is vital that the world,
particularly the United States, realize that the direction China
finally takes is dependent not solely on autonomous decisions
made in Peking but on a broader world situation in whose
determination the United States plays a crucial role. The worse
the war in Vietnam becomes, the more it confirms the Chinese
Communist ideological conception of the world.

The failures of the Great Leap Forward, the reluctance of
the Soviet Union to return to "true Marxism-Leninism," and the
turn to the right in so many countries of the third world have
done harm to Mao Tse-tung's conceptions of the world. It
would be one of the great ironies of history if Washington and
Peking collaborated to make Mao's vision come true in the
contemporary world.

MAO TSE-TUNG *

from *On Contradiction*

TWO KINDS OF WORLD OUTLOOK

In the history of human knowledge, there have been two different views on the laws of development of the world, two

* Mao Tse-tung, *On Contradiction* [abridged] (Peking: Foreign Languages
Press, second edition, 1960).

mutually opposed world outlooks: the metaphysical view and the dialectical view. Lenin said: "The two basic (or two possible? or two historically observable?) conceptions of development (evolution) are: development as decrease and increase, as repetition, *and* development as a unity of opposites (the division of the one into mutually exclusive opposites and their reciprocal relation)." Here Lenin was referring to these two different kinds of world outlook.

In China as well as in Europe, metaphysics has for a long time formed part of the idealist world outlook and occupied a dominant position in human thought. In the early days of the bourgeoisie in Europe, materialism was also metaphysical. The Marxist materialist-dialectical world outlook emerged because in many European countries social economy had entered the stage of highly developed capitalism, the productive forces, the class struggle, and the sciences had all advanced to a level unprecedented in history, and the industrial proletariat had become the greatest motive force in historical development. Then among the bourgeoisie, besides idealism which sheds all disguise and flaunts its reactionary tendency, there also emerged vulgar evolutionism to oppose materialist dialectics. . . .

Contrary to the metaphysical world outlook, the materialistic-dialectical world outlook advocates the study of the development of a thing from the inside, from its relationship to other things, or in other words teaches that the development of a thing should be regarded as its internal and necessary self-movement, that a thing in its movement and the things round it should be regarded as interconnected and interacting upon each other. The basic cause of development of a thing is not external but internal and lies in its internal contradictions. A thing moves and develops because of such contradictions within itself. Contradictions within a thing are the basic cause of its development, while its relationship with other things, their interconnection and interaction, is a secondary cause. Thus materialist dialectics effectively combats the theory of external causes, or of propulsion, advanced by metaphysical mechanistic materialism and vulgar evolutionism. It is evident that purely external causes can only lead to mechanical motion, that is, to changes in size and quantity, but cannot explain why things are qualitatively different in a thousand and one ways and why one thing changes into another. . . .

The dialectical world outlook had already emerged in ancient times both in China and in Europe. Ancient dialectics, however, has something spontaneous and naïve about it; based upon the product of the social and historical conditions then prevailing, it could not develop into an adequate theory to offer a comprehensive explanation of the world and was consequently supplanted by metaphysics. The famous German philosopher Hegel, who lived from the late eighteenth to the early nineteenth century, made very important contributions to dialectics, but his dialectics is idealist. It was not until Marx and Engels, the great men of action in the proletarian movement, summed up the positive achievements in the history of human knowledge and, in particular, critically absorbed the rational elements in Hegelian dialectics, and created the great theory of dialectical and historical materialism that an unprecedented revolution took place in the history of human knowledge. This great theory has received further development at the hands of Lenin and Stalin. Once introduced into China, it immediately brought about tremendous changes in Chinese thought.

The dialectical world outlook teaches us primarily how to observe and analyze skillfully the movement of opposites in various things and, on the basis of such an analysis, to work out solutions of the contradictions. It is therefore of paramount importance for us to understand concretely the law of contradiction in things.

THE UNIVERSALITY OF CONTRADICTION

For convenience in exposition, I shall start with the universality of contradiction, and then proceed to the particularity of contradiction. The universality of contradiction can be briefly dealt with because the concept has been widely accepted ever since the great creators and continuators of Marxism—Marx, Engels, Lenin, and Stalin—established the materialist-dialectical world outlook and applied materialist dialectics with remarkable success in analyzing human history and natural history, and in changing society and nature (as in the Soviet Union); but many comrades, especially the doctrinaires, are still not clear about the problem of the particularity of contradiction. They do not understand that the universality of contradiction resides in the particularity of contradiction. Nor do they understand the importance of studying the particularity of contradiction in things confronting us in order to guide us further in revolutionary practice. Therefore, this problem calls for special attention and needs to be explained fully. Accordingly, in analyzing the law of contradiction in things, we start with the universality of contradiction, then proceed with special care to the particularity of contradiction, and finally return to the universality of contradiction.

The universality or absoluteness of contradiction has a two-fold meaning. One is that contradiction exists in the process of development of all things and the other is that in the process of development of each thing a movement of opposites exists from beginning to end. . . .

THE PARTICULARITY OF CONTRADICTION

As has been shown, the universality and absoluteness of contradiction means that contradiction exists in and runs through the whole process of development of all things. Let us now take up the particularity and relativity of contradiction.

This problem should be studied from several angles.

First, the contradiction in each form of motion of matter has it particularity. Our knowledge of matter is a knowledge of the forms of its motion, because there is nothing in the world except matter in motion and this motion must assume a certain form. In considering each form of motion, we must take into account the features common to all forms. But what is especially important and constitutes the basis of our knowledge is that we must take note of the distinguishing features, namely, the qualitative difference between one form of motion and other forms. Only when we have done this can we distinguish between things. Any form of motion contains within itself its own particular contradiction. This particular contradiction constitutes the particular quality which distinguishes one thing from all others. This is the internal cause or, as it may be called, the basis of the thousand and one ways in which things are different from one another. Many forms of motion exist in nature, mechanical movement, sound, light, heat, electricity, decomposition, combination, and so on. All these forms are interdependent and each is qualitatively different from the other. The particular quality of a form of motion is determined by the particular contradiction inherent in that form. This holds good not only with nature but also with society and with thinking. Every form of society, every way of thinking has its particular contradiction and particular quality. . . .

The relation between the universality and the particularity of contradiction is one between the common character and the individual character of contradictions. By the former we mean that contradictions exist in and run through all processes from beginning to end: contradictions are movements, things, processes and thoughts. To deny contradiction is to deny everything. This is a truth applicable to all times and all countries without exception. Hence the common character or absoluteness. But this common character is contained in all individual characters; without individual character there can be no common character. If all individual characters were removed, what common character would remain? Individual characters arise because each contradiction is a particular one. All individual characters exist conditionally and temporarily, hence they are relative.

This principle of common character and individual character, of absoluteness and relativity, is the essence of the problem of the contradiction in things; to fail to understand it is tantamount to abandoning dialectics.

THE PRINCIPAL CONTRADICTION AND THE
PRINCIPAL ASPECT OF A CONTRADICTION

As regards the particularity of contradiction, there are still two points which require special analysis, the principal contradiction and the principal aspect of a contradiction.

Many contradictions exist in the development of a complex

thing; among these, one is necessarily the principal contradiction whose existence and growth determines or influences the others.

For instance, in capitalist society, the two opposing forces, the proletariat and the bourgeoisie, form the principal contradiction; the other contradictions between the remnant feudal class and the bourgeoisie, the rural petty bourgeoisie and the bourgeoisie, the proletariat and the rural petty bourgeoisie, the liberal bourgeoisie and the monopolistic bourgeois democracy and bourgeois fascism, the capitalist countries themselves, imperialism and the colonies, are determined and influenced by this principal contradiction.

In semi-colonial countries like China, the relationship between the principal contradiction and non-principal contradictions presents a complicated problem.

When imperialism wages a war of aggression on such a country, the various classes in that country, except for a handful of traitors, can temporarily unite in a national anti-imperialist war. At such a time, the contradiction between imperialism and that country becomes the principal one, while all the contradictions among the various classes within that country—including the principal contradiction between the feudal system and the masses of the people—are relegated for the time being to a secondary or subordinate position. Such was the case in China in the Opium War of 1840, the Sino-Japanese War of 1894, the Boxer War of 1900, and is also the case in the present Sino-Japanese War [1937].

In a different situation, however, contradictions change their relative positions. When imperialism does not force a war on the semi-colonial countries, but carries on its oppression in the milder political, economic, and cultural forms, the ruling classes in these countries will capitulate to imperialism and ally themselves with it to oppress the masses of the people. Then the masses will often resort to civil war to oppose the alliance of imperialism and the feudal class, while imperialism will avoid taking direct action but employ indirect methods to help the reactionaries in these countries to oppress the people, and the internal contradiction will thus become very much sharper. This happened in China in the Revolutionary War of 1911, the Revolutionary War of 1924–1927, and the ten years' Agrarian

Revolutionary War since 1927. An analogous situation can also be found in the internecine wars of the reactionary ruling blocs in the semi-colonial countries, for instance, the wars between the warlords in China. . . .

THE IDENTITY AND STRUGGLE
OF THE ASPECTS OF A CONTRADICTION

Having understood the universality and particularity of contradiction, we must proceed to study the identity and struggle of the aspects of a contradiction.

Identity, unity, coincidence, interpermeation, interpenetration, interdependence, interconnection, or cooperation—all these different terms mean the same thing and refer to the following two conditions: first, each of the two aspects of a contradiction in the process of development presupposes its existence in the other aspect and both aspects coexist in an entity; second, each of the two contradictory aspects, according to given conditions, tends to transform itself into the other. This is what is meant by identity. . . .

All contradictory things are interconnected, and they not only coexist in an entity under certain conditions, but also transform themselves into each other under certain conditions; this is the whole meaning of the identity of contradictions. This is exactly what Lenin meant when he discussed "how *opposites* . . . are (how they become) *identical*—under what conditions they are identical, transforming themselves into each other. . . ."

Why should we conceive these opposites not as things dead and rigid, but as living, fluid things, conditioned by circumstances, and transforming themselves into each other? Because that is just what objective things are. The unity or identity of the opposites in objective things is never dead or rigid, but living, fluid, temporary, relative, and conditioned by circumstances; all contradictory aspects transform themselves, under certain conditions, into their opposites. Reflected in human thought, this becomes the materialist-dialectical world outlook of Marxism. Only the reactionary ruling classes, past as well as present, and the metaphysicians in their service, do not regard opposites as living, fluid things, conditioned by circumstances, and transforming themselves into each other, but as dead and rigid things, and propagate this fallacy to delude the masses of the people, seeking thus to perpetuate their rule. The task of the Communists is precisely to expose such wrong reactionary and metaphysical ideas, to propagate the dialectics inherent in things, to hasten the transformation of things, and thus to bring about the Revolution. . . .

Such is the problem of identity. What then is struggle? What is the relation between identity and struggle? Lenin said:

The unity (coincidence, identity, resultant) of opposites is conditional, temporary, transitory, relative. The struggle of mutually exclusive opposites is absolute, just as development and motion are absolute.

What does this quotation from Lenin mean?

All processes have a beginning and an end and transform themselves into their opposites. The stability of all processes is relative, but the mutability manifested in the transformation of one process into another is absolute.

The movement of all things assumes either one of the two forms: relative rest and conspicuous change. Both forms are caused by the struggle of the opposites within a thing. When the movement assumes the first form, it only undergoes a quantitative but not a qualitative change and consequently appears in a state of seeming rest. When it assumes the second form, it has already reached a certain culminating point of the quantitative change of the first form, caused the dissolution of the entity, produced a qualitative change, and consequently appears as conspicuous change. Such unity, solidarity, amalgamation, harmony, balance, stalemate, deadlock, rest, stability, equilibrium, coagulation, attraction, as we see in daily life, are all the appearances of things in the state of quantitative change. On the other hand, the dissolution of the entity, the breakdown of such solidarity, amalgamation, harmony, balance, stalemate, deadlock, rest, stability, equilibrium, coagulation, and attraction, and the change into their opposites, are all the appearances of things in the state of qualitative change during the transformation of one process into another. Things are constantly transforming themselves from the first into the second form, while the struggle within the contradictions exists in both forms and reaches its solution through the second form. We say therefore that the unity of opposites is conditional, temporary and relative, while the struggle of mutually exclusive opposites is absolute. . . .

THE ROLE OF ANTAGONISM IN CONTRADICTION

One of the questions concerning the struggle within the contradiction is: What is antagonism? Our answer is: Antagonism is one form of struggle within the contradiction, but not the only form.

In human history, class antagonism exists as a particular manifestation of the struggle within the contradiction. There is contradiction between the exploiting class and the exploited class, the two classes which, opposed as they are, coexist for a long time in the same slave, feudal, or capitalist society, and struggle with each other; but it is not until this contradiction has developed to a certain stage that the two classes adopt the form of open antagonism which develops into revolution. The transformation of peace into war in a class society is also a case in point.

Before its explosion, a bomb is an entity in which contradictory things coexist because of certain conditions. The explosion takes place only when the new condition of ignition is present. An analogous situation exists in all natural phenomena when they finally assume the form of open antagonism to solve old contradictions and to produce new things.

It is very important to grasp this fact. It enables us to understand that in a class society revolutions and revolutionary wars are inevitable, that apart from them the leap in social development cannot take place, the reactionary ruling classes cannot be overthrown, and the people cannot win political power. Communists must expose the deceitful propaganda of the reactionaries that social revolution is unnecessary and impossible, and firmly uphold the Marxist-Leninist theory of social revolution so as to help the people to understand that social revolution is not only absolutely necessary but also entirely possible, and that this is a scientific truth already confirmed by the whole history of mankind and the triumph of the Soviet Union.

However, we must study the specific conditions of various kinds of struggle within the contradiction and should not inappropriately impose this formula on everything. Contradiction and struggle are universal, absolute, but the methods of solving them, that is, the forms of struggle, differ according to the nature of the contradictions. Some contradictions are characterized by open antagonism, others are not. Based on the specific development of things, some contradictions, originally not yet antagonistic, develop and become antagonistic, while others, originally antagonistic, develop and become non-antagonistic.

As we have pointed out, the contradiction between correct and incorrect ideas within the Communist Party reflects in the Party the class contradictions so long as classes exist. In the beginning, or with regard to certain issues, such a contradiction need not immediately manifest itself as antagonistic. But with the development of the class struggle, it can also develop and become antagonistic. The history of the Communist Party of the Soviet Union shows us that the contradiction between the correct ideas of Lenin and Stalin and the incorrect ideas of Trotsky, Bukharin, and others, was in the beginning not manifested in an antagonistic form, but subsequently developed into antagonism. A similar case occurred in the history of the Chinese Communist Party. The contradiction between the correct ideas of many of our comrades in the Party and the incorrect ideas of Ch'en Tu-hsiu, Chang Kuo-tao and others, was also in the beginning not manifested in an antagonistic form, but subsequently developed into antagonism. At present the contradiction between the correct ideas and the incorrect ideas in our Party is not manifested in an antagonistic form and, if comrades who have committed mistakes can correct them, it will not develop into antagonism. Therefore, the Party on the one hand must carry on a serious struggle against incorrect ideas, and on the other must give the comrades who have committed mistakes sufficient opportunity to become aware of them. Under such conditions, it is obviously wrong to push the struggles too far. But if those who have committed mistakes persist in and aggravate them, then such contradictions may quite possibly develop into antagonism.

Economically, in capitalist society where the town under

bourgeois rule ruthlessly exploits the countryside and in the Kuomintang-controlled areas in China where the town under the rule of foreign imperialism and the native big comprador bourgeoisie most savagely exploits the countryside, the contradiction between town and country is one of extreme antagonism. But in a socialist country and in our revolutionary bases, such an antagonistic contradiction changes into a non-antagonistic one, and will disappear in a Communist society.

Lenin said: "Antagonism and contradiction are not in the least identical. Under socialism, the former will disappear while the latter will remain." That is to say, antagonism is one form of struggle within the contradiction but not the only form, and cannot be applied as a universal formula.

CONCLUSION

A few remarks by way of summing up.

The law of the contradiction in things, that is, the law of the unity of opposites, is the fundamental law of nature and society and therefore also the fundamental law of thought. It is opposed to the metaphysical world outlook. It means a great revolution in the history of human knowledge.

According to dialectical materialism, contradiction exists in all processes of objective things and subjective thought and runs through all processes from beginning to end; this is the universality and absoluteness of contradiction. Contradictory things and each of their aspects have respectively their specific features; this is the particularity and relativity of contradiction. Contradictory things, according to specific conditions, are characterized by identity, and consequently can coexist in an entity and transform themselves each into its opposite; this again is the particularity and relativity of contradiction. But the struggle within the contradiction is ceaseless, and goes on when the opposites coexist as well as when they are transforming themselves into each other, especially in the latter case; this again is the universality and absoluteness of contradiction.

In order to avoid mistakes, we must, in studying the particularity and relativity of contradiction, endeavor to distinguish between the principal and the non-principal in contradictions as well as in contradictory aspects, and in studying the universality and the struggle of contradiction, to distinguish between various forms of struggle.

If, after study, we have really grasped the essentials mentioned above, we shall be able to smash those doctrinaire ideas which are opposed to the fundamental principles of Marxism-Leninism and detrimental to our revolutionary cause, and our experienced comrades will be able to systematize their experiences and arrive at certain principles, thereby avoiding the mistakes of empiricism.

These are a few simple conclusions we have reached in the study of the law of contradiction.

Two Different Types of Contradictions*

Never has our country been as united as it is today. The victories of the bourgeois-democratic revolution and the socialist revolution, coupled with our achievements in socialist construction, have rapidly changed the face of old China. Now we see before us an even brighter future. The days of national disunity and turmoil which the people detested have gone for ever. Led by the working class and the Communist Party, and united as one, our six hundred million people are engaged in the great work of building socialism. Unification of the country, unity of the people and unity among our various nationalities—these are the basic guarantees for the sure triumph of our cause. However, this does not mean that there are no longer any contradictions in our society. It would be naïve to imagine that there are no more contradictions. To do so would be to fly in the face of objective reality. We are confronted by two types of social contradictions—contradictions between ourselves and the enemy and contradictions among the people. These two types of contradictions are totally different in nature.

If we are to have a correct understanding of these two different types of contradictions, we must, first of all, make clear

* Mao Tse-tung, "On the Correct Handling of Contradictions" (Peking: Foreign Languages Press, 1957), pp. 1–4.

what is meant by "the people" and what is meant by "the enemy."

The term "the people" has different meanings in different countries, and in different historical periods in each country. Take our country for example. During the War of Resistance to Japanese Aggression, all those classes, strata, and social groups which opposed Japanese aggression belonged to the category of the people, while the Japanese imperialists, Chinese traitors, and the pro-Japanese elements belonged to the category of enemies of the people. During the War of Liberation, the United States imperialists and their henchmen—the bureaucrat-capitalists and landlord class—and the Kuomintang reaction-aries, who represented these two classes, were the enemies of the people, while all other classes, strata, and social groups which opposed these enemies, belonged to the category of the people. At this stage of building socialism, all classes, strata, and social groups which approve, support, and work for the cause of socialist construction belong to the category of the people, while those social forces and groups which resist the socialist revolu-tion, and are hostile to and try to wreck socialist construction, are enemies of the people.

The contradictions between ourselves and our enemies are antagonistic ones. Within the ranks of the people, contradictions among the working people are non-antagonistic, while those between the exploiters and the exploited classes have, apart from their antagonistic aspect, a non-antagonistic aspect. Contradic-tions among the people have always existed. But their content differs in each period of the revolution and during the building of socialism. In the conditions existing in China today what we call contradictions among the people include the following: contradictions within the working class, contradictions within the peasantry, contradictions within the intelligentsia, contradic-tions between the working class and the peasantry, contradic-tions between the working class and peasantry on the one hand and the intelligentsia on the other, contradictions between the working class and other sections of the working people on the one hand and the national bourgeoisie on the other, contradic-tions within the national bourgeoisie, and so forth. Our people's government is a government that truly represents the interests of the people and serves the people, yet certain contradictions do exist between the government and the masses. These include contradictions between the interests of the state, collective interests; and individual interests; between democracy and centralism; between those in positions of leadership and the led, and contradictions arising from the bureaucratic practices of certain state functionaries in their relations with the masses. All these are contradictions among the people. Generally speaking, underlying the contradictions among the people is the basic identity of the interests of the people.

In our country, the contradiction between the working class and the national bourgeoisie is a contradiction among the people. The class struggle waged between the two is, by and large, a class struggle within the ranks of the people. This is because of the dual character of the national bourgeoisie in our country. In the years of the bourgeois-democratic revolution, there was a revolutionary side to their character; there was also a tendency to compromise with the enemy, this was the other side. In the period of the socialist revolution, exploitation of the working class to make profits is one side, while support of the Constitution and willingness to accept socialist transformation is the other. The national bourgeoisie differs from the imperialists, the landlords and the bureaucrat-capitalists. The contradiction between exploiter and exploited, which exists between the national bourgeoisie and the working class, is an antagonistic one. But, in the concrete conditions existing in China, such an antagonistic contradiction, if properly handled, can be transformed into a non-antagonistic one and resolved in a peaceful way. But if it is not properly handled, if, say, we do not follow a policy of uniting, criticizing and educating the national bourgeoisie, or if the national bourgeoisie does not accept this policy, then the contradiction between the working class and the national bourgeoisie can turn into an antagonistic contradiction as between ourselves and the enemy.

Since the contradictions between ourselves and the enemy and those among the people differ in nature, they must be solved in different ways. To put it briefly, the former is a matter of drawing a line between us and our enemies, while the latter is a matter of distinguishing between right and wrong. It is, of course, true that drawing a line between ourselves and our enemies is also a question of distinguishing between right and wrong. For example, the question as to who is right, we or the reactionaries at home and abroad—that is, the imperialists, the feudalists and bureaucrat-capitalists—is also a question of distinguishing between right and wrong, but it is different in nature from questions of right and wrong among the people. . . .

THE CENTRAL COMMITTEE
OF THE CHINESE COMMUNIST PARTY *
Proposal Concerning the General Line
of the International Communist Movement

June 14, 1963

The Central Committee of the Communist
Party of the Soviet Union

Dear Comrades,

The Central Committee of the Communist Party of China has studied the letter of the Central Committee of the Communist Party of the Soviet Union of March 30, 1963.

All who have the unity of the socialist camp and the international Communist movement at heart are deeply concerned about the talks between the Chinese and Soviet Parties and hope that our talks will help to eliminate differences, strengthen unity, and create favorable conditions for convening a meeting of representatives of all the Communist and Workers' Parties.

It is the common and sacred duty of the Communist and Workers' Parties of all countries to uphold and strengthen the unity of the international Communist movement. The Chinese and Soviet Parties bear a heavier responsibility for the unity of the entire socialist camp and international Communist movement and should of course make commensurately greater efforts.

* *Peking Review,* VI, 25 (June 21, 1963), pp. 6–22.

A number of major differences of principle now exist in the international Communist movement. But however serious these differences, we should exercise sufficient patience and find ways to eliminate them so that we can unite our forces and strengthen the struggle against our common enemy. . . .

(1) The general line of the international Communist movement must take as its guiding principle the Marxist-Leninist revolutionary theory concerning the historical mission of the proletariat and must not depart from it. . . .

It is true that for several years there have been differences within the international Communist movement in the understanding of, and the attitude toward, the Declaration of 1957 and the Statement of 1960. The central issue here is whether or not to accept the revolutionary principles of the Declaration and the Statement. In the last analysis, it is a question of whether or not to accept the universal truth of Marxism-Leninism, whether or not to recognize the universal significance of the road of the October Revolution, whether or not to accept the fact that the people still living under the imperialist and capitalist system, who comprise two thirds of the world's population, need to make revolution, and whether or not to accept the fact that the people already on the socialist road, who comprise one third of the world's population, need to carry their revolution forward to the end. . . .

(2) What are the revolutionary principles of the Declaration and the Statement? They may be summarized as follows:

Workers of all countries, unite; workers of the world, unite with the oppressed peoples and oppressed nations; oppose imperialism and reaction in all countries; strive for world peace, national liberation, people's democracy and socialism; consolidate and expand the socialist camp; bring the proletarian world revolution step by step to complete victory; and establish a new world without imperialism, without capitalism, and without the exploitation of man by man.

This, in our view, is the general line of the international Communist movement at the present stage.

(3) This general line proceeds from the actual world situation taken as a whole and from a class analysis of the fundamental contradictions in the contemporary world, and is

directed against the counter-revolutionary global strategy of U.S. imperialism.

This general line is one of forming a broad united front, with the socialist camp and the international proletariat as its nucleus, to oppose the imperialists and reactionaries headed by the United States; it is a line of boldly arousing the masses, expanding the revolutionary forces, winning over the middle forces and isolating the reactionary forces.

This general line is one of resolute revolutionary struggle by the people of all countries and of carrying the proletarian world revolution forward to the end; it is the line that most effectively combats imperialism and defends world peace.

If the general line of the international Communist movement is one-sidedly reduced to "peaceful coexistence," "peaceful competition," and "peaceful transition," this is to violate the revolutionary principles of the 1957 Declaration and the 1960 Statement, to discard the historical mission of proletarian world revolution, and to depart from the revolutionary teachings of Marxism-Leninism. . . .

(4) In defining the general line of the international Communist movement, the starting point is the concrete class analysis of world politics and economics as a whole and of actual world conditions, that is to say, of the fundamental contradictions in the contemporary world.

If one avoids a concrete class analysis, seizes at random on certain superficial phenomena, and draws subjective and groundless conclusions, one cannot possibly reach correct conclusions with regard to the general line of the international Communist movement but will inevitably slide on to a track entirely different from that of Marxism-Leninism.

What are the fundamental contradictions in the contemporary world? Marxist-Leninists consistently hold that they are:

> the contradiction between the socialist camp and the imperialist camp;
> the contradiction between the proletariat and the bourgeoisie in the capitalist countries;
> the contradiction between the oppressed nations and imperialism; and
> the contradictions among imperialist countries and among monopoly capitalist groups.

The contradiction between the socialist camp and the imperialist camp is a contradiction between two fundamentally different social systems, socialism and capitalism. It is undoubtedly very sharp. But Marxist-Leninists must not regard the contradictions in the world as consisting solely and simply of the contradiction between the socialist camp and the imperialist camp.

The international balance of forces has changed and has become increasingly favorable to socialism and to all the oppressed peoples and nations of the world, and most unfavorable to imperialism and the reactionaries of all countries. Nevertheless, the contradictions enumerated above still objectively exist.

These contradictions and the struggles to which they give rise are interrelated and influence each other. Nobody can obliterate any of these fundamental contradictions or subjectively substitute one for all the rest.

It is inevitable that these contradictions will give rise to popular revolutions, which alone can resolve them.

(5) The following erroneous views should be repudiated on the question of the fundamental contradictions in the contemporary world:

(a) the view which blots out the class content of the contradiction between the socialist and the imperialist camps and fails to see this contradiction as one between states under the dictatorship of the proletariat and states under the dictatorship of the monopoly capitalists;

(b) the view which recognizes only the contradiction between the socialist and the imperialist camps while neglecting or underestimating the contradictions between the proletariat and the bourgeoisie in the capitalist world, between the oppressed nations and imperialism, among the imperialist countries and among the monopoly capitalist groups, and the struggles to which these contradictions give rise;

(c) the view which maintains with regard to the capitalist world that the contradiction between the proletariat and the bourgeoisie can be resolved without a proletarian revolution in each country and that the contradiction between the oppressed nations and imperialism can be resolved without revolution by the oppressed nations;

(d) the view which denies that the development of the

inherent contradictions in the contemporary capitalist world inevitably leads to a new situation in which the imperialist countries are locked in an intense struggle, and asserts that the contradictions among the imperialist countries can be reconciled, or even eliminated, by "international agreements among the big monopolies"; and

(e) the view which maintains that the contradiction between the two world systems of socialism and capitalism will automatically disappear in the course of "economic competition," that the other fundamental world contradictions will automatically do so with the disappearance of the contradiction between the two systems, and that a "world without wars," a new world of "all-round cooperation," will appear.

It is obvious that these erroneous views inevitably lead to erroneous and harmful policies and hence to setbacks and losses of one kind or another to the cause of the people and of socialism.

(6) The balance of forces between imperialism and socialism has undergone a fundamental change since World War II. The main indication of this change is that the world now has not just one socialist country but a number of socialist countries forming the mighty socialist camp, and that the people who have taken the socialist road now number not two hundred million but a thousand million, or a third of the world's population. . . .

The question of what is the correct attitude toward the socialist camp is a most important question of principle confronting all Communist and Workers' Parties.

It is under new historical conditions that the Communist and Workers' Parties are now carrying on the task of proletarian internationalist unity and struggle. When only one socialist country existed and when this country was faced with hostility and jeopardized by all the imperialists and reactionaries because it firmly pursued the correct Marxist-Leninist line and policies, the touchstone of proletarian internationalism for every Communist Party was whether or not it resolutely defended the only socialist country. Now there is a socialist camp consisting of thirteen countries, Albania, Bulgaria, China, Cuba, Czecho-slovakia, the German Democratic Republic, Hungary, the Democratic People's Republic of Korea, Mongolia, Poland, Rumania, the Soviet Union, and the Democratic Republic of Vietnam. Under these circumstances, the touchstone of proletarian internationalism for every Communist Party is whether or not it resolutely defends the whole of the socialist camp, whether or not it defends the unity of all the countries in the camp on the basis of Marxism-Leninism and whether or not it defends the Marxist-Leninist line and policies which the socialist countries ought to pursue.

If anybody does not pursue the correct Marxist-Leninist line and policies, does not defend the unity of the socialist camp but on the contrary creates tension and splits within it, or even follows the policies of the Yugoslav revisionists, tries to liquidate the socialist camp or helps capitalist countries to attack fraternal socialist countries, then he is betraying the interests of the entire international proletariat and the people of the world.

If anybody, following in the footsteps of others, defends the erroneous opportunist line and policies pursued by a certain socialist country instead of upholding the correct Marxist-Leninist line and policies which the socialist countries ought to pursue, defends the policy of split instead of upholding the policy of unity, then he is departing from Marxism-Leninism and proletarian internationalism.

(7) Taking advantage of the situation after World War II, the U.S. imperialists stepped into the shoes of the German, Italian, and Japanese fascists, and have been trying to erect a huge world empire such as has never been known before. The strategic objectives of U.S. imperialism have been to grab and dominate the intermediate zone lying between the United States and the socialist camp, put down the revolutions of the oppressed peoples and nations, proceed to destroy the socialist countries, and thus to subject all the peoples and countries of the world, including its allies, to domination and enslavement by U.S. monopoly capital.

Ever since World War II, the U.S. imperialists have been conducting propaganda for war against the Soviet Union and the socialist camp. There are two aspects to this propaganda. While the U.S. imperialists are actually preparing such a war, they also use this propaganda as a smokescreen for their oppression of the American people and for the extension of their aggression against the rest of the capitalist world. . . .

(8) The various types of contradictions in the contemporary world are concentrated in the vast areas of Asia, Africa, and Latin America; these are the most vulnerable areas under imperialist rule and the storm centers of world revolution dealing direct blows at imperialism.

The national democratic revolutionary movement in these areas and the international socialist revolutionary movement are the two great historical currents of our time.

The national democratic revolution in these areas is an important component of the contemporary proletarian world revolution.

The anti-imperialist revolutionary struggles of the people in Asia, Africa, and Latin America are pounding and undermining the foundations of the rule of imperialism and colonialism, old and new, and are now a mighty force in defense of world peace.

In a sense, therefore, the whole cause of the international proletarian revolution hinges on the outcome of the revolutionary struggles of the people of these areas, who constitute the overwhelming majority of the world's population.

Therefore, the anti-imperialist revolutionary struggle of the people in Asia, Africa, and Latin America is definitely not merely a matter of regional significance but one of over-all importance for the whole cause of proletarian world revolution.

Certain persons now go so far as to deny the great international significance of the anti-imperialist revolutionary struggles of the Asian, African, and Latin American peoples and, on the pretext of breaking down the barriers of nationality, color, and geographical location, are trying their best to efface the line of demarcation between oppressed and oppressor nations and between oppressed and oppressor countries and to hold down the revolutionary struggles of the peoples in these areas. In fact, they cater to the needs of imperialism and create a new "theory" to justify the rule of imperialism in these areas and the promotion of its policies of old and new colonialism. Actually, this "theory" seeks not to break down the barriers of nationality, color, and geographical location but to maintain the rule of the "superior nations" over the oppressed nations. It is only natural that this fraudulent "theory" is rejected by the people in these areas. . . .

The attitude taken toward the revolutionary struggles of the people in the Asian, African, and Latin American countries is an important criterion for differentiating those who want revolution from those who do not and those who are truly defending world peace from those who are abetting the forces of aggression and war.

(9) The oppressed nations and peoples of Asia, Africa, and Latin America are faced with the urgent task of fighting imperialism and its lackeys.

History has entrusted to the proletarian parties in these areas the glorious mission of holding high the banner of struggle against imperialism, against old and new colonialism and for national independence and people's democracy, of standing in the forefront of the national democratic revolutionary movement and striving for a socialist future.

In these areas, extremely broad sections of the population refuse to be slaves of imperialism. They include not only the workers, peasants, intellectuals, and petty bourgeoisie, but also the patriotic national bourgeoisie and even certain kings, princes, and aristocrats who are patriotic.

The proletariat and its party must have confidence in the strength of the masses and, above all, must unite with the peasants and establish a solid worker-peasant alliance. It is of primary importance for advanced members of the proletariat to work in the rural areas, help the peasants to get organized, and raise their class consciousness and their national self-respect and self-confidence.

On the basis of the worker-peasant alliance the proletariat and its party must unite all the strata that can be united and organize a broad united front against imperialism and its lackeys. In order to consolidate and expand this united front it is necessary that the proletarian party should maintain its ideological, political, and organizational independence and insist on the leadership of the Revolution.

The proletarian party and the revolutionary people must learn to master all forms of struggle, including armed struggle.

They must defeat counter-revolutionary armed force with revolutionary armed force whenever imperialism and its lackeys resort to armed suppression. . . .

(10) In the imperialist and the capitalist countries, the proletarian revolution and the dictatorship of the proletariat are essential for the thorough resolution of the contradictions of capitalist society.

In striving to accomplish this task the proletarian party must under the present circumstances actively lead the working class and the working people in struggles to oppose monopoly capital, to defend democratic rights, to oppose the menace of fascism, to improve living conditions, to oppose imperialist arms expansion and war preparations, to defend world peace and actively to support the revolutionary struggles of the oppressed nations.

In the capitalist countries which U.S. imperialism controls or is trying to control, the working class and the people should direct their attacks mainly against U.S. imperialism, but also against their own monopoly capitalists and other reactionary forces who are betraying the national interests.

Large-scale mass struggles in the capitalist countries in recent years have shown that the working class and working people are experiencing a new awakening. Their struggles, which are dealing blows at monopoly capital and reaction, have opened bright prospects for the revolutionary cause in their own countries and are also a powerful support for the revolutionary struggles of the Asian, African, and Latin American peoples and for the countries of the socialist camp.

The proletarian parties in imperialist or capitalist countries must maintain their own ideological, political, and organizational independence in leading revolutionary struggles. At the same time, they must unite all the forces that can be united and build a broad united front against monopoly capital and against the imperialist policies of aggression and war. . . .

(11) On the question of transition from capitalism to socialism, the proletarian party must proceed from the stand of class struggle and revolution and base itself on the Marxist-Leninist teachings concerning the proletarian revolution and the dictatorship of the proletariat.

Communists would always prefer to bring about the transition to socialism by peaceful means. But can peaceful transition be made into a new worldwide strategic principle for the international Communist movement? Absolutely not.

Marxism-Leninism consistently holds that the fundamental question in all revolutions is that of state power. The 1957 Declaration and the 1960 Statement both clearly point out, "Leninism teaches, and experience confirms, that the ruling classes never relinquish power voluntarily." The old government never topples even in a period of crisis, unless it is pushed. This is a universal law of class struggle.

In specific historical conditions, Marx and Lenin did raise the possibility that revolution may develop peacefully. But, as Lenin pointed out, the peaceful development of revolution is an opportunity "very seldom to be met with in the history of revolution."

As a matter of fact, there is no historical precedent for peaceful transition from capitalism to socialism. . . .

(12) All social revolutions in the various stages of the history of mankind are historically inevitable and are governed by objective laws independent of man's will. Moreover, history shows that there never was a revolution which was able to achieve victory without zigzags and sacrifices.

With Marxist-Leninist theory as the basis, the task of the proletarian party is to analyze the concrete historical conditions, put forward the correct strategy and tactics, and guide the masses in bypassing hidden reefs, avoiding unnecessary sacrifices and reaching the goal step by step. Is it possible to avoid sacrifices altogether? Such is not the case with the slave revolutions, the serf revolutions, the bourgeois revolutions, or the national revolutions; nor is it the case with proletarian revolutions. Even if the guiding line of the revolution is correct, it is impossible to have a sure guarantee against setbacks and sacrifices in the course of the revolution. So long as a correct line is adhered to, the revolution is bound to triumph in the end. To abandon revolution on the pretext of avoiding sacrifices is in reality to demand that the people should forever remain slaves and endure infinite pain and sacrifice. . . .

In the last few years the international Communist movement and the national liberation movement have had many experiences and many lessons. There are experiences which people should praise and there are experiences which make people grieve. Communists and revolutionaries in all countries should ponder and seriously study these experiences of success and failure, so as to draw correct conclusions and useful lessons from them.

(13) The socialist countries and the revolutionary struggles of the oppressed peoples and nations support and assist each other.

The national liberation movements of Asia, Africa, and Latin America and the revolutionary movements of the people in the capitalist countries are a strong support to the socialist countries. It is completely wrong to deny this.

The only attitude for the socialist countries to adopt toward the revolutionary struggles of the oppressed peoples and nations is one of warm sympathy and active support; they must not adopt a perfunctory attitude, or one of national selfishness or of great-power chauvinism. . . .

(14) In the last few years much—in fact a great deal—has been said on the question of war and peace. Our views and policies on this question are known to the world, and no one can distort them.

It is a pity that although certain persons in the international Communist movement talk about how much they love peace and hate war, they are unwilling to acquire even a faint understanding of the simple truth on war pointed out by Lenin. . . .

As Marxist-Leninists see it, war is the continuation of politics by other means, and every war is inseparable from the political system and the political struggles which give rise to it. If one departs from this scientific Marxist-Leninist proposition which has been confirmed by the entire history of class struggle, one will never be able to understand either the question of war or the question of peace.

There are different types of peace and different types of war. Marxist-Leninists must be clear about what type of peace or what type of war is in question. Lumping just wars and unjust wars together and opposing all of them undiscriminatingly is a bourgecis-pacifist and not a Marxist-Leninist approach.

Certain persons say that revolutions are entirely possible without war. Now which type of war are they referring to—is

it a war of national liberation or a revolutionary civil war, or
is it a world war?

If they are referring to a war of national liberation or a
revolutionary civil war, then this formulation is, in effect, opposed to revolutionary wars and to revolution.

If they are referring to a world war, then they are shooting
at a nonexistent target. Although Marxist-Leninists have pointed
out, on the basis of the history of the two world wars, that world
wars inevitably lead to revolution, no Marxist-Leninist ever has
held or ever will hold that revolution must be made through
world war. . . .

In order to overcome the present ideological confusion in
the international working-class movement on the question of
war and peace, we consider that Lenin's thesis, which has been
discarded by the modern revisionists, must be restored in the
interest of combating the imperialist policies of aggression and
war and defending world peace.

The people of the world universally demand the prevention
of a new world war. And it is possible to prevent a new world
war.

The question then is, What is the way to secure world peace?
According to the Leninist viewpoint, world peace can be won
only by the struggles of the people in all countries and not by
begging the imperialists for it. World peace can only be effectively defended by relying on the development of the forces of
the socialist camp, on the revolutionary struggles of the proletariat and working people of all countries, on the liberation
struggles of the oppressed nations and on the struggles of all
peaceloving people and countries.

Such is the Leninist policy. Any policy to the contrary definitely will not lead to world peace but will only encourage the
ambitions of the imperialists and increase the danger of world
war.

In recent years, certain persons have been spreading the
argument that a single spark from a war of national liberation
or from a revolutionary people's war will lead to a world con-
flagration destroying the whole of mankind. What are the facts?
Contrary to what these persons say, the wars of national liberation and the revolutionary people's wars that have occurred since
World War II have not led to world war. The victory of these

revolutionary wars has directly weakened the forces of imperialism and greatly strengthened the forces which prevent the imperialists from launching a world war and which defend world peace. Do not the facts demonstrate the absurdity of this argument?

(15) The complete banning and destruction of nuclear weapons is an important task in the struggle to defend world peace. We must do our utmost to this end.

Nuclear weapons are unprecedentedly destructive, which is why for more than a decade now the U.S. imperialists have been pursuing their policy of nuclear blackmail in order to realize their ambition of enslaving the people of all countries and dominating the world.

But when the imperialists threaten other countries with nuclear weapons, they subject the people in their own country to the same threat, thus arousing them against nuclear weapons and against the imperialist policies of aggression and war. At the same time, in their vain hope of destroying their opponents with nuclear weapons, the imperialists are in fact subjecting themselves to the danger of being destroyed.

The possibility of banning nuclear weapons does indeed exist. However, if the imperialists are forced to accept an agreement to ban nuclear weapons it decidedly will not be because of their "love for humanity" but because of the pressure of the people of all countries and for the sake of their own vital interests.

In contrast to the imperialists, socialist countries rely upon the righteous strength of the people and on their own correct policies, and have no need whatever to gamble with nuclear weapons in the world arena. Socialist countries have nuclear weapons solely in order to defend themselves and to prevent imperialism from launching a nuclear war. . . .

(16) It was Lenin who advanced the thesis that it is possible for the socialist countries to practice peaceful coexistence with the capitalist countries. It is well known that after the great Soviet people had repulsed foreign armed intervention the Communist Party of the Soviet Union and the Soviet Government, led first by Lenin and then by Stalin, consistently pursued the policy of peaceful coexistence and that they were

forced to wage a war of self-defense only when attacked by the German imperialists.

Since its founding, the People's Republic of China too has consistently pursued the policy of peaceful coexistence with countries having different social systems, and it is China which initiated the Five Principles of Peaceful Coexistence. . . .

In our view, the general line of the foreign policy of the socialist countries should have the following content: to develop relations of friendship, mutual assistance, and cooperation among the countries in the socialist camp in accordance with the principle of proletarian internationalism; to strive for peaceful coexistence on the basis of the Five Principles with countries having different social systems and oppose the imperialist policies of aggression and war; and to support and assist the revolutionary struggles of all the oppressed peoples and nations. These three aspects are interrelated and indivisible, and not a single one can be omitted.

(17) For a very long historical period after the proletariat takes power, class struggle continues as an objective law independent of man's will, differing only in form from what it was before the taking of power. . . .

To deny the existence of class struggle in the period of the dictatorship of the proletariat and the necessity of thoroughly completing the socialist revolution on the economic, political, and ideological fronts is wrong, does not correspond to objective reality and violates Marxism-Leninism.

(18) Both Marx and Lenin maintained that the entire period before the advent of the higher stage of communist society is the period of transition from capitalism to communism, the period of the dictatorship of the proletariat. In this transition period, the dictatorship of the proletariat, that is to say, the proletarian state, goes through the dialectical process of establishment, consolidation, strengthening and withering away. . . .

When we look at the economic base of any socialist society, we find that the difference between ownership by the whole people and collective ownership exists in all socialist countries without exception, and that there is individual ownership too. Ownership by the whole people and collective ownership are two kinds of ownership and two kinds of relations of production in socialist society. The workers in enterprises owned by the whole people and the peasants on farms owned collectively belong to two different categories of laborers in socialist society. Therefore, the class difference between worker and peasant exists in all socialist countries without exception. This difference will not disappear until the transition to the higher stage of communism is achieved. In their present level of economic development all socialist countries are still far, far removed from the higher stage of communism in which "from each according to his ability, to each according to his needs" is put into practice. Therefore, it will take a long, long time to eliminate the class difference between worker and peasant. And until this difference is eliminated, it is impossible to say that society is classless or that there is no longer any need for the dictatorship of the proletariat.

In calling a socialist state the "state of the whole people," is one trying to replace the Marxist-Leninist theory of the state by the bourgeois theory of the state? Is one trying to replace the state of the dictatorship of the proletariat by a state of a different character?

If that is the case, it is nothing but a great historical retrogression. The degeneration of the social system in Yugoslavia is a grave lesson.

(19) Leninism holds that the proletarian party must exist together with the dictatorship of the proletariat in socialist countries. The party of the proletariat is indispensable for the entire historical period of the dictatorship of the proletariat. The reason is that the dictatorship of the proletariat has to struggle against the enemies of the proletariat and of the people, remold the peasants and other small producers, constantly consolidate the proletarian ranks, build socialism and effect the transition to communism; none of these things can be done without the leadership of the party of the proletariat.

Can there be a "party of the entire people"? Is it possible to replace the Party which is the vanguard of the proletariat by a "party of the entire people"?

This, too, is not a question about the internal affairs of any particular party, but a fundamental problem involving the universal truth of Marxism-Leninism.

In the view of Marxist-Leninists, there is no such thing as a non-class or supra-class political party. All political parties have a class character. Party spirit is the concentrated expression of class character.

The party of the proletariat is the only party able to represent the interests of the whole people. It can do so precisely because it represents the interests of the proletariat, whose ideas and will it concentrates. It can lead the whole people because the proletariat can finally emancipate itself only with the emancipation of all mankind, because the very nature of the proletariat enables its party to approach problems in terms of its present and future interests, because the party is boundlessly loyal to the people and has the spirit of self-sacrifice; hence its democratic centralism and iron discipline. Without such a party, it is impossible to maintain the dictatorship of the proletariat and to represent the interests of the whole people. . . .

(20) Over the past few years, certain persons have violated Lenin's integral teachings about the interrelationship of leaders, party, class, and masses, and raised the issue of "combating the cult of the individual"; this is erroneous and harmful.

The theory propounded by Lenin is as follows:

(a) The masses are divided into classes;

(b) Classes are usually led by political parties;

(c) Political parties, as a general rule, are directed by more or less stable groups composed of the most authoritative, influential, and experienced members, who are elected to the most responsible positions and are called leaders.

Lenin said, "All this is elementary." . . .

The Communist Party of China has always disapproved of exaggerating the role of the individual, has advocated and persistently practiced democratic centralism within the Party and advocated the linking of the leadership with the masses, maintaining that correct leadership must know how to concentrate the views of the masses.

While loudly combating the so-called cult of the individual, certain persons are in reality doing their best to defame the proletarian party and the dictatorship of the proletariat. At the same time, they are enormously exaggerating the role of certain individuals, shifting all errors on to others and claiming all credit for themselves.

What is more serious is that, under the pretext of "combating the cult of the individual," certain persons are crudely interfering in the internal affairs of other fraternal parties and fraternal countries and forcing other fraternal parties to change their leadership in order to impose their own wrong line on these parties. What is all this if not great-power chauvinism, sectarianism, and splitism? What is all this if not subversion?

It is high time to propagate seriously and comprehensively Lenin's integral teachings on the interrelationship of leaders, party, class, and masses.

(21) Relations between socialist countries are international relations of a new type. Relations between socialist countries, whether large or small, and whether more developed or less developed economically, must be based on the principles of complete equality, respect for territorial integrity, sovereignty and independence, and non-interference in each other's internal affairs, and must also be based on the principles of mutual support and mutual assistance in accordance with proletarian internationalism.

Every socialist country must rely mainly on itself for its construction.

In accordance with its own concrete conditions, every socialist country must rely first of all on the diligent labor and talents of its own people, utilize all its available resources fully and in a planned way, and bring all its potential into play in socialist construction. Only thus can it build socialism effectively and develop its economy speedily.

This is the only way for each socialist country to strengthen the might of the entire socialist camp and enhance its capacity to assist the revolutionary cause of the international proletariat. Therefore, to observe the principle of mainly relying on oneself in construction is to apply proletarian internationalism concretely. . . .

In relations among socialist countries it would be preposterous to follow the practice of gaining profit for oneself at the expense of others, a practice characteristic of relations among capitalist countries, or go so far as to take the "economic integration" and the "common market," which monopoly capitalist groups have instituted for the purpose of seizing markets and grabbing profits, as examples which socialist countries ought to follow in their economic cooperation and mutual assistance.

(22) The 1957 Declaration and the 1960 Statement lay down the principles guiding relations among fraternal Parties. These are the principle of solidarity, the principle of mutual support and mutual assistance, the principle of independence and equality and the principle of reaching unanimity through consultation—all on the basis of Marxism-Leninism and proletarian internationalism.

We note that in its letter of March 30 the Central Committee of the CPSU says that there are no "superior" and "subordinate" Parties in the Communist movement, that all Communist Parties are independent and equal, and that they should all build their relations on the basis of proletarian internationalism and mutual assistance.

It is a fine quality of Communists that their deeds are consistent with their words. The only correct way to safeguard and strengthen unity among the fraternal Parties is genuinely to adhere to, and not to violate, the principle of proletarian internationalism and genuinely to observe, and not to undermine, the principles guiding relations among fraternal Parties—and to do so not only in words but, much more important, in deeds.

If the principle of independence and equality is accepted in relations among fraternal Parties, then it is impermissible for any Party to place itself above others, to interfere in their internal affairs, and to adopt patriarchal ways in relations with them.

If it is accepted that there are no "superiors" and "subordinates" in relations among fraternal Parties, then it is impermissible to impose the program, resolutions, and line of one's own Party on other fraternal Parties as the "common program" of the international Communist movement.

If the principle of reaching unanimity through consultation is accepted in relations among fraternal Parties, then one should not emphasize "who is in the majority" or "who is in the minority" and bank on a so-called majority in order to force through one's own erroneous line and carry out sectarian and splitting policies.

If it is agreed that differences between fraternal Parties

should be settled through inter-Party consultation, then other fraternal Parties should not be attacked publicly and by name at one's own congress or at other Party congresses, in speeches by Party leaders, resolutions, statements, etc.; and still less should the ideological differences among fraternal Parties be extended into the sphere of state relations.

We hold that in the present circumstances, when there are differences in the international Communist movement, it is particularly important to stress strict adherence to the principles guiding relations among fraternal Parties as laid down in the Declaration and the Statement. . . .

(23) In order to carry out the common program of the international Communist movement unanimously agreed upon by the fraternal Parties, an uncompromising struggle must be waged against all forms of opportunism, which is a deviation from Marxism-Leninism. . . .

Over the past few years, the revisionist trend flooding the international working-class movement and the many experiences and lessons of the international Communist movement have fully confirmed the correctness of the conclusion in the Declaration and the Statement that revisionism is the main danger in the international Communist movement at present.

However, certain persons are openly saying that dogmatism and not revisionism is the main danger, or that dogmatism is no less dangerous than revisionism, etc. What sort of principle underlies all this?

Firm Marxist-Leninists and genuine Marxist-Leninist parties must put principles first. They must not barter away principles, approving one thing today and another tomorrow, advocating one thing today and another tomorrow.

Together with all Marxist-Leninists, the Chinese Communists will continue to wage an uncompromising struggle against modern revisionism in order to defend the purity of Marxism-Leninism and the principled stand of the Declaration and the Statement.

While combating revisionism, which is the main danger in the international Communist movement, Communists must also combat dogmatism. . . .

(24) A most important lesson from the experience of

the international Communist movement is that the development and victory of a revolution depend on the existence of a revolutionary proletarian party.

There must be a revolutionary party.

There must be a revolutionary party built according to the revolutionary theory and revolutionary style of Marxism-Leninism.

There must be a revolutionary party able to integrate the universal truth of Marxism-Leninism with the concrete practice of the revolution in its own country.

There must be a revolutionary party able to link the leadership closely with the broad masses of the people.

There must be a revolutionary party that perseveres in the truth, corrects its errors and knows how to conduct criticism and self-criticism.

Only such a revolutionary party can lead the proletariat and the broad masses of the people in defeating imperialism and its lackeys, winning a thorough victory in the national democratic revolution and winning the socialist revolution.

If a party is not a proletarian revolutionary party but a bourgeois reformist party;

If it is not a Marxist-Leninist party but a revisionist party;

If it is not a vanguard party of the proletariat but a party tailing after the bourgeoisie;

If it is not a party representing the interests of the proletariat and all the working people but a party representing the interests of the labor aristocracy;

If it is not an internationalist party but a nationalist party;

If it is not a party that can use its brains to think for itself and acquire an accurate knowledge of the trends of the different classes in its own country through serious investigation and study, and knows how to apply the universal truth of Marxism-Leninism and integrate it with the concrete practice of its own country, but instead is a party that parrots the words of others, copies foreign experience without analysis, runs hither and thither in response to the baton of certain persons abroad, and has become a hodgepodge of revisionism, dogmatism, and everything but Marxist-Leninist principle;

Then such a party is absolutely incapable of leading the proletariat and the masses in revolutionary struggle, absolutely incapable of winning the Revolution, and absolutely incapable of fulfilling the great historical mission of the proletariat.

This is a question all Marxist-Leninists, all class-conscious workers and all progressive people everywhere need to ponder deeply.

(25) It is the duty of Marxist-Leninists to distinguish between truth and falsehood with respect to the differences that have arisen in the international Communist movement. In the common interest of the unity for struggle against the enemy, we have always advocated solving problems through inter-Party consultations and opposed bringing differences into the open before the enemy.

As the comrades of the CPSU know, the public polemics in the international Communist movement have been provoked by certain fraternal Party leaders and forced on us.

Since a public debate has been provoked, it ought to be conducted on the basis of equality among fraternal Parties and of democracy, and by presenting the facts and reasoning things out.

Since certain Party leaders have publicly attacked other fraternal Parties and provoked a public debate, it is our opinion that they have no reason or right to forbid the fraternal Parties attacked to make public replies.

Since certain Party leaders have published innumerable articles attacking other fraternal Parties, why do they not publish in their own press the articles those parties have written in reply? . . .

We hope that the public debate among fraternal Parties can be stopped. This is a problem that has to be dealt with in accordance with the principles of independence, of equality and of reaching unanimity through consultation among fraternal Parties. In the international Communist movement, no one has the right to launch attacks whenever he wants, or to order the "ending of open polemics" whenever he wants to prevent the other side from replying.

It is known to the comrades of the CPSU that in order to create a favorable atmosphere for convening the meeting of the fraternal Parties, we have decided temporarily to suspend, as from March 9, 1963, public replies to the public attacks directed by name against us by comrades of fraternal Parties. We reserve the right of public reply.

In our letter of March 9, we said that on the question of suspending public debate "it is necessary that our two Parties and the fraternal Parties concerned should have some discussion and reach an agreement that is fair and acceptable to all."

The foregoing are our views regarding the general line of the international Communist movement and some related questions of principle. We hope, as we indicated at the beginning of this letter, that the frank presentation of our views will be conducive to mutual understanding. Of course, comrades may agree or disagree with these views. But in our opinion, the questions we discuss here are the crucial questions calling for attention and solution by the international Communist movement. We hope that all these questions and also those raised in your letter will be fully discussed in the talks between our two Parties and at the meeting of representatives of all the fraternal Parties. . . .

We hope that events which grieve those near and dear to us and only gladden the enemy will not recur in the international Communist movement in the future.

The Chinese Communists firmly believe that the Marxist-Leninists, the proletariat, and the revolutionary people everywhere will unite more closely, overcome all difficulties and obstacles and win still greater victories in the struggle against imperialism and for world peace, and in the fight for the revolutionary cause of the people of the world and the cause of international communism.

Workers of all countries, unite! Workers and oppressed peoples and nations of the world, unite! Oppose our common enemy!

With communist greetings,

The Central Committee of the Communist Party of China

LIU SHAO-CH'I *

From *How To Be a Good Communist*

WHY COMMUNISTS MUST
UNDERTAKE SELF-CULTIVATION

Why must Communists undertake to cultivate themselves?

In order to live, man must wage a struggle against nature and make use of nature to produce material values. At all times and under all conditions, his production of material things is social in character. It follows that when men engage in production at any stage of social development, they have to enter into certain relations of production with one another. In their ceaseless struggle against nature, men ceaselessly change nature and simultaneously change themselves and their mutual relations. Men themselves, their social relations, their forms of social organization, and their consciousness change and progress continuously in the long struggle which as social beings they wage against nature. In ancient times, man's mode of life, social organization, and consciousness were all different from what they are today, and in the future they will again be different.

Mankind and human society are in process of historical development. When human society reached a certain historical stage, classes and class struggle emerged. Every member of a class society exists as a member of a given class and lives in given conditions of class struggle. Man's social being determines his consciousness. In class society the ideology of the members of each class reflects a different class position and different class interests. The class struggle constantly goes on among these classes with their different positions, interests, and ideologies. Thus it is not only in the struggle against nature but

* Liu Shao-ch'i, *How To Be a Good Communist* (Peking: Foreign Languages Press, 1964), pp. 1–9, 45–47.

in the struggle of social classes that men change nature, change society and at the same time change themselves.

Marx and Engels said:

> Both for the production on a mass scale of this communist consciousness, and for the success of the cause itself, the alteration of men on a mass scale is necessary, an alteration which can only take place in a practical movement, a *revolution;* this revolution is necessary, therefore, not only because the ruling class cannot be overthrown in any other way, but also because the class *overthrowing* it can only in a revolution succeed in ridding itself of all the muck of ages and become fitted to found society anew.

That is to say, the proletariat must consciously go through long periods of social revolutionary struggles and, in such struggles, change society and change itself.

We should therefore see ourselves as in need of change and capable of being changed. We should not look upon ourselves as immutable, perfect and sacrosanct, as persons who need not and cannot be changed. When we pose the task of remolding ourselves in social struggle, we are not demeaning ourselves; the objective laws of social development demand it. Unless we do so, we cannot make progress, nor fulfill the task of changing society.

We Communists are the most advanced revolutionaries in modern history; today the changing of society and the world rests upon us and we are the driving force in this change. It is by unremitting struggle against counter-revolutionaries and reformists that we Communists change society and the world, and at the same time change ourselves.

When we say that Communists must remold themselves by waging struggles in every sphere against the counter-revolutionaries and reformists, we mean that it is through such struggles that they must seek to make progress, and must enhance their revolutionary quality and ability. An immature revolutionary has to go through a long process of revolutionary tempering and self-cultivation, a long process of remolding, before he can become a mature and seasoned revolutionary who can grasp and skillfully apply the laws of revolution. For in the first place a comparatively immature revolutionary, born and bred in the old society, carries with him remnants of the various ideologies of that society (including its prejudices, habits, and traditions), and in the second he has not been through a long period of revolutionary activity. Therefore he does not yet have a really thorough understanding of the enemy, of ourselves, or of the laws of social development and revolutionary struggle. In order to change this state of affairs, besides learning from past revolutionary experience (the practice of our predecessors), he must himself participate in contemporary revolutionary practice, and in this revolutionary practice and the struggle against all kinds of counter-revolutionaries and reformists, he must bring his conscious activity into full play and work hard at study and self-cultivation. Only so can he gradually acquire deeper experience and knowledge of the laws of social development and revolutionary struggle, acquire a really thorough understanding of the enemy and ourselves, discover and correct his wrong ideas, habits and prejudices, and thus raise the level of his political consciousness, cultivate his revolutionary qualities and improve his revolutionary methods.

Hence, in order to remold himself and raise his own level, a revolutionary must take part in revolutionary practice from which he must on no account isolate himself. He cannot do so, moreover, without subjective effort, without self-cultivation and study, in the course of practice. Otherwise, it will still be impossible for him to make progress.

For example, several Communists take part in a revolutionary mass struggle together and engage in revolutionary practice under roughly the same circumstances and conditions. It is possible that the effect of the struggle on these Party members will not be at all uniform. Some will make very rapid progress and some who used to lag behind will even forge ahead of others. Other Party members will advance very slowly. Still others will waver in the struggle, and instead of being pushed forward by revolutionary practice will fall behind. Why?

Or take another example. Many members of our Party were on the Long March; it was a severe process of tempering for them, and the overwhelming majority made very great progress indeed. But the Long March had the opposite effect on certain individuals in the Party. After having been on the Long

March they began to shrink before such arduous struggles, and some of them even planned to back out or run away and later, succumbing to outside allurements, actually deserted the revolutionary ranks. Many Party members took part in the Long March together, and yet its impact and results varied very greatly. Again, why?

Basically speaking, these phenomena are reflections in our revolutionary ranks of the class struggle in society. Our Party members differ in quality because they differ in social background and have come under different social influences. They differ in their attitude, stand, and comprehension in relation to revolutionary practice, and consequently they develop in different directions in the course of revolutionary practice. This can clearly be seen in your Institute as well. You all receive the same education and training here, and yet because you differ in quality and experience, in degree of effort and self-cultivation, you may obtain different or even contrary results. Hence, subjective effort and self-cultivation in the course of revolutionary struggle are absolutely essential, indeed indispensable, for a revolutionary in remolding himself and raising his own level.

Whether he joined the Revolution long ago or recently, every Communist who wants to become a good, politically mature revolutionary must undergo a long period of tempering in revolutionary struggle, must steel himself in mass revolutionary struggles and all kinds of difficulties and hardships, must sum up the experience gained through practice, make great efforts in self-cultivation, raise his ideological level, heighten his ability and never lose his sense of what is new. For only thus can he turn himself into a politically staunch revolutionary of high quality.

Confucius said, "At fifteen, my mind was bent on learning. At thirty, I could think for myself. At forty, I was no longer perplexed. At fifty, I knew the decree of Heaven. At sixty, my ear was attuned to the truth. At seventy, I can follow my heart's desire, without transgressing what is right." Here the feudal philosopher was referring to his own process of self-cultivation; he did not consider himself to have been born a "sage."

Mencius, another feudal philosopher, said that no one had

fulfilled "a great mission" and played a role in history without first undergoing a hard process of tempering, a process which "exercises his mind with suffering and toughens his sinews and bones with toil, exposes his body to hunger, subjects him to extreme poverty, thwarts his undertakings, and thereby stimulates his mind, tempers his character, and adds to his capacities." Still more so must Communists give attention to tempering and cultivating themselves in revolutionary struggles, since they have the historically unprecedented "great mission" of changing the world.

Our Communist self-cultivation is the kind essential to proletarian revolutionaries. It must not be divorced from revolutionary practice or from the actual revolutionary movements of the laboring masses, and especially of the proletarian masses. Comrade Mao Tse-tung has said:

> Discover the truth through practice; and again through practice verify and develop the truth. Start from perceptual knowledge and actively develop it into rational knowledge; then start from rational knowledge and actively guide revolutionary practice to change both the subjective and the objective world. Practice, knowledge, again practice, and again knowledge. This form repeats itself in endless cycles, and with each cycle the content of practice and knowledge rises to a higher level. Such is the whole of the dialectical materialist theory of knowledge, and such is the dialectical materialist theory of the unity of knowing and doing.

Our Party members should temper themselves and intensify their self-cultivation not only in the hardships, difficulties and reverses of revolutionary practice, but also in the course of smooth, successful, and victorious revolutionary practice. Some members of our Party cannot withstand the plaudits of success and victory; they let victories turn their heads, become brazen, arrogant, and bureaucratic and may even vacillate, degenerate, and become corrupted, completely losing their original revolutionary quality. Individual instances of this kind are not uncommon among our Party members. The existence of such a phenomenon in the Party calls for our comrades' sharp attention.

In past ages, before proletarian revolutionaries appeared

on the scene, practically all revolutionaries became corrupted and degenerated with the achievement of victory. They lost their original revolutionary spirit and became obstacles to the further development of the revolution. In the past hundred years of China's history, or to speak of more recent times, in the past fifty years, we have seen that many bourgeois and petty-bourgeois revolutionaries became corrupted and degenerated after gaining some success and climbing to power. This was determined by the class basis of revolutionaries in the past and by the nature of earlier revolutions. Before the Great October Socialist Revolution in Russia, all revolutions throughout history invariably ended in the supersession of the rule of one exploiting class by that of another. Thus, once they themselves became the ruling class, these revolutionaries lost their revolutionary quality and turned around to oppress the exploited masses; this was an inexorable law.

But such can never be the case with the proletarian revolution and with the Communist Party. The proletarian revolution is a revolution to abolish all exploitation, oppression, and classes. The Communist Party represents the proletariat which is itself exploited but does not exploit others, and it can therefore carry the Revolution through to the end, finally abolish all exploitation and sweep away all the corruption and rottenness in human society. The proletariat is able to build a strictly organized and disciplined party and set up a centralized and at the same time democratic state apparatus; and through the Party and this state apparatus, it is able to lead the masses of the people in waging unrelenting struggle against all corruption and rottenness and in ceaselessly weeding out of the Party and the state organs all those elements that have become corrupt and degenerate (whatever high office they may hold), thereby preserving the purity of the Party and the state apparatus. This outstanding feature of the proletarian revolution and of the proletarian revolutionary party did not and could not exist in earlier revolutions and revolutionary parties. Members of our Party must be clear on this point, and—particularly when the Revolution is successful and victorious and when they themselves enjoy the ever greater confidence and support of the masses—they must sharpen their vigilance, intensify their self-cultivation in proletarian ideology and always preserve their pure proletarian revolutionary character so that they will not fall into the rut of earlier revolutionaries who degenerated in the hour of success.

Tempering and self-cultivation in revolutionary practice and tempering and self-cultivation in proletarian ideology are important for every Communist, especially after the seizure of political power. The Communist Party did not drop from heaven but was born out of Chinese society. Every member of the Communist Party has come from this society, is living in it today, and is constantly exposed to all its evils. It is not surprising then that Communists, whether they are of proletarian or non-proletarian origin and whether they are old or new members of the Party, should carry with them to a greater or lesser extent the thinking and habits of the old society. In order to preserve our purity as vanguard fighters of the proletariat and to enhance our revolutionary quality and working ability, it is essential for every Communist to work hard to temper and cultivate himself in every respect. . . .

A PARTY MEMBER'S PERSONAL INTERESTS MUST BE UNCONDITIONALLY SUBORDINATED TO THE INTERESTS OF THE PARTY

Personal interests must be subordinated to the Party's interests, the interests of the local Party organization to those of the entire Party, the interests of the part to those of the whole, and temporary to long-term interests. This is a Marxist-Leninist principle which must be followed by every Communist.

A Communist must be clear about the correct relationship between personal and Party interests.

The Communist Party is the political party of the proletariat and has no interests of its own other than those of the emancipation of the proletariat. The final emancipation of the proletariat will also inevitably be the final emancipation of all mankind. Unless the proletariat emancipates all working people and all nations—unless it emancipates mankind as a whole —it cannot fully emancipate itself. The cause of the emancipation of the proletariat is identical with and inseparable from the cause of the emancipation of all working people, all oppressed nations, and all mankind. Therefore, the interests of the Communist Party are the emancipation of the proletariat and of all mankind, are communism and social progress. When a Party member's personal interests are subordinated to those of the Party, they are subordinated to the interests of the emancipation of the class and the nation, and those of communism and social progress.

Comrade Mao Tse-tung has said:

> At no time and in no circumstances should a Communist place his personal interests first; he should subordinate them to the interests of the nation and of the masses of the people. Hence, selfishness, slacking, corruption, striving for the limelight, etc., are most contemptible, while selflessness, working with all one's energy, wholehearted devotion to public duty, and quiet hard work are the qualities that command respect.

The test of a Party member's loyalty to the Party, the Revolution, and the cause of Communism is whether or not he can subordinate his personal interests absolutely and unconditionally to the interests of the Party, whatever the circumstances.

At all times and on all questions, a Party member should give first consideration to the interests of the Party as a whole, and put them in the forefront and place personal matters and interests second. The supremacy of the Party's interests is the highest principle that must govern the thinking and actions of the members of our Party. In accordance with this principle, every Party member must completely identify his personal interests with those of the Party both in his thinking and in his actions. He must be able to yield to the interests of the Party without any hesitation or reluctance and sacrifice his personal interests whenever the two are at variance. Unhesitating readiness to sacrifice personal interests, and even one's life, for the Party and the proletariat and for the emancipation of the nation and of all mankind—this is one expression of what we usually describe as "Party spirit," "Party sense" or "sense of organization." It is the highest expression of Communist morality, of the principled nature of the party of the proletariat, and of the purest proletarian class consciousness.

Members of our Party should not have personal aims which

are independent of the Party's interests. Their personal aims must harmonize with the Party's interests. If the aim they set themselves is to study Marxist-Leninist theory, to develop their ability in work, to establish revolutionary organizations, and to lead the masses in successful revolutionary struggles—if their aim is to do more for the Party—then this personal aim harmonizes with the interests of the Party. The Party needs many such members and cadres. Apart from this aim, Party members should have no independent personal motives such as attaining position or fame, or playing the individual hero, otherwise they will depart from the interests of the Party and may even become careerists within the Party. . . .

Mao Tse-tung

DESPITE THE concern of Western social science with the impersonal aspects of power and the Marxist denial that personality plays any role in social power, many modern movements and nations have been led and shaped by great men. Perhaps the French intellectual Amaury de Riencourt is right when he claims that "as society becomes more equalitarian, it tends increasingly to concentrate absolute power in the hands of one single man." We might add that as societies, and particularly their governments, become more highly organized, the power to shape policy, set forth goals, and make awesome decisions tends to become concentrated in the hands of one individual. This has been particularly true of China. The figure and personality of Mao Tse-tung has dominated Chinese Communism from the late 1920s to the present.

Both Westerners and Chinese have always been deeply concerned with the personalities of great men. Biography is a favored vehicle of Western literature; it is not uncommon for Chinese to spend entire evenings dissecting the qualities of individuals, both great and small, familiar and unfamiliar. A common tradition in Chinese plays is to stereotype people as ambitious, clever, arrogant, wise, and so on. The stereotypic conception of men from Hunan, Mao's native province, is that they are hot-tempered, emotional, militaristic, heroic, upright, and unyielding (Wolfram Eberhard, "Chinese Regional Stereotypes," *Asian Survey,* 12 [December 1965], 605). Such characterizations would seem to apply to Mao, whose temper and disinclination to yield to Soviet pressure have been evident in the Sino-Soviet dispute. Mao's capacity as a soldier and his ability to withstand hardship are known from his days in Kiangsi and

Yenan. Mao, like many Chinese, has an extraordinary gift for maintaining personal friendships, including some with foreigners. From those who have known him and from his poetry we get the impression of a man whose feelings surface easily; laughter and anger are quick in his relations with other people. Yet the man's character, formed in a Hunan peasant village and later in Hunan schools, tells us little about his greatness and personal role in Chinese Communism. The two following selections portray Mao Tse-tung through the eyes of two Western journalists who have spoken with him at length.

Mao was born on December 26, 1893, in a Hunan peasant village. Until 1918, when he graduated from the Changsha Normal School, he had never been out of his native province. Though a provincial, he read widely in the literature of the West, like so many of his contemporaries who, in the early twentieth century, were beginning to break out of China's traditional intellectual isolation. In Peking, an impoverished intellectual, he worked in the Peking University library. In 1921 he became one of the founding members—though far from the leading one—of the Chinese Communist Party. Until the White Terror of April 1927 he spent much of his time organizing in Hunan, editing Kuomintang political publications, and giving advice as a regional specialist to Kuomintang and Communists alike. His chance for leadership came in the spring of 1927 when he joined with Chu Teh to form the Red Army. From the mountains of Kiangsi and Hunan he led the formation of the Chinese Soviet Republic. By 1935 he had weathered all challenges to his leadership and become the undisputed leader of Chinese Communism. For the subsequent period Edgar Snow, novelist, journalist, biographer, and personal friend of Mao, and author of the classic *Red Star Over China,* states in that work (p. 175):

> Mao Tse-tung's account had begun to pass out of the category of "personal history," and to sublimate itself somehow intangibly in the career of a great movement, in which, though he retained a dominant role, you could no longer see him clearly as a personality.

Hunanese appear to be born leaders, and so it is not surprising that Mao was able to inspire, lead, and, as the Chinese

Communists put it, "solidarize men." But what of the quality of that leadership, the ideas which shaped Chinese Communism? Chinese Communist ideology has been marked by a concern with theory and practice, that is, unified conceptions about China and the world and effective methods for achieving its goals. Theory and practice are also the titles of Mao's two major philosophical works: *On Contradiction* and *On Practice.* We must therefore go beyond his basic personality and look at the man of ideas and of action.

Mao has often been derided by Chinese and Westerners alike as a simplistic Marxist who, in contrast to Lenin and Trotsky, added nothing original to Marxist theory. Reading his canonical works does little to dispel this impression, for many of them have been so edited and shaped by his hagiographers that they resemble the painstakingly carved but dull ivories of earlier days. We get a better idea of the power of Mao's thought by looking at the Chinese documents of the Sino-Soviet dispute. It matters not who wrote them: the ideas are clearly Mao's. What does matter is not the originality of Mao's thinking, but its quality and conceptions. As both Edgar Snow and Mark Gayn, correspondent for the *Toronto Star,* indicate in the following selections, Mao's thinking is schematic but not dogmatic. Dogmatism (the fault the Soviets have accused the Chinese of) means rigid adherence to ideas as such; Mao's response has been "dogma is more useless than cow dung." For Mao, theory (Marxism-Leninism) is truth and hence sacrosanct, but that does not mean that practice can be mechanically derived from theory (such would be dogmatic thinking). Practice must remain flexible and changing. When a particular policy fails, one must be ready to try something else.

The schematism is evident in Mao's philosophical writings of the late 1930s, his analysis of the domestic and foreign situation of China during the Sino-Japanese War, his writings on organization, his formulation of the global Cold War in the late 1940s, and, of course, in the grandiose schemes which guided China from 1949 to the present. Of the latter, three are of major importance. First, his vision of how Chinese society would break out of backwardness, notably through the transformation of the peasantry, a scheme finally implemented in the Great Leap Forward. Gayn notes that "Mao's preoccupation with rural China is almost obsessive. To me, he spoke of the peasant with knowledge and passion, with pride and sympathy. He spoke in generalities, but each generality had behind it the recollection of a specific event." The last observation seems to have been true of so many of Mao's ideas: from a set of events, the experiences of the Chinese Revolution for example, Mao has often moved to the most macroscopic generalizations. Second, from the time of the Civil War, Mao developed conceptions about the global confrontation between socialism and imperialism, particularly between the Soviet Union and the United States, and, from the mid-1950s, about the proper policies of and relations between the countries of the socialist camp. Third, largely as a consequence of the Sino-Soviet dispute but with roots in the 1940s, Mao evolved a grand conception of the process of world history, particularly the revolutionary rise of the poor nations, a conception most clearly expressed in Lin Piao's recent article "On People's War" (see pp. 347–359).

Although the Chinese Communists have acted on all three of these grand visions, the results have not always been as predicted. Yet regardless of success or failure, these visions have inspired, stimulated, and unified the Party. Vision is a necessary ingredient for all complex revolutionary movements.

The core of Mao Tse-tung's thinking is the notion of contradiction or a juxtaposition of opposites as the essential mark of all human and social process (see pp. 32–46). This dialectic thinking, rooted both in traditional Chinese philosophy and in Marxism, leads Mao to search out juxtapositions of opposites everywhere, from within the soul of man to the world at large. (Marx wrote that "the socialism of China may have the same relationship to that of Europe as that of Chinese philosophy to the Hegelian" [*Neue Rheinische Revue,* January 31, 1850].) If Trotsky and Stalin dogmatically taught that revolution could come only from the proletariat, Mao sought out revolutionary contradictions wherever he could find them, maintaining that one must take sides in the struggle and be committed. Above all, a revolutionary must side with the masses, live among them. Mao's greatest discovery was the organized power of the poor, their capacity to make and sustain revolution, and to build a revolutionary country. One must remember that Mao grew up at a time when China's traditional authority figures—officials, landlords, scholars—were being stripped of their traditional robes and were standing naked before the country; not only their cruelty and corruption, but their ineptness, timidity, and inability to lead men had driven the revolutionary intellectuals to the workers and peasants. Mao's contempt for intellectuals and bureaucrats, often expressed with references to human dung, continues to this day.

Mao is old and will soon pass away. In many ways he has already passed into history. His legacy is his theoretical ideas and his practical experiences, one aspect of which may not be sufficiently appreciated in the West: he has been careful, often cautious, and built slowly from the bottom up over long periods of time. As Edgar Snow says, "he knows that [the edifice he has been building] will be long in the creation but he does believe that it will create everlastingly." Mao built carefully during the Yenan Period, and during the Civil War he was not optimistic about a rapid victory. He has also taken great risks, but only, as his guerrilla writings tell us, when he felt victory was certain. Sometimes he was right, as in the onslaught against the cities during the Civil War, but at other times he was wrong, as during the Great Leap Forward. In times of failure or overextended efforts, however, he has been quick to retreat: the careful organizer has usually quickly superseded the one-shot gambler.

EDGAR SNOW *
Power Personality

Mao's childhood resentments seem to have been well-founded protests against tyranny and ignorance, but we have only his side of the story. On his later years there is much more information. It is difficult to separate Mao's adult behavior or writing from the whole Chinese Revolution. Should that be considered

* Edgar Snow, *The Other Side of the River* (New York: Random House, 1961), pp. 144–152.

one vast delusion of persecution? Is everyone who disdains to compromise with the intolerable a paranoid? That would put Patrick Henry in the vanguard. If, after a nation has been exploited, robbed, opium-soaked, plundered, occupied, and partitioned by foreign invaders for a century, the people turns upon its persecutors and drives them from the house, along with the society whose weakness permitted the abuses, is it suffering from paranoia? Or would it be schizoid if it did otherwise? Some grave miscalculations in Mao's later years suggest delusions of grandeur. Could they not readily be matched by blunders of bigoted "normal" statesmen elsewhere which are rationalized as bad judgment? Erik Erikson recently described Martin Luther as a great man whose personality found maximum stability only when he discovered his *adult* "identity" in reasonable heresy; in his rebellion against Rome he found truth in a fully justified, good cause. Thus far, Mao has had little difficulty in uniting his personality as leader of a "just war" of liberation, but it may be a long time before historians or psychoanalysts can agree on final verdicts.

It is not my intention to offer that judgment here, nor to attempt any amateur analysis to resolve the "personal contradictions" of Mao's character. A man who has made a career of nonconformism, he demands from the nation a degree of conformism unsurpassed anywhere. He is as aggressive as any civilized leader alive, and, like the rest of them, not above wanting a bomb of his own. He would never slap his soft-soled shoe on the table to demand attention, but he is not entirely free of the exhibitionism that affects other power personalities. The father of any nation must reflect at least some of the paradoxes of its children as well as those of the outside world.

It was Mao's ability to analyze the experience common to his generation—rather than the uniqueness of his own experience—plus his messianic belief in the correctness of his own generalizations of that experience, which distinguished him from compatriots who became his followers.

There is nothing neutral or passive about Mao, but neither is there any record that he has ever advocated a war of foreign conquest. His concept is that revolutionary war is essentially an offensive-defensive action. When people are held in subjection by armed oppressors they repel them by force. Having "liberated" China by means of "struggle," Mao views the world to-day as divided between two camps in which justice and right will finally prevail after more struggle. Class war everywhere continues in the capitalist countries; they threaten humanity with imperialist war which can be prevented or defeated only by struggle, as Mao sees it. Because he is the product of a land repeatedly hit by foreign invasion and civil war, and was him-self a near-victim of counter-revolutionary violence, life has taught him to rationalize all revolutionary actions as "blows for peace."

"War," he wrote at the time of the Japanese invasion, "this monster of mutual slaughter among mankind, will be finally eliminated through the progress of human society, and in no dis-tant future, too. But there is only one way of eliminating it, namely, to oppose war by means of war, to oppose counter-revolutionary war by means of revolutionary war, and to oppose counter-revolutionary class war by means of revolutionary class war. All counter-revolutionary wars are unjust, all revolutionary wars are just. Our study of the laws of revolutionary war starts from our will to eliminate all wars—this is the dividing line be-tween us Communists and all exploiting classes."

Generations of Western dominance in Asia had brought not peace but a sword, and Mao summarized the lesson for many of his countrymen when he said, "All political power grows out of the barrel of a gun." Not until China had learned to use modern guns effectively did the West begin to respect and fear her. It is therefore not likely, alas, that China will be first to lay down her arms.

To Mao Tse-tung, Western observers who expect China to commit suicide by launching aggressive wars of conquest are hypocrites or fools. "Sooner or later," he said, "these gentlemen will take a look at a map. Then they will notice that it is not China that is occupying Western territory, not China that has ringed Western countries with military bases, but the other way round."

To a man sincerely convinced that revolutions are "blows for peace"—and who has actually seen revolution bring internal peace to China—the question of war and the nature of its causes is bound to look very different from the way it looks to those who believe that counter-revolutions are "blows for peace."

Whatever objective results Mao's policies may have in an infinitely complex world, there is in my own mind little doubt that he wishes to avoid war but greatly fears it may not be possible. Still less does he believe that a general holocaust would hasten the construction of socialism—and certainly not in time for him to receive congratulations. Mao is not mad. Anyone who talks to him for a few hours sees in Mao an aging warrior deeply conscious of his mortality and aware that he must soon step aside, leaving behind him the still unfinished edifice of which he has merely laid the foundations. He knows that it will be long in the creation but he does believe that it will create everlastingly. Even without the cataclysm of nuclear war the task will take many years. Fifty? A hundred? What is that, he asks, in the life of nations—and especially in the life of China?

There is evidence that Mao has understood his own country better than any national leader in modern times, but his grasp of the Western world is a schematic one based on methods of Marxist analysis of classes as they exist in backward economies like the one he grew up in. He lacks sufficient understanding of the subtle changes brought about in those classes in advanced "welfare states" by two hundred years of the kind of transformation China is only now entering; just as many well-fed American congressmen consistently fail to understand that starving have-not majorities of poor nations will not wait for two hundred years to see their children fed and educated.

Is Mao a blind and rigid dogmatist? "Dogma is more useless than cow dung," he has said. He stresses the importance of concrete analysis derived from specific and concrete conditions. Does he hold that *only* material conditions determine social behavior and that there is no such force as the spiritual, which preoccupies the idealistic philosophers? No; what Mao said in *On Contradiction* was ". . . while we recognize that in the development of history as a whole it is material things that determine spiritual things, and social existence that determines social consciousness, at the same time we also recognize and must recognize the reaction of spiritual things and social consciousness on social existence, and the reaction of the superstructure on the economic foundation." Between them contradictions are bound to exist.

Chinese Communists appear to us to hold extremely dogmatic positions from which no logic can budge them. That is because, once a Party line is formulated, all members parrot it with the same uniformity and seeming lack of individual thought or will. But the line is constantly subjected to re-examination in terms of old and new data. There are repeated examples of changes and reversals of tactical or even strategical approaches to many questions—often accompanied by "rectification" movements and downgrading of "anti-party" elements too slow to move with the times. Chinese Marxists, in kinship with all Marxists, do not disbelieve in change but regard nothing as immune to change. Although they are often slower to modify their analysis to accommodate minor changes than are politicians who lack a basic doctrine—and hence depend more upon improvisation and pragmatism—they can make very sudden and dramatic policy shifts. They may leave an obsolete line hanging on a cliff, to the embarrassment of non-Party sympathizers who supported it for reasons of personal interest or ideals without understanding its transitory character. Acceptance of the new line—which may directly contradict the old—presents no problem to the experienced Party member, however, whose disciplined faith enables him to proclaim the reconstructed "only truth" on any question with the same zeal and uniformity as he did the old.

In the past few years Communists have been going through an "agonizing reappraisal" of the "inevitable imperialist war" thesis—one of the very fundamental formulations of Lenin—based on changed world conditions. Mao has been denounced as a backward dogmatist in this dispute. We shall see, farther on, that experiences of China to date give more logical support to his views than many persons living in another milieu can readily comprehend.

Inside China, Mao's record as a prophet is very good but not without blemish. As a recent example of an amazing lapse: his promise made in June 1958, when he set goals "attainable within one or two years," namely: "that there should be available each year for each person 1,650 pounds of food grains" and "110 pounds of pork." In 1960 he told Marshal Montgomery that such Western standards of diet would not be realized for "fifty years." How to reconcile the two remarks? Mao is a complex man. Neither he nor China yields to any simple analysis, be it by Freud or by Marx.

Serious miscalculations in planning have been attributed to Mao, and he has undoubtedly ignored some good advice. Yet he was not too conceited to adopt the ideas of a trenchant critic by incorporating them into the national "eight-point charter for agriculture." In their original aims the people's communes were the most radical attempt to uproot man and remake his environment since the Paris Commune. Observers afar tend to blame the entire current food shortage on the communes (which is erroneous) and to hold Mao responsible. The communes were not Mao's idea alone, as we shall presently see, yet he cannot avoid responsibility for the costly haste of their beginnings.

Foreign critics accuse Mao of indifference to the possible loss of millions of lives in nuclear war. It is said that Mao regards his own "blue ants"—a fashionable substitute nowadays for the "yellow peril," which conjures up the same ancient racist fears and hates—as expendable. Yet under Mao's regime very great and systematic efforts have been made to preserve and prolong human life and to educate it for constructive effort.

Mao has been called stubborn, quick-tempered, egotistical, and ruthless. Yet some Chinese intellectuals who have used these terms are still walking around free men. At a moment when Mao stood at the summit of power Liu Shao-ch'i was named his successor and today works as closely with him as formerly. It has been said abroad that Mao's vanity surpasses Stalin's. But in a period when Khrushchev was still dancing jigs to amuse Stalin (according to his own report to his Twentieth Party Congress) and doubtless looking for new rivers to name for the boss, Mao Tse-tung initiated a Central Committee decision to forbid the naming of provinces, cities, or towns for himself or other living leaders, and banned birthday celebrations in his honor.

In order to hold power Stalin had to kill or remove nearly all the old Bolsheviks left behind by Lenin, and now Khrushchev has removed every member of the 1953 Politburo except Anastas Mikoyan. Mao has worked with much the same Central Committee for nearly twenty years. Except for Kao Kang and

Jao Shu-shih, who were accused in the mid-fifties of attempting to set up an independent state in Manchuria (possibly backed by Stalin), there has been no split in the top leadership since 1937. The Politburo is composed exclusively of close comrades of a lifetime, but Mao has at times been bitterly opposed and occasionally defeated. He has not shot his opposition. Following his own advice to others, to "use means of persuasion," he has either accepted his defeat or recovered by winning a majority in the Central Committee.

Three men who were Mao's bitterest opponents and rivals for Party leadership are all alive. One of them, Li Li-san, fought Mao for years, with Comintern backing. When Mao formed his government he made Li Li-san Minister of Labor. Li is still a member of the Central Committee. Wang Ming, who earlier tried to wrest control from Mao (with Comintern support, also) and is still denounced as "anti-Party" in the official records of the period, is today a Central Committee member and Mao still calls him "comrade."

Mao's treatment of Chang Kuo-t'ao offers a dramatic contrast to Stalin's vengeful pursuit of Trotsky. At the time, Chang led an armed revolt and schism which almost destroyed the Party during the most critical phase of the Long March. He allegedly executed "hundreds" of Mao's partisans who disagreed with him. At the end of the Long March he was expelled by the Central Committee in Yenan but retained his post as vice-chairman of the Northwest "border" government. In 1938 Chang crossed the border, unopposed, and joined the Kuomintang. Later he alleged that his bodyguard had been shot to prevent his escape. According to Mao the bodyguard is today an army officer.

After the war Chang became a refugee in Hong Kong. When Mao heard that Chang was impoverished and in poor health he sent for Mme Chang Kuo-t'ao, who was still living in China with her children. He told her that a wife's place was beside her husband in adversity and advised her to join Chang in Hong Kong. Mme Chang agreed, was provided with funds, and went to Hong Kong, taking her children with her. In confirming these facts to me, Mao concluded with a smile, "Yet Mr. Dulles complained that we Communists were separating husbands and wives and breaking up families!"

Although Chang Kuo-t'ao has harshly attacked him, Mao spoke of his former adversary with a seeming absence of rancor. He even appeared concerned for Chang's welfare and not displeased when he learned that Chang was being paid for his memoirs by an American institution. Chang had made his contributions to the Revolution in the past, and even his recent writing was "not all bad." Mao's remarks about Chiang Kai-shek revealed no personal bitterness either. Once Chiang had accepted the role of a protectee he was regarded less as a serious contender for Mainland leadership than as a latter-day P'u Yi, a victim of fate and a kind of secundine of the Revolution. (If Americans find this difficult to understand we might ask ourselves how much chance Jefferson Davis would have had to be elected to the White House if he had established the defeated Confederate government under British protection on Staten Island.) Mao and other Chinese continued to respect Chiang Kai-shek for one thing, however: he had declined to support the "two-Chinas" plan aimed at removing Taiwan from the sovereignty of China. On this point the fallen leader and his successor are united.

"No man can rule guiltlessly," said Saint-Simon, and least of all can men in a hurry. If the successes of China's Revolution may be personified by one man so must its crimes and its failures. Mao has not held power by devouring his closest comrades, as Stalin did, but he is not without blood on his hands. The amount of killing during a revolutionary change of power varies with the intensity of the counter-revolution, and in China that was of long duration. Throughout his twenty-two years of power Chiang Kai-shek was held responsible for the execution of countless rebels and sympathizers, as well as four fifths of the Communist Party membership during his 1927 *coup d'état*. In the same sense Mao is responsible for sanguinary excesses no less severe. During the Revolution Mao sanctioned "necessary" executions of "archcriminals." His repeated admonitions against killing without "fair trials" and emphasis on "the less killing the better" are not indicative, however, of a sadist or a man with a personal blood lust.

"Revolution is not the same thing as inviting people to tea or writing an essay or painting a picture or doing fancy needlework," Mao discovered years ago on his first encounter with rebel peasants in action. "It cannot be anything so refined, so calm and gentle, or so mild, kind, courteous, restrained and magnanimous."

Today's image of Mao among the masses is hardly that of an executioner. What makes him formidable is that he is not just a Party boss but by many millions of Chinese is quite genuinely regarded as a teacher, statesman, strategist, philosopher, poet laureate, national hero, head of the family, and greatest liberator in history. He is to them Confucius plus Lao-tzu plus Rousseau plus Marx plus Buddha. The "Hundred Flowers" period revealed that he has enemies as well, yet Mao was the only Party boss who ever dared open the press and forum to give voice to that popular resentment.

Some of the hero worship of Mao may express much the same kind of national self-esteem as British idolatry of Queen Victoria in days when the Empire was shouldering the white man's burden. Victoria did no more to discourage that, it may be recalled, than the press is doing to demolish the Kennedy "image" of today. Insofar as the Mao "cult" is reminiscent of the synthetic beatification of Stalin when he was alive, it is to any Westerner nauseating in the same degree. No public building, no commune, no factory or girls' dormitory is complete without its solemn statue or plaster bust of the man with the mole on his chin. They are as much a part of the furniture in any reception room as the inevitable green tablecloth and bowls of boiling tea. In Szechwan I even saw a towering simulated bronze statue of Mao made of lacquer so light that a schoolgirl could easily shift it from pedestal to pedestal as occasion demanded. The extravagance of praise nowadays heard in Moscow for Stalin's successor, however, does not seem to give Mr. K. much advantage in a modesty contest. Consider a sample from the speeches of party delegates to the October 1961 Congress which hailed the new Oracle:

> The planting of corn in 1961, in comparison with 1953, increased almost 7.5 times. We all know that this is the great service of Nikita Sergeyevich Khrushchev. He revealed to the country the valiant strength of corn, made us love it. . . . (Deputy Chairman Ignatov, U.S.S.R. Council of Ministers)

The value of a state father image in the "democratic dictatorship" is clearly recognized by the Chinese Party. With the breakup of large families as a result of industrialization of both town and country, as well as the replacement of family paternalism by Party paternalism, the mantle of national patriarch would inevitably have descended on the shoulders of any leader in a country not far removed from ancestor worship and emperor worship. Mao has now become an Institution of such prestige and authority that no one in the Party could raze it without sacrificing a collective vested interest of first importance. Probably no one knows that better than Mao himself.

He has also been his own best propagandist by practicing the rule of "physician, heal thyself." Consider this significant passage:

> If you want the masses to understand you and want to become one with them, you must be determined to undergo a long and even painful process of remolding. I began as a student and acquired at school the habits of a student; in the presence of a crowd of students who could neither fetch nor carry for themselves I used to feel it undignified to do any manual labor such as shouldering my own luggage. At that time it seemed to me that the intellectuals were the only clean persons in the world and peasants seemed rather dirty beside them.
>
> Having become a revolutionary I found myself in the same ranks as the workers, peasants and soldiers of the revolutionary army, and gradually I became familiar with them and they with me, too. It was then and only then that a fundamental change occurred in the bourgeois and petty-bourgeois feelings implanted in me by bourgeois schools. I came to feel that it was those unremodeled intellectuals who were unclean while the workers and peasants are after all the cleanest persons even though their hands are soiled and their feet smeared with cow dung. This is what is meant by having one's feelings transformed, changed from those of one class to those of another.

Early in life Mao understood the obvious but neglected facts which brought him to power: 1) that the vast majority of the Chinese people were poor and illiterate; 2) that China's greatest reservoir of creative energy lay in this majority; 3) that the man who succeeded in winning its confidence and effectively organized it could gain political ascendancy; 4) that in this massive labor power lay all the "capital" necessary to industrialize China and make of it a wealthy and mighty nation.

Unlike many Chinese intellectuals who looked upon the huge, illiterate, spawning population as their country's greatest liability, Mao saw their "economically poor" and "culturally blank" condition as China's greatest assets. Because they were so very poor, he said, things could hardly be worse; any party which brought even a modest improvement would win their support and hold their loyalty. Because they were so "culturally blank" they were like a clean new sheet of paper. Whoever made the effort to remold their lives for the better would leave sharp, clean, and lasting impressions.

"Ninety per cent of the people," Mao often said, "are without culture and education." What distinguished him from all previous Chinese leaders, with the exception of Sun Yat-sen, was that he did not mean merely to utilize the peasants in order to attain power, and then drop them back into the mud. The ex-teacher proposed to end the misery and stupidity of illiterate and invertebrate peasant life itself by lifting the peasants onto high levels of education and access to tools of a new environment.

To convince the peasants that by determined struggle they could own the land they tilled, and then to convert that sense of ownership into energetic participation in the mastery of their fate through the "construction of socialism"—these were the not inconsiderable tasks which Mao and his followers assumed, and the results of which are here being examined.

MARK GAYN*
Mao Tse-tung Reassessed

We sat in a cave, Mao Tse-tung and I, and we were arguing about the state of the United States's economy.

There may be a strong touch of unreality to this scene, but the time was 1947 and the place was Yenan, and the unreal was commonplace. In a few weeks, Yenan would fall to the Nationalists, encamped just the other side of the mountains. At night, Party officials were already slipping into the hills to bury documents and equipment, and in a corral next to the Central Committee headquarters a hundred ponies waited to take the leaders on a speedy flight. But from this improbable capital, Mao and his companions still governed more people than there were in France and Britain put together; still debated doctrinal matters; still attended theater plays and held weekly dances at the Party headquarters; and still received the infrequent visitor.

We sat in Mao's dimly lighted cave, shivered in the February cold, and he insisted that the United States was on the eve of a shattering depression.

"Our radio station," he said, "monitors the American news broadcasts from Treasure Island [in San Francisco Bay]. These reports are brought to me, complete with stock market quotations. I study the market reports very closely. One day soon I'll find in them the first signs of the coming depression. That'll be the beginning of the end for the capitalist system."

We argued. I suggested that no economic collapse could be expected while there was such a huge postwar demand for cars and washing machines, for radios and baby carriages. Mao said a little impatiently,

* Mark Gayn, "Mao Tse-tung Reassessed," unpublished working paper for The China Conference (Chicago, February 8–12, 1966).

The trouble with you liberals in the West is that you misunderstand the social and political currents in the United States. The American toiling masses have had enough of capitalist oppression and injustice. They want a better life, a democratic system. When the next depression comes, they'll march on Washington and overthrow the Wall Street government. Then they'll establish a democratic regime that will cooperate with democratic forces all over the world, including China.

I told Mao that the picture of the American toilers marching on Washington to overthrow the Wall Street government did not fully agree with what I knew of American society.

Mao said, "I'll give you an example that will prove my point. Have you read *Thunder Out of China* by Theodore White and Annalee Jacoby?"

I said I had.

"Would you agree," he asked, "that this book is quite critical of Chiang Kai-shek and of the Kuomintang misrule and corruption?"

I agreed.

"Don't you think," he asked again, "that it's quite fair to us?"

I did think so.

"Who published the book?"

I told Mao it had been distributed by the Book-of-the-Month Club, and when Mao asked if this was a capitalist enterprise, I conceded that, Yes, indeed the book club was very much a capitalist undertaking.

"All right then," Mao said triumphantly, "there you have the answer! Why would a capitalist firm publish a book critical of Chiang Kai-shek and fair to us but for the pressure of the American toiling masses who are friendly to China and who demand to know the truth?"

Last spring, eighteen years after this encounter, I returned to China. Yesterday's rebels in Yenan were now policymakers in a world capital. The press in Peking was full of reports of American reverses in Vietnam, and of unrest and turbulence in U.S. cities. There was also a great deal on the teach-in in

Washington. As the newspapers depicted it, this was a descent on the capital by the American toiling masses which realized that the imperialist aggression in Vietnam was directed against them no less than against the Vietnamese people.

The American toilers, the press said, were led by intellectuals at last aware of the true feelings of the working masses. And, of course, the gangster government of President Johnson was quaking in its jackboots before this powerful display of popular anger.

I felt as if I was back in Mao's cave, and he was telling me of the imminent Marxist revolution in Main Street, U.S.A.

This unchanged doctrinal approach is an essential fact in any new assessment of Mao Tse-tung. It is as if time has stood still for him and his companions, and they were still totally isolated from all reality except that of their own limited domain.

On the mountain terrace outside of one of his caves back in 1947, Mao had a small kiosk in which he used to read, write, or contemplate nature. On a return visit to Yenan last year, I stood in the kiosk and looked out, as he must have for so many years. What I saw was a small and austere world—the vegetable patch Mao once cultivated, the gully that was really a narrow cleavage in the mountains, and then a view of the villagers in the fields, the Yen River, and more treeless and brown mountains beyond.

Almost symbolically, the mountains hemmed in Mao's field of vision, and reduced it to the sights of rural and primitive China. With the exception of a two-day visit to Chungking in 1945, Mao had seen no city lights in the twenty-two years preceding his triumphal entry into Peking. For twelve of these twenty-two years he lived in caves.

The isolation was intellectual as well as physical. Even in Yenan, Mao had an opportunity to meet a good many Westerners. Only seldom did he seek from them knowledge of the strength, complexity, or social change in the West. Nor would he summon, from Peking, Shanghai, or Hong Kong, those informed Chinese who could have told him of other lands and peoples. Instead of seeking such first-hand counsel, Mao relied on the contents of the rickety bookcase I saw in his cave. Apart from Chinese classics and books on history, it also held the works of Marx and Lenin.

In effect, Mao saw the complex and ever-changing world beyond China's borders through the eyes of these Westerners— the German who lived in the nineteenth century and concerned himself with the social and economic currents in Europe when the Industrial Revolution was still young, and the Russian who dealt with the developments in the early years of this century.

Both saw the history of modern man in terms of a merciless struggle between the capitalist oppressors and the rebellious toiling masses. For Mao and his companions this was a meaningful picture, for it seemed to parallel what they saw in the rural China they knew so well.

It may be argued that what Mao thought in 1947 did not matter. But it does matter that Mao's thinking has not changed, and that the concepts and analyses he employs today do not explain the world as it really is. For this is not the world that Marx and Lenin knew, but one of changed Western societies and of yesterday's colonies that are now free and rambunctious; of automation, cybernetics, multimegaton bombs, and men preparing to journey to the moon; and, indeed, of the Communist camp itself torn by internecine feuds and of the Soviet Union engaged, with a fair degree of success, in an almost Kennanian campaign to "contain" China.

Washington is often blamed for walling China and her leaders off from the world without. It has certainly tried. But China today is ringed not with one wall but with two, and the taller one was erected by the nation's governors themselves. This wall is in plain sight—in propaganda posters, which are such a part of the Chinese landscape, in the press, the theater and the movies, in the popular song and even the children's comics. And, of course, in state policy and in the unchanging political faith.

This continuing isolation is part of the legacy of Yenan. Another part is Mao's preoccupation with the village. Like any traditional Marxist, he speaks now and then of the urban proletarians as the driving force of the Revolution. But neither he nor his companions seem to believe this. It is the peasant who dominates their dreams, their theories, and their policies.

In 1947 Mao described to me the uprising he led as the latest—and the last—of the many peasant revolutions that run through the weave of Chinese history. He spoke with intimate knowledge and with compassion of the revolts that began in the countryside, gathered strength, scored triumphs—and then were drowned in their own blood because their leaders lacked strength or wisdom.

Mao saw these revolts as mileposts of China's social and political development. And he saw his own revolution as a lineal successor to the great peasant upheavals of the past—from the first revolt of Ch'en Sheng and Wu Kuang nearly twenty-two hundred years ago, to the Red Eyebrows and the Yellow Turbans of the Han Dynasty, to the Taiping Heavenly Kingdom and the Boxers. And as he spoke, it became difficult to decide where, in his own mind, the orthodox Marxist ended and the leader of a peasant revolution took over.

Last spring [1965] I went through the magnificent historical museum in Peking's Square of Heavenly Peace. It is a vast building filled with priceless relics, dummies of historic figures, ancient farm tools and weapons, and models of palaces and peasant huts. Dominating the exhibits are huge paintings depicting historic violence—and endless quotations from the works of Mao Tse-tung.

As I moved along it suddenly dawned on me that what the pretty guide was telling me was what Mao told me in Yenan. China's entire history was being portrayed as a succession of peasant uprisings, heroic, cruel, glorious, and futile. Along with this presentation came the assurance that Mao's revolution would not fail like the others, for it was led by a strong and wise leader at the head of a tightly knit party.

The same idea is expounded outside of the museum walls. Day in and day out, the people are told that they must be brave and steadfast, that they must make sacrifices and obey, lest this revolution fail like the peasant revolts of the past. Mao has called it "the uninterrupted revolution," and the people are warned it may not be completed for fifty or a hundred years.

To an outsider the class enemy may seem to have been liquidated, but the faithful are exhorted to continue the class struggle, in town and in country, in politics and the arts. The village is shown as a repository of most virtues, as well as the source and the unconquerable bastion of Mao's revolution. And everyone is enjoined to emulate the spirit of the People's Liberation Army, the glorious army of peasants that carried the Revolution to victory.

All tools and agents of persuasion are engaged. The artists are kept busy painting posters that glorify the villager—or the young urban intellectual who has gone back to the land. The choreographers are working on pseudo-peasant dances, and I saw these danced not only on the stage but also in parks, factory clubs, and, by five- and six-year-olds, in kindergartens.

The writers, moviemakers, playwrights, composers, journalists, and even philosophers are told to go to the villages to learn at first hand the strength and beauty of the peasant spirit. And, currently, the young are urged to emulate those typical traits of the "poor and lower middle peasant"—"bravery, steadfastness, diligence, and simplicity."

As one studies Mao or reads *The People's Daily,* one begins to detect nostalgia for the heroic and uncomplicated days of Yenan. This nostalgia is part of what might be called the "Yenan Complex"—a state of mind, a faith, a political philosophy. Into its shaping went many influences—the ideas of Marx and Lenin, bitter memories, decades of isolation from the mainstream of world history, the conviction that the village is the only dependable stronghold of revolution, and the belief that the hour has come for a violent rural revolution to destroy both the decaying imperialism and the timid revisionism.

Out of the Yenan Complex flow problems. Few observers can fail to be impressed by China's leadership. It has ability, intelligence, toughness, a singleness of purpose, and superb skill in the uses of power. It has given China political stability many European states could envy.

But this is also a company of men resistant to change. Although the world, China, and the Chinese have all changed, the leaders' favorite point of orientation is still the village crossroads. Some of this may be justified because China remains a nation of half a billion peasants or more—and the countryside has been slow to change. But the village orientation hinders Mao and his companions in understanding some of the powerful currents at home and abroad.

Because of this, Peking abounds in paradoxes. Primitive village yardsticks are being used in the policymaking of what, after all, is one of the three major powers of our day. They are also being applied to a society a growing segment of which is becoming urbanized. And what is avowedly a revolution of tomorrow, of the young and the intellectual, is being run by oldsters who deny the young any political voice. For the young this is a land of challenge and exciting opportunity in many fields—but decidedly not in politics.

China today has three echelons of power. The first is formed by Mao and his six companions, whose portraits are sold in every department store, and displayed in every office, school, barrack, and village commune. These are the Founding Fathers, the men of the Long March and of Yenan, the makers of faith and policy. Their average age is sixty-seven.

The second echelon consists of perhaps a hundred men, who sit on the Central Committee, run senior ministries, hold key posts in the Party headquarters, or serve as Party, state, and army leaders outside of Peking. This group includes such men as Po I-po, an ex-guerrilla organizer and now an economic specialist; Lu Ting-i, the intense propagandist who is now Minister of Culture; Yang Shang-k'un, an affable man with a phenomenal memory who oversees the Party cadres; Lo Jui-ch'ing, now Chief of the Army General Staff who once headed the secret police; and T'ao Chu, who runs the Party's Central-South regional bureau and who increasingly speaks for the Party on village problems. The average age of the second echelon is about sixty-one. (See pp. 388–400, 608–610.)

The third echelon holds key posts a shade lower than those of the second. These are the provincial secretaries of the Party, army commissars, key men in the army's powerful General Political Department, provincial governors. Many of them were university students in 1937, when Japan attacked China proper. Fired by patriotism, they walked out of Peking, Tientsin, and Shanghai into the countryside to fight the invaders. But the countryside in North China was already dominated by the Communists, and these youngsters soon found themselves swallowed in the Communist movement.

On a truck journey across the great plain of North China in 1947 I interviewed many of these young men, and obtained their autobiographies. At that point they were serving as mayors, police chiefs, or Party secretaries in small towns, as propagandists and junior army commissars.

They were intelligent, literate, and dynamic. They were also zealots—dogmatic, intolerant, impatient and ruthless. If the old men in Yenan were the makers of the faith, these were the disciples eager to convert and, if necessary, ready to die. Below these men, now averaging in age between fifty and fifty-two, there is today no discernible echelon of power. In this regime of the oldsters, no Sorensens sit in the inner councils, and none seemingly are being groomed for the responsibilities of power.

The men of the three echelons are veterans of the Civil War and of Yenan. By and large they have held the same or comparable posts for a decade or more, thus denying room at the top to younger men. Indeed, this elite distrusts all those unlucky enough to have been too young to live and fight in the years of glory and bloodletting.

From Mao down, the elite makes no effort to conceal its distrust. It reproaches the young, sharply and incessantly, for their softness. It ships them by the hundreds of thousands into the villages to put calluses on their hands and spirits. It demands of them discipline, loyalty, and self-sacrifice. And it frightens them with the horrible specter of the moral decay that, it insists, now afflicts the young of the Soviet Union.

Back in Yenan, Mao told me China needed a powerful industry that would produce machines and motor cars, cannon, tanks, and aircraft—all she needed to "defend her sacred boundaries." The industrial revolution that he initiated in 1949 has given China all this—and atomic devices as well.

To make the industrial revolution possible, the Party brought millions of peasants into the cities and gave skills and education to them and their children. But the Party leaders have obdurately refused to recognize that industrialization brings with it a profound *social* change. And when, in consternation, they discovered that yesterday's peasants—and especially the peasants' sons—have become a changed breed, the leaders began to demand that the new urbanites return to the country to rediscover its virtues and its patterns of thought.

A wide gap is thus developing between the graybeards and

the young. For if the young bear no scars of the civil war in which their fathers fought, they are discovering worlds their fathers never knew—the worlds of automation, computers, electronics, and, yes, missiles and atomic bombs. They look at the world from a city boulevard and not a village crossroads, and Yenan for them is a historic town and not a philosophy of life.

Because the Yenan Complex is fundamentally anti-urban and anti-intellectual, it is beginning to hinder the nation's progress. Examples are beyond number. In Sian an intellectual complains that this large city's administration comes to a halt at certain periods because the officials are required to work in the countryside ("One doesn't even try to transact official business during such times"). Newly graduated engineers put away their new degrees and are assigned to jobs as common laborers for at least a year, and in some plants for as long as five years. Factory managers leave their proper and urgent tasks to become ordinary workers for varying periods, "so as to be as one with the masses."

A current movie hit extols trained army officers who wash their soldiers' socks and underwear to demonstrate their oneness. Writers, poets, playwrights, musicians, and choreographers are pressed to go to the country to work in the fields and thus imbibe the true peasant spirit. And even nuclear physicists are expected to do manual work for the same political reason.

Such exertions may help to maintain the revolutionary fervor of the city worker or the intellectual. But they also represent a significant loss to the nation. No improvement, however, is in sight. Under the "cultural revolution" now being planned, all education by 1990, if not by 1975, is to be given in "part-work, part-study" schools. This is how Huang Hsin-pai, a senior officer in the Ministry of Higher Learning, justified it to me:

> We want to enable our students to have the same steely revolutionary spirit that moved the men who fought in the struggle for liberation. To insure such revolutionary spirit we shall make students engage in productive work through the half-study, half-work schools. This will cover all fields, including medicine and nuclear research. This is a cultural revolution based on Chairman Mao's thinking.

This "reform" is not really new. Premier Nikita Khrushchev initiated it in the Soviet Union in the late fifties, ostensibly to make the young respect manual labor but actually to meet the need for trained manpower. Mr. K.'s successors dropped this innovation as a result of protests from universities which were getting a huge crop of ill-prepared applicants.

One of the aims of the Chinese "reform" is to produce speedily the technicians the villages need so desperately. But as the Russians found, part-study can produce only part-literates. And this is a fearful price to pay for revolutionary spirit in a nation that must have an intellectual elite to advance.

A visitor to China is impressed by the signs of industrial revolution. The sleepy provincial towns I knew so well in the thirties and the forties are no longer dozing. Today, they are boom cities, with bustle and disorder, with unpaved streets reaching out for miles into the countryside, and with each street flanked with new factories and company housing. China today makes thousands of items she never made before.

But much of this industrial plant was built by the Russians before they pulled out of China in two dramatic days in July 1960. Notably also, this is now an obsolescent and inefficient plant.

The huge truck works in Changchun—twenty thousand workers, four hundred thousand square meters of floor space —still turns out the four-ton, 90-horsepower vehicle the Soviet Army used in the war a quarter of a century ago (the Chinese call it "Liberation lorry"). The blast furnaces in the great steel city of Anshan were installed by the Russians in the early fifties and were probably designed in the thirties. The new Chinese-built machines I saw in the Shanghai cable factory were copies of older machines stamped GENERAL ELECTRIC—1934.

For the moment, this industry meets some of the country's demands. But the day must come when China will feel the need for a second industrial revolution. This will not be attained without a radical change in the attitudes of the aging leaders to the new, young, urban, intellectual class.

Mao's revolution has nowhere had a more shattering impact than in the countryside. The old system of landownership, of authority, of social relationships has been destroyed. In its place has come the commune—a superb device for mobilizing manpower and for political control.

But this violent change has not ended the economic backwardness. Touring villages last year, it was difficult for me to believe that seventeen years had elapsed since my previous visit. I saw the same mud huts; families pushing the same heavy millstones to grind their grain; men, women, and children pulling the same ploughs. Not once in my two months of travel did I see a tractor at work in the fields.

Two senior officials of the Agriculture Ministry told me China has a hundred and twenty thousand "standard" tractors (that is, estimated in 15-horsepower units). Since most of the tractors are larger, their actual number may be no more than eighty thousand—for seventy-four thousand communes and more than half a billion peasants.

But even this may not offer a faithful picture of rural want. At the celebrated Nan Fan Commune in South Shansi, I was told this story by its young Communist leader. One recent summer the cottonfields were invaded by insects which were destroying the crop. A mass meeting was called to discuss the problem. As is the custom, an appropriate essay by Mao Tse-tung was read and discussed, and the answer was found between its lines.

"We organized a force of two hundred and fifty youngsters," the chairman said, "and sent them up the mountain to the fields. They remained there for seven days and seven nights. They ate and slept there, and they killed the bugs. By the time they came down, they had destroyed seventy thousand insects."

The crop was saved, and the village was proud of its youngsters' feat. But to me this image of two hundred fifty children crawling on all fours and hunting for bugs became a symbol not only of the strength of will but also of the stark backwardness of rural China.

Nothing preoccupies Mao as much as this backwardness. He knows and feels acutely the peasant's miseries. And possibly more than any man in Chinese history he has sought to end the inequity of rural life. No one in the village today prospers while someone else goes unfed.

But it is also true that like all the Soviet leaders up to and including Mr. Khrushchev, Mao Tse-tung never understood that the tired earth will give a high yield only if it is sown with a generous investment.

Billions of dollars have gone into the building of the atomic establishment. At the same time, wherever I went the commune officials complained about the shortage of farm tools and fertilizer; and for lack of pesticide, the children of the Nan Fan Commune crawled on all fours in a hunt for insects. In countless villages, men still dream of getting rubber tires for the heavy carts they pull. And thousands of villages, for lack of funds, go without schools, and their children go without education.

In the Great Leap Forward, the village was given verbal honors—and a low budgetary appropriation. It took the disastrously lean years of 1959–1961 to raise the priority of agriculture. But these have still been half measures. Sooner or later, Mao or his successors will learn, like the Soviet leaders, that the village requires not only love but also cash and care.

Meanwhile, however, China remains on her precarious course. For Mao's premise that underlay the Great Leap Forward was that it was possible to build a twentieth-century industry atop a countryside still barely emerging from the eighteenth. Both economically and politically this is an invitation to trouble. Today, the village is getting a more generous largesse from the state than, say, a half dozen years ago. But the basic premise of the Great Leap remains unchanged.

But to end the assessment of Mao and his work at this point would be neither fair nor accurate. For, with all his shortcomings, Mao is a subtle and brilliant thinker, and a leader whose achievements have been historic.

One of the most famous paintings in new China shows Mao Tse-tung reading the proclamation that established the People's Republic in 1949. On that day, the nation was still prostrate after a quarter of a century of civil war and external aggression. There was no money in the treasury, what industry there was lay disorganized, and many regions faced hunger.

Mao overcame these obstacles. He unified China and enabled her to speak with a vigorous voice. He gave the country a government more competent and uncorrupted than any China

ever had. He initiated an industrial revolution that made China
the second strongest industrial power in Asia. He also led a
psychological revolution that could best be compared to the religious revivals of the Middle Ages.

A conversation with Mao is a memorable experience. He is
not a spellbinder. But he is a fluent speaker with a disciplined
mind that rejects the extraneous and automatically relates the
isolated episode to the broad picture.

Mao's preoccupation with rural China is almost obsessive.
To me, he spoke of the peasant with knowledge and passion,
with pride and sympathy. He spoke in generalities, but each generality had behind it the recollection of a specific event. He
spoke of happenings in Hunan, where he was born in 1893;
of Kiangsi, in whose mountains he established a short-lived
soviet in the early thirties; and of northern Shensi, the harsh
and unfriendly country where I met him in 1947.

In Yenan, where life was so lean that a brown steamed
bun, issued twice a month, was regarded as a luxury, each
leader had his own field to cultivate. And Mao and his companions made it a practice to visit nearby villages to hear what
the peasants had to say, and to help in the daily chores. This
experience also became a strand in the fabric of Mao's thought.

In his conversation, Mao customarily used the standard
Marxist terminology. But, easily, he switched to the earthy
language of the peasant. As one listened to him, one gradually
felt himself immersed in the life of the Chinese village, its lore,
its superstitions, its hopes, fears, angers, and weaknesses. And
it became easy to imagine this man, in his padded cotton suit,
small cap, and a ridiculously short scarf, as the personification
of China's peasantry.

Mao's second preoccupation is with history. He sees his
revolution as an integral part of the entire experience of the
Chinese people. Thus, a conversation with Mao can be un-
settling, for the visitor may quickly lose all sense of time. Mao
may be speaking of an ambush in which his armies caught an
enemy column, and suddenly the visitor becomes aware that
the battle that is being described is not the recent one but one
much like it a thousand years earlier.

With me, Mao crisscrossed history, until I began to feel
that the great men and the villains of the past were familiar and

contemporary, and that what was happening now was indeed a natural sequel to a much older drama.

Most revolutionaries seek a link with the past, if only to establish a claim to historical respectability and native roots. But with Mao I came to feel that history was his habitat, from the first Chinese dynasty on, and that he felt close kinship to all the great rebels of the past. This sense of historic continuity seemed to give depth to his ideas and policies.

A fierce debate is raging among the Sinologists in the West on whether Mao is an innovator or merely a borrower of ideas first expounded by Marx and Lenin. Those who see in him no more than an able imitator are a little naïve. What Lenin said in 1922 about the role of a peasant in the revolutionary drama or a Comintern resolution passed in 1924 is largely irrelevant. What *is* relevant is that Mao tested, revised, changed, and carried out in the Chinese countryside ideas that before him were merely words on paper. In any sober assessment of Mao, he must be given credit for bold and original ideas.

One of these, of course, is the notion that it is not the worker but the discontented peasant who will bear the banners—and the guns—of the revolution in Asia. Mao may be wrong in insisting that his theory is universal; the experience of the Chinese peasant cannot be equated with that of the Watusi tribesman. But the experience in Asia seems to support some of his key ideas on revolution-making on that continent. In Vietnam, what is crucial is not the infiltration of the South by Northern units, nor the smuggling of guns to the Viet Cong, but the simple fact that without a measure of peasant support the rebellion could not last for four weeks.

Indeed, the war in Vietnam is a textbook illustration of the dangerous effectiveness of Mao's doctrine of the "people's war" and violent revolution. The West has as yet found no effective response to this type of revolution. In fact, some of its current responses—as Mao had foreseen—merely help to fan the flames of the insurrection.

One does not know what role Mao himself has played in the revision of Maoism that has been in progress in Peking since last spring. His imprint, however, is clear on Marshal Lin Piao's picture of the great industrial states being strangled by the revolutionary peasantry on other continents—as once in China the

Communist-held countryside strangled the Kuomintang-controlled cities.

This idea is anything but absurd. For what the marshal, or Mao, is saying is that, once much of Asia, Africa, and Latin America has gone Communist, the sensitive Western economies would collapse. Not even the United States could easily endure the loss of world markets and sources of raw materials.

What Mao and his companions have been saying to the malcontents of the have-not continents is, "Rise up in arms, and if there are enough of you, the American imperialists will not have enough strength to fight you." One of the crucial questions for the West today is whether Mao can make it come true. If he can, all the power relationships in the world will be altered.

Another of Mao's important ideas involves nuclear war. In 1947, Mao told me that "we're too primitive to fear the atomic bomb." He also described the bomb as a "paper tiger"—an expression he coined the previous summer.

Mao has since been depicted, notably by Mr. Khrushchev, as a warmonger who does not fear the nuclear holocaust because he does not understand it. But Mr. K. may have been distorting Mao's position. For if Mao knew little of the devastating effect of the A-bomb, and especially of radioactivity, he was also the first leader to detect, only a year after the tragedy in Hiroshima, the one striking flaw in nuclear power. The atomic bomb is awesomely effective against major centers of population and industry. Nuclear war could conceivably knock out Britain, France, West Germany, or, for that matter, the United States and the Soviet Union. But its effectiveness against primitive countries is limited—unless the user wanted to do the unthinkable and erase the target country with all its life off the map.

Furthermore, the atomic deterrent may be effective against a major nuclear power, but it is no deterrent against the kind of a revolution Mao has been preaching. The trouble with the A-bomb is that it has no sense of discrimination. It cannot tell apart the revolutionaries whom one may want to incinerate and the good people who must be spared. Mao has, thus, probably been right all along in insisting that the bomb could not be employed to prevent an Asian revolution—and, therefore, it *is* a "paper tiger" that need not be feared.

Since last spring, the Chinese leaders have been preparing their people for the possibility of a U.S. nuclear attack. Beyond doubt, the first such hours of such a war would see China's atomic installations, missile plants, and key industries destroyed. But this would hardly end the conflict, for what survives of Mao's revolution would take to the hills and the villages.

The land would lie poisoned and devastated, but this would give victory to no one. Mao perceived this in the days when the political and military strategists in the West saw the A-bomb as the ultimate, the unanswerable weapon.

Mao believes in violent revolution, but he is not likely to want to involve China in another war like that in Korea. Today, as he was in 1947, he seems confident the Revolution will triumph if only stout-hearted men everywhere rise up in arms against the *status quo,* local authority, and, above all, that champion of world imperialism, the United States. Mao's disciples have made clear their belief that China herself need do no more than help these revolutionaries in other lands with guns, supplies, and the magic of Maoism.

No black or white assessment of Mao as a political leader is possible. He understands his own world, but neither his experience nor his political philosophy equips him to understand the incredibly complex world of the industrial states. He set into motion forces that are changing China's society, but he neither trusts nor understands the new urbanite. And if he has launched China's renaissance, he remains anti-intellectual. A system that favors intellectuals encourages a free interplay of ideas. Except for the brief experiment in which Mao "let a hundred flowers bloom together and a hundred schools of thought contend," he has suppressed all ideas that did not serve his revolution.

Mao's political theories will remain explosive so long as there are backward continents and peoples determined to better their lot, with violence if necessary. Men as yet unborn will die because they had been inspired by his ideas. But Mao's genius lies more in wrecking the established order than in building a more sophisticated society. With China changing, Mao may already be outliving his time—as Stalin outlived *his* years before his death.

After he dies, Mao may come to be regarded, along with Lenin, as one of the two political giants of this century. But, like Lenin, he may also be venerated, exalted, and eventually quoted in support of policies he would have fought tooth and spear while alive.

𝕽 *Mao the Poet*

OF THE great leaders of the world, only Mao is a poet. Some of his best poems have been published in China and have become required reading. Official commentaries have already appeared which, as in past centuries, interpret each phrase as an allusion to some larger, impersonal event. Yet despite the formalism that once marked so much Chinese poetry, it always remained a vehicle for the deepest personal expression.

The first poem, written during the middle of the Long March, speaks of the exaltation in reaching the top of a mountain pass—the whole world in all its splendor stretches out before one's eyes. But Mao reminds us that it takes time to reach the top, as the horses laboriously make their way up the ever steeper slopes. The second, written in April 1949, speaks of friendship, mutual sorrow, and the nostalgia for past friends and time gone by. The third was written in one of China's darkest periods (1962), a time of economic crisis and of conflict with an old ally, the Soviet Union. There is a sense of hope, but it is shrouded in a grim panorama of "winter clouds" and "cold currents."

In the West, Mao is usually pictured as the archetypal unemotional impersonal Communist leader. Thus the Westerner who reads Mao's poetry is always surprised to find that as well as writing dry tracts on ideology and politics, he is capable of writing with great feeling and sensitivity about human matters.

MAO TSE-TUNG *

From *The Poems of Mao Tse-tung*

LOUSHAN PASS

Cold is the west wind;
Far in the frosty air the wild geese call in the morning moonlight.
    In the morning moonlight
The clatter of horses' hooves rings sharp,
And the bugle's note is muted.

Do not say that the strong pass is guarded with iron.
This very day in one step we shall pass its summit,
    We shall pass its summit!
There the hills are blue like the sea,
And the dying sun like blood.

TO MR. LIU YA-TSE

I cannot forget how at Canton we were drinking tea to-
    gether,
And at Chungking exchanging verses just when the leaves
    were yellow.
Thirty-one years have passed, we are back in the old capital;
At the season of falling flowers I am reading your beautiful
    lines.
Take care not to break your heart with too much sorrow;
We should ever take far-sighted views of the ways of the
    world.

* Mao Tse-tung, *Nineteen Poems* (Peking: Foreign Languages Press, 1958),
pp. 16, 24. "Winter Clouds" was translated by Franz Schurmann in 1964.

Do not say that the waters of Kunming Lake are too
  shallow;
For watching fish they are better than Fuchun River.

WINTER CLOUDS

Snow presses winter clouds, white cotton flies,
  Thousand flowers take confused leave, suddenly so few.
High heaven—the cold current rushes in boiling,
  Great earth—a warm breath blows just a bit.
If only the heroes chase away tigers and panthers,
  None of the brave need fear the bears.
Plum blossoms sing out happy of snow that fills the heaven,
  Who cares about the flies that have frozen to death!

✿ Party and Government:
The Organizational Instruments of Rule

THE CHINESE COMMUNISTS' greatest achievement has been the unification of a vast country which had degenerated into anarchy, regional satrapies, and incessant internecine conflict. Winning the Civil War was only the first step toward unification. The one valuable instrument at their disposal in 1949 was the army with which they achieved victory. With the support of the general population, which saw in the Communists hope of escape from the interminable cycle of war and poverty, it had defeated all military opposition on the Chinese Mainland. But Party and government, two pillars of rule today, were not yet organizational instruments adequate to the task of ruling a great country.

The administrative systems which the Communists had set up earlier in the Northwest were crude, albeit efficient governments, hardly suited to the task of running large modern cities like Peking and Shanghai. The disciplined, loyal, effective body of men which constituted the Chinese Communist Party had formed the political nucleus of victory, but with its preponderant membership of illiterate peasants, it was hardly in a position to assume rule over an entire country. To make matters worse, China's biggest regions, Manchuria and Sinkiang, came under powerful Soviet influence. A Nationalist blockade at sea cut off the coast from the outer world, and behind the Nationalists stood a hostile America. From late 1950 to 1953, China waged a bloody war in Korea.

The seeming ease with which the Chinese Communists unified their country, proclaiming a new constitution in 1954 (the symbol of unity rather than legality), makes us forget the tremendous obstacles they faced in 1949. How did they achieve unity?

The key is the Communist Party's remarkable organization. It is difficult for Westerners, accustomed to parliamentary-
type political parties, to grasp the nature of a Communist
Party in a socialist country. On paper it is a hierarchical organization whose apex is a central committee, and more narrowly a politburo, with levels of provincial and local organizations descending to the basic units of social organization: factories, farms, schools, stores, and offices. The Party is an alter
ego to society. At top, middle, or bottom, wherever there is an
organized group of men, for example, an office or a factory,
inside of that group will be a committee or team of Party members. These Party members hold positions in the larger organization, but at the same time work in the Party, and they work
hard. They must undergo thought reform, read and discuss policy
documents, hammer out work plans, and analyze the men with
whom, and the environment in which, they operate. Since the
early 1950s literacy has been a firm requirement for Party membership. In short, the Party embraces the active leadership elite
of the country.

Equal credit belongs to the type of government the Chinese
Communists set up, which was and remains modeled on that of
the Soviet Union. The Chinese Communists, learning from
their Soviet mentors, quickly realized that one way to assure
national unity and launch development was to gain comprehensive control over the economy. The economy was divided
into many sectors, property was nationalized, and specialized central ministries were established which took command over each
sector. An example of this approach is the centralized banking
system, which rapidly gained control over all money and credit
in China by creating a nationwide network of branch banks to
monopolize all monetary transactions. Aside from these ministerial empires, Peking set up various coordinating agencies, such
as the State Planning Commission, to work out national economic balances and design developmental plans.

In the following selection the senior author of this reader
points out that "China today is governed by a structure of organization that consists of three great arms: *Party, Government,
Army.*" Since the army is dealt with elsewhere, he focuses on
Party and government. The main argument is that despite attempts at tight centralization in the early 1950s, the administra-

tive system of China is today partially decentralized. This is particularly true of the economy. That unity remains strong despite some provincial autonomy, indicating that the Chinese Communists have found a way of combining central control with regional flexibility. But as the author notes, decisive in this picture of rule is the Party's role: "With all of the trials it has endured over the years, the Party has emerged as a permanent institution in the country. It is everywhere, penetrates everything, and keeps its mind on its chief task: maintaining the national integrity of the country."

FRANZ SCHURMANN *
Party

When the Chinese Communists triumphed in 1949, they faced not only the chaos of a decade of war, but all the immense problems confronting China as a consequence of a long revolution. The three great problems Peking faced were the classical problems facing all backward countries, but on a magnitude surpassing those of all other countries. The first was national integration. China may have had a long history of national unity, but fifty years of internal war had torn the fabric of unity. Since 1911 no Chinese government had been able to create a working administrative system to hold the country together. The Communists had won a war, but so had the Kuomintang in 1927. The second was economic development. China had only the most rudimentary beginnings of a modern economy, and what there was of modern industry had been damaged and despoiled by war and Soviet occupation. Since the 1870s Chinese governments had attempted to emulate Japan and enter the modern economic world, but all attempts had failed. The third was population growth, which posed several challenges, the simplest and most difficult of which was the fact that more food had to

* Franz Schurmann, *Party and Government* (unpublished paper).

be extracted from an agriculture that in many respects had reached its limits of productivity. But there were other population problems: the cities were growing fast and new opportunities had to be created for the immigrants; the spread of education was already creating new demands in excess of the society's capacities to satisfy them. These, of course, were macroscopic problems that could not be resolved in the immediate period following victory. More pressing problems, which had to be dealt with immediately, arose from the chaos of war. Rural China was in the throes of a revolutionary land reform. More than a million individuals left the cities to join the Nationalists on Taiwan. They constituted an important segment of China's small middle class which had contributed badly needed administrative and professional talent.

The first challenge to be faced was the need for national unity. The Chinese Communists entered the cities as revolutionary occupiers with armies made up largely of peasant cadres and soldiers. Despite the existence of governmental organization in what were called the "old liberated areas," the Chinese Communists had little experience in managing large metropolitan centers. There was not much of an administrative structure for them to take over even if they had so intended. They had scored a series of brilliant military victories over Kuomintang armies that were not always as disorganized and corrupt as has subsequently been alleged. But battlefield success has little relationship to success in administering a country. Despite the monumental difficulties the Chinese Communists faced, they succeeded in a short time in creating a government able to administer without military force. It took five years to create the government, for it was not till October 1954 that a new constitution was proclaimed and a *de facto* government given *de jure* legitimation. In 1955 China's wartime armies were largely demobilized and its veterans sent home. There have been significant changes in China's administrative system during the fifteen-year history of the Chinese People's Republic, yet in all this time the governmental system has remained intact and functioning. Internal unity was not created without threats to it: in the early 1950s there was still serious resistance from nationality groups, notably in Sinkiang; Manchuria, in the words of the Chinese Communists, was turning into "an independent kingdom" until those tendencies were decisively eradicated in 1954; the Tibetan Rebellion of 1959 was the last and greatest of the revolts of non-Chinese nationalities against Han rule. During the serious economic crisis of 1960–1961 whole areas degenerated into lawlessness and had to be governed militarily. Despite the seriousness of these challenges to national unity, they are hardly comparable to the *de facto* secession of whole provinces that took place during the Nationalist era. There can be no doubt that if there had been real disintegration, Kuomintang armies would have intervened from Taiwan to realize Chiang's dream of a return to the Mainland. The Chinese Communists succeeded in creating a fabric of national unity unprecedented in Chinese history.

The world forgets rapidly what China was like before 1949. Mao Tse-tung has not. In his declining years Mao's greatest concern is transforming national unity into steel bonds that will never again break. He is well aware of the lessons of Chinese history, and of the Chinese people's tendencies toward self-absorption. Regionalism remains a centrifugal factor in the country. Chinese parochialism can be seen in the Overseas Chinese, most of whom seem quite prepared at the moment to accept any political rule over them which allows them freedom to "do business."

It has always been something of a paradox that Japan, which until 1868 was governed by a rickety bureaucracy and divided into feudal regions, should so suddenly have achieved national unity, while China, with its centuries-old tradition of unity, fell apart. Unification in early Meiji Japan was greatly helped by the Emperor's symbolic role. The young radical *samurai,* who led Japan into modernization, saw in the Emperor a powerful anti-feudal force who could pull the nation together until adequate new institutions had been created.

Chinese Emperors have traditionally been different from their Japanese counterparts. For centuries the Japanese Emperor was powerless, yet the institution of Imperial rule persisted. The Emperor of China, a different figure, exercised power and used it to make and enforce policy; he was a leader, not a symbol. But China did have a human symbol comparable to the Japanese Emperor—Confucius, who was called the "uncrowned king." Confucius was the symbol of the moral and ethical order that pervaded agrarian China. Recently there has been something like an apotheosis of Mao Tse-tung. The Russians have accused the Chinese of practicing the personality cult, and they are right: the writings of Mao Tse-tung have become scripture for almost every aspect of human life. But in this apotheosis Mao resembles Confucius more than Stalin. Now that he is old and incapable of the direct leadership of earlier days, he has become China's modern sage. Chinese intellectuals are often cynical about Mao's apotheosis, but one must remember that the symbolic importance of Confucius was greatest on the land, among the peasantry—the class from which Mao is recruiting a large number of his young Red cadres. Mao realizes that national unity cannot rely on organization alone, that in the long run organization must have a social basis. If the peasants and the workers are that basis, then China's tradition suggests the need for a popular ethos. In the past the ethos centered on a human symbol—Confucius. (See pp. 628–632 on Mao's more active leadership role as a consequence of the "Great Proletarian Cultural Revolution.")

Regardless of the recourse to political symbolism, China's rulers are a practical, hard-headed group of individuals. Organization holds the country together, and most of the efforts of the leadership are directed to using, directing, and solidifying the remarkable structure they have created. China today is governed by a structure of organization which consists of three great arms: *Party, Government, Army.* These three organizations are intimately interrelated, and each plays a significant role in the governing of society.

This trinitarian system of state differs from that of the Soviet Union, where the army remains segregated from civil society and is a highly professional force, performing the classical functions of an army: national defense (though Stalin's purges of Tukhachevsky and Blücher, and Khrushchev's ouster of Zhukov suggest that the army was involved in political struggles). The Chinese were not always committed to the idea of making the army a part of national life. In the early 1950s they followed the Soviet model of building a small professional army more or less segregated from civil society, except for public works projects it undertook and in border areas where it was permanently encamped. But from the late 1950s on, policy changed. The Great Leap Forward and the ouster of P'eng Te-huai saw a far-reaching deprofessionalization of the army and the rise of the popular militia as a major part of the military system. There can be no doubt that the army's enhanced role in civil life is bound up with Mao's concern for national unity. Mao is determined that this triple structure of government, Party, and army shall continue to govern China. So far, this approach has been remarkably successful in holding a sprawling country together.

Though a full discussion of Communist China's political system requires careful consideration of the role the army plays in both Party and government (and vice-versa), we shall here restrict ourselves to Party and government. In any case, beyond the broad outlines of the army's important position in the political system, we know few details about the concrete interpenetration of these three arms of the state.

Westerners often see all Communist Parties in the Soviet image. Thus the accusation of Stalinism has been easy to hurl at the Chinese; in fact, the Russians themselves have made it. The Communist Party of the Soviet Union is a body different from its Chinese counterpart. It was born in Russian Social Democracy, triumphed in the struggle of the October Revolution, and was decimated by Stalin. It still carries the revolutionary ideology of its origins, but in fact it is a collectivity of the country's elite. All who govern or excel in this highly industrialized and professionalized country are in the Party. In Stalin's day, it became as bureaucratized as the country as a whole.

The Chinese Communist Party was reborn in the mid-thirties in the remote periphery of China from a band of ten thousand who survived the Long March. The Long March has the symbolic importance to the Chinese that the October Revolution has to the Russians: it is the beginning of their road to victory. The Chinese Communist Party has undergone periodic purges and has faced deep internal crises, yet has held together. Its solidarity is symbolized by the continuity of its leadership from Yenan times to the present. The Chinese Communist Party is an organization of combat leaders and cadres. Ever since Yenan times the Chinese Communists have been concerned with leadership, with finding young men who could take command of groups of human beings and direct them in work and battle. The cadre ideal remains basic to the Party, and is expressed by the preferential recruitment of young poor workers and peasants.

The membership of the Chinese Communist Party today is about seventeen million, according to the most recent statements (released in July 1961); the vast majority of its members were recruited since 1953. Since the attrition rate appears to be fairly low, the average age of members must be approaching the late thirties. The recent campaign to train a new revolutionary generation is intended to bring new, young, proletarian cadres into the Party. The generational problem is serious in China, not only between the old and the middle-aged, but between the middle-aged and the young. Leadership capacity often turns into administrative ability as men grow older; hence, given the Chinese Communists' deep fear of bureaucratization, one can understand their desire to keep the emphasis on youth. In the summer of 1964 a Communist Youth League held a congress in Peking, at which were present all the top leaders of the country. Mao told them that the reins of the Revolution must remain in their hands during the decades that would be needed to make China into a rich and powerful country. The current emphasis on learning from the People's Liberation Army also stresses the role of youth, since continual turnover has kept the army young in years. Without corrective measures the Party could easily turn into the kind of middle-aged elite club the Soviet Party has become. It is in this aging process more than anything else in which the seeds of revisionism lie. Aging and bureaucratization often appear to go hand in hand. Whether the process that Max Weber has called routinization will win out in the long run remains to be seen. It is here that the militarization of society, symbolized by the army's active role in civil life, plays a powerful part. The Party may grow old, but the army will remain young, as long as it does not go too far on the road to professionalization. Professional training demands years of study and intellectual investment, and as a result, highly professionalized armies tend to develop corps of middle-aged cadres. Conscript armies, popular militias, young infantry officers who need little technical training keep the emphasis on youth. If the Party rules China today, the army is assuming the increasingly important task of keeping militancy, leadership, and youthful attitudes alive.

The organizational structure of the Communist Party is easily described. It stands as an alter ego alongside every unit of organization in the country. Factories, communes (and their production brigades), schools, government bureaus, military companies, and so on—all have their Party committees. The Party committees contain most of the important leaders of the counterpart organizational unit. In a factory top management, leading staff personnel, supervisors down to the work-team level, and outstanding workers are members of the Party committee or of some lower-echelon Party organization. These are called basic-level organizations of the Party, and at times they may be so large that they have to be broken down into smaller units, called branches and teams. Party committees which exercise authority at the top may also be large, so that the old device of standing committees is used to facilitate decision-making. Whatever form their activities take, the Party organizations group together all the important people in an organization. Within this collective context problems can be thrashed out with all the key people present and arguing. A common type of meeting is actually called a "knock-heads-together meeting" (p'eng-t'ou-hui).

These basic-level Party organizations constitute the building blocks of a pyramid of organization that follows the territorial lines of administrative divisions. The factory Party committee is subject to a district committee, which in turn is subject to a city committee, and so on up the ladder to the Central Committee, which, despite its name, more resembles the large delegates' meetings that take place at various levels of organization. Such meetings may include hundreds of members. The Central Committee contains close to two hundred members, but when it meets, hundreds of others may be invited to attend. Large bodies cannot make decisions; they can only discuss them, and this is in fact what the Central Committee does. When it meets in plenary session, which is not too frequent, it discusses basic policy lines that have been decided on by the Politburo. Discussions are by no means mechanical. The Politburo may have worked out a general line, but specific policies as well as operational details still have to be thrashed out. Plenary meetings of the Central Committee are often attended by provincial

Party secretaries and their deputies who know best what local conditions are and how general policy can be adapted to them. Central Committee sessions begin with reports read by leaders who have had a major voice in making the decisions for the sector concerned. The meeting then splits up into small group sessions, in which vigorous discussion takes place. In this crucial process of verbalization, the members get a firm grip on what the new line is. Plenary sessions are resumed, at which members ask questions, demand clarification, and perhaps on occasion even suggest modification. Again, small group sessions are held. Finally, the plenum agrees on the wording of draft proposals which are to be submitted to the State Council for promulgation or constitute policy statements to be made known to the country at large. We have no detailed descriptions as to how the Central Committee works, but we do have descriptions of lower-echelon meetings. The conjecture is justified that the consultative process at the highest level more or less follows the general pattern.

The Party's top decision-making body is, of course, the Politburo. Unlike the Russians, who changed the name of this body to Presidium, the Chinese have retained the traditional name. The term "political" connotes policy-making in Chinese, in contrast to the more managerial-sounding "presidium." The Politburo's composition has always held the keenest interest of outside observers, as giving an indication of policy trends. No changes in membership have been announced since May 1958, although there are several members who, like Ch'en Yün and P'eng Te-huai, have lost power and influence. Judging from positions known to have been taken by various Politburo members, it is doubtful that there is ever monolithic agreement on all questions. The men around Mao Tse-tung are not yes-men, as were those surrounding Stalin. The Chinese Communists have not hesitated to denounce their internal and external opponents, yet on the other hand they have not liquidated them in Stalin fashion. Opponents purged during the great anti-rightist movements of 1957–1958 have been rehabilitated. Ch'en Yün, who is known to have opposed Mao's radical plans for agriculture, reappeared in public life in January 1965. (See pp. 607–615 for changes in leadership positions as a consequence of the "Great Proletarian Cultural Revolution.")

There is also a standing committee consisting of seven old men of the revolution: Mao Tse-tung, Liu Shao-ch'i, Chu Teh, Chou En-lai, Ch'en Yün, Lin Piao, and Teng Hsiao-p'ing. There is a powerful secretariat headed by Teng Hsiao-p'ing which is the Party's top administrative arm. The secretariat has the important role of maintaining direct contact with the provincial Party chiefs, and thus constitutes a strong link in the chain between center and province. There also are two other committees directly attached to the Politburo: one is in charge of Party discipline, and has played major roles during rectification movements; the other is called the General Political Department for Military Affairs. Political departments constitute the Party structure in the military and are under the control of the General Political Department. Although nothing is known about this committee's membership and functions, it undoubtedly has the extremely important task of maintaining tight linkage between the party and the military.

The Chinese Communist Party is the real key to China's present-day unity. Its threads run through every organized segment of society. It consists of individuals who have undergone long processes of political training. Party membership is not easily won, and candidates must demonstrate leadership ability, education, some professional talent, and above all evidence of political skill and loyalty. Candidate members have to participate in long sessions during which they are subject to intense criticism whose purpose is not merely to ferret out disloyal tendencies but to test leadership ability. Men lead by talk as well as by action, and the highly articulate and expressive Chinese Communists put great stress on the verbal ability of their Party members. No matter what a man's loyalty, if he cannot function as a leader in his place of work, his chances for Party membership are poor. Once membership is granted, participation in what is called Party life is obligatory. Members must give reports, which is a test of their ability to gather information and express it, to focus on problems, as well as to add to the constant flow of political, social, and economic data transmitted upward. The Party measures the pulse of the nation. Rigorous self-discipline is an inevitable consequence of this training.

It is significant that there have been very few defections of

Party members to the outside world, indicating that the Party is a powerful body able to retain its members' loyalty. The rewards and motivations for membership are not easy to assess. For the sons of workers and peasants, it is a channel of mobility where their leadership talents can be utilized. Semi-educated Party members are given chances to attend higher schools and get an education which they would have difficulty getting in ordinary civil life. The incentives for membership among professionals and the intellectuals is probably less, inasmuch as many feel they have more to gain in the long run from higher technical training. One must not underestimate in all this the appeal of a powerful ideology which teaches sacrifice for a higher cause.

The Chinese Communist Party did not acquire its leadership position in a matter of days after victory. In fact, it showed signs of shame at its crude peasant background. In 1949 the Party changed its recruitment policy from emphasis on peasant membership to workers and intellectuals, mostly city people. Peasant cadres won the Civil War, but they were also responsible for the bloody excesses of land reform. High standards of membership were set, with the result that the Party remained organizationally weak for a number of years. Professionals and intellectuals moved into top positions. In Manchuria and perhaps also Shanghai, factionalist tendencies began to appear. Party organization was spotty in many areas. It is not accidental that when bureaucratic rule was strongest in China, the Party was relatively weak. Things changed radically in 1955. With demobilization, millions of veterans returned to their villages, joined the Party, and led the collectivization movement. Party membership doubled in the space of about a year, after which Party power grew until it ran the country from top to bottom during the Great Leap Forward. Just about the only leadership exercised in the country during 1958–1960 came from the Party. Local Party cadres were mostly workers and peasants, fanatic and enthusiastic in their newly acquired power roles. Since early 1961 the scope of Party power has been reduced, and a kind of collaboration-cum-conflict relationship exists between them and the professionals, somewhat the same situation as during the mild years 1956–1957. With all the trials it has endured over the years, the Party has emerged as a permanent institution in the country. It is everywhere, penetrates everything, and keeps its mind on its chief task: maintaining the national integrity of the country.

Government

Let us begin this discussion with the governmental bureaucracy. As in every country, there is a hierarchy of state administration from local to national levels. The smallest unit is called the *hsiang,* an administrative entity comprising a number of villages and usually based on a market town. For all practical purposes, *hsiang* and the people's commune are identical, although the pattern varies somewhat by region. Above the *hsiang,* there is the county or *hsien,* traditionally the lowest level of state administration in Imperial times. The *hsien* is a fairly large administrative unit with an average population of over 215,000; by contrast, the average population of a *hsiang* is around 7,000. Above the *hsien* level, there are often the special districts. Above the *hsien* and the special district is the province. There are in all twenty-nine provinces or regions comparable to provinces, including Peking and Shanghai. There are other types of administrative districts, but they exist mainly in the nationality areas.

During the early 1950s the Chinese Communists tried to create a centralized administration, following the Soviet model, wherein provinces, districts, counties, and *hsiang* were largely rungs on a continuous ladder. But policy changed, probably as early as 1955. The leaders in Peking realized that to govern effectively they had to allow some degree of autonomy at subnational levels; the question was, at which level. In 1949 the country was divided into seven Large Administrative Regions governed by civil-military committees with far-reaching autonomous powers. It was clear that Peking was not yet in a position to govern from the center. The most autonomous of these regions was Manchuria. In the summer of 1954 the Large Administrative Regions were abolished, and the province re-established as the highest subnational level of administration. In 1956 discussions on decentralization began in political and academic circles. Late in 1957 Peking issued a series of decentralization decrees which granted provincial governments greater autonomy, notably in the economic field. As is apparent from a variety of evidence, the provinces assumed far greater administrative importance than they had in the early 1950s, when a provincial bureau was often little more than a branch of a central ministry. From the mid-1950s on, the provincial bureau became a part of a highly active provincial government, and to the extent that it can be judged, has remained so to the present time.

What this means is that the two crucial levels of administration are national and provincial. In this sense China's administrative system somewhat resembles that of the United States and Brazil, where state governments enjoy a wide area of autonomy. The similarities are, of course, functional and not legal. Peking can always, if it wishes, withdraw any powers it has granted provincial governments. There is no real counterpart to the Chinese province in the Soviet Union where republics are delineated on nationality grounds; several are actually artificial creations of the Soviet period. China has no counterpart to the RSFSR in the Soviet Union, which is almost as big as the country itself. Despite some minor redrawing of boundary lines, the present-day Chinese provinces are much the same as those of the Kuomintang period. In the early 1950s the Chinese Communists created a new province call P'ingyüan in Central China, but abolished it not long thereafter; it is clear that there is an historical unity to the provinces that the Communists were unable or unwilling to change, and only in Manchuria, in one sense China's newest region, have there been significant redrawings of provincial boundary lines. The Chinese provinces were first laid out by the Mongols in the thirteenth century. Since the Ming Dynasty provincial boundaries have remained essentially as they were then. In the course of time the provinces have acquired a marked cultural character. Kwangtung, for example, is mostly Cantonese-speaking, though it contains the Swatow region in the north which speaks a different dialect. Kwangsi consists of two major dialect areas, one close to Kwangtung and the other close to what the Chinese call "the common speech," or the language of North China. The provinces are areas of traditional administrative unity that contain populations which identify themselves in provincial terms (to a Chinese, for example, Mao is clearly a Hunanese). The provincial identification appears to be much stronger in China than in Japan, where the "provinces" were abolished in 1870 and have for the most part vanished from popular memory.

In the period after 1911, many provinces, under the control of warlords, fell out of central control. How is it that the Chinese Communists have once again allowed provincial autonomy, without fearing a recurrence of the centrifugal forces that plagued China after 1911? The Chinese Communists have not been indifferent to this problem. At the very time when the government announced its decentralization measures late in 1957, a high-ranking Party official from Chekiang warned: "We must not allow the slogan 'regionalization of cadres' to be used to develop regionalism; we must not allow those other-minded individuals to use this slogan to alienate outside cadres from local cadres." Early in the 1950s the Chinese Communists encouraged local recruitment of cadres to avoid the appearance of being a foreign occupation army. By late 1957, when the leaders began to fear that "regionalization of cadres" might have gone too far, that local cadres were committed more to local than to national goals, an internal Party purge rooted out some of the most "regionalistic" Party leaders.

The answer to the question about unity with decentralization lies in the Communist Party. Decentralization gives the provinces scope to act within the context of local conditions, but the Party acts as a link between the center and the region. It is in this linkage role that one can see one of the Chinese Communist Party's most important present-day functions.

Let us look at central government. The most striking thing is the proliferation of government agencies, particularly those concerned with economic problems. Over the years there has been some reduction in the number of government agencies, but the structure of administration at the central level has not changed fundamentally. Organization charts give an idea of the complexity of the governmental structure, and details need not be given here. In general, one might say that governmental agencies fall into three general types: policymaking, coordinative, and administrative. As a whole, the Chinese Communists have tended fairly clearly to separate policymaking from policy-executing functions, a phenomenon called in the Western literature the policy-administration dichotomy. The extremely large numbers of ministries indicate a high degree of functional specialization, yet one must remember that few ministries have broad policymaking powers. The decisions governing the operations of the economic ministries, for example, are not made in the ministry but by higher-level committees.

There have been many changes of ministry chiefs and department directors over the years, but in the politically less sensitive ministries staff personnel has remained quite stable. The Minister and two Deputy Ministers of Foreign Trade, for example, have been in since 1952 (another came in in 1955, and two others in 1956). The same pattern holds true for a number of other ministries. On the other hand, there have been politically sensitive ministries, such as the Ministry of Commerce, where there has been almost a complete personnel turnover at the top levels since 1958. For a long time the Ministry of Commerce was headed by Ch'en Yün, known for his cautious approach to economic development. Under his leadership, the Ministry of Commerce acquired vast powers over the supply and allocation system.

During the anti-rightist movement of the latter half of 1957 a number of staff individuals from certain ministries were attacked and removed from their posts. There are grounds for believing that these attacks were actually directed against top-level individuals whose opinions were not acceptable. It has been argued by Western observers that there is a growing corps of professionals at the next-to-highest levels of the governmental apparatus, and that this group might eventually accede to leadership. This may be so, but it is equally possible that this group might simply continue on in terms of its present qualifications and experience, and that the new policymaking group may arise from a completely different context. The practice of keeping policy and administrative functions separate is an old Chinese habit. In Imperial times the local magistrate was always surrounded by a staff of experts who continued on for years in the yamen, while magistrates were regularly transferred from district to district. Similarly, in pre-1949 Chinese business concerns, the boards of directors rarely bothered with managerial problems, leaving them to be resolved by experts in whom they had full trust.

A second type of agency performs essentially coordinative functions. Western observers have noted the Chinese Communist predilection for committee government. There are many reasons for this. In the period immediately after victory there was no choice but to govern by committee. Military administration was carried out largely by committees which contained a broad range of political, military, and civil individuals. Even after the establishment of regular bureaucratic rule, the committee system continued. In fact, one might say that all Chinese policymaking bodies are committees rather than specialized agencies. A committee groups together individuals from different agencies, and so permits decision-making in a context in which broad knowledge is available. But committees and comparable bodies also have coordinative functions, particularly necessary in the Chinese government, in which there are so many specialized agencies. The most important coordinative agencies in the government are the Offices of the State Council. There were six of these: agriculture and forestry, culture and education, finance and trade, foreign affairs, industry and communications, and political and legal affairs. These coordinative offices seem to be headed by experts in the field concerned. Thus, the Office for Foreign Affairs is headed by Ch'en Yi, and includes four Deputy Directors, of whom the most notable are Liao Ch'eng-chih and Liu Ning-i. None of the latter can be considered as being in the top policymaking group as far as foreign affairs are concerned, yet each is involved in a different area of foreign work and thus can be considered to have specialized knowledge and experience. In fact, one might hazard the guess that the work of these offices is far more important than the State Council's collective deliberations. The vice-premiers of the State Council are for the most part full or candidate members of the Politburo. The secretariat of the State Council, on the other hand, consists mostly of administrative personnel whose main tasks appear to be administration of the great bureaucratic structure attached to the State Council.

A third type of body performs essentially policymaking functions. Top policymaking functions are, of course, vested in the Politburo. Nevertheless the Chinese Communists make a basic distinction in regard to policy. There are two words for policy in Chinese: *fang-chen* and *cheng-ts'e,* which together may be translated as "line and policy." *Fang-chen* literally means "line," but in fact refers to general policy. *Cheng-ts'e,* on the other hand, refers to specific policy. The Politburo may lay down a general line on economic development to be followed during a given period, but these decisions still have to be translated into more specific terms to make action possible. The specific policies derived from the general line are called *cheng-ts'e.*

When the Chinese Communists instituted decentralization in late 1957, they empowered provincial authorities to make decisions on specific policies. Peking, however, determined the line. Enough has been written in Western organizational literature to make clear that basic policymaking can occur at many levels of an organizational system, and that highest-level policy decisions do not always produce one-for-one consequences at lower echelons, and conversely that lower-level operational decisions often have a forcing effect on top-level policy. This, in fact, turned out to be one of the serious difficulties during the Great Leap Forward, when provincial authorities made specific policy decisions that ultimately worked against the general line adopted by Peking. This was openly expressed late in 1958, when members of the State Planning Commission voiced alarm at the extent to which unregulated economic activity at the provincial level was leading to a breakdown of the state economic plan.

Perhaps the three most important bodies in the State Council responsible for specific policy decisions are: (1) the State Planning Commission, which, following the Soviet pattern, concerns itself with long-range economic planning; (2) the State Economic Commission, which works out annual and short-range plans, and in general is in charge of current economic activity; and (3) the Scientific-Technological Commission, which is in charge of basic scientific and technological work, and probably directs China's nuclear program. In addition, many of the ministries have far-reaching specific policymaking powers, among which the Ministry of National Defense, the Finance Ministry, and the Ministry of Commerce can be singled out. The first was headed for years by P'eng Te-huai and appears to have pursued military professionalization policies which, in September 1959, led to P'eng's removal and subsequent replacement by Lin Piao. The Ministry of National Defense makes specific policy on military programs, and has influence on industrialization programs. The Ministry of Finance is also an extremely important agency, headed since 1954 by Li Hsiennien, who has been known for his policies of fiscal responsibility and balanced budgets. He almost certainly opposed the free-spending tendencies of the Great Leap Forward, and there is evidence that he had been indirectly attacked. But he returned to prominence late in 1958 when the regime retreated from the excesses of the Great Leap Forward. Since early 1961, the power of the Ministry of Finance has grown even more, until now it plays a major role in the direction and regulation of the economy. The Ministry of Commerce, headed until the late 1950s by Ch'en Yün, a well-known moderate, operates the far-flung supply system, and so has always played a strong role in the matter of allocation.

"Who makes the decisions?" is one question that bedevils all organization, not just the state system of China. Decision-making is hard enough to study when the workings of organization are known, let alone when it is shrouded in secrecy as in the case of China. Some general trends seem to be visible over the years, however. During the early 1950s the Chinese Communists pursued a policy of creating strong central bureaucracies, notably ministries and economic agencies. Although this was done partly in emulation of the Soviet system, another reason lies in the type of central planning the Chinese were instituting. Central planning is impossible without bureaucratic networks, and so it is not surprising that basic decisions were made in the ministries and agencies. The State Planning Commission, organized late in 1952, must have had far-reaching powers. Headed by Kao Kang, it consisted to a surprising extent of individuals who were later dismissed from or lost influence in the leadership. Since Manchuria was the core area of economic development during the First Five Year Plan, it is not likely that any decisions could have been made without Kao Kang's concurrence. The trend toward growing ministerial power was reversed in 1955, with the ouster of Kao Kang and the initiation of an anti-bureaucratic movement know as *Su-fan*. Ministerial power appears to have increased again during the years of stabilization, 1956 and 1957; but the late-1957 decentralization measures deprived the central ministries of broad areas of jurisdiction. Almost all light industry, for example, was removed from central jurisdiction and put into the hands of provincial authorities. An anti-ministerial mood prevailed simultaneously in the Soviet Union, but the power shift in China appears to have been farther-reaching. In its most general sense, the struggle may be seen as one between the reds and the experts, as the Chinese put it. The reds won out in late 1957, and with that victory came greater emphasis on government by committee, both at national and provincial levels.

The present situation is difficult to judge. There can be little doubt that many of the ministries have recovered powers lost during the Great Leap Forward. The recent emphasis on financial control has expanded the Finance Ministry's and People's Bank's functions. On the other hand, the tendency to keep policymaking functions in committee hands has continued. Early in 1964 a number of "political departments" were set up directly under the Central Committee, the most publicized of which is the Political Department for Finance and Trade. This hierarchy of political departments is parallel to the ministerial branches, and despite their political and even military character, there has been a distinct emphasis on putting professionals in charge. The main purpose of the political departments appears to be coordinative, in particular to iron out frictions arising between the national ministries and local Party committees, the latter having acquired much power during the Great Leap Forward. The fact that the political departments are attached to the Central Committee gives them an authority to arbitrate conflicts which any other kind of body would not have.

A final word might be said on the policy-administration dichotomy. One of the most striking aspects of nineteenth-century Western, notably British, diplomatic contact with China was the British insistence that they have direct contact with Chinese policymakers, whereas the Chinese insisted that the British channel their contacts through the policymakers' agents. Neither, of course, understood the other's ways. It has long been Chinese practice to insulate policymakers from negotiational situations. The general line is laid down, and the operational agent, traditionally a man of high and respected stature, carries on negotiations with his counterpart, and at times can even make policy decisions, though of the nature of *cheng-ts'e* rather than *fang-chen*. The point is, he who holds ultimate authority never negotiates, which creates flexibility and inflexibility on the part of the Chinese professional negotiator, who has enough delegated authority to make decisions on technical points, yet cannot make basic decisions on major matters. Here, China's pattern of diplomatic negotiation differs from that of the Soviet Union, whose major decision-makers have been directly involved in negotiations, whereas China's top leaders, Mao and Liu, have not been. In fact, Liu Shao-ch'i's late-1960 journey to Moscow, where he was actively involved in the polemic with the Russians, was a fiasco.

This deep-rooted practice of separating policy and operational matters is undoubtedly a factor responsible for the existence of two different power groups in China, the red cadres and the professional experts. Despite efforts to merge the two during the Great Leap Forward, this old phenomenon in China is appearing once again, but with a difference arising from the nature of the modern world. In Imperial China the experts were usually in the category of local lawyers, and not very highly esteemed; in fact, they often appeared as villains in popular dramas. The modern world, however, has put a great premium on professional expertise, hence the professionals can no longer be relegated to the role of technical advisers, as the Chinese tried to do with the many foreign experts they hired in the nineteenth century.

There are implications in this peculiar pattern of politics which the West would be well advised to take into consideration. For one thing, negotiations will normally be carried out by professionals; they are men who are not only esteemed but who have considerable decision-making power. As was the case with internal decentralization, the local cadres acquired far-reaching power to move ahead on their own, on the assumption that they were completely loyal to the center; autonomy was possible because of the unshakeable bonds of loyalty between leaders and cadres. On the other hand, the professional can suddenly lose that autonomy, as a highly sensitive matter is broached or as some new policy line is inaugurated. To the outside negotiator this can often appear to be inexplicable inconsistency, a discontinuity appearing almost from nowhere. It is not impossible that this pattern has also been a factor in Sino-Soviet relations.

The Central Government is a structure whose arms reach throughout the country. Until the decentralization of late 1957, many ministries had branch bureaus in different parts of the country, particularly the economic ministries which directly administered a vast empire of state-owned enterprises. Some of the largest industrial complexes, such as Anshan, are subject not to ministries but directly to the State Council. The People's Bank runs a nationwide network generally immune from local control.

The early 1950s, in general, were a period of extreme centralization. Since late 1957 provincial governments have acquired some control over these provincially located central agencies by virtue of a principle called "dual rule," which essentially means a sharing of authority between a central and a local agency or between two different branch agencies. The emphasis on dual rule, as contrasted to vertical rule, has gone hand in hand with trends toward decentralization. The linkage between central and provincial government is greatly facilitated by the fact that, structurally, provincial governments are copies of the Central Government. There is direct communication between a central ministry and its counterpart in local government.

If information on the Central Government is scarce, that on provincial governments is even scarcer. Structurally, as we have said, provincial governments are modeled on the Central Government; functionally, their activities also resemble the Central Government's. Published reports of provincial economic activity are available which read like small-scale versions of national economic reports. Such reports were published with particular frequency during the years of the Great Leap Forward, when provincial governments undertook major economic programs. Political changes at provincial levels have occasionally been very important.

In the absence of careful studies of provincial government, few generalizations can be made beyond the assertion that this is an extremely important level of administration in China. The late-1957 decentralization measures greatly increased the provincial governments' economic resources, thus making them an important power factor in the government. There is no evidence that independent political machines have been built up, as was the case under the Kuomintang. A look at the leading personnel in provincial government indicates a balance between insiders and outsiders, that is, individuals from within and without the province. Most provincial Party secretaries are outsiders, but the governors are mostly from the province itself. There has been considerable continuity of rule in many of the provinces: most provincial Party secretaries have been in power since the early or mid-1950s. A critical turning point in the organizational history of the Chinese Communist Party came around 1954 and 1955, when the Kao Kang and Jao Shu-shih factions were eliminated and a new Party solidarity forged. Also in 1955 the Party began to expand rapidly and take over greater powers at provincial and lower levels. There can be little doubt that, organizationally, the Party has functioned as a very effective mechanism, to prevent provincial satrapies from forming and to assure continuity of rule. There are strong indications that the Party as an organization exercises far greater power at the provincial than at the national level. Peking, as the capital of the country, has the heaviest concentration of professionals. As might be expected, there are far fewer professionals at the provincial level, although this probably does not apply to such provinces that are relatively developed economically and culturally. The fateful decisions made in late 1957 gave much power to the Party committees, and it was inevitable that this would enlarge the political role of the provincial Party committees.

🔄 Thought Reform: The Ideological
Transformation of the Individual

NO ASPECT of Chinese Communism has aroused such dread fascination in the United States as "brainwashing." When brainwashing tales began to come out of the Korean War, many believed that the Chinese Communists had discovered some demonic psychological device which could transform individuals with free will into fanatic slaves to the new system. By now the "aura of fear and mystery" has abated, however, and we are able to look at "thought reform," the Chinese Communist term for the process, with objectivity. One must begin by discarding the word brainwashing, which is never used in China.

Thought reform, as Dr. Robert J. Lifton, Professor of Psychiatry at Yale University and a scholar both of China and Japan, states, is "a special form of group psychotherapy." Individuals, particularly those belonging to the elites, have to participate in Party-organized group sessions in which their entire personal backgrounds are exposed, analyzed, criticized, and finally put together in the terms of the new ideology. Thought reform serves two basic functions. First, by raising his entire personal life to critical consciousness, the individual cuts his psychological and emotional ties to past authority. A most important part of self-criticism, as Lifton points out, is the denunciation of the father. Since awesome respect for the father was one of the core values of Traditional China, cutting that tie is essential for the inculcation of new attitudes. One might remember that personal denunciation of the individual landlord and his final humiliation before the peasants was a crucial part of land reform (see Volume II). Once the individual has broken with the past, he moves to the second purpose of thought reform; reintegration into the new society. The same comrades

135

who mercilessly attacked him during criticism now "help" him regain a new identity.

In training their new elites, the Chinese Communists, unlike the Russians, have put great stress on individual psychological transformation. Where and when this approach arose is difficult to say. A part of it lies in Chinese tradition, with its emphasis on personal relationships, but as Lifton indicates, it is mainly a practice developed by the Chinese Communists, particularly during the Yenan Period. Some aspects of thought reform are similar to practices in some Protestant sects.

Lifton is careful in judging the effects of thought reform: "much more time is needed before we can evaluate the extent of 'change' which thought reform has brought about in individual Chinese intellectuals." Yet there can be no doubt that the constant exercise of thought reform is one of the most important practical tools of Chinese Communist ideology. It serves as a channel for transmitting the new values and goals from the leaders to the people, in particular to the cadres, and it provides the Chinese Communist leaders a way of combating their opponents without bloodshed. Though there has been a continuous current of opposition in China from 1949 to the present, not since the early 1950s have the Communists resorted to terror. Thought reform and related devices of psychological control have given the Party a much more effective weapon than the conventional and dangerous firing squad.

ROBERT J. LIFTON *
Peking's "Thought Reform"—
Group Psychotherapy To Save Your Soul

Perhaps more than any regime in history, Communist or other-wise, the present Chinese government has energetically and in-geniously devoted itself to the "changing" of human beings. Its methods for altering individual thoughts and emotions have been popularly termed "brainwashing"—a word which has become surrounded with an aura of fear and mystery, leaving in its wake a loose body of comment, polemic, and tongue-in-cheek humor.

But the process which gave rise to this concern and con-fusion is very much a reality. Known by the Chinese themselves as *szu-hsiang kai-tsao* (variously translated as "ideological re-molding," "ideological reform," and "thought reform"), it com-bines a remarkably widespread dissemination with a focused emotional power. Even a brief examination of this basic in-gredient of Chinese Communism reveals much about the nature of the regime, something about Chinese culture, and perhaps a bit about human beings in general.

Thought reform has received most publicity when applied, often accompanied by physical abuse, to such groups as Ameri-can prisoners of war and other incarcerated Westerners. Yet far more important is its use among the Chinese people them-selves—in universities and schools, in special "revolutionary colleges," in government and business offices, in prisons, and in labor and peasant groups. There are probably few persons throughout Mainland China who have not in some way partici-pated in it; but the intellectuals have been subjected to its most intensive and elaborate versions, and it is their experiences that I will discuss here.

* Dr. Robert J. Lifton, "Brainwashing in Perspective," *New Republic*, May 13, 1957.

What is the "philosophy," the Communist justification of thought reform? Although Chinese Communist theorists rarely refer to details of manipulative techniques, they do put forth an elaborate rationale, which is forcefully presented to every participant during a preliminary stage in his personal "reform."

In brief, the argument runs this way: the "old society" (everything predating Communist rule, but particularly the Nationalist period) was evil and corrupt; this was so because it was dominated by the "exploiting classes"—the landowners and the bourgeoisie; most intellectuals come from these "exploiting classes" (or from the closely related petty bourgeoisie) and therefore retain "evil remnants" of their origins and of the old regime; each must now rid himself of these "ideological poisons" in order to become a "new man" in the "new society." Mao Tse-tung has compared the process to a medical problem, referring to "diseases in thought and politics" which require "an attitude of saving men by curing their diseases." What we see as a set of coercive maneuvers, the Communists present as a morally uplifting, harmonizing, and therapeutic experience.

But the program has also had immediate goals of a highly practical nature: the consolidation of the new regime and the rallying of the Chinese people behind its policies, the training of new personnel, the undermining or conversion of all opposition (real or imagined—past, present, or potential); and in the service of these, the establishment of close control over individual behavior and thought. Here is clearly an expression of totalitarianism, an arbitrary policy in a monolithic state; but it is at the same time the product of a powerful ideological movement, a pseudo-religious mystique which creates both the demand and the emotional fervor.

Whatever its setting, thought reform consists of two closely related elements: *confession,* the detailed recitation of past evil accompanied by the promise of humble service to the regime in the future; and *re-education,* the attempt of remaking a man in the Communist image. Both are always present, although one may take precedence over the other. During the national Ideological Remolding Movement of 1951–1952, the old professor was required to recant, but not necessarily expected to "change"; the young student in the same campaign had not as much to confess—more important for him was his re-education. Confession and re-education were combined with greatest intensity in the "revolutionary colleges," unique indoctrination centers set up all over China for diverse groups of intellectuals at the time of the Communist takeover.

What are the most important psychological features of thought reform? I have drawn most of my illustrations from the six-month course conducted at the revolutionary college, but the basic principles apply wherever the process takes place.

The *control of the milieu* is the psychological foundation upon which thought reform always operates. So complete is the manipulative power of the Communist officials running a revolutionary college that they can not only control all events, but also create and change at will the general atmosphere which prevails. They set up at the beginning an open, democratic milieu which encourages free discussion and contributes to a high *esprit de corps*. When they feel the moment is at hand, they bring about a gradual closing in of the environment, greater pressures upon the students for full confessions and "progressive" (or Marxist) expression. They accomplish this atmospheric change through their instructions to the student leaders of the small study groups who report to them daily, and to other "activists" whose relationship to them is more covert.

In the face of these manipulations, the student finds the emphasis shifting from the intellectual to the personal, such that he, rather than the Marxist doctrine, becomes the object of study. Everything he says, does, or even feels may be noted by his fellow students and reported back to faculty officials, who may in turn use this information to devise specific measures geared to his personal susceptibilities. All of the information which he receives is increasingly limited to the Communist point of view. More important, the entire environment becomes so mobilized that it will psychologically nourish him only when he is meeting its demands, and consistently undermine him when he fails to do so. He finds, more and more, that his own inner life becomes indistinguishable from the message of his environment. As one student described it:

> Using the same pattern of words for so long, you are
> so accustomed to them that you feel chained. If you make

a mistake, you make it within that pattern. Although you don't admit that you have adopted this kind of ideology, you are actually using it subconsciously, almost automatically. . . . Such was the state of confusion in my own mind that I couldn't tell or make out what were the things I believed.

It is this airtight control of communication which gives thought reform its awesome effect upon the individual. It is in many ways similar to what George Orwell so brilliantly envisioned in his novel *1984*. Orwell, with the mind of a Westerner, saw milieu control accomplished through mechanical means, the two-way "telescreen." But the Chinese have here established an entirely *human* recording and transmitting apparatus, one which therefore reaches more deeply into the student's intellectual and emotional life. It is this human form of milieu control, practiced throughout China on a less intensive basis, which explains the Communists' ability to maintain such intimate individual supervision over their sprawling population without benefit of an advanced mechanical communication system.

Crucial also to thought reform is the stimulation of both a *sense of guilt* and a *sense of shame*. Each student is constantly criticizing others and being criticized himself; each is required to lay himself bare—to state verbally and in writing his political, social, and personal attitudes, past and present. He must particularly dig out his "errors," his "reactionary" tendencies and affiliations, his maltreatment of others. One student vies to outdo the other in lurid details; one group challenges another to match its collective confessions.

The man who fails to confess fully, or in any way resists his reform, is labeled a "lagging-behind element." He soon finds himself the special target of heated rebuke from the other members of his group, and a victim of social ostracism. He may in some cases be offered a special opportunity for public repentance: a prearranged, revivalist-like gathering at which he dramatically recites his past evils, expresses relief at "washing away all of my sins," and gratitude toward the government for allowing him to "become a new man." The rare student who is truly recalcitrant, hopelessly "backward," is subjected to the ultimate indignity: denunciation by faculty members, cadres, and fellow students at a mass "struggle" meeting, before hundreds or even thousands of people. It becomes clear that his future in Communist China is indeed precarious: the ceremony serves as a grim warning for other students of questionable standing.

This accusatory atmosphere and stress upon personal evil brings out feelings of sinfulness and expectations of punishment—or a sense of guilt. The pressures toward isolation and public humiliation cause a loss of "face"—of social recognition, prestige, and self-esteem—all contributing to a sense of shame. As a student expressed it to me, "You are alone and you suffer if you do not believe."

In other words, however ethical and honest a man has been, thought reform can make him feel guilty and shamed. It can revive the store of guilt and shame present in all of us, as a consequence of both our childhood transgressions and our adult limitations. It is an environment specially geared to mobilize such feelings, as *everyone* is made to experience them—and indeed one *must* experience them if one is to be accepted.

All of this produces one particularly important result: as guilt and shame mount within, the student comes to feel that his fears and conflicts, in fact all of his emotional pain, are caused by his own evil and worthlessness. He begins to believe that he is deserving of any punishment the group may impose, and feels really in need of reform. At this point, he can solve his dilemma only through the prescribed confession method—finding in it an outlet for the pressure valves of guilt and shame, and at the same time a necessary act of self-surrender, in coming to terms with a demanding milieu.

As a means of furthering this adjustment, the Communists apply their own system of *psychological analysis*. Since this is conducted in small six-to-ten-man study groups (known throughout China as *hsüeh-hsi*), the individual student finds himself involved in a special form of group psychotherapy. Not only is he expected to express "spontaneously" all of his shortcomings, but also to seek interpretations for them or accept the interpretations of others. He must search for their origins in his own family, educational, and social background. His "insight" in such a *self-criticism* is of course highly slanted and virtually the same in all cases. He finds that his deficiency—

whether it is the character trait of "individualism," "erroneous" political thinking, or rude manners—is caused by "ruling class" or "bourgeois" influences derived from early life, and especially from his class origin.

As in most situations where a man is under psychological "treatment," he must be willing to expose himself completely and hold nothing back. He is expected to go beyond mere mouthing of Communist views and become emotionally involved in the process, lest he be exposed as a "false progressive." Even his relations with the opposite sex must be discussed in the group and evaluated in terms of their effect upon the treatment goal —his personal reform. If a relationship, in the judgment of the group, enhances his "progress," it is encouraged; if it seems to hold him back, he is advised to break it off.

The student who shows signs of confusion or of resistance is said to have a "thought problem." He is likely to be approached by more progressive students or by faculty representatives who urge him to "talk it over" and offer him help in working it out. Similarly, should he show signs of stress and report to the school physician with such symptoms as insomnia, headache, or fatigue, these will probably be recognized as psychosomatic in origin. He will be told, as was a student I interviewed: "There is nothing wrong with your body. It must be your thoughts that are sick. You will feel better when you have solved your problems and completed your reform." In all cases, inner conflict is encouraged, as long as it is solved in a reform-oriented manner.

The *hsüeh-hsi* group is thus armed with a psychological theory which attributes all personal traits to class origin. It is a theory with questionable validity in our eyes, but when supported by the entire environment, it can be made an effective weapon. The group is also fortified by a highly charged morality and an absolute doctrinal authority for the "correctness" of all of its solutions. In the face of this combined approach, the individual student must inevitably find it very difficult to maintain a dissenting opinion, especially in a Chinese culture which has always stressed group harmony at the expense of individualistic achievement. Again, he begins to interpret any confusion or disagreement with the group as *his* problem, and accepts the principle that it is *he* who must give way and "change."

It would be highly misleading to assume that thought reform consists exclusively of painful experiences; it contains powerful *emotional appeals* and meaningful psychological satisfactions as well. If a Chinese intellectual is able to accept its principles, it can supply him with a profoundly binding set of group affiliations—in his small group and in the vast Communist movement. It encourages and mobilizes nationalistic sentiments, and can for many restore pride in being Chinese. The student may experience great relief at giving up his individual struggles, merging with an all-powerful force, and thereby sharing its strength. He is fortified by an ideology which justifies all that is done, answers all questions, leaves no problem unsolved. And perhaps most important of all, he shares the powerful bond of participation in a great "moral crusade"— reforming himself, reforming others about him, reforming society, joining in the "struggle for peace," "the brotherhood of man," and "the great Communist future."

In its pressures and appeals, thought reform seeks to do more than impose a set of authoritarian rules. It aims at bringing about a profound inner change in the individual student, particularly in his feeling of who and what he is in relationship to people around him, or in his *sense of inner identity*. The events of the twentieth century, and particularly during the years prior to the Communist takeover, had placed a great strain upon the Chinese intellectual, and had caused him much confusion concerning his position in the family and in society. The old stress upon absolute family loyalty and filial piety had been long under attack, and many Chinese intellectuals found themselves wavering between the conflicting roles of the modern rebellious reformer and the more traditional filial son. This conflict was magnified for most of them by their disaffection from the former regime.

Thought reform supplies each student with a dramatic solution to this dilemma through the symbolic climax of the process—the denunciation of the father. Each must expose and attack his father's political, social, and economic abuses, as well as his individual shortcomings, denouncing him both as a person and as a representative of the exploiting classes. He is likely to find this the most painful demand of his thought reform, and may require endless prodding, persuasion, or indirect

threat before he is able to take the crucial step. But he has little
choice and he almost invariably complies. In this act he is renouncing the symbol of the old order and the mainspring of his
traditional identity—that of the filial son—in order to make
way for a new allegiance and a new identity—that of the
zealous adherent of the Communist regime. And to his new
affiliation he is expected to bring his old sense of loyalty and
"correct" behavior.

This shift is most readily accomplished in younger students,
those in their post-adolescence or early adulthood, as this is
normally a period of identity crisis and a time when the individual is most susceptible to ideological or religious conversion. But every student is expected to undergo a symbolic
death—a break with his family and his past—and a near-
mystical rebirth, his union with The Government and The
People. Only through such an emotional experience—through
some shift in inner identity—is he likely to experience a true
change in his beliefs.

In sum, thought reform makes use of a powerful combination of emotional forces in the total manipulation of the individual participant. It employs no theologians, but it closely
resembles an attempt at induced religious conversion—saving
souls, stressing guilt and shame, demanding atonement, recanta-
tion, and rebirth. It makes use of no psychiatrists, but is certainly a coercive form of psychotherapy—focusing upon cathar-
sis, analytic interpretations, and causative influences from early
life. It is a unique form of "treatment," which supplies both the
disease and the cure.

But where did the Chinese learn to be such master psychologists? Is this their process or is it a Russian import? Is it
compatible with, or in direct opposition to, traditional Chinese
cultural forms? There are no simple answers to any of these
questions, but a brief consideration of them is necessary in
order to obtain some perspective. By and large, the forms
(criticism, "struggle," and confession) as well as most of the
content (the allegedly scientific Marxist doctrine) appear to be
carried over from Russian Communist practice. But it is the
Chinese who have molded these into a comprehensive process,
and carried it out on a broad national scale; and it is they who

have developed the emphasis upon *reform* rather than *purge,* as well as the nuances of group and individual psychological pressures which make it work.

Despite its borrowings, then, thought reform is essentially a Chinese Communist process. Its history can be traced back to the early days of the Chinese Communist movement (late 1920s or early 1930s) when rather simple reform methods were first applied to captured enemy soldiers. Later, during the Yenan Period (1937–1945) more sophisticated techniques were developed for intellectuals recruited to the movement, and at the time of the Communist takeover in 1948–1949 these had evolved into an extensive thought-reform apparatus. (The process is rather an economical one as the participants reform themselves, and relatively few people are needed to direct a particular reform operation; also, the man who has just been reformed can readily be recruited to work toward reforming others.)

All evidence suggests that the Chinese have evolved their programs on a pragmatic, trial-and-error basis, rather than through the deliberate use of any known psychiatric techniques, or, as is so frequently asserted, of Pavlovian theory.

One is struck at first glance with thought reform's bold attack on traditional Chinese cultural forms: the open denunciation of the father in a culture steeped in filial piety, the lack of consideration of "face" in the humiliating public demonstrations, and the violations of codes of loyalty in criticizing family and friends. But it is important to point out that the traditions violated had been under steady assault for more than fifty years, and in this sense the Communists have been riding the wave of the broad intellectual rebellion of modern China.

There are also aspects of the process that are quite consistent with the Confucian tradition, particularly its thesis that man can and should be re-educated, its emphasis upon following the "correct" ideological path as a guide to human conduct, its stress upon "self-cultivation." We see then that it in some ways violates, and in other ways reflects, long-standing Chinese cultural patterns. It also would seem to contain Christian, and possibly Buddhist, influences, indirectly derived. And it no doubt makes use of certain common denominators which exist in all attempts to reach and influence profound human emotions.

But there is one additional factor which I think important in explaining the Chinese Communists' development of this psychologically astute process. Chinese culture has—possibly at the expense of technological advance—always emphasized the *human* aspects of life, and particularly the nuances of personal relationships. Children are taught to be sensitive to psychological currents about them, in order to learn how to behave appropriately toward others. In the educated adult, this sensitivity is expected and required. Most Chinese intellectuals whom I knew, as subjects or as friends, impressed me with their consistent skill in perceiving the emotion at play between one person and another, as well as their tendency to make use of this understanding in seeking their life objectives. They conducted human relationships as one practices a highly refined art. In this sense, I believe that thought reform could be viewed as the totalitarian expression of a national genius.

Does thought reform succeed in achieving its aims? Is it worth all the trouble which the Chinese Communists expend upon it? These are questions which no one can now answer with certainty. The specific cases at my disposal were only the "failures"—those who fled—but from everything I have been able to learn I would delineate three types of response: the zealous "converts," the most successful products, particularly among the young; the resistors who feel suffocated by the process, some of whom break away; and the great majority of people, the in-between group, partially convinced, but essentially concerned with adapting themselves to this stress and assuring their future under the new regime. Some in the first and third groups feel "purified" and helped by the experience; others, in the second group, have a reverse response, less sympathetic to the regime after their "reform" than they had been before.

On the whole, we can say that thought reform seems to develop in most people intellectual and emotional responses which are useful to the Communist regime. These responses continue to be supported and demanded by the general environment of Communist China long after the particular course has been completed. This, and the great receptivity which many intellectuals felt for the Communist program even before their reform, are crucial factors in the program's effectiveness.

Thought reform has played a large part in superimposing a

new Chinese Communist "culture," particularly in the intellectual and ideological spheres. It was most actively applied during the first five years of the Communist regime. Now, as the younger intellectuals emerge with their educations increasingly limited to Communist teachings, there seems to be less emphasis upon "reform" and more focus upon continuing indoctrination. (Most revolutionary colleges, for instance, have been converted into more conventional Marxist schools and training centers.) A modified type of thought reform—"the correction of ideological errors"—is still very much present, receiving periodic waves of emphasis, and will no doubt be a permanent feature of the Chinese Communist regime.

Much more time is needed before we can evaluate the extent of "change" which thought reform has brought about in individual Chinese intellectuals. We must await its longer-term interplay with Chinese cultural forces, and we cannot now judge the extent to which the rebelliousness of the modern Chinese intellectual—so effectively made use of—may ultimately work against the process. We do know that psychological forces do not operate in a vacuum. What matters most for Chinese intellectuals, as they pass beyond the stage of initial ideological fervor, is the extent to which they can achieve a workable personal identity and a satisfying way of life under their new and demanding masters.

ℜ The Intellectuals:
The Dilemma of the Educated

IN HIS WRITINGS Mao Tse-tung has been continually pre-occupied with two major classes of Chinese society: intellectuals and peasants. Aside from doctrinal references to the Party as the vanguard of the proletariat, Mao says little about the working class. After all, the Chinese industrial proletariat was small and did not play a major part in the Revolution, and, after 1949, acquired a favored position in society. The reasons are obvious for Mao's preoccupation with the peasants. Less obvious is the persistent concern with the intellectuals. The Chinese Communists refer to the intellectuals as the "learned elements" (*chih-shih fen-tzu*), by which they mean anyone with a higher degree, generally from upper-middle school on up. In the mid-1950s China had about four million intellectuals in a total population of some six hundred million.

In a country as backward as China the demand for talent is high, thus the intellectuals easily found positions in the new system. By and large they supported the new government; even the most severe criticisms of the "blooming and contending" period of May 1957 did not demand a destruction of the system. Why, then, Mao's worry and why the ferocious reaction of the anti-rightist movement of June 1957 which followed the "blooming and contending"? This can be understood only in terms of the role traditionally played by educated men in China. The traditional official was an educated man, whose position gave him the power of command but whose education gave him an even greater authority founded on the respect held by all Chinese for the man of learning. Despite strenuous efforts to train a worker-peasant intelligentsia, by the mid-1950s the Party, at middle and lower levels, was still dominated by men of inferior learning. Intellectuals had been welcomed into the Party, but by and large, as Mao admitted in his famous speech on contradictions of February 1957, the intellectuals still stood to one side—in but not a part of the new system. As the graduates of the higher schools entered administrative and technical positions, Mao feared that a modern version of the old literati-officials was developing. Would the people finally come to look for authority to these men rather than to the Party? The severity and extent of criticism which erupted in May 1957 convinced Mao that the gap between Party and intellectuals was too great to leave untended. The intellectuals had to be criticized, "struggled against," reformed, thrown together with the masses, and turned into new socialist men.

The first selection, by Vidya Prakash Dutt, Professor of East Asian Studies at the Indian School of International Studies at New Delhi, recounts with vividness the rise and fall of the "blooming and contending" period. Dutt, one of the outstanding authorities on Chinese foreign policy, was in Peking at the time and thus writes from direct experience. He regards the anti-rightist movement as having directly contributed to that ideological orthodoxy which is still a characteristic of China's leaders. Disappointed and chastened by their experiences with the intellectuals, the Chinese Communists turned once again to the masses, from which change of approach came the Great Leap Forward. Dutt writes that henceforth "they saw no reason for, and showed no inclination to make conciliatory gestures toward others." Today Mao harbors suspicions that the intellectuals are strongly revisionist. Lately even such stalwart supporters of the Party as Kuo Mo-jo, whom one might call China's Ilya Ehrenburg, and the Marxist historian Chien Po-tsan have had to confess their errors. Mao seems to regard the Soviet "revisionist" leaders in much the same way as he sees his own intellectuals: both are talented, hard-working, and essential for revolution and socialism; but both are motivated by self-interest, cannot be trusted, want the good life, and will sell out if it serves their interests (see also p. 81).

The second selection is an interview by the senior author with a young Chinese student in Hong Kong on August 23, 1958. The student was about twenty-four, a graduate of Peking University in the field of chemistry. He had worked in the Northeast

Chemical Institute in Mukden for a few months, and had been allowed to go to Hong Kong in December 1957. His experiences supply some further details on the "blooming and contending" period. His personal attitudes toward the new system are indicative of a large group of "bourgeois" youth in China.

The third selection presents a recent confession by one of China's leading mathematicians, Hua Lo-keng. Hua begins by admitting that were it not for the Thought of Mao Tse-tung, he would have been contented "with a pot of tea and a cigar, [occupying] myself in my study with mathematical problems which were so dear to me." Chinese intellectuals, like their colleagues everywhere, enjoy the ivory tower. Mao Tse-tung, the man who suffered, failed, and finally led a people to victory, is determined to pull them out of the tower and put them into service for the Revolution. Hua was asked to do some programming, a useful operation but one involving simple mathematics. His intellectual pride made him disdain such work, but the Thought of Mao Tse-tung made him change his mind. But, "to be quite honest, I have not yet quite passed the ideological test. I am still far from the required state of 'selflessness.' " As for Hua, so also for thousands of other Chinese intellectuals and cadres: all still fall short of the goal of ideological purity which can only be achieved by ceaseless thought reform.

VIDYA PRAKASH DUTT *
From China's Foreign Policy

On April 27, 1957, the Central Committee of the Chinese Communist Party passed a formal resolution calling for a new rectification campaign in order to mobilize all the "positive forces" and "uniting with all elements it was possible to unite" for the building of a "great Socialist country." The objective was to

* Vidya Prakash Dutt, China's Foreign Policy (New York: Asia Publishing House, 1964), pp. 9–20.

rectify in the Party members and cadres the threefold evils of "bureaucratism," "sectarianism," and "subjectivism," and the novelty was that the movement was not confined to the Party but that the people were asked to criticize and cure the Party members and cadres of their defects. It was the hope of the Party that as a result of rectification the relations between the Party and the people would be greatly strengthened and that the "wall" between the two, particularly between the Party and the intellectuals, would be demolished.

BLOOMING AND CONTENDING

The Communist Party now solicited open criticism from the people and exposures of mistakes. The *Jen-min jih-pao,* official organ of the Chinese Communist Party, explaining the need for rectification, deplored the fact that many Communists were not good at dealing with "contradictions among the people" and that bureaucracy, sectarianism, and subjectivism within the Party had had "new growth after the victory of the Revolution." Many cadres were prone to "solve problems through purely administrative orders" and were very fond of their special powers and position. They did not share the joys and sorrows of the people; some did not identify themselves with the workers and peasants, intellectuals, and members of other democratic parties and did not allow them to speak out their minds.

The Communist leaders and the Press urged the people to speak out their minds and freely criticize their mistakes. They spoke of *Ta Fang* (Great Release) and asked the people to unburden their minds and spotlight government and Party shortcomings. This urging and soliciting was needed, for the response of the people was slow in coming. They were bewildered by the rapidity of the change and baffled by the scope and intent of rectification. They were uncertain of its objectives and of what lay at the back of the Party's mind, and they were afraid of a "mousetrap." The area of freedom had not been well defined and it was not clear how far criticism could go. Many people preferred to keep their fingers crossed rather than risk getting them burnt. A powerful member of the Politburo and Mayor of Peking, P'eng Chen, said at a meeting in

Peking that there was still not enough of criticism and asked for more, so that a new unity would be achieved as a result of the struggle between different views and contradictions. He declared that even strikes were not something to be afraid of, as they were a manifestation of serious bureaucratism and lack of democratic functioning on the part of the cadres. The Party would stand to gain if such defects came to light.

While the people were responding uncertainly, some of the leaders of the non-Communist groups like Lo Lung-chi and Chang Po-chün came forth and appealed to the people to cast off their doubts and speak out freely. They themselves made scathing criticism of the Communist Party's ways and policies; and it was this which sharpened the edge of disapprobation among the intellectuals, the teachers, the students, the government functionaries, who all rushed to "raise their opinions," and with each passing day the crescendo of criticism rose higher and opinions became sharper. Wall posters appeared in hundreds and all aspects of state policy came under attack from some quarter or the other. The month of May saw the movement at its height. Not all the critics were agreed among themselves, nor did all the criticism relate to the same issues; criticism at the top was concerned more with fundamental issues, while criticism at the lower level generally touched upon lesser issues.

Many of the non-Communist leaders directed their guns at the Communist monopoly of power. They bitterly complained that the non-Party people did not wield sufficient power. Power must go with position, they demanded. The Communists did not respect their position. There could be no real freedom and equality as long as they had to wait for a nod from the Party member before arriving at any decision; consequently, they asked for "political freedom," "organizational independence," and "equality of position." Others demanded that there should be some distinction between the government and the Party. They wanted a definite line to be drawn between the functions and powers of the administration and those of the Communist Party. At the moment, they alleged, these were completely blurred and many decisions of the Party did not go through regular administrative channels. This gave the non-Communists the feeling of being "outsiders." Some critics demanded early

formulation of civil and criminal codes and held that the rectification campaign was no substitute for a legal system; others
suggested that the system of Communist Party committees in
government departments and educational institutions be replaced
by that of administrative committees, composed of both Communists and non-Communists and vested with the power and
authority of management and control.

There were complaints against the attitude and behavior of
Communist Party members. They looked down upon all but
the Communists and were high-minded and arrogant. They
kept themselves aloof and would not mix with non-Party
people. Chang Hsi-jo, Chairman of the People's Institute for
Foreign Affairs, acidly remarked that many Party members
thought that they had "conquered the empire" and that their
attitude toward others was: "We have given you a bowl of
rice and official position and that is enough, but all this is for
the sake of unity, not because you have really any ability."
The Timber Minister in the Central Government and one of
the non-Communist leaders, Lo Lung-chi, denounced the movement for suppressing counter-revolutionaries as having involved
many innocent people and asked for a "Review Committee" for
a thorough re-examination of all the cases. Some critics went
further and questioned the need for the continuance of the dictatorship of the proletariat in China. Since classes had been
abolished and class struggle "basically resolved," there was no
more justification for proletarian dictatorship which, they
claimed, was the real cause of dogmatism, sectarianism, and
bureaucratism.

The Party attitude toward intellectuals also came under
heavy fire. Many asked for a free scope for intellectuals and
for academic divergencies, and an end to Party fiats on every
academic matter. The critics in the literary and art circles complained of Party censorship and dogmatism, and wanted freedom
to write and publish what they liked. The Party control over
the Press also came in for considerable criticism, and the editor
of *Chung-kuo Ch'ing-nien Pao* (*China Youth Paper*) complained that newspapers had become "notice boards, gramo-
phone records or photostat editions of books."

Significantly, criticism of the Soviet Union figured prominently during this period. Critics held that some of the dog-

matism resulted from following Soviet methods, and there were many references to the Yugoslav and Polish paths being superior to the Soviet practice and as worthy of emulation by China. Translations of Khrushchev's hitherto unpublished speech on Stalin at the Twentieth Party Congress (text taken from the Communist newspapers from the West which were still available at many libraries!) appeared on wall posters. It was alleged that there was often blind imitation of the Soviets and that not infrequently it was deemed sufficient to clinch the argument by saying that this was how it was done in the Soviet Union. A plucky girl student from the People's University in Peking created a nationwide sensation by alleging that the Soviet Union was the source of all dogmatism, that the Hungarian blood had not been shed in vain, that Mao Tse-tung wanted to take the country toward the Yugoslav way but that he was in a minority in the Party, 80 per cent of whom were opposed to the rectification movement.

By the end of May and beginning of June the "blooming and contending" movement, as it was elegantly called, had reached its climax. The gathering storm of criticism had burst and opinions had come like floodtide. As the movement snowballed, criticism became sharper and more violent. Its tone became more and more menacing. Even many Communist Party members joined in and denounced many aspects of state policy. There were scattered reports of disturbances and minor riots in many parts of the country, particularly in some educational institutions. Where was all this leading to? The movement seemed to be getting out of hand and taking a threatening turn. Frightened and dismayed, the Chinese leaders decided to crack down on the critics, suppress all "blooming" and "contending" and launch a furious anti-rightist struggle. On June 8 the *Jen-min Jih-pao* published an editorial claiming that one of the members of the Revolutionary Kuomintang Party had received a threatening anonymous letter for defending Communists and Communist policies. The paper declared that this menacing letter was of special political significance because it was a warning to the "broad masses" that "certain people" were using the rectification campaign to continue the class struggle. They thought of capitalism in their hearts, and their minds were full of European politics. "These are the people," the paper said, "whom today we call rightists." Under the excuse of helping the Communist Party in rectification they were attacking the Party and "proletarian dictatorship" in order to overthrow the rule of the Party and the proletariat. The editorial declared that "their threats are a warning to us that the class struggle is still going on and that we must adopt the class struggle point of view and review the present-day phenomena and matters and thus arrive at correct conclusions."

ANTI-RIGHTIST STRUGGLE

This was the signal for a counter-attack that followed and shook the country for many months. For the greater part of the second half of 1957, the struggle against the rightists was conducted with full fury. If the first phase of the rectification movement came as a storm, the anti-rightist campaign was thunder and lightning itself. Endless, nerve-wrecking meetings were held to accuse and denounce the rightists, and, finally, most of them were removed from their offices and positions of responsibility, and the younger and less known among them were sent to villages or labor camps to "reform" themselves through labor. Among the most serious charges against the rightists was that their real aim was to destroy the socialist system and overthrow the leadership of the Communist Party. Many non-Communist leaders were accused of harboring political ambitions and of plotting to seize political power in order to establish the capitalist system of society. It was alleged that they were trying and hoping for a repetition of the Hungarian episode in China. The critics were accused of "glorifying" the special characteristics of the intellectuals with a view to snatching the leadership of the intellectuals from the hands of the Communists in the universities, especially with their proposals for the substitution of the Party committee system by the system of administrative committees, and that they wanted to seize the press and turn it into a "class instrument of the bourgeoisie" by demanding that the non-Communist press should be free of Communist direction. The rectification movement, declared the Party supporters, was not meant to weaken the central role of the Communist Party nor to replace Marxism by "revisionism."

The rightists were accused of using the movement against the "three evils" (bureaucratism, sectarianism, and subjectivism) to turn it into a question of the whole system as such. Under the cover of opposing dogmatism, it was said, they were really propagating "revisionism."

For the Chinese Communists the rectification campaign was a harrowing, nightmarish experience. It was almost unbelievably stupefying. The crestfallen look of dismay and agony on the faces of the cadres one saw during the "blooming and contending" period was evidence, if evidence were really needed, that they were surprised by and unprepared for the nature and volume of the criticism and that it had gone beyond their wildest fears. The Party high command had hoped for the rectification movement to be conducted like a "mild breeze" and "gentle rain"; actually it was shaken by the storm that came in its wake. It had become overconfident of its own achievements. It seemed almost incredible to the leaders that people should want to say all the bad things they did say about the Party's policies and behavior. Mao had expected only minor criticism about lapses here and there, which could be rectified without substantial overhaul of the system; that fundamental issues of state structure and of the Party's power would be raised and aired had not been considered a serious possibility, for in that case the rectification movement would never have been launched. From complacency the reaction of Mao and his colleagues switched to fright and anger at the critics that they should have been so "ungrateful" as to ignore all that the Party had achieved for the country and make such nasty criticisms, that after having so obsequiously eulogized the Party role and policies (thus encouraging the Party leadership to believe that the bulk of the intellectuals had been successfully "brainwashed"), they should be roaring like a lion when the rectification campaign gave them the freedom to speak out their minds. The Party luminaries were frightened out of their wits at the thought of the consequences not only for the political structure of the country but also for the economic plans of the Communist Party if the critics were allowed to continue to spread disaffection. So far the debate and contention had been confined to the critics, to the intellectual class, but what would happen if these were to spread to the working class and the peasantry, particularly if the peasantry came to be infected with this disaffection. That could threaten and upset all the blueprints and plans for rapid economic growth. The troublemakers had to be suppressed before they could do any further damage.

LESSONS OF THE RECTIFICATION CAMPAIGN

For Mao, who is fond of summing up experiences into general principles and guidelines, the lessons of this unforgettable and unsavory experience were clear and he seemed to have made the following deductions:

(1) That in the present stage of her development, China could not afford to relax. The short-lived experiment in liberalization had proved to be a miserable failure. In the singleminded drive toward economic construction and in the race for catching up with the most powerful nations of the world, there was to be no let-up or hindrance. No real criticism would be allowed, no deviation tolerated. China was now in the grip of a most rigid and dogmatic climate and Mao shifted to a position of a most uncompromising struggle against the critics.

(2) That the "bourgeois intellectuals" remained "bourgeois," ready to foul the air and corrupt the atmosphere the moment a chance was provided to them. Notwithstanding years of ideological remolding, and beneath the thin socialist veneer, they remained the same old unrepentant, unreformed "intellectuals." No trust could be placed in them and while they need not be physically liquidated, they were to be regarded with the utmost circumspection and had to be constantly watched; the Party must needs rear and nurture its own elite which would gradually supplant older "bourgeois intellectuals" or their offspring.

Significantly, Mao seemed to have transferred the domestic experience on to the international plane. It was not a fortuitous conjunction that dogmatic policies at home were quickly followed by dogmatic policies abroad. The internal hardening had an organic connection with the subsequent external hardening.

If despite the iron rule of the Party for the last ten years and continual, persistent ideological re-education, the "bourgeois rightist critics" showed such tenacity in clinging to their bourgeois views, what better could be expected of the bourgeoisie and the rightists of other countries of the world where power lay in the hands of those very classes? Surely no gradual transformation or peaceful conversion could be expected of the ruling bourgeois groups in other countries when such expectations had been belied in the case of Chinese "rightists." It now appeared obvious to the Chinese Communist leadership that struggle, constant struggle, was the *only* correct method of dealing with all the "rightists" of the world. Of course, no one could argue with Mao Tse-tung that many of the so-called "rightists" in China were not really asking for the restoration of capitalism in China but only for structural changes in the Communist system (somewhat on the lines of Poland and Yugoslavia) and that a large number of the critics, especially in the lower echelons, had no political ambitions and no intention of shaking the citadels of Communist political power.

One additional experience reinforced this new understanding of the Communist high command. That was the Tibetan Revolt of late 1958 and early 1959. For Mao and his associates it substantiated what they had already come to believe; it was clear evidence that if the Tibetan rightists and "reactionaries" could be so desperate as to dare start an open, violent rebellion under the very nose of the Red Army, it was foolish to imagine that the reactionaries in non-Communist countries would relinquish their power peacefully and gracefully; the Communists and the progressive forces in those countries could only expect violent and protracted struggles in their quest for power. That was—for Peking—the meaning and significance of the Tibetan revolt.

Disappointed and chastened by their experience of the rectification campaign, Peking switched over from political experimentation to economic experimentation. The "Hundred Flowers" movement was followed by the Great Leap and the People's Communes. The Chinese leaders were now in a hurry; they wanted quick results. They hoped to telescope the time of several decades that were normally required for industrialization and economic development into three or four—at the maximum, five years. This they hoped to achieve by making the people work harder and by undertaking simultaneous development of industry and agriculture—in short, through the Great Leap and the institutional reorganization of agriculture in the People's Communes.

The Great Leap and the People's Communes got into full swing by the fall of 1958. The fancied phenomenal success of the new policies and reports of fantastic increases in production—highly exaggerated as they later turned out—generated an atmosphere of overweening confidence in Peking. It served to reinforce the dogmatic trend. The Chinese leaders believed that they had found the key to the solution of their problems and hoped to catch up with the advanced countries of the world in a short period. They saw no reason for, and showed no inclination to, making conciliatory gestures toward others. Consequently, Peking's foreign policy attitudes further stiffened and the rigidity in internal politics was carried over to the Chinese stance in foreign policy.

The formulation of foreign policy is always the result of the interplay and interpenetration of a complex of forces and a variety of factors, and it is not being suggested here that the domestic experience was the only explanation for the changes in Chinese foreign policy. There were so many other factors playing an important role . . . but the domestic experience was without doubt one significant factor in a whole set of factors influencing Chinese thinking. And it was certainly in the Chinese tradition for the Chinese leaders to regard their own experience as having universal validity. China has always functioned, consciously or subconsciously, on the assumption that the truth as seen in China was the universal truth and that whatever happened in China was significant for every other part of the world. In this regard the thinking of Mao was little different from that of the previous rulers of the Universal Empire—that China had a central position in the world and that what was true of China was true of the rest of the world. While the international context had no doubt changed and Mao was not necessarily looking upon the rest of the world as barbarians, the influence of traditional thinking remained strong in regarding Chinese ex-

perience as having unique relevance for the rest of the world
and in looking at the world almost exclusively through the Chinese prism.

FRANZ SCHURMANN *
A Student from Peking University

The Hungarian Uprising had two important consequences in
China: the raising of workers' wages and the rectification movement. The former failed because of the weakness of China's
economic base. Here I shall speak of the rectification movement. It had been planned early in 1957, but was officially announced only on May 1, 1957. The newspapers began to ask the
people to offer criticisms of the Party. What they wanted, however, were not fundamental criticisms, but criticisms of the
"shortcoming" type: wastage, high living, incompetence, and
so on.

On May 4, the time of the celebration of the thirty-eighth
anniversary of the May Fourth Movement, a leading Party
cadre addressed eight thousand members of the Youth League,
giving them an outline of the kind of rectification movement the
Party expected. He deliberately exaggerated "corruption" and
"shortcomings" in order to get people to make criticisms of this
sort. On May 18 the Youth League held a big meeting with delegates from the entire country attending. The meeting was in
connection with the name change from New Democratic Youth
League to Communist Youth League. The following day posters
began to appear in all of Peking's schools announcing the results of the meeting and urging criticism. However, sometime
between May 5 and May 10 posters of a unique kind began to
appear on the bulletin boards of the semi-secret Aviation College, which was located in the northwestern part of Peking along

* This article is based on an interview by Franz Schurmann with a Chinese
student in Hong Kong on August 23, 1958.

with other universities and schools (this section of the city has a student population of two hundred thousand). These posters contained sharp criticisms of the Communist Party. We quickly learned that posters of this kind had appeared. May 18 can be said to have marked the end of the first period of the rectification campaign.

The second period began on May 19. The Party and the League called upon the students to offer criticisms. The posters which appeared were mostly signed. So much excitement arose as a result of the campaign that examinations were postponed. This was the first time in four years that studies had been interrupted. The initial type of criticism was mainly of the concrete sort: such and such a cadre lived too well, was a poor administrator, and so on. However, another type soon appeared which leveled fundamental criticism of the Communist Party.

This second type began to ask: "Why should the Communist Party develop such bad aspects?" The fundamental criticisms came largely from fourth-year physics students who were the most intelligent students in all of China. Their criticisms were political. For example, they published a complete translation of Khrushchev's denunciation of Stalin at the Soviet Twentieth Party Congress. Hundreds of poems were posted to incite students' emotions. About a hundred physics seniors formed the core group of critics. They had no organization. Criticism was spontaneous. Posters were put up by individuals or a couple of roommates, but rarely by larger groups.

As time went on these two types of criticism became more sharply defined. The first type asked: "How can we help the Party carry out the rectification movement?" The second asked: "Why are the Communists bad?" Though there were many in the second group who had earlier been criticized during the *Su-fan* movement of 1955, there were no clear-cut social divisions between the two. Party members, of course, tended to make the first type of criticism. More than half of all the physics students, however, made fundamental criticisms.

Toward the second week of this second period, a rudimentary organization appeared: the Hundred Flowers Study Group (*Pai-hua hsüeh-she*). The organization had no real leadership, though the most active members were also members of the Youth League. It had, however, very few Party members.

Everything was completely democratic. Since all they did was discuss, they had no need for a real organizational structure. Some wanted to expand the organization to other schools, but their general purposes, aside from discussion, were unclear. Such leaders as there were were not important. Individual Communists joined, but most of them followed the Party's orders. For the first time, the Communists were on the defensive and their critics were on the offensive. One day a heavy rain washed away all the posters, putting a temporary halt to the campaign. We were all very excited. Every day students ran out to read the latest posters. News spread of the happenings at Peking University to other schools.

The students began to ask: "Where should we go from here? (*Wo-men tsou shen-mo fang-hsiang?*). Should we go the way of Poland?" Yet, though there were grave doubts about the new system, no one criticized it openly or directly. In general, there were no fundamental objections to Communism as such (that is, to the ideology) but to the present state of affairs. I myself began to develop doubts as to whether a planned economy could ever succeed only after I went to Manchuria to work.

This second period, which began on May 19, lasted for two weeks. It was a time of intense discussion and criticism. We all felt that the Party center had not taken any definite position on the criticism; it was a period of uncertainty and "confusion." Thus, on the second day of this period (May 20), the vice-president of the University (a Party member) praised us and urged us to put up more posters. The movement began to spread to other universities. A few students went to cities like Tientsin, to launch a movement there. We printed up many mimeographed pamphlets. None of us wanted to go back to our studies, so the examinations were postponed a second time. The fundamental criticisms emphasized the following points: (1) there is no freedom and democracy under Communism; (2) how could Stalin, who killed so many people, exist under Communism?; (3) China should have a more democratic electoral system with free choice among different candidates.

Many students thought that a new era had dawned. Some gave the following dialectical description of the coming era: Marx's first international was positive, and its negation was the second international; Lenin's third international was positive, and Stalin's Cominform was its negation. Now Mao Tse-tung should take over the leadership of a new Communist movement which would again be positive.

Discussions were very democratic. Soapboxes, just like in Hyde Park, were set up everywhere [Hyde Park was the term actually used]. While we ate in the great mess halls, students would gather in the open spaces outside and give speeches on soapboxes. Posters would announce that at such and such a time a student would talk on such and such a subject. Professors, in general, did not participate in these discussions.

The second period ended when an editorial appeared in *The People's Daily,* around June 8, warning the students not to go too far. Thus the third period began with a slow and gradual attack on the "rightists." Opposition began to die down. As long as we felt that the attitude of the Party was unclear, we felt we could take advantage of the situation to make some fundamental criticisms. The anti-rightist movement began democratically, and was, of course, led by the Party. But it soon got fiercer. Sometimes Party members would surround a "rightist" and debate with him. Although the rightists were still encouraged to talk freely, most became less and less interested in doing so. I do not remember the anti-rightist criticisms because they were not convincing to me (*mei yu shuo-fu-li*). It became the practice of the Party to single out "bad" elements and brand them typical rightists. Thus they tried to discredit the entire criticism movement.

Let me now state to you what I think the good and bad points of Communism in China are. First the good points:

(1) The Communists have faith. They believe in a future society, in an eventual good world. They believe that they are moving toward such a good world. This gives them strength (*kei t'a-men li-liang*). In their hearts, they are good (*hsin-li hao*). They believe they have a good social system.

(2) They have united China. We now have no more bandits and enjoy complete security. Everything is clean.

(3) Human relations are much better. People freely help

each other. There is no corruption. The spirit of mutual help is much better than before, in great contrast to the selfishness of Hong Kong.

(4) The Communists have started great economic development.

(5) The Communists have introduced a work spirit. Chinese now work all the time just like Americans. Before, they worked to consume, to enjoy themselves. Now they work for the sake of work. They are no longer lazy.

Now the bad points:

(1) Communism is like an absolute religion. Communists always think they are right. But what they do is not always in accordance with what they preach. If you accept their religion, you can be very happy, as it is with Catholics. But if you cannot accept it, you are unhappy. So many of my fellow students who accepted the new faith were happy, for they had a mission in life. Those who were outside felt isolated, lonely, and unhappy.

(2) The Communists believe superstitiously in the use of force. Lenin says that all great social changes come with violence. So many people were killed during the land reform. They say: "If you do not kill, then you cannot succeed" (*"ju pu t'u-sha, pu ch'eng"*). They killed so as to prevent their enemies from arising. Even though the killing has stopped, they use force in ruling. The collectives are a kind of forced structure.

(3) They believe superstitiously in the possibility of a propertyless society. I do not believe that the system of private property can be changed.

(4) The Communists dictatorially dominate the country. They allow no opposition, and will not share power with anyone.

Let me now tell you why I could not accept Communism. My father is a Christian pastor, and I was educated in a Christian school in Hong Kong. Because he worked so much among human beings, my father could not neglect them as Communists do. Knowledge of the Trotsky question, the Yugoslav question, the Hungarian Uprising, the revelations of the Twentieth Party

Congress and all that I knew about their cruelties and injustices made it impossible for me to believe in Communism. I also do not believe in a planned economy. I think the Communists interfere with the natural workings of the economy. The economy has its own laws. It is like a river which always flows downward. Economic development has its own laws; human activity is subject to these laws and must go along with it. But the Communists forcibly turn economic laws into manmade laws. They force men to become planners. Since human beings themselves have limitations, the plan too must necessarily have limitations. This results in great economic loss and stoppages. I think that a planned economy is wasteful and will result in a precarious, unbalanced economy. We shall overtake Britain [one of the slogans of the Great Leap Forward], but at the cost of great economic instability.

HUA LO-KENG *

Remolding of Intellectuals

Had it not been for the guidance of the Thought of Mao Tse-tung, I dare say that I would surely have been contented with what I was. With a pot of tea and a cigar, I would occupy myself in my study with mathematical problems which were so dear to me and with which I was familiar, oblivious to the buffeting of the four seas and the storm over the five continents. Without exerting undue effort, I would write so many learned treatises a year, so that my name might be known and I might live in peace and comfort. I would teach a little, give guidance to students, and hand my specialized knowledge without reservation (and without discrimination) to the younger generation. In this way, it appears that I would have done my duty. But would I really? No. . . .

* Hua Lo-keng, "Remolding of Intellectuals," *Atlas* (Magazine of the World Press), April 1966.

I am, after all, a "self-made man" from the old society. My efforts made me deeply attached to the science which I had studied. But this attachment prevented me from seeing the situation as a whole. Sometimes I even asked that the realities of the motherland be adapted to my favorite specialty, instead of letting the requirements of the Revolution determine the direction of research that would be most beneficial to the people. Of course, I do not mean to say that we should no longer cherish any affection for our specialties. What I mean is that attachment to a specialty should be determined by the interests of socialism, the Revolution and the people.

Chairman Mao has said, "Some of the things with which we are familiar will soon have to be laid aside, while we are being compelled to do things with which we are not familiar. . . . We must overcome this difficulty by learning what we do not know."

When it comes to actual work, obstacles still continue to frustrate us at every step and ideological problems continue to crop up without end. Had it not been for the illumination provided by the brilliance of Chairman Mao's thinking, and the timely help rendered by the basic Party organization, I must frankly admit that I would have been completely at a loss as to how to overcome these difficulties.

When I first came in touch with the method of programming, I had a mind to turn it down. Was I not a quite good mathematician even if I never bothered myself with the method of programming? Since the method originated in capitalist countries, was it not tainted with the odor of the bourgeoisie? If I engaged myself in working on this method, I might easily get myself contaminated. Why should I do that?

However, the Thought of Mao Tse-tung influenced me. Since I realized that this method might be useful to socialist construction and helpful to the implementation of the general line calling for "greater, quicker, better and more economical results," I felt it my duty to make some suggestions.

Accordingly, the idea of "passing it on" gave way to the idea of "having a try." I felt that I ought to tackle the subject, but I was also afraid that I might not be able to shoulder such a heavy burden.

Fortunately for me, the Party immediately came to my aid.

From now on I should take more initiative in doing my work, put myself in an even less important position, and strive to work hard for the Revolution with no care for my personal well-being.

The second barrier was "fear." The first time I went to a selected spot to make a trial, I was daring and full of confidence.

Arriving at the spot, I saw what an enormous and complex project it was. There were many things that I did not understand. All of a sudden I was struck by fear, like "Mr. Yeh who took a fancy to dragons," but who was frightened out of his wits when a real dragon came to him. Fortunately for us, the local Party organization did some timely ideological work on us. It arranged for us to go deep into the construction site to find out facts for ourselves and listen to stories about exemplary persons and exemplary deeds. It gave us encouragement. When I saw how my comrades, defying difficulties, worked with an awareness of the threat from the enemy and with class hatred in mind, I was able to overcome my "fear."

I had another "fear." I was afraid of what other mathematicians might say of the popularization of the science. They might say that this work involved no advanced mathematics, was "uninteresting," was simple "mathematics," or even that it was no mathematics at all. Such imagined criticism was in fact an illusion. I was judging a new generation of people by standards of my old self.

Recently I have visited many cities and construction sites. I have found that under the leadership of the Party and the influence of the Thought of Mao Tse-tung, mathematicians have changed. Many of them have gone to the forefront of socialist construction. "Empty talk and high-sounding theories" have given way to "practical and hard work." . . .

My work during a recent period has enabled me to realize even better the necessity of uniting myself with workers, peasants, and soldiers. Of course, owing to personal reasons I have not yet gone deep into the masses, but even the brief contact with them has given me an indescribable class education.

In practical work I personally experienced the possible tragedy of injury or death to our class brothers and losses to the state as a result of a miscalculation. Very often what a class brother and revolutionary fighter strives to secure at the risk of his life is a matter of decimal zero, something which we may ignore in our calculations. These living facts have enabled me to see many problems in teaching which must be considered in relation to the threat from the enemy and to class distinctions. . . .

What I have learned could never have been imagined in my study or in the classroom. When a drop of water falls into the sea, it will discover that its demands have changed. It is now no longer concerned solely with preserving itself against evaporating, but must conform to the requirements of the vast ocean.

The habit of practicing what one has learned and applying what one has practiced, and of combining learning with application, is vastly different from the way of study of "going round in circles among concepts and indulging in empty discussion of terms," with which I was familiar. This enables me to realize profoundly that class struggle, production struggle, and scientific experiment are united in an integral whole, that there cannot be a new-type scientific worker who can carry out scientific experiment well but whose idea of class is indifferent and whose production practice is vague. There might have been such scientists in the past, but they are no more. They could not be compared with the scientists who have grown up with the help of Mao Tse-tung's thoughts and who combine in themselves redness and expertness.

To be quite honest, I have not yet quite passed the ideological test. I am still far from the required state of "selflessness." However, when I see my comrades working selflessly, my "egoistic" considerations become less intense and will gradually vanish.

As it has been said, "Raspberry that grows among hemp will grow straight without support, and white sand will become black in mud, because they are influenced by the soil and their upbringing." Since I have come from the "mud" of the old society, how can I avoid being black! I am glad to see that now it is possible for me to grow straight like "raspberry among hemp." . . .

"I will do what Chairman Mao tells me to do." This famous saying of Comrade Wang Chieh rings in my ears. Although my youth is gone and there is little time left, Chairman Mao's thinking has "stayed the sun" for me. Under the brilliance of this sun that never sets, I will resolutely and ceaselessly walk on the road of revolution!

❧ The Peasants: Organization
and Reorganization of Rural Society

WE KNOW that China is an overwhelmingly peasant country. Yet we can only grasp the magnitude of that fact if we realize that her urban population exceeds a hundred million, greater than the population of industrialized Japan. The remaining six hundred million are peasants.

Let us also remember that Chinese agriculture long ago reached limits of expansion within the traditional framework of economy and society (see Volume I). How can China simultaneously feed a growing urban population, on which her modern industry depends, a growing peasant population, whose expectations have risen as a result of modern influence, and export farm products to import needed capital goods? China's rulers are not just visionary utopians. They know that unless they can resolve the food problem, China will die and with her their system.

Agriculture can be developed technologically. Japan stands as a remarkable example of a traditional rural economy transformed by modern technological inputs: fertilizer, electrification, small-scale farm machinery, and so on. But how could China, with her primitive modern industry, get sufficient modern products to invest in an agriculture employing six hundred million people? Mao Tse-tung and his colleagues believed that they had discovered a substitute for technique—the power of organization and the liberated energies of spiritual transformation—and that if the way the peasant worked, the arrangement of his lands, the forms of division of labor, and, most important, the peasant's attitudes could be drastically changed, output and productivity would rise. Eventually, a developed industry could take over and help agriculture attain even greater heights.

The land reform with its revolutionary terror had destroyed the peasant's awe of the gentry and cut his spiritual bonds to ancient ways. Having experimented with mutual-aid teams and small-scale cooperatives, in 1955 the Chinese Communist leaders began rapidly to collectivize Chinese agriculture: lands were joined together so that crops could be rationally farmed; peasants surrendered their property to the common weal. By 1957 even rich peasants and remnant landlords had been brought into the Agricultural Producers Cooperatives (APCs), thus making the village into an integrated socioeconomic unit.

Yet Mao was not satisfied. Collectivization still left the village isolated from the larger polity, and it had not basically changed the peasant's way of working. In 1958, with the Great Leap Forward in full momentum, the communes were formed: large entities spanning many villages, politically and economically linked to county, province, and finally nation. The commune period was above all one of emotional frenzy; the peasant appeared to have experienced a second liberation, which would soon lead him into full communism (three years of suffering and a thousand years of happiness!).

The communes as conceived in 1958 failed, but they remain in a modified form today. Mao knows that the transformation of the peasant is a slow process, that it cannot be done by organization and spiritual transformation alone. Education and capital investment are necessary. The world would do well to remember, however, that China is not only the world's largest peasant society, but the one which has made great efforts to turn the peasant into a modern producer. India's present tragic position must make us refrain from too severe criticism of the commune period in China.

In this selection the senior author of this reader traces the organizational changes in the Chinese village from land reform through collectivization to communization, concluding that today "the state persuades rather than commands the peasants to raise crops which the state needs." Thus, despite the ideological fanaticism reigning in the country, the Chinese approach to their rural economy, as to other sectors of the economy, combines pressures from the top with tolerance from below.

Their present treatment of agriculture and the peasant may indicate an ultimate recognition that progress must be slow but sure. Yet the ideology of the Great Leap Forward remains, thus not excluding the possibility of another attempt to speed up the transformation of agriculture.

FRANZ SCHURMANN *
Peasants

The greatest problem facing China today is the transformation of her huge peasant population into modern producers able to raise enough food to meet the rapidly growing needs of China's population. No government in China's history has been more acutely concerned with this challenge than the present government in Peking. In contrast to Stalin, who regarded the peasantry mainly as a source of surplus for industrialization, Mao Tse-tung believes that the spiritual transformation of the peasantry and the material transformation of agriculture are vital to China's survival and growth. Recognizing the slowness of technological transformation, Mao was convinced that organization could change the peasant's attitudes and so pave the way for the technological revolution on the land. The history of cooperativization, collectivization, and finally communization must be understood in the context of this supreme belief in the power of organization. Here we shall examine the course of this social transformation from the time of the revolutionary land reform in the late 1940s to the abandonment of the extremes of communization in the late 1950s.

* Franz Schurmann, *Ideology and Organization in Communist China* (Berkeley and Los Angeles: University of California Press, 1966). An adaptation.

THE LAND REFORM AND ITS RESULTS

The magnitude of the social revolution that struck the Chinese countryside remains yet to be studied. China's vast population alone made the land reform one of the greatest social revolutions of modern times. In July 1950 the Communists announced that land reform, by the fall of 1950, would have affected 100,000,-000 peasants, of whom the landlords constituted 4 per cent or 4,000,000 individuals. This left another 364,000,000 peasants, according to the population calculations of the time, among whom land reform was to be carried through, and some 10,000,-000 landlord elements to be eliminated. Land reform in substance was said to have been completed by the end of 1952, which meant presumably that the bulk of landlord and rich-peasant land had been redistributed by that time. Land reform did not lead to an economic revolution, for production patterns in the village did not change fundamentally. But as a social revolution, land reform succeeded in destroying the traditional system of social stratification in the rural areas. The old rural gentry, whether based on the villages or residing in towns, was destroyed. A social element, which had exercised leadership in the village by virtue of its status, its ownership of land, and its access to power had ceased to exist. That class which traditionally had formed a link between local society and the state—the gentry—was wiped out in the process of land reform. Land reform did not bring about complete leveling, for "rich peasants" and apparently even some former landlord elements continued to exercise power and influence within the villages themselves. But a return to the *status quo ante* was impossible. (See Volume II.)

The local landlord gentry was destroyed, and in its place came the arms of the state apparatus—in the form of *hsiang* government. The drive to increase agricultural production during the early 1950s was accompanied by rapid bureaucratization at the *hsiang* levels and above. In 1950 the government issued a series of decrees outlining the structure of government at all levels of national life. The basic-level unit of administration was henceforth to be the *hsiang* or the administrative village. Late in 1950 formal rules for *hsiang* people's government were issued.

In many areas, the *hsiang* people's congresses were simply the old peasant councils transformed into a more formal body. The new *hsiang* governments were staffed by rural cadres who had remained in the good graces of the leadership. As throughout China, much administration was carried out by committees, some permanent, some *ad hoc*. The formal *hsiang* people's government committee, having one head and several deputy heads, took on the following form: civil administration work committee, finance and food work committee, production cooperation committee, education and hygiene work committee, work committee for public order and security, work committee for the people's armed forces, and several *ad hoc* committees.

Each *hsiang* government had attached to it units of the people's militia and a local public security-police station. In theory, *hsiang* government was subject to the *hsiang* people's congresses, which were periodically held; there, *hsiang* government officials reported on their work, announced policy, and solicited criticisms and suggestions. The different sections of *hsiang* government accurately reflected the major interests of the state in the rural areas: the maintenance of order and control, the collection of taxes, and the desire to extend the network of organization over the rural areas. The first two functions are little different from those of earlier Chinese governments, but the Communists were determined not simply to exercise control over the rural areas but to transform them.

The pace of rural reorganization was to remain slow for a number of years. The first stage in rural reorganization took the form of the creation of mutual-aid teams. By late 1952, 40 per cent of China's rural households were organized in one or another form of mutual-aid teams. Still, "though the mutual-aid teams were certainly organized on a massive scale, many of those, however, appeared to have produced only pro forma results." Whatever the results of these early attempts to organize mutual-aid teams, the structure of *hsiang* government already reflected the intention of the leadership to concern itself with positive steps aiming at the reorganization of Chinese agriculture. . . .

THE CREATION OF AGRICULTURAL
PRODUCERS COOPERATIVES (APCS)

Though during the early 1950s Peking encouraged the development of mutual-aid teams and agricultural producers' cooperatives, the campaign had only limited success. . . . Peking's
main instrument for handling the villages was still bureaucratic
administration exercised through the *hsiang*. However, the pace
of cooperativization gradually speeded up. In January 1954 the
Central Committee issued a directive on "developing agricultural
producers cooperatives"; by the end of the year 114,165 APCs
had been organized in the country.

But the great change came in the summer of 1955 when
Mao Tse-tung in his famous July speech (made public in October) "On the Question of Cooperativization in Agriculture"
urged a decisive speedup in the campaign of organizing APCs.
The anger expressed in speeches and editorials which appeared
in 1955 against rightist and counter-revolutionary elements,
landlords, and rich peasants "who have wormed their way into
the cooperatives" indicates that traditional leaders were reappearing in China's villages. As happened in earlier periods of
China's history, these village leaders resisted encroachments from
the state. The only way the Chinese Communists saw to pene-
trate the fabric of village organization was once again to do
what they had done during the Yenan Period, namely make
use of the Party cadre. But neglect of rural Party organization
during the early 1950s had meant that there had not been
enough village Party cadres to perform this task. Thus, Party
recruitment policy changed. Early in 1955, before a decision
to cooperativize had been made, China's leaders launched a program of building up Party organization in all rural areas of
China.

During the early 1950s the leadership had succeeded in
creating an administration which gradually covered the entire society. However, it was essentially oriented to the classic functions of control and exploitation. As the state intensified its exploitation of the peasantry, local administration
played an ever more important role in "planned purchase"

and "centralized purchase" of farm products, as well as in the task of taxation. But as exploitation functions increased, so did those of control. A rural police system was introduced in the early 1950s. Public security squads were organized. A people's militia remained on the scene, in the form of a "permanent militia" and a "supporting militia." The latter consisted of young peasants normally engaged in production, but the former was a permanent militia, either not engaged in production at all or only part of the time. The combination of rural police, public security teams, and people's militia formed a kind of latter-day *paochia,* though far better organized and more effective than any known earlier in Chinese history. By 1955 the countryside was under control and the state's mechanisms for collecting surplus were effective.

But more was needed than control and exploitation. Agricultural output had to be increased, and the policy adopted by Peking to achieve this was full-scale cooperativization. Economic considerations played an important part in the decision to speed up the pace of cooperativization in late 1955. The 1954 harvest had been bad, providing a diminished surplus for industrial investment. . . .

Collectivization seemed to be the answer to the problem of increased needs for agricultural surplus. Land reform had given the peasant land, but did not lead to an improvement of the over-all agricultural situation. The average landholding of the peasant did not increase greatly as a result of land reform. The prospects for a rapid technological revolution in agriculture were not good. As Mao said, "to complete, fundamentally, the technological revolution in agriculture on a national scale, I reckon that four or five five-year plans will be necessary, or twenty to twenty-five years." This meant that little capital could be diverted to agriculture during the period of intensive industrialization. Organized hand labor alone would have to be used to achieve greater agricultural output.

Mao was aware of the fact that there was widespread reluctance to intensify the pace of cooperativization, that "it goes beyond the realistic possibilities" and "goes beyond the level of consciousness of the masses." True, there was the example of the Soviet Union's difficulties with collectivization, but, Mao said, the "error of 'dizziness with success' was quickly rectified."

Their own experience and that of the Soviet Union undoubtedly made the leadership quite aware of the adverse consequences that could ensue from collectivization. They were perhaps not aware, though, that the technological revolution could not be postponed, for as the social revolution created new forms of production organization, it also created new capital needs in agriculture.

Why did the Communists decide to move so quickly and drastically on the agricultural front? Probably because there was no inevitable evolutionary process leading from land reform through mutual aid to cooperativization. Mao reported that in Chekiang "at one blow" fifteen thousand out of fifty-three thousand cooperatives had been dissolved, and admitted that in 1953 there had been "the error of large-scale dissolution of cooperatives." Aside from the open dissolution of cooperatives, there was reason to question how cooperative many of the cooperatives really were. . . .

Mao made clear that, though land reform had done away with "feudal" forces (the landlord gentry), new "capitalist" forces (rich peasants) had arisen. During the early 1950s Peking had decided to rule the countryside administratively, and so had retreated from the natural village. The result was a resurgence of the rich peasants who, in a manner familiar from traditional times, once again took over village leadership. Reports pointed out that in some instances rich peasants often refused to join the cooperatives, leaving the poor peasants in an association that had only limited land and tools. But in many other instances, landlords and rich peasants had infiltrated the cooperatives and diverted them to the particularistic interests of the village. The greater the resurgence of traditional village leadership, the less effective the actions of the Party and Youth League cadres. Rural Party organization still suffered from the abrupt change in recruitment policy in 1950. Organization was poor; cadres were of a low caliber; and central support was often lacking for a powerful organizational drive. The result of all this was growing apprehension on the part of the leadership that the social revolution initiated by land reform would start moving in reverse. Village self-sufficiency would reassert itself, making it increasingly difficult to crack the shell of village organization. Already "some comrades" felt that the village cadres had trouble enough organizing small-scale cooperatives; how much greater the problems in organizing them on a large scale! The leadership decided that the time had come to take a bold step to accelerate the social revolution.

The social revolution could be carried out in the villages only through the Party and its auxiliary mass organizations like the Youth League. . . . The social revolution was to be undertaken by cadres from the villages themselves. The old technique of sending down "operations squads," *kungtso-tui,* from higher echelons was to be used only in a limited way. . . .

THE PACE OF COOPERATIVIZATION

The year 1955 was significant in the organizational history of Communist China. It was a year of rural class struggle, even if it did not assume the violent character of the land-reform period. Organizationally, it saw the transformation of the mutual-aid teams into APCs. Once the APCs had been created, the move from an "early stage" to a "higher stage" was not difficult. Although the "early-stage" APCs did not affect property rights to the extent that the "higher-stage" APCs would, the initial stage of cooperativization had introduced the principle of property amalgamation. Though there was considerable resistance to cooperativization, it appears to have mainly taken the form of passive noncompliance, withdrawal of effort, slaughter of farm animals, and the like. As a whole, however, the resistance to the APCs was far less violent than that in the Soviet Union at the time of original collectivization. The revolutionary terror was still fresh in the minds of the rural population. Neither the peasants nor the leaders wished to risk a repetition of those events. Though various forms of compulsion were used, the leaders were reluctant to use force which would have had a disastrous impact on production. Membership in the APCs was still based on voluntary assent, for even in later years the press reported instances of peasants quitting the APCs.

After the fall 1955 harvest was assured, the pace of cooperativization was rapid. By the end of 1955 seventy-five million peasant households (63.3 per cent of the total peasant population) had been enlisted in one or another form of cooperative; by the end of 1956, 83 per cent, and by the summer of 1957, 97 per cent.

Not only the speed of cooperativization but the rapidity of the conversion of "early-stage APCs" to "higher-stage APCs" were remarkable. By the middle of 1957 more than 96 per cent of all peasant households were in "higher-stage APCs." These were fully socialized, and in essence comparable to the Soviet *kolkhozes.* Some writers have used the word "cooperative" to designate the earlier-stage APCs, and the word "collective" to designate the higher-stage APCs. Full collectivization meant not only the socialization of all property, but the creation of a unified village economy. In its September 14, 1957, directive on the reorganization of the APCs, the Central Committee declared that "as the experiences of the previous year have shown, under most conditions, one APC per village is relatively correct." Thus the transition to the higher stage involved not merely the complete socialization of peasant property, but the amalgamation of smaller APCs into larger units covering an entire village.

In conclusion one can say the transition from early-stage APCs to higher-stage APCs did not have the clear-cut character of the 1955 cooperativization, thus making it difficult to label the first stage cooperativization and the later stage collectivization. However, the basic purpose of the leaders in aiming at the higher-stage APCs is clear. As we said, full collectivization meant both the socialization of all property and the creation of a unified village economy. A higher-stage APC was to be a cooperative identical with the natural village and comprising all land, including that formerly owned by landlords and rich peasants. Such an all-village cooperative would make possible the development of a planned all-village economy, particularly for the basic grains. It also would create a socioeconomic organization based on the natural village, but politically responsive to the state. Thus, the early-stage APCs must be regarded as a transitional form designed mainly to break the socioeconomic power of the traditional village leaders. Once their power had been broken, they and their valuable property could then, and only then, be integrated into the APCs, thus permitting a transition to the higher stage. . . .

THE EMERGENCE OF THE COMMUNES

Two policy changes during the latter part of 1957 had a decisive influence on village policy. One was the anti-rightist movement and the other was decentralization. Two aspects of the anti-rightist movement had a direct effect on the rural areas. One was the "socialist education movement" which brought about a revival of attacks on landlord and capitalist elements; the other was *hsiafang,* which saw thousands of city intellectuals sent to the villages. The "socialist education movement" and *hsiafang* brought about an increasingly radicalized atmosphere in the country. Though decentralization had been planned as early as 1956, the growing radicalization during the summer of 1957 influenced the form decentralization would take. Instead of moving in the direction of a market economy, decentralization took the form of locally directed social mobilization. . . . The revival of Mao Tse-tung's twelve-year plan for the development of agriculture early in October was the signal that a radical step forward was going to be taken in the area of land policy.

Residents in Peking at the time reported a sudden change in the atmosphere which occurred in December 1957 or January 1958. The intense, hard-driving pace of the Great Leap Forward was said to have begun at that time. It was reported that the Politburo held a secret meeting in Hangchow in December in which it decided to call for a Great Leap Forward in production and to institute a policy of amalgamating APCs into larger units. These same problems were discussed again and decided on in two later secret Politburo meetings, one in January in Nanning and the other in Chengtu in March. A decision to amalgamate the APCs must have been made at the highest level, for it is hardly likely that the experimental communes, some of which dated back to the spring of 1958, could have been established without a fundamental policy decision at the top. All the more so because the basic policy in regard to the APCs, made clear as late as September 1957, had been to keep the APCs relatively small in size. . . .

As the Great Leap Forward grew in intensity, it began to spread to the entire society. What had started as a movement

aimed at "overtaking England in fifteen years in industrial production" quickly became a gigantic nationwide mass movement
which affected city and country alike. The mounting *hsiafang*
campaign saw millions of city people pour down into the villages
to engage in agricultural work. The growing atmosphere of "high
speed" also affected the villages. As 1957 went into 1958 a
"fermentation" was developing in the rural areas which soon
would cause the words of the September directives, which had
promised no further changes in rural social organization, to be
completely forgotten.

One new policy already had a direct effect on the APCs.
On September 24, 1957, a joint resolution of the Central Committee and the State Council announced a new movement to
build and improve waterworks. By the end of the year, the
movement had become a "high tide" with "six hundred million
people throughout the country hurling themselves into a campaign to build waterworks." The movement intensified as
it became clear that a decision had been made to press forward
with a great leap during the coming year. A large-scale irrigation
and waterworks program had been successfully carried through
during the winter of 1955 and the spring of 1956. This time an
even larger program was carried out during the winter months
between the fall harvest and spring plowing. Small waterworks
were emphasized. Rather than have the work done by detailed
planning, in keeping with the decentralization policy of the time,
the basic planning was done at the lowest level, namely the
APCs. Irrigation projects became a part of the APCs' production
plans. Though some support was forthcoming from the state, the
APCs provided the bulk of the labor. . . .

The great waterworks brigades organized during the winter
and spring of 1957–1958 were forerunners of the production
brigades that were to arise under the communes. There was an
essential difference between these waterworks brigades and the
production brigades of the APCs. The latter were work groups
that consisted largely of people who lived in the same general
area and had had experiences of cooperation on more or less
common land. The former were more in the nature of military
units, moved from place to place as construction needs changed.
The waterworks brigades could be organized along lines of
rational division of labor, which was difficult for the production

brigades to do. The idea of mobilization and rational division of labor began to take hold in the villages, and particularly in the minds of the cadres. Methods used for the organization of waterworks brigades were increasingly applied to other work sectors. As the pressures of the Great Leap Forward became more intense, the idea arose that a radical change in the organization of work must be brought about.

During the spring and summer it became apparent that in many APCs, under the impetus of the irrigation movement, attempts were being made to create a new work order. On July 4, 1958, an article in the *Jen-min jih-pao* described an APC "which was being administered like a factory." APC No. 38 in Su-hsien, Anhwei, had 1,065 households, and was therefore already larger than the earlier APCs. Under the impact of the Great Leap Forward, APC No. 38 found itself caught in a number of "contradictions." First, there were the conflicting demands of agricultural work and those arising from the new policy of building small-scale industries to serve agriculture. Second, "the original simple division of labor was no longer able to satisfy the needs of the present comprehensive leap forward in agriculture." Third, original production technology was no longer adequate. And fourth, "the contradiction of a labor shortage had become particularly apparent." After considerable discussion, the cadres and masses decided that "there must be a further leap forward in work organization."

Clearly, the Great Leap Forward was beginning to make heavy demands on the peasantry. Irrigation work had already drawn off considerable labor from the fields. The drive to increase fertilizer resources demanded additional labor, as did the drive to set up small farm-servicing industries. The bumper summer crop intensified the need for labor even more. The labor shortage, occurring in an increasing mobilizational atmosphere, gave rise to the idea that the existing work order must be broken up and a new division of labor created. In retrospect now, it was at this point that the leadership and its cadres were at the verge of introducing an even more profound social revolution into the village. The collectivization of land in 1955–1956 in China seems to have had a less disruptive effect on the Chinese peasant than Soviet collectivization of the late 1920s and early 1930s had on the Soviet peasant. Many Chinese poor and middle peasants did not have time to develop strong proprietary relationships to the land they received during the land reform carried out only a few years earlier. By contrast, Soviet peasants had actively seized land during the Russian Revolution. What proved to be far more disruptive in China was this attempt to transform the organization of work. . . .

If work was to be rationally organized, then the leadership was faced with a new limitation: the small size of the APCs. Although the average size of the APCs had grown in 1956 and 1957, as a rule the APC still was the equivalent of a "natural village" or of several small "natural villages." In fact, as we have said, in 1956 the leadership discouraged the formation of excessively large APCs. This made sense as long as the traditional work order was to remain unchanged. But by the spring and summer of 1958, because of the large-scale irrigation brigades, village labor was increasingly working beyond the confines of the APC. The original directives on the organization of irrigation work had encouraged APCs to cooperate in collective efforts. As the Great Leap Forward imposed new tasks on the APCs, such as the setting up of small industries, it became increasingly obvious that the administrative framework of the APCs was too small to allow for rational management. It was necessary to establish these industries at a broader level and draw labor from several villages or APCs to operate them. When the summer harvest came and the crop was good, the labor shortage became apparent. It was even more necesary to shift work teams from village to village, and throw them into the production front as the needs arose. Crops do not ripen at exactly the same time, and there is always a slight time difference from village to village, and indeed often from field to field, in the optimal time for harvesting. It thus became common practice at this time to set up "specialized brigades" which were shifted from village to village as the need arose. . . .

Although by the spring of 1958 the waterworks campaign and the experimental policy of amalgamating APCs were bringing about significant changes in village organization, there was no direct, predetermined path from the policy decisions of late 1957 to the formation of APCs in the summer of 1958. The adoption of Mao Tse-tung's twelve-year plan for the development of agriculture by the Third Plenum of October 1957 meant a general decision in favor of social mobilization as against material incentives. But no one in Peking was quite certain about what concrete form the new social mobilization policy would take. Despite the victory of the Mao-Liu advocates of social mobilization, the debate over agricultural policy continued into the spring of 1958. However, the second session of the Eighth Party Congress (May 1958), held to rectify the first session's moderate tone with the new radical line, appears to have given a new impetus to radicalization.

During the summer of 1958 a labor shortage developed in many farm areas, due partly to the good harvest and partly to the draining off of able-bodied workers to irrigation and construction projects. The labor shortage undoubtedly suggested to rural Party cadres that a new form of work organization, based on the specialized team idea, would be more effective than the old forms of work organization in bringing in the harvest.

Here, we must look at the word "commune," which first appeared in July to designate the new amalgamated APCs. All Communists remember the Paris Commune; Russian Communists remember their war communes following the October Revolution; Chinese Communists remember the short-lived Canton Commune of December 1927. All three were armed egalitarian workers' communities—work, struggle, and administration were carried out by the workers themselves. Thus, in essence, commune meant an armed community.

Reports of an arming of the peasantry began to appear in July, notably from provinces like Honan and Liaoning which had come under radical provincial leadership. Though it is not known how many arms were distributed to the peasantry, we know that the popular militia (*minping*) was revived on a large scale at this time. APCs were required to organize armed groups of young men and women attached both to the APCs and to units of the People's Liberation Army. At the same time, peasants were recruited into military-type brigades and teams. In fact, in many APCs military terminology was used to designate the different organizational units. Again it is not clear why the summer was chosen as the time for reviving the militia. It is not likely that Peking had international aims in mind, for the militia, with its largely defensive potential, would have been of little use in any possible attack on the offshore islands. More likely is the explanation that the formation of the militia was bound up with the struggle between political and professional orientations in the PLA, a struggle which reached one climax in October 1958 with the dismissal of Su Yü, Chief of Staff and a known proponent of professional policies in the armed forces.

It was the militarization of the APCs that gave Party leaders the idea of calling them communes, for which the Russians, for the first time, openly criticized their Chinese allies. It is not clear whether it was Peking which decided on the name or local Party leaders who independently started using it. Late in July the Party's top leaders undertook wide-ranging and well-publicized trips throughout the country; it appeared that they wanted to see with their own eyes what was occurring. Beginning on August 17 the Politburo met for thirteen days in enlarged session in the resort town of Peitaiho to discuss the commune problem. The communiqué which emerged from these meetings announced the high tide of a communization movement already in progress, yet was remarkably cautious in its tone.

Despite the caution voiced in the communiqué, the pace of communization was incredibly rapid. At the end of August there were 8,730 communes covering 30.4 per cent of the total peasant population; by the end of September there were 26,425 communes, covering 98 per cent of the peasant population. The ideological tone accompanying communization was utopian: the mass media loudly proclaimed that final communism was imminent, that three years of suffering would be followed by a thousand years of happiness.

What was the commune as social organization? Since communes differed widely from area to area, it is difficult to point to a single "ideal type." Nevertheless, general organizational policy was uniform throughout the country. In some instances the amalgamated APCs were totally transformed along the new lines. In other cases amalgamation meant little more than the creation of a new overarching administrative framework over the discrete APCs. The official literature of the period singled out the advanced communes as models for others to follow.

But no matter how radical the reorganization, the communes did not represent a completely new creation. There was an existing social organization with which the cadres had to reckon. In fact, there are indications that the leaders were concerned over the tendency of the local cadres to move too fast and too radically in transforming existing social organization. The communiqué of the Central Committee on the establishment of communes, which was issued on August 29 but not published until September 10, is a surprisingly cautious document full of advice not to do this and that. The communiqué warns the cadres not to go too far in tampering with existing organization and not to jeopardize agricultural production, as is evident in the following paragraph:

> One must combine the amalgamation of large APCs into communes with existing production [conditions]. Not only must it not adversely affect existing production, but this movement must be made into a great force to bring about an even greater leap forward in production. Therefore, in the early period of amalgamating APCs it is well to adopt the policy of "moving at the top but not at the bottom."

It is apparent that the leadership was already worried over the radicalism of the communization movement. The fall harvest was impending, and the leadership was not willing to risk jeopardizing what promised to be another bumper crop. The policy of "moving at the top but not at the bottom" meant that the cadres must not go too far in disturbing existing social organization. Better to move radically at the commune level and more carefully at the village level. The August 29 communiqué made clear that the communes must take as their nuclear elements the preexisting APCs. . . .

Communization aimed at something broader than the creation of a larger administrative framework for the APCs. As we have said, communization was meant to revolutionize the entire conception of agricultural work. Mobilization was to become a permanent part of village life. The degree of permanent mobilization differed from village to village, but the essence of commune organization was mobilization.

What did permanent mobilization mean? The following description of a commune in remote Chinghai province describes mobilization in one multinational commune:

> The Red Flag people's commune [of Lotu *hsien* in

Chinghai province] was formed out of seven APCs. . . .
Now it has 524 households and 3,003 individuals. Among
them there are 408 Han households, or 2,494 individuals,
113 households of local peoples or 500 individuals, and
three households of Tibetans with 9 individuals. There are
12,000 *mou* of land consisting of 700 *mou* of high mountain land, 4,400 *mou* of mountain stream land, and 6,900
mou of shallow mountain dry lands. Each laborer on the
average was able to take responsibility over twelve *mou*
of land; there were somewhat over a thousand workers,
male and female. In addition there were 3,000 head of
sheep, some 50 fruit trees (apricot, *shakuo,* pear). Geo-
graphically, there are stream areas, stream lands. From
east to west the commune covers more than 30 *li.* . . .

Before the commune was established, the seven APCs
had an average of twenty–thirty households. The largest
hardly numbered a hundred. The population was scattered,
and there was a shortage of labor. Though irrigation was
practiced, land was leveled, schools and factories were set
up—all was difficult. The land was fragmented into small
parcels. It was impossible to use machinery to till the land,
nor was it possible to use large implements. The local people who lived in the mountain regions subsisted on millet
and were never able to eat wheat. The Han people living in
the stream regions found it difficult to consume milk. As
long as production materials such as forests, fruit trees,
houses, sheep, small plots of land were still under private
ownership, it was impossible to carry out unified planning
and unified use, something which affected the development
of production and construction. Private ownership of these
production materials and small collectivity ownership (the
small APCs) came into contradiction with productive forces
which since the Great Leap Forward have demanded
rapid development. The setting up of a people's commune
was the best way of resolving these contradictions.

The Red Flag Commune can prove this point. Since
the commune was established, within the short space of one
month, there came about a great change. Through the
unified allocation of the work force, when wheat was being
harvested in the stream areas, more than two hundred peo-

ple were recruited from among the local hill people to assist. Work which before took twenty days to do was accomplished in five days. Now when the millet ripens in the hills, the commune members in the stream areas take their tents to the hills.

Recently several specialized brigades have been set up which operate industry, agriculture, and supplemental enterprises, and work with a division of labor. Since the forests now belong to the commune, the lumber problem for building a wood-track railroad has been resolved. Recently iron and coal ore have been found in the hills, making it possible for the commune to smelt iron. The iron foundries, winemaking plants, medicine-processing shops, red-and-expert school, after-hours middle school, clinic, maternity room, nursery, mess hall, barber shop, sewing teams which have been set up by the commune—all are unifiedly run by the commune.

The Red Flag Commune of Lotu *hsien* was different from the usual Chinese commune. Since Chinghai province has a large minority population, the commune was ethnically mixed, in contrast to the population of the usual commune solidly Han. The settlement patterns in Lotu *hsien* were typical of areas of ethnically mixed habitation in China. The Han peoples occupied the lowlands adjacent to the streams; the aboriginal peoples lived in the hills. Traditionally, the different races did not mix. Though there always were existing relationships between them, social organization never united Han and non-Han. The original APCs in Lotu *hsien* had been set up along ethnic lines. But the new commune aimed at uniting something that tradition had kept apart. Thus, Chinese were sent into the hills to help the local people harvest millet, and local people were mobilized to help the Chinese with their wheat harvest.

The Red Flag Commune provides an example of what communes throughout China tried to do, namely to break through the barriers of traditional and territorial limitations—break through from the village to the *hsiang* to the *hsien* and link up with the larger world. Here in Chinghai not only territorial limits were broken through but traditional ethnic boundaries. . . .

THE RETREAT

The great assault on agricultural production lasted only to the end of 1958. From November 28 to December 10, 1958, the Central Committee held its Sixth Plenum on the Wuchang side of the triple city of Wuhan. The communiqué issued marked the first step in the retreat from the extremes of the summer before. It called for moderation and consolidation in implementing communization. During the spring and summer of 1959 repeated reference was made to the "three-level system of ownership" in the communes. These references indicated, as we can now say in retrospect, that Peking was increasingly adopting a policy of retreat from the extremes of commune centralization during the summer of 1958. The Seventh Plenum, held April 1959 in Shanghai, discussed the communes but did not issue any definitive policy statement. The communiqué of the Eighth Plenum, held in Lushan from August 2 to 16, 1959, made the now famous admission of the exaggeration of the 1958 crop figures. It also made clear that the basic unit of ownership in the communes was the brigade, that is, the second of the three levels of ownership. Though the Eighth Plenum was followed by a partial return to the mobilizational policies of 1958, by the summer of 1960 it became clear that Peking was continuing its retreat. On November 20 and 25, 1960, the *Jen-min jih-pao* published two major policy editorials on the communes, which, in effect, made the team (that is, the third or the smallest of the three levels) the *de facto* unit of ownership. Although the editorial made clear that the legal ownership rights remained within the brigade, it differentiated between rights of ownership and rights of use. The team was given full rights of use over labor, land, animals, tools, and equipment. It was formally made the basic-level unit of accounting in the commune. In January 1961 the communiqué of the Ninth Plenum of the Central Committee announced a far-reaching reversal of economic policy which ended the Great Leap Forward and inaugurated a period of economic consolidation and liberalization.

Retreat would thus appear to have begun in December

1958, only a few months after the communes were launched. However, in view of the cautious notes already evident in the Peitaiho communiqué of late August, one might even suggest that the retreat started at the very time that communization was launched. By the summer of 1959 Peking, for all practical purposes, had gone back to the old higher-stage APCs which were the same as the large production brigades of the communes. By autumn 1960 it had retreated even further. Since the small production brigades or teams were the equivalent of the early-stage APCs, that is, parts of the natural village, Peking had even abandoned the idea of an operationally unified natural village. Of course, the all-village collective economy was still directed at the brigade level. However, the teams, though they were required to contribute labor to the collective economy, had full rights of disposition over ways to do so.

Liberalization set in in force after the great policy reversal of early 1961. On the one hand, organizational pressure on the peasant was reduced—for example, by expanding the free market. On the other hand, both heavy and light industry were reoriented to fulfilling some of the consumer needs of the peasant. Peking, at that time, abandoned its policy of social mobilization on the land and tried a campaign of selective capital investment in agriculture. Since then, the food situation has gradually improved until, at present, most food items appear to be plentifully available in the cities. Peasant income has apparently risen, and peasant life, particularly in the vicinity of the great urban and industrial areas, has improved. The main beneficiaries of the new land policy have been the more productive peasants, just as the professionals have gained from the new policy toward industry. Rich peasants are appearing again, which suggests that "kulakization" may be endemic to an imperfectly collectivized rural economy such as that of China.

Yet the ebb and flow of policy continues, and so one sees today an intensification of political and ideological pressures. Since the late summer of 1962 a new socialist education movement (the first, it will be recalled, was launched in August 1957 as a part of the anti-rightist campaign) has been in progress. It differs from the earlier campaign in that the movement is not marked by peaks of political intensity. It has now been going on for three years with a steady drumfire of ideological indoctrination. There have been the expected attacks on "capitalistic vestiges," which is to say attacks on the wealthier and more individualistic peasants. But, so far, "socialist education" has not been followed by concrete action. As in so many other areas of life in China, a gap between ideology and organization has been developing.

In the face of this new situation, what is the state of social organization on the land? It is now certain that Peking has given up its attempts to create a rural economy transcending the limits of the natural village. The peasant may still be called on to do labor outside of his village, but it is usually for emergency tasks, such as flood control. For the most part he works within the confines of his village, as he always has done. The real social unit appears to be a small team of twenty or thirty households who live close to each other; given the nature of Chinese villages, they may be related to each other by kinship. Though the team must contribute to the collective economy of the village, it devotes a considerable part of its labor to the raising of "supplemental crops." What is left of the peasant's time is given to his private holdings which, as in Russia, constitute an important part of the rural economy. The state pays better prices for farm output, thus increasing the income of the peasant. A portion of the collective output is left to the peasants to be disposed of on the now legal open market. Peasants who live close to cities bring in their produce and sell it individually to urban consumers. The official literature indicates that "old peasants" have again assumed leadership in the villages. The "old peasants" are not the young Party cadres who led the Great Leap Forward. Some are probably new rich peasants; others are probably peasants who enjoy local prestige for traditional reasons.

The popular militia remains, and is important for maintaining public order; in the exposed coastal regions it has been a major instrument for capturing subversives landed from abroad. The young cadres have an unchallenged part to play in the popular militia. Party cadres continue to exercise power and influence at commune and village administrative levels, though, under the new policy, they have been instructed not to lead or dominate the work life of the peasant. The communes remain as an administrative framework—not surprising since they are the latter-day version of the earlier *hsiang* administration. If the *hsiang* is indeed the equivalent of a standard marketing area, as G. William Skinner has suggested, then the commune has an important role to play in rural trading. The communes continue to operate some of the small industries that are still functioning. And, most important, the commune directs disaster relief and emergency work. The natural village has come into its own again; it is the unit of the collective economy. Party cadres still sit in the committee of the production brigade, but they may no longer impose plans from above. Procurement plans for farm products are worked out as a compromise between the state's demands and the peasant's capabilities. The state persuades rather than commands the peasants to raise crops which the state needs.

𝕰 Economic Development

DESPITE THEIR inexperience in economics, the Chinese Communists were determined from the outset to launch a grandiose program of economic expansion. During the early years after 1949 the Soviet Union was their general model for industrialization and modernization, a model calling for rapid expansion of heavy industry with savings extracted largely from agriculture. This developmental strategy became the core of the First Five Year Plan (1953–1957). Choh-ming Li, Vice-Chancellor of the Chinese University of Hong Kong and Professor of Business Administration at the University of California, notes that "be it 7, 6.5, 6 or thereabouts, China's rate of growth during this period was quite high—more than double, if not three times, the average annual rate of natural increase of the population, officially estimated at 2.2 per cent." The exact growth rate of the Chinese economy has been widely disputed in Western economic literature, but even low estimates, as Li shows, compare favorably with the growth rates of other countries such as the Soviet Union and Japan during similar periods of development.

The "phenomenal industrial growth" of this period can be attributed to two key factors: Soviet aid and agricultural savings. As Choh-ming Li points out, although 97 per cent of the investment for basic development came from the Chinese people themselves, without Soviet aid the First Five Year Plan could not have been realized. Far more important than the relatively meager credits furnished China were the plants, blueprints, technical assistance, and training of students in Soviet universities. The Soviet aid program to China must be reckoned as the most successful effort by an advanced nation to lay the

193

foundations of basic industrialization in a backward nation. China's heavy industrial economy, despite some Japanese industrialization in Manchuria, still rests on Soviet-built foundations.

Although Soviet aid was efficiently administered and given in liberal quantities, the Chinese people had to pay for it all. Here the thorny problem of agriculture enters. As Li indicates, "by the end of 1956 it had become increasingly clear that economic growth was closely tied to agricultural output. The amount of savings from which all industrial and other investments are made depends heavily on the harvests of the preceding year." Chinese agricultural output has its ups and downs: a sharp drop in one year means fewer materials for industry, less food for the cities, lower monetary revenues for the state, and less available for export to pay for needed capital goods. Thus in 1957, following the poor 1956 harvest, investment, output, and trade declined.

Since the Chinese, unlike other developing countries, refused (or were not given) outright economic aid, they had no choice but to confront the problem of agriculture directly. They collectivized, as the Soviets had, but in 1958 they went a step further and created the communes. The Chinese leaders appeared to have had great confidence that farm productivity would leap forward; for example, they cut cultivated acreage devoted to food production by one third—and had their illusions shattered by the food crisis of 1959. At the same time they were struck by a second blow: in August 1960, as a result of the intensifying Sino-Soviet dispute, the Soviets withdrew their technicians, for all practical purposes ending their program of assistance to China; henceforth, Sino-Soviet trade dropped sharply.

Li concludes his analysis of the First Five Year Plan with the observation that "barring a violent outburst of general discontent, a change in Party leadership, or war, continuous and rapid industrialization of the country may be expected." In the short run, Li appears not to have been entirely correct. Because of the stoppage of Soviet assistance and the economic crisis, Chinese industrial growth seriously slumped, and some economists, in fact, have described the crisis period as a capitalist depression. In the mid-1960s, however, we can see that China's industrial development has once again picked up. We would do well to remember that today China is not only industrializing, but is paying for it by herself. Her guiding slogan is self-reliance (*tzu-li keng-sheng*). Though she purchases foreign capital goods with her limited foreign-exchange holdings, her technology and industry are now mainly her own. Agriculture remains a serious bottleneck, but the last years have seen a slow but steady growth in output. Thus, in the long run, we would agree with Li's estimations of China's prospects for economic development.

CHOH-MING LI *
Economic Development

In the ten years of Communist rule since late 1949 a thorough-going revolution has taken place on the Chinese Mainland in economic organization, savings and investment, and distribution, with profound effects on the daily lives of the people. Peking has claimed that immense progress has been made on all economic fronts, including the real income of industrial and agricultural workers. It has felt confident enough to shorten from fifteen to ten years (beginning 1958) the target period at the end of which its output of electric power and certain major industrial goods would match or exceed that of Britain. In the non-Communist world, commentators vary greatly in their judgments; they range from those who reject all the official statistics and consider no important progress to have been made during the period, to those who not only accept the claims *in toto* but have advanced all sorts of arguments to defend even those claims that Peking has later had to repudiate.

There are, indeed, serious problems connected with the official statistics, and the early claim of a 105-per-cent increase in food output for 1958 over 1957 was so unreasonable as to cast grave doubt on the reliability of all official data in the minds of

* Choh-ming Li, "Economic Development," *China Quarterly*, 1, January–March 1960, pp. 35–50.

objective investigators. But, despite the domestic and international fanfare given to these "Great Leap Forward" achievements, Peking later saw fit to announce a drastic downward revision of them as well as of the targets for 1959. This lends strong support to the view that the regime has not been operating with two different sets of statistics, one for confidential use and the other for public consumption; that in the need of reliable data for planning purposes it demands accurate information from junior officials whose psychological bias and incompetence are the major source of error; and that provisional data must be sharply distinguished from final figures, which, however, particularly in respect of agricultural statistics, represent at best the considered judgment of the State Statistical Bureau and therefore have to be used with care.

Statistical differences notwithstanding, there can be no doubt that the economy was able to sustain continuous growth in national product during the period under review at an annual rate much higher than the rate of population increase. This performance has greatly impressed many of the underdeveloped countries and has caused India, for example, to shift its emphasis from agriculture in its First Five Year Plan to heavy industry in the Second, and more recently to introduce "cooperative farming" on the Chinese model. To the West, the crucial question is whether this growth will continue and China will thus become a World Power. It is important, therefore, to examine the record carefully: to evaluate the over-all rate of growth, to find out how it was achieved, to understand the background that led to the Great Leap Forward and the people's communes and their current status, and to realize the sacrifices the people have been called upon to make.

THE FIRST FIVE YEAR PLAN

The ten-year period falls into three phases, namely, rehabilitation (1950–1952), the First Five Year Plan (1953–1957), and the Great Leap Forward (1958–1959). The first phase saw the rehabilitation of the war-torn, inflation-infested economy, the completion of the land redistribution program, and the beginning of socialization of private trade and industry—a process which was destined to be consummated, together with that of agriculture, in 1956. The cessation of civil strife, Soviet aid toward restoring the industrial base in Manchuria, and the Korean War all contributed to the rapid economic recovery. Deliberate economic development began in 1953 when the First Five Year Plan was launched. Evaluation of Peking's performance must start from this point. The third phase, covering the first two years of the Second Five Year Plan, witnessed such a radical change in economic organization and in the nature of data that it is best treated separately.

How fast did the economy grow from 1953 to 1957? According to official calculations, the net domestic material product (that is, the total values added by all the materially productive sectors minus depreciation) increased from 61.1 billion yuan in 1952, 70 billion in 1953, to 93.8 billion in 1957, all at 1952 market prices. This gives an annual rate of 8.9 per cent with 1952 as the base and 7.6 per cent with 1953 as the base. It is interesting to note that a recent Western estimate of China's gross national product for the seven-year period from 1950 to 1957, made by William W. Hollister, who made use of official raw data together with independent calculations, gives an annual growth rate of 8.6 per cent with 1952 as the base and 7.4 per cent with 1953 as the base. Thus, the choice of the base year makes a great deal of difference to the growth rate. It is important to realize that 1952 is not a representative base, because for a good part of the year trade and industry were at a low ebb due to the dislocation caused by the "three anti" and "five anti" movements. For this reason, 1953 is a much better choice as the base year.

Taking 1953 as the base, the 7.6-per-cent annual rate as obtained from official statistics is still an exaggeration. Among the factors contributing to the exaggeration are the pricing of new products in industry, the low pricing of agricultural products on the constant price list, and above all, the understatement of the gross agricultural value product from 1952 to 1954 and overstatement in the subsequent three years. What the actual growth rate was during this period has not yet been satisfactorily determined. Professor Ta-chung Liu of Cornell University has recently published the summary results of his estimation of China's net domestic product (that is, the net domestic material product plus the values added by government administration and other service sectors). They show an annual growth rate of 6.8 per cent with 1953 as the base. The details of his calculation have not been published, but when computed in 1952 prices, a growth rate of this magnitude is probably closer to reality than any of the others.

Be it 7, 6.5, 6, or thereabouts, China's rate of growth during this period was quite high—more than double, if not three times, the average annual rate of natural increase of the population, officially estimated at 2.2 per cent. One is tempted to compare it with those of other countries which were or are at a similar stage of development. But such a comparison is fraught with difficulties; for example, methods of estimation, bases of calculation, length of period, and degrees of accuracy, all vary a great deal among different national estimates. For general interest, however, the following annual growth rate (all computed in constant prices) may be cited: for the Soviet Union, about 7 per cent during the period 1928–1937; for Japan, 4.6 per cent during the period 1898–1914 and 4.9 per cent from 1914 to 1936; and for India, 3.3 per cent during its First Five Year Plan period from 1950–1951 to 1955–1956.

SOVIET AID AND THE RATE OF INVESTMENT

What made this growth possible was a massive investment program which was financed almost completely through compulsory savings in the form of taxes, profits, and depreciation reserves of state-controlled enterprises, and reserve funds of the farm units. In Peking's national income accounting, the total savings (net of current replacement costs) of the economy are designated as "accumulation" and may be regarded also as that part of net national material product (that is, net domestic material products, adjusted to international balances) devoted to increasing fixed capital assets in the entire economy, working capital of the materially productive sectors, commercial inventories, and stockpiles of the state. According to the latest official data, the rate of accumulation at 1952 prices had increased from 19.7 per cent of the net national material product in 1952 to 23.7 per cent in 1957, with an average rate of 23 per cent for the five-year period.

Although the underlying concepts are different, it may be pertinent to mention three other estimates, all based on 1952 prices. Hollister found the rate of gross domestic investment to gross national product to be 18.5 per cent for the five years; and Liu gave the rate of net domestic investment to net domestic expenditures to be 21.8 per cent. Taking only fixed capital investment and working capital for industry and agriculture into account, I have estimated that for the same period the rate of capital formation to net capital product averaged 11 per cent.

Whatever the precise rate of investment was, it is certain that virtually all investments were made with internal savings. Financial assistance from abroad was not substantial. Since 1950, only two Soviet loans for economic development purposes have been announced; one, contracted in 1950, was for 1,200 million rubles, and the other, in 1954, was for 520 million. Together they were only enough to pay for 31 per cent of the necessary equipment and supplies for the original 156 industrial and other projects which the Soviet Union agreed to help China construct, or to cover but 11 per cent of China's total imports for the eight years from 1950 to 1957. During the First Five Year Plan, the amount of Soviet credit available for new investment (1.57 billion yuan) constituted merely 3 per cent of the total state investment (49.3 billion yuan). By the end of 1957, all outstanding Soviet credit was exhausted, and since then no new loan has been announced. Meanwhile, amortization payments have been mounting since 1954.

Of course, the Soviet contribution cannot be evaluated in terms of financial assistance alone. In respect of the Soviet-aid projects, not only the supply of machinery and equipment is assured, but all ancillary services are made available, including installation and operation of the plants and training of personnel. At the end of 1957 the total number of these projects already agreed upon came to 211, a figure which was subsequently increased by 125 through the agreements of August 1958 and February 1959. Equally important, if not more so, is the Soviet supply, virtually gratis, of whole sets of blueprints and related technical materials giving direction for the layout of a plant, its construction, and pilot manufacturing in various heavy and light industries. From 1954 to 1957, over 3,000 items of such information were provided. In the field of training, during the period from 1951 to 1957, some 6,500 Chinese students were sent to the Soviet Union for higher education and 7,100 workers for acquiring experience in Soviet factories. For basic research, significant Soviet assistance has been given in both personnel and equipment, the latter including such facilities as electronic computers and a 6,500-kilowatt atomic reactor pile and rotating accelerator. Indeed, Soviet experience and experts were made readily available to Peking in perhaps all state endeavors. Premier Chou En-lai revealed in a tenth-anniversary article in the *People's Daily* on October 6, 1959, that the Soviet Union had sent over 10,800 experts and the East European satellites over 1,500 to China during the previous decade.

Technical assistance of this scope must have contributed greatly to the efficiency of investment—which probably meant as much to the country as capital supply, especially in view of the shortage of engineering and management personnel. But the fact remains that for the five-year period, 97 per cent of the investment for basic development came from the Chinese people themselves.

PHENOMENAL INDUSTRIAL GROWTH

The investment program centered around 156 Soviet-aid engineering projects. In the words of the Chairman of the State Planning Commission, the underlying objective of economic development is "the marshaling of all efforts and resources for the development of heavy industry so as to lay down a foundation for an industrialized state and a modernized national defense." It is anticipated that by the end of the Third Five Year Plan the country will be capable of producing all machinery and equipment needed for further economic development. This objective gives over-all guidance to the allocation of state investments. From 1953 to 1957 the total amount of realized state investment for basic development came to 49.3 billion yuan, of which three quarters went to industry (56 per cent) and transportation and communications (18.7 per cent), and only 8.2

per cent to agriculture, forestry, and water conservation. And out of the 27.6 billion yuan of investment in industry 87 per cent was for heavy industry, leaving 13 per cent for light industry.

As a result, heavy industry grew at a phenomenal and sustained rate. To cite a few examples: rolled steel output increased from 1.1 million metric tons in 1952 to 4.5 million in 1957, coal from 64.7 million tons to 130 million, electric power from 7.3 billion kilowatt hours to 19.3 billion, and cement from 2.9 million tons to 6.9 million. For the first time and in quantity, the country was able to produce trucks and automobiles, merchant ships, tractors, and jet airplanes, and to export whole sets of cotton textile machinery, sugar-refining machinery and paper-making machinery. By the end of 1957, expansion of the iron and steel complex in Manchuria was virtually accomplished, and new centers of comparable size were being built at Wuhan in Central China and Paotow in Inner Mongolia. In light industry, production capacity was also rapidly enlarged, especially in the paper, textile, and sugar industries, but production was repeatedly held back by shortages of raw materials.

To support this development, the educational system was completely revamped to give primary emphasis to technical subjects. Polytechnical schools and short courses for industrial and agricultural techniques were introduced everywhere. On-the-job training and apprenticeship were introduced on a national scale. It is reported that the engineering and technical personnel in industry had increased 200 per cent from 58,000 in 1952 to 175,000 in 1957, while industrial employment (including mining and construction) grew 66 per cent from 6.15 million to 10.19 million.

The development of agriculture presents a different picture. It is true that in addition to state investment, the independent peasants, the agricultural cooperatives and collectives did set aside, as required, a small percentage of their annual output for expansion. But this amount, together with the state investment, was, at best, equal to about one half of the state funds spent for industry. During this period, mobilization of the masses for construction was practiced every year, but never on such a gigantic scale as in the spring of 1958. This neglect of agricultural development was reflected in agricultural output.

According to official statistics, the output of food grains (not including soyabeans) increased from 154.4 million to 185 million tons over the five years, at an annual rate of increase of 3.7 per cent. If this rate of increase were correct, there would have been an ample supply of food for various purposes. But by the beginning of 1956, the number of draft animals, essential for farm work, had been drastically reduced, owing, among other reasons, to the lack of feed. It is certain that the rate of increase in food production was exaggerated in official data, due to underestimates of output from 1952 to 1954 and over-estimates from 1955 to 1957. One cannot help drawing the conclusion that "the average annual rate of increase in food production during the First Five Year Plan was very close to but perhaps somewhat higher than the natural rate of population increase." In this connection, it is of interest to note that Hollister, in his estimate of the output of basic food crops and animal products, came out with an annual rate increase of 2.65 per cent—which is much closer than the official rate of 3.7 per cent to the natural rate of population increase (2.2 per cent).

Thus, as one might expect from the shape of the investment program, it was "the marshaling of all efforts and resources for the development of heavy industry" that accounted mainly for the economic growth of this period.

PROBLEMS OF COLLECTIVIZATION

The "high tide" of collectivization of agriculture and socialization of all other sectors of the economy came after the autumn harvest of 1955, when a nationwide movement for the "liquidation of counter-revolutionaries" had just concluded with huge numbers of people either executed or put in labor camps. The change in economic organization was so sweeping that although the changeover was successfully completed by the end of 1956 as the authorities claimed, it would have been logical for them to devote the next few years to consolidating these new gains in the interest, at least, of economic development. How then can one explain the Great Leap Forward movement that began in the winter of 1957 and the people's commune system which was introduced in the summer of 1958? Could it be that the changeover had not been as successful as claimed and that it was felt that if the resultant difficulties were not promptly corrected, economic growth and perhaps political stability would be jeopardized?

What were these difficulties? I believe the key to this question lies in the agricultural situation, which, contrary to Peking's expectations, deteriorated rapidly because of collectivization. Slaughter of farm animals and destruction of farm implements were widespread. Many collectives existed only in name because the members were attracted to trading in the "free markets." As a result, even though the cultivated area affected by natural calamities was only 14.7 million hectares in 1957 against 15.3 million in 1956, the total cropping area was reduced by 2 million hectares, and the cropping area for food by 3.4 million hectares. The multiple cropping index also fell from 141 to 139; the amount of fertilizers collected was smaller; and the rate of increase in irrigated areas stood lower than that of 1956. What was even more alarming was that food output increased only 1.3 per cent, from 182.5 million to 185 million tons, over the year, a rate which was far below the natural rate of population increase. Collectivization thus turned out to be a great failure— more so than the provisional statistics had led one to believe. When collectivization was first introduced nationally, there was already strong opposition to it within the Chinese Communist Party on the ground that the step was too hastily taken. Now the architects of the plan had to find an immediate solution for both political and economic reasons.

The situation was all the more serious because agricultural development could no longer be neglected in favor of concentrated development of heavy industry. By the end of 1956 it had become increasingly clear that economic growth was closely tied to agricultural output. The amount of savings from which all industrial and other investments are made depends heavily on the harvests of the preceding year. A good crop permits large capital investments in the subsequent twelve months while a poor crop reduces them. In fact, the whole economy follows closely the fluctuations in agricultural output with about a one-year time lag. But this was not appreciated by the leaders in

Peking until the latter half of 1957 when the summer and winter harvests fell far short of what the proponents of collectivization insisted that they should be.

Recognition of the basic importance of agriculture immediately raised the issue of whether the state investment program for the Second Five Year Plan be changed to favor agriculture at the expense of heavy industry. Such a change would, of course, have run completely counter to Peking's primary objective in economic development and also to the ideological tenets of the Communist world. What could Peking do?

To deal with the situation, a series of directives were issued in the name of the Central Committee of the Party. Two stood out as the most significant. One, dated September 14, 1957, concerned improving the management of agricultural collectives. It said, in part (Article 6):

> The size of collectives and production teams is crucial to the success of management. Because of the various characteristics of agricultural production at the present and because the technological and managerial levels of the present collectives are not high, experiences in different localities during the last few years have proved that large collectives and large teams are generally not adaptable to the present production conditions. . . . Therefore, except the few that have been well managed, all those that are too big and not well managed should be divided into smaller units in accordance with the wishes of members. Henceforth, a collective should generally be of the size of a village with over 100 households. . . . A much larger village may become one collective or be organized into several collectives. . . . As to the size of production teams, twenty neighboring households is the proper number. . . .
>
> After the size of the collectives and production teams has been decided upon, it should be publicly announced that this organization will remain unchanged in the next ten years.

Thus, one of the immediate steps taken was to reorganize the collectives and production teams by reducing their size. The ten-year period of no further change was obviously intended as a device to appease the peasants and to give the regime a chance to consolidate its position in the rural areas. The reasons given for the reorganization were based on practical experiences. All this seems to indicate strongly that the later development of "people's communes" was not a preconceived, ideological move on the part of the Party leadership, although as early as 1955 Mao did remark on the operational superiority of large cooperatives on the basis of actual observation.

The second was the revised draft of the national agricultural development program from 1956 to 1957, released on October 25, 1957. This, together with an earlier directive of September 24, seemed to have given rise to the slogan "Great Leap Forward." Moreover, it sparked a national movement to mobilize the farming population to repair and build irrigation works of various sizes (chiefly small) and to collect all sorts of organic fertilizers throughout the countryside and in the hills. It was reported that from November 1957 to well into the spring of 1958 tens of millions of peasants were mobilized every day, often working long hours at places far away from home. This started the establishment of common mess halls. When the time for spring planting arrived, a labor shortage began to be felt. Utilization of idle labor time as a form of capital formation had reached a limit. Additional manpower had to be found if full advantage was to be taken of the investment. The dispatch of people to the villages from overcrowded cities and overstaffed offices and factories was one expedient. More important was the other—the induction of women into the labor force by freeing them from housework through further development of mess halls and the introduction of tailoring teams, nurseries, old folks' homes, etc. Since peasants working in large groups needed discipline to insure punctuality and a good work pace, something akin to military organization was needed. In sum, it was against this background that the communes were developed—with Mao's personal blessings and encouragement.

Although this development was diametrically opposed to the Party's directive issued a few months previously, the chain of events that led up to it seemed to the leadership a justification for taking a bold step which would not only wipe out responsibility for the failure of collectivization but offer a new and rational solution to the baffling agricultural problem. To them, low man-hour productivity was not so important as high unit-area productivity which was the crucial factor for accelerating industrialization.

Thus, in 1958, out of a total basic development investment (not including investment by the communes for their own purposes) of 26.7 billion yuan, 78 per cent went into industry (65 per cent) and transportation and communication (13 per cent), and only 10 per cent into agriculture, forestry, and water conservation. In the original plan for 1959, which called for a total investment of 27 billion yuan, only 7 per cent was allocated for the latter three related fields.

THE GREAT LEAP FORWARD

Just as collectivization produced a strong psychological bias on the part of the rank and file to overreport the agricultural output of 1956 and 1957, so the harvests of 1958 were grossly exaggerated as a result of the Great Leap Forward and the formation of the communes. Whether food output actually increased from 185 million tons in 1957 to 250 million (instead of 375 million) in 1958, as the officially revised statistics show, remains a question to which perhaps even the State Statistical Bureau itself is not in a position to give a definite answer. Admittedly, such measures as the building of irrigation facilities and the introduction of various labor-intensification methods (deep plowing, close cropping, etc.) might have increased unit-area productivity and therefore total output. Moreover, the area devastated by flood and drought—only 6 million hectares as compared to 14.7 million in 1957—was the smallest in five years. It was naturally a bumper crop year. But the reasons officially given for the overreporting in the first instance refer to the methods of estimating which are still being used and in which a high margin of error is always present, regardless of how carefully the results are checked.

If the 35-per-cent increase were accepted, it would be difficult to understand the severe food shortage in both rural and urban areas during 1958 and 1959. Perhaps part of the explanation is to be found in the 1-per-cent increase in food output in 1957, which affected the supply situation the following year. Then there is the question of the composition of the 35-per-cent increase in 1958. According to the original, unrevised claim, a 103-per-cent increase had taken place in food output, reflecting an increase of 70 per cent in wheat, 73 per cent in rice, 76 per cent in coarse grains, and 320 per cent in sweet potatoes. No such breakdown has yet been given for the revised figures.

Is it possible that sweet potatoes accounted for so much of the 35-per-cent increase in food output that the other food crops did not register any significant improvement? That the population on the Mainland have been forced to accept the unwelcome sweet potatoes as their regular diet lends plausibility to this speculation.

Toward the end of autumn harvest in 1958 and at the height of the commune movement, there was another nationwide mobilization of the masses, especially in the countryside, for producing pig iron and steel. With the great majority of women drawn into the labor force, the end of the agricultural season brought in its train the pressing problem of how to keep the working population fully occupied without the state having to make any investment. The "backyard furnace" scheme seemed to be the answer. As usual, the cadres carried it too far with a resulting disruption of regular transportation and the neglect of irrigation and other field work. In the meanwhile, a large majority of the so-called furnaces were not able to produce, and most of those that could came up with products so poor in quality that for modern mills raw materials were of more use. Both manpower and materials were misused. The project was finally abandoned in the spring of 1959 as a movement, although industrial production by indigenous methods was allowed to continue to grow in localities where limited success with good prospects had obtained.

For 1958, the regime thus claimed a great leap in industrial output, pointing especially to an increase in the output of steel by 101 per cent, coal by 107 per cent, and pig iron by 130 per cent. Only in August 1959 was it made clear that these output figures for 1957 and 1958 were not comparable and that when production from indigenous sources was omitted, the increase in each case was reduced to about one half of the original claim —a still quite impressive record. It is not clear if the modern factory output and the production by indigenous methods had been properly segregated and if the quality of factory output was as uniform as it was before. However, a substantial increase in factory output was credible because some of the major projects built under the First Five Year Plan were now bearing fruit.

The downward revision of the official claims for 1958 was accompanied by a scaling down of the plan for 1959. To cite a few examples, the planned increase in the production of food was reduced from 40 to 10 per cent, raw cotton from 50 to 10 per cent, coal from 40 to 24 per cent, metal-cutting lathes from 40–50 to 20 per cent. In each of these cases, the planned increase was far less than the increase in 1958 over 1957. According to the definition given by Chou En-lai, the "Great Leap Forward" had now petered off to a "Leap Forward." It was reported that floods and drought had occurred over a large area of the country in the late spring and summer of the year. The drastic reduction in the goals for food and cotton output, made public in August, must have taken their effects into account. Nevertheless, if the innovations, plus excellent weather, had accounted for the 35-per-cent increase in food in 1958, thus advancing the level of output to a new plateau, and if the experience of other countries is any guide, one may legitimately express doubt whether the 10-per-cent planned increase in the output of food as well as cotton in 1959 could be realized—without mechanization and large-scale use of chemical fertilizers. Perhaps a 10-per-cent increase or a higher rate will be reported, but the 1958 episode should teach us to be extremely cautious in respect of such claims.

DEVELOPMENT AND THE CONSUMER

At the end of the decade of Communist rule, the economy would seem so well launched on the path of development that further growth would be easier. This would have been the case if the process had been carried through under a leadership that inspired popular support or at least consent. But the development program, calling for heavier and heavier sacrifices, was determinedly imposed upon the people from above. Discontent was growing and widespread. The regime may indeed face an internal situation far more serious than at any other time since 1949.

To be sure, Peking has long instituted certain socioeconomic measures designed to gain the support of the workers. As early as 1951, a system of social security was inaugurated by which state enterprises were required to contribute annually an amount equivalent to about 15 per cent of the wage bill to various welfare purposes such as workmen's compensation, medical assistance, cost-of-living subsidies, and trade union activities. Private enterprises, when still in existence, were required to enter into contract with their employees to provide similar obligations. For workers in governmental and educational institutions, a system of free medical benefits was established in addition to welfare and educational benefits. It was reported that from 1953 to 1957 the actual outlay for all these purposes equaled about one quarter of the national wage bill. Then in 1958 a system of retirement was put into effect for workers in industrial and business enterprises and governmental and civil institutions. All these measures were innovations introduced into the country for the first time on such a large scale.

As against these benefits, however, the workers have completely lost their freedom of choice of jobs. They are subject to deployment from factory to factory and from locality to locality. Direction of labor is practiced extensively to support the growth of new industrial cities in the hinterland. Moreover, workers are not secure in their jobs, because especially after 1957 they are liable to be assigned to the countryside to become a part of the agricultural labor force, thus losing a great deal of the benefits accruing to them in the cities. While technical skill enhances security in industrial employment, the determining factor is poltical attitude and "socialist consciousness."

As was foreseeable, social security benefits have not been extended to the peasants. The early official justification that their position had already improved as a result of land redistribution no longer held true under collectivization and the communes. They have been required to take care of their welfare collectively out of their own annual output, and even primary education in the countryside is financed out of agricultural taxes. Mass mobilization projects often take them far away from home.

And during the Great Leap Forward movement they were driven to labor such long hours that the Party at the end of 1958 had to reaffirm the principle of giving them eight hours of sleep and four hours of mealtime and rest every day except in the busy agricultural seasons. As compared with the urban workers who were also pressed into emulative and overfulfillment-of-the-plan drives, the peasants are the worse off by far because their work is all physical exertion unmitigated by mechanical assistance.

Changes in the real income of workers and peasants are among the subjects yet to be carefully investigated. During the period from 1952 to 1957, "per capita consumption of food, cloth and housing services had declined in absolute terms, with the exception of staple food grains, the total consumption of which probably had increased a little for the country as a whole, owing primarily to the growing need for energy work by those not used to work on the farm and to the leveling process of collectivization." The slight increase in staple food consumption, however, was in terms of weight, and there was strong evidence that the composition of staple food had been rapidly changing in favor of sweet potatoes and coarse grains. In 1958 and 1959, per capita consumption as a whole took a deep dive. The severe shortage of staple (rice and wheat) and subsidiary food and cloth was nationwide.

The situation was particularly bad in the rural areas. According to the many instances reported in the Mainland newspapers, in 1958 the communes were generally required to set aside, as "accumulation," 50 to 70 per cent of their total output, net of production and management costs. Now a survey made by Peking's State Statistical Bureau of 228 collectives in the country reveals that in 1957 consumption accounted for 89 per cent of the net output, with only 11 per cent for accumulation. The collectives investigated were better than the average, so that the share of consumption must have been higher for the country as a whole. Assume conservatively that consumption took 90 per cent in 1957 and that accumulation was raised to 50 per cent in 1958. It does not take much calculation to see that the net agricultural output must increase 80 per cent if consumption in 1958 was to be maintained on the same level as in 1957. Obviously the 50–70-per-cent accumulation rate was decided upon in accordance with an expected increase in gross agricultural output of about 80 per cent. However, since the gross agricultural output in fact increased only 25 per cent (according to officially revised data), if one assumes that the net output had grown at the same pace, consumption must have declined by about one third when one half of the net output went into accumulation. It is not surprising that the peasants became restive.

The causes of discontent were not confined to economic factors. Many of the national movements, coming on each other's heels, were in the nature of purges. Countless numbers of people were executed, imprisoned, or placed in labor camps. The threat to personal safety was ever present, and the atmosphere of insecurity must have been tense and oppressive. This was enough to generate unrest. A further major blow was the disintegration of the family system in the communes. It may well be true, as the document issued by the Party in December 1958 stated, that husband and wife had not been forcibly separated in different quarters. But when people had to eat in common mess halls and both husband and wife had to work long hours outside and the children were in nurseries, the family ceased to have any common bond or unity of interest and purpose. It was no longer the place where material rewards were shared together or occasionally with friends; nor was it a place for enriching personal cultural heritage. Even the Soviet Union had never gone this far.

Thus discontent had been growing and widespread. One needs only to read Deputy Premier Teng Hsiao-p'ing's report of September 1957 on the "Rectification Movement" to realize the extent of it among intellectuals, peasants, industrial workers, minority nationalities, armed forces, and Party members. The situation deteriorated even further after that date, not only because of the further decline in per capita consumption, but because of the Great Leap Forward and the people's communes. Resentment was particularly strong among the peasants, as attested by the official acknowledgment that the bumper crop of 1958 suffered heavy losses from poor reaping, threshing, collecting, and storing. This feeling was quickly communicated to the armed forces, whose recruits came chiefly from the rural areas. Therefore, it was not unexpected that opposition to the present leadership stiffened within the Chinese Communist Party, as clearly revealed in the *People's Daily* editorial of August 27, 1959.

Peking, of course, had already taken steps to cope with the situation. Since March 1959, many of the radical features of the commune system had been gradually altered. Accumulation in the communes was generally scaled down from 50–70 per cent to about 30 per cent for 1959; participation in common mess halls became voluntary; ownership of most of the means of production was reverted back from the commune to the "production brigades"—the old collectives; small plots of land were returned to individual households for private cultivation; "free markets" were partially reopened. Thus by the end of 1959 the people's communes existed very much in name only, although each still retained a share of accumulation funds for developing local industries. On the political scene, perhaps the most important move was the strengthening of the present leadership through an extensive reshuffle of Party personnel in the government, and the appointment of General Lo Jui-ch'ing, who had long been Minister of Public Security, as Chief of Staff of the Army.

How the future will shape up is, of course, a hazardous guess, for much depends on how well the widespread discontent is contained. There is, however, no indication that the present leadership has any desire to give up the commune system—a step that would vindicate the opposition. Perhaps, for some time to come, the commune will continue primarily as an administrative unit, engaging more and more in industrial activities supported by the farming units operating as collectives. But even under *de facto* collectivization, the agricultural problem still awaits urgent solution. In the economic picture proper, two developments should ease somewhat the regime's effort in this direction—the extensive construction of irrigation works in 1958 and 1959 which, if properly maintained, will raise agricultural productivity to a new level, and the increasing flow of capital goods from the major projects built in the last few years. Thus, barring a violent outburst of general discontent, a change in Party leadership, or war, continuous and rapid industrialization of the country may be expected.

🙋 The Military System

FROM 1927 to the present the army has been a major part of Chinese Communism. Party and army have continuously been closely linked: during the Long March, the Yenan Period, the Civil War, and since 1949. Almost all the top leaders have records of military command. During the Yenan and Civil War periods, soldiers and peasants alternated roles, fighting one day and tilling the land the next. After 1949 the situation changed when, under Soviet influence, the Chinese began to build up a professional armed force serving purely military purposes. During the Great Leap Forward, however, the Chinese Communists began to return to their earlier traditions. They revived the popular militia. With the cutoff in Soviet military aid, as a result of the Sino-Soviet conflict, the Chinese Communists began to put even greater stress on the militia. Though the militia was initially as disorganized as the Great Leap Forward itself, the Party undertook a thorough reorganization. Today apparently all youths not conscripted into the People's Liberation Army join the militia, which plays a major part in the life of the country and in the defense planning of the leadership.

In the following selection General Samuel B. Griffith, a retired Marine Corps officer who served in China, discusses the organization and capability of the People's Liberation Army. With its stress on political awareness, on mixing of officers and men, on lower-echelon decision-making, the PLA is unique among the world's armies, which tend generally to function according to a straight-line chain of command. The basic Chinese premise is that, as Lin Piao put it, men are more important than weapons. Though this may partly be due to China's inferiority in military technology, it also is in accord with the entire tradition of the Chinese Communist Party. Thus, as Griffith points out, a constant process of ideological remolding, criticism and self-criticism, and study of the works of Mao Tse-tung goes on. To make certain that the PLA gets soldiers with correct attitudes, it conscripts largely youths who are ideologically reliable and from untainted family backgrounds. Of equal importance is the stress on the unity of officers and men: officers must "go down to the company and become soldiers" (*hsia-lien tang-ping*). The influence of the guerrilla tradition is unmistakable: guerrillas fight in isolated bands in which morale, loyalty, and mutual understanding among soldiers are of primary importance.

The doctrine that men are more important than weapons has not found universal acceptance in China. Griffith points out that during the Korean War there often were conflicts between political officers and their military counterparts, which impaired decision-making. At the highest levels the conflict between the "reds" and the "experts" (the latter being advocates of military professionalism with stress on modern weaponry) reached a climax with the dismissal of General Su Yü, Chief of Staff, in October 1958, and the ouster of Marshal P'eng Te-huai, Minister of Defense, in September 1959. Nevertheless, Peking retreated from the Great Leap Forward extremism, with its fetishism of guerrilla approaches, and has resumed stressing the need for professionalism. Today Peking is trying to combine these two "contradictory" approaches, but still recent accounts indicate that the polemic continues. Perhaps the most striking sign of Peking's awareness of the importance of modern weaponry is its development of nuclear arms.

After examining the capabilities of the Chinese armed forces, Griffith's main judgment is that "Chinese capability for sustained conventional action on a major scale outside her own borders is poor." However, "China's capabilities for defense against conventional attack are of a different order entirely." Moreover, "Chinese capabilities in the paramilitary field—the entire spectrum of insurgency, of which guerrilla warfare is but a part—are high, particularly in Southeast Asia." Thus he argues that while China's defensive capabilities are great, her offensive capabilities are generally restricted to paramilitary action: "from areas contiguous to her borders, the Chinese can easily exfiltrate selected young men and women for intensive political indoctrination and training . . . [who] can then be put back as nuclei for cells." Griffith discusses their combat doctrine, which is "viable" and "adaptable to modern war," and he lists the doctrine's key elements: morale, fight only when victory is certain, prudence, the importance of military intelligence, indirect rather than direct approaches, and the element of surprise.

During the last decade and a half China fought one major foreign war (if we do not count as a war the Sino-Indian border conflict of October 1962): in June 1950 North Korean armies invaded South Korea; in October, Chinese armies entered the Korean War, and all of China was mobilized in a "Resist America and Aid Korea" campaign. It is not clear why North Korea, entirely a Soviet satellite, launched the war in the first place; that China entered the war when she felt her Manchurian border threatened seems clear. The war proved to be costly in human casualties for the Chinese, and its lessons have played a major part in subsequent Chinese military thinking.

The Chinese tactics in that war, notably the "human sea" attacks, seem to be at variance with those Griffith describes. The "human sea" tactics were a standard feature of Russian warfare in both World Wars, and their use by the Chinese in Korea may have been a reflection of the rapid Sovietization of the Chinese Army which began with the "Liberation" in 1949. The Chinese had preferred to build their Civil War victories by "multiplying many minor successes," as Lieutenant Colonel Rigg pointed out (see Volume II), the key to which was the small combat team. During the late 1950s the Chinese Communists once again stressed small-combat-team tactics, and they probably will not repeat the tactics used in the Korean War in any future war beyond their borders.

SAMUEL B. GRIFFITH *

The Military Potential of China

One hundred and sixty-six years ago, a political writer on the staff of a respected journal—the *Philadelphia Monthly Magazine*—devoted a column to reports of a civil war then said to be raging in China. This anonymous and unpretentious commentator, unlike some who follow the trade today, admitted that his analysis was almost entirely speculative, for he wrote: ". . . our knowledge of that nation is very little, and that little, too obscure to be trusted."

Since 1798, this situation has not improved much, if at all, and there is small prospect that it will. Thus, any lay estimate of current Communist Chinese military capabilities, or her future potential, is likely at best to be but partially correct; at worst, flagrantly inaccurate. "It is extremely important," Mao Tse-tung wrote in *On Protracted War*, to keep the enemy "in the dark about where and when our forces will attack." This, he goes on, creates a basis "for misconceptions and unpreparedness on his part. . . . In order to achieve victory we must as far as possible make the enemy blind and deaf by sealing his eyes and ears, and drive his commanders to distraction by creating confusion in their minds."

Even those whose primary professional concern it is to assess Communist Chinese military capabilities have made egregious mistakes. History has qualified the late General of the Army Douglas MacArthur, Commander-in-Chief, United Nations Command in Korea, as an expert witness to the truth of this statement. At the Wake Island conference with the President (October 15, 1950), Mr Truman asked his General

* Samuel B. Griffith, "The Military Potential of China," in Alastair Buchan, *China and the Peace of Asia* (New York: Frederick A. Praeger, 1965), pp. 65–91.

what he thought of Chinese capability to intervene in the Korean War. MacArthur was not perturbed. He viewed this as a remote contingency. He replied:

> Very little. Had they intervened in the first or second months it would have been decisive. We are no longer fearful of their intervention. We no longer stand with hat in hand. The Chinese have 300,000 men in Manchuria. Of these probably not more than 100,000 to 200,000 are distributed along the Yalu River. Only 50,000 to 60,000 could be gotten across the Yalu River. They have no Air Force. Now that we have bases for our Air Force in Korea, if the Chinese tried to get down to Pyongyang there would be the greatest slaughter.

Forty-eight hours before the meeting on the peaceful mid-Pacific atoll, advance elements of Lin Piao's Fourth Field Army of almost a quarter of a million men began to cross the Yalu, and to disappear, without trace, in the rugged mountains of North Korea.

On Saturday, June 2, 1951, at a Senate hearing relating to the relief of General MacArthur, Secretary of State Dean Acheson read MacArthur's Wake Island appreciation into the record, and added: "That turned out to be an error—that they could only get fifty to sixty thousand across the river, and if they tried to get down to the south there would be great slaughter. They did it, and in considerably larger numbers."

> SENATOR SALTONSTALL: They really fooled us when it comes right down to it, didn't they?
> SECRETARY ACHESON: Yes, sir.

This secret concentration of overwhelming force in the zone of operations preceded attacks that brought the United Nations Command in Korea suddenly face to face with disaster. The unfortunate episode should exert a salutary effect on all of us who in discussion of the present and future capabilities of the People's Liberation Army (PLA) are too frequently inclined to make dogmatic statements and to draw subjective— and therefore unwarranted—conclusions. . . .

The mystique of the army is unique. It was well summarized in the September 7, 1962, issue of *China News Analysis*, a weekly newsletter published in Hong Kong:

> A Communist Army, certainly the Army of China, is run in a very different way from the "capitalist" armies, at least as they were before psychoanalysis, unfortunately, was applied to the life of soldiers. In the good old days the sergeant shouted at the top of his voice, and all obeyed; the sergeant was not much interested in knowing your *Weltanschauung,* or whether you had one. In the Liberation Army things are different; at the company level, and it is there that human beings are encountered, the real commander is not the commander of the company; he is the political guide, a comrade whose curiosity has no limits. He wants to know, it is his duty to know, not only what you do but—and primarily—what you think, whether you think the thoughts of Mao Tse-tung. It is his business to see to it that you do.
>
> He is not alone in his job. He is helped by men called "kanpu," cadres, who are, or should be, specialized in the job; but all others must give a helping hand. Indeed everybody, officer and soldier, must help everybody else to think the thoughts of Chairman Mao and report it if someone has kept a little private ownership in a corner of his mind. That would be a dangerous thing. A general of high authority declared that such things must be detected at their first appearance, before the evil is done; it is a kind of mine detecting work, in the minds of men.

In October and November 1961, after a detailed countrywide investigation of PLA units at all levels, the General Political Department issued a series of directives designed to correct the ideological situation in the armed forces. These deal with the functions of the Company Political Guide, the Party Branch Committees in Companies, the Youth Corps Branch in Companies, and the Revolutionary Soldiers' Committees in Companies.

These four regulations are designed to ensure predominance of the Party at the basic level in the PLA, where the Party Branch is the "Combat Fortress."

This emphasis is consistent with the Party's views of the correct nature of the political-military relation. Many years ago Mao laid down the basic guidelines for these views. "The Party commands the gun; the gun will never command the Party," and "In war, man, not material, is decisive." We find these themes echoed constantly by members of the hierarchy.

Here, for instance, is General Hsiao Hua, Deputy Director of the General Political Department, PLA, in an address to the PLA's "Political Work Conference" on February 14, 1963:

> Although the role of weapons and technical equipment has become more important in modern warfare, man—not materials—is the determining factor in war. In the end, victory or defeat in combat depends on the courage of man, his awareness, and his willingness to sacrifice.
>
> The decisions of the Military Affairs Committee pointed out that while the material atom bomb is very important, the atom bomb of the spirit is even more important.
>
> A revolutionary army is not afraid of the enemy, no matter how powerful he is. It is not afraid of any weapon, no matter how strong it is. What a revolutionary army is really afraid of is political backwardness, isolation from the people, and loss of determination to fight.
>
> Mao Tse-tung has taught us that politics is the commander and the soul. If our political and ideological work is carried out well, then other activities will fall into their proper places. Therefore, to develop a force with strong combat powers, it is first necessary for the cadres to profoundly learn the thinking of Comrade Mao on people's war—and to be guided by the thinking of Comrade Mao in all activities. The most basic tasks in political-ideological work are to raise the great Red Banner of Mao's thought, to use this thought to arm the combat commanders, to have everyone study his writings, work according to his directions, and become a good soldier of Mao Tse-tung. . . . We must all look up to the Party Central Committee, to Comrade Mao and to the Military Affairs Commission. . . .

The question is: Are the tasks summarized in the four regulations cited, and outlined by Comrade General Hsiao Hua, being successfully accomplished? I venture to say they are. During the last three years repeated ideological "remolding" campaigns have no doubt located and weeded out the "remnant bourgeois" and "lurking counter-revolutionary elements" of the officer and non-commissioned officer groups, together with "Russified" officers, followers of former Defense Minister Marshal P'eng Te-huai, and other dissidents and malcontents.

The control postulated by the MAC is comprehensive. It is wide and deep; vertical and horizontal. Activists in platoons, squads, sections, gun crews, air crews—*i.e.*, at the very lowest levels in the armed forces—are alert to discover signs of "wrong thoughts." Should these be discovered, or indeed imagined, to exist, "remolding" is in order.

A good example of how the Party operates on a selected group is provided by the *Hsia Lien Tang Ping*—"Go down to the companies and soldiers"—campaign as applied to the officer corps between 1959 and 1962. During this operation, which involved every officer from Lin Piao down to the most junior lieutenant, officers served in the ranks for stated periods, and performed every menial task, including cleaning spittoons and lavatories, washing dishes, policing barracks and grounds, and so on. The purpose of this was stated by the Party to be to insure the "unity" of officers and enlisted men. Possibly. But the punitive aspect of the campaign cannot be overlooked.

Undoubtedly some officers objected to this sort of "remolding." If they did vocally, they are no longer officers. As one does not now hear anything of the *Hsia Lien* movement, it may be assumed that this rite of purification was consummated to the satisfaction of the "Central Authorities."

Several other mechanisms are used in the "remolding" process. Possibly the best known of them is the "criticism" meeting. Here officers and soldiers are encouraged publicly to reveal their innermost thoughts and confess their ideological shortcomings to the group. "Before I read and studied the works of Chairman Mao, I was arrogant and bureaucratic and treated the soldiers in my platoon too harshly. But now that I have studied our revered Chairman's inspirational and illuminating essays, I am greatly enlightened." Etc., etc.

Another favored type of mental and emotional therapy is the "recollection of past bitterness, contemplation of present sweetness" meeting. At these gatherings, which are essentially "hate meetings," the soldiers are encouraged to work themselves into a state bordering on hysteria as older men recount the outrages perpetrated pre-1949 by landlords, merchants, other bourgeois elements, and imperialists. On this subject the Work Bulletins state that the cadres should not "enforce" mass weeping! The clear inference is that paroxysms of enraged grief should be encouraged, but not demanded! After the wailing sessions, the soldiers reflect (aloud, of course) on "present sweetness."

A third device currently in favor in the PLA is the "emulation" campaign. Such campaigns were common enough in agriculture and industry, but were not applied to the PLA until 1962. Here a particular individual, a squad, section, company, battery, or other unit (some of which have no doubt been fictitious—their reported virtues and accomplishments are really unbelievable) is selected as a model of frugality, industry, "loving the people," "loving the Party," or studying the works of Chairman Mao. When an emulation campaign is launched, all stops are pulled. One of the purposes of these various campaigns is to keep the revolutionary fervor of the soldiers at a high level. We see, in press reports, many references to the necessity for the PLA to maintain the revolutionary élan which distinguished the Eighth Route Army.

Still another mechanism which can be manipulated by the Party to ensure a high level of ideological commitment is the conscription process. Since 1959, the Party has been much more selective than it was previously. To induct 750,000 young men a year (the current rate), the PLA need only choose one from every seven or eight of the approximately six million young men who reach the age of eighteen each year. Thus, the Party is able to insure, during the annual draft, that only ideologically reliable youngsters with untainted family backgrounds are taken. Additionally, quite rigid mental, physical and emotional standards can be applied to them, as to officer aspirants.

For these reasons, it is not realistic to assume a crisis of morale in the PLA, or to entertain the hope that the armed forces, or really significant elements of them, will prove disloyal to the Party. Now, it is an article of faith on Taiwan that the PLA is on the verge of disintegration. This I believe to be wishful thinking. There may be schisms in the command hierarchy in the future. There may be occasional defectors. But the notion that the PLA harbors important anti-Party elements is illusory. The PLA, or the People's Armed Police, might be the decisive factor should there be a split in the hierarchy after the death of Mao. But that the PLA could act independently to deprive the Party of control of the state apparatus appears an extremely remote possibility indeed.

If the PLA were not now considered entirely "safe" we should not have it held up, which it is at present, as a model worthy of emulation on a national scale. The Chinese people today are constantly adjured: "Learn from the PLA!" Learn what? Frugality, industry, implicit obedience, love of the Party, reverence for Chairman Mao.

Work Bulletins reveal that the quality of leadership at lower levels has been a source of concern. Very few officers junior to lieutenant colonel—that is, to battalion commanders— have actually participated in combat. Hence the present emphasis on schooling and training. Politics has not taken a back seat, but has been considerably de-emphasized. The PLA operates an elaborate graded school system, and there is no reason to believe that the officer corps is not rapidly gaining professional competence.

As the political orientation (or lack of it) of junior officers in 1960–1961 was considered unsatisfactory by the Party, steps were taken in the ground forces at least to find officer material in the ranks. This policy was announced by General Hsü Li-ch'ing, a Deputy Director of the GPD, in 1961: ". . . from now on, platoon leaders, in the main, are to be promoted from rank-and-file soldiers, and not to be recruited from middle school graduates." (There was no indication that this program was to be applied to the navy and air force.) In the long run, this may prove to have been a poor decision. It does illustrate the Party's dogmatic dedication to the thesis that "redness" is more to be desired than "expertness," and causes one to wonder just how serious the Chinese are when they talk of technical modernization of the ground forces.

The substantive question is to what degree, if any, pervasive Party control affects the morale and operational flexibility of the armed forces. Certainly, in combat, situations will frequently arise in which military and political commanders find themselves deadlocked.

Theory holds that in a combat "emergency" the military commander's view prevails. In all conditions other than "emergency" differing points of view should be presented to the next higher echelon for resolution. We know, in fact, that in Korea political officers and their military counterparts at lower echelons frequently did reach just such an impasse, with the result that critical decisions were often not taken when they should have been.

For instance, General Mark Clark refers to this:

> . . . The system resulted in a weakness in military leadership at lower levels, and forced the Chinese to sacrifice flexibility in their operations. Individual initiative during action was rare in the Chinese Army.

This lack of flexibility on platoon, company, and battalion levels was noticed by U.S. Marine officers, and is documented in official Marine Corps reports. It is true that the Chinese apparently took steps to correct this situation, but no evidence is available to me as to what, precisely, the measures were. Nor is there the slightest evidence of lack of initiative on the part of lower commanders during the Sino-Indian fighting. Indeed, the contrary seems to be the case.

Certainly, there seems to be no doubt in the minds of top leadership that the system is effective both in peace and war, and that it is a decisive factor in promoting and maintaining very high standards of loyalty, morale, and discipline. . . .

Chinese Communist dogma postulates certain axioms fundamental to long-term grand strategy. Principal among these is the stereotyped concept of a bipolar world in which the forces of "imperialism" are inexorably arrayed against the forces of "socialism." This concept specifically excludes the possibilities of "non-alignment" and neutralism. There can be no middle way, no third road, no fence straddling. A nation must, in Mao's word, "lean" to one side or the other.

According to Lenin's theories, at least as the Chinese leadership interprets them, conflict between the two irreconcilable forces of "progress" and "decay" is inescapable, and although it may be postponed, victory of the socialist camp is inevitable. The struggle to hasten this consummation must be waged constantly, at all levels, in all susceptible areas, and by all appropriate means. In this context, *Panch Shila* is, as the Indians discovered, a tactic.

The Chinese Communists believe, or pretend to believe, that Mao Tse-tung discovered a basic law of war: Man is superior to material; the strength of the true believer is as the strength of ten. "We," said Liu Shao-ch'i, "have the spiritual atomic bomb." It follows that the PLA is "invincible and impregnable." By definition, armed forces of imperialist countries lack this unique mystical quality, which can only exist in dedicated revolutionists who have soaked up Marxism-Leninism and Chairman Mao's inspiring thought.

A corollary is: "All imperialists are paper tigers." Since their demise is inevitable, they may be "despised strategically," but must be "taken seriously tactically." The meal, in Mao's analogy, will be eaten, but one must still chew each mouthful deliberately. There may be bones in the fish.

In a speech in 1959, on the tenth anniversary of the founding of the People's Republic, Marshal Lin Piao seemed concerned with the possibility that "imperialism" might "dare to attack" China. If so, he said, the entire population would be turned into a military force, and "in co-ordination with the standing army, this militia force can overwhelm the enemy in the flames of an all-out people's war." In practical terms this concept may seem totally irrelevant to the contemporary context. But obsessive fear that Chiang Kai-shek, backed by the U.S., might attack the Mainland still seems to dominate Chinese military thinking. The Work Bulletins do reveal some concern about a surprise atomic/nuclear attack on military, urban, and economic targets. The military leadership sees this, however, as but a first and indecisive phase. The ultimate conclusion, they say, must be reached on the ground. And here man, not weapons, will decide.

Since the earliest days in China, military theorists and commentators (and in the course of twenty-three centuries they have produced quite a number of these) have placed great emphasis on morale of the people. This was one of the secrets of Communist success in mobilizing the masses before and during the Civil War, and it is a key point of doctrine today.

Another traditional precept finds favor in Peking. This relates to the creation of "a victorious situation" before battle is joined. According to the ancient military writers, victory must be assured before shots are exchanged. Victory thus derives from the situation. We find in Mao's writings constant admonitions not to fight unless victory is certain. A great deal of maneuvering to gain a favorable position is a necessary preliminary to battle. This maneuvering takes place on political and strategic levels, before guns are brought to bear.

Prudence is another principle. Adventurism and opportunism in military matters are roundly condemned, as is rashness in generals. Confucius is said to have remarked that he did not want a general who would "rush a river." He preferred one who could "succeed by strategy."

Long experience has led the Communists to place great emphasis on intelligence, and, at the same time, to deny information to the enemy. In Korea as well as in the brief border war with India, they were highly successful on both counts.

Generally the Chinese are predisposed to indirect, rather than direct, means, an approach summarized in the phrase *"Sheng tung; chi hsi"* ("Uproar in the East; strike in the West"). This was a basic ingredient in the successful operations carried on by the Eighth Route Army and its predecessor and successor armies. Obviously, the principle is not confined to tactical application.

The Chinese lay great store by surprise, and always seek to attain it. In the past, the Communist armies have proved adept at gaining the advantage conferred by strategic and tactical surprise. When estimating Chinese capabilities, this predilection must invariably be taken into account.

This brief summary suggests that the Chinese have a viable body of combat doctrine, one adaptable to modern war, and to future developments.

Chinese capability for sustained conventional action on a major scale outside her own borders is poor. Her present military impotence stems largely from the stoppage of Soviet aid. The result has been that for the last five years she has been deprived of the military hardware, technical assistance, and professional advice which were essential if she was to create a balanced defense establishment. Still, when appraising possible Communist military actions we must not, as Mao says, take "a purely military viewpoint," but must relate them to the contexts of domestic and external situations. Should the Party feel that national morale needs a massive injection, the leadership might tie renewed intensive bombardment of Quemoy and Matsu to a xenophobic anti-U.S. campaign, or it might so provoke the Indians that another "self-defense counter-attack" would be in order.

Today, the PLA does not have even a primitive capability for operations involving combined land, sea, and air arms. In the ground forces, training emphasis during the past few years has apparently been directed to the individual, to squads, and to companies, with special attention given to night marches, infiltration, night fighting, and techniques of close combat. One may conjecture that regimental and divisional maneuvers involving close coordination of the infantry-tank-air-artillery team are confined to élite units, if indeed they are held at all, which I doubt. A campaign to conserve fuel oil, coal, electric power, and materials of all descriptions—including ragged garments and soles of shoes—has been applied to the PLA across the board, and it is most unlikely that the Party would encourage the PLA to conduct expensive live firing exercises on the scale required to achieve battle proficiency when so many other requirements cannot be met. However, concern with small unit training has distinct relevance to situations which may develop in Southeast Asia.

China's geographical position is such that she can only attack her avowed enemy, the United States, indirectly, in South Korea. That she would provoke conventional hostilities in this quarter is no more than a remote contingency, but cannot be dismissed completely. She might react here to pressures in other areas, or she might stir up trouble along the 38th Parallel as a distraction operation. In the context of her split with Russia, unilateral action in Korea would apparently constitute an unacceptable risk. But on the other hand, such an action might be a deliberate catalytic attempt designed to involve the Russians, and so precipitate a general war from which the Chinese feel they stand to gain.

Conventional forces could be used in Southeast Asia, but again the risk would be great. In that area the United States and its allies enjoy incomparably more strategic and tactical flexibility, and thus many more options than would be available to the Chinese, who would additionally be faced with staggering logistic problems. Too, her opponents, with carrier aircraft, highly mobile amphibious striking power, and a significant airlift capability, could strike targets of their choice along her southeast coast, or in other rear areas. The fear of a major Nationalist landing on the southeast coast, or on Hainan, would be a further, and perhaps decisive, deterrent to conventional adventurism to the South.

In the unlikely event that she were to engage in limited conventional hostilities with the Soviet Union, China could probably cut off the maritime provinces and at least temporarily eject the Russians from areas adjacent to northern Manchuria. Border hostilities would no doubt be signaled by a series of small-scale "testing" actions. We may recall that the Japanese tried this and discovered that the Soviets were more than a match for them.

However, the Chinese are aware that it takes two to limit a war in terms either of geography or arms, and in this situation the question of whether the Russians would have many inhibitions as to selective use of tactical atomic weapons is at least speculative. In fact, the Russians could respond conventionally by hitting the Chinese in central Asia, where they could amputate Sinkiang from Mao's empire without too much trouble.

Military action to recover Mongolia—which Mao has claimed to be Chinese territory—is also unlikely in the foreseeable future. Sedition, subversion, and support of other treasonable activities would no doubt be her policy in any attempt to influence and gradually assimilate this area. The Russians are, however, quite as skilled in these forms of activity as are the Chinese. The same applies to Sinkiang, where there is no well-defined natural boundary between Chinese and Soviet territories, and where until fairly recently there was a constant ebb and flow across relatively open borders.

The Chinese could take over Nepal, Bhutan, Sikkim, and Assam should they wish to do so. Troop strength in the Tibetan area is of the order of five-six acclimatized, well-equipped mountain divisions, plus some separate task groups of regimental size. Over-all strength is possibly 160,000.

India can by no means match Chinese capabilities for action in the Himalayan states. She may be able to hold present precarious positions in Ladakh, but I doubt if she can regain much of the territory already lost. Here, the controlling factor for both sides is supply, and while the Indians are rapidly improving their capabilities for defense, the Chinese have been similarly engaged. The situation there appears to be a stalemate, which will probably persist for some years.

There is no reason why the Chinese would be particularly interested in physically occupying Nepal, Bhutan, and Sikkim. And, in any case, it would not be fear of India which might discourage the Chinese from committing the PLA here in furtherance of her imperial ambitions.

China's capabilities for defense against conventional attack are of a different order entirely. In these circumstances, Mao's theories of nationwide, protracted war would be applied. The vastness of China, and, with the exception of Manchuria and the Northern provinces, the nature of her terrain, rule out any attempt of conquest by conventional means.

Chinese capabilities in the paramilitary field—the entire spectrum of insurgency, of which guerrilla warfare is but a part —are high, particularly in Southeast Asia. With relatively slight investment of resources, and at very little risk, she stands to receive a disproportionate return.

From areas contiguous to her borders, the Chinese can easily exfiltrate selected young men and women for intensive political indoctrination and training as propagandists, organizers, terrorists, saboteurs, and guerrillas. These agents can then be put back as nuclei for cells. Several such training centers are said to be in Yunnan. These reports are probably correct; the procedure is a logical one, for Southeast Asia provides a target area suitable in all respects for the application of Mao's theories of protracted insurgent war.

One may suspect that when Chinese troops pulled out of the North East Frontier Area (NEFA), they took with them a number of candidates for this schooling, and it should come as no surprise to the Indian government if, in say 1967, it finds itself suddenly faced with this very threat in NEFA. We know —and the Indians may be given an opportunity to learn—what an arduous and costly task it is to attempt to cope with these situations, in which technical superiority is essentially nullified by the environment, and in which Mao's theory that man, and not weapons, is decisive is rather difficult to disprove.

Burmese terrain is favorable to quiet insurgent organization and buildup; North and East Burma are remote and sparsely populated areas which can be supplied from China. Local takeovers in the North by puppets supported by "People's Volunteers" would give the Chinese a number of bases for small-scale infiltration and attacks on Assam from the south. The area east of the Salween is also particularly suitable. A similar type of operation can be run from Laos against susceptible eastern Thailand along the Mekong.

How many North Vietnamese units are now in Laos under Pathet Lao cover would be difficult to estimate. One figure is as high as fifteen six-hundred-man battalions. Possibly we are inclined to overestimate, but, in general context, it is only prudent to assume that there are some troops present and that the Pathet Lao is receiving material aid (to say nothing of vociferous moral encouragement) from Peking. We are sure, for example, that the Chinese are building jeep tracks in northern Laos. There is thus a decided potential capability to "put the bite" on Thailand from two directions.

Operations of the nature, and on the level described, are most difficult for the United States, or anyone else, to counter directly. The Chinese might calculate that we would be inhibited from a conventional response elsewhere by the specter of escalation. However, should they commit conventional units to operation along the Mekong (a most unlikely but possible course of action) they would, of course, be inviting intervention elsewhere.

Release of the "Work Bulletins" (or "Bulletins of Activities," as some prefer to describe these papers) gave us new insights into the Party–PLA relationship. They substantiated the supposition that morale problems as of 1960–1961 were quite serious. They validated the opinions of some analysts that the combat efficiency of the air force was steadily deteriorating, that the navy (such as it is) was practically immobilized because of lack of fuel and spare parts, and that the ground forces were suffering from shortages of automotive transport, heavy weapons, and essential spare parts.

Nevertheless, in many areas of interest we lack (and no doubt shall continue to lack) specific information on which reasonably accurate estimates of Communist China's military potential must be based. Consequently, our appraisals tend to swing wildly from one extreme to the other. This has been characteristic of Western (particularly U.S.) estimates of Soviet capabilities, which periodically are unreasonably upgraded only to be later similarly downgraded.

Frequently in the American press, the Chinese leadership is represented as a group of almost superhuman Machiavellis. But these men, and the members of the authoritarian bureaucracy over which they preside, can make mistakes. They have made serious errors in the past, and they will make them in the future.

Nevertheless, of one thing we may be certain: they are determined to extend their influence, at the least risk and cost to themselves, to susceptible areas. If a limited military adventure offers a handsome pay-off at very low risk, they will probably embark on it. It is part of our business to narrow the field of choices open to them and thus to deny them strategic options from which they may reap large returns on small investments.

2. CHINA'S FOREIGN POLICY: "LEAN TO ONE SIDE"

᪄ᣠ Just as she adopted the Soviet Union as her model for internal development, China allied herself unreservedly with the Soviet Union in foreign policy. "Lean to one side" meant that in the struggle between the two great world camps (the socialist camp led by the Soviet Union and the capitalist camp led by the United States), China made her decisive choice to go with the Soviet Union. Thus, like our other section titles, this one also contains a duality: friendship for the Soviet Union and hostility to the United States.

During the first decade of the People's Republic, Chinese foreign policy, like its internal policy, passed through several stages. During the mid-1950s, after a period of close relations with the Soviet bloc and isolation from the non-Communist world, the People's Republic gradually began to extend the scope of its foreign policy and enter the world community. It cultivated relations with many countries and even held out an olive branch to the United States. From late 1957, however, Chinese foreign policy began to harden again. As the 1950s drew to a close a dramatic change developed in China's most important foreign relationship: the Sino-Soviet dispute broke out; a decade begun with unconditional alliance with the Soviet Union ended with growing bitterness and hostility.

A nation's foreign policies are normally thought to be multifaceted, reflecting the varied issues inherent in relations between different states. In the case of China, however, we maintain that the keystone of all of her foreign relations, from 1949 to the present, has been her relationship to the Soviet Union and to the United States. We maintain furthermore that there is a triangle of relationships between these three great powers, so that change in the relationship between two of them will have a direct effect on relationships with the other. This has been most apparent in the Sino-Soviet dispute, in which the growing détente between the United States and the Soviet Union was the major factor in splitting the Soviet Union and China.

Whereas the Sino-Soviet relationship clearly changed during the first decade, on the surface it appears there was no change in the Sino-American relationship: China and America began and ended the decade with mutual hostility. We might reflect here on the different meanings of "relation" and "relationship": the former denotes an action of relating, the latter a state of being related. Sino-American relations have been minimal, marked mainly by the ambassadorial talks at Geneva and then at Warsaw, and occasional joint participation at international conferences. But since both nations have been key factors in each other's foreign policies, a Sino-American relationship has been real and highly significant.

During the 1950s China's foreign policy was determined almost completely by her relationship to the Soviet Union. China supported every Soviet foreign-policy position, and her closest diplomatic ties were with the Soviet bloc countries. When the Soviet Union softened its attitude to the West, China similarly took a more moderate stance, as revealed during the Bandung Conference of 1955. In 1956 China made overtures to the United States to improve relations. When Khrushchev denounced Stalin, the Chinese leadership was shaken. When Poland and Hungary began to loosen their ties with the Soviet Union, the Chinese encouraged them behind the scenes. When the Soviets put down the Hungarian Rebelion, the Chinese came out in full support of the Soviets. Late in 1957, when Mao Tse-tung felt confident that the ostensible Soviet breakthrough in the weaponry field had changed the world balance of power, he was encouraged to risk the Great Leap Forward in China and follow a different policy line abroad.

Even when friendship turned into hostility, China's fate was still closely linked to that of the Soviet Union. Each time the Soviet Union moved closer to the West, China denounced it with vehemence. Today, Soviet moves still produce a Chinese counter-action. The Chinese—now leaning on no one and boldly proclaiming their self-reliance—speak of Soviet-American plots to rule the world and encircle China. Yet despite the bitterness of the dispute, China still considers herself a member of the socialist camp. Thus in love and in hate, the two countries are still linked.

When China was an empire, she refused to acknowledge any other nation as an equal. In the period of decline and collapse, she reverted to the old tactics of "barbarian management," trying to play off one foreigner against the other. Thus, even in degradation, she retained some command over her fate, and until 1949 never voluntarily linked her fate with any other nation's. After 1949, however, China chose to become part of a disciplined bloc of nations led by the Soviet Union, accepting bloc interests as her own. Unless we assume that China had indeed become a "Slavic Manchukuo," as Dean Rusk said years ago, we might ask why a sovereign and independent nation should tie itself to another great power so far beyond the requirements of a normal alliance.

Ideological affinities and Party-to-Party relations bound the two countries together, but in themselves did not account for the close Sino-Soviet entente. We must remember that when the Chinese "leaned to one side," the world was locked in a bitter cold war. The Chinese believed that, sooner or later, the two blocs would collide violently. China watched the United States organizing a series of alliances and building a ring of military bases on the perimeter of the Eurasian continent. Since China was one of the main targets, only complete solidarity with the Soviet Union could afford her protection against the American threat. Under the terms of the 1950 alliance the Soviet Union extended a protective nuclear shield over China—a shield for which China paid the price of complete subordination to the Soviet Union.

In our selection on Sino-American relations we point out that, from the beginning, Taiwan has been the outstanding issue between America and China. The Taiwan question has two aspects to it: on the one hand, it is a major piece of Chinese irredenta. Peking regards Taiwan as a province of China and claims that it will never compromise on that score; on the other

hand, Taiwan represents a potential threat against the Mainland as the seat of a government sworn to destroy Peking, and
as a real and symbolic part of the chain of American armed
power directed at China. If America were to make a concession
on Taiwan, China would probably regard this as a first step
toward allaying one of her greatest fears: attack by the United
States.

The Soviet shield and the American threat have been and
still are key factors in Chinese foreign policy, Thus it follows that
if one or both of these factors change, so would Chinese
foreign policy.

In June 1959 the Soviets abrogated the nuclear sharing
agreement concluded with the Chinese in October 1957. To
Mao Tse-tung, when Khrushchev visited Eisenhower at Camp
David in September, this meant only one thing: in return for
peaceful coexistence, Khrushchev was willing to betray his
alliance with China. To make matters even worse, Khrushchev
is reported to have asked Mao to accept the status quo regarding Taiwan. With the Soviet nuclear shield and Soviet support
for Chinese claims to Taiwan in jeopardy, the Chinese began
to reconsider the entire relationship. Thus the fraternal relations of the 1950s became the bitter hostility of the 1960s.

Our triangular conception of the relationships between the
three great powers would suggest that something should have
changed in the Sino-American relationship. Neither China nor
America appeared to have made any move toward each other to
establish relations. Both China and America participated in the
Geneva Conference on Laos of 1961–1962, but the chief protagonists were the Soviet Union and the United States, not
China; China, despite the dispute with the Soviet Union, followed its lead at Geneva. Was it ideology that prevented China
from making new approaches to America? Or was it China's
conviction that, freed from the Soviet threat in Europe because
of the détente, America was more than ever determined to pursue a policy in Eastern Asia of implacable hostility to China?

In the early years of the Sino-Soviet dispute China still
thought that world events and her own political and ideological
pressures could force the Soviets to abandon peaceful coexistence. In other words, China appeared to wish for a return to
relations as they were between 1954 and 1956, when the Soviet

Union and China, as equal partners, were locked in a close and friendly alliance, hostile to the United States but willing to act pragmatically toward it. But as the 1960s rolled on, China began to lose hope in the Soviet Union and sought friends and allies in the "Asian, African, and Latin American" world. Today, as a result of recent reverses, she sees herself encircled by a ring of hostile nations: the United States, the Soviet Union, India, and Japan.

But let us return to our question: was there a change in the Sino-American relationship as a result of the Soviet-American détente and the Sino-Soviet split? Without suggesting a direct causality, we might note that the American commitment to South Vietnam began to grow steadily from 1961 on; on August 2, 1961, for example, President Kennedy declared that the United States would do all it could to save South Vietnam from Communism. Soviet interest in North Vietnam and Laos was strong (probably much stronger than Chinese) and in the spring of 1961 Premier Khrushchev had proclaimed a policy of supporting national liberation movements. So the initial American commitment to South Vietnam may be seen as a part of the Soviet-American conflict. However, in the end, the immense buildup of American power in Eastern Asia revived China's fear that she was the real target of American actions.

If Taiwan and the American military perimeter in Eastern Asia represented a potential threat, the exacerbation of the Vietnam war appeared to turn a potential threat into a real one. Thus one can say that a change in the Sino-American relationship did occur.

There is much confusion as to what foreign policy is. Countries have patterns of relations with each other, and these can be said to constitute the foreign policy of each. But there is more to foreign policy. In subsequent discussions of Chinese foreign policy we shall distinguish between ideological and pragmatic policies: the former are derivative from a larger world view, while the latter are generally based on prospects of tangible gain and self-interest. The distinction is comparable to the one we have made between relationship and relation. Relations between countries are the product of a series of past interactions. A relationship, however, is more complex, involving attitudes, states of mind, a general view of the other, and constituting the framework within which specific policies toward another country are made; but such a framework, the product of historical development into which many factors have gone, does not easily change.

When the Chinese speak of "American imperialism" and the Americans speak of "Chinese expansionism," they mean the frameworks of thought which guide the actions of each toward the other. Theory and practice, as the Chinese admit, may often be rather different, and so it does not always follow that specific policies directly reflect the world view, although the world view always enters into the decision-making process.

When a government is marked by ideological thinking, such as when it holds to certain fixed views of the world, then its foreign policy includes such thinking. In our opinion, not only the Soviet Union and China but also the United States has developed an ideological foreign policy.

Let us end with a few additional remarks on the triangle of relationships between the three great powers. All three have developed conceptions as to the course of world historical trends in which the other two play a major role. The Soviet view of the peaceful transformation of capitalism, the Chinese view of the inevitability of violent revolution in the third world, and the American view on Soviet embourgeoisement and Chinese expansionism are key elements in the world views of each, and constitute the basis of the triangular relationship. But the relationship is more than an ideological state of mind: it is a conception of long-term power balances. As we have indicated, the two crucial material elements in China's relationships to the Soviet Union and the United States were the Soviet nuclear shield and the American military threat—two elements obviously closely associated. Every nation, whatever its positive goals abroad may be, is first and foremost concerned with its national security. For China, the overriding threat comes from the ring of power America has thrown around her. One should not be surprised that this has been and remains a key part of the framework in which the Chinese work out their foreign relations, not only to the big powers but to the remainder of the world.

❦ Sino-Soviet Relations:
Alliance, Friendship, Hostility

LET US begin our analysis of the alliance and the split between China and Russia by noting that there are two types of relations among Communist countries: the conventional state-to-state relations, expressed in the usual manner—treaties, pacts, trade, diplomatic relations; second, the Party-to-Party relations, the contact between the two dominant political bodies, their Communist Parties, bound together by ideology and historically regarding themselves as part of a worldwide movement. (The differences have been well described by Ruth Fischer in *Stalin and German Communism,* in which official Soviet relations with the Weimar Republic were one thing and political relations with the German Communist Party another.) Sometimes the two lines of relations have been dichotomous; at other times they have intersected.

Until 1949, as A. Doak Barnett, Professor of Government at Columbia University and one of America's foremost scholars on contemporary China indicates, Soviet relations with the Chinese Communist Party were of the Party-to-Party type. State-to-state relations were exclusively with the Nanking government, from 1928 to 1949, when Ambassador Roshchin was the last foreign ambassador to follow that government down to Canton.

Since the foreign policies of all countries have roots in history, let us briefly describe Russian-Chinese relations up to the early part of the twentieth century. Until the coming of Western and Japanese imperialism, Russia's main interests vis-à-vis China were to secure her Central Asian and Siberian borders. Thereafter, Russia began to press for "special rights in China," notably in Manchuria, Sinkiang, and in Korea. From the early twentieth century until 1945 the Russian Far Eastern provinces were threatened by an aggressive expansionist power, Japan. Thwarted by her defeat in the Russo-Japanese War, Russia periodically resumed her attempts to extend her zone of power and influence into Manchuria, Sinkiang, and Korea. At the Yalta Conference of February 1945 Stalin extracted Western agreement for the extension of Soviet power into these zones. In August 1945 the Nanking government, as Barnett notes, "acquiesced in these terms." In 1950 the Chinese Communist government agreed, in substance, to the same extension of Soviet influence, though subject to much stricter time limitations. Though the Central Manchurian Railroad was returned to China late in 1952, shortly before Stalin's death, the Soviets did not fully liquidate their special position in China until the fall of 1954, when Khrushchev visited Peking.

State-to-state relations between Russia and China also had a more positive side. Until 1945 Russia regarded China as a bulwark against Japanese expansionism. Though the help the Soviet government gave the Kuomintang between 1922 and 1927 was largely bound up with Comintern judgments about the world revolutionary situation, it also served traditional Russian foreign-policy interests to build up China against Japan; one must remember that Japanese pressure against China continued after the conclusion of the Versailles Conference. As the Sino-Japanese War threatened in the mid-1930s, Stalin indicated his interest in strengthening the Nanking government as early as 1938, when he signed a mutual assistance treaty with Chiang Kai-shek. In August 1945 Moscow again concluded a pact with Nanking, promising "to give moral and military support only to the Nationalist government." Obviously, the defeat of Japan did away with one of the major determining factors of Russian foreign policy since the late nineteenth century.

The history of Party-to-Party relations between the Soviet and Chinese Communist Parties is "still obscure in many respects." The Chinese Communist Party was founded with Comintern support, but after the debacle of April 1927, Soviet Party support went to the Shanghai Central Committee. What the relations between Moscow and the Chinese Communist Party were during the Kiangsi Soviet Period is unclear. Stalin is reputed to have played a role in the decision to release Chiang

Kai-shek from captivity during the Sian Incident, but there is little evidence of close contact between the two Parties during the Yenan Period. The nature of Party-to-Party relations during the post-Yenan Period (the Civil War of 1946 to 1949) is even more unclear. Barnett notes that "there is substantial evidence that during and immediately after the war Soviet leaders were uncertain about the Chinese Communists' prospects," but this "did not deter them from giving substantial material assistance to the Chinese Communists during 1945–1946." Though he cites the State Department White Paper of August 1949 to support this point, it is still not clear whether this was actually the case. That the Chinese Communists acquired great quantities of supplies from Japanese stocks in Manchuria is known. But as our selections on the Civil War indicate (see Volume II), even anti-Communist observers are not certain to what extent Soviet cooperation was a decisive factor in the Communist takeover of Manchuria.

Assuming that it was international, notably American pressure which impelled the Soviets to withdraw their troops from Manchuria, the traditional thrust of Russian foreign policy indicates their interest in having a Chinese government in control which would reaffirm Soviet rights laid down in the 1945 treaty. Given the ambiguous relations with the Chinese Communist Party, Stalin could hardly have felt any assurance that a Red government in Peking would automatically grant the Russian demands. Moreover, the inferior position of the Chinese Communists in 1945 did not appear to promise a forthcoming Communist victory in the Civil War. On the other hand, the growing ties between Republican China and America reduced the chances of fruitful collaboration between Moscow and Nanking. The conclusion would appear warranted that Russia's best interests would have been served by a protracted Chinese Civil War, with Moscow committed either to both sides simultaneously or to neither.

Aside from the indirect material assistance the Soviets may have given the Chinese Communists during the Civil War, Party-to-Party relations between the two were mainly ideological and political, that is to say, positions taken on major theoretical and practical issues facing the Communist movement. During the Yenan Period, the two parties were in general agreement on practical issues (with the possible exception of the Sian Incident) because of general Soviet support for the Nanking government. In regard to theory, however, the Chinese Communists appeared to have taken a somewhat independent direction, as evidenced in the publication in 1940 of Mao Tse-tung's essay "On the New Democracy." Although the wording was couched in strict Marxist-Leninist terms and none of the ideas were entirely new, a theme appeared which was to be taken up again in future years: the uniqueness of the Chinese Revolution and the applicability of its experiences to other backward countries. Mao Tse-tung was credited with having formulated new theory, as would later be reaffirmed at the Seventh Party Congress in the spring of 1945.

It is the peculiar nature of Chinese Communist rhetoric, evident in the exceedingly careful adherence to canonical Marxist-Leninist modes of expression, that sheds light on the nature of the ideological relationship between the Soviet and Chinese Communist Parties, a matter very difficult for Westerners to understand. From the time of the founding of the Communist Party until recently, the Chinese Communists had consistently regarded themselves as part of a worldwide movement whose center was the Soviet Union. Since from 1936 to 1945 no significant practical issues linked the Soviet and the Chinese Communist Parties, the ties between the two were almost entirely in the realm of ideology or theory. That the Chinese Communists veered from the doctrinaire positions on theory set down by the Soviets is clear for several periods before and after 1949. But, one must ask, what is this ideological link between the two parties, and why, when the Chinese Communists do deviate from Soviet theory, they do so within the accepted Marxist-Leninist framework, so much so that even during times of the most intense dispute the outside observer fails to see much overt difference between the two positions.

Even if one accepts the idea that ideology is mainly an instrument for holding an organized movement together, one still wonders why, during the Yenan Period, Mao Tse-tung and his followers did not go all the way and proclaim their own world view as canonical. Similarly, one can ask why now, at a time when the Sino-Soviet dispute has reached unprecedented heights of bitterness, the Chinese Communists still do not proclaim their own brand of Marxism-Leninism as the sole valid theory and proceed to organize a new international movement on that basis. There is no simple answer. One would do well to remember that basic to the Communist world outlook (at least up to the time of "modern revisionism") is the view that class conflict, from the smallest human community to the entire world, is the fundamental fact of life. In that conflict the gap between the revolutionaries and the reactionaries is fundamentally unbridgeable. Thus, if the struggle between peasant and landlord is unbridgeable, so too is the struggle between Communists and Nationalists, and, on a worldwide scale, between the Soviet Union and the imperialist powers. No matter how self-seeking, degenerate, misguided the Soviet Union may be, by the facts of history it is the movement's leader. Though it may betray fraternal parties at certain times, at the inevitable moment of crisis, conjured up by the attacks of international imperialism and capitalism, it will be forced back into the revolutionaries' camp. Therefore, loyal commitment to "theory" not only serves internal organizational purposes, but it provides the revolutionaries with an additional future option to invoke Soviet support—an option they would surrender by declaring their ideological independence.

When did the Chinese Communists begin to take up the option provided by the ideological link? Since that option presumably would become operational only when the global struggle between socialism and imperialism came out into the open, one might ask when the Chinese Communists first envisaged the possibility of a war between the Soviet Union and the United States. In a short document dated April 1946 but not published till December 1947, Mao declared: "The reactionary forces of the world are now preparing World War III; the danger of war thus exists." He repeated the statement a few months later, in August 1946, during his famous interview with Anna Louise Strong. By the spring of 1946, particularly after Winston Churchill's Fulton speech, the Cold War, already threatening to turn into a hot war, had become reality. Whether coincidence or not, it is significant that the Chinese Civil War was entering its hot phase at the same time; by July, Communists and Nationalists were locked in full-scale battle, with the Communists accusing the United States of supporting their Nationalist opponents.

Though, as Barnett points out, Stalin had told the Chinese Communists that "the development of the uprising in China had no prospect," Mao Tse-tung continued to press on. In December 1947 he declared: "Those dregs spat out by the people form the imperialist and anti-democratic camp; they oppose all democratic forces led by the Soviet Union and are preparing to make war against them." In 1948 the Chinese Communists openly supported Stalin's break with Tito (although in 1956 they were to criticize it). In July 1949 Mao proclaimed his celebrated "lean to one side" doctrine. When the Civil War ended, the Chinese Communists stood solidly on the Soviet side and in uncompromising opposition to the United States. They had chosen their side in the Cold War.

With Soviet recognition of the new Communist government in China and the conclusion of the thirty-year Treaty of Friendship, Alliance, and Mutual Assistance in 1950, the Soviet Union for the first time entered into full state-to-state and Party-to-Party relations with the Chinese Communists. Peking made major concessions to Moscow in areas of traditional foreign-policy concern to Russia (Manchuria and Sinkiang), and in return became the beneficiary of one of the greatest international assistance programs in modern history. Whether the Soviets hoped to regain their material investments by acquiring *de facto* control over Manchuria through Kao Kang remains a disputed question. Peking unreservedly recognized the ideological primacy of the Soviet Communist Party; all references to Mao Tse-tung as the creator of new "theory" were deleted from the Chinese Communist ideological lexicon.

As we sketch out briefly some of the broader patterns in the picture of Sino-Soviet relations, we will do well to remember that one of the Chinese Communists' cardinal operational principles is their attempt always to have at least two different options available. For example, while consistently adhering to the need for a disciplined Party based on Marxist-Leninist ideology, the Chinese Communists have also continuously maintained the principle of the united front, that is to say, a broad coalition with non-Communist elements, whether at home or abroad. Following the first option to its extreme point in the international field meant unreserved alliance with the Soviet Union, but following the second to its extreme point would have meant accommodation with the United States. There are signs that as final victory became evident in 1949, the Chinese Communist leaders were at least considering this second option (see Volume II). Thus, while they veered toward the Soviet Union during the bitterness of the Civil War, in the summer of 1949 they seemed again to be considering the possibility of a Sino-American accommodation. By late 1949, however, Peking had made its final choice. The Korean War which broke out in June 1950 finalized the breach between Peking and Washington.

Mao's perception of the global struggle between the Soviet Union and the United States, the latter's role in the Chinese Civil War, and the ideological trends within the Chinese Communist Party during this time suggest that the attitudes and actions of the United States form a crucial part of the equation from which the Chinese Communist Party's particular ideological and practical stance arises. From then on, as well as for the years following 1949, we may speak of a triangle of relationships between the Chinese Communists, the Soviets, and the Americans, as we have indicated in our introduction to this section.

From late 1949 until Stalin's death in March 1953 Sino-Soviet state-to-state relations were marked by wrangling over Soviet "special rights" in China and the degree of Soviet material assistance to China. What transpired between the two Parties is again obscure; no revelations of the later Sino-Soviet split have shed any detailed light on this period, aside from oblique references. Within China the Soviet Union was extolled and emulated as the model for China to follow in every walk of life, but at this same time struggle began between what was later to be called an anti-Party clique, headed by Kao Kang, the Party boss of Manchuria, and the men of Yenan who ruled in Peking. We do not know whether Stalin had a hand in that struggle, but examples from other Communist countries and parties suggest that he probably did. In view of the fact that the great majority of Soviet-supplied complete industrial plants were in Manchuria, that Soviet advisers played a prominent role in Manchuria, and that the Soviets had control over that region's crucial railroad network, it is not unlikely that Stalin thereby sought to acquire leverage over the Chinese Communist Party.

One of the great turning points in Sino-Soviet relations came with the death of Stalin. By the late summer of 1954 Khrushchev had consolidated his position against Malenkov in the Soviet Union, and Mao Tse-tung had eliminated his opponent, Kao Kang (the fall of Malenkov from the Premiership was announced in February 1955 and Kao Kang's suicide was announced in March 1955, though the decisive power shifts had occurred during the previous year). Khrushchev's visit to Peking in the fall of 1954 inaugurated what in retrospect can be regarded as the warmest period of Sino-Soviet relations. The Soviets completely liquidated their "special rights" in China, offered new material assistance, and expressed unqualified support for China's foreign-policy goals. The Chinese reciprocated with full support for Soviet policies and unreserved recognition of the Soviet Union as the leader of the socialist camp.

With the liquidation of Soviet "special rights" in China an important qualitative change came about in the state-to-state relations between the two countries: henceforth they were to deal with each other as two sovereign and equal nations. On the Party-to-Party level an amicality not evident in the Stalin era appeared throughout Russia and China, symbolized by what seemed to be a personal friendship between Mao and Khrushchev.

In contrast to late 1949, when the nature of state-to-state relations was the principal subject of Sino-Soviet negotiation, after the fall of 1954 Sino-Soviet relations shifted mainly to the Party-to-Party level. Thus it was to be expected that Khrushchev's denunciation of Stalin at the Soviet Twentieth Party Congress of February 1956 would have a powerful impact on the Chinese Communist Party. The Stalin issue was one of the principal subjects of discussion at the April 1956 Politburo meeting of the Chinese Communist Party (which decided also to launch a consolidation period after the collectivization drive of the winter of 1955–1956).

One of the effects of Khrushchev's denunciation of the cult of personality was a perceptible downgrading of Mao Tse-tung in China; his unique position in China was not particularly stressed at the Chinese Eighth Party Congress of September 1956. Harry Gelman, an American specialist on Communist affairs, suggests in our second selection that the issue in 1956 between the two parties was "over the authority to define (and redefine) the proper relationships between the CPSU and other bloc Communist Parties," but a reading of contemporary Chinese documents, particularly the April and December 1956 articles on "the historical experiences of the dictatorship of the proletariat," does not bear out this interpretation. Since the Chinese had already acquired *de facto* equality with the Soviets in 1954, their main worry in 1956 appeared to be that the denunciation of Stalin would lead to weakened international Communist unity. For example, they criticized Stalin's break with Yugoslavia and supported Soviet efforts to re-establish good relations with that country. At the end of their April statement they warned: "All the world's reactionaries are laughing at this event [*i.e.,* the Congress] . . . but what will be the result of this laughter? There is no doubt that they shall face the great camp of peace and socialism headed by the Soviet Union greater and more invincible than ever before."

Chinese worries about a breakdown in camp solidarity came true in Poland, Hungary, in the continuing intra-Party struggle within the Soviet Union, and even in China during the "blooming and contending" of May 1957. But by June 1957 the Polish and Hungarian positions had been stabilized, Khrushchev had decisively emerged as the undisputed Soviet leader, and Mao Tse-tung had launched a counter-attack against his opponents which culminated in the triumph of the Third Plenum of October 1957. By late 1957, with Sputnik and the ICBM breakthrough, the Soviet Union appeared to have reached a new pinnacle of international power. In November, Mao Tse-tung paid his second and last visit to Moscow. The Soviets and the Chinese had just concluded a nuclear sharing agreement, and the subsequent remarkable jump in Sino-Soviet trade (from 1958 through the summer of 1960) suggests that general understanding along these lines must also have been achieved. For whatever he received, Mao declared: "The socialist camp must have a head and this head is the USSR."

The Twentieth Party Congress is cited by Gelman as the

dispute's starting point and the November 1957 meeting as its second stage, but there was a considerable difference in the issues. As Gelman indicates, the issues in the former case were intra-bloc, but in the latter case moved into the international field. Mao's insistence that the phrase "U.S. imperialism is the center of world reaction and the sworn enemy of the people" be included in the conference resolution indicates that America was again to be a major element in Sino-Soviet relations. That America was on the minds of Chinese Communist leaders is indicated by the increasingly sharp attacks during the latter half of 1957 on America's "two-China intrigues," in contrast to the friendlier attitude prevailing as late as the fall of 1956, when the Chinese proposed to the Americans, at ambassadorial talks, that all travel restrictions be lifted and cultural exchanges be arranged.

During the Civil War and in the early 1950s and in the summer and fall of 1957, a domestic swing to the left was accompanied by a turning to the Soviet Union and violent hostility against the United States. The anti-rightist movement, succeeding the calmer Hundred Flowers period, led to the most radicalized era since 1949. Whatever the disagreements at that time between Mao Tse-tung and Khrushchev, the resolution emerging from the Moscow Conference of twelve Communist Parties signified broad agreement between the Soviets and the Chinese on major issues of state and Party relations. The main difference appeared to be Chinese insistence that the Soviets, using their breakthrough in the weaponry field, pursue a more aggressive anti-American policy. As Gelman puts it, the difference was over "whose national interests—Moscow's or Peking's —should be accorded greater weight in the formulation of Communist policy."

Gelman cites three areas of disagreement between Moscow and Peking in 1958: the military relationship between the two powers, Soviet conduct over Taiwan, and Peking's radical new economic programs. Soviet displeasure over the communes was already obliquely expressed in 1958, but the key issues of conflict appear to have been the first two. Indeed, they were related, for the questions of Taiwan and of military (*i.e.,* nuclear) aid to China tied in directly to America. The Quemoy crisis of August 1958 sharpened this issue because of Soviet fear of being dragged into a nuclear conflict with the United States over a foreign-policy issue not directly related to its national interests. Behind this fear lay an apparent Soviet decision "to forego the substantial additional expense required to make [their ICBMs] operational in large numbers" (Myron Rush, "Soviet Policy and International Tensions," *Beyond the Cold War,* p. 142). In other words, the Soviets refused to carry through on the momentum achieved by the breakthrough.

The decisive period in Sino-Soviet relations, which can be identified as the point of eruption of the Sino-Soviet split, was in the summer of 1959. In June the Soviets tore up the October 1957 nuclear sharing agreement. In October, during his last visit to Peking, Khrushchev hinted that "Peking ought to accept a 'two-Chinas' solution." As the Chinese documents on the Sino-Soviet dispute indicate repeatedly, the Camp David meeting of Eisenhower and Khrushchev in September 1959 was regarded in Peking as the *cause célèbre.* While what transpired at Camp David is still not fully known, there can be little doubt that it started a process of Soviet-American accommodation which reached its culmination in the 1963 Test-Ban Treaty.

Reaction in China to these new developments was swift. The social mobilization program which had ebbed somewhat earlier in 1959 was put in high gear again. More important, the Party launched a campaign against "rightist tendencies" within the Party. In September, Marshal P'eng Te-huai was dismissed from his position of Minister of National Defense. In retrospect, it appears that this was the beginning of the domestic campaign against "modern revisionists."

By the spring of 1960 the inter-Party split began to be made public when the Chinese indirectly criticized the Soviets in an article praising "Leninism," and then more openly criticized them in international meetings at Peking and Bucharest, but until July or August the dispute remained within Party-to-Party bounds. Suddenly in August 1960, however, the Soviets withdrew all technicians from China and terminated technical assistance programs—an act that must be regarded as one of the major causes of the industrial depression that struck China late in 1960. Everywhere factories closed down, imported machinery rusted at railroad stations, and projects halted because of Soviet refusal to leave the blueprints behind.

August 1960 constitutes another turning point in Sino-Soviet state-to-state relations. Two-way trade fell drastically late in 1960 and has continued to decline. Soviet military assistance practically ended, which of course put into question the Soviet nuclear shield guaranteed by the thirty-year pact of 1950. By the early 1960s Soviet diplomatic and economic relations with China were little different from those of some non-Communist countries. Nonetheless, Party-to-Party relations have remained in force, albeit marked by an almost unbelievable acrimony whose focus is policy toward the United States. In August 1960 the Soviets proclaimed that "peaceful coexistence represented the general foreign-policy line of the *entire* Communist bloc." The Chinese proclaimed America the mortal foe of all peoples.

The split worsened through the winter of 1961. Early in 1962, apparently at the urging of the North Vietnamese, there was a temporary lull in the dispute, but it became heated again in the summer of 1962. Khrushchev's ambivalent attitude during the Sino-Indian border dispute intensified the quarrel. In time, however, the Soviet and Chinese positions on bloc solidarity began to change. Whereas in the early days of the split the Chinese were most eager to restore bloc solidarity, in the later period it was the Soviets who began to make overtures to heal the rupture (this was evident, as Gelman points out, during the Sino-Indian border dispute). But, despairing of convincing the Soviets to return to a "true Marxist-Leninist course," the Chinese went on an ideological and political offensive. In a torrent of documents, often brilliant and persuasive, the Chinese unleashed an ideological barrage against the Soviets unheard of since the Comintern and Soviet Party disputes of the 1920s. Politically, the Chinese set about encouraging pro-Peking elements in Communist Parties throughout the world. The downfall of Khrushchev in November 1964 led to a temporary lull, but the Chinese soon resumed the offensive against "Khrushchevism without Khrushchev."

Today the dispute remains where it has been for years except that the Chinese ideological and political offensive has not been particularly successful; the Soviets have managed to regain the adherence of the overwhelming majority of the world's Communist Parties, as evidenced in the Twenty-third

Party Congress (April 1966). (On the present state of the Sino-Soviet relationship, see pp. 491–502.)

In the history of Sino-Soviet relations two major questions arise: Why have the Chinese Communists continued to profess their fundamental ideological links with the Soviet Union? Why does the United States play so central a role in those relations?

To this day, the Chinese Communists have not tried to create a new international of pro-Peking Parties or to make Peking into the modern center of world revolution. An international of Communist Parties requires a revolutionary theory. Although the Chinese Communists have made some attempts to proclaim Mao Tse-tung the canonical theoretician of modern revolution, as in Lin Piao's September 1965 article, "People's War" (see pp. 347–359), they are still reluctant to label "the Thought of Mao Tse-tung" as universal theory or to designate Mao the true successor of Marx, Engels, Lenin, and Stalin. As long as this is the case, the tie, no matter how tenuous, to the Soviet Union and to the international Communist movement born from the Moscow Comintern remains. The rage and fury of the Chinese polemics, many of which probably come directly from Mao's pen, have caused foreign observers time and time again to predict the final break, but as yet it has not come. The history of Sino-Soviet relations, particularly from the Yenan and Civil War periods, suggests that, despite everything, the Chinese Communists still regard the Soviet Union as a potential option which, under the right circumstances, can again be tapped in China's own interests. In the absence of meaningful state-to-state relations, it is only through maintaining the Party links that the option remains. Young Chinese today are taught to study "the Thought of Mao Tse-tung," with little concrete reference to the works of Marx, Engels, Lenin, or Stalin. The Chinese Communist Party's ideology has for all practical purposes become the thinking of Mao Tse-tung, yet theory is still proclaimed to be Marxist-Leninist. Clearly, it is through continued adherence to universal theory that the Chinese Communist Party retains its international linkages and significance.

If theory is a bond to the international movement, and particularly to the Soviet Union (the Soviets invited the Chinese to attend the Twenty-third Party Congress), what is its practical function? As during the Civil War period, this brings us to the role of the United States, to which, since late 1957, the Chinese Communists have maintained an attitude of uncompromising hostility. This attitude rests in sum on the conviction that the United States is the modern successor to German and Japanese imperialism, and sooner or later will attack China. To understand the depth and persistence of this fear, one must remember the conviction of "capitalist encirclement" which the Soviet leaders held from the late 1920s until the advent of "peaceful co-existence" after Stalin's death. But one must also remember that ever since Korea, the United States has been building a perimeter of armed power around China. The island bastion of Okinawa, with its air and sea power aimed directly at China, serves as a symbolic example. The war in Vietnam has convinced the Chinese that the United States has moved from threat to action.

If the Chinese are convinced that an eventual armed confrontation between China and the United States will come about, they appear equally convinced that American power will ultimately be hurled against the Soviet Union as well. In 1946 Mao Tse-tung spoke of the dangers of a Soviet-American war. Today, despite his contempt for Soviet softness and appeasement, and charges that the two great powers are conspiring to rule the world, he undoubtedly still believes that a Soviet-American war is inevitable. Mao has lived in an age of wars: experience has no reason to teach him that peace is likely.

In the dispute's early days the Chinese urged the Soviets to return to a militant anti-American policy for which they would regain the solidarity of the socialist camp, an approach which agreed with Mao's "lean to one side" policy. China's recent simultaneous hostility both to the Soviet Union and the United States, however, conjures up the possibility that the Chinese may be faced with either a two-front war or a one-front war with the Soviets refusing to aid them. The Sino-Soviet border is not peaceful: there have been incidents in Sinkiang (mass exodus of Kazakhs, for example) and the Chinese have alluded to their ancestral lands in the Soviet Far East lost through "unequal treaties." But Chinese national interests in those regions are hardly comparable to their overriding interest in Taiwan and to the military threat deriving from the Vietnam war. Thus the state-to-state issues dividing them from the United States are far more serious than any with the Soviet Union. Despite the border incidents, the Chinese are not likely to feel that the Soviet Union threatens China's national integrity, nor is it likely that the recovery of Outer Mongolia and the Soviet Far Eastern provinces are major Chinese foreign-policy goals. If they have little reason to fear Soviet encroachment or attack for national reasons, they have even less to fear for political or ideological reasons. Short of a final break, the Sino-Soviet ideological and political tie has been strained as far as it can go.

It has often been said that the Chinese Nationalists hope for World War III (and lately, for a Sino-American war over Vietnam; see pp. 569–576) to enable their return to the Mainland. It is undoubtedly also true that Mao Tse-tung hopes for a deteriorating worldwide political-military situation which will bring the Soviet Union and America back into conflict, for in such a situation the Soviets will need China. If the second phase of the Sino-Soviet dispute, marked by a Chinese ideological and political offensive, aims at this, how does Mao calculate that China's actions will help bring this about?

In the tragic war in Vietnam we may find an answer. However that war came about, the triangular relationship of the Soviet Union, China, and the United States meets in that small country. The Soviets appear anxious to see the war ended (and have been so accused by the Chinese), yet are not willing to have it end at any price. Through Hanoi the Soviets have a presence and a stake in Vietnam. China opposes negotiations and argues for a protracted war lasting years and decades. The United States simultaneously, and with what the Chinese Communists call a "two-handed policy," escalates the war and proposes negotiations. The Chinese argue that only one hand means business, namely, escalation. They look at Moscow and see the agonizing dilemma of the Soviets. Chinese accusations of appeasement, cowardice toward the United States, and insufficient help to North Vietnam have been followed by greater Soviet efforts to show loyalty to their small fraternal brother. Whether they are right or wrong, the Chinese believe that their own actions, the continuing war in South Vietnam, and American mili-

tary escalation are gradually shattering peaceful coexistence.
The Sino-Soviet dispute has played a major part in American foreign-policy formation. There has been a torrent of writing on the subject, in and out of government. It is of interest to point out what the Communist side believes to have been the role of the dispute in American foreign policy. In February 1966 *Akahata*, organ of the pro-Peking Japanese Communist Party, published a long article (reprinted in *The People's Daily*) claiming that the split had encouraged "American imperialism" to aggressive actions in the Far East, because of the inability of the Soviet Union and China to mount common resistance. Both Moscow and Peking in effect agree at this point, except that Moscow seeks a renewed solidarity more or less without preconditions, while Peking demands the much higher price of a united policy of resistance to the United States.

Vietnam now has become the focal point of the Sino-Soviet relationship, as it is rapidly becoming the focal point of the Sino-American relationship. It is important to realize that the problem, as in the past, is triangular: what one protagonist does affects the other two.

A. DOAK BARNETT *
The Sino-Soviet Alliance

During the past decade the Sino-Soviet alliance has become a crucial factor in world politics, and it is no longer realistic to examine the power and aims of either the Soviet Union or Communist China in isolation. These two powers, ruling some 850 million people and comprising the strategic "heartland" of Eurasia, have forged an intimate association—ideological, military, political, and economic—and now pursue joint or coordinated policies toward the non-Communist world. The support

* A. Doak Barnett, *Communist China and Asia* (New York: Random House, 1961), pp. 337–351.

which they give each other adds greatly to the capacities of both nations to pursue their common aims.

Numerous common interests have welded the two partners into a strong alliance. However, beneath the façade of monolithic unity, the relationship between Peking and Moscow has by no means been a static one. It has, in fact, been undergoing constant adjustment and change. It is necessary, therefore, in evaluating the strength and purposes of Communist China to take a careful look at the nature of the bonds which link the two countries, the ways in which each partner is influenced by its own outlook and interests, and the sources of actual or potential friction and divergence between them.

The questions most frequently asked about the future of the Sino-Soviet alliance are generally formulated in terms of extremes. Will Peking and Moscow maintain a monolithic unity? Or will the Chinese Communists eventually break with the Russians as the Yugoslavs did in 1948? These questions are certainly relevant, but they may not reveal the practical issues which are likely to be most important during the period immediately ahead. The limited evidence which we have suggests that, like all alliances, even strong ones, the Sino-Soviet partnership has not been completely monolithic. The evidence available also indicates that in recent years the alliance has grown stronger rather than weaker, and there appears to be little immediate prospect of an open split between the two allies. Probably the most meaningful question now is whether, within the framework of a continuing alliance, there are likely to be significant shifts in relationships, or important strains and tensions, which may affect the alliance and the policies of the two partners. To approach this question realistically, it is necessary to examine how the partnership has evolved in recent years, to define the nature of possible problems, tensions, or divergent interests which may arise within the alliance in the years ahead, and to assess the significance that possible future changes in relations between the two allies may have for the non-Communist world.

EARLY RELATIONS BETWEEN THE CHINESE
COMMUNISTS AND MOSCOW

Although the Sino-Soviet alliance came into formal existence only in 1950 with the signing of a Treaty of Friendship, Alliance, and Mutual Assistance, its origins must be traced to links which were formed thirty years earlier, when the first Comintern representatives reached China. These agents helped a handful of Chinese intellectuals to organize the Chinese Communist Party in 1921, and throughout the 1920s Moscow played a decisive role both in selecting the local leadership and in determining the domestic strategy of the Chinese Party. During this early period Soviet policies toward China were extremely complex. While maintaining diplomatic relations until 1927 with the weak Chinese National Government in Peking, the Russians also supported, with advisers and material aid, the revolutionary efforts of both the Nationalist Party and the Communist Party, which cooperated in a revolutionary alliance from 1923 until 1927. The relationship of the Chinese Communists to Moscow was further complicated by the bitter struggles then going on within the Soviet Party, particularly by the Stalin-Trotsky contest for power. These struggles were intimately related to debates over the correct revolutionary strategy to follow in China, and they had a profound impact upon the Chinese Party.

Following the Nationalist-Communist split of 1927 within China, Soviet advisers were forced to leave the country, and the Chinese Communists themselves were repressed by the Nationalists and driven underground. Then, after a confused period of shifting policies and leadership, the Chinese Party, thrown largely onto its own resources, developed an indigenous strategy of armed revolution organized from rural bases. It established revolutionary bases first in the East China province of Kiangsi and later, after the "Long March," in Shensi province in the Northwest. Mao Tse-tung, who favored a peasant-based revolutionary strategy, emerged from this period of confusion as the Party's chief strategist. Mao, who had never been in Moscow, had gained his leadership without Soviet assistance, and his power was based, therefore, on internal rather than Soviet support.

The relationships which developed between the Chinese Communists and Moscow during the 1930s and 1940s, up to the end of World War II, are still obscure in many respects. However, there is no definite evidence that Moscow seriously attempted to intervene in the internal politics of the Chinese Communists, who were then isolated in remote rural areas. In their struggle to expand the area under their control, first in the Northwest, and then, after the start of the Japanese war, throughout the North China countryside—where a vacuum had been created by the Nationalist military withdrawal and the Japanese failure to consolidate control in rural areas—the Chinese Communists fought their own battles, with no significant outside material support. Guidance from Moscow no longer played a decisive role, as it had in earlier years, in determining the leadership and in shaping the domestic strategy of the Communist Party in China. The Chinese Communists developed their own unique strategy of guerrilla warfare and built up their own revolutionary strength.

Even in this period, however, the ideological, personal, and other intangible bonds which had linked the Chinese Communist Party to Moscow from the start remained strong. According to a top Chinese Communist leader writing in 1949, Mao himself had not made any systematic study of Stalin's many works on China before World War II but had "been able to reach the same conclusions as Stalin on many fundamental problems through his own independent thinking." Still, a large proportion of the top Chinese Communist leaders had received some training in the Soviet Union, and there was never any serious doubt about the fidelity of the Party to Moscow. On all major international issues the Chinese Communists adhered faithfully to the line emanating from Moscow, and they supported every major shift in Soviet foreign policy. In their own major policy shifts—for example, in their decision in 1936–1937 to form a second temporary alliance with the Nationalists to fight the Japanese—the Chinese Communists closely followed shifts which had previously taken place in the Russian and Comintern line. Soviet material aid to China during the Sino-

Japanese War was channeled to the Nationalist government rather than to the Communists, but there is no significant evidence that the Chinese Communists did not give consistent allegiance to Moscow or that Moscow lost faith in their loyalty.

During the last two years of the war, it is true, Stalin and Molotov made certain deprecatory remarks about the Chinese Communists to American diplomatic representatives. According to Ambassador Patrick J. Hurley, they said that "the Chinese Communists are not in fact Communists at all" and that the "Soviet Union is not supporting the Chinese Communist Party." But these statements may well have been deliberately calculated to mislead the United States. At the same time, however, they may also have reflected a certain lack of confidence on the part of the Soviet leaders in the ability of the Chinese Communists to play a primary role in the conflict with Japan, as well as a feeling that Chinese Communist interests had to be subordinated in Soviet policy because of the immediate need for a unified anti-Japanese war effort in China under Nationalist leadership.

POSTWAR DEVELOPMENTS

There is substantial evidence that during and immediately after the war Soviet leaders were uncertain about the Chinese Communists' prospects. Certainly, at that time the Russians did not rely on the Chinese Communist Party as the principal instrument of their policy in China. With almost no reference to the Chinese Communist movement, the Soviet leaders pressed for the re-establishment of Russia's special rights in China, such as had existed under past Tsarist regimes. At the Yalta Conference in February 1945 Stalin extracted from Great Britain and the United States the promise that, in return for Soviet entry into the war with Japan, the Soviet Union would recover "the former rights of Russia violated by the treacherous attack of Japan in 1904" (including the re-establishment of joint Sino-Soviet control over the major railways in Manchuria, a lease on Port Arthur as a naval base, and the internationalization of Dairen, as well as recovery of the Kurile Islands and the southern part of Sakhalin from Japan). He also insisted that China agree to recognize the *status quo* of Outer Mongolia—that is, its separation from China and its status as a nominally independent satellite of the Soviet Union. The Chinese Nationalist government acquiesced in these terms, and in August 1945 it signed a treaty and exchanged several notes with the Soviet Union in which China agreed that the major Manchurian railways should be placed under joint Sino-Soviet ownership for thirty years, Port Arthur should be jointly used as a naval base, and Dairen should be turned into a free port, with half of its port facilities leased free of charge to the Russians. The Nationalists also agreed to recognize the independence of the "Mongolian People's Republic" if a plebiscite confirmed the Mongolians' desire for this status. In return, the Russians reaffirmed their recognition of China's full sovereignty in Manchuria, pledged noninterference in Chinese internal affairs, and promised to give moral and military support only to the Nationalist government.

Despite Moscow's political pledges, the Soviet troops which occupied Manchuria began immediately after the war to remove a large portion of the Japanese-built industries and equipment in that region, claiming it as "war booty." Although the Russians' own pressing need for industrial equipment was undoubtedly one motive for this policy, the dismantling of industries in Manchuria also seemed to suggest either a lack of confidence that the Chinese Communists could soon achieve control of Manchuria or a belief that an industrially strong Manchuria under the control of any Chinese regime, whether Nationalist or Communist, was not desirable from the Soviet viewpoint.

Top-ranking Yugoslav Communists have claimed that there was a basic disagreement between Moscow and the Chinese Communists on strategy in China in the immediate postwar period. In his authorized biography of Tito, Vladimir Dedijer asserts that in 1948 Stalin told a Yugoslav delegation that, after the war, "we told them [the Chinese Communists] bluntly that we considered the development of the uprising in China had no prospect and that the Chinese comrades should seek a *modus vivendi* with Chiang Kai-shek, that they should join the Chiang Kai-shek government and dissolve their army." Reportedly, Stalin added: "The Chinese comrades agreed here with the views of the Soviet comrades but went back to China and acted quite otherwise." There are several aspects of Stalin's statement as quoted by Dedijer, including his alleged advice to the Chinese Communists to disband their army, as well as his reported admission that "we were wrong," which are not wholly credible. Nevertheless, the Yugoslav Communists' belief that in this period there was a basic difference between Soviet advice and Chinese Communist actions may have a basis in fact.

Whatever doubts or lack of confidence the Soviet leaders may have felt about the Communists in China immediately after the end of the war did not deter them from giving substantial material assistance to the Chinese Communists during 1945–1946. Immediately after Soviet troops occupied Manchuria and a part of Inner Mongolia, the Chinese Communists shifted an important segment of their Party leadership and military forces to that region, where they received extremely valuable assistance from the Russians in their revolutionary struggle. The Soviet troops delayed their evacuation from several key points and then timed their departure so that Chinese Communist forces were able to move in before the Nationalists and take possession of large stocks of surrendered Japanese arms and equipment. Even with these arms, it is true, the Communists were still inferior in military strength to the Nationalist forces which eventually moved into Manchuria, and the reasons for ultimate Communist success must be sought in the complex development of political, economic, and social, as well as military, forces in China. Nevertheless, the indirect military aid which the Russians gave the Chinese Communists in Manchuria after the war had an important and direct effect on the situation in China and helped the Communists substantially in building up their strength.

There is no indication that the Chinese Communists questioned the basic importance of close alignment with Moscow at any time during this period, and more than a year before they came to power in 1949 they defined their commitment to accept Soviet leadership in very clear terms. One of the most important statements of this commitment was made in November 1948 by Liu Shao-ch'i. In his article "On Internationalism and Nationalism," Liu expressed the Chinese Communists' unequivocal support for the Soviet leaders' world view and international policies and endorsed the crackdown on Tito which had taken place earlier in the year. "Communists will be betraying the proletariat and Communism and playing the game of the imperialists all over the world and will make themselves pawns of the imperialists," Liu said, "if, after their own nation has been freed from imperialist oppression, the Communists . . . reject the international unity of the proletariat and working people and . . . oppose the Socialist Soviet Union." Then, in an essay, "On People's Democratic Dictatorship," published in July 1949, Mao Tse-tung proclaimed his celebrated "lean to one side" doctrine. "The gunfire of the October Revolution sent us Marxism-Leninism," he said. "Travel the road of the Russians—this was the conclusion." Mao rejected the idea of accepting aid from the non-Communist countries even if it should be offered. "Internationally, we belong to the anti-imperialist front, headed by the U.S.S.R.," he said, and "we can only look for genuine and friendly aid from that front and not from the imperialist front."

By early 1949, some months before Mao had set up a national government, the Chinese Communist authorities in Manchuria had begun dealing with the Russians on a formal intergovernmental level. Kao Kang, top Communist leader in the region, headed a Chinese industrial and commercial mission to Moscow and signed an agreement to regulate Manchurian trade with the Soviet Union. The Russians continued to maintain diplomatic relations with the Nationalists during this period, however, and even though the Communist victory in the Chinese Civil War was clearly imminent, they negotiated with the Nationalists throughout 1949 to secure special Soviet economic rights in Sinkiang. Stalin was apparently still determined to guarantee Russian, as distinct from Communist, interests in China, and this ambition, which he continued to press even after 1949, had a significant influence on Sino-Soviet relations throughout the period of Stalin's rule.

THE ALLIANCE AND STALIN'S POLICIES

When the Chinese Communist government was formally established on October 1, 1949, the Soviet Union immediately recognized it, with the satellites following suit, and in the next few months the initial framework of Sino-Soviet relations was worked out in detail. In December, Mao Tse-tung paid his first visit to the USSR, and during his nine-week stay a number of important Sino-Soviet agreements were concluded. Most important was the thirty-year Treaty of Friendship, Alliance, and Mutual Assistance, signed in February 1950. In this political and military alliance the Chinese and Russians agreed that if either ally were "attacked by Japan or any state allied with it" (the latter phrase clearly referred to the United States), the other partner would "immediately render military and other assistance by all means at its disposal." This treaty gave Communist China strong, though not unqualified, military backing. By a separate agreement the Russians gave Communist China economic backing through a five-year $300-million loan. During the same period important trade and other economic arrangements were also worked out.

In return for Soviet support, Communist China had to make major concessions. Stalin was still concerned about establishing Russia's "special rights" in China, even though China was now under Communist rule. An agreement signed in February 1950 provided for joint Sino-Soviet administration of the principal railways in Manchuria, as well as for joint use of the naval base at Port Arthur, either until a peace treaty with Japan could be concluded or, at the latest, until the end of 1952. Later agreements called for the establishment of several long-term joint stock companies, to operate mostly in China's borderlands, where the Russians had traditionally pressed for special rights. These included: two companies to exploit petroleum and nonferrous metals in Sinkiang, a company to build and repair ships in Dairen, and a civil aviation company to provide services between Communist China and the USSR. The Chinese Communists also agreed, in an exchange of notes in February, to accept the *status quo*—that is, Soviet-dominated "independence"—in Outer Mongolia. At Moscow, Stalin and Mao probably also discussed plans for bringing South Korea under Communist control—although there was no indication of this at the time.

The first real test of the Sino-Soviet alliance came less than a half year later with the outbreak of the Korean War, and, whatever pullings and haulings may have taken place behind the scenes, the partnership weathered the test successfully. Entering the war to make good Soviet miscalculations and rescue the North Korean regime, the Chinese Communists did the bulk of the fighting to preserve the Communist bloc's interest. Peking's willingness to bear the brunt of the conflict enabled the Russians to avoid direct involvement, and in return Moscow poured in large amounts of military supplies and equipment, which helped the Chinese Communists not only to fight the war but also to modernize and build up their army and air force. Furthermore, Peking's alliance with the Soviet Union and the Russians' possession of atomic weapons were undoubtedly major factors which deterred the West from direct attacks against Communist bases in Manchuria, and the war remained a limited one. (The United States' desire to avoid an all-out war, and the unwillingness of its allies to support attacks beyond the Yalu, were other important factors, of course, which contributed to the decision to limit the war.) It is clear, however, that the major risks and costs of the war had to be borne primarily by the Chinese Communists, and this may have been less than wholly satisfactory to Peking.

In the autumn of 1952 Chinese Communist and Russian leaders again sat down together to discuss a wide range of problems, in their most important meeting since Mao's 1949–1950 visit. In September, while Premier Chou En-lai was in Moscow, the two governments announced that the Manchurian railways would be returned to sole Chinese management by the end of 1952, as agreed in 1950. They also revealed, however, that the Russians would stay on beyond 1952 in joint control of the naval base at Port Arthur, allegedly at Peking's "request." Because the Korean War was still going on and Communist China had no strong navy of its own, Peking may genuinely have wished the Russians to continue using and maintaining the base, but Chinese Communist leaders probably had mixed feelings about prolonging the special Russian rights on Chinese soil.

A large delegation of Chinese experts, whom Chou left behind in Moscow, continued negotiating with the Russians until mid-1953. Liu Shao-ch'i attended the Nineteenth Congress of the Soviet Communist Party in October 1952 and stayed on in Russia until January 1953, and he may also have taken part in the negotiations. Apparently, there was hard bargaining, particularly over economic matters, and the aid offered by the

Russians may have fallen considerably short of what the Chinese Communists hoped for. Peking had formally launched its First Five Year Plan at the start of 1953, while the negotiations were still in progress, and it could not determine the scope of the Plan until it knew how much economic assistance would be forthcoming from the Russians. Finally, after the negotiations had dragged on for many months, the results were announced in the autumn of 1953. The Russians committed themselves to help the Chinese by providing equipment and technical assistance for a large number of key development projects, which made it possible for Peking to proceed with its Five Year Plan. But there was no announcement of any new financial aid to supplement the Soviet loan of 1950. (An agreement on the construction of a new railway linking China and the Soviet Union was also signed in this period, in late 1952, but it was not publicly announced until 1954.)

The Moscow discussions must also have dealt with the problem of terminating the Korean War. Later developments suggest that the Chinese Communists were probably more eager than Stalin to end the war and extricate themselves from it. Until Stalin's death in March 1953 the truce talks in Korea had remained deadlocked, but only four days after Stalin's death Chou En-lai put forth new proposals, very similar to the proposals previously advanced by India and rejected by the Communist powers, which made possible a solution of the main issues still outstanding.

Throughout Stalin's last years, although the alliance remained solid and a public posture of monolithic unity and enthusiastic cooperation was carefully maintained, there clearly must have been strains and frictions beneath the surface. Soviet primacy and superiority were highlighted at all times by both partners in the alliance. The Chinese Communists, on their part, engaged in enthusiastic adulation of Stalin and of almost everything about the Soviet Union, going to extraordinary lengths to indoctrinate their people in Stalinism and pro-Soviet feelings. At the same time, however, Peking was paying a sizable price for Soviet support, and apparently Stalin withheld both the level of assistance and the political status which the Chinese Communists wished for. According to Polish sources, Khrushchev, in a speech in Warsaw made after his decision to promote "de-

Stalinization," specifically accused Stalin of having been responsible for serious strains in Sino-Soviet relations.

AFTER STALIN

Mao Tse-tung's prestige within the Communist bloc started to rise even before Stalin's death, but, perhaps because of domestic and international uncertainties, Stalin's successors began almost immediately to show increasing deference to the Chinese Communists. Over a period of time they made a number of important concessions to China and granted it some additional economic aid. Undoubtedly, the Russians' steps to improve relations since the spring of 1953 have helped to strengthen the Sino-Soviet alliance by removing some of the previous sources of friction. They have also contributed to a steady rise in Peking's influence and prestige within the Communist bloc.

An increased Soviet sensitivity to Chinese Communist pride was apparent at Stalin's funeral, at which Chou En-lai marched in a place of honor, along with top Soviet leaders. Almost immediately a perceptible change in tone began to creep into Soviet statements about the "great Chinese people." Even more important to the Chinese, the Russians found it desirable to make definite concessions.

The first visit of any top-level Soviet leaders to Communist China took place in the autumn of 1954. Khrushchev and Bulganin, soon to emerge in the top positions in Moscow, paid unprecedented deference to Communist China when they went to Peking in September-October of that year. Khrushchev called Communist China a "great power" and declared that "after the Great October Socialist Revolution, the victory of the Chinese people's revolution is the most outstanding event in world history," one which has "immense" significance for the "peoples of Asia." He praised the Chinese Communists for having "creatively applied" Marxism-Leninism and proclaimed that "the Soviet Union and the People's Republic of China are the invulnerable bastion of the camp of peace, democracy, and socialism."

During Khrushchev's 1954 visit the Russians agreed to sell China all their shares in the Sino-Soviet joint-stock companies and to return Port Arthur to sole Chinese control by the end of 1955. They announced a second Soviet loan of $130 million as well as an increase in the number of "Soviet aid" projects in China. They also agreed to cooperate in constructing another major railway, to link China and the Soviet Union through Sinkiang. And in two major joint declarations they gave strong endorsement to many of Peking's objectives, including the recovery of Taiwan. Somewhat over a year later, in the spring of 1956, Mikoyan visited Communist China and promised a substantial increase in the number of Chinese industrial projects to be built with Russian help.

These developments were tangible signs of a significant adjustment which appeared to be taking place in Sino-Soviet relations after 1953. The Russians began to pay more attention to Chinese Communist feelings and interests, and Peking started to assume greater independence and initiative in Communist bloc affairs. This process gained a startling momentum following Khrushchev's dramatic attack on Stalin at the Twentieth Party Congress of the Soviet Party in February 1956.

PEKING AND "DE-STALINIZATION"

Khrushchev's decision to "de-Stalinize" the Soviet Party set in motion a process which soon led to a loosening of controls throughout the Communist bloc, and it marked the beginning of a critical period of instability in bloc affairs. Stalin's heavy-handed dominance and his insistence upon tight Soviet control, particularly in the East European satellites, had created numerous fundamental tensions within the bloc, which had been clearly revealed by Tito's struggle against Moscow after 1948, the Berlin uprising in 1953, and many less obvious signs. By 1955 Khrushchev had apparently decided to meet these problems by relaxing Moscow's controls, denouncing the symbol of past Soviet dominance, and seeking a reconciliation with Yugoslavia. But the unprecedented violence of Khrushchev's denunciation of Stalin and Stalinism sent a shock throughout the entire world Communist movement and gave a sudden impetus to the development of what Italian Communist leader Togliatti called "polycentric Communism." It touched off the Poznan riots, the crisis in Soviet-Polish relations, and the Hungarian uprising. Finally, it raised the whole issue of the future unity of the Communist boc.

At almost every stage in these turbulent events the Chinese Communist leaders gave evidence that, instead of being content merely to parrot Moscow's line, they were determined to make their own independent evaluations and to define their own position. Despite the obscurity which surrounds most Communist bloc affairs, it is clear that during 1956–1957 Peking assumed a new and very significant political role as a mediator or conciliator between Moscow and the East European satellites. Apparently, Communist China took considerable initiative in defining political and ideological positions for the bloc as a whole. And as a result it emerged into a position much closer to parity with the Soviet Union in the leadership of the bloc, at least in political and ideological terms.

From the start Peking's reaction to Khrushchev's February 1956 denunciation of Stalin was somewhat cool. Its leaders and press were slow in reacting at all, but finally the Chinese Politburo's views were made known in an article entitled "On the Historical Experience of the Dictatorship of the Proletariat," published in early April. These views differed considerably from those which Khrushchev had revealed at the Twentieth Congress. Although, the article stated, Stalin had "exaggerated his own role" and had made "unrealistic and erroneous decisions on certain important matters" (including "in particular a wrong decision on the question of Yugoslavia"), he had nonetheless "creatively applied and developed Marxism-Leninism." "Some people," it said, "consider that Stalin was wrong in everything; this is a grave misconception. Stalin was a great Marxist-Leninist, yet at the same time a Marxist-Leninist who committed several gross errors without realizing they were errors." The article went on to criticize Stalin for maintaining that the principal target of Communist revolutionaries should be "middle-of-the-road" social and political forces; this formula, it said, had been "crudely applied" in China until the Chinese Communists worked out their own program calling for "winning over" and "neutralizing" the "middle-of-the-road" forces. But, the article continued, "Stalin's works should, as before, still be seriously studied and . . . we should accept as an important historical legacy all that is of value in them, especially those many works in which he defended Leninism and correctly summarized the experience of building up the Soviet Union."

There were undoubtedly many reasons why the Chinese Communists decided to take this middle position, instead of accepting Khrushchev's initial, general condemnation. In 1956 the Chinese Communists were, in a sense, passing through a Stalinist stage of their own. They had explicitly modeled many of their policies on Stalin's, and an outright repudiation of Stalin could have led to the questioning of many of their own current policies. Peking may also have feared that the attack on Stalin could have repercussions affecting Mao Tse-tung's position within China, since for many years Mao had played a comparable, although by no means identical, role as the foremost Party leader. In addition, the Chinese Communist leaders, then and subsequently, seem to have shown a greater concern than Stalin's successors in the Soviet Union about the prime importance of doctrine and ideology in the Communist system. This may have deterred them from approving any blanket condemnation of the man who for years had been idolized as the principal oracle of world Communism. And, unlike Khrushchev, the Chinese Communists had no compelling domestic reasons to discredit Stalin's past leadership. By the end of 1956 Khrushchev, too, had apparently come to the conclusion that his initial condemnation of Stalin was too sweeping; in any case, he began moderating his extreme stand and moved closer to the Chinese position.

HARRY GELMAN *
The Sino-Soviet Conflict

Eight years have now gone by since the Twentieth Congress of the CPSU touched off the momentous struggle between the Soviet and Chinese Communist Parties, and nearly four since the conflict passed—in the spring of 1960—from the stage of concealed behind-the-scenes argumentation and veiled public criticism to that of open vituperation. Looking back over the whole course of events, particularly in the light of what both sides revealed during 1963 of their past confidential dealings, one is struck above all by the continuity and steady growth of the conflict. Despite periodic lulls in the intensity of its public expression, the Sino-Soviet struggle has gone on unceasingly since 1956, and each successive year has brought important new developments—some publicly known at the time, others not—which progressively expanded and exacerbated it.

From the beginning, the struggle has been fundamentally a dispute over authority: since 1956, over the authority to define (and redefine) the proper relationships between the CPSU and other bloc Communist Parties; since 1957, over the authority to fix unified policy lines for the bloc and the international Communist movement; and, since 1958 particularly, over the authority to determine whose national interest—Moscow's or Peking's—should be accorded greater weight in the formulation of Communist policy. Conflicts of national interest between the disputants have involved such questions as whether the Soviet Union should assist Communist China to attain a nuclear capability; what risks the USSR should be willing to take in order to support Chinese Communist ambitions re-

* Harry Gelman, "The Sino-Soviet Conflict: A Survey," in *Problems of Communism* (Washington, D.C.: U.S. Government Printing Office, March-April, 1964).

garding Taiwan; the desirability of moves to reduce tensions with the United States; how far the Communist bloc should go in encouraging and backing revolutionary armed struggles in underdeveloped areas; and what attitude should be taken toward "national-bourgeois" regimes in these areas, especially where—as in India—the regime appears hostile to Chinese Communist but not to Soviet interests.

BEGINNING OF THE CHINESE CHALLENGE

While it is appropriate to trace the Sino-Soviet struggle from the Twentieth CPSU Congress, which Peking now claims to have been its starting point, it should be noted that the CCP had already had important policy disagreements with Stalin before, during, and after its advent to power in 1949. The point, however, is that not until Stalin's death did the Chinese Party dare to make such conflicts the occasion for challenging the authority and prerogatives of the CPSU—and eventually denying them altogether. It so happened that the first new policy divergence of importance folowing Stalin's death arose with the Twentieth Congress and the positions it took regarding the Stalin cult and the possibility of "peaceful transitions" to socialism. Confronted once again, as it had been in the past, with Soviet decisions of policy with which it strongly disagreed, the CCP leadership now for the first time felt itself in a position to press for their modification and, in so doing, to contest the paramount authority of the Soviet Party.

In its major statement on the dispute last September [1963], the CCP referred back to its April 1956 pronouncement "On the Historical Experience of the Dictatorship of the Proletariat" (*Jen-min jih-pao* [*People's Daily*], April 5, 1956) as having "tactfully but unequivocally criticized the erroneous propositions of the Twentieth Congress." This pronouncement did, in fact, seek to defend Mao's own position in the Chinese Party by revising what the CCP regarded as the one-sided appraisal of Stalin at the Congress, at the same time presenting a Marxist "explanation" of how Stalin's "mistakes" had occurred and how they could be prevented from recurring in the future. In brief, the CCP held that Stalin had indeed committed "serious mistakes," but that his merits were more important; that his errors had reflected contradictions "between the individual and the collective in a socialist society"; and that such contradictions, although they might recur, could be minimized, and mistakes averted, if the "leaders of Communist Parties and socialist states" exercised sufficient prudence.

This document, representing the first in a long series of Chinese efforts to correct the errant CPSU and provide guidance for all those who had heretofore looked to Moscow for direction, made an immediate and widespread impression in the international Communist movement. Moreover, the Chinese disclosed last September that they had followed up the April 1956 pronouncement with a series of private protests conveyed by Mao, Liu Shao-ch'i, and Chou En-Lai in conversations with Soviet leaders in Moscow and Peking in April, October, and November 1956, and January 1957. In these talks, according to the Chinese, they maintained that "the basic policy and line during the period when Stalin was in power were correct," and that the CPSU leadership had shown a "total lack of over-all analysis" of Stalin, a "lack of self-criticism," and (apparently most serious of all in Peking's view) a "failure to consult with the fraternal parties in advance."

THE EAST EUROPEAN CRISES

Besides questioning the propriety of the Soviet repudiation of Stalin, the CCP apparently undertook to intervene directly in Moscow's relations with its East European satellites before and during the crises of late 1956. Chinese statements and credible press reports at the time indicated that the Peking leadership gave support to the Polish Communist demands for greater autonomy from Moscow; and the Chinese have charged in their more recent statements on the dispute that the Soviet Union "committed the error of great power chauvinism . . . by moving up troops in an attempt to subdue the Polish comrades by armed force," intimating that the CCP had then stepped in to warn Moscow against using force. At the same time, the Chinese claim that it was also they who pressured the CPSU into abandoning an altogether different sort of "grave error" in the

handling of the Hungarian revolt. The Peking statement of last
September says:

> At the critical moment when the Hungarian counter-
> revolutionaries had occupied Budapest, it [the CPSU] in-
> tended for a time to adopt a policy of capitulation and to
> abandon socialist Hungary to counter-revolution. . . . We
> insisted on the taking of all necessary measures to smash
> the counter-revolutionary rebellion in Hungary and firmly
> opposed the abandonment of . . . Hungary.

Although it is quite likely that the Chinese have greatly
exaggerated their part in determining the course ultimately taken
by the Soviet Union in both the Polish and Hungarian crises,
the essential point is that Peking apparently did intervene in an
attempt to influence decisions that hitherto had been accepted
as Moscow's sole prerogative. Further, the Chinese now claim
(since last year) that it was likewise at their suggestion that the
Soviet government issued its declaration of October 30, 1956,
in which—as the Chinese put it—the Soviet leaders re-examined
"some of their own past mistakes in handling their relations
with fraternal countries" and recognized the need for "mutual
respect," "equality" and "independence" in intra-bloc relations.
On November 1, 1956, Peking published a statement supporting
the Soviet declaration, but also voicing direct approval of the
Polish Communist position and warning against further mani-
festations of "great power chauvinism."

In their statements last year, the Chinese piously professed
to be saddened by the fact that the actions they took in 1956
in the best interests of Communism had caused the Soviet
leadership to "nurse rancor against us" and to regard the CCP
as its "biggest obstacle." That such rancor arose was hardly
surprising, however, in view of the fact that Peking was now
asserting its independent right to provide doctrinal guidance to
the Communist world, to judge the propriety of Soviet policy
innovations, and even to prescribe the correct framework of
relationships between the USSR and other members of the
Communist bloc.

MAO AT MOSCOW, 1957

At the conference of Communist leaders held in Moscow in November 1957, with Mao himself attending as chief spokesman for the CCP, the Chinese vigorously renewed their efforts to shape over-all Communist policy, although with a perceptible shift in direction. Whereas in 1956 Peking had stressed autonomy and inveighed against "great power chauvinism," its representatives now urged unity and deference to the leading role of the Soviet Union. Speaking publicly at Moscow University on November 17, Mao declared that "the socialist camp must have a head and this head is the USSR," and that "the Communist Parties of all countries must have a head and this head is the CPSU."

It is now clear from the information made public by Peking last year that Mao's attendance at the Moscow parley followed less than a month after the signature of an agreement providing for Soviet assistance to China in the area of "new technology for national defense." Hence, the Chinese leader's insistence upon a special status for the CPSU, together with the strong Chinese stand taken in the conference against revisionism and emphasizing the value of Soviet experience for all members of the bloc, may well have been partly intended as a repayment by Peking for the military aid agreement. However, it seems equally likely that the Chinese position on bloc unity and doctrinal orthodoxy was, in any case, a necessary complement to the CCP's effort at the Moscow meeting to force acceptance of a more vigorous and aggressive Communist strategy toward the West in the light of Soviet weapons developments. In 1963 Moscow and Peking published differing versions of portions of Mao's conference speech dealing with this point, but both versions indicated that the Chinese leader had sought to impress upon the delegates that nuclear war was neither so likely, nor its consequences—if it came—so unacceptable, as to justify Communist hesitancy to adopt a more militant international policy.

Thus, the Chinese line at the 1957 conference by no means signified Peking's submission to CPSU discipline or Soviet policy dictates. On the contrary, Mao apparently insisted upon the prerogatives of a kingmaker. While publicly proclaiming the USSR and CPSU to be the "center" and "head" of world Communism, he met privately with Soviet Party leaders and—so the Chinese claim—"where necessary and appropriate, waged struggle against them in order to help them correct their errors." Prominent among the errors which Mao "struggled" to correct, according to the Chinese, was the CPSU's draft of the passage in the conference resolution relating to the modes of acquiring power. The Chinese claim that this draft "said not a word about non-peaceful transition [to power], mentioning only peaceful transition" and emphasizing the "parliamentary road." They admit that they did not obtain everything they wished, but claim to have forced the Soviets to accept counterbalancing phrases on the possibility of "non-peaceful transition" which were embodied in a joint CPSU-CCP draft declaration and later incorporated in the published conference resolution.

The CCP also claims that it succeeded in wresting other concessions from the CPSU at the 1957 meeting, and certain of these testify to Peking's desire at the time for a harsher bloc foreign policy. Notably, Peking asserts that its representatives secured additions to the conference resolution embodying the notions that "U.S. imperialism is the center of world reaction and the sworn enemy of the people," and that "if imperialism should unleash a world war, it would doom itself to destruction."

NEW AREAS OF FRICTION

In 1958 the Sino-Soviet struggle took on broader dimensions as new conflicts of national interest arose on several fronts. The three most important mattters at issue were the military relationship between the two powers, the related question of Soviet conduct during the Taiwan Straits crisis, and Peking's radical new economic programs and the claims associated with them.

On the military issue, Peking's statement of last September, though not saying so explicitly, seeks to convey the impression that the Soviet Union, in the October 1957 defense assistance agreement, gave a firm commitment to help China retain an atomic weapons capability. This appears doubtful, however, particularly in view of the campaign launched by the CCP in the summer of 1958 against Chinese military leaders charged with overemphasizing the importance of both atomic weapons and outside aid. The same Chinese statement further alleges that sometime (unspecified) in 1958 "the CPSU put forward unreasonable demands designed to bring China under Soviet military control," and that these demands were "firmly rejected by the Chinese government." It is conceivable that the demands were linked by the Soviets to the question of atomic assistance to China, and that they were advanced by Khrushchev when he visited Peking in early August, at which time Soviet military assistance was reportedly discussed in the context of China's requirements for the impending Taiwan Straits venture. In any event, the absence of any Soviet agreement to supply nuclear weapons to China was suggested shortly after Khrushchev's departure by an article in the CCP organ *Hung Ch'i* (August 16) prominently reasserting Mao's dictum that "the atomic bomb is a paper tiger."

If the Chinese were embittered by the evident Soviet reluctance to satisfy them in regard to the sharing of the USSR's nuclear might, that bitterness was further intensified by the hesitant backing China received from Moscow in the ensuing crisis in the Taiwan Straits. Confronted by American nuclear power, Peking apparently sought to obtain an early public commitment by the Soviet Union that would enable it to face down the United States and thus would make feasible Chinese military action to "liberate" the offshore islands. The Chinese government statement of September 1, 1963, charged that the Soviet Union had perfidiously withheld such a commitment until Moscow was sure that it could be given without risk—in other words, until it was too late to be of any assistance to the original Chinese goal.

The slow and deliberate course taken by Moscow in the Taiwan Straits crisis does, indeed, suggest that the Soviet leadership feared the possibility of being dragged into a nuclear conflict with the United States as a result of precipitate Chinese action taken in pursuit of interests not shared by the USSR. This interpretation would appear to derive support from the Chinese claim made last September (denied, unconvincingly, by Moscow) that Khrushchev, in his talks with Mao at Peking in October 1959, sought to remove Taiwan as "an incendiary factor in the international situation" by hinting that Peking ought to accept a "two Chinas" solution. At the same time, it seems likely that the Chinese Communist challenge to the United States in 1958 further reinforced Soviet reluctance to assist China in acquiring nuclear weapons.

A third new area of friction developed in connection with the radical turn in Chinese domestic policy during 1958, manifested in the launching of the communes program and the economic Great Leap Forward. Chinese spokesmen exuberantly claimed that the communes, with their system of partial distribution according to need, contained "shoots" of communism, signifying that the final attainment of communism in China was no longer far off; that they represented an unprecedented achievement as well as a useful model for other countries. In these claims and the policies of the Great Leap as a whole, the CPSU saw a new and dangerous Chinese challenge to its leadership of the Communist world. As a Soviet comment stated in 1963, "things were depicted as though only they (the Chinese) were really engaged in communist construction, leaving other countries behind," and the Chinese leaders tried to present their "totally unsound and harmful policy . . . as an objective law" and "as a prescription or recipe for other countries."

According to one of the official Soviet statements issued last fall, Khrushchev personally protested these "innovations" in his talks with Mao in early August 1958. For some time afterward, however, the Soviet leaders continued to ignore the communes publicly, although their attitude was reflected in Soviet press comments criticizing the lack of material incentives characteristic of the commune system and emphasizing that the attainment of full communism required a level of production which was much closer to realization in the Soviet Union than in Communist China. Later, as the Sino-Soviet rift widened and as deteriorating economic conditions in China forced abandonment of the communes in all but name, Khrushchev repeatedly gibed at the Chinese with thinly veiled references to Communist leaders who had become "estranged from the masses," disobedient "children" who had "burned their finger," and to the fatuity of those who desired "pantsless communism."

WIDENING OF THE BREACH

The year 1959 saw the deterioration of Sino-Soviet relations proceed at a markedly faster pace as dissensions over Soviet moves toward an easing of tensions with the United States and over Communist China's involvement in a border conflict with India still further widened the gap between the two Communist powers.

Moscow's intent to pursue more vigorously the "peaceful coexistence" strategy toward the West was signaled in January by Soviet Deputy Premier Anastas Mikoyan's exploratory visit to the United States, and was underlined later the same month by the ruling handed down by the Twenty-first CPSU Congress that war between the capitalist and socialist states not only was not inevitable but might even be permanently avoided while capitalism still remained. Khrushchev's visit to the United States and his meeting with President Eisenhower followed in the fall, while Soviet propaganda during and after the visit took the softest line toward the West that it had displayed since World War II—or has taken since.

All this was naturally anathema to Peking, which considered the United States the principal obstacle to its ambitions in Asia and viewed the exertion of maximum Communist revolutionary pressure against the U.S. in all parts of the world as essential to China's national interests. Accordingly, Chinese Communist propaganda in the fall of 1959, while paying lip service to the principle of "peaceful coexistence," became more and more shrill in its warnings against perfidious American intentions to use negotiations and a relaxation of international tensions as a "smokescreen" to lull the peoples of the world into a false sense of security and thus facilitate U.S. "aggression" against the national liberation movements in underdeveloped areas.

Other Soviet actions during the year aggravated old Chinese grievances or created new ones. Speaking publicly on July 18 at Poznan, Poland, Khrushchev—without referring to China by name—recalled the failure of the Soviet experiment with communes during the period of "war communism" and remarked that those who had wished to set them up "had a poor

understanding of what communism is and how it is to be built."
Inasmuch as the CCP Central Committee was at that very moment meeting at Lushan to re-examine the communes program,
Khrushchev's comment was regarded by the Chinese as a gra-
tuitous attempt to intervene in Chinese internal affairs. There
is also reason to suspect that the Soviets tried to intervene more
directly by encouraging Chinese Communist Defense Minister
Marshal P'eng Te-huai, during his visit to Eastern Europe in
the spring of 1959, to oppose Maoist policies. It is believed that
P'eng did challenge Mao's program at the Lushan meeting, and
that this was responsible for his dismissal shortly thereafter, in
September 1959.

Meanwhile, Moscow continued to turn a deaf ear to Chinese appeals for assistance in the acquisition of nuclear weapons.
According to the CCP, the Soviet Union in June 1959 finally
rejected Peking's request that China be provided with "a sample
of an atomic bomb" and thereby "unilaterally tore up" the 1957
Sino-Soviet agreement concerning "new technology for national
defense."

On top of all this, the refusal of the Soviet leadership to
stand beside Communist China in her border conflict with non-
socialist, bourgeois India was viewed in Peking as an outright
betrayal of the obligations of "proletarian internationalism."
Following the outbreak of hostilities in late August, the Soviet
government on September 9 issued a public statement taking a
neutral stand toward the conflict—this, the Chinese have since
claimed, in spite of frantic last-minute efforts by themselves to
dissuade Moscow from such action. Not only did Moscow refuse
to heed this appeal, but it later accused the Chinese of having
deliberately timed their military action against India so as to
embarrass Khrushchev on the eve of his trip to the United States.

Khrushchev's visit to Peking at the end of September, on
the heels of his U.S. trip, apparently did more to accentuate than
to assuage the grievances on both sides. Regarding the Sino-
Indian conflict, Peking claims that the Chinese leaders "personally gave Comrade Khrushchev an explanation of the true
situation" but that he "did not wish to know the true situation";
on the other hand, according to Moscow, the Soviet leader took
the occasion to warn the Chinese that their course of action was
"fraught with negative consequences not only for Sino-Indian

relations, but also for the entire international situation." It was also at this time, as noted earlier, that Khrushchev allegedly suggested to Mao the desirability of accepting a two-Chinas solution of the Taiwan problem. Moreover, the Soviet leader further outraged his hosts by warning them, in a public address on September 30, against "testing by force the stability of the capitalist system."

THE WAR OF WORDS

As the Chinese saw it, Khrushchev's actions during 1959 had set virtually a new record of error and betrayal: he had rebuffed them on the question of atomic military assistance, sought to interfere in Chinese internal affairs, hobnobbed with the leaders of "U.S. imperialism," betrayed them in the Sino-Indian conflict, intimated that they should renounce their claim to Taiwan, and upbraided them publicly for their domestic and foreign policies. It is little wonder, therefore, that in April 1960 the CCP unleashed a massive propaganda assault aimed at the policies—and, implicitly, the authority—of the Soviet Communist Party.

Central to the many indirect but unmistakable indictments of Khrushchev's policies published in the leading organs of the CCP was the contention that the peaceful coexistence line as applied by the Soviet Party was eroding the militancy of revolutionaries throughout the world. Now, for the first time, the Chinese systematically elaborated their objections to the arguments that the advent of nuclear weapons necessitated a change in Communist revolutionary strategy, that local wars involving the great powers would inevitably lead to world war, and that revolutionary armed struggles should not be so vigorously cultivated as to create a danger of nuclear conflict. While it was possible that world war could be averted, the Chinese contended, local anti-colonial or anti-imperialist wars of liberation could not, and the Communist policy should be to encourage and support such struggles without being inhibited by exaggerated fears of nuclear destruction or by a misguided desire to facilitate negotiations with the capitalist West.

Soon after the CCP campaign began, the position of the CPSU to defend its policies against the Chinese criticisms was measurably weakened as a result of the Soviet decision to publicly exploit the U-2 incident of May 1 whereas previous overflights had been ignored. This decision set in motion a train of events which apparently led the Soviet leadership to conclude, after anguished debate, that it would be politically harmful, in view of the Chinese offensive, to allow the scheduled summit conference with the Western leaders at Paris to take place. There is now substantive evidence that the CPSU leaders had the Chinese very much on their minds during the sixteen-day interval between the U-2 incident and Khrushchev's dynamiting of the summit parley. The Soviet Party disclosed in April last year that on May 12, 1960—four days before the Paris meeting was to open—Mao had been urgently invited to come to Moscow, but had refused. Instead, on May 14, he made his first officially reported statement in two years, in which he professed to support a summit meeting but simultaneously gloated over the U-2 incident and implicitly taunted Khruschev for having displayed "illusions" about imperialism.

In early June the Chinese Party carried its fight against the CPSU a step farther by utilizing the opportunity afforded by a meeting of the General Council of the World Federation of Trade Unions in Peking to conduct a campaign against the Soviet line among both Communist and non-Communist delegates. Shortly thereafter, according to the Chinese, the CPSU privately proposed to the CCP that steps be taken to organize a conference of all Communist Parties for the purpose of ironing out differences, suggesting that a preparatory exchange of views take place in closed multiparty meetings during the impending Rumanian Party Congress.

When the CCP representatives went to Bucharest in the latter part of June, they were shocked to find themselves the target of a "surprise assault" allegedly concocted by the CPSU in order to browbeat them into submission. Khrushchev, according to the Chinese, first circulated a CPSU letter to the CCP, dated June 21, which attacked the Chinese Party "all along the line." Then, in their speeches to the congress, Khrushchev and his supporters among the East European Party leaders denounced the Chinese as Trotskyites and "madmen" seeking war, and further accused them of pursuing a selfishly "nationalistic" course in the Sino-Indian border conflict. The Soviet leader is also alleged to have belittled Chinese military knowledge and the militia system, and to have criticized the purge of Marshal P'eng Te-huai. The CCP delegation, according to Peking, responded to the attacks with a "tit-for-tat struggle" and distributed a written statement of defiance at the close of the congress proceedings.

New Soviet acts of retaliation followed soon afterward. According to the Chinese statements of last September, it was in July 1960 that Moscow "suddenly took a unilateral decision recalling all Soviet experts in China within one month." In addition, the Soviet government unilaterally canceled the reciprocal publication of friendship magazines in both countries and demanded the recall of a member of the Chinese Embassy in Moscow. It also appears from last year's statements by both sides that incidents began occurring on the Sino-Soviet border about this time, each side charging the other with having provoked them.

Meanwhile, the war of words continued with mounting intensity. In early August, Soviet Party journals began claiming for the first time that peaceful coexistence represented the general foreign-policy line of the *entire* Communist bloc, thus implicitly asserting the authority of the CPSU to define bloc foreign policy and the obligation of bloc members to accept such definition as a matter of Communist discipline. This was to be a recurrent Soviet motif in the Sino-Soviet polemic of subsequent years, receding in periods of Soviet retreat but reappearing when Moscow returned to the attack.

On September 10, the CCP replied to the CPSU letter of June 21 with a letter of rebuttal which called upon Moscow to restore bloc unity by abandoning not only its "erroneous" policy line but all efforts to exert its authority over Peking. That same month a Chinese delegation went to Moscow for fruitless private talks with CPSU leaders, and in Hanoi, Soviet and Chinese Party representatives again vied for support among the delegates to the Vietnamese Party congress.

THE 1960 COMMUNIST CONFERENCE

In October 1960 there was another skirmish between the two antagonists in the twenty-six-party committee which met in Moscow to prepare a draft declaration for submission to the scheduled November conference of Communist Parties. Agreement was eventually reached on the bulk of a draft text, but not on certain key issues. In connection with this meeting, the Chinese claimed last September that Khrushchev, upon returning from the United Nations session in New York, "even scrapped agreements that had already been reached on some questions"—suggesting that some of the CPSU leaders were more willing than Khrushchev to make concessions to the Chinese for the sake of unity.

When the conference proper convened, according to Peking, the Soviets again started things off, as at Bucharest, by distributing among the delegates a new sixty-thousand-word CPSU "letter" attacking the CCP (and the Albanian Party) "more savagely than ever." In the conference debate also, the Chinese claim, the CPSU mustered its adherents and "engineered converging assaults on the CCP" in an attempt to force it to yield. In the end, an ambiguous document was produced and signed, embodying the mutually contradictory positions of the two parties on many issues. While the CPSU perhaps succeeded in getting more of its points included than did the Chinese, it nevertheless suffered a major defeat on the central issue of authority in that it failed to obtain either a condemnation of (Chinese-Albanian) "factional activities" or an endorsement of the Soviet thesis that peaceful coexistence was the "general line" of bloc foreign policy. The Chinese have since boasted that this was "an event of great historical significance" because it "changed the previous highly abnormal situation in which not even the slightest criticism of the errors of the CPSU leadership was tolerated and its word was final."

The signature of the conference declaration was accompanied by the customary public pledges of undying solidarity and mutual affection, but privately neither Moscow nor Peking regarded the compromise as anything but a temporary makeshift, nor did either intend to abandon the struggle. Right after the conference, in fact, Khrushchev renewed his attack on the Chinese position at what he evidently regarded as its weakest point—Albania. The Albanians, who had been the most vociferous supporters of the Chinese at Bucharest and the November Moscow conference, were now subjected to an extension of the Soviet economic pressures that had been initiated in the summer of 1960. These reprisals culminated in the withdrawal of all Soviet technicians and the complete termination of Soviet economic aid to Albania in April 1961, followed by the withdrawal of Soviet naval units from Vlore in May. An acrimonious exchange of messages between Moscow and Tirana was climaxed by a violent letter addressed to the Albanian Party by the CPSU Central Committee on August 24, 1961. The Chinese, fully conscious of the fact that the Soviet pressures against Albania were aimed as much against themselves, countered by providing their East European ally with economic aid and technicians to replace those withdrawn by Moscow. Peking has since revealed that the CCP urged the Soviet Party early in 1961 to take steps to improve Soviet-Albanian relations, and that it repeated this advice on the eve of the Twenty-Second CPSU Congress in October, apparently in an effort to head off the all-out Soviet attack on Albania that seemed foreshadowed by the August 24 CPSU letter to Tirana.

THE TWENTY-SECOND CONGRESS AND AFTER

As events soon proved, however, the Soviet leadership was determined to force the Albanian issue into the open, evidently hoping thereby to recoup the damage done to its authority by the Chinese at the November 1960 conference of Communist Parties. Thus, the Twenty-second Congress witnessed an unprecedented torrent of abuse hurled publicly at the Albanians by CPSU spokesmen, most of all by Khrushchev, who in his speech of October 27 went so far as to call explicitly for the overthrow of Albanian Party leaders Hoxha and Shehu.

Besides the assault on the Albanians, there were other moves at the congress which appeared aimed, at least implicitly, at various aspects of the Chinese position. The first was the renewed attack on Stalin, which flouted the position taken by the CCP ever since the Twentieth Congress. The second was the new, intensified offensive unleashed against the "anti-Party group," and particularly against Molotov, who—it was repeatedly intimated by congress speakers—had been encouraged by the Chinese to attack Khrushchev's policies on two occasions, once in April 1960 (when Molotov was still Ambassador to Outer Mongolia) and again just before the Twenty-second Congress. The third was the effort to present the new CPSU Program, which the congress was to ratify, as a "new Communist Manifesto" justifying the claim of the Soviet Party to world Communist leadership. On top of all this, the Chinese claim that Khrushchev, in his private meetings with Premier Chou En-lai during the congress, "expressed undisguised support for anti-party [*i.e.,* revisionist] elements in the CCP."

As leader of the Chinese delegation, Chou responded to the Soviet moves by reproving Khrushchev before the congress for his open attack on the Albanian Party, by demonstratively laying a wreath on Stalin's tomb, and by suddenly leaving for Peking before the conclusion of the congress. According to Chinese statements, he also "frankly criticized the errors of the CPSU leadership" in private conversations with Khrushchev and other Soviet leaders.

Following the congress, the CPSU stepped up its campaign to mobilize the bulk of the world's Communist Parties in a solid front against the Albanians—and hence, implicitly, against the Chinese. Although all the East European parties and some of the non-bloc parties had backed the Soviet attack on Albania at the congress, many of the latter—as well as the North Korean and North Vietnamese parties—had failed to do so. During the next three months, however, in response to evident Soviet pressures, the great majority of the non-Asian Communist Parties went on record with some form of rebuke to the Albanians. The Soviet press avidly republished these statements, as it did the statements (after mid-November) of some of the foreign Parties mildly but explicitly criticizing the Chinese for opposing criticism of the Albanians. In December, diplomatic relations between Moscow and Tirana were, in effect, ruptured.

Meanwhile, the Chinese Communist press maintained a spurious Olympian attitude, reprinting both the attacks on

Albania and the ferocious Albanian replies—but of course giving greater prominence to the latter. Ample publicity was also given to statements by various Asian parties which declined to follow the Soviet lead. The North Vietnamese Party, alarmed at the drift of events, took the initiative in January 1962 in privately urging the combatants to agree to the holding of a new world Communist conference "to settle the discord" and in proposing that "pending such a meeting the parties cease attacking one another in the press and over the radio." Similar proposals were put forward, apparently also privately, by the Indonesian Party, and publicly by the New Zealand CP.

JOCKEYING FOR POSITION

By February 1962 it was evident to the CPSU that its campaign not only had failed to isolate the Albanians and Chinese but even had resulted in setbacks to its position, primarily among the Asian Parties but also to some extent elsewhere. On February 21, the Soviet Party climaxed its drive with an imposing two-page spread in *Pravda* summarizing the support it had received, citing Lenin on the necessity of subordination "to the international discipline of the revolutionary proletariat," and insisting that "only open, uncompromising criticism of the anti-socialist, nationalist actions of the Hoxha-Shehu group can secure the unity of our movement. "

The very next day, February 22, the CPSU dispatched a secret letter to Peking which—as discreetly summarized by the Russians last July—"drew the attention of the CCP" to the dangerous consequences of disunity and urged "more effective measures" for coordinating the positions of the two Parties in the various world front organizations and elsewhere. According to the more outspoken Chinese summary, the CPSU letter accused the Chinese of taking "a special stand of their own" in opposition to the world movement, "even made a crime" of the CCP's support for the Albanians, and demanded that Peking abandon its position and embrace Moscow's "erroneous line" as "preconditions" for an improvement of Sino-Soviet relations.

In April the CCP replied with a letter favoring a new general conference of Communist Parties, concurring with the

North Vietnamese proposal for a truce in polemics, and calling for bilateral or multilateral talks to prepare for a world meeting. The Chinese also blandly advised the Soviet Party to "take the initiative" in seeking a settlement of its differences with the Albanians. Late in May, the CPSU again returned the ball to Peking with a note which, according to Moscow, reiterated the main points of the February 22 letter. The Soviet Party also claimed last year that it had agreed in May 1962 to the convocation of a new Communist conference; but the Chinese assert that the CPSU made an Albanian surrender the "precondition" for such a conference.

Meanwhile, Moscow and Peking seemed to have agreed, at least for the time being, to heed the North Vietnamese appeal and apply the brake to public polemics against each other. Mutual recriminations were, in fact, greatly toned down during the spring of 1962—although never quite eliminated. Public pronouncements on both sides sought to convey to the West an impression of restored harmony and unity—an effort which, as an American scholar of Communist affairs has noted, was assisted by Communist news correspondents in Moscow, and which was rather naïvely taken at face value by some sections of the Western press.

Again, the reality was very different. According to the Chinese statement of last September 6, it was precisely during this period of seeming calm (April-May 1962) that "the leaders of the CPSU used their organs and personnel in Sinkiang, China, to carry out large-scale subversive activities in the Ili region, and enticed and coerced several tens of thousands of Chinese citizens into going into the Soviet Union," subsequently refusing to return them to Chinese territory despite Peking's protests. These events were presumably related to the subsequently reported action of the CPSU government closing Soviet consulates in China. Soviet press reports last September confirmed that a mass flight of Chinese across the Sino-Soviet border had in fact taken place, adding further lurid details which contradicted the Peking version.

RENEWAL OF HOSTILITIES

At the end of the summer of 1962, the Chinese fired the opening salvos in a renewed anti-Soviet campaign which has gone on continuously ever since. On three separate occasions, at the Rumanian (August 23), Vietnamese (September 1), and Bulgarian (September 8) national anniversary receptions held in Peking, Foreign Minister Ch'en Yi alluded to socialist countries which attempted to "forcibly impose . . . [their] views on others" and "replaced comradelike discussions . . . with interference in [others'] internal affairs." Soon afterward, in mid-September, the Chinese and Albanian press launched an obviously coordinated and violent assault on "modern revisionism," timed to coincide with the visit of Leonid Brezhnev, Chairman of the Presidium of the USSR Supreme Soviet, to Yugoslavia.

Curiously, Soviet propaganda displayed remarkable restraint as the Chinese attacks continued, and there was even an attempt to appease Peking. In meetings with the departing Chinese Ambassador Liu Hsiao on October 13 and 14, Khrushchev, according to Soviet statements last year, asked that Mao forget the past and "start our relations with a clear page." Moreover, according to the Chinese, the Soviet leader expressed complete sympathy for Peking's stand on the border conflict with India, implicitly endorsed the Chinese intention to use force in that conflict, and promised to stand by Peking if hostilities again arose. These private statements by Khrushchev were followed on October 25 by an equally remarkable editorial in *Pravda* which, for the first and last time in the three yeas of the Sino-Indian border controversy, sided with Peking. One can only speculate that the adoption by Moscow of a conciliatory posture was motivated by the approach of the Cuban crisis, which erupted into the open on October 22—that is, by Soviet desire to assure bloc solidarity at a time of military crisis and also, perhaps, to buy Chinese forbearance if it should become necessary to back down over the issue of Cuba.

As it turned out, the Soviets did have to back down, but the Chinese did not forbear and instead proceeded to belabor Khrushchev unmercifully for his "betrayal" of Castro. Placed on the defensive, Moscow edged back toward its previous neutral position vis-à-vis the Sino-Indian border conflict and then organized a thoroughgoing counterattack against the Chinese Party.

The counterattack was pressed with mounting intensity throughout November and the first week of December at the successive congresses of the Bulgarian, Hungarian, Czechoslovakian, and Italian Communist Parties, each of these meetings witnessing the dragooning of a still larger number of the CPSU's foreign adherents into joining a chorus of denunciation first against the Albanians and later against the Chinese as well. The climax was reached in early December with the extremely violent anti-Albanian and Chinese speeches delivered by the Czechoslovak and Italian Party secretaries, Koucky and Pajetta. There followed the elaborate state visit of Tito to the Soviet Union, where on December 12 the Yugoslav leader heard Khrushchev deliver an angry speech before the Supreme Soviet impugning Chinese motives and policies.

Mao's response was to open the sluice gates. In a succession of articles published between mid-December 1962 and March 1963, the CCP completed the process it had begun in 1956, gradually making explicit its past grievances and present ambitions. The Chinese Party called on the Communists of the world to revolt against the "baton" of the CPSU; it derided the Soviet "temporary majority"; and it challenged Moscow to convene a meeting of the world movement, thus repeating publicly the demand made privately early in 1962. At last, Peking attacked, by name, the CPSU and its leading adherents in the West as betrayers of the Revolution, simultaneously elaborating its 1960 thesis that the real focus of revolutionary struggle against "imperialism" was now in the underdeveloped areas of the world and that the real leader of this struggle was the Chinese Communist Party.

In response, Moscow began in February 1963 to intimate that its adversary was seeking to divide the revolutionary movement along geographical and racial lines—a complaint which was eventually expanded into thunderous denunciations of Chinese "racism," coupled with charges that Peking was attempting to isolate the European "socialist" states from the "national liberation movement" and to distort reality by claiming that imperialism's main conflict was now with the underdeveloped world (led by Peking's rhetoric) rather than with the bloc (led by Soviet military might).

In the meantime, however, it became clear early in 1963 that the Chinese public demand for a world Communist meeting had embarrassed the CPSU. In his January address to the East German Party congress, Khrushchev not only proposed—as if it were his own idea—a suspension of polemics between the two factions, but also acknowledged the existence of pressure on him from "some comrades" to convene a world conference. He insisted, however, that the time was not ripe for such a meeting. The Soviet leader then went on to declare that he had no desire to excommunicate the Albanians from the bloc and challenged the Chinese to treat the Yugoslavs similarly. But even while extending this olive branch to Mao, Khrushchev could not forbear striking him with it: the East German congress was made the occasion for new attacks on the Albanians and the Chinese, and the CCP delegate was interrupted and subjected to apparently well-organized booing and hissing, an unprecedented insult to the Chinese Party. Nevertheless, in February, the CPSU retreated a step further and sent Peking a fairly mild letter agreeing in principle to a world meeting and proposing bilateral talks to prepare for it.

The Chinese, however, were in no conciliatory mood and —as the Soviets later said—took Moscow's offer as a sign of weakness. They were by then in the midst of a vast new offensive against the CPSU and were vigorously proselytizing in every part of the world. To this end, the various CCP statements and editorials were being assembled in brochures and distributed in many languages. In February, the Chinese openly attacked Soviet influence at a Tanganyika meeting of the Afro-Asian Solidarity Organization (using racial arguments, the Soviets said), and at the same time they began setting up counterparts to the existing world front organizations, excluding the Soviets from participation in the new bodies.

After receiving the CPSU letter of late February, the Chinese Party responded with new public attacks of still greater violence. It was at this time that the CCP initiated the practice of publishing its current communications to the CPSU (forcing the Soviet Party to do likewise), so that even the exchanges between the two Central Committees, hitherto kept in the form of confidential letters, now became a part of the open polemic. Thus, in spite of a promise given on March 9 that it would desist from further public attacks, Peking clearly had no intention of doing so.

MOVING TOWARD SCHISM

This was dramatically demonstrated on the eve of a CPSU Central Committee plenum and three weeks before the scheduled opening of bilateral Sino-Soviet talks in Moscow, when the Chinese distributed in the Soviet capital—and subsequently throughout the rest of the world—the CCP letter of June 14, 1963, explicitly indicting Soviet domestic policies for the first time and announcing Peking's intention to split every Communist Party whose leadership continued to support Moscow. In this proclamation of Peking's "general line" for the Communists of the world, the Chinese also promised to anoint as honorary Marxists-Leninists all revolutionaries now *outside* the Communist movement who would carry their banner.

The Soviet leadership now reacted forcefully. The Chinese officials who had distributed the CCP letter in the Soviet Union were formally expelled, and after the Central Committee had pondered its course at the mid-June plenum, the Soviet case against the CCP was placed before the world in the form of a CPSU "Open Letter" released on July 13. A highly emotional speech delivered by Khrushchev six days later, on July 19, made it clear that he regarded the Chinese action as nothing less than an attempt to subvert his position at home and abroad.

Meanwhile, CPSU and CCP representatives opened their scheduled bilateral talks in Moscow, but even as the talks ground on toward eventual fruitless suspension, the Soviet government concluded a partial nuclear test-ban agreement with the United States on terms which it had previously rejected. Throughout the summer and autumn Soviet propaganda heavily exploited this agreement in an effort to isolate the Chinese, who were placed in the vulnerable position of having to defend before world opinion their determination to acquire nuclear weapons and their refusal to adhere to the Test-Ban Treaty.

Sino-Soviet relations had now reached a point where both sides were caricaturing and attacking each other's leaders by name, and where both proceeded to publish statements revealing hitherto secret aspects of their dealings with each other since the beginning of the dispute. The Soviets spoke of Mao as a senile "Trotskyite" tyrant and racist who sought world war, who had made monumental blunders in domestic policy, and whose government maintained "concentration camps" and massacred minority peoples, forcing them to seek haven in the USSR. The Chinese, in turn, characterized Khrushchev as a cowardly traitor allied with "imperialism" who was striving to restore capitalism in the Soviet Union and to undermine Marxism-Leninism throughout the world.

In September-October 1963 there were reports in the Western press, supported circumstantially by hints in Soviet propaganda, which suggested that the CPSU was almost reconciled to the consequences of a schism and was now considering the convocation of a world Communist meeting at which the Chinese and their supporters would be called upon to recant their factional activity or depart. In late October, however, the CPSU—apparently again under pressure from members of its own camp—temporarily abandoned this intention and instead began calling once again for an end to public polemics.

The CCP, however, would not relent, and by late January 1964 Peking had begun to announce formal recognition of pro-Chinese factions which had rebelled and seceded from the established Communist Parties of such countries as Ceylon, Peru, Belgium, and Switzerland as *the* official Communist Parties in those countries. These ominous organizational measures were followed in early February by a new Chinese pronouncement— the most outspoken to date—which proclaimed Peking's intention to recognize and support such "revolutionary" Communist Parties everywhere.

The formalization of the worldwide Communist schism had now begun.

✪ Sino-American Relations:
The Confrontation of Two Great Powers

[*We are indebted for much of the material used in this introduction to chapters from the late Robert Blum's study of United States China policy, made available to us in manuscript form.*]

UNITED STATES relations with China are of more immediate concern to Americans than most of the other subjects treated in this reader. Again and again people ask: What should our China policy be? We have often been told that there is some special emotional relationship between America and China, going back to the days of the China trade and the missionaries. There is some truth to this, particularly if one contrasts American interest in Russia with that in China. During the height of the Cold War there was great public interest in Russia but mostly in the form of a curiosity to know what the fatherland of Communism was like. As Russia opened up wider and the news spread of its embourgeoisement, public interest began to wane. On the other hand, Americans have generally been curious about China as China, and not just as the second fatherland of Communism.

During the height of the McCarthy period many Americans thought that a Communist cancer was eating away at the body of China. Today the public is less concerned about Communism in China and once again about its "Chineseness"; travel films on China, for example, have been highly popular among American movie audiences. We would suggest a reason for the contrasting attitude toward Russia and China: Russia was traditionally a distant land, vaguely associated with Europe, and beyond the perimeter of American historical interests; China, on the other hand, was in many ways the westernmost point in the expansion of the American land. American movement has been from east to west, away from Europe toward the Pacific. America's territorial acquisitions, aside from continental North America and Puerto Rico, have been entirely in the Pacific: Hawaii, Samoa, Philippines, the islands of Oceania, and now Okinawa. In the period following the Civil War thousands of American missionaries and businessmen went westward, and China was one of their main targets. Accounts of life in China formed a major part of the vast missionary literature that appeared during the late nineteenth century in America (see Volume II). Whatever the anti-Oriental feeling on the West Coast, to the established upper and middle classes of New England and the Middle West, China appeared to be America's special responsibility in the world. Europe had its own destiny and Latin America was an area of economic and military interest, but China was a moral problem that America appeared to be uniquely destined to resolve.

Yet if this moral concern about China, reflected even today in earnest discussions about how we should relate to China, characterizes popular attitudes to China, it does not help explain what the relations between the United States and China actually were. As John K. Fairbank states in his classic work *The United States and China* (p. 249), "none of our ideas and attitudes about China can quite account for the facts of American policy there. Our diplomacy has had several other sources." Fairbank sees two stages in American Far Eastern policy. During most of the nineteenth century "the real American policy . . . was usually to acquiesce, sometimes querulously, in British policy." But in the last year of the nineteenth century the United States assumed a more independent policy known as the Open Door, which was essentially aimed at preventing any outside power from acquiring a dominant position in China. As long as there was a pluralism of foreign powers in China without any shattering infringement on China's sovereign rights, the United States felt that its interests in China would be ensured. The assumption by the United States of a more independent role in the Far East was, of course, tied in with the growth of America's military power in the Pacific. In substance, however, the policy's two stages had the same aims. England was historically opposed to any single power becoming dominant in Europe; she followed the same policy in the Far East. The growing congruence of British and American world histories is one of the major developments of the nineteenth and twentieth centuries. In the nineteenth century America became a participant in the British world empire. In the early twentieth century it lent its new power to pursuing that empire's pluralistic interests, that is, preventing any rival great power from arising and keeping the channels of the developing world market system open and free. In World War I the United States helped save Britain from the German threat. In World War II the United States saved the British Empire from a mortal onslaught coming from the West and the East. After World War II, as Dean Rusk indicates in his historical review of American policy on Vietnam (see pp. 581–587), America took over from Britain the responsibilities of world leadership.

America's oft-repeated concern about the territorial integrity of China and the need to make China into a modern nation rested on a deep conviction that China was so poor and backward that it would take decades and centuries before she could reach the levels of the great world powers, a conviction arising perhaps from the missionary writings of the period. China was portrayed as weak, degenerate, starving, disorganized, incapable of doing anything; so long as she was in this state, she remained prey for any avaricious nation, notably Germany, Japan, and Russia, seeking what wealth she had. A strengthened China would keep out the wolves but would also threaten no one. After all, the basic values of China were harmony, gentleness, and submission.

America's most serious involvement in the Far East since the arrival there of the first Americans resulted from the festering problem of Japanese expansionism. Even during the early years of the twentieth century, when relations with Japan were good, America interposed herself against Japanese expansionism. The Japanese occupation of Manchuria in 1931 marked a turning point in American Far Eastern policy, for there was no longer any doubt that Japan intended to make herself the dominant power in the Far East, and to achieve this dominance by conquering or at least forcing the submission of China. Pearl Harbor shocked Americans, but viewed in broader historical perspectives, it marked America's inevitable entry into armed conflict with Japan. It is difficult to believe that America would have allowed Japan to gain dominance in the Far East while beating down Nazi Germany together with all other powers who had Far Eastern interests, notably Russia and Britain.

When the war ended, America's supreme foreign-policy goals all appeared to have been achieved. True, Britain was enfeebled, but America's might stood behind her in peace as in war to prevent collapse. Moreover, America could now proceed to suggest a more reasonable arrangement of the British Empire: colonialism had to be replaced by national freedom and a true commonwealth of free and independent nations linked by the bonds of political and economic exchange. The United Nations arose as the dream of this new "one world." Germany and Japan had been so decisively smashed that their resurrection was out of the question. Russia had been devastated by the war and, despite Winston Churchill's warnings, did not seem to be in any position to make trouble.

China too was in shambles, but then she had been for a century. America extended to her the hand of friendship and material aid as she did to so many other shattered nations. China, however, had a particular problem: her dormant Civil War erupted only weeks after the conclusion of the war against Japan. To make peace between the two sides, the United States dispatched the Marshall mission to China, but it failed. American policy toward China at this time cannot be disassociated from an even more momentous development: the beginning of the Cold War between the United States and the Soviet Union.

By the spring of 1946 the world, still accustomed to the Soviet-American friendship of World War II, began to hear talk of an impending war between the two countries. In 1948 the Soviet Union and the United States had their first major confrontation over Berlin. In Greece and in the Philippines the United States became involved in civil wars against Communist insurgents. The threat was said to be Communist expansionism led by movements subservient to Moscow. There can be little doubt that the Soviet-American Cold War influenced American actions in China: When the Chinese Communists began to move closer to the Soviet Union, pressure was put on the American government to increase aid to Nationalist China to prevent her falling under Communist domination. (We refer the reader to the selections on the Civil War in Volume II on American involvement.) By July 1949, when the State Department White Paper on China was published, Secretary of State Dean Acheson charged: "The Communist leaders have foresworn their Chinese heritage and have publicly announced their subservience to a foreign power, Russia, which during the last fifty years under Czars and Communists alike, has been most assiduous in its efforts to extend its control in the Far East."

A relationship between the United States and Communist China began in the summer of 1949. The White Paper marked the transition from a period of commitment to the Nationalist government to a period when a new relationship had to be worked out with China. By the summer of 1949 Communist China was a reality, even though the new government was formally established only in October of that year.

Before we review the course of that relationship, let us take Acheson's statement and fit it into the traditional picture of American foreign policy in the Far East. America had just destroyed Japan and freed China from the fear of foreign domination; now, barely four years later, Russia appeared to have taken control of China through her chosen instrument, the Chinese Communist Party. What Britain and America had feared most for an entire century had come to pass. But who could say how secure the Communist hold on China was? Perhaps the new regime would be a transient phenomenon to be succeeded by a more palatable government. This line of thinking suggested one logical course of action: the U.S. should make every effort to shake the base of Communist rule in China. There was another line of thinking, however, which suggested that the Chinese Communists were not simply tools of Moscow, and that they were basically Chinese whose primary interests were those of China and not the international Communist movement. This line of thinking is reflected in words of Dean Acheson uttered in January 1950: "We must not undertake to deflect from the Russians to ourselves the righteous anger, the wrath, and the hatred of the Chinese people which must develop. . . . Anyone who violates the integrity of China is the enemy of China and is acting contrary to our own interest." Acheson said this when the serious concessions the Chinese had made to the Russians in Moscow were already known. The course of action following from this line of thought was quite the opposite of the first. If China was a potential Yugoslavia, then recognition and even potential support from America would have been the proper policy.

What Acheson and all of Washington wanted to know was, are they Chinese or are they Communist? In and out of Washington one found exponents of both sides: the old China-hands tended to take the position that the Chinese were Chinese; the rising specialists on international Communism saw the Chinese Communist movement as an appendage of the international Red conspiracy.

The White Paper of July 30, 1949, a detailed review of a century of American policy in China, closed the book on the past, but it was also a major policy document pointing to the future. Acheson made this clear in the last paragraph of his introduction:

> In the immediate future, however, the implementation of our historic policy of friendship for China must be profoundly affected by current developments. It will necessarily be influenced by the degree to which the Chinese people come to recognize that the Communist regime serves not their interests but those of Soviet Russia and the manner in which, having become aware of the facts, they react to this foreign domination. One point is, however, clear. Should the Communist regime lend itself to the aims of Soviet Russian imperialism and attempt to engage in aggression against China's neighbors, we and the other members of the United Nations would be confronted by a situation violative of the principles of the United Nations Charter and threatening international peace and security.

Acheson's point was clear: if Peking should move away from Moscow, she would find America receptive; if she moved closer to Moscow, she would find America hostile, even to the point of using armed force.

The White Paper caused an immediate reaction in China, and within the space of a month starting on August 14, Mao Tse-tung wrote five short pieces on it, filled with ridicule, anger, summations of Chinese humiliations over the previous century, accusations of insincerity, reminders that the United States had aided Chiang Kai-shek, and so on. There are a few thin strands in Mao's writing, however, which indicate that the Chinese Communists may not yet have finally committed themselves to an irrevocable course. In a farewell to the American Ambassador, John Leighton Stuart, Mao accused the United States of a global strategy intended to secure its Far Eastern flank so as better to deploy its forces in Europe, namely against Russia. But in contrast to some of his earlier writings on the global situation, he said very little about Russia. At one point, he noted that "some ties between the Chinese and American peoples still remain, and, through the efforts of both peoples, these ties in the future could develop to the point of 'very close friendship,' but because of the obstruction of reactionary elements in both China and America, these relationships, in the past and now, are being greatly hampered." One of the obstructions Mao had in mind came out when he brought up the issue of Canton (then still under Nationalist control), Taiwan, and the Nationalist naval blockade of the coast. He implied quite openly that America should cease all support to the "reactionary elements," *i.e.,* the Nationalists, who were still fighting the last few futile battles on the Mainland.

Once the remainder of the Mainland had fallen to the Communists, the great issue became Taiwan. Acheson appeared to demand that Mao make some sign of his independence from Russia. Mao appeared to say, First give us Taiwan. In the complex picture of "two-handed policies," there are two mysteries. First, why did the Chinese Communists not take Taiwan? The Nationalists were disorganized, the Taiwanese population remembered the bloody insurrection of 1947, and the Communists could have probably found enough junks in Fukien to transport a small army. The second relates to the matter of American disengagement from Taiwan. Acheson seemed at times to imply that the United States would not use armed force to interfere in the Chinese Civil War (then meaning a possible Communist attack on Taiwan). On the other hand, many leading Republicans were pressing the administration to use force to keep Taiwan out of Communist hands. The probable answer to these mysteries is, assuming the Communists had the capability to invade Taiwan, they were not sure what the Americans would do.

The Sino-American relationship was still ambivalent in the summer of 1949. But by that winter the Chinese had taken a firm position: they concluded an alliance with the Soviet Union. In January 1950, Washington recalled all American diplomats from China, and during the first half of 1950 the atmosphere changed both in China and in America. As Chinese friendship for Russia became more apparent, the United States adopted an increasingly harder line toward the new government of China. But more significant perhaps, in early 1950 the figure of Senator Joseph McCarthy appeared on the American political scene.

The Korean War put a final seal on the course of events from the summer of 1949 on. President Truman ordered the Seventh Fleet to neutralize the Taiwan Straits on June 27, 1950. From then on, Communist China lost all hope of regaining Taiwan without the acquiescence of the United States.

So far we have dealt mainly with American policy toward China. What about Chinese policy toward America? Before 1949 Chinese policy toward America was made by the Kuomintang. Despite frictions during the wartime period, Sino-American relations were cordial. Even during their anti-imperialist period before 1927, the Kuomintang was not particularly anti-American. But beginning in 1945 cordiality became dependence. The Kuomintang looked increasingly to America to save it from destruction, and after 1950 the Kuomintang government on Taiwan depended entirely on America for political and military survival: American military aid resurrected the Nationalist Army and still supports it today; American economic aid revived the economy of Taiwan. Since it is doubtful that the Kuomintang government on Taiwan can independently influence American policy toward China and since Taiwan's international position is so closely linked to the Sino-American relationship, we have felt that a separate treatment of relations between Taipei and Washington was not warranted in this reader.

Until the publication of the White Paper there were in effect, no state-to-state relations between the Chinese Communists and the United States. The Communists, of course, took

positions toward America, but in the absence of direct contact
with the United States, these positions were largely ideological.
It was only in the summer of 1949, when Americans and Chinese Communists began making probes at each other, that there
was the beginning of a relationship.

The Korean War brought the United States and China to
the brink of a shooting war. As United Nations forces were
being driven back by the Chinese, General MacArthur called
for an extension of the war to China. But Washington did not
concur with his proposals, and by the summer of 1951 cease-
fire negotiations had begun. Though a shooting war was averted,
the events pushed American policy toward China into an uncompromising position. The United Nations embargo against
North Korea and China was followed by Congressional legisla-
tion prohibiting all trade with China and threatening sanctions
against nations who violated it. The new China policy was then
clearly stated by Dean Rusk, then Assistant Secretary of State
for Far Eastern Affairs:

> We do not recognize the authorities in Peiping for what
> they pretend to be. The Peiping regime may be a colonial
> Russian government—a Slavic Manchukuo on a larger
> scale. It is not the government of China. It does not pass
> the first test. It is not Chinese. . . . We recognize the na-
> tional government of the Republic of China, even though
> the territory of its control is severely restricted. We believe
> it more authentically represents the views of the great body
> of the people of China, particularly their historic demand
> for independence from foreign control. That government
> will continue to receive important aid and assistance from
> the United States.

The new China policy appeared at first sight to threaten
intervention to bring about the collapse of the Peking government, an impression reinforced by the decision to "unleash
Chiang Kai-shek" taken in 1953 by the new Eisenhower Administration. In retrospect, however, we can now see it for what
it was: a policy of hostile containment. The United States had
indicated that the line running through the Taiwan Straits was
one of a series of demarcation lines running from Europe to
Eastern Asia, separating the Communist and non-Communist

worlds. Any movement across that line by whatever political or military means would be met with force. That doctrine remains in effect as of 1966, and is the basis of American policy in Vietnam.

The concrete expression of the policy of containment with hostility was a series of alliances ringing China: with Japan, Australia, New Zealand, South Korea, Formosa, and finally the setting up of the Southeast Asia Treaty Organization. Despite some statements, notably by Walter Robertson, Rusk's successor as Assistant Secretary of State for Far Eastern Affairs, that America was always ready to use armed force against China (January 26, 1954), general policy appeared to be to solve "the problem of the mainland of China . . . not through attack upon the mainland but rather by actions which would promote disintegration from within." The Chinese have for years alleged intrusions by American planes and ships, U-2 flights, landings of saboteurs, air drops of arms to dissident groups in China and in Tibet (notably the Khampas), support for the marauding armies of General Li Mi on the Yunnan-Burma frontier. It seems clear that a large part of these Chinese allegations are true. In the diplomatic arena the United States used all its power and influence to prevent the Peking government from entering the United Nations and any other world organization. The American press, still in the grip of the McCarthyite spirit, took an extremely hostile view toward Communist China. At a time when the American attitude toward China has softened, at least in words, and that of the Chinese has hardened, it would be well to remember the period of the early 1950s.

Late in 1954, when a defense pact was signed between Washington and Taipei, the split between America and Communist China seemed to have reached a new point of finality. But at Bandung in April 1955 Chou En-lai sounded a softer note from the Chinese side. He reiterated China's friendship for the American people, and said China did not want war with the United States and that China was prepared to enter into discussions with the American government to remove tensions in the Taiwan Straits. The United States responded by demanding that China first renounce the use of force in the Taiwan Straits before any meaningful negotiations could take place; this remained a standard American demand at the later diplomatic talks. In July 1955 the United States government proposed to the Chinese that talks which had been going on at a consular level be raised to the ambassadorial level. The Chinese accepted and from this grew the ambassadorial talks (first at Geneva and after September 1958 at Warsaw) which continue to this day. Although agreement was reached over some minor issues (*e.g.,* exchange of prisoners), the talks soon bogged down over the issue of Taiwan as both sides made demands which the other could not accept.

There can be no doubt that first steps toward an improvement of relations were taken in 1955 and 1956. But here again it appears that changes in Sino-American relations were a reflection of changing relations between the United States and the Soviet Union. The Geneva Accords of 1954 settled the Indochina war. In May 1955, the Austrian State Treaty was signed. The Bandung Conference, during which Chou En-lai made his first proposals for an improvement in Sino-American relations, had taken place in April 1955. The Summit Conference at Geneva that summer gave rise to the "Geneva spirit." And it was at this same time that the Sino-American ambassadorial talks began in Geneva.

By 1957 Sino-American relations worsened again, as the Chinese began to accuse the United States of plotting to create "two Chinas." The ambassadorial talks, suspended in December 1957, were not resumed until September 1958, in Warsaw, under the impetus of the worsening Quemoy crisis. That crisis served only to reveal the key issues in the conflict on both sides. The United States made clear to Chiang Kai-shek that it would prefer his withdrawing from the offshore islands and that he should abandon hope of using military force to return to the Mainland. In substance, the United States wanted a *de facto* "two Chinas" situation. Chou En-lai stated the Chinese position: the Sino-American conflict over Taiwan and the Chinese people's liberation of Taiwan were two separate matters. In other words, if the United States would accept the principle of withdrawal from Taiwan, then the actual matter of how Taiwan would rejoin the Mainland could subsequently be resolved. In fact, the Chinese, from that time on, have indirectly indicated that they would be willing to accept some autonomous status for the island as long as Peking's sovereignty was recognized.

The overtures made by Chou En-lai early in 1955 were also related to the new position China gained within the socialist camp, as we point out in our discussion of Sino-Soviet relations (see pp. 237–252). Thus, at that time, China was able to turn to full pursuit of her major national goals, notably the recovery of Taiwan. In 1949 and early 1950 the main issue between China and America was Taiwan and from 1955 until the early 1960s it remained the sole major issue of contention. During the 1957 ambassadorial talks the Chinese proposed cultural exchanges, presumably in the hope of improving relations to the point where America might make some concessions on the Taiwan issue. The Americans responded consistently with demands that the Chinese renounce the use of force in the Taiwan Straits. In its simplest terms, China demanded formal recognition by the United States of her sovereignty over Taiwan; America was intent on creating "two Chinas." For China, reunification was the paramount issue; for America, maintaining the historic lines of division between the Communist and the non-Communist worlds was the paramount issue.

Was there a change in the Sino-American relationship during the Kennedy Administration? Apparently not in the early years. The dominant Chinese line was that Kennedy's election had changed nothing, and if anything, references to Kennedy's "olive branch and the sword" policy were interpreted as meaning a harsher line toward China paired with a softer line toward the Soviet Union. Toward the end of Kennedy's Presidency, however, there were signs that American thinking on China policy was changing. The Cuban missile crisis had led to a new understanding with the Soviet Union, which later culminated in the Test-Ban Treaty of 1963. Now that a détente with the Soviet Union was under way, was Kennedy thinking of a similar approach toward China? The most tangible evidence of such a trend was the speech of Roger Hilsman, Assistant Secretary of State for Far Eastern Affairs, on December 13, 1963. Though delivered three weeks after Kennedy's assassination, it obviously reflected ideas that had been worked out before his death. There had already been a few actions which hinted at a changed policy. In the spring of 1962, when the Nationalists were threatening to use the economic crisis to attempt a landing, the American government reportedly informed the Chinese through the Warsaw channel that they would not favor such an attack (*New York Times,* June 27, 1962).

How far the new thinking had gone is difficult to say, particularly since Hilsman reaffirmed America's commitment to the Nationalists, and thus implicitly to a "two China" policy, anathema to Peking. Early in 1964, however, shortly after the Johnson Administration came to power, Hilsman resigned his position. It was just at that time that Washington was pondering a new and stronger commitment to Vietnam, in particular the possibility of bombing North Vietnam (*Newsweek,* March 9, 1964).

Not only did U.S. China policy remain unchanged, but a new and far more dangerous issue was added to the old one of Taiwan: Vietnam. Now, as became abundantly clear after the Tonkin Bay incident and the first bombings of North Vietnam in August 1964, the resolution of the Sino-American conflict was bound up with two issues.

The Sino-American conflict over Taiwan has been ideological as well as practical, thus making it virtually insoluble. With the exacerbation of the Vietnam war through American escalation, Vietnam has joined Taiwan as both an ideological and practical issue between China and the United States. The Chinese Communists obviously have an ideological image of America: "American imperialism," *i.e.,* an expansionist America seeking to control the non-Communist world and preparing to wage war against the socialist camp, first China and then Russia. But the Chinese have had this image for a long time and have not always let their foreign policy be narrowly determined by it. Moreover, they accept the distinction between theory and practice, hence, regardless of their fulminations about "American imperialism," it is likely that they would react to any significant American concession on Taiwan, one of the overriding issues of their practical national interest. (Symbolic of this ideological approach is the persistent use by the State Department and other American government agencies of "Peiping" instead of Peking.)

The American ideological picture of China is more complex and has changed over the years. In the early 1950s China was regarded as a "Slavic Manchukuo." In the late 1950s, as the image of a Soviet puppet waned, she turned into a stumbling giant, one which hopefully would fall into a "descending spiral," in the words of Joseph Alsop (the persistent old hope that maybe, after all, she would collapse). In the 1960s the American image of China began to assume a different shape. China was seen as an increasingly dangerous enemy, the new center of revolutionary Communism, and the source of subversive contagion, as Russia had been in earlier days. The current official American images of Russia and China are the reverse of what they were in the early 1950s, when Russia was the evil monster and China was bullied by it. Now it is a monstrous China which tries to deflect Russia from her embourgeoisement.

We are told that China is aiming at step-by-step domination of all of Asia. The Chinese have repeatedly denied that they have any expansionist interests in Southeast Asia, and point out that not a single Chinese soldier is stationed beyond China's borders. Washington, however, regards Chinese expansionism as the chief threat in Southeast Asia and has justified its Vietnam policy on those grounds. In the issue of "Chinese expansionism" we can see the reappearance of an old strain in American Far Eastern policy: allow no one nation to achieve dominance in Asia. Since Washington sometimes invokes its earlier policy against Imperial Japan to justify its present Far Eastern policy, the analogy is questionable. Expansionism means the gaining of control over other nations by military, political, economic, or other means. Imperial Japan used all means to gain control over China or parts of her territory. An examination of China's foreign policy toward the Southeast Asian nations from the mid-1950s to the present indicates a desire to create neutralist buffer zones. China has signed border agreements with Afghanistan, Pakistan, Nepal, and Burma (not to mention Mongolia, an ancient part of the Chinese Empire). Moreover, as U Thant has indicated, the Chinese have given no support to the insurgent movements still threatening the neutralist Burmese government. Finally, we might mention North Korea and North Vietnam, two Asian Communist countries ideally suited to become Chinese puppets: as of 1966 both countries have swung back toward a more pro-Soviet line. If this be Chinese expansionism, the record is dismal.

Although it appears difficult to make a persuasive case for "Chinese expansionism," Washington is apparently convinced that a new and powerful Far Eastern empire which aspires to control large parts of Asia is again emerging. For over half a century the aim of American Far Eastern policy has been to prevent this. American military power is rapidly building up in the Far East; one war is in progress, and a bigger one threatens. The historical framework of American foreign policy and China's legacy from the past bode ill for the future relationship between these two great countries.

In the preceding discussion we have traced the development of the Sino-American relationship to the present time. Following are two selections which state the American and the Chinese positions on the important issues between the two countries. The first selection (published in 1959), by Ralph N. Clough, an American diplomat of long service in China, states the major premises and positions of the United States government vis-à-vis China. He begins by stating that United States policy toward China is part of a global foreign policy aimed at containing Communism and is particularly bound up with the recognition that Eastern Asia is peculiarly vulnerable to Communist expansion, notably from Communist China. Clough speaks of "the ominous shadow of Communist China," and the aims of her leaders to extend revolution and subversion beyond her borders, by force if necessary. He describes United States policy as a reaction against this threat, and proceeds to outline the containment policy followed in Eastern Asia, a policy in which Taiwan occupies "territory vital to the defense of the area." If Taiwan were to fall, so would all remaining resistance to the Peking government on the part of Chinese inside and outside the Mainland, notably in the Overseas Chinese communities. Clough explores the "two China" policy proposals and concludes that it is not feasible, given "today's realities." He argues, in effect, for a continuation of United States policy toward China as it was in the mid-1950s: "In time, if we hold steadfast, we can confidently look forward to a relaxation of the pressures."

The second selection details an interview which Edgar Snow had with Chou En-lai late in 1960 on the subject of Sino-American relations. Snow notes that "Chou gave me the most comprehensive exposition of Sino-American problems and statement of China's policy yet offered in a public interview," and he notes further that "nearly all of Chou's arguments depend on the logic of nationalism, quite apart from communism." Chou argues strongly that the Chinese do accept and practice the idea of peaceful coexistence, and cites agreements which the Chinese concluded with their neighbors. He then proceeds to review the course of Sino-American relations, making it entirely clear that the crucial issue between the United States and China is Taiwan. Chou indicates that a major turning point in Sino-American relations came when the United States ordered the Seventh Fleet into the Taiwan Straits, thus changing an apparent policy of non-interference earlier advocated by Dean Acheson. He reports that the Chinese had warned the United States during the Korean War, through the Indian Ambassador, not to press on toward the Yalu River, but that the warning was disregarded. He observes that Chinese policy toward America began to change at the time of the Bandung Conference and that China made overtures to America to improve relations, but that the United States did not respond. Chou then proposes two courses of action by which the United States could improve relations: first, accept the principle of negotiations with the Peking government (which he spoke of elsewhere as bilateral talks); second, accept the principle of withdrawal from Taiwan. Once these are accepted, concrete details could be worked out. Chou's statement that "there is no conflict of basic interest between the peoples of China and the United States, and friendship will eventually prevail" strongly implies that in his view a solution of the Taiwan question would remove the major stumbling block between the two countries.

In reflecting on the course of Sino-American relations over the past decade and a half and looking at the positions presented by both sides, two conclusions can be drawn: first, until the escalation of the Vietnamese war, Taiwan was the major specific issue between the United States and China; second, both America and China saw Taiwan as part of a larger global picture—America saw it as part of a necessary defense perimeter against Communist expansion, China saw it as part of an American plan to secure control over the entire non-Communist world, with the aim of eventually starting hostilities against the Communist camp itself.

Given this interlocking of the global and the regional issues centering on Taiwan, it is not difficult to see why neither side could make any concessions. For China, more was involved than just securing the return of one of her provinces. An American concession on Taiwan would mean a change in America's entire military posture in the Far East and a guarantee to China that her national security would not be threatened by American attack. America has proclaimed many times that she has no intention of attacking China, yet the Chinese are understandably unconvinced as long as the ring of bases remains around them, and as long as Taiwan plays a major role in this defense perimeter. The same argument prevails in regard to America: as long as America remains committed to a strong military posture in Eastern Asia, the abandonment of Taiwan would be interpreted as undermining that posture.

As Clough implies, such a state of ambivalent uncertainty in the relations between China and America could have gone on for a long time. But, as we have already indicated, Vietnam has entered the picture and has added a new and dangerous element to the pattern of the Sino-American relationship.

RALPH N. CLOUGH *
United States China Policy

The basic premises which underlie the policy of the United States toward China are easily understood and generally accepted by the American people. They are: that the Soviet bloc, of which Communist China is a part, is engaged in a long-range struggle to destroy the way of life of the free countries of the world and bring about the global dominion of Communism; and that East Asia, where eight of the eleven countries are newly

* Ralph N. Clough, "United States China Policy," *Annals of the American Academy of Political and Social Science* (Philadelphia, 1959), pp. 21–28.

independent since World War II, is peculiarly vulnerable to the Communist offensive.

THE COMMUNIST THREAT

The Communist movement has taken full advantage of East Asia's vulnerability. Since 1945 it has seized control in territories where live 660,000,000 people, close to 70 per cent of the population of the area. Today Asian Communist armies totaling over 3,000,000 men, well equipped with Soviet weapons, many of their soldiers seasoned in battle in China, Korea, or Vietnam, pose a constant threat to their weaker neighbors. Communists are active throughout the non-Communist countries of the region, ranging in importance from the legally sanctioned, rapidly growing Communist Party of Indonesia to the proscribed, isolated infiltrators who are discovered from time to time in Taiwan or the Republic of Korea. Armed Communist aggression has been halted since 1954. The free countries of the area have made progress in reducing the internal Communist threat. Yet the ominous shadow of Communist power remains. No statesman or politician can omit it from his daily calculations. The writings of Lenin, Stalin, and Mao on the Communization of Asia stand as a constant reminder to the free countries of Asia that the struggle to maintain their freedom may be long and grim.

The giants of Asian Communism are the Chinese Communists. Rulers of 640,000,000 people and proud originators of the "classic type of revolution for colonial and semi-colonial countries," they lend encouragement, moral and material, to their sister Communist Parties. Their policy is, as Mao Tse-tung has declared, to "give active support to the national independence and liberation movement in countries in Asia, Africa, and Latin America." This "active support" has manifested itself in the form of armed aggression in Korea, provision of arms and supplies in Indochina, and less overt means of assistance elsewhere.

The Chinese Communists' demonstrated military strength, underwritten by the still more powerful USSR, inspires both fear and respect. Reports—frequently inflated—of their rapid industrial development evoke admiration among those ignorant of or unconcerned with the cost in human lives. Chinese Communist propaganda blankets the area. Even where it is prohibited in written form, the ubiquitous radio broadcast in the local language gets through. Peiping's "peoples' democracy" brings thousands of influential Asians to Peiping annually for red carpet treatment. Offers of trade and economic aid have provided an effective means of gaining or expanding a political toehold. Where diplomatic relations exist, contacts are multiplied, encouragement of the local Communist and Communist-front opposition facilitated, and the use of Chinese financial institutions such as the Bank of China for subversive purposes made possible. Overseas Chinese communities then come under the domination of pro-Communist elements. For, in the long run, the Chinese Communists are not interested in the development of good relations with existing governments and peoples. Their object is revolution and they promote it where and as it is possible without excessive risk, adapting their methods to local conditions. Their goal is to lead Asia to Communism. As the Peiping *People's Daily* declared on December 29, 1956, in an article prepared on specific instructions from the Chinese Communist Party's Politburo, "The issue is the future. However many twists and turns may await us on our forward journey, humanity will eventually reach its bright destiny—Communism. There is no force that can stop it."

An appreciation of the Chinese Communist revolutionary commitment is essential to an understanding of United States policy. There is ample evidence that we must deal, not with leaders whose aim is to promote the welfare of their people and live at peace with their neighbors, but with a group of men in power who are dedicated to extending revolution beyond their own borders, by force where necessary and feasible. As Liu Shao-ch'i phrased it in a book still regarded in Peiping as one of the Chinese Communist classics, "The most fundamental and common duty of Communist Party members is to establish Communism and transform the present world into a Communist world." With Mainland China now in their hands and with Communist allies in every country of East Asia, they are in a good position from which to promote what they consider to be the inevitable victory of Communism.

UNITED STATES POLICY

Our China policy has been, in part, a reaction to the hostile acts of the Peiping regime toward American citizens and American property. The American people have not forgotten the 142,000 casualties in Korea, the brutalities committed against American prisoners of war, the continued refusal to account for our personnel missing in Korea, the jailing and torture of American civilians in Communist China, the violation of the Chinese Communist commitment in September 1955 to release American civilians, four of whom are still held today, the confiscation of American property in China, and the indignities to which American officials were subjected. No other regime in modern times, not excepting other Communist countries, has demonstrated such violent, prolonged, and calculated hostility toward this country and its citizens. This grim record would, in itself, make it difficult to accept the Chinese Communist professions that they seek only "peaceful coexistence."

But the more fundamental reason why our policy has developed as it has lies in the threat, described above, of Chinese Communist aggression, direct and indirect, against its neighbors. United States policy in East Asia, as in other parts of the world, is aimed at promoting mutually beneficial progress in the free countries which can only take place so long as the Communist threat is neutralized. Therefore, our policy must, first, deter Communist military aggression; second, strengthen the economies and the internal security of the free nations; and, third, oppose any action which would contribute to the Chinese Communist power to conquer or subvert.

In order to deter Chinese Communist aggression, it is essential to maintain sizable ground forces in the immediately threatened areas: the Republic of Korea, Taiwan, and Vietnam. It would be risky to rely on nuclear retaliatory power alone to protect these areas. These countries gladly supply the soldiers and a portion of the other requirements for the forces necessary to defend themselves. But because Communist military power is so great, the forces must be far larger than the economies of the countries can support, and the United States makes up the difference. It is a cooperative and mutually advantageous arrangement. The East Asian countries achieve the self-respect derived from making the major contribution to their own defense, while the United States is relieved of the burden of maintaining equivalent forces for the defense of these territories and peoples, the conquest of which by Communist power would have serious implications for the security of the United States.

The Communists are deterred from military action not only by the United States-supported indigenous forces in the area but also by the knowledge that the United States has entered into security commitments with most of the free nations of East Asia. They know that we would consider any attack upon one of these nations as endangering our own peace and safety and that we would respond accordingly.

Behind the collectively created military shield which protects the free nations of East Asia from aggression, political, economic, and social progress is taking place. The United States through its mutual security programs has encouraged such progress by helping to maintain economic stability and contributing to economic development. From 1949 through fiscal year 1957, $3,737,000,000 was expended for these purposes, most of the total necessarily going to the three countries with the heaviest defense burdens. American assistance to police forces has contributed to the improved internal security in most of the countries of East Asia and the diminished Communist capability for creating disorder within these countries.

The fact that the Chinese Communists, deterred from further employment of military force, have resorted to a complex program of political action to achieve their ends, makes it more essential than ever that the United States oppose any action which would increase their prestige and influence. Their program relies heavily on convincing the people of each country that the United States is an unreliable ally and that Communist triumph is inevitable. Their task would be greatly facilitated were the United States to agree to the seating of the Chinese Communist regime in the United Nations, or should the United States itself recognize the Peiping regime, trade with it, or enter into cultural exchanges with it.

UNITED STATES SUPPORT
FOR THE REPUBLIC OF CHINA

An essential part of United States policy aimed at limiting the
external political effectiveness of the Peiping regime is our continued support of the government of the Republic of China as
the legitimate representative of the Chinese people. This government, which is recognized as the government of China by
forty-five countries, has diplomatic relations in East Asia with
Japan, Korea, the Philippines, Vietnam, and Thailand. Communist China has diplomatic relations with only Burma, Indonesia,
and Cambodia in the area. The government of the Republic of
China occupies territory vital to the defense of the area—the
loss of Taiwan to the Chinese Communists would gravely
threaten the Philippines to the south and Okinawa to the north.
It also stands as a symbol of freedom to the restive Mainlanders
under Communist dominion.

The accomplishments since 1950 on the island of Taiwan
and the smaller islands administered by the government in Taipei are in many respects a model of Asian-American cooperation. The Chinese government—taking advantage of a higher
proportion of experienced, capable administrators and technicians than are available in most East Asian countries, a largely
literate population (93 per cent of children of primary-school
age are now in school), and the rich resources of Taiwan—has
made effective use of United States military and economic aid
to progress in many fields. The armed forces—some 600,000
men—bear little resemblance to the disorganized, demoralized
units which managed to escape from the Mainland in 1949.
Since 1953, by means of a universal conscription system, the
average age of the troops has been brought down to twenty-six.
About one third of the forces is now composed of young Taiwanese draftees. The Republic of China's forces today, well
equipped, highly trained, with the fourth largest jet air force
in the Free World, and a small but efficient navy, are an important part of the free world deterrent force in the Far East.
On the economic side, gross national product increased 66 per
cent between 1950 and 1956, agricultural production 32 per

cent, and industrial production 132 per cent. One of the most successful land reforms in Asia has broadened the social base. The great extremes of wealth and poverty which existed on the Mainland are not present in Taiwan, and the standard of living is higher than that of any East Asian country except Japan and Malaya.

In recent years the Republic of China has made vigorous efforts to maintain its international position in the face of heavy Communist assaults upon it. During 1957 free China's diplomats reached agreement on the establishment of diplomatic relations with five countries with which it had previously not maintained diplomatic relations: Paraguay, Uruguay, Liberia, Saudi Arabia, and Jordan. Taipei has increasingly played host to free world leaders such as the Shah of Iran, the Premier of Turkey, and the Prime Minister of Japan, as well as many parliamentary and trade delegations.

The progress which has been made on Taiwan is still relatively little known, but it is more and more coming to be recognized. That is not to say that no problems exist. The undiminished Communist threat, the heavy strain resulting from military expenditures, the rapid growth of the population, the scarcity of funds for capital investment, and the discouragement felt by many Mainland Chinese at the continued domination of their homeland by Communism all impose their limitations. Nevertheless, the dominant note is activity and progress. The United States is not simply helping to support a military bastion in Taiwan, but ten million energetic, resourceful, resilient people, whose vigorous development and growing ties with the rest of the free world make them increasingly effective contributors to our common objectives.

Our policy toward the Republic of China has a vital bearing on the influential overseas Chinese communities, some ten million people scattered throughout Southeast Asia who are today divided in their allegiance and among whom there is continued strong resistance to efforts by pro-Communists to seize control. The Chinese Communists have directed their political activity particularly toward gaining control of overseas Chinese schools, newspapers, business organizations, and financial institutions. However, their failure to win general diplomatic recognition and oust the Republic of China from its international position has seriously hampered their efforts. Large numbers of business associations, banks, newspapers, and schools continue to look to Taipei as the temporary seat of the government of China and reject Peiping's efforts to assume that role. Particularly in the key field of education has Taipei scored striking successes, with more than eight thousand overseas Chinese studying in Taiwan's high schools and colleges as compared to fewer than one hundred seven years ago. If the United States and its Asian associates were to deny the right of the Republic of China to represent Chinese abroad and were to acquiesce in the claim of the Communist regime to do so, the resistance to Communism in the overseas Chinese communities could not long continue.

ARE THERE ACCEPTABLE ALTERNATIVES?

United States policy toward China has received strong support from the American people. They have been willing to assume the heavy burdens necessary in order to prevent further Communist aggression in East Asia and to promote the peaceful development of the free countries. There has also been general support for opposing acts which would enhance the prestige and influence of Communist China. Yet, there have been expressions of doubt as to the long-term validity of the policy. Critics do not usually attempt to prove that the policy to date has not served the interests of the United States reasonably well; they tend to concentrate on the alleged weakness of such a policy if continued into the indefinite future.

Of course, the future is obscure in East Asia, as it is in most of the rest of the world. It is not possible to predict with any degree of precision what the shape of the future will be if we continue generally along our present lines or, alternatively, if we should effect radical changes in our policy. However, when a given policy has been reasonably effective, the burden of proof must rest on the proponents of change that an acceptable alternative exists and that this alternative would be a better instrument for accomplishing our aims.

It is not feasible here to examine the many possible permutations of a policy toward China and their probable effects. One general category of proposal, probably the one which has at-

tracted most attention, will be examined. This is the so-called
"two Chinas" concept. There are many variants of this concept,
but in essence it is intended to provide a formula whereby the
Chinese Communist regime would obtain general international
recognition and seating in the United Nations as the representative of the Chinese people, while the government of the Republic
of China would be reduced to representing only the people of
Taiwan and the Pescadores, either as a new independent state or
under some form of United Nations trusteeship.

The "two Chinas" concept is designed as a means of obtaining international sanction for the perpetuation of the present
division of the Chinese people into two separate political units.
One glaring flaw in the scheme, which invalidates the claim of
"realism" advanced for it, is the fact that it has been vehemently
denounced by both Peiping and Taipei. No Chinese leader on
either side has given the slightest indication that it would be
acceptable.

"TWO CHINAS" CONCEPT VIS-À-VIS
TODAY'S REALITIES

In the absence of any disposition on the part of the Chinese
themselves to accept the "two Chinas" concept, it becomes academic to discuss the advantages and disadvantages of applying
the concept in practice. It becomes necessary to assume, at the
very least, that the Chinese Communists would agree to the
establishment of diplomatic relations with the United States,
despite our continued maintenance of close relations with Taipei, and that they would join the United Nations, despite the
continued presence of representatives from Taiwan. It is also
necessary to assume that the United States would take this step
over the vehement protests of its friend and ally, the government
of the Republic of China, and that we were willing to risk the
consequences of what to that ally and other allies in the area
would appear a betrayal for the sake of appeasing the Chinese
Communists.

The fact that the requisite assumptions appear fanciful
when held up against today's realities has not prevented advocates of the "two Chinas" concept from discussing its advan-

tages and disadvantages as if it were a practicable policy now or in the near future. Therefore, a brief commentary on the pros and cons may be in order here, bearing in mind that the essential conditions for placing such a policy into effect do not exist today.

The arguments for the "two Chinas" concept fall generally into two categories: (1) that it is "realistic" to establish formal diplomatic relations with those in actual control of Mainland China and that it is inevitable anyway, sooner or later; and (2) that there are definite advantages to be gained from such a step, such as reducing tension in the Far East, influencing the Chinese Communist leaders, driving a wedge between Moscow and Peiping or improving the relations between the United States and those Asian countries where a vocal element of the population is critical of present United States China policy.

Neither so-called realism nor alleged inevitability constitutes a persuasive argument for the "two Chinas" concept. The final test must be whether the acceptance of such a concept would serve the enlightened self-interest of the United States. It is realistic to deal, when necessary, with those actually governing an area. We dealt with the Japanese administrators of Manchuria for years, but never recognized "Manchukuo." We have dealt with the Chinese Communists in Korea, and have held eighty-three meetings with them in Geneva and Warsaw at the ambassadorial level, but we have not considered it necessary nor desirable to accord them the advantages which would accrue from diplomatic recognition. As to the inevitability argument, it smacks strongly of the Communists' own thesis that their system of government will endure forever and will inevitably take over the world. They may well consider recognition of the Peiping regime by the United States inevitable (and if they do, it would be naïve to expect them to make any concessions in order to bring it about), but there is no need for the United States to succumb to this argument.

EFFECTS OF DIPLOMATIC CONCESSIONS
TO COMMUNIST CHINA

There remain the arguments that there are positive advantages to be gained from establishing our diplomats in Peiping and bringing Communist China into the United Nations.

Would recognition of Red China by the United States, under the conditions mentioned, lead to a reduction of tension in East Asia? Only if one were to make the unrealistic assumption that the Communists would thereupon give up their designs on the free countries of the area. It is certainly far more likely that the Chinese Communists would take advantage of the severe blow to the people of free China and the sudden enhancement of their own power and influence to redouble their subversive activities directed toward Taiwan and the other free peoples of East Asia. Communists and pro-Communists in each of these countries would exploit to the utmost this telling evidence that even the United States was bowing to the inevitable and recognizing Communism as the wave of the future. As Communist power grew throughout the area, tension would rise, not decrease.

Would seating in the United Nations exert a beneficial effect on the Chinese Communists and make them easier to deal with? It would be disastrous to the United Nations system and to the role of the United Nations as a guardian of the collective security to seat a regime which stands condemned as an aggressor by that very institution, which defies the United Nations itself and refuses to admit its competence to play any part in Korea. For Red China to be seated under these circumstances would prove to the Chinese Communist leaders the effectiveness of their present strategy, rather than temper their hostile attitude toward the free world.

Would recognition of the Peiping regime by the United States and its seating in the United Nations contribute to the weaning of Peiping from Moscow? There is no evidence that the bonds between the two chief Communist powers are so weak that a broadening of Chinese Communist diplomatic contacts with the free world could have any perceptible effect on them.

On the contrary, the evidence available to us since the Hungarian revolt indicates that the two powers' primary concern is to maintain the solidarity of the Communist bloc and that their ties today are probably as strong or stronger than they have ever been. They view the world through the same ideological frame and hold common objectives. So long as Communist China remains heavily dependent on the Soviet Union for its military strength and so long as Mao and his lieutenants remain satisfied that "the east wind is prevailing over the west wind," only the gravest sort of crisis between Peiping and Moscow could lead to significant alienation.

It is hard to conceive of any inducement the free world could offer which would at this time attract Mao toward what he regards as the losing side in the world struggle. Only growing disillusionment at the top as a result of the failure of Communism to make further headway in free world areas, to resolve the problems of intrabloc relationships and to overcome internal problems in China could create the conditions favorable to such a shift. Far from promoting such disillusionment, recognition of Communist China by the United States or seating it in the United Nations would be much more likely to confirm to the Peiping leadership the correctness of their present course and the advantages of continued close cooperation with the USSR.

Would recognition of Red China by the United States and our support for its seating in the United Nations improve our relations with the neutralist countries of Asia? It is true that there are many advocates of such action in these countries. However, most such advocates would not be satisfied unless the United States also agreed to withdraw its support from the Republic of China and permitted the ten million Chinese in Taiwan to be taken over by the Chinese Communists, a disastrous betrayal of a free people which few Americans would accept. Whether any significant improvement in our relations with these countries would result from the lesser step of embracing the "two Chinas" concept is questionable. United States policy is not a major issue affecting the state of our relations with the neutralist states. Whether these relations are good or bad depends far more upon other issues much closer to home than how the United States regards China. On the other hand, in such countries as the Philippines and Thailand, and even more so in

Korea, Vietnam, and the Republic of China, under the immediate threat of Communist armed might, United States China policy is a vital issue. We could not adopt the "two Chinas" concept without causing the most serious and far-reaching repercussions in these countries. We certainly have much more to lose by demoralizing our close allies, who live under the shadow of Communist guns and whose military strength is vital to the maintenance of the Free World position in East Asia, than we could possibly gain in the more distant areas where the China problem is not a matter of life and death to the people.

THE FUTURE

Looking toward the future, the American people would like to see an early settlement of some kind, a relaxation of the tension between the free world and the Communist world, so that the threat of war would be diminished and a larger share of our resources could be turned to the uses of peace. But in East Asia, as elsewhere, there is little prospect that this will happen so long as the Communist movement has the will and the power to seek further accessions to its empire. The Chinese Communists hope that we will tire of the continual struggle and the cost of supporting our friends of the Free World against their pressures. They hold that the United States will inevitably, sooner or later, give in. But there are currents within the Communist world which, far from sweeping Communism on to inevitable victory, are sapping the strength of the Communist system. In time, if we hold steadfast, we can confidently look forward to a relaxation of the pressures. In the meantime, we must cleave staunchly to our friends and resist any move which would increase the ability of those hostile to us to do them harm.

Our China policy, although it has so far served us well, is not, of course, a perfect instrument. There are doubtless many improvements which can be made. The policy, like other policies, is under constant review to see where it could be improved. But proposed improvements must be able to meet the tests of practicability and realism and must clearly serve the long-term interest of the United States.

EDGAR SNOW *
Chou En-lai and America

There is no such thing as a "pro-foreign" Chinese, and even if there were, one would still have to expect a continuing ideological antagonism against the United States among Communists for many years to come. What is probably not comprehensible from abroad is the extent to which even anti-Communist Chinese support Peking on any *nationalistic* issue. The fact that the United States has for a decade followed a policy of armed intervention in China's affairs, that this policy has served to discredit influential Chinese on the Mainland once friendly to America and has added great force to Peking's ideological attacks on imperialism—which might otherwise seem as obsolete to Chinese intellectuals as they do to Mr. Nehru—is little understood by those Americans most anxious to bring about the downfall of the Communists.

I shall later have something of my own to say about the contribution which China's policies have made to the embitterment of Sino-American relations. Here I merely act as a reporter, whose job it is accurately to record answers, not to lead a debating team.

Premier Chou considered that my first seven questions were all related and said that he would answer them in a general discussion of the background of Sino-American problems involved, and then in terms of solutions. (These interviews took place on August 30, 1960. The italics are added to express Premier Chou's original emphasis.) The seven questions, in slightly condensed form:

(1) Would China take the initiative in summoning a conference to discuss Chou En-lai's proposal for a non-

* Edgar Snow, *The Other Side of the River, op. cit.,* pp. 86–92.

aggression pact to create a nuclear-free zone in the Pacific? (This proposal was first publicized by Nikita Khrushchev in 1958 and in March of that year supported by Chinese Foreign Minister Ch'en Yi.)

(2) What could be the main points covered by such a pact?

(3) If the President were to invite Chou to the United States to discuss such a pact, would he accept?

(4) Would China welcome any envoy the President might designate to visit Peking for the same purpose?

(5) Would it be possible for China to sign such a pact as long as the United States pact with the Taiwan regime existed?

(6) If China was resolutely opposed to the extension of nuclear arming of the world, why was she striving to make nuclear weapons?

(7) It was said that China considered that successful negotiation with the United States would be possible only when China possessed the means of manufacturing nuclear weapons. Please comment.

"The [Pacific Peace Pact] proposal I made at the National Day reception of the Swiss Embassy" [on August 1, 1960], Premier Chou began, "was not a new one. But to mention it again in August had its new significance. Western opinion has been spreading rumors to the effect that China has given up the policy of peaceful coexistence.

"As one who follows political developments in this country, you must have noted that China signed treaties of peace and friendship with three Asian countries this year. A treaty of friendship and mutual nonaggression was concluded with the Union of Burma in January. A treaty of peace and friendship was signed with the Kingdom of Nepal during my visit to that country in April. In August, when Vice-Premier and Foreign Minister Ch'en Yi visited Afghanistan, a treaty of friendship and mutual nonaggression was concluded with the Kingdom of Afghanistan. These add up to three already, not to mention the earlier treaty of friendship with the Mutawakelite Kingdom of the Yemen and the joint statements on peaceful coexistence with India, Indonesia, Cambodia, and Ceylon.

"The main content of the three treaties this year is based on the Five Principles of peaceful coexistence, which China has all along advocated. You know these principles: (1) Mutual respect for sovereignty and territorial integrity; (2) mutual nonaggression; (3) noninterference in each other's internal affairs; (4) equality and mutual benefit and (5) peaceful coexistence.

"A peace pact of mutual nonaggression among the countries of Asia and those bordering on the Pacific involves the questions of Sino-Soviet relations and of relations between the four countries of China, the USSR, Japan, and the U.S.A.

"It is inconceivable that a peace pact can be concluded without diplomatic relations between China and the United States.

"It is also inconceivable that there can be diplomatic relations between China and the United States without a settlement of the dispute between the two countries in the Taiwan region.

"These are two important facts. That is why I said that prolonged efforts were necessary to realize this proposal. Since prolonged efforts are required, why have we repeatedly made this proposal? It demonstrates that the Chinese people and the Chinese government desire to settle disputes between China and the United States through peaceful negotiations, and are opposed to the U.S. policy of aggression against China. But I would like first to cite one proof of this. After the liberation of China the U.S. government declared that it would not interfere in the internal affairs of China, and that Taiwan was China's internal affair. [Dean] Acheson said so in the White Paper and it was also admitted by Truman later. As a matter of fact, Taiwan was restored to the then government of China in 1945, after the Japanese surrender. It was taken over and administered by the then Governor of Taiwan, General Ch'en I, who was later killed by Chiang Kai-shek.

"After war broke out in Korea in June 1950 Truman changed the policy and adopted a policy of aggression toward China. While sending troops to Korea the United States at the same time dispatched the Seventh Fleet to the Taiwan Straits and exercised military control over Taiwan. *Beginning from that time the United States started new aggression against China.* The Chinese government sternly condemned United

States aggression in Taiwan and the Taiwan Straits. Shortly afterward United States troops in Korea showed the intention of crossing the 38th Parallel and pressing on toward the Yalu River [China's frontier], and, because of this, the Chinese government could not but warn the United States government that we would not stand idly by if United States troops crossed the 38th Parallel and pressed on toward the Yalu River. This warning was conveyed to the United States through the Indian Ambassador. The United States government disregarded this warning and United States troops did indeed cross the 38th Parallel and press on toward the Yalu River.

"The Chinese people could only take the action of volunteering support to Korea in its war of resistance against the United States. But this action *was not taken until four months after the United States stationed its forces in the Taiwan Straits and exercised military control over Taiwan*, and not until United States troops had crossed the 38th Parallel and approached the Yalu River. Truman made many statements during these four months to explain this act of aggression against Korea; of course, they were futile. Moreover, he could not justify aggression in Taiwan, nor the stationing of United States forces in the Taiwan Straits. Furthermore, Truman failed to heed China's warning conveyed through the Indian Ambassador.

"After two years of negotiations an armistice was at last reached in Korea. *By 1958 Chinese troops had withdrawn completely from Korea*. But up to now United States troops are still hanging on in South Korea and will not withdraw. Moreover, the United States is still controlling Taiwan with its land, sea, and air forces, and the United States Navy and Air Force are still active in the Taiwan Straits. Isn't this the best proof that the United States government continues to pursue policies of aggression and war toward China? It is not necessary to cite in addition the numerous military bases maintained by the United States in Asia and the many aggressive military pacts which have China as their main target. *China, on the other hand, has not a single soldier abroad, and the treaties it has concluded with Asian countries are all treaties of peace and friendship*.

"Though the United States committed these acts of aggression against China, *would we use force to settle disputes with*

the United States? No! I declared already during the Bandung
Conference in 1955 that the Chinese people were friendly to
the American *people* and the Chinese government was willing
to sit down and enter into negotiations with the United States
government to discuss existing disputes between the two countries, though the two countries had not recognized each other
and had no diplomatic relations. This proposal of ours resulted, through the good offices of Britain, in ambassadorial
talks between China and the United States which started
August 1, 1955, in Geneva.

"In order to create a favorable atmosphere China released,
before the talks began, eleven so-called 'prisoners of war,' following the mediation of Krishna Menon and UN Secretary-
General Dag Hammarskjöld's visit to Peking. Why are they
referred to as so-called 'prisoners of war'? Because they were
not captured on the Korean battlefield. With the exception of
a few who chose, of their own will, to stay behind, all prisoners
of war captured on the Korean front were repatriated after the
armistice. Later, among those who stayed behind, some returned
also of their own will. But the eleven so-called 'prisoners of
war' were on a United States plane which intruded into China's
air space, and were captured after their plane was hit. Both
China and the United States had declared that the Korean War
was restricted to Korea and did not extend to China. This plane
was shot down in China. So China did not recognize them as
'prisoners of war.' Nevertheless, China released them—to create
a favorable atmosphere for the ambassadorial talks at Geneva.

"That was the end of the so-called 'prisoners of war' issue.

"Besides the so-called 'prisoners of war,' however, there
were two other categories of United States nationals in Chinese
prisons. First were United States citizens, guilty of such crimes
as sabotage and espionage, or who had in other ways violated
the laws of China. Since 1955, we have released twenty-five
such United States criminals when their terms were fully served
or were granted clemency and released ahead of time for good
behavior. One of the twenty-five chose to remain in China after
his release. Of this category only three are now still serving
sentences in China.

"There are two United States nationals in Chinese prisons
of another category—a very special one. They are airborne

secret agents sent by the United States to China, namely, the very famous Downey and Fecteau. Allen Dulles of the United States Central Intelligence Agency could give you all the details, but perhaps he wouldn't want to give the information in such detail as we would. In early 1955, when Hammarskjöld came to Peking to discuss the question of the United States nationals in Chinese prisons, even he found it inconvenient to bring up their case for discussion. These two were in no way related to the Korean War, but were on a mission of pure espionage and secret-agent activity. If you are interested, I could show you some portions of the notes of my talks with Hammarskjöld for your reference. The notes have never been published.

"Five years have elapsed since the start of the Chinese-United States talks in August 1955. At the very outset, we proposed that disputes between China and the United States, including the dispute between the two countries in the Taiwan region, should be settled through peaceful negotiations, without resorting to the use or threat of force. The United States blocked all news of this proposal, but China later published it. Why did [John Foster] Dulles reject it? Because Dulles realized that reaching such an agreement implied that the next step would be discussions on how and when United States armed forces were to withdraw from Taiwan and the Taiwan Straits.

"We hold that the dispute between China and the United States in the Taiwan region is an international question; whereas military action between the Central Government of New China and the Chiang Kai-shek clique in Taiwan is an internal question. The United States has maintained that the two questions are inseparable. We hold that they can and must be separated. Since it has been possible for China and the United States to hold ambassadorial talks in Geneva and Warsaw, talks can also be held at the same time between the Central Government of China and the Chiang Kai-shek clique. The former is an international question while the latter is an internal question. Parallel talks can be conducted and solutions reached separately.

"In the talks between China and the United States, agreement on principle must after all be reached first before concrete issues can be settled. The two points of principle on which agreement should be reached are:

"(1) All disputes between China and the United States, including the dispute between the two countries in the Taiwan region, should be settled through peaceful negotiations, without resorting to the use or threat of force; and

"(2) The United States must agree to withdraw its armed forces from Taiwan and the Taiwan Straits. As to the specific steps on when and how to withdraw, they are matters for subsequent discussion. If the United States government ceases to pursue the policy of aggression against China and of resorting to threats of force, this is the only logical conclusion which can be drawn.

"This is the crux of the dispute between China and the United States. The activities and direction of United States policy toward China have been aimed at manufacturing 'two Chinas.' In this respect, both the Republican and the Democratic Parties aim at the same thing. . . . This scheme would probably be opposed not only by Mainland China, but also by the Kuomintang in Taiwan and the Chinese in Taiwan. Therefore such an approach would lead nowhere, but in the solution of Sino-U.S. relations it would tie things up in knots.

"We believe that a solution to Sino-U.S. relations will ultimately be found; it is only a question of time. But there is one point: if the United States does not give up its policy of aggression and the threat of war against China, no solution is possible. We do not believe that the people of the United States will allow their government indefinitely to pursue such a policy. *There is no conflict of basic interest between the peoples of China and the United States, and friendship will eventually prevail."*

I asked Chou whether the two principles he spoke of had been the topic of discussion for a long time in the Sino-American ambassadorial talks held at Warsaw.

THE PREMIER: Yes. The first principle was put forward by China at the end of 1955. The second principle was put forward in the autumn of 1958 at Warsaw.

QUESTION: Does the second principle include as well the question of the time and manner of the withdrawal from Taiwan?

ANSWER: The United States government must first agree on the principle before concrete matters can be taken up.

Q: The United States government has insisted that no agreement is possible without a declaration from the Chinese government to refrain from the use of force in the Taiwan area, has it not?

A: The United States government has insisted that the United States and Chiang Kai-shek have "the inherent right of individual and collective self-defense" in the Taiwan region. In other words, it would also legalize United States aggression in Taiwan and the Taiwan Straits, and create the objective reality of "two Chinas." This is opposed by the entire Chinese nation. Suppose someone occupied the Hawaiian Islands and dispatched a fleet to the waters between the mainland of the United States and the Hawaiian Islands, or supposing someone occupied Long Island and sent a fleet to the straits north of Long Island, how would the people of the United States feel in such a situation? You can thus imagine how the Chinese feel. Did not the people of the United States rise up against the Japanese after Pearl Harbor was attacked? . . .

For some minutes a white-jacketed waiter had been hovering discreetly at the door of the salon. When he had finished speaking, Chou looked around and saw him.

"Hungry?" he asked me.

Here was at least one concrete matter we were able to settle at once. I followed him into the dining car, where a table was set for about twenty guests—and one historian.

II. China Today:
The 1960 s

෫ᢒ In Part I of this volume we presented material on the basic framework of the People's Republic. In this part we shall look at the internal and external problems of China today. By "today" we mean, broadly speaking, a period of time which began in 1961. The winter of 1960–1961 was a turning point: the economic crisis was at its worst, Sino-Soviet relations had deteriorated, and China's leaders decided on a radical change in domestic policy. The year 1961 was a turning point on the international front as well. The Kennedy Administration came to power, and within six months announced its firm commitment to fight Communism in South Vietnam, thus paving the way for the formation of a new and grave issue between China and the United States.

In the darkest hours of crisis in January 1961, the Central Committee of the Chinese Communist Party met in plenary session and decided on a far-reaching switch in domestic policy. By the fall of 1960 Peking had realized that it again faced a disastrous crop failure; industrial production had fallen; food was everywhere in short supply; the already limited transportation system was crippled by bottleneck after bottleneck. The people, tired and overworked, lost confidence in the Party's magic. Liu Shao-ch'i had just returned from Moscow, where the Chinese had been sharply rebuffed in their dispute with the Russians. The Chinese Communists, as so often in the past, had once again come close to disaster.

Instead of clamping down on the grumbling discontent, the Chinese leaders loosened controls: Peasants were given greater freedom to grow what they wanted; officials and managers were relieved of bothersome ministerial interference and Party haranguing, and instructed to use whatever means they could to rescue the economy; students were allowed to devote more of their time to study rather than physical labor. The leaders took another risky step when they ordered a "rectification" movement against the lower-echelon Party cadres who

just a few years earlier had been the driving force behind the
Great Leap Forward. The gamble paid off: the peasant turned
with alacrity to his private plots and within a few years supplied
the cities once again with vegetables and meat in abundance;
industrial production picked up; the quality of education again
rose, and the pace of scientific and technological development
was resumed.

Over the last five years the Chinese have followed a sensible approach to economic problems. They have generally retained the decentralization introduced in 1958, though they
strengthened regulatory controls, evident particularly in the
monetary field. Monetary stabilization has always been of prime
concern to the leaders who well remember the inflation they had
to combat when they came to power. One of the first measures
undertaken in 1961 when they changed their economic policy
was a strengthening of the banking system. Loosening of controls and the allowance of a free market brought about infla-
tionary dangers, but through a sophisticated price policy the
Chinese Communists were able to prevent the development of a
serious inflation. So important has the regulation of money and
credit become in China that the leading economic policymaker
in the government today seems to be Li Hsien-nien, Minister of
Finance since 1954.

The Chinese, in contrast to the Russians of Stalin's day,
have taken the position that all three major sectors of the economy—agriculture, light industry, and heavy industry (this is the
order in which they are listed in Chinese publications)—must
develop simultaneously. The government has made significant
capital investments in agriculture, though largely in a few select
regions: electrification, mechanized water works for pumping
and irrigation, and chemical fertilizers. Great attention has been
given to peasant education, though usually under the cloak of
a politically oriented "socialist education movement." Agricultural output has improved steadily. The increasing number
of foreign tourists to China report no signs of food shortage in
the cities, and they gain the same impression in those rural areas
they have visited. China continues her grain-purchase programs
from abroad, using scarce foreign exchange for the purpose.
Economists are generally in agreement that China gains more

this way than by overloading her transportation system with bulk-food shipments from distant inland areas to the coastal cities.

The continuing stress on agriculture indicates that long-term Chinese economic strategy sees China's industrialization as directly tied up with the resolution of the agricultural problem. China neither wants to nor can rely on foreign aid as a source of capital. Ultimately her sole source of capital is agriculture, whose modernization will be a slow and arduous task, which means that she must be satisfied with a moderate rate of industrial growth for a long time to come. The Chinese attitude to agriculture gives a clue to Chinese thinking in general: they see development as a matter of decades of intensive effort. In 1958 Mao Tse-tung may have thought that he would live to see the day of China's economic greatness. It is apparent that he no longer thinks so.

Despite the absence of official data, we know that Chinese industry has made a remarkable comeback after the Great Leap Forward. New types of strategic industries have been born in such fields as aircraft and nuclear weapons. The Chinese appear able to produce a surprisingly large range of machine tools, including precision instruments. Light industry is providing an increasing output of both producer and consumer goods. Despite her still-limited foreign trade, China is beginning to exhibit manufactured products of a scope that indicate that sometime in the not too distant future she will be able to compete with some of the more advanced industrial nations in the export market.

This sensible approach to economic development contrasts with the official Chinese ideological pronouncements that have defended the wisdom of the Great Leap Forward. Several times during the past years talk about a "leap forward" has appeared in China, but nothing happened. Today, during the "cultural revolution," the anti-Party elements are bitterly assailed for having reviled the Great Leap Forward. Only the future will tell whether economic theory and practice will continue to remain separate.

Rather than try to divine the future, let us see what the present trends are. What little we know indicates that the Third Five Year Plan is building on economic policies pursued during the last five years, with a stepped-up rate of growth. Why haven't the Chinese said more about the Third Five Year Plan? We must remember that economic plans are strongly influenced by political factors and other exogenous variables over which the economic policymakers may have no control. One of the critical exogenous variables, we suggest, is war. Obviously, if the Vietnam war spreads, economic policies will take a different turn. A second variable is the political situation within China. Significant changes in the power structure could have a major influence on economic policies. As of the summer of 1966 there have been no signs of major changes in current economic policies.

Persuasive signs that the Chinese have assumed a peace-time economy can be seen in the nature of their trade patterns. Their trade relations with the non-Communist world have been expanding rapidly in the last years, particularly with the advanced industrial nations of Europe and with Japan. Since all of the imports from these countries come to China by sea, war and a consequent blockade of Chinese ports by American sea power would completely end this source of imports. The Chinese have been careful not to become too dependent on foreign trade, and so a blockade would not have the devastating effect which the Soviet withdrawal of August 1960 had, even though it would hurt the Chinese seriously.

Long-range economic plans take years to work out, and basic investment decisions, particularly with regard to foreign imports, must also be made considerably in advance. In December 1964 Mao Tse-tung had told Edgar Snow that he did not think that the United States would expand the war to North Vietnam. One of the questions that has concerned students of Chinese military strategy is whether the Chinese really believed that they were in danger of American attack and whether they had made operational decisions on the basis of that belief. In the spring of 1962 the United States had reportedly assured the Chinese through Warsaw that it would not support a Nationalist attack on the Mainland (see pp. 301–302). If Mao's brief statements to Edgar Snow were indicative of the general thinking in Peking, then as late as early 1965 the Chinese must still have believed that while war eventually might come, it did not threaten in the near future. We suggest that the few facts we know about Chinese economic planning over the past years bears out the impression that the Chinese had been counting on peace during the period of their Third Five Year Plan.

While economic policy during this period has moved in a generally pragmatic direction, political policy clearly has moved in an ideological direction. The Party "rectification" movement ended late in 1961, and by the summer of 1962 a campaign was under way once again to strengthen Party organization and discipline. As the succession crisis appeared to be approaching, ideological pressure steadily increased. By early 1966 the daily newspapers stressed "the Thought of Mao Tse-tung" as the sole guideline for action. In this intense political campaign two trends may be noted: increasing emphasis on youth and on the army.

Mao Tse-tung won the Revolution with the young and the poor, and he believes that they will guarantee China's survival in the future when he is gone. He has called for a "revolutionary successor generation." Thousands of young people have been sent to the rural areas to teach the peasants. Militia training for the youth has been stepped up. The Communist Youth League appears, at times, to be playing a role almost similar to the Party's. Newspapers and magazines constantly publicize the activities of youth. Older cadres have been told that they must learn from the masses, and have been instructed to "go down deep" and work with the masses. It is not known whether growing numbers of young people have joined the Party or what the degree is of mobility within the Party. Nevertheless, from the low attrition rate in the Party, it is a fair guess that the Party membership is gradually becoming middle-aged.

The army's growing importance may also be tied to the policy on youth. The army remains young, due largely to the high turnover rate arising from conscription. Moreover, the militia, made up largely of young people, plays an important role in Chinese defense planning. At higher levels as well, the army has been playing an increasingly important role in civil life; there is evidence that army officers have assumed important economic positions at middle-echelon administrative levels.

The army's growing role is indicated not only by the enhanced stature of Marshal Lin Piao, but by the fact that the "Great Proletarian Cultural Revolution" was, in effect, launched by the army newspaper *Liberation Daily* in April 1966. For several years prior to this, an "Emulate the People's Liberation Army" campaign had been under way. It was particularly stressed that the army was the true custodian of the "Thought of Mao Tse-tung." The establishment of army-type economic agencies, the so-called "general political departments," which were to supervise policy in the fields of finance, trade, communications, and industry, indicated the growing power of the military in the state administration. Though the conflict between "red and expert" continued during the early 1960s within the army, the apparent purge of Lo Jui-ch'ing and the triumph of Lin Piao imply that the "reds" have finally won out. Likewise, the purge of P'eng Chen, the leader of the Party apparatus within the central government, and the downgrading of Liu Shao-ch'i, suggest basic policy and power struggles between a major segment of the Party and the People's Liberation Army.

From past experience, Mao undoubtedly feels that elements of serious conflict still remain within the higher ranks of Party, government, and army. Nothing could more threaten China's unity in a time of political transition than such conflicts. It may be that Mao feels that the army, headed by Lin Piao, who shares his views and is supported by ideologically loyal young cadres, will be the instrument to ensure that these potential conflicts do not erupt.

The strange contrast between sensible economics and radical politics is mirrored in Chinese daily life. Foreign visitors report that material needs are adequately available, that people do not work too hard, that men can be seen enjoying their leisure, that, until recently, few overt signs of war preparation were visible. Yet at the same time, the pace of "study" and ideological indoctrination has quickened.

The contrast between economics and politics is equally visible in China's foreign policy. Since 1961 China has pursued both ideological and pragmatic foreign policies. As already noted, her trade relations with non-Communist nations have greatly expanded. Cultural contacts with "bourgeois" nations have increased: Chinese students have been sent to Western Europe to study and foreign students have again been welcomed in China; Chinese cultural groups have even visited Canada a number of times; tourism has been on the upswing, particularly since the inauguration of new air routes through the Pakistan International Airlines. Over a decade ago the Chinese divided the world into four tiers: the United States and its allies, the Soviet Union and its allies, the uncommitted "bourgeois" nations, and the neutralist backward countries. Today, China has shown herself quite prepared to carry on business relations with the uncommitted and even committed "bourgeois" nations, like France, West Germany, and the Scandinavian countries. Relations with these countries are carried on in the framework of pragmatic foreign policy. The Canton Fair, one might note, is a perfect example of this pragmatism: thousands of foreign buyers and sellers go to China to make deals in good capitalist fashion.

As might be expected, the Soviet Union and the United States lie within the framework of Chinese ideological foreign policy. The Sino-Soviet dispute has worsened over the last five years, and even when Soviet polemics against the Chinese softened after Khrushchev's fall from power, the Chinese replied with increased hostility and bitterness. The reasons for this must be understood in terms of a new direction in Chinese foreign policy: the application of ideological politics to the third world. The Chinese appear to have had two aims in this: to gain new support for themselves and apply pressure on the Soviet Union.

Generally speaking, until the 1960s Chinese relations with the countries of Asia, Africa, and Latin America were businesslike. Despite talk, even before 1949, that the Chinese Revolution provided a model for colonial countries to follow, the Chinese did not appear to be counting on "wars of liberation" as a major factor in their foreign policy. But as the Sino-Soviet dispute worsened and the Chinese became more concerned over their national security, they turned their attention increasingly to "Asia-Africa-Latin America" (they usually refer to that part of the world in a single phrase). On the one hand, China sought to acquire support from the more radical wings of the Communist Parties of those countries; on the other, she tried to turn those left-leaning countries sympathetic to the Soviet Union in a pro-Chinese direction. In short, she sought support within the international Communist movement in her struggle against the Soviet Union and from among the poorer nations in her dual confrontation with both the Soviet Union and the United States.

China's ideological politics toward the third world appear

to have been based on one of Mao Tse-tung's global visions: the revolutionary process China had experienced would have its analogue on the world scene. Cuba, for example, was seen as the harbinger of a revolutionary movement which would sweep Latin America; indeed, for years the Chinese press carried an extraordinary amount of news on Latin America, where, Mao believed, was American imperialism's Achilles heel. Similarly, Africa would enter the phase of national liberation and so undermine capitalist Europe's economies.

The Chinese actually gave little material help to these movements. They sent advisers to give instruction in the theory and practice of revolution, sent quantities of propaganda, and gave some financial support. They stated openly that "revolution could not be exported," that it had to arise independently in each country according to concrete conditions, and that it could be fought only by the local revolutionaries with their own means.

Until the latter part of 1965 the Chinese were able to keep their various foreign-policy lines from becoming entangled with each other. The attack on India in October 1962, despite its roots in a real border issue, was mainly prompted by ideological reasons and was unilaterally terminated by the Chinese before it got too serious, but it had little effect on China's relations with other Afro-Asian nations. Chinese support for the Congo rebels did not spoil their relations with most other African nations, though later it caused Burundi to expel the Chinese. Growing Afro-Asian unity appeared to provide China with new world leadership possibilities without endangering her relations with the advanced "bourgeois" nations. By late 1965, however, Mao's dream of a rising tide of revolution in the third world seemed to grow increasingly far from reality: several African nations underwent rightist coups, the Congo revolt collapsed, the Indonesian Communist Party was destroyed, and Castro denounced Peking. Within the international Communist movement, one could see the same swing to the right: Moscow once again became the center of the movement. China's failures in 1965 have been almost entirely in the area of ideological foreign policy. In the area of pragmatic policy China has been generally quite successful.

As of the date of writing (August 1966), the most critical

issue facing the world is Vietnam. The United States has indicated repeatedly that Vietnam is a testing ground for Chinese-inspired wars of national liberation and "Chinese expansionism." Thus Washington claims that Vietnam is a place where China's ideological and practical interests converge. As a Communist "power" she uses the Viet Cong as a weapon against "American imperialism"; as a modern version of Imperial China she seeks to draw Vietnam and eventually all of Southeast Asia into her sphere of influence.

Available evidence does not indicate that North Vietnam has become a Chinese satellite. This is even accepted by the United States government, as one can see in the selection from a speech by William P. Bundy presented below. In the dispute North Vietnam has generally taken an ambivalent position, somewhere between Moscow and Peking, though by the summer of 1966 it appeared to be leaning once again toward Moscow (note that North Korea and North Vietnam have recently swung away from a doctrinaire Chinese position). It is strange that China's most loyal ally in the Communist world is Albania—a tiny nation so distant from her borders.

The relationship between the South Vietnamese National Liberation Front and Peking is even more ambiguous. The NLF did not set up an office in Peking until September 1964 (it set one up in Moscow in January 1965). Though Chinese-made weapons have appeared in South Vietnam, they have not come directly from China but from North Vietnam. China has given considerable foreign aid to North Vietnam, but so has the Soviet Union, and today North Vietnam appears equally dependent on China and the Soviet Union for military supplies. There is a rail link to China, but a sea route through Haiphong links North Vietnam with the Soviet Union. By mid-1966 there was still no evidence of the presence of Chinese troops in that country. China's influence in North Vietnam and on the NLF may be great, but it is far from absolute.

Some observers of Chinese foreign policy have maintained that a major change took place in 1965. We suggest that this is true and that the Chinese began to believe that there was acute danger of a war with the United States over Vietnam. In December 1964 Mao told Edgar Snow that he thought there was hope for improving Sino-American relations, and doubted that

the United States would extend the war to North Vietnam. In
September 1965 Foreign Minister Ch'en Yi declared in evident
anger: "it is up to the U.S. President and the Pentagon to decide
whether the United States wants a big war with China *today*"
[our italics]. But, Ch'en Yi appeared careful to make these remarks not in discussing Vietnam directly, but on the question
of Hong Kong as a base for the American war in Vietnam.
Similarly, in his discussion of United States China policy in the
selection presented below, Dean Rusk appears careful not to
link the Vietnam and the China issues too closely. This same
indirect linking of Sino-American relations with the Vietnam
issue, as evident in Ch'en Yi's remarks, can be seen in Chou
En-lai's four-point statement of April 10, 1966, on China's
policy toward the United States.

The change in Chinese foreign-policy thinking on Vietnam
is obviously bound up with American escalation of the war into
North Vietnam, but also with increasing talk in the United
States about China as America's main enemy, and with suggestions from some military quarters that China's nuclear installations be bombed. The growing buildup of American military power in the western Pacific and in Southeast Asia has
heightened the risks of an armed conflict with China; increased
references by leading Americans to a "collision course with
China" are perfectly well known in Peking.

There has been a guessing game in some American official
quarters as to what point of escalation might bring China into
the war. The Chinese have made it clear in a number of statements that they would "send their own people to fight together
with the Vietnamese people . . . in the event that U.S. imperialism continues to escalate its war of aggression and the
Vietnamese people need them" (see p. 600). Obviously,
they refuse to say what the point of no return is. In December
1965 Chou En-lai predicted a significant escalation of the
Vietnam war leading possibly to war with China. The Chinese
statements have been obvious warnings to Washington to desist
from further escalation.

The Vietnam war is the overriding issue today in Chinese
foreign policy, and specifically in China's relations with the
Soviet Union and the United States. If the war gets worse, the
dangers of Chinese intervention increase, and with it the pros-

pects of a general war on the Asian mainland. China's internal and external policies over the last five years do not indicate that she expected war. Perhaps the Chinese tendency to think in long-term spans made them unable to realize the rapidity with which a relatively limited American involvement in South Vietnam could have been escalated, politically and militarily, to one which has become the focus of almost all of present-day American foreign policy. On the other hand, if the war danger should subside, it is possible that China might once again turn inward. Several American students of Chinese foreign policy have maintained that rather than expansionist, China has been concerned primarily with her domestic problems which are far from resolved.

As of the proofreading of this introduction (November 1966), China is still involved in a volcanic movement known as the "Great Proletarian Cultural Revolution." As a consequence of that movement, a large number of prominent leaders have fallen from power, many organizational sectors, including the Party, have been subjected to "rectification," and a new mass force, the Red Guards, has appeared on the political scene. Reading the Chinese press and listening to Chinese radio stations indicate a preoccupation with internal problems. Since Chinese foreign and domestic policies have been intimately linked in the past, it would appear that now too Vietnam and the "cultural revolution" are related factors in current Chinese policy. How they are related remains a matter of dispute.

There can be no doubt about the grave problems China faces both at home and abroad. The summer of 1966 would seem to represent a turning point for both sets of problems. What happens in Vietnam will have a profound effect on Chinese foreign policy, particularly in her relationships with the Soviet Union and the United States. Similarly, the eventual outcome of the "cultural revolution" will influence the course of China's domestic political, economic, and social policies.

1. IDEOLOGY
🕉 World Views of China
and the United States

IT IS EVIDENT from our earlier selections that in addition to the chess game of practical national interests, the relationship between the United States and China is governed to a great degree by the image each has of the other. In both cases, however, the image is but part of a larger world view of the fundamental trends of contemporary history. This sense of global mission is relatively new for both countries. In the nineteenth century America seldom ventured out of the Western Hemisphere. Until the end of World War II she felt a responsibility to help prevent the rise of new world empires, but after World War II, she took over the leadership of the non-Communist world, and as the Cold War began, started to think ideologically and operationally in global terms. In the eighteenth century China was indeed the center of an empire, but her thinking could hardly be called global. Global thinking implies a conception of the world as a unified entity. Eighteenth-century Imperial Chinese thinking saw the outer limits of the world as sinking away into vague and uninteresting barbarities. Unlike Moscow, which for centuries saw itself as a Third Rome destined eventually to save the world, Imperial China could not have cared less about its distant subjects; even the thought of a Chinese global mission during the nineteenth century and the first half of the twentieth century was ridiculous. During the last years of the war against Japan, however, the Chinese Communists began to see their Revolution as a model for others to follow. Chinese global thinking, always present since the founding of the Chinese

Communist Party, assumed major dimensions after the beginning of the Sino-Soviet conflict.

Few ideological documents from China have aroused such attention in the United States as Marshal Lin Piao's article "Long Live the Victory of the People's War," published on September 3, 1965. High official American sources have referred to it as the Chinese blueprint for world conquest, comparable to Hitler's *Mein Kampf*. There can be no doubt that the article expresses a strain in Chinese global thinking which goes back into the Yenan Period, and that it directly reflects the global thinking of Mao Tse-tung. The article was actually the third and last in a series of major articles on global and military problems which appeared in 1965. The first, by Lo Jui-ch'ing, appeared in May, celebrating the twentieth anniversary of VE Day, and more specifically the Soviet Union's victory over Germany. The second, by Ho Lung, appeared in August 1965 and announced the abolition of all ranks in the Chinese Army. Lin Piao's article celebrated the twentieth anniversary of the defeat of Japan in World War II.

Lin Piao, who appears to be playing an increasingly significant role in Chinese leadership circles, was born in 1908 in eastern Hupei province. He was one of Mao Tse-tung's most loyal supporters during the Long March, and was the conqueror of Manchuria and North China during the Civil War. In September 1959 he replaced P'eng Te-huai as Minister of National Defense. In the ranking of China's ten marshals he comes third after Chu Teh and P'eng Te-huai; today, with the inactivity of the former and the fall from power of the latter, he is China's leading military figure. He is reputed to be a quiet and careful man; his motto is "think carefully and act decisively."

Lin Piao's previous major article was published in October 1960, at the time of the appearance of Volume IV of Mao Tse-tung's *Selected Works* (containing documents from the Civil War). In view of the close association of the two men, the present article may be seen as a statement of Mao Tse-tung's global thinking on matters of strategy and tactics, written in the context of an expanding war in Vietnam.

Lin Piao clearly places the Chinese Revolution in the

revolutionary current emanating from the Russian October Revolution. However, the focal point of world revolution has moved from the advanced industrialized capitalist countries to the backward semi-feudal and semi-colonial countries, namely to Asia, Africa, and Latin America. Moreover, the nature of the revolutionary process has changed: whereas the October Revolution was won by armed uprisings led by the proletariat, the revolutions in the third world will be won by protracted struggles in the rural areas, gradually closing in on the cities. Contemporary revolutions must be based on a broad popular front led by the Communist Party but directed against the foreign ruler, rural landlords, and those urban officials and capitalists in alliance with reactionary governments and imperialist forces.

Lin Piao foresees growing confrontations between the United States and national liberation movements which will break out in different parts of the world. Though he conceives of the possibility of a total nuclear war, he appears to see as more likely a series of protracted struggles all over the world which will increasingly overextend and finally sap the strength of the United States. On tactics, Lin Piao notes: "Everything is divisible. And so is this colossus of U.S. imperialism. It can be split up and defeated." Specifically, in his account of the war against Japan, he suggests: "In order to annihilate the enemy, we just adopt the policy of luring him in deep and abandon some cities and districts of our own accord in a planned way, so as to let him in. It is only after letting the enemy in that the people can take part in the war in various ways and that the power of the people's war can be fully exerted." He emphasizes that no national liberation movement must rely on external support: "The common victory was won by all the peoples, who gave one another support and encouragement. Yet each country was, above all, liberated as a result of its own efforts." Lin Piao obviously had Vietnam in mind when he wrote this. His advice to the Vietnamese would appear to be: Fight a protracted war, do not hastily try to take cities, keep your organization disciplined and intact, try to gain alliances with non-Communist anti-imperialist groups in the cities, and force the enemy to commit his forces, particularly land forces, ever wider, ever deeper, and ever longer. Tactically, the enemy is superior and must be respected, as Mao teaches in his paper tiger theses, but in the long run, he will falter from overextension.

The crux of Lin Piao's military thinking is that men are superior to weapons. In other words, no matter how great the level of technological superiority on the part of the enemy, "in the final analysis the outcome of the war will be decided by the sustained fighting of the ground forces, by the fighting at close quarters, by the political consciousness of the men, by their courage and spirit of sacrifice."

If we may be allowed a comment on the nature of the Vietnam war, we might note that Lin Piao pictures a war which, in the final analysis, is fought solely between one side relying almost entirely on men and the other relying almost entirely on technology. If that war should finally become one where the leading combatants on the South Vietnamese side are Americans relying mainly on air power, then we have a testing ground for Lin Piao's thesis: which are more powerful, weapons or men.

To argue that Lin Piao's article is a modern *Mein Kampf* confuses two basic philosophies. Hitler argued that goals can be achieved only through "will": history is made by men. Communists, by contrast, have a deep belief in the inevitable course of history. Lin Piao does not argue that China must make these revolutions, or else they will not occur. On the contrary, in good Marxist fashion, he argues they will occur, regardless of what China chooses to do. In fact, with his emphasis on nationalism and self-reliance, he implies that the less outside interference there is in these revolutionary processes, the better their chances of rallying broad popular support and winning final victory.

Since we are so accustomed to see the world views of the protagonists in the struggles of the modern world through their official ideological statements, we here present a different kind of document, the summary of an interview Edgar Snow had with Mao Tse-tung in December 1964. Westerners have often wondered, though we cannot know, whether Communists speak to each other in high policy meetings in the same jargon they use in their official documents. In their talks with "bourgeois" representatives Communist leaders, both in East and West, have been capable of speaking in understandable common-sense language, as is evident in the Mao interview. Rather surprising is the tone of practicality and even of caution in Mao's words, and the fact that he is well-read and informed about the details of world events. On the other hand, there is no mistaking the global sweep of his thinking. This is not so surprising if we remember that Mao has always taught that one must walk on two legs: practice (*i.e.*, action in concrete realities) is as important as theory (see pp. 24–25). In contrast to Lin Piao's clear-cut statement that contemporary revolutionary struggles center in the third world, Mao wonders whether "contradictions between the capitalist countries themselves" still might not be a major cause of war. Nevertheless, Mao clearly believes in his estimations of the revolutionary possibilities in the third world. It is also evident that he does not share the Russians' great fear of the destructiveness of nuclear weapons, though he adds: "if one must fight, one should confine oneself to conventional weapons."

Mao's remarks on Vietnam were made before the beginning of major American air raids on North Vietnam. He doubted that the Americans would invade China. When asked whether the United States would expand the war to North Vietnam, he replied: "Mr. Rusk has now made it clear that the U.S. would not do that." He dismissed the idea of Chinese expansionism. He thought that in Vietnam "fighting would go on perhaps for one or two years. After that the United States troops would find it boring and might go home or somewhere else." He ended the interview with reflections on his own coming death.

The reader must be confused at the sharply different tone of Mao Tse-tung speaking through Lin Piao and the same Mao Tse-tung speaking to Edgar Snow. James Reston, *New York Times* Washington correspondent, reports another kind of confusion about China in his article "Washington: The Two Concepts of China," which we present below. There are the Pentagon and State Department geopoliticians who take Lin Piao's statements at face value and want to step up the war in Vietnam. Then there are those who take it equally seriously but would not risk war with China. We refer the reader to the statements of Dean Rusk and Roger Hilsman (see pp. 581–592) which, respectively, illustrate these two lines of thought. Then there are others, particularly in the governments of other countries, who dismiss the whole thing and see it as "nothing more than a theoretical argument aimed at the Soviet Union, and/or a propaganda line designed to influence the Chinese workers." The Asians in particular prefer to see the problem in terms of China's real capabilities rather than in terms of her ideological pronouncements. This attitude would appear to be shared by John K. Fairbank, as indicated in his testimony before the Senate Foreign Relations Committee (see pp. 527–531).

Official Washington still asks: Which is the real thinking of China; is it the apocalyptic picture drawn by Lin Piao reflecting Mao's views, or is it the common-sense responses Mao gave to Snow's questions? The first answer to this question must be that the question itself is stated incorrectly. Unless we fall into the trap of ideological thinking ourselves which imputes to the enemy a fixed way of thinking from which all his actions arise or can be explained (see pp. 22–24), then we must recognize that Lin Piao's theories, Mao's down-to-earth comments, Ch'en Yi's acid and often humorous remarks, and the Chinese leader's grand visions, expressed at one time or another and in one form or another, all form part of the whole that constitutes the thinking of China's leadership. That there are contradictions in that thinking should surprise no one, for the Chinese Communists have stated time and time again that everything without exception is made up of contradictory elements.

We must also remember, however, that ideological and counter-ideological thinking tend to reinforce each other. Lin Piao did not project his ideas in an isolated vacuum, but predicted what would happen, specifically what the United States would do. Thus if the United States reacts to this "blueprint for global conquest" with a counter-blueprint and proceeds to act according to it, then this not only reinforces the Chinese world view but forces them to a counter-action. Thus, in time, theory and practice come closer and closer together, with both sides contributing to the convergence through ideologies and counter-ideologies, and through actions and counter-actions.

In the selection from a speech by William P. Bundy, Assistant Secretary of State for Far Eastern Affairs, who succeeded Roger Hilsman early in 1964, and whom *Newsweek* (March 9, 1964) described as a "Pentagon intellectual who is one of Washington's most knowledgeable men on Southeast

Asia," we have an expression of what might be called the American world view, particularly in its relation to China. Bundy forthrightly states America's major aim in the Far East is to create in effect a plurality of independent nations. "In harsh conflict with these objectives," he states, "is any situation in which a single nation or combination of nations sets out to control others in the region or to exercise political domination over other nations in the area or any major part of it."

Bundy makes it clear that America's actions in Eastern Asia are directly linked to her conception of Chinese objectives and actions in that part of the world. Bundy regards Communist China both as "Communist" and as "Chinese." As a Communist nation, it "is dedicated to the promotion of Communism by violent revolution." As a new version of the old Imperial China, "the present leaders in Peking also seek to restore China to its past position of grandeur and influence." As a new empire, it aspires to control Eastern Asia, but as a center of Communism, "their vision of this Communist mission extends to countries far from China—including . . . Africa and even Latin America." He regards the Lin Piao article as one of the latest and most widely publicized of "Peking's plans for carrying out its objectives." In sum, Bundy indicates that the Lin Piao article must be taken seriously as a statement of Chinese objectives, and that it therefore must constitute a part of the over-all American conception of the world situation and influence concrete American policy.

Attacking arguments that "the ambitions of Communist China in the areas contiguous to it do not mean outright control," Bundy then proceeds to discuss Chinese tactics and strategy and American counter-policies. He does not appear to agree with the analogy that paints "the picture of another Hitler, building a vast military machine with the aim of conquest by conventional warfare on a timetable backed at some point, in the Chinese case, by a nuclear capability." Rather, we "are dealing here not with the power of ideas but with the power of subversive organization—perhaps the one field in which Communist China has shown real innovation and skill." He admits that the "Chinese are patient and think in long historical terms." He cites as the main instance of Chinese-supported subversion in Southeast Asia the so-called "Thai Patriotic

Front." On Vietnam, however, he admits that "what is now happening in Vietnam is basically the result of Hanoi's own ambitions and efforts." But he adds, "Peking might wish eventually to dominate North Vietnam or a unified Vietnam under Hanoi's initial control." In other words, though North Vietnam is not yet entirely a Chinese puppet, in time it will become so if Chinese expansionism is not checked. He then proceeds to an analysis of American policy, which we omit since essentially the same points were made by Dean Rusk in his testimony before the Senate Foreign Relations Committee.

It is clear from Bundy's speech that the Chinese world view, specifically in the form of Lin Piao's article, has been woven into the American world view, and thus constitutes a basis for American policy in Southeast Asia. One cannot avoid the fatalistic impression that world view and counter-world view, bit by bit, confirm each other, making each a self-fulfilling prophecy.

LIN PIAO *
Mao Tse-tung's Theory of People's War

The Chinese Revolution is a continuation of the great October Revolution. The road of the October Revolution is the common road for all people's revolutions. The Chinese Revolution and the October Revolution have in common the following basic characteristics: (1) Both were led by the working class with a Marxist-Leninist party as its nucleus. (2) Both were based on the worker-peasant alliance. (3) In both cases state power was seized through violent revolution and the dictatorship of the proletariat was established. (4) In both cases the socialist system was built after victory in the Revolution. (5) Both were component parts of the proletarian world revolution.

Naturally, the Chinese Revolution had its own peculiar

* Lin Piao, "The International Significance of Comrade Mao Tse-tung's Theory of People's War" (Peking: Foreign Languages Press, 1965), pp. 42–59.

characteristics. The October Revolution took place in imperialist Russia, but the Chinese Revolution broke out in a semi-colonial and semi-feudal country. The former was a proletarian socialist revolution, while the latter developed into a socialist revolution after the complete victory of the new democratic revolution. The October Revolution began with armed uprisings in the cities and then spread to the countryside, while the Chinese Revolution won nationwide victory through the encirclement of the cities from the rural areas and the final capture of the cities.

Comrade Mao Tse-tung's great merit lies in the fact that he has succeeded in integrating the universal truth of Marxism-Leninism with the concrete practice of the Chinese Revolution and has enriched and developed Marxism-Leninism by his masterly generalization and summation of the experience gained during the Chinese people's protracted revolutionary struggle.

Comrade Mao Tse-tung's theory of people's war has been proved by the long practice of the Chinese Revolution to be in accord with the objective laws of such wars and to be invincible. It has not only been valid for China, it is a great contribution to the revolutionary struggles of the oppressed nations and peoples throughout the world.

The people's war led by the Chinese Communist Party, comprising the War of Resistance and the Revolutionary Civil Wars, lasted for twenty-two years. It constitutes the most drawn-out and most complex people's war led by the proletariat in modern history, and it has been the richest in experience.

In the last analysis, the Marxist-Leninist theory of proletarian revolution is the theory of the seizure of state power by revolutionary violence, the theory of countering war against the people by people's war. As Marx so aptly put it, "Force is the midwife of every old society pregnant with a new one."

It was on the basis of the lessons derived from the people's wars in China that Comrade Mao Tse-tung, using the simplest and the most vivid language, advanced the famous thesis that "political power grows out of the barrel of a gun."

He clearly pointed out:

> The seizure of power by armed force, the settlement of the issue by war, is the central task and the highest form

of revolution. This Marxist-Leninist principle of revolution holds good universally, for China and for all other countries.

War is the product of imperialism and the system of exploitation of man by man. Lenin said that "war is always and everywhere begun by the exploiters themselves, by the ruling and oppressing classes." So long as imperialism and the system of exploitation of man by man exist, the imperialists and reactionaries will invariably rely on armed force to maintain their reactionary rule and impose war on the oppressed nations and peoples. This is an objective law independent of man's will.

In the world today, all the imperialists headed by the United States and their lackeys, without exception, are strengthening their state machinery, and especially their armed forces. U.S. imperialism, in particular, is carrying out armed aggression and suppression everywhere.

What should the oppressed nations and the oppressed people do in the face of wars of aggression and armed suppression by the imperialists and their lackeys? Should they submit and remain slaves in perpetuity? Or should they rise in resistance and fight for their liberation?

Comrade Mao Tse-tung answered this question in vivid terms. He said that after long investigation and study the Chinese people discovered that all the imperialists and their lackeys "have swords in their hands and are out to kill. The people have come to understand this and so act after the same fashion." This is called doing unto them what they do unto us.

In the last analysis, whether one dares to wage a tit-for-tat struggle against armed aggression and suppression by the imperialists and their lackeys, whether one dares to fight a people's war against them, means whether one dares to embark on revolution. This is the most effective touchstone for distinguishing genuine from fake revolutionaries and Marxist-Leninists.

In view of the fact that some people were afflicted with the fear of the imperialists and reactionaries, Comrade Mao Tse-tung put forward his famous thesis that "the imperialists and all reactionaries are paper tigers." He said:

> All reactionaries are paper tigers. In appearance, the reactionaries are terrifying, but in reality they are not so

powerful. From a long-term point of view, it is not the reactionaries but the people who are really powerful.

The history of people's war in China and other countries
provides conclusive evidence that the growth of the people's
revolutionary forces from weak and small beginnings into strong
and large forces is a universal law of development of class struggle, a universal law of development of people's war. A people's
war inevitably meets with many difficulties, with ups and downs
and setbacks in the course of its development, but no force can
alter its general trend toward inevitable triumph.

Comrade Mao Tse-tung points out that we must despise
the enemy strategically and take full account of him tactically.

To despise the enemy strategically is an elementary requirement for a revolutionary. Without the courage to despise
the enemy and without daring to win, it will be simply impossible
to make revolution and wage a people's war, let alone to achieve
victory.

It is also very important for revolutionaries to take full
account of the enemy tactically. It is likewise impossible to win
victory in a people's war without taking full account of the
enemy tactically, and without examining the concrete conditions, without being prudent and giving great attention to the
study of the art of struggle, and without adopting appropriate
forms of struggle in the concrete practice of the revolution in
each country and with regard to each concrete problem of
struggle.

Dialectical and historical materialism teaches us that what
is important primarily is not that which at the given moment
seems to be durable and yet is already beginning to die away,
but that which is arising and developing, even though at the
given moment it may not appear to be durable, for only that
which is arising and developing is invincible.

Why can the apparently weak newborn forces always triumph over the decadent forces which appear so powerful? The
reason is that truth is on their side and that the masses are on
their side, while the reactionary classes are always divorced
from the masses and set themselves against the masses.

This has been borne out by the victory of the Chinese

Revolution, by the history of all revolutions, the whole history of class struggle, and the entire history of mankind.

The imperialists are extremely afraid of Comrade Mao Tse-tung's thesis that "imperialism and all reactionaries are paper tigers," and the revisionists are extremely hostile to it. They all oppose and attack this thesis and the philistines follow suit by ridiculing it. But all this cannot in the least diminish its importance. The light of truth cannot be dimmed by anybody.

Comrade Mao Tse-tung's theory of people's war solves not only the problem of daring to fight a people's war, but also that of how to wage it.

Comrade Mao Tse-tung is a great statesman and military scientist, proficient at directing war in accordance with its laws. By the line and policies, the strategy and tactics he formulated for the people's war, he led the Chinese people in steering the ship of the people's war past all hidden reefs to the shores of victory in most complicated and difficult conditions.

It must be emphasized that Comrade Mao Tse-tung's theory of the establishment of rural revolutionary base areas and the encirclement of the cities from the countryside is of outstanding and universal practical importance for the present revolutionary struggles of all the oppressed nations and peoples, and particularly for the revolutionary struggles of the oppressed nations and peoples in Asia, Africa, and Latin America against imperialism and its lackeys.

Many countries and peoples in Asia, Africa, and Latin America are now being subjected to aggression and enslavement on a serious scale by the imperialists headed by the United States and their lackeys. The basic political and economic conditions in many of these countries have many similarities to those that prevailed in old China. As in China, the peasant question is extremely important in these regions. The peasants constitute the main force of the national-democratic revolution against the imperialists and their lackeys. In committing aggression against these countries, the imperialists usually begin by seizing the big cities and the main lines of communication, but they are unable to bring the vast countryside completely under their control. The countryside, and the countryside alone, can provide the broad areas in which the revolutionaries can maneuver freely. The countryside, and the countryside alone, can provide the revolutionary bases from which the revolutionaries can go forward to final victory. Precisely for this reason, Comrade Mao Tse-tung's theory of establishing revolutionary base areas in the rural districts and encircling the cities from the countryside is attracting more and more attention among the people in these regions.

Taking the entire globe, if North America and Western Europe can be called "the cities of the world," then Asia, Africa, and Latin America constitute "the rural areas of the world." Since World War II, the proletarian revolutionary movement has for various reasons been temporarily held back in the North American and West European capitalist countries, while the people's revolutionary movement in Asia, Africa, and Latin America has been growing vigorously. In a sense, the contemporary world revolution also presents a picture of the encirclement of cities by the rural areas. In the final analysis, the whole cause of world revolution hinges on the revolutionary struggles of the Asian, African, and Latin American peoples who make up the overwhelming majority of the world's population. The socialist countries should regard it as their internationalist duty to support the people's revolutionary struggles in Asia, Africa, and Latin America.

The October Revolution opened up a new era in the revolution of the oppressed nations. The victory of the October Revolution built a bridge between the socialist revolution of the proletariat of the West and the national-democratic revolution of the colonial and semi-colonial countries of the East. The Chinese Revolution has successfully solved the problem of how to link up the national-democratic with the socialist revolution in the colonial and semi-colonial countries.

Comrade Mao Tse-tung has pointed out that, in the epoch since the October Revolution, anti-imperialist revolution in any colonial or semi-colonial country is no longer part of the old bourgeois, or capitalist world revolution, but is part of the new world revolution, the proletarian-socialist world revolution.

Comrade Mao Tse-tung has formulated a complete theory of the new-democratic revolution. He indicated that this revolution, which is different from all others, can only be, nay must be, a revolution against imperialism, feudalism, and bureaucrat-capitalism waged by the broad masses of the people under the leadership of the proletariat.

This means that the revolution can only be, nay must be, led by the proletariat and the genuinely revolutionary party armed with Marxism-Leninism, and by no other class or party.

This means that the revolution embraces in its ranks not only the workers, peasants, and the urban petty bourgeoisie, but also the national bourgeoisie and other patriotic and anti-imperialist democrats.

This means, finally, that the revolution is directed against imperialism, feudalism, and bureaucrat-capitalism.

The new-democratic revolution leads to socialism, and not to capitalism.

Comrade Mao Tse-tung's theory of the new democratic revolution is the Marxist-Leninist theory of revolution by stages as well as the Marxist-Leninist theory of uninterrupted revolution.

Comrade Mao Tse-tung made a correct distinction between the two revolutionary stages, *i.e.*, the national-democratic and the socialist revolutions; at the same time he correctly and closely linked the two. The national-democratic revolution is the necessary preparation for the socialist revolution, and the socialist revolution is the inevitable sequel to the national-democratic revolution. There is no Great Wall between the two revolutionary stages. But the socialist revolution is only possible after the completion of the national-democratic revolution. The more thorough the national-democratic revolution, the better the conditions for the socialist revolution.

The experience of the Chinese Revolution shows that the tasks of the national-democratic revolution can be fulfilled only through long and tortuous struggles. In this stage of revolution, imperialism and its lackeys are the principal enemy. In the struggle against imperialism and its lackeys, it is necessary to rally all anti-imperialist patriotic forces, including the national bourgeoisie and all patriotic personages. All those patriotic personages from among the bourgeoisie and other exploiting classes who join the anti-imperialist struggle play a progressive historical role; they are not tolerated by imperialism but welcomed by the proletariat.

It is very harmful to confuse the two stages, that is, the

national-democratic and the socialist revolutions. Comrade Mao Tse-tung criticized the wrong idea of "accomplishing both at one stroke," and pointed out that this utopian idea could only weaken the struggle against imperialism and its lackeys, the most urgent task at that time. The Kuomintang reactionaries and the Trotskyites they hired during the War of Resistance deliberately confused these two stages of the Chinese Revolution, proclaiming the "theory of a single revolution" and preaching so-called "socialism" without any Communist Party. With this preposterous theory they attempted to swallow up the Communist Party, wipe out any revolution, and prevent the advance of the national-democratic revolution, and they used it as a pretext for their non-resistance and capitulation to imperialism. This reactionary theory was buried long ago by the history of the Chinese Revolution.

The Khrushchev revisionists are now actively preaching that socialism can be built without the proletariat and without a genuinely revolutionary party armed with the advanced proletarian ideology, and they have cast the fundamental tenets of Marxism-Leninism to the four winds. The revisionists' purpose is solely to divert the oppressed nations from their struggle against imperialism and sabotage their national-democratic revolution, all in the service of imperialism.

The Chinese Revolution provides a successful lesson for making a thoroughgoing national-democratic revolution under the leadership of the proletariat; it likewise provides a successful lesson for the timely transition from the national-democratic revolution to the socialist revolution under the leadership of the proletariat.

Mao Tse-tung's Thought has been the guide to the victory of the Chinese Revolution. It has integrated the universal truth of Marxism-Leninism with the concrete practice of the Chinese Revolution and creatively developed Marxism-Leninism, thus adding new weapons to the arsenal of Marxism-Leninism.

Ours is the epoch in which world capitalism and imperialism are heading for their doom and socialism and communism are marching to victory. Comrade Mao Tse-tung's theory of people's war is not only a product of the Chinese Revolution, but has also the characteristics of our epoch. The new experience gained in the people's revolutionary struggles in various countries since World War II has provided continuous evidence that Mao Tse-tung's Thought is a common asset of the revolutionary people of the whole world. This is the great international significance of the Thought of Mao Tse-tung.

DEFEAT U.S. IMPERIALISM
AND ITS LACKEYS BY PEOPLE'S WAR

Since World War II, U.S. imperialism has stepped into the shoes of German, Japanese, and Italian fascism and has been trying to build a great American empire by dominating and enslaving the whole world. It is actively fostering Japanese and West German militarism as its chief accomplices in unleashing a world war. Like a vicious wolf, it is bullying and enslaving various peoples, plundering their wealth, encroaching upon their countries' sovereignty and interfering in their internal affairs. It is the most rabid aggressor in human history and the most ferocious common enemy of the people of the world. Every people or country in the world that wants revolution, independence, and peace cannot but direct the spearhead of its struggle against U.S. imperialism.

Just as the Japanese imperialists' policy of subjugating China made it possible for the Chinese people to form the broadest possible united front against them, so the U.S. imperialists' policy of seeking world domination makes it possible for the people throughout the world to unite all the forces that can be united and form the broadest possible united front for a converging attack on U.S. imperialism.

At present, the main battlefield of the fierce struggle between the people of the world on the one side and U.S. imperialism and its lackeys on the other is the vast area of Asia, Africa, and Latin America. In the world as a whole, this is the area where the people suffer worst from imperialist oppression and where imperialist rule is most vulnerable. Since World War II, revolutionary storms have been rising in this area, and today they have become the most important force directly pounding U.S. imperialism. The contradiction between the revolutionary peoples of Asia, Africa, and Latin America and the imperialists headed by the United States is the principal contradiction in the contemporary world. The development of this contradiction is promoting the struggle of the people of the whole world against U.S. imperialism and its lackeys.

Since World War II, people's war has increasingly demonstrated its power in Asia, Africa, and Latin America. The peoples of China, Korea, Vietnam, Laos, Cuba, Indonesia, Algeria, and other countries have waged people's wars against the imperialists and their lackeys and won great victories. The classes leading these people's wars may vary, and so may the breadth and depth of mass mobilization and the extent of victory, but the victories in these people's wars have very much weakened and pinned down the forces of imperialism, upset the U.S. imperialist plan to launch a world war, and become mighty factors defending world peace.

Today, the conditions are more favorable than ever before for the waging of people's wars by the revolutionary peoples of Asia, Africa, and Latin America against U.S. imperialism and its lackeys.

Since World War II and the succeeding years of revolutionary upsurge, there has been a great rise in the level of political consciousness and the degree of organization of the people in all countries, and the resources available to them for mutual support and aid have greatly increased. The whole capitalist-imperialist system has become drastically weaker and is in the process of increasing convulsion and disintegration. After World War I, the imperialists lacked the power to destroy the newborn socialist Soviet state, but they were still able to suppress the people's revolutionary movements in some countries in the parts of the world under their own rule and so maintain a short period of comparative stability. Since World War II, however, not only have they been unable to stop a number of countries from taking the socialist road, but they are no longer capable of holding back the surging tide of the people's revolutionary movements in the areas under their own rule.

U.S. imperialism is stronger, but also more vulnerable, than any imperialism of the past. It sets itself against the people of the whole world, including the people of the United States. Its human, military, material, and financial resources are far from sufficient for the realization of its ambition of dominating the whole world. U.S. imperialism has further weakened

itself by occupying so many places in the world, overreaching
itself, stretching its fingers out wide and dispersing its strength,
with its rear so far away and its supply lines so long. As Comrade Mao Tse-tung has said, "Wherever it commits aggression,
it puts a new noose around its neck. It is besieged ring upon ring
by the people of the whole world."

When committing aggression in a foreign country, U.S.
imperialism can only employ part of its forces, which are sent
to fight an unjust war far from their native land and therefore
have a low morale, and so U.S. imperialism is beset with great
difficulties. The people subjected to its aggression are having a
trial of strength with U.S. imperialism neither in Washington nor
New York, neither in Honolulu nor Florida, but are fighting for
independence and freedom on their own soil. Once they are
mobilized on a broad scale, they will have inexhaustible strength.
Thus superiority will belong not to the United States but to the
people subjected to its aggression. The latter, though apparently
weak and small, are really more powerful than U.S. imperialism.

The struggles waged by the different peoples against U.S.
imperialism reinforce each other and merge into a torrential
worldwide tide of opposition to U.S. imperialism. The more
successful the development of people's war in a given region,
the larger the number of U.S. imperialist forces that can be
pinned down and depleted there. When the U.S. aggressors are
hard pressed in one place, they have no alternative but to loosen
their grip on others. Therefore, the conditions become more
favorable for the people elsewhere to wage struggles against U.S.
imperialism and its lackeys.

Everything is divisible. And so is this colossus of U.S.
imperialism. It can be split up and defeated. The peoples of
Asia, Africa, Latin America, and other regions can destroy it
piece by piece, some striking at its head and others at its feet.
That is why the greatest fear of U.S. imperialism is that people's
wars will be launched in different parts of the world, and particularly in Asia, Africa, and Latin America, and why it regards
people's war as a mortal danger.

U.S. imperialism relies solely on its nuclear weapons to
intimidate people. But these weapons cannot save U.S. imperialism from its doom. Nuclear weapons cannot be used
lightly. U.S. imperialism has been condemned by the people of

the whole world for its towering crime of dropping two atom bombs on Japan. If it uses nuclear weapons again, it will become isolated in the extreme. Moreover, the U.S. monopoly of nuclear weapons has long been broken; U.S. imperialism has these weapons, but others have them too. If it threatens other countries with nuclear weapons, U.S. imperialism will expose its own country to the same threat. For this reason, it will meet with strong opposition not only from the people elsewhere but also inevitably from the people in its own country. Even if U.S. imperialism brazenly uses nuclear weapons, it cannot conquer the people, who are indomitable.

However highly developed modern weapons and technical equipment may be and however complicated the methods of modern warfare, in the final analysis the outcome of a war will be decided by the sustained fighting of the ground forces, by the fighting at close quarters on battlefields, by the political consciousness of the men, by their courage and spirit of sacrifice. Here the weak points of U.S. imperialism will be completely laid bare, while the superiority of the revolutionary people will be brought into full play. The reactionary troops of U.S. imperialism cannot possibly be endowed with the courage and the spirit of sacrifice possessed by the revolutionary people. The spiritual atom bomb which the revolutionary people possess is a far more powerful and useful weapon than the physical atom bomb.

Vietnam is the most convincing current example of a victim of aggression defeating U.S. imperialism by a people's war. The United States has made South Vietnam a testing ground for the suppression of people's war. It has carried on this experiment for many years, and everybody can now see that the U.S. aggressors are unable to find a way of coping with people's war. On the other hand, the Vietnamese people have brought the power of people's war into full play in their struggle against the U.S. aggressors. The U.S. aggressors are in danger of being swamped in the people's war in Vietnam. They are deeply worried that their defeat in Vietnam will lead to a chain reaction. They are expanding the war in an attempt to save themselves from defeat. But the more they expand the war, the greater will be the chain reaction. The more they escalate the war, the heavier will be their fall and the more disastrous their defeat. The people in other parts of the world will see still more clearly that U.S. imperialism can be defeated, and that what the Vietnamese people can do, they can do too.

History has proved and will go on proving that people's war is the most effective weapon against U.S. imperialism and its lackeys. All revolutionary people will learn to wage people's war against U.S. imperialism and its lackeys. They will take up arms, learn to fight battles, and become skilled in waging people's war, though they have not done so before. U.S. imperialism like a mad bull dashing from place to place, will finally be burned to ashes in the blazing fires of the people's wars it has provoked by its own actions.

EDGAR SNOW *
Interview with Mao

Peking

In a rare interview which lasted about four hours, Mao Tse-tung conversed with me on topics ranging over what he himself called *shan nan hai pei,* or "from south of the mountains to north of the seas." With China's bountiful two-hundred-million-ton 1964 grain harvest taxing winter-storage capacities, with shops everywhere offering inexpensive foods and consumer-goods necessities, and with technological and scientific advances climaxed by an atomic bang that saluted Khrushchev's political demise, Chairman Mao might well have claimed a few creative achievements. I found him reflecting on man's rendezvous with death and ready to leave the assessment of his political legacy to future generations.

The seventy-two-year-old warrior greeted me in one of the spacious Peking-decor rooms of the Great Hall of the People, across the wide square facing T'ien An Men, the Heavenly Peace Gate of the former Forbidden City. During our conversation he

* Edgar Snow, "Interview with Mao," *New Republic,* January 20, 1965.

repeatedly thanked foreign invaders for speeding up the Chinese Revolution and for bestowing similar favors in Southeast Asia today. He asserted that China has no troops outside her own frontiers and has no intention of fighting anybody unless her own territory is attacked. He observed that the more American weapons and troops brought into Saigon, the faster the South Vietnamese liberation forces would become armed and educated to win victory. By now they did not need the help of Chinese troops.

At the start of our conversation Chairman Mao agreed to be photographed informally in a film I believe to be the first ever made of him for foreign television. From this film political clinicians may make their own diagnosis of his condition, lately rumored to be much deteriorated. On January 9, coming at the end of strenuous weeks of daily and nightly conferences with many regional leaders drawn to the capital for the annual National People's Congress, his talk with me might have been more speedily terminated by a sick man. He seemed wholly relaxed throughout our conversation, which began before six, continued during dinner and went on for about two hours after.

One of the chairman's doctors informed me that Mao has no organic troubles and suffers from nothing beyond the normal fatigue of his age. He ate moderately of a peppery Hunanese meal shared with me and drank a glass or two of wine, rather perfunctorily.

It was reported abroad that other "government officials" were present during my interview. These officials were two friends from pre-revolutionary days in China: Mme Kung P'eng, now an assistant to the Chinese Foreign Minister, and her husband, Ch'iao Kuan-hua, an Assistant Minister in the same department. I submitted no written questions and took no notes during the interview. Fortunately I was able to refresh my memory by reviewing the conversation with one of those present who had kept a written record. It was agreed that I might publish, without direct quotation, such of the Chairman's comment as is given below.

"Some American commentators in Saigon have compared the strength of the Viet Cong there with the 1947 period in China, when the People's Liberation Army began to engage in large-scale annihilations of Nationalist forces. Are the conditions comparable?"

The chairman thought not. By 1947 the People's Liberation Army already had more than a million men, against several million troops on Chiang Kai-shek's side. The PLA had then used divisional and group army strength, whereas the Vietnamese liberation forces were now operating at battalion or at most regimental strength. American forces in Vietnam were still relatively small. Of course, if they increased they could help speed up the arming of the people against them. But if he should tell that to United States leaders they would not listen. Had they listened to Diem? Both Ho Chi Minh and he (Mao Tse-tung) thought that Ngo Dinh Diem was not so bad. They had expected the Americans to maintain him for several more years. But impatient American generals became disgusted with Diem and got rid of him. After all, following his assassination, was everything between heaven and earth more peaceful?

"Can Viet Cong forces now win victory by their own efforts alone?" Yes, he thought that they could. Their position was relatively better than that of the Communists during the first Civil War (1927–1937) in China. At that time there was no direct foreign intervention, but now already the Viet Cong had the American intervention to help arm and educate the rank and file and the army officers. Those opposed to the United States were no longer confined to the Liberation Army. Diem had not wanted to take orders. Now this independence had spread to the generals. The American teachers were succeeding. Asked whether some of these generals would soon join the Liberation Army, Mao said yes, some would follow the example of Kuomintang generals who had turned to the Communists.

THE "THIRD WORLD"

"United States intervention in Vietnam, the Congo, and other former colonial battlefields suggests a question of some theoretical interest as seen within Marxist concepts. The question is whether the contradiction between neocolonialism and the revolutionary forces in what the French like to call the 'third world'

—the so-called underdeveloped or ex-colonial or still colonial nations of Asia, Africa, and Latin America—is today the principal political contradiction in the world? Or do you consider that the basic contradiction is still one between the capitalist countries themselves?"

Mao Tse-tung said that he had not reached an opinion about that but he recalled something that President Kennedy had said. Had Kennedy not declared that as far as the United States, Canada, and Western Europe were concerned, there was not much real and basic difference? The President had said that the problem was in the Southern Hemisphere. In advocating "special forces warfare" training for "local [counter-subversive?] warfare," the late President may have had my question in mind.

On the other hand, contradictions between imperialists were what had caused two world wars in the past, and their struggles against colonial revolutions had not changed their character. If one looked at France one saw two reasons for de Gaulle's policies. The first was to assert independence from American domination. The second was to attempt to adjust French policies to changes occurring in the Asian-African countries and Latin America. The result was intensified contradiction between the capitalist nations, but was France part of its so-called "third world"? Recently he had asked some French visitors about that and they had told him no, that France was a developed country and could not be a member of the "third world" of undeveloped countries. The matter was not so simple.

"Perhaps it could be said that France is in the third world but not of it?"

Perhaps. This question which had engaged the interest of President Kennedy had led Kennedy, Mao had read, to study Mao's own essays on military operations. Mao had also learned from Algerian friends during their struggle against France that the French were reading his works and using his information against them. But he had told the Algerian Prime Minister, Abbas, at that time, that his own books were based on Chinese experience and would not work in reverse. They could be adapted only to the waging of people's wars of liberation and were rather useless in an anti-people's war. They did not save the French from defeat in Algeria. Chiang Kai-shek had also studied the Communists' materials but he had not been saved either.

Mao remarked that the Chinese also study American books. For instance, he had read *The Uncertain Trumpet* by General [Maxwell D.] Taylor, the United States Ambassador in Saigon. General Taylor's view was that nuclear weapons probably would not be used, therefore non-nuclear arms would decide. Taylor wanted priority given to the army. Now he had his chance to test out his theories of special warfare. In Vietnam he was gaining some valuable experience.

The chairman had also read some articles issued by U.S. authorities to their troops on how to handle guerrillas. These instructions dealt with the shortcomings and military weaknesses of the guerrillas and held out hopes for American victory. They ignored the decisive political fact that whether it was Diem or somebody else, governments cut off from the masses could not win against wars of liberation.

Since the Americans would not listen to Chairman Mao, his advice would do nobody any harm.

"In Southeast Asia as well as in India and certain countries of Africa and even Latin America, there exist some social conditions comparable to those that brought on the Chinese Revolution. Each country has its own problems, and solutions will vary widely, yet I wonder if you agree that social revolutions will occur which may borrow much from the Chinese?"

Anti-feudal and anti-capitalist sentiments combined with opposition to imperialism and neocolonialism, he replied, grew out of oppression and wrongs of the past. Wherever the latter existed there would be revolutions, but in most of the countries I was talking about, the people were merely seeking national independence, not socialism—quite another matter. European countries had also had anti-feudal revolutions. Though the United States had had no real feudal period, still it had fought a progressive war of independence from British colonialism, and then a civil war to establish a free labor market. Washington and Lincoln had been great men of the time.

"Among the roughly three fifths of the earth which belongs in the third world category, very acute problems exist, as we know. The gap between the ratio of population growth and growth of production is growing more disadvantageous. The gap between their ever falling standard of living and that of the affluent countries is rapidly widening. Under such conditions, will time wait for the Soviet Union to demonstrate the superiority of the socialist system—and then wait a century for parliamentarianism to arise in the underdeveloped areas and peacefully establish socialism?"

Mao thought that it would not wait so long.

I asked whether that question did not perhaps touch upon the nexus of China's ideological dispute with the Soviet Union. He agreed that it did.

"Do you think it would be possible to complete not only the national liberation of emerging nations of the third world, but also their modernization, without another world war?"

Use of the word "complete" must give one pause, he said. Most of the countries concerned were still very far from socialist revolutions. In some there were no Communist Parties at all, while in others there were only revisionists. It was said that Latin America had twenty Communist Parties and of these eighteen had issued resolutions against China. One thing was certain. Where severe oppression existed there would be revolution.

CHINA AND THE BOMB

"Do you still believe that the bomb is a paper tiger?"

That had just been a way of talking, he said, a kind of figure of speech. Of course the bomb could kill people. But in the end the people would destroy the bomb. Then it would truly become a paper tiger.

"You have been quoted as saying that China had less fear of the bomb than other nations because of her vast population. Other peoples might be totally wiped out, but China would still have a few hundred millions left to begin anew. Was there ever any factual basis to such reports?"

He answered that he had no recollection of saying anything like that but he might have said it. He did recall a conversation he had had with Jawaharlal Nehru, when the latter visited China (in 1954). As he remembered it, he had said China did not want a war. They didn't have atom bombs, but if other countries wanted to fight there would be a catastrophe in the whole world, meaning that many people would die. As for how many, nobody could know. He was not speaking only of China. He did not believe one atom bomb would destroy all mankind, so that you would not be able to find a government to negotiate peace. He mentioned this to Nehru during their conversation. Nehru said that he was Chairman of the Atomic Energy Commission of India and he knew about the destructiveness of atomic power. He was sure that no one could survive. Mao replied that it would probably not be as Nehru said. Existing governments might disappear but others would arise to replace them.

Not so long ago, Khrushchev said that he had a deadly weapon capable of killing all living things. But then he immediately retracted his statement—not only once but many times. Mao would not deny anything he had said, nor did he wish me to deny for him this so-called rumor (about China's millions' power of survival in a nuclear war).

Americans also had said very much about the destructiveness of the atom bomb and Khrushchev had made a big noise about that. They had all surpassed him in this respect, so that he was more backward than they, was not that so? Yet recently he had read reports of an investigation by Americans who visited the Bikini Islands six years after nuclear tests had been conducted there. From 1959 onward research workers had been in Bikini. When they first entered the island they had had to cut open paths through the undergrowth. They found mice scampering about and fish swimming in the streams as usual. The well water was potable, plantation foliage was flourishing, and birds were twittering in the trees. Probably there had been two bad years after the tests, but nature had gone on. In the eyes of nature and the birds, the mice and the trees, the atom bomb was a paper tiger. Possibly man has less stamina than they?

"Nevertheless, you would not exactly consider nuclear war to be a good thing?"

Certainly not, he replied. If one must fight, one should confine oneself to conventional weapons.

Indonesia had withdrawn from the United Nations, I observed, accompanied by applause from China. Did Mao Tsetung think the move would set a precedent and that other withdrawals would follow?

Mao said that it was the United States which had first set

the precedent, by excluding China from the United Nations. Now that a majority of nations might favor restoring China's seat despite U.S. opposition, there was a new scheme to require a two-thirds majority instead of a simple majority. But the question was, did China gain or lose by being outside the UN during the past fifteen years? Indonesia had left because she felt that there was not much advantage to remaining in the UN. As for China, was it not in itself a United Nations? Any one of several of China's minority nationalities was larger in population and territory than some states in the UN whose votes had helped deprive China of her seat there. China was a large country with plenty of work to keep her busy outside the UN.

"Is it now practicable to consider forming a union of nations excluding the United States?"

Mao pointed out that such forums already existed. One example was the Afro-Asian conference. Another was GANEFO—Games of the New Emerging Forces—organized after the United States excluded China from the Olympics.

(Preparations for the Afro-Asian conference scheduled to open in Algiers in March had been plagued by many problems. These included the Indonesia-Malaysia dispute, and insistence on the part of the pro-China Bandung powers that the USSR must be excluded from the conference, as a strictly European power. There is reason to believe that China regards the Afro-Asian organization as the potential center of planned development of a third world largely independent of neocolonial or Western capital. Following Chinese principles of "self-reliance" in internal development, and of mutual help between the Afro-Asian states, the process of modernization might be so speeded up as to bypass the slow and painful method of capital accumulation by traditional bourgeois means. Such a theoretical alternative would of course imply more rapid and radical political evolution and an earlier arrival at pre-socialist conditions in the capital-poor Afro-Asian states. Outside the context of this interview, it may be added that it has been obvious for some time that the Afro-Asian conference is also viewed as a potential permanent assembly of the have-not nations, to exist independently from the American-dominated United Nations from which China and her closest allies have long been excluded and which Indonesia has recently left.)

"In fact, Mr. Chairman, how many people are there inside

China's own 'United Nations'?" I asked. "Can you give me a population figure resulting from the recent census?"

The chairman replied that he really did not know. Some said that there were 680 to 690 million, but he did not believe it. How could there be so many? When I suggested that it ought not to be difficult to calculate, on the basis of ration coupons (cotton and rice) alone, he indicated that the peasants had sometimes confused the picture. Before liberation they had hidden births and kept some off the register out of fear of having them conscripted. Since liberation there had been a tendency to report greater numbers and less land, and to minimize output returns while exaggerating the effects of calamities. Nowadays a new birth is reported at once, but if someone dies it may not be reported for months. (His implication seemed to be that extra ration coupons could be accumulated in that way.) No doubt there had been a real decline in the birth rate, but the peasants were still too slow to adopt family planning. There had been a decline in the birth rate but the decline in the death rate was even greater. Longevity had increased from about thirty years of age to a life expectancy of around fifty.

That was the kind of answer, I said, which was calculated to give foreign professors lots of work to do. What kind of professors were those, Mao asked?

He was interested to hear that I had attended a conference where professors had debated whether he had or had not made any original contributions to Marxism. I told him that I had asked one professor, at the close of such a conference, whether it would make any difference in their controversy if it could be shown that Mao himself had never claimed to have made any creative contribution. The professor said, "No."

Mao was amused. More than two thousand years ago, he remarked, Chuang Chou wrote his immortal essay on Lao Tzu (called the *Chuang Tzu*). A hundred schools of thought then arose to dispute the meaning.

MAO'S WRITINGS

In 1960, when I had last seen Mao Tse-tung, I asked him whether he had ever written or had any intention of writing an "autobiography." He had replied in the negative. Nevertheless, learned professors had discovered "autobiographies" written by Mao. The fact that they were fraudulent did not in the least affect their documentary terminology.

A question currently exercising the professors was whether Mao had in fact written his celebrated philosophical essays "On Contradictions" and "On Practice" in the summer of 1937, as asserted in his collected works, or whether they had really been composed later.

He replied that he had indeed written them in the summer of 1937. During the weeks preceding and immediately following the Lukouch'iao incident, there had been a lull in his life in Yenan. The army had left for the front and Mao had found time in which to collect materials for some lectures on basic philosophy for use in the anti-Japanese academy. Some simple and yet fundamental text was needed for the young students being prepared, in brief, three-month courses, for political guidance during the years immediately ahead. At the insistence of the party Mao prepared "On Contradictions" and "On Practice" to sum up the experiences of the Chinese Revolution, by combining the essentials of Marxism with concrete and everyday Chinese examples. Mao wrote most of the night and slept during the day. What he had written over a period of weeks he delivered in lecture form in a matter of two hours. Mao added that he himself considered "On Practice" a more important essay than "On Contradictions." As for a treatise entitled "On Dialectical Materialism," which has been attributed to Mao's authorship by foreign Sinologists, he said that he had no recollection of having written any such work and he thought he would not have forgotten it had he done so.

"Youths who heard you lecture at Yenan later learned about revolution in practice but what could be the substitute for youths in China today?"

Mao said that of course those in China now under the age of twenty had never fought a war and never seen an imperalist or known capitalism in power. They knew nothing about the old society at first hand. Parents could tell them, but to hear about history and to read books was not the same thing as living it.

"Is the current emphasis on indoctrination of students with revolutionary principles and manual labor practice intended primarily to safeguard the future of socialism inside China or to teach Chinese youth that that security can never be guaranteed until socialism is victorious everywhere? Or are both aims inseparable?"

For the moment he did not directly answer the question. He asked what nation could really be said to have security? All the governments were talking about it and at the same time talking about complete and total disarmament. China herself had proposed general disarmament since a long time past. So had the Soviet Union. The U.S. kept talking about it. What we were getting instead was complete rearmament.

"President Johnson may find it difficult to settle problems in the East one by one," I said. "Perhaps if he desired to expose the world to the real complexity of those problems he might do worse than cut to the heart of the matter by accepting China's proposal to hold a summit conference to consider the total destruction of nuclear weapons."

Chairman Mao agreed but concluded that it would be quite impossible. Even if Mr. Johnson himself desired such a meeting, he was after all but a steward for the monopoly capitalists, and they would never permit it. China had had only one atomic explosion and perhaps it had to be proved that one could divide into two, and so *ad infinitum*. Yet China did not want a lot of bombs, which were really quite useless, since probably no nation dared employ them. A few would suffice for scientific experiments. Even one bomb was not liked in China's hands, however. Mao feared that his reputation was against him. The imperialists did not like him. Yet was it really right to blame China for everything and start anti-Chinese movements? Did China kill Ngo Dinh Diem? And yet that had happened. When the assassination of President Kennedy occurred, the Chinese were quite surprised. They had not planned that. Once more, they were quite surprised when Khrushchev was removed in Russia.

THE VIEW OF KHRUSHCHEV

"Western commentators, and especially the Italian Communists, severely criticized the Soviet leaders for the conspiratorial and undemocratic way in which Khrushchev was thrown aside. What is your view?"

He replied that Mr. K. had not been very popular in China even before his fall. Few portraits of him were to be seen. But K.'s books were for sale in the bookstores before the fall and they were still for sale here but not in Russia. The world needed Khrushchev: his ghost would linger on. There were bound to be people who liked him. China would miss him as a negative example.

"On the basis of your own 70/30 standard—that is, a man's work may be judged satisfactory if it is 70 per cent correct and only 30 per cent in error—how would you grade the present leadership of the Soviet Party? How far is it still below passing?" I asked.

Mao said he would not choose to discuss the present leaders in those terms. As for any improvement in Sino-Soviet relations, there was possibly some but not much. The disappearance of Khrushchev had perhaps only removed a target for polemical articles.

"In the Soviet Union," I said, "China has been criticized for fostering a 'cult of personality.' "

Mao thought that perhaps there was some. It was said that Stalin had been the center of a cult of personality, and that Khrushchev had none at all. The Chinese people, critics say, have some (feelings or practices of this kind). There might be some reasons for saying that. Was it possible, he asked, that Mr. K. fell because he had no cult of personality at all?

"Naturally I personally regret that forces of history have divided and separated the American and Chinese peoples from virtually all communication during the past fifteen years. Today the gulf seems broader than ever. However, I myself do not believe it will end in war and one of history's major tragedies."

Mao said that forces of history were also bound, eventually, to bring the two peoples together again; that day would surely come. Possibly I was right that meanwhile there would be no war. That could occur only if American troops came to China. They would not really get much out of it. That simply would not be allowed. Probably the American leaders knew that and consequently they would not invade China. Then there would be no war, because the Chinese certainly would never send troops to attack the United States.

"What of the possibilities of war arising over Vietnam? I

have read many newspaper stories indicating that the United States has considered expanding the war into North Vietnam."

No, Mao said, he thought otherwise. Mr. Rusk had now made it clear that the U.S. would not do that. Mr. Rusk may have earlier said something like that, but now he had corrected himself and said that he had never made such a statement. Therefore, there need not be any war in North Vietnam.

"I do not believe that the makers and administrators of United States policy understand you," I said.

Why not? China's armies would not go beyond her borders to fight. That was clear enough. Only if the United States attacked China would the Chinese fight. Wasn't that clear? The Chinese were very busy with their internal affairs. Fighting beyond one's own borders was criminal. Why should the Chinese do that? The Vietnamese could cope with their situation.

"American officials repeatedly say that if United States forces were withdrawn from Vietnam, then all Southeast Asia would be overrun."

The question was, said Mao, "overrun" by whom? Overrun by Chinese or overrun by the inhabitants? China was "overrun," but only by Chinese.

NO TROOPS OUTSIDE CHINA

In reply to a specific question, the Chairman affirmed that there were no Chinese forces in Northern Vietnam or anywhere else in Southeast Asia. China had no troops outside her own frontiers.

(In another context, it was said that unless Indian troops again crossed China's frontiers, there would be no conflict there.)

"Dean Rusk has often stated that if China would give up her aggressive policies then the United States would withdraw from Vietnam. What does he mean?"

Mao replied that China had no policies of aggression to abandon. China had committed no acts of aggression. China gave support to revolutionary movements but not by sending troops. Of course, whenever a liberation struggle existed China would publish statements and call demonstrations to support it. It was precisely that which vexed the imperialists.

Mao went on to say that on some occasions China deliberately makes a loud noise, as for example around Quemoy and Matsu. A flurry of shots there could attract a lot of attention, perhaps because the Americans were uneasy so far away from home. Consider what could be accomplished by firing some blank shells within those Chinese teritorial waters. Not so long ago the United States Seventh Fleet in the Taiwan Straits was deemed insufficient to reply to the shells. The U.S. also dispatched part of its Sixth Fleet in this direction and brought over part of the navy from San Francisco. Arrived here, they had found nothing to do, so it seemed that China could order the American forces to march here, to march there. It had been the same with Chiang Kai-shek's army. They had been able to order Chiang to scurry this way and then to hurry off in another direction. Of course when Navy men are warm and have full bellies they must be given something to do. But how was it that shooting off empty guns at home could be called aggression, while those who actually intervened with arms and bombed and burned people of other lands were not aggressors?

He continued: some Americans had said that the Chinese Revolution was led by Russian aggressors, but in truth the Chinese Revolution was armed by Americans. In the same way the Vietnamese revolution was also being armed by Americans, not by China. The liberation forces had not only greatly improved their supplies of American weapons during recent months but also expanded their forces by recruiting American-trained troops and officers from the puppet armies of South Vietnam. China's liberation forces had grown in numbers and strength by recruiting to their side the troops trained and armed by the Americans for Chiang Kai-shek. The movement was called "changing of hats." When Nationalist soldiers changed hats in large numbers because they knew the peasants would kill them for wearing the wrong hat, then the end was near. "Changing hats" was becoming more popular now among the Vietnamese puppets.

Mao said that the conditions of revolutionary victory in China had been, first, that the ruling group was weak and incompetent, led by a man who was always losing battles.

Second, the People's Liberation Army was strong and able and people believed in its cause. In places where such conditions did not prevail the Americans could intervene. Otherwise, they would stay away or soon leave.

"Do you mean that the circumstances of victory for the liberation front now exist in South Vietnam?"

Mao thought that the American forces were not yet ready to leave. Fighting would go on perhaps for one to two years. After that the United States troops would find it boring and might go home or somewhere else.

"Is it your policy now to insist upon the withdrawal of United States forces before participating in a Geneva conference to discuss the international position of a unified Vietnam?"

The chairman said that several possibilities should be mentioned. First, a conference might be held and United States withdrawal would follow. Second, the conference might be deferred until after the withdrawal. Third, a conference might be held but United States troops might stay around Saigon, as in the case of South Korea. Finally, the South Vietnamese front might drive out the Americans without any conference or international agreement. The 1954 Geneva Conference had provided for the withdrawal of French troops from all Indochina and forbade any intervention by any other foreign troops. The United States had nevertheless violated the convention and that could happen again.

"Under existing circumstances," I asked, "do you really see any hope of an improvement in Sino-American relations?"

GOING TO SEE GOD SOON

Yes, he thought there was hope. It would take time. Maybe there would be no improvement in his generation. He was soon going to see God. According to the laws of dialectics all contradictions must finally be resolved, including the struggle of the individual.

"Judging from this evening you seem to be in good condition," I said.

Mao Tse-tung smiled wryly and replied that there was perhaps some doubt about that. He said again that he was getting ready to see God very soon.

"I wonder if you mean you are going to find out whether there is a God. Do you believe that?"

No, he did not. But some people who claimed to be well informed said that there was a God. There seemed to be many gods and sometimes the same god could take all sides. In the wars of Europe the Christian God had been on the side of the British, the French, the Germans, and so on, even when they were fighting each other. At the time of the Suez Canal crisis God was united behind the British and French, but then there was Allah to back up the other side.

At dinner Mao had mentioned that both his brothers had been killed. His first wife had also been executed during the Revolution and their son had been killed during the Korean War. Now he said that it was odd that death had so far passed him by. He had been prepared for it many times but death just did not seem to want him. What could he do? On several occasions it had seemed that he would die. His personal bodyguard was killed while standing right beside him. Once he was splashed all over with the blood of another soldier, but the bomb had not touched him. There had been other narrow escapes.

After a moment of silence Mao said that he had, as I knew, begun life as a primary-school teacher. He had then had no thought of fighting wars. Neither had he thought of becoming a Communist. He was more or less a democratic personage such as myself. Later on, he sometimes wondered by what chance combination of reasons he had become interested in founding the Chinese Communist Party. Anyway, events did not move in accordance with the individual human will. What mattered was that China had been oppressed by imperialism, feudalism, and bureaucratic capitalism.

"Man makes his own history, but he makes it in accordance with his environment," I quoted. "You have fundamentally changed the environment in China. Many wonder what the younger generation bred under easier conditions will do. What do you think about it?"

He also could not know, he said. He doubted that anyone could be sure. There were two possibilities. There could be continued development of the Revolution toward Communism, the other possibility was that youth could negate the Revolution, and give a poor performance: make peace with imperialism, bring the remnants of the Chiang Kai-shek clique back to the Mainland, and take a stand beside the small percentage of counter-revolutionaries still in the country. Of course he did not hope for counter-revolution. But future events would be decided by future generations, and in accordance with conditions we could not foresee. From the long-range view, future generations ought to be more knowledgeable than we are, just as men of the bourgeois-democratic era were more knowledgeable than those of the feudal ages. Their judgment would prevail, not ours. The youth of today and those to come after them would assess the work of the Revolution in accordance with values of their own. Mao's voice dropped away, and he half closed his eyes. Man's condition on this earth was changing with ever increasing rapidity. A thousand years from now all of them, he said, even Marx, Engels, and Lenin, would possibly appear rather ridiculous.

Mao Tse-tung walked me through the doorway and, despite my protests, saw me to my car, where he stood alone for a moment, coatless in the sub-zero Peking night, to wave me farewell in the traditional manner of that ancient cultured city. I saw no security guards around the entrance, nor can I now recall having seen even one armed bodyguard in our vicinity all evening. As the car drove away I looked back and watched Mao brace his shoulders and slowly retrace his steps, leaning heavily on the arm of an aide, into the Great Hall of the People.

JAMES RESTON *

Washington: the Two Concepts of China

Washington, January 18, 1966

Behind the present debate on America's future strategy in Vietnam lie two fundamentally different arguments about modern China.

* James Reston, "Washington: The Two Concepts of China," *The New York Times,* January 19, 1966.

One is that she means what she says and is now embarked on a worldwide revolutionary movement to weaken and if possible destroy Western authority in a series of guerrilla wars.

The other is that she may mean what she says but does not have the power or influence to carry out her designs. Accordingly, the debate inside the government here increasingly encompasses questions that extend well beyond the geographical confines of Vietnam and even beyond the confines of this decade.

THE QUESTIONS

Is China capable of conquering all of Southeast Asia and threatening Japan and India? Is this her intention? If so, how can her expansion be contained and what nations, if any, will help take on the task?

The only thing that is clear is that this government and the allies seldom face up to these questions and when even a few of the leaders do, they differ fundamentally in their answers.

Some of them read the writings of Mao Tse-tung and his Defense Minister, Marshal Lin Piao, as if they were as important as Hitler's *Mein Kampf*. America and Europe, according to Chinese Communist doctrine, are the central urban area of the world which can be destroyed in an endless series of guerrilla wars waged by the rural peoples of Asia, Africa, and Latin America.

THE APOCALYPTIC VIEW

"When the U.S. aggressors are hard pressed in one place," Marshal Lin writes, "they have no alternative but to loosen their grip on others. Therefore, the conditions become more favorable for the people elsewhere to wage struggles against U.S. imperialism and its lackeys."

Nobody in the West has been more frank about the objective of these Communist wars of national liberation. "Everything is divisible," says Lin, "and so is this colossus of U.S. imperialism. It can be split up and defeated. The peoples of Asia,

Africa, Latin America, and other regions can destroy it piece by piece, some striking at its head and others at its feet. . . ."

The geopoliticians at the Pentagon and the State Department are fascinated by this sweeping and brutal call to war. Some of them take it seriously and would step up the war in Vietnam in order to demonstrate while China is comparatively weak that this doctrine cannot succeed.

Others take it seriously and would do exactly the opposite. That is to say, they would not risk war with China because they think China would fight rather than see the Viet Cong and the North Vietnamese Army destroyed.

And there are experienced men in this government and in the governments of our allies who think the whole vicious Chinese line is nothing more than a theoretical argument aimed at the Soviet Union, and/or a propaganda line designed to influence the Chinese workers.

The Premier of one of our Asian allies said to this reporter: "You Americans puzzle me. You taught us everything we know about pragmatism, but you are not approaching China pragmatically. You are operating on what China says and not on what China does."

He was not worried about China conquering Southeast Asia or getting into the Vietnamese war unless faced with the imminent collapse of North Vietnam. "China's problem is that she cannot conquer herself. She is not winning but losing the propaganda war with the more moderate Communists. She is not even convincing her own young people let alone the rest of the Communist world. Production is her problem and she is not doing very well at it. She is using the war in Vietnam to scare her own people into working harder. She may want to do all these revolutionary things in the world, but she cannot even deal with her problems at home."

There is very little clarity in the present debate in Washington because there is very little agreement on what the menace is, and until there is more clarity about modern China, the Vietnam debate is likely to remain in a state of confusion.

WILLIAM P. BUNDY *
The United States and Communist China

Communist China is without doubt the most serious and perplexing problem that confronts our foreign policy today. Peking's foreign-policy objectives, and the tactics it employs to achieve these objectives, sharply focus for us the issues of war and peace in Asia and the freedom and lives of millions of people, not only in Asia but throughout the world.

U.S. OBJECTIVES

The key questions we must ask at the outset are: What are our objectives, in Asia and in the world as a whole? What are Communist China's objectives? and What kind of policy is best for the United States in the light of those basic assessments?

And, viewed in this light, the unfortunate fact is that the kind of world that we seek and the kind of world our Asian friends seek is totally antithetic to the kind of Asia and the kind of world that Communist China seeks. What we seek is a situation where small as well as large nations are able to develop as free and independent countries, secure from outside aggression or subversion. We look toward their economic, political, and social development and growth; we hope their development will be in the direction of increasingly democratic institutions, but we recognize that these nations must develop as they themselves see fit, in accordance with their own traditions and customs. Their rate of progress, we believe, will vary according to individual situations, but progress will inevitably take place and

---

* William P. Bundy, "The United States and Communist China," address before the Associated Students of Pomona (California) College, February 12, 1966 (Washington, D.C.: U.S. Government Printing Office, 1966).

toward goals which are deeply rooted in individual aspirations.

In harsh conflict with these objectives is any situation in which a single nation or combination of nations sets out to control others in the region or to exercise political domination over other nations in the area or any major part of it.

Our objectives are consistent with the spirit of the Charter of the United Nations and, I believe, with the aspirations of the peoples and the governments of the area and of the nations in contiguous and other areas that share with us a concern for what happens in Asia in this and in the next generation. We believe, too, that our objectives accord with the whole tide of history at the present time. They are not abstract principles. They are the bedrock of our policy throughout the world. Governed by what the nations themselves wish to do and by practical factors, what we seek is to assist the nations that are trying to preserve their independence, trying to develop themselves, and, therefore, necessarily trying to resist forces working in the contrary direction.

CHINESE COMMUNIST OBJECTIVES

There is today in Communist China a government whose leadership is dedicated to the promotion of Communism by violent revolution.

The present leaders in Peking also seek to restore China to its past position of grandeur and influence. Many of Peking's leaders today, now grown old, are proud and arrogant, convinced that they have been responsible for a resurgence of Chinese power. The China of old exercised a degree of control over Asia that waxed and waned according to the power of the ruling emperor. Under strong rulers this meant a type of overlordship, sometimes benign but frequently otherwise, over the countries around its borders. And the restoration of that image and controlling influence is certainly a part of Communist China's foreign policy today.

In the 1930s Mao Tse-tung called attention to areas controlled by China under the Manchu Empire but since removed from Chinese control: Korea, Taiwan, the Ryukyus, the Pescadores, Burma, Bhutan, Nepal, Annam, and Outer Mongolia. In more recent years, Chinese Communist leaders have added to that list parts of Soviet Central Asia and eastern Siberia. I think we can take this as valid evidence of Peking's Asian ambitions. As Professor Oliver Edmund Clubb, in his *Twentieth Century China*, says: "The urge to revolutionary empire is fortified by the feeling drilled into all Chinese since the beginning of the Republic that all territory ever included in the vast Manchu Empire rightfully belongs to China."

In addition to these historically rooted aspirations, the present leadership is inspired by a Communist ideology still in a highly militant and aggressive phase. This phase is ideologically akin to that in the Soviet Union in the 1920s or early 1930s. It coincides, however, with a situation in which the opportunities for expansion are, or appear to Peking, more akin to those available to the Soviet Union at a much later phase in its ideological development—in 1945 and the immediate postwar years. This Communist element includes the advocacy of change through revolution and violence throughout the world and particularly in China's neighboring areas—not revolution seeking the fruition of the national goals of the people of these areas, but revolution supplied or stimulated from outside and based on a preconceived pattern of historical development.

Their vision of this Communist mission extends to countries far from China—including, as we all clearly have seen, Africa and even Latin America. Peking's plans for carrying out its objectives have been delineated in a series of pronouncements issued by its leaders, one of the latest and most widely publicized having been that issued last September by Marshal Lin Piao, top military leader in Communist China, in which Lin Piao offered Chinese Communist experience in the war against Japan as a lesson to be emulated by the less developed countries in Asia, Africa, and Latin America in their pursuit of "revolution."

As you know, the Lin Piao article draws an elaborate analogy based upon the domestic experience of Mao and his cohorts in taking over China: the organization of the rural areas against the urban ones. It extends that analogy to the thesis that the less developed areas of the world are all in the rural category which will be mobilized in order to destroy "the cities";

that is to say, all the Western, more advanced centers—ourselves, of course, at the head.

I mention this article because it is a clear and comprehensive indication that there has not taken place any moderating, but if anything a solidifying at least at this stage, of this virulent revolutionary policy that is central to our discussion of Communist China. And, of course, we have seen it in action over and over again.

THE CHINESE THREAT IN ASIA

I shall not speak at length of the problems created by Communist Chinese policy in Africa and Latin America. The recent reaction even of Castro suggests that Latin America is reacting adversely to the heavy-handedness of these policies. In Africa, too, there is every sign that the new nations of the area, themselves carrying out nationalist revolutions of their own design, know full well what is meant when Chou En-lai, for example, referred last June to Africa being ripe for a second stage of revolution. The new leaders of Africa have shown no desire to be Kerenskys.

But it is in Asia itself that the major thrust of Communist Chinese policy is felt and must be countered by their neighbors. It is sometimes argued that the ambitions of Communist China in the areas contiguous to it do not mean outright control; and it can certainly be argued that they are tactically cautious in pursuing these ambitions. They have not wished to seek a confrontation of military power with us, and in any situation that would be likely to lead to wider conflict they are tactically cautious. But in looking at the extent of their ambitions one cannot, I think, simply take the historical picture of tributary governments that would be tolerated as long as they did roughly what China wished. That indeed was the historic pattern in many periods when powerful governments ruled in the mainland of China. It is also, perhaps, the pattern one might draw abstractly from the desire any major power might feel not to have hostile military power based in areas adjacent to it. Those two logics, historic Chinese logic and "great power" logic, might appear to point to something less than total political domination as the Chinese Communist objective around their borders.

And yet we must recognize, I think, because of the Communist element in the thinking and practice of the leaders of Peking today, that there is another factor that raises strong doubts whether their ambitions are in fact this modest. We have seen, for example, in the contrast between what the Soviets have done in Eastern Europe and the behavior of predecessor Russian regimes, that there is a Communist logic that does insist on total control, that will not tolerate anything other than the imposition of the full Communist totalitarian system. The experience of Soviet control in Eastern Europe suggests that this same kind of Communist logic does and would apply to the behavior of Communist China.

That it would is further strongly suggested by the way that the Communist Chinese regime has treated Tibet. The fact that Tibet was within the historic limits of Chinese suzerainty does not explain why Communist China has virtually obliterated the culture of Tibet in seizing control of it. One cannot rationalize this on grounds of history or of the need of a great power not to have hostile forces adjacent to it. So I suggest that we must give great weight to the probability that the ambitions of Communist China do extend, not necessarily to the degree of obliteration of the local culture that we have seen in Tibet, but at least to a fairly total form of domination and control in areas contiguous to it.

What, then, would be the consequences if Communist China were to achieve the kind of domination it seeks? Here again one is tempted to look for analogy to Eastern Europe, where there is a growing will to pursue national and independent policies and to adopt domestic policies that differ sharply from the original Communist model. Yet it has taken twenty years of virtual subjugation for the nations of Eastern Europe to move this far, and their nationalism, traditions of independence, and capabilities for independent development were in general far more highly developed than those of the smaller nations on China's borders. To accept Mainland Chinese domination in Asia would be to look forward to conditions of external domination and probably totalitarian control, not merely for twenty years but quite possibly for generations.

Moreover, the spread of Chinese domination would inevitably create its own dynamic and in the end threaten even the most securely based and largest nations within the area of that threat, such as India and Japan. One does not need to subscribe to any pat "domino" formula to know from the history of the last generation, and indeed from all history, that the spread of domination feeds on itself, kindling its own fires within the dominant country and progressively weakening the will and capability of others to resist.

PAST MISTAKES AND THEIR RELEVANCE TO PRESENT

This is what we are dealing with. We can all think, as we look back at the history of China, of errors that we as a nation have made and that other nations of the West have made—errors in justice and conduct in our relationships with China. We should search our souls on these and set our objectives and our principles to avoid repeating them ever again. In Asia, at least, the colonial era is for all significant purposes at an end.

But to say that the West itself bears a measure of historical responsibility for the strength of the feelings of Communist China does not deal with the present problem any more than discussion of the inequities of Versailles dealt with the ambitions of Hitlerite Germany. Whatever the historic blame may be, we have to deal with the present fact of a Chinese Communist government whose attitudes are very deeply rooted in China's national history and ambitions to revive its past greatness, and in an extremely virulent Communist ideology.

In the words of a recent article by Professor [John K.] Fairbank:

> We are up against a dynamic opponent whose strident anti-Americanism will not soon die away. It comes from China's long background of feeling superior to all outsiders and expecting a supreme position in the world, which we seem to thwart.

TACTICS AND STRATEGY

I would like to emphasize that up to this point I have been speaking of the basic objectives of Peking's policy. To describe these objectives as deeply expansionist is by no means to paint the picture of another Hitler, building a vast military machine with the aim of conquest by conventional warfare on a timetable backed at some point, in the Chinese case, by a nuclear capability.

This has not been the historical Chinese way, and there is every reason to believe that it is not their present preference. Chinese are patient and think in long historical terms. Military force is important and they would like to think that their nuclear capability may at some point be useful in backing the picture of an overwhelmingly strong China whose will must be accepted. But the doctrinal statements of Lin Piao and others speak rather in terms of what they call "people's war," which plainly means the instigation and support of movements that can be represented as local movements, designed to subvert and overthrow existing governments and replace them by regimes responsive to Peking's will.

This is what we are seeing today in Thailand in the form of a so-called "Thai Patriotic Front" established and supported from Mainland China. This is the direct form of Communist Chinese tactic that must be met. A variant tactic was reflected in the Communist Chinese role in support of the PKI [Communist Party of Indonesia] in Indonesia.

But equally important to Peking is its encouragement and support of the parallel efforts of the other Communist Asian regimes in North Korea and North Vietnam. What is now happening in Vietnam is basically the result of Hanoi's own ambitions and efforts. Peking might wish eventually to dominate North Vietnam or a unified Vietnam under Hanoi's initial control. But if this were resisted by the Vietnamese in the classic historical pattern of relations between the two areas Peking would still gain enormously from the success of Hanoi's effort, which would clear the way for Peking to expand and extend the kind of action it is undertaking on its own in Thailand. It takes no vivid imagination to visualize what Peking would do in Malaysia, Singapore, and Burma if Hanoi were to succeed in Vietnam and Peking itself succeed in Thailand.

This, then, is the preferred Communist Chinese tactic and strategy. Ideas are a part of it, although Communist China's image as a successful model of social and political organization is hardly as attractive today as it may have been before the disastrous mistakes of the Great Leap Forward and the uneven progress of the years since. Few Asians today think of the Communist Chinese structure as a model, although individual ideas such as land reform and attacks on "feudal" social structures are a part of Peking's tactical efforts.

But essentially we are dealing here not with the power of ideas but with the power of subversive organization—perhaps the one field in which Communist China has shown real innovation and skill. In mainland Southeast Asia, as today in South Vietnam, what we could expect to see as the spearhead of the subversive effort would be terrorism, selective assassination, guerrilla action, and finally, if it were required, conventional military forces largely recruited by the tactics of the earlier phases.

These tactics might be varied if Communist China were to decide again to threaten India directly. There the element of conventional forces would play a greater part but would still be backed and reinforced by major political efforts to disrupt the cohesion and strength of India. . . .

2. DOMESTIC DEVELOPMENTS

❦ Succession and Generational Change: The Quest for Revolutionary Continuity

THE GREATEST concern of the Chinese leaders today is the preservation of China's future political unity and stability. The leaders of China are old and dying: in the past year they have mourned several of their old comrades; in the months and years to come they will mourn even more. Mao Tse-tung knows well, from Chinese history and from the history of other Communist movements, that the great leader is the indispensable man, for he alone can hold contending groups together. China's political system has vast institutionalized strength at its middle and lower levels, but at the top political men struggle with each other for different interests and ideas. Mao Tse-tung is determined that when he dies, factionalism shall not erupt at the top and endanger the entire structure.

The Chinese Communists won the Revolution with ideology and organization. Today, through one of history's most intensive indoctrination campaigns, they are seeking to imbue all Chinese with the revolutionary spirit and the Thought of Mao Tse-tung. The young are taught that the Revolution is far from being won, that internal and external danger still threaten, that economic progress gives an illusion of stability. They are also told that the hope of the continuing Revolution lies in their hands, and not in the men at the top. As Michel Oksenberg, Professor of Political Science at Stanford University, points out, the Chinese leaders are determined to fight the growing power of entrenched bureaucracy. Mao's contempt for the bureaucracy is well known, but Mao also knows that Chinese history is replete with revolts against officials who settled down in their high positions indifferent to the challenges of society.

Chinese tend to think in terms of three generations. The oldest generation still holds the reins of power today, reluctant to let the generation below it take over. But it is this second generation, men in their forties and fifties, who have assumed entrenched positions in China's immense bureaucracy. Mao does not trust them. His hope for the future lies in the young and the poor, the same kind of people who furnished the Revolution's combat cadres. Mao knows that the masses are often more radical than the leaders; men in positions of responsibility become cautious and careful, as Mao himself has been on many an occasion.

It is youth today which is being glorified in China. The models the young are exhorted to follow are the Lei Fengs (see pp. 450–456) and the Wang Chiehs, young men who died serving the people. With the abolition of military rank, famous generals now must serve for a period of time as privates with their men; managers and officials must go "deep down" and work with the masses. As can be noted in our selection on the Taiping Rebellion of the mid-1800s (see Volume II), Taiping decline began with decay among its leaders. Mao fears the same, and hopes that the organized younger generation will put such pressure from below on their new leaders that they dare not risk disunity through internecine strife. Young Chinese are today told that their fatherland is in mortal danger, from within as well as from without. The worsening world situation, of course, confirms the correctness of Mao's teachings. (On more recent changes in the structure of leadership, see pp. 607–610.)

MICHEL OKSENBERG *
Communist China:
A Quiet Crisis in Revolution

Efforts to maintain revolutionary momentum provide the unifying theme for analysis of Chinese politics in 1965. The strong
continuity with the policies established the previous year means
that analyses of broad political trends on the Mainland in 1964
are generally applicable to 1965. The Chinese Communist Party
(CCP) continued to face two fundamental problems. Can it
cultivate a political environment which is conducive to rapid,
planned social and economic change? To what extent and how
can the CCP channel and give direction to the social forces
which it has unleashed?

Peking's preoccupation with continuing the revolutionary
momentum was reflected not only by the specific measures
calculated to deal with the issue directly, but also by the policies
adopted toward two concrete issues which received primary
attention—military preparedness and foreign affairs. These policies were clearly intended, in part, to facilitate Party-directed
social change.

By 1965, it was evident that the CCP leadership was facing
a quiet crisis in its attempt to keep the revolutionary fires burning. Forcing the pace of economic and social change through
Party-organized mass campaigns and rigorous Party ideological
control invites the disasters of the Great Leap. Party failure to
force the pace invites bureaucratic calcification and causes the
Party to surrender authority, particularly in the economic realm,
to technicians. Neither alternative is desirable. Before outlining
the dimensions of the difficulties and some of the steps the
Party took, it is wise to state what the "quiet crisis" does *not*
include.

* Michel Oksenberg, "Communist China: A Quiet Crisis in Revolution,"
Asian Survey, VI, 1, January 1966, pp. 3–11.

There is no crisis in rule. Barring China's involvement in a war, when new considerations could enter the picture, the supremacy of the Communist Party is secure. The CCP continued to display its dominance over the one conceivable rival group, the professional soldiers, when it abolished the system of military rank.

Within the party, the problem of succession appears to be settled, if the sixty-seven-year-old heir apparent, Liu Shao-ch'i, outlives seventy-two-year-old Mao Tse-tung. Liu's position was further consolidated during the year. The standard phrase, "Under the leadership of Chairman Mao . . ." was altered upon occasion to read, "Under the leadership of Chairman Mao and Chairman Liu. . . ." In perhaps the supreme accolade, Liu's calligraphy graced the pages of major government publications when they reprinted his message commemorating the tenth anniversary of the Bandung Conference. Finally, Liu was named to head the prestigious committee which will direct the November 1966 celebrations of the one hundredth birthday of Sun Yat-sen.

The only visible problem surrounding succession is the lack of a clearly designated "Number Three." While factional strife quite conceivably could erupt following Mao's death, with Liu presiding over an interregnum, there are no signs that any power struggle would affect the basic stability of the regime. In its forty-four-year history, the CCP has displayed a remarkable ability to engage in bitter intra-Party disputes without directly benefiting bystanders.

Moreover, there is no crisis in the economy. With a few exceptions, the year saw a continuation of the recovery and growth which began in 1963, after three years of deep economic depression. Unavailability of firm data precludes giving precise production statistics and growth-rate percentages. Nonetheless, visitors to the Mainland were impressed with the variety of consumer goods available in the major cities which they were allowed to visit. Early indications are that grain production dropped slightly due to drought in the North. But, the government was able to resume its program of stockpiling grain in warehouses for emergency use, a program pursued during the midfifties and drawn upon during the "three lean years." Hog production increased considerably, which, as the authorities recognized, was largely due to incentives provided to private hog producers. The light and heavy industry sectors also appear to have recovered from the slump. The recovery has enabled the regime to proclaim throughout the year that it was on the eve of launching another "high tide" of production increase. What this means specifically will be revealed in the Third Five Year Plan, to be launched in 1966. Early indications are that the plan will continue the policies of emphasizing agricultural improvements and stressing quality, quantity, and variety of goods. Ambitious but rational targets will probably be set. Thus, while there are some lagging sectors in the recovery, and some bottlenecks in the economy (principally transportation and chemical fertilizers, and perhaps oil).

The urgent problem which the regime does face, however, and of which the rulers are well aware, is the maintenance of the set of conditions which gave the Revolution its earlier impetus. When the People's Republic was established in 1949, the government was in a political climate hospitable to the development of the Chinese economy and the change of Chinese society. The new leadership was young and vigorous, composed of bold visionaries who had displayed a talent in their guerrilla experience for arriving at pragmatic solutions to the problems they faced.

The new government had wide appeal among many sectors of society: intellectuals, students, peasants, white-collar workers, and laborers. A large proportion of the population, while not completely aware of the new leadership's ultimate social aims and certainly unaware of the inevitable demands which rapid economic development exact from the population, was prepared to join in the building of the "New China."

In addition to the quality of the leadership and its mass support, the Communist Party and the army provided effective revolutionary instruments. They were composed of men and women steeled in a bitter guerrilla struggle, disciplined by thorough rectification movements, and whose interests tended to coincide with the Party's program. In its early years, moreover, the revolutionary government could, within limits, structure a new bureaucracy; it did not face a government bureaucracy to whom it owed political debts.

Sixteen years after the assumption of power, many of these

initial advantages have eroded. The top leadership is aged and presumably not as vigorous as in 1949. In a difficult matter to judge, it appears that the regime has alienated some of its initial supporters, particularly intellectuals, and lost the active support of others, particularly in the countryside. (Whether the people would rally to support the government in case of war is, of course, another matter.) With the expansion of its membership to nearly eighteen million, the Party has attracted not only people interested in implementing the Party's program, but also those primarily interested in advancing their own careers. The interests of lower level Party functionaries no longer closely coincide with the policies advocated by the top leadership. Bureaucracy has become entrenched. Throughout 1965, the leaders devoted their attention to these difficulties.

Personnel changes and promotions have led to the introduction of slightly younger personnel into the higher echelons of the government and Party, in a leadership where fifty-five to sixty years of age must be considered "slightly younger." For example, Ho Wei, fifty-seven, replaced the sixty-nine-year-old Yang Hsiu-feng as Minister of Education; Yang, in turn, replaced the eighty-five-year-old Hsüeh Chüeh-ts'ai as head of the Supreme People's Court. In the past two years, twelve men in their fifties, relatively new faces, have become Ministers of industrial departments. These men will probably play a crucial role in directing the Third Five Year Plan. T'ao Chu, the energetic fifty-nine-year-old First Secretary of the Party's Central South Bureau, continued his rapid ascent by becoming Vice-Premier. Fifty-two-year-old Hu Yao-pang, longtime holder of the important post of First Secretary of the Young Communist League, stepped into Party work when he became First Secretary of Shensi province and Third Secretary of the Northwest Bureau.

The regime's effort to widen its popular support probably was a major reason for the establishment of Poor and Lower Middle Peasants' Associations (PLMPA) throughout the countryside, a form of organization which harked back to the Peasants' Associations established to assist in land reform. These prestige associations first began to appear in late 1964, and reports of their meetings and activities have received considerable attention in regional radio broadcasts. Membership in the brigade and commune PLMPA is limited to peasants of the lower

economic classes; indirect elections successively select the delegates to county and provincial PLMPAs. The purposes of the
PLMPA are numerous—to continue the Party's class policy
in the countryside, to keep an independent check upon lower
level cadres, and to create another "transmission belt" by which
policy directives can elicit a mass response. These purposes indicate that the regime is aware that many of its lower level
officials have become estranged from the peasantry. Establishment of these prestige associations is designed to recapture
positive commitment from the Party's most enthusiastic initial
supporters.

Peking also was concerned with the disenchantment its class
policy was causing among children of upper-class parents. Many
such offspring apparently have become alienated because they
have little future in a society where careers are heavily influenced
by one's class origins. The Party campaigned strongly, particularly in the pages of publications aimed at youth, to convince
these youths that their background would not influence their
career opportunities, providing they clearly renounced the influence of their parents. Further, local branches of the Young
Communist League were urged to consider the character of applicants for membership, and not to reject outright people from
upper-class background.

An important editorial in *People's Daily* on June 21, 1965,
entitled "Coordination Between Labor and Leisure" also reflected the regime's desire to capture and maintain the active
support of the working man. The editorial points out that workers must have leisure time which they can dispose of freely. Non-
working hours should not be devoted entirely to organized spare
time activities such as study, production conferences, and sport
activities. One may question the effectiveness of these editorials
and organizational measures. They do, however, indicate the
leadership's awareness and concern.

Moreover, the higher echelons apparently have debated
the policy of seeking wider support. The scanty evidence available indicates that while the government is willing to take limited
measures, it is not prepared to sacrifice important aspects of its
program. Apparently some, possibly including the dismissed
head of the United Front Work Department, Li Wei-han, have
advocated policies with more appeal. Premier Chou En-lai re-

vealed this in his report to the First Session of the Third National People's Congress, when he stated:

> In domestic affairs, quite a number of people actively advocated the so-called "three self and one undertaking" (*i.e.,* increasing the size of private plots, extending free markets, and increasing small enterprises with sole responsibility for their own profits and losses, and the fixing of output quotas at the household level), "going it alone" (*i.e.,* the restoration of individual economy), "liberalization," "reversal of previous correct decisions," and capitulationism in United Front Work.

Thus, the regime is reluctant to provide further material incentives to win popular support. It feels that this would divert resources from investment and would cause the nation to turn away from building a communist society.

The top leadership displayed its concern for maintaining a dynamic, vital Party apparatus by continuing to call for the intensive study of the works of Chairman Mao, study which is intended to heighten the dedication, resolve, and initiative of the reader; by continuing the socialist education campaign, which applies to both Party and non-Party members; and by calling for renovation and reform in specific Party apparatus. For example, in September, *People's Daily* began a series of articles which spelled out weaknesses in the *hsien* (county) Party committee apparatus ("divorced from reality," "too much paper shuffling," and "topheavy in organization"). They indicate that a major "rectification campaign" and perhaps a reorganization of the *hsien*-level Party apparatus is in the offing.

The concern of the top leadership with maintaining the vitality of the Party pales, however, in comparison with its fight against the growing power of entrenched bureaucracy. Interviewing refugees and reading the Mainland press indicate that the zeal for achieving social change has been sapped by a penchant for bureaucratic behavior: the desire to maximize status while minimizing responsibility, the ability to postpone decision and action until the decision or action is no longer required, and the capacity to build an organizational position impregnable to attack.

Admittedly, the evidence for this picture of Chinese bureaucracy is impressionistic. The top leadership views the problem in the commercial arena in this way:

> The tendency to ignore politics and to cling to purely professional viewpoints is a kind of habitual force which has long occupied a ruling position in commercial departments. When commercial departments at various levels hold conferences, announce directives, and report on work, the leadership cadres often emphasize only commodities, targets, systems, and professional techniques. . . . Very often they see things, but not people. . . .
>
> The manifestations of the above-mentioned purely professional viewpoints exist to a large extent in commercial departments. Many comrades take this state of affairs for granted, and are not surprised by it. They are satisfied with the *status quo*. They refuse to seek improvements. They have not yet realized that the tendency to ignore politics and to cling to purely professional viewpoints, to be satisfied with the *status quo,* and to be blindly complacent without seeking improvements are big obstacles to the further improvement of socialist commercial work in our country.

Examples abound of this behavior and the government's determination to deal with it.

The T'ang-shan Special Administrative District (SAD) experiment in commodity distribution is a case in point. *Hsien* commercial organs required all commodities purchased or distributed in the area under their jurisdiction to be shipped first to its central warehouse, usually located in the county seat. Goods were then reshipped to the ultimate destination. Such a distribution system resulted in considerable double-shipping. Often, merchandise transported to the warehouse in the county seat was then carried back over the same route to the ultimate destination. Moreover, production brigades were to buy and sell all commodities in their *hsien;* they were not to transact business in neighboring *hsien,* even if transportation or prices were more advantageous.

In effect, these practices were the means by which the *hsien*-level commercial units played a prominent part in, and justified their role in, distribution. The proposals arising from the experiment in commodity distribution were, when appropriate and when the transportation system makes it economical, to bypass the *hsien*-level distribution apparatus, and to allow SAD-level commercial units to deal directly with the lowest level commercial units. The network for the purchase and supply of commodities would be based on "natural economic conditions" —transportation routes, traditional marketing patterns, etc.— rather than forcing the trading network to conform to the less suitable *hsien* boundary. The proposals make economic sense, and would help to solve the rather serious transportation bottlenecks in rural China. The reform is now spreading to other regions of China.

The initiative for the experiment apparently should be traced to a Central Committee "Directive on Some Questions Concerning Commercial Work," issued in September 1962. The present spread of the system is apparently the result of considerable pressure and propaganda work. One is led to ask, have organizations such as *hsien*-level trading companies become so entrenched that the center must exert tremendous effort before reforms can occur? Has periodic reorganization become a major method for enabling the center to maintain a responsive bureaucracy? One is tempted to answer "yes" to both of these questions.

Another example of bureaucracy protecting its vested interests can be found in the history of the Poor and Lower Middle Peasants' Association described above. One of their purposes was to check on the performance of lower level cadres. However, when the chairmen of the various provincial PLMAs were announced, they usually were the Provincial First Party Secretaries, while the associations' permanent organization was dominated by the leading provincial Party figures. It would be surprising if these men would welcome vigilance over the Party apparatus they led. Moreover, when the occupations of delegates to PLMAs were disclosed, typically the delegates were heads of production brigades, accountants, and/or Party members. Lower level officials appear to have captured control of an organization intended to supervise them.

There are more examples of bureaucracy in the pejorative sense: the ceaseless flow of forms and reports which lower level units must supply to their superiors; and a clearly demarcated

civil service grading system in which people of different status
are entitled to different housing accommodations, transportation, and office furniture.

Such behavior resembles that of organizations and bureaucrats everywhere. But such practices cannot be tolerated by a
ruling elite dedicated to the implementation of such a social
revolution. An urgency exists, lest bureaucracy becomes so committed to the *status quo* that no momentum for change can be
generated. On the other hand, an excessive attack upon bureaucratic practices, such as occurred during the Great Leap, will
disrupt the day-to-day administration required to order society
and direct the economy.

The regime's most recent solution to this problem is the
establishment of offices in charge of political affairs, located in
organizations dealing with finance and trade, industry and communications, and agriculture and forestry. This major administrative innovation, modeled after the system of political training
and supervision in the People's Liberation Army (PLA), began
in 1964 and spread to lower level organizational units and the
agricultural and forestry administrative system in 1965. The
political offices are responsible for implementing the Party's
ideological program within the bureaucracy. Organizations have
been created to secure attitudinal change among government
and enterprise personnel.

The reform has also entailed a reorganization of the departments under the CCP Central Committee. The exact nature
of the Party reorganization remains vague, since the Mainland
press rarely discusses the internal organization of the CCP. However, it appears that these departments have been given the job
of providing personnel for and supervising the activities of the
political offices in enterprises and government agencies. For
example, the CCP's Finance and Trade Political Department,
which previously was called the Finance and Trade Department, is in charge of the political offices in financial and trade
organizations.

The programs of "red and expert" and "combining education with labor" are also inextricably intertwined with the fight
against the development of a bureaucratic mentality. "Redness"
might be translated as being sensitive to the general needs of society, as defined by the CCP. "Expert" refers to technical pro-

ficiency. The Party believes that in order for one's technical proficiency to be well employed, personal sacrifices must inevitably be made. Thus, one must possess a certain degree of altruism and idealism in addition to technical skill. A series of articles dealing with design work, which appeared in *People's Daily,* provide examples of the continued emphasis upon "Red and expert." The theme of these articles was that designers must not strive solely for artistic quality, as their professional commitment requires; rather, they should stress functional design, for that is all their society can afford.

Thus, a number of measures underline a continuation and perhaps even an intensification of the effort to recapture the advantages which the regime possessed when it came to power— vigorous leadership, mass appeal, a Party and army ready to serve as revolutionary instruments, and (after the Three-Anti, Five-Anti Campaigns in 1951–1952) a bureaucracy relatively unencumbered by vested interests. In addition, Peking's concern with maintaining revolutionary momentum was reflected in its handling of two of the year's dominant issues, military preparedness and foreign affairs.

Due largely to the conflict in Vietnam, military preparedness was of paramount importance. A number of steps were taken to ready the nation for war, both physically and psychologically. First, even prior to the constant U.S. bombardment of North Vietnam, the length of service in China's armed forces had been increased by one year, bringing the total to four years in the army, five years in the specialized troops, security forces, and air force, and six years in the navy. It is estimated that, if the annual draft quotas remain the same, the change will result in a 25-per-cent expansion of the armed forces. Longer tenure, in any case, enables fuller utilization of skills.

Second, there were persistent reports of Chinese troops massing on the Sino-North Vietnamese border, and of major cities on the Mainland girding for war. Reportedly, civil defense exercises were held, some of the population was being evacuated, and plans were made to disperse industries. Third, the portion of Kwangtung province bordering on North Vietnam was transferred to Kwangsi, a province also bordering on North Vietnam. Defense strategy and control of communications thereby came under more unified military command.

It would seem that the Chinese people have been carefully prepared for involvement in Vietnam. Night after night, domestic radio described the "dastardly acts" of "American imperialism" in Vietnam. Pamphlets, posters, and short stories about the "brave struggle of the people of South Vietnam" have flooded the Mainland. The stakes which Peking thinks are involved were clearly repeated and explained. In addition, physical fitness, particularly in the form of a mass swimming campaign that had distinct military overtones, became a major preoccupation.

Two other measures to secure China's defense were connected with the maintenance of revolutionary momentum. The abolition of military rank was intended, in part, to improve morale in an army which conceivably could soon be involved in combat. But it also was calculated to curb a narrow professional military loyalty from spreading among the officer corps. It therefore can also be considered as part of the campaign against bureaucracy. Members of the PLA now no longer hold a rank independent of their command post. One effect of such a military system is to increase the dependency of the careerist upon those people who assign the command post. Without one, all privileges are lost; no ranks exist which help to establish priorities in the assignment of command posts. Since personnel cadres probably have close Party connections, the net effect of the abolition of rank seems to be an increase in the power of the Party over the army.

The role of the People's Militia received increased emphasis. The militia has received varying attention over the past decade, but periods of emphasis have been correlated with dangers of war. Thus, the 1958 campaign to make "every man a soldier" fell in the same year as the Quemoy-Matsu crisis, while the 1962 revival of the militia coincided with a period when the regime apparently believed attack by the Republic of China (Taiwan) was imminent. In addition to military preparedness, the leadership believes that the militia serves revolutionary purposes:

> Turning all people into soldiers has been a basic measure for consolidating national defense and the dictatorship of the proletariat, and an important guarantee for . . . preventing a capitalist restoration during the new period of socialist revolution and socialist construction.

Organizing and training of the people's militia . . . is
also an important measure to guarantee that the guns will
be forever in the hands of the Party and the people, and
will never become the tool of careerists.

Military preparedness shared the headlines with China's
involvement in world affairs. The year was highlighted by successes in the United Nations and Vietnam, and failures over the
Afro-Asian Conference and in Indonesia. The 47–47 vote to
seat the People's Republic in the General Assembly was Peking's
highest total to date. From the leadership's perspective, success
was being achieved in the long-run strategy of isolating, harassing, and overextending the United States while committing a
minimum amount of Chinese power and prestige. In Vietnam,
over 165,000 U.S. troops are entangled in an expensive jungle
war. America's efforts are receiving little active support from
her allies and produce student demonstrations at home. Thus far,
all this has occurred without China's direct involvement.

On the other hand, the inability to convene an Afro-Asian
Conference under China's leadership was a serious setback.
China was confident that the underdeveloped areas were hers
to lead. She seriously underestimated the divisions within the
Afro-Asian world and the influences of the USSR and USA.
Undoubtedly, the most serious blow occurred in Indonesia. The
anti-Communist movement which developed in reaction to the
unsuccessful September 30th coup has placed Peking in a position similar to the one Stalin faced in 1927 over China. It is the
problem of the United Front. How long can Peking continue
to pay homage to the United Front, and particularly to a Su-
karno who appears to be the captive of the military? Will China
stand idly by while the Indonesian Communist Party (PKI)
is systematically decimated? Or, will she risk deterioration of
Sino-Indonesian relations and support the PKI? In effect, will
she choose the revolutionary road, or the road of cooperation
with nationalist non-Communists, and hence the road to Afro-
Asian unity? Peking confronts such unpleasant alternatives that
choice will probably be postponed as long as possible.

China's foreign policy is best explained in terms of the
leadership's projection of their guerrilla experiences to the
world arena. It is also related to her economic base, to the
opportunities she perceives, and to such intangibles as the leader-

ship's personalities and knowledge. It is also important to ask, however, whether the foreign policy is suited to the rulers' domestic needs. If it is, then it is unlikely that domestic forces will prevail to change it.

In one respect, it does meet the leadership's needs: it helps sustain the Revolution. Emphasis upon "self reliance" in economic development and a willingness to do without firm allies in foreign affairs enables the regime to appeal to nationalistic and patriotic sentiments and to make heavier demands upon the population. Attributing China's industrial collapse largely to the USSR's withdrawal of technical advisers, or arousing hostile feelings toward the United States may focus domestic discontent upon foreign powers, rather than upon the top leadership.

Domestic political needs also help to explain the difference between China's verbal militancy and her actual cautiousness in foreign affairs. As their widespread coverage in domestically oriented publications indicate, foreign-policy statements are directed as much toward domestic as they are toward foreign audiences. By stressing its militant foreign posture, the leadership is probably better able to convince its citizens that domestically it is determined to "carry out the Revolution to the end."

The stated objectives of China's ruling elite are to change China rapidly: to build an industrialized nation, to instill among its people new values derived from Marxism-Leninism and the CCP's guerrilla heritage, to provide its citizens with a higher standard of living, and to enable China to have a strong and perhaps even dominant voice in the council of nations. Not all of these ambitious goals are compatible. Often, pursuit of one involves temporary and perhaps permanent surrender of another. The leadership does not wish to abandon any of its ambitious dreams.

In 1965, moderate progress was registered in the economy; China's voice in world affairs was listened to more attentively. It was a normal, predictable year, with few innovations in policy. To the average ruling elite, these results would have been satisfactory. But China's revolutionary elite must ask themselves another question. How many years such as 1965 can be tolerated before the social system becomes so settled that rapid, directed change is nearly impossible? The Third Five Year Plan should indicate their answer to this question.

❧ Economy and Trade:
Recovery and Development

AS THE Great Leap Forward moved into high gear early in 1958, the Chinese began to believe that they had really unlocked a secret source of energy which in a few short years would transform China from a backward into a modern nation: here was a gigantic nation with an immense potential labor force. During the First Five Year Plan the Chinese, with the help of Soviet economic advisers, built up an impressive modern industry. Yet as new factories went up in Manchuria, the leaders in Peking looked over China's vast lands where peasants were still working the fields in age-old fashion. Why not tap the peasants' energies to build small factories? Why not use the underemployed city population for productive work to supplement the production of the modern factories? If everyone were taught to do a few simple industrial tasks, the aggregate output would add immensely to China's economic potential. The key, it seemed, lay in mobilizing the population.

From early 1958 on, all of China was in a fever pitch of work. Everywhere backyard steel furnaces were erected; roads, dams, reservoirs, small-scale factories were built. Steel, symbol of Stalin's industrialization, had been the preserve of a few modern plants; now everyone could make his own steel. Just as the masses were the foundation of politics, now they would become the foundation of the economy. Behind all the frenzy there was a rational program. Industry was concentrated in a few key areas, mainly Manchuria and East China, while the other provinces remained overwhelmingly agricultural. Why not mobilize the provincial population, bring in a few simple modern techniques, unearth ancient techniques that might still be useful, and start building small factories which could at least supply local needs, thus relieving the distant modern industries of the burden? Moreover, economists in and out of China had long argued that a backward country with a vast labor force could not afford capital-intensive projects. Why not substitute labor for capital? If you cannot afford to build a machine, have hundreds of men do the machine's work until such time as the machine can be built.

As the organized masses hurled themselves into the front line of production, their cadre leaders became dizzy with success. As products rolled out of the factories and production figures climbed, the cadres felt that for years they had been subject to a gigantic swindle which they called the fetishism of technology. Industrial work was not so complicated as the educated technicians had told them. Who needed complex blueprints when a simple drawing sufficed? Economists had told them they must keep careful records. Why, when a few figures were enough to tell the planners what the masses were doing. In any case, the need for planners was not so great any longer. Planning work was sitting in offices, and that was bureaucratism. The state would soon wither away, the cadres were told, and so thousands of trained economists were fired from their jobs.

The Great Leap Forward was magnificent madness. The Russians, who had helped draft the original Second Five Year Plan, went home in despair. Chinese economists, if they were not "*hsiafang*ed" (sent down to the villages and the factories) kept discreetly quiet. After all, so respected an old economist as Ma Yin-ch'u, President of Peking University, had been bitterly criticized for having said that China's vast population might put a brake on its economic growth. For a while during 1958 it appeared that the Chinese had succeeded: output figures for industry and agriculture soared. But by December 1958 the leaders were becoming cognizant of the need to bank down the fires somewhat. The pace of development continued, but an effort was made to coordinate the millions of projects. The new slogan was "All the Country Is a Single Chessboard." But by the fall of 1959 the drive was put into high gear again, not with the elation of 1958 but with a dogged determination to make it work.

By the late summer of 1960 full disaster had set in. The reckless communization of agriculture had sent the rural economy into a tailspin. At the same time, China suffered some of the worst natural disasters in hundreds of years. The termination of Soviet economic assistance paralyzed the industrial economy. The dramatic reversal of all the progress of just a few years earlier caused a number of Western observers to see a "descending spiral" in the Chinese economy in which chaos would multiply until, hopefully, the Communist regime would topple. These were terrible years for Mao Tse-tung. In many parts of the country he was blamed for the terrible turn of events. Though mass starvation was avoided, hunger swept the land. Factory after factory closed down, just as in the Great Depression of the United States. The dream of a fully industrialized China vanished.

Kang Chao, Professor of Economics at the University of Wisconsin, describes the disastrous effects of the Great Leap Forward. There was enormous waste of resources and a disastrous decline in the quality of output. Useless machines were produced in great quantities. The system of economic statistics, on which a modern economy depends, had broken down. In 1958 cadres had sent up inflated production figures, caring little whether they were right or wrong. In 1960, when the government proceeded to clean up the mess, the planners did not know what kind of economy they faced. The limited and overstrained transportation system developed structural bottlenecks that greatly impeded shipment from surplus to deficit areas. During the Great Leap Forward the Communists urged plants to diversify their production, making use of waste materials to produce supplemental products which could reduce the dependency of the factories on outside sources of supply. But production costs rose so much that the advantages of diversification over the earlier specialization were practically nullified. Not least important was the drop in workers' morale. The short supply of food was destroying the incentive to work hard.

There was undisguised satisfaction in many Western circles that the arrogant Communists were finally being faced with their just deserts after subjecting society and economy to such a drive. But the "descending spiral" did not result in collapse. In January of 1961, when the Central Committee decided on a reversal of economic policy, the country's top economic leaders came back into prominence. They turned to the technicians, managers, and administrators, so berated only a short time ago, and asked their aid in pulling the pieces together again. The "experts" responded, and within a few years China was back on the road to recovery. This time, however, the Chinese vowed never to depend on anyone again. The slogan was *tzu-li keng-sheng*—self-reliance.

To this day the Chinese Communists feel the effects of the economic crisis. As Alexander Eckstein, Professor of Economics at the University of Michigan and one of the foremost American experts on Chinese economics, states: ". . . unless there is a miraculous boon in the form of unusually good harvests or foreign aid on a large scale, further economic growth and advance in China may be expected to be significantly slower than in the 1950s. Correspondingly, the Chinese Communist vision of becoming a top-ranking industrial nation may have to be postponed for a long time to come." The Chinese Communists appear to agree with this estimation, now speaking of decades of hard effort before China can reach the industrial level of the Soviet Union, let alone the United States.

The Chinese have a strong practical streak. Having recognized the failure of ideological economics, they went back to practical economics. As Eckstein points out, they realized that food and population were their two serious economic bottlenecks. In effect, they accepted the counsel of economists like Ma Yin-ch'u whom they had previously scorned, and made birth control and agricultural development the keystones of their socioeconomic policy. No one outside of China, and perhaps even no one in China, knows what the precise size and growth rate of the Chinese population is. China's one nationwide census (1953) is regarded by most foreign observers as faulty. United Nations calculations project a "high estimate" population of over a billion in 1978, and a "low estimate" of some 770,000,000. Since June 1966 the Chinese officially admit to a population of 700,000,000. Population has been growing in China for a long time, but ironically it has been the improved health standards, longer life expectancy, and a dramatic decline in death rates all brought about by Communist rule that have been major factors in the recent population explosion.

China's first birth-control campaign began late in 1956. It

was interrupted during the Great Leap Forward, at least in official theory, when the Chinese Communist leaders appeared to have literally accepted the Marxian teaching that the solution to the Malthusian dilemma was not reduction of population but increase in production. The birth-control campaign was revived in 1962, and since then has been major official policy. Thus, regardless of high or low population-growth projections, the Chinese government is clearly determined to take radical measures to keep the birth rate down.

On agricultural policy Eckstein notes that, in general, they "have pursued a prudent and more or less conservative economic policy—easing the tax and collection pressure on the peasantry, trying to foster a generally more favorable incentive system for agriculture, keeping the savings burden down, and channeling a large share of investment to agriculture and agriculture-supporting industries." Obviously, a policy which redirects investment to agriculture and cuts down on rural savings will have the effect of slowing industrial growth, particularly in view of the relatively minor role of foreign trade and the total absence of foreign aid in the Chinese economic picture.

Despite the reduced rate of growth, however, the Chinese economy gives the impression of slow but steady progress. The number and quality of manufactured products have increased, as has been evident at recent Canton trade fairs. Visitors report well-stocked department stores in the country. Their nuclear energy industry indicates an economic and technological capability of no mean dimension. While a few highly developed manufacturing plants do not tell how developed the economy is as a whole, basic industries have undergone obvious development, and the Chinese appear able to manufacture a whole range of machines which they formerly imported. It is quite conceivable that China could develop a sophisticated modern industry while the bulk of her economy is still backward.

Economic growth has military potential, and Eckstein concludes that the "economy—as underdeveloped as it is—is capable of providing Communist China with a military potential which can, and indeed has, significantly altered the power balance on the Asian continent despite the fact that it may not permit the Chinese to challenge the Soviet Union and the United States in other parts of the world." Still, he foresees that in the near future China may only reach the level of power of Japan in the 1930s, a position of relatively greater inferiority considering the extraordinary advances made by other countries.

Aside from its significance as a model for development, the outside world is interested in the Chinese economy mainly for its military and trading potential. While Eckstein does not speculate on the prospects of the "China market" for international trade, he does make it clear that foreign trade is hardly likely to be used by the Chinese Communists as an instrument of foreign policy. He notes that "from China's point of view, the primary function of trade is to facilitate the maintenance of economic stability and to foster economic development at home." Yet China's two-way trade, though still at a low level compared to other nations, has been growing rapidly in recent years. For the west, "the ever present lure of a 'market with hundreds of millions of customers' seems to be just as strong today as it was in the nineteenth century."

Eckstein concludes with an examination of American trade policy toward China. The United States has imposed a total embargo on all trade with Communist China since 1950 and has tried to persuade as many nations as possible to join in that embargo, whose aim was to cripple the Chinese economy which had formerly depended heavily on foreign trade. But the embargo had little effect in hampering Chinese economic development. During the 1950s China obtained from the Communist world most of what she needed in imports; since the breakdown in Sino-Soviet economic relations, the Chinese have been able to acquire almost anything they needed, except military matériel, from non-Communist nations other than the United States. Moreover, the Chinese have also been able to obtain all the short- and medium-term credits they need. China's excellent repayment record has gone a long way in improving her international credit standing. In view of the failure of the embargo and China's easy access to foreign credits, Eckstein urges a removal of the embargo and "some experimentation in the field of credit policy" as a first step in improving Sino-American relations.

Barring a major war in the Far East, the prospects are for continued economic growth in China and further expansion of Chinese trade with the outside world, particularly with the non-

Communist nations. Since the United States is neither in a position to hinder the former nor slow down the latter, the United States would be eminently sensible in starting to break down the economic walls separating it from China.

In January of 1966 the Chinese began their Third Five Year Plan, of whose details we know next to nothing. The indications are that it will be largely a continuation of those economic policies in force in recent years. They could be changed by a decision of the leadership to launch a new "leap forward" or by a major international war.

KANG CHAO *
The Great Leap

In 1958 the Chinese Communist leadership launched the so-called Great Leap movement with the aim of increasing production on all economic fronts at an unprecedentedly high rate. As a result, the nation plunged rapidly into a deep economic quagmire.

Under the new program, production targets for many commodities were repeatedly adjusted upward, and maximum pressure was applied on production units to achieve assigned output quotas by whatever means necessary. Another salient feature of the Great Leap movement was a greater emphasis on indigenous methods of production and labor-intensive investment projects. This policy, officially called "walking with two legs," represented a sharp departure from previous development strategy which had stressed only modern production techniques and large-scale investment projects. The technical dualism introduced in 1958 was based on the assumption that native and small plants require less capital and a shorter construction period and that such plants can make use of local resources and labor that might

* Kang Chao, "Economic Aftermath of the Great Leap in Communist China," *Asian Survey*, IV, 5, May 1964, pp. 851–858.

otherwise be unemployed. These arguments were even more persuasive because of the discontinuation of Soviet loans which led to restraints on the importation of modern equipment for the ambitious economic development plans. Theoretically, the technical dualism envisaged by the Great Leap program is not inherently unreasonable. In a country like Communist China, the rate of economic growth could be maximized, assuming a fixed amount of investment, by developing labor-intensive production. Misallocation of resources would occur only if this strategy were carried too far and conducted in a chaotic fashion.

The Great Leap movement, lasting about two years, was abandoned in 1960 after the country had been afflicted by a prolonged and serious agrarian crisis. The economic situation made continued industrial expansion impossible. The most obvious consequence of the Great Leap was the enormous waste involved. Indigenous production methods often proved either too costly in comparison with their counterparts in the modern sector or capable of producing only low-quality goods. A large number of the backyard furnaces hastily built in 1958 dissolved into piles of mud and brick after a few rains. Others were given up by the local authorities because of prohibitively high operation costs. Only a small portion of the indigenous blast furnaces survived and then only after some renovation. Similar situations prevailed in other industries, such as the small coal pits utilizing primitive methods of production that had been opened in 1958.

Another serious form of wastage was created as a result of inter-industry imbalance. Because the Great Leap movement was improvised rather than well planned in terms of inter-industry coordination, and because bottlenecks came sooner in some industries than in others as the movement proceeded, the economy was completely off-balance toward the end of 1958 and during 1959. Stocks piled up in those industries which had overproduced, while production capacities could not be fully utilized in other fields due to material shortages.

Resource misallocation due to industrial imbalance may be only temporary since the Communist leadership can avoid further waste of this type by altering or discontinuing the program. However, from official statements and non-official disclosures, we know that in addition to the waste of resources incurred in the Great Leap movement, there were more profound shocks to the economy, some of which lasted for a considerable period after the movement was discontinued and which could be corrected only through serious readjustments.

Unfortunately, it is very difficult to make a full assessment of these more fundamental factors even today, four years after the Great Leap movement was abandoned. However, certain preliminary evaluations can be made. The Great Leap followed immediately after nationwide decentralization in industry, commerce, finance, and other areas in the economy. It was also at this time that the commune system was introduced. All these drastic institutional changes in Mainland China have had profound effects. Moreover, some of the damaging effects became noticeable only after 1959 when extremely unfavorable weather conditions and other natural calamities were also devastating the country. Since 1960, the Communist authorities in China have withheld all economic information so that an outside observer is unable to evaluate these developments in quantitative terms.

Clearly, one far-reaching result of the Great Leap movement was the statistical confusion that ensued, creating new difficulties for future planning. Since the founding of the State Statistical Bureau in 1952, the Chinese Communists had striven to establish a workable statistical system over the whole nation to facilitate economic planning. The avowed objective of the State Statistical Bureau was to collect reliable and comprehensive data by standardizing statistical schedules, methods of computation, and definitions of terms and designations. Undoubtedly, the statistical system was greatly improved during the First Five Year Plan period. However, these efforts were partially nullified in 1958 and 1959 by decentralization and the Great Leap. Under the decentralization policy, more than 80 per cent of the centrally controlled enterprises were transferred to provincial jurisdiction. Local Party cadres, who had been given greater responsibility and independence in handling production statistics, did not always follow the rules set by the State Statistical Bureau. Standard statistical schedules, computation methods, and commodity designations were frequently changed by the local governments to suit their own needs and purposes.

The Great Leap movement, on the other hand, created additional burdens for the State Statistical Bureau. Under the "walking with two legs" policy, more than seven hundred thousand tiny industrial units emerged throughout the country in 1958. These native industries utilizing indigenous methods produced non-standardized goods. The lack of well-trained accountants and statisticians to provide regular statistical reports was common. In some small-sized industries, there were not even instruments to measure output. More serious was the tendency among production units to exaggerate output because of the intense pressure to fulfill targets. Local cadres, hoping that the glowing reports would stimulate other units to accomplish spectacular results, were unwilling to check on, and in some cases connived in, the statistical exaggerations made by individual enterprises.

The statistical confusion reached its climax in 1959 when the Central Government openly admitted surprisingly large errors in some of the 1958 figures, and consequently adjusted the planned targets for 1959. However, this confession merely exposed the chaotic situation; it did not change it. Several years were required for the Communist planners to remove fully the statistical confusion created. Meanwhile, massive statistical errors increased the difficulties of economic planning. Communist planners have been deprived of reliable current production data from which to work out consistent plans for the future. To formulate the so-called material balance tables, moreover, the planners need fairly accurate technical coefficients indicating how much of one commodity will be required as material input in producing one unit of another commodity. However, with the technical dualism that rapidly developed in 1958–1959, most technical coefficients or input-output ratios had so greatly diverged between modern and native industries that national averages became less meaningful. As a result, it became more difficult for the planners to maintain inter-industry balance even when production figures were well controlled.

QUALITY CONTROL

One universal phenomenon in the Great Leap era was the drastic decline in the quality of commodities. A number of factors were responsible. Shortages of raw materials existed in varying degree in practically all manufacturing plants during this period.

As a remedy, producers were asked to use inferior materials, poor substitutes, or scrap materials, which would inevitably lower the quality of finished products. At the same time, a larger number of new workers were recruited by industries from the countryside and were immediately put to work without having received sufficient training in production techniques. Deterioration in quality was also attributed to the fact that in many plants the normal process of production and technical requirements were not strictly observed. But, more important was the tendency for some producers to deliberately lower quality as the only possible means of fulfilling the unreasonably high output quotas. The deterioration in the quality of products reached such an alarming level that six nationwide conferences were held by various industrial ministries in June 1959 to correct the situation.

Except for a few cases, this problem may have been a temporary one without any long-lasting impact on the economy. One might expect the quality of production to return to normal when the production drive was discontinued, shortages of materials were relieved, normal production processes and technical requirements were carefully observed, and regular quality control was reinstated.

One probable exception, however, is machine production in which the quality of output may have been affected for a number of years. Machines of inferior quality tend to make poor products. Some plants in Communist China have reported that they constantly have difficulty in stabilizing the quality of their products because they are using non-standard machinery built in the Great Leap period.

Still worse is the problem of quality in water-conservation projects. The inferior quality of ordinary goods at most makes them defective or useless articles. Even the injurious effects of defective medicines can be prevented by not using them. But the poor quality of water conservation projects can be far more serious and their damaging effects can hardly be prevented, once construction has been completed. In 1958, more than a hundred million people were mobilized to construct dams, reservoirs, and other irrigation projects. Most of these were small projects hurriedly approved without adequate advance surveys or proper designs. During that period, even for large-scale, well-planned projects, normal construction procedures were altered under the pressure of speeding up the work. Precautionary measures were often labeled "superstition" and were abandoned. As hydraulic engineers know, unsatisfactorily designed and poorly constructed flood-control projects may make the control of floods more difficult and the results of floods more disastrous. Improperly built water reservoirs may raise the underground water level in the neighboring area above its critical point resulting in the land becoming too alkaline. Similarly, irrigation systems with inadequate drainage may also cause alkalinization or salinization. In fact, some hydraulic engineering experts had warned the Communist cadres before and during the Great Leap about the dangers of building water conservation projects without careful planning, survey, and design. Since 1959, articles have appeared in leading Communist journals and newspapers condemning the heavy damage in agricultural production caused by realkalinization and other manmade disasters. Today, certain observers on both sides of the bamboo curtain are inclined to believe that the abnormal weather conditions in the past few years would have been less disastrous if the Chinese Communists had not built so many indigenous and defective water-conservation projects during the Great Leap period.

LACK OF MAINTENANCE

Under heavy pressure to increase output during the Great Leap, all industrial enterprises overused or abused their machinery and equipment. Regular maintenance and checkups were reduced to a minimum in order to gain more time for operation. Some machines were operated at such a high speed as to exceed the technically permissible limit. It was also very common in the transportation system that vehicles were overloaded and kept running with little or no normal maintenance.

Repair and maintenance departments in large enterprises were converted into manufacturing workshops. This was partly because an illusion had been created that maintenance services could be abandoned without affecting the conditions of the machinery. Since workers in the repair and maintenance departments knew more than the newly recruited workers about the equipment and production skills, those departments were frequently converted into production units as a very convenient way to increase production. These conversions were euphemistically termed the promotion of repair and maintenance departments. In this period, a great number of independent repair shops in the cities were also encouraged to become production units by local authorities.

The impact of reduced maintenance and repair activities was extensively felt only after a period of time; conversely, it will also take time to reverse the trend. Unfortunately for the Communists, the corrective measures taken after 1959 were modified by another factor, that is, a shortage of spare parts. Great Leap targets assigned to machine-producing enterprises were assigned only on the basis of major machine parts; the output of accessories and attachments was usually not taken into account. Hence, individual enterprises naturally concentrated all their efforts on increasing the production of the essential machine parts at the expense of the output of appurtenances and accessories. Consequently, in many large enterprises, workshops producing spare parts and accessories were converted into units manufacturing machines proper. One Communist source has reported that almost all iron and steel enterprises established in 1958 lack inspecting devices, spare parts, and other necessary accessories.

A very serious impact was first felt in the transportation system in the latter part of 1959 when official reports disclosed that thousands of motor vehicles could hardly be kept in normal operational condition due to the abovementioned difficulties. Within approximately one year, similar problems arose, with varying intensity, in other industries. As a result, beginning in 1961, the Communist leadership launched a new campaign urging all production and transportation units to place a higher priority on maintenance than on production. They were ordered to restore their repair departments or to establish new ones, and were also instructed to observe strictly the normal maintenance schedules and regular checkups of equipment. In 1961 and 1962, a coordinated plan was mapped out among three machine-industry ministries to produce more parts and accessories. All parts-producing units which had changed their production lines during the Great Leap period were ordered to shift back to their original line, or to be re-equipped with new lathes or machines for the production of spare parts.

DIVERSIFICATION OF PRODUCTION

Another undesirable result of the Great Leap movement was an unnecessary diversification of production in most large enterprises. One of the main features of industrial development in Communist China prior to 1958 was the emphasis on specialization. Most state enterprises were so designed as to specialize in one or several products, and each was subject to the direct control of the industrial ministry concerned. However, this principle was somewhat negated in 1958 by more diversified production or what the Chinese Communists called "multiple-lines of business."

Diversification of production is not necessarily bad if carried out properly. Indeed, it is quite common in large enterprises in the Western world. There is some savings in cost if a manufacturer produces several commodities which are joint products of the same materials or are related to each other in the production processes or in the requirements of machinery, laboratory equipment, and technical personnel. This type of diversification, which may be called horizontal diversification, provides some protection for the producer against the risk of a sudden decline in the market demand for the commodity in which he might otherwise have specialized. However, except for certain giant industries such as the iron and steel complexes, it is less common to find vertical diversification—*i.e.,* the production of all kinds of raw materials required in making industrial end products. This type of diversification may not provide any appreciable cost-saving, and even little or no protection for the firm in case of a sudden decline in demand for the end product.

Industries in Communist China pursued vertical diversification after 1958. This was a consequence of the failure by most plants to obtain sufficient quantities of materials needed for production during the Great Leap period. As a result, factories were inclined, under the decentralized administration, to establish a number of subsidiary units, known as satellite plants, around each main plant in order to supply materials needed by the main plant. Thus, railway bureaus began to run cement plants and steel mills in order to make their own cement and rails. Cement mills began to establish paper mills to supply paper bags. Paper mills began to produce sulphuric acid and caustic soda in their satellite plants. This development was further encouraged by a speech of Mao Tse-tung in September 1958, in which he applauded the operation of multiple businesses as an ingenious idea to make plants self-sufficient and to overcome the shortage of raw materials. In about one year, thousands of complex industries had been formed, each trying to produce whatever materials were in short supply.

Since the satellite plants were quite different from the main plant in capital and technical requirements, there was little cost saving. In fact, a great number of satellite plants were hurriedly built to meet exigent needs without any serious consideration being given to the geographical distribution of natural resources and other relevant conditions. Consequently, production costs in such plants were abnormally high. Of course, cost considerations had been relegated to secondary importance during the Great Leap period and it seemed justified for an enterprise to fulfill its assigned target even at a high expense. It was only when the Great Leap was over that the Communist planners began to worry about the disequilibrium caused by the undesirable diversification in industries. It has subsequently been suggested that the principle of industrial specialization should be restored, that waste in satellite plants should be eliminated, and that diversification should be confined only to those industries where cost savings may be induced by diversified production.

LABOR MORALE

Finally, the Great Leap caused a demoralization among workers, managerial, and technical personnel that has also had a long-lasting effect. A large number of new workers were recruited into industry in 1958. They differed from the old workers in that most of them were so-called contract workers, hired on a contract basis for a specified period of time. They lacked a feeling of security. Most important, they were not entitled to all of the benefits enjoyed by the old workers such as free medical care, compensation for injury and disability, retirement pensions, and special allowances for dependents. On the other hand, the number of work accidents greatly increased during the Great Leap period due to the relaxation of safety measures under the pressure of the production drive. Demoralization among workers became even worse when the Communist authorities began to repatriate superfluous workers to the countryside in late 1959.

The factors that impaired the morale of managerial and technical personnel were different. Under the slogans "politics takes command" and "reliance on the mass line," the administrative system within an enterprise underwent considerable disruption. Technicians and engineers were humiliated by the existence of a situation under which experts had to listen to non-experts in technical matters, scientific laws were replaced by political demands, and production fell into the hands of a group of "fanatics."

Several years after the Great Leap era, the situation has still not returned to normal in many enterprises. The Communist leadership has recently repeated the necessity to overcome management chaos in those enterprises in which there is no one person responsible for any specific job or assignment. Emphasis is again being placed upon a managerial system in which the entire factory is subordinate to the unified leadership of a general manager, and each staff member is responsible only for those tasks assigned to his post. Workers have been instructed to respect the professional opinion of the engineers and technicians and to observe strictly the normal order and technical requirements in each production process.

The above problems represent some consequences of the Great Leap movement on the subsequent economic development of Mainland China. However, one should not describe the Great Leap as a total failure. It is undeniable that output increased remarkably in that period even after official claims have been subjected to an intensive and skeptical scrutiny. More important from a long-run point of view perhaps is the fact that the Great Leap movement, like most blunders made by men, has had its educational effect. Chinese Communist planners must have learned a lesson from it and, presumably, they will try to avoid the same mistakes in the future.

ALEXANDER ECKSTEIN *
Economic Growth and Foreign Trade

Undoubtedly the most fundamental and intractable problem facing economic policymakers in China is that of population and food. On the basis of highly fragmentary and rather unreliable data, Mainland China's population in 1964 was estimated to be about 730 million. This vast population is supposed to be growing at an average annual rate of 2 per cent or more. Thus, about fifteen million people are added each year. Maintaining such a rapidly growing population just at the prevailing standards of living entails heroic efforts. It requires an average annual rate of growth in food supply of 2–3 per cent; it places a heavy demand on investment resources for housing, school construction, hospitals, and other educational, health, and welfare facilities.

This population has high birth rates and fairly high death rates—*i.e.,* it is a preponderantly young population with a high ratio of consumers to producers. These characteristics are conducive to high consumption and low saving. Furthermore, a sizable share of savings needs to be channeled into investment in social overhead rather than production facilities.

These relationships pose a series of dilemmas, which are common to all economies subject to acute population pressure. At the end of the First Five Year Plan period (1957), it seemed that China might be on the way to breaking out of this vicious circle of backwardness. Seen from the perspective of 1965, one can be much less certain of this.

There is no doubt that the Chinese Communist leadership

* Alexander Eckstein, *Communist China's Economic Growth and Foreign Trade* (New York: McGraw-Hill, 1956), pp. 245–259, 267–274.

is fully conscious of the problem and is trying to attack it from two directions simultaneously . . . it has in recent years accorded high priority to agricultural development. At the same time, it has embarked on a program of family planning, thus far largely confined to the urban areas.

Present indications are that this two-pronged attack has produced some recovery and progress. However, unless there is a miraculous boon in the form of unusually good harvests or foreign aid on a large scale, further economic growth and advance in China may be expected to be significantly slower than in the 1950s. Correspondingly, the Chinese Communist vision of becoming a top-ranking industrial nation may have to be postponed for a long time to come.

This prospect could be altered if Communist China were to gain access to foreign credits or grants. In this respect, China is in a unique situation, for it is perhaps the only underdeveloped country today that has no long-term credits or foreign aid to draw upon. On the contrary, since 1955 it has been a net exporter of capital. These capital exports have been used to amortize the Soviet loans and to finance Chinese foreign-aid programs. It would seem that in contributing to rising Sino-Soviet tensions, the Chinese Communist leadership must have chosen to buy increasing self-reliance and freedom of action in foreign affairs at the price of economic development at home.

China's development prospects could also be altered markedly by changes in domestic policy. In recent years, the Chinese Communists have pursued a prudent and more or less conservative economic policy—easing the tax and collection pressure on the peasantry, trying to foster a generally more favorable incentive system for agriculture, keeping the savings burden down, and channeling a large share of investment to agriculture and agriculture-supporting industries. However, this policy yields a pattern of resource allocation which runs strongly counter to the ideological and programmatic commitments of the leadership. It tends to produce a lower rate of investment and a lower rate of industrial growth. Therefore, the current economic policies are in many ways distasteful to the regime— so much so that they become a continuing source of tension between what the leadership desires and hopes for and what it considers possible and necessary. This tension may in turn tempt the leadership to resort once more to bold measures to break out of the vise of backwardness. Such attempts could easily lead to another economic breakdown and crisis. Consequently, one of the most serious problems for the leadership is to curb its own sense of impatience.

According to some assessments, the very intractability of the population-food dilemma might drive the Chinese Communists into adventurism, particularly in Southeast Asia. The adherents of this view maintain that Communist China's current interest in Vietnam is at least partly motivated by a desire to gain access to the rice surpluses and the rich mineral resources of Southeast Asia. However, it is difficult to see what the economic gains of conquest would be. What could China obtain through conquest of this region that she cannot now get through the normal processes of international trade?

Implicit in this view is an assumption that the Chinese Communists could move in and confiscate the rice and other commodities. This region, however, depends on rice and mineral exports for essential imports. If Communist China conquered the region, she would have to assume responsibility for maintaining economic and political stability. This task would mean assuring a modicum of incentives to farmers to induce them at least to maintain, if not expand, production. Forced confiscation might yield some produce for a year or two but would unquestionably be counter-productive in the long run. The Chinese Communists have a great deal of difficulty with their own peasantry. It is hard to believe that they would expect to overcome these difficulties with a conquered peasantry.

For these reasons one probably has to look to historical, cultural, ideological, and strategic considerations rather than to economic motivations for the primary explanation for Communist China's interest in Southeast Asia.

THE ECONOMIC BASE FOR MILITARY POWER

In terms of total size, Mainland China's economy definitely is among the ten largest in the world. According to the data in Table 1, China in 1962 was outranked in total production by the United States by a ratio of nearly 14:1, by the Soviet Union

by about 6:1, by Germany, Britain, France, and Japan by about
1.8–2.3:1, and by Italy barely at all.

Taken by themselves, however, these figures are misleading,
for they overstate China's economic capabilities as compared to
those of the more highly developed and more industrialized
countries. Roughly 40 per cent of Mainland China's national
product never enters marketing channels, while in the United
States the figure is only about 5 per cent. The other countries
listed in Table 1 lie between these two extremes. Therefore,

Table 1: *The Gross National Product of
Communist China and Selected Countries
(in billions of U.S. dollars)*

Country	1962 GNP (at 1961 prices)
United States	551.8
USSR	256.3
Germany (Federal Republic)	96.2
United Kingdom	91.5
France	83.6
Japan	77.0
Italy	52.8
China	
1957	40.0
1960	50.0
1962	42.0

a sizable share of the goods and services produced in China are
"frozen" within the household and cannot readily be mobilized
or reallocated to alternative uses. *Pari passu* resources are "tied"
to specific patterns of use which cannot easily be shifted into
the military sector.

Bearing this fact in mind, we may perhaps better approach
an analysis of relative capabilities by comparing the size of the
industrial product of China with that of the other countries. This
measure encompasses only "modern" economic sectors which are
fully commercialized and monetized. Within industry, therefore,
factors can be more rapidly reallocated between branches in

response to changing needs. Moreover, military capability is more directly related to industrial production than to any other branch of the economy. Analyzing the data in Table 2, then, we find that the conclusions emerging from Table 1 are indeed modified. That is, the gap between China and the other countries is significantly greater in terms of industrial product alone than it is if gauged by national product as a whole.

While in terms of the foregoing indicators, China is outranked by all the large industrial countries, her economy seems

Table 2: *Comparative Industrial Production of Communist China and Selected Countries, 1962 (in billions of U.S. dollars)*

Country	Industrial Product
United States	180.2
USSR	86.7
United Kingdom	39.3
Germany (Federal Republic)	32.8
France	21.3
Japan	18.4
Italy	15.0
China	
1957	8
1960	13
1962	10

vast indeed in relation to other underdeveloped areas—that is, all of Asia (except Japan), Africa, and Latin America. The implications of size are further underlined by the apparent fact that pre-World War II Japan was capable of engaging in a major world conflict and sustaining it more or less successfully for four-five years with a total industrial product which probably was smaller than Communist China's is today. Admittedly, Japan was even then much more advanced technologically and much more highly industrialized than China is now. Furthermore, prewar Japan had a much smaller population to care for than China does, so it could allocate a much larger share of its total industrial product to expanding the military and closely related sectors. Therefore, one certainly could not conclude from this comparison that what Japan was capable of doing then, China could do now. Nevertheless, the comparison does suggest that if China continues on her industrialization path, it may not be too long before her warmaking power may match that of Japan in the 1930s.

One of the most critical questions is whether population size should be treated as a source of weakness or strength. If one compares Communist China with her immediate continental neighbors, who are roughly at the same stage of development as she is, there is no doubt that population size represents an element of strength and power. If one compares Communist China with the United States and Russia, population size might represent an element of strength in the context of conventional warfare waged on the Asian continent. Within certain limits, sheer manpower might serve as a substitute for firepower. In a nuclear confrontation, however, it might have no effect at all, except in the macabre sense that a vast population has a somewhat better chance of leaving behind survivors.

Viewed in the above light, the economy—as underdeveloped as it is—is capable of providing Communist China with a military potential which can, and indeed has, significantly altered the power balance on the Asian continent despite the fact that it may not permit the Chinese to challenge the Soviet Union and the United States in other parts of the world.

TRADE AND AID AS INSTRUMENTS
OF FOREIGN POLICY

While China's size alone—its land area, population, and economy—gives it a significant weight in international affairs, this very size combined with the country's relative backwardness has tended to reduce its participation in world trade and thereby to reduce the importance of international trade as an instrument of Chinese Communist foreign policy. A vast country necessarily will tend to be more self-sufficient and to rely principally on internal markets and sources of supply. For this reason, its exports and imports will tend to be small relative to the total flow of goods and services produced in the economy. At the same time, the absolute level of foreign trade, regardless of its share in the national product, will tend to be a function of the country's stage of development. Thus, of two countries with roughly the same size of population, the one with the higher per capita income will tend to have the larger trade volume. It is not surprising, therefore, that even in its peak trade year of 1959, Communist China ranked only twelfth in world imports and thirteenth in world exports. A number of smaller but highly developed countries outranked her. West Germany and the United Kingdom, with gross national products about twice as large as that of Mainland China, carried on a volume of trade that was four to five times as large. Even a country as small as the Netherlands carried on a volume of foreign trade twice as large.

These discrepancies were greatly magnified in the 1960s by the sharp slump in China's foreign trade under the impact of the economic crisis. As a result, by 1962 China slipped to eighteenth place in world rank with respect to exports and thirtieth place with respect to imports. This slump further curtailed the effectiveness of trade as a tool of foreign policy.

Foreign trade can provide a country with maximum power leverage if that country serves as the market for a vast share of another country's exports without itself being too dependent on these or, alternatively, if that country becomes a major source of its trading partner's supplies of imports without being too dependent on this market. Short of these circumstances, however, economic power can still be translated into political power via foreign trade when a country serves as a major market for another's principal exports or as a leading source of vital raw materials for the other's industries. For example, various agreements for a guaranteed market or for preclusive purchase can be of significant aid to particular industries or economic interests. Such a situation can be used to gain influence and to exercise pressure—if need be by threatening a sudden trade rupture with its attendant dislocations.

In the Chinese case . . . only for one country—namely, the Soviet Union—did Mainland China constitute both a truly major market for exports and an important source of supply. Yet even in this instance, China's trade dependence on the Soviet Union during the 1950s was two to three times greater than vice versa. Moreover, the disparity in trade dependence increased in the 1960s, for China's share in Soviet foreign trade dropped to around 5 per cent while the Soviet Union's share in Mainland commerce was still around 20 per cent. Before 1960, about 30–60 per cent of Russia's exports to China consisted of plant and transport equipment and machinery. The drastic curtailment in the purchase of these items in the 1960s might have led to some disruption in the Soviet machine-building industry. One cannot, for example, rule out the possibility that this curtailment of purchases may in the short run have placed a considerable burden of adjustment on individual factories producing for the China market. Nevertheless, the effect on the industry as a whole could not have been too serious, for by 1962–1963 less than 1 per cent of its output was exported to China.

The only other area with a major trade orientation toward China has been Hong Kong. The latter obtains about 20 per cent of its imports from China, while the Mainland now buys only a negligible share of its supplies from the colony. In and of itself, this situation gives the Chinese Communist regime limited leverage over Hong Kong, for the colony can find alternative sources of supply for its food and raw materials, although some inconvenience and possibly higher costs might be involved. Moreover, Hong Kong's dependence on Chinese supplies is counterbalanced by China's dependence on the colony as its principal source of foreign exchange. What this situation suggests is not that Communist China has no power or influence in Hong Kong but rather that its influence rests primarily on military and political—not economic—factors.

In addition, for several countries trade with Mainland China has been of considerable importance to particular sectors rather than to the economy as a whole. Such, for instance, is the case with respect to grain exports from Canada and Australia. Both these countries had accumulated large grain surpluses, so Chinese purchases on a large scale offered definite relief to the farmers and traders of the two countries. The significance of these purchases can best be illustrated by the fact that since 1961 China has absorbed large shares of Australian and Canadian wheat exports. Although the Chinese are quite dependent on this grain, they have neutralized some of the effects of this dependence by fostering among the suppliers a spirit of competition for the China market. For example, they opened negotiations to buy a million tons of wheat from the French, who in

1964 were reported to have about two million tons of surplus wheat for export. . . .

What are the implications of this analysis for China's ability to use trade as an instrument in the conduct of its foreign relations? It is evident from these cases that the moderate size of total Mainland exports and imports makes it difficult for China to impose a pattern of economic dependence and thereby to gain dominance over a country through trade. From China's point of view, the primary function of trade is to facilitate the maintenance of economic stability and to foster economic development at home. If at the same time trade can open new channels of communication for the spread of propaganda and political influence, so much the better. In other words, imports must be purchased from countries which can provide them on the most favorable terms, and exports must be sold in such a way as to maximize earnings of foreign exchange.

Therefore, China cannot afford to use import orders or export supplies just to impose patterns of economic dependence. I do not mean that trade cannot be used as a weapon in special cases where the additional costs incurred might be modest— either because economic and foreign policy considerations happen to coincide or because the country concerned is small (*e.g.*, Cambodia). Occasionally, for example, China may engage in preclusive buying at prices higher than world market prices or sell in specific markets at prices lower than world market prices. To the extent that China uses the trade weapon in one place, however, her capability of using it in other places is correspondingly reduced.

For all these reasons combined, trade is best suited to perform a supporting rather than independent role in the Chinese Communists' pursuit of their foreign-policy objectives. It is really of importance in two rather different contexts. In countries where China has already made heavy inroads through the use of a whole arsenal of weapons, trade may serve to reinforce and accelerate an ongoing trend. In highly industrialized countries, it can serve as a prime avenue for gaining a certain measure of influence by creating the illusion of enormous trading potentials even in the face of currently modest trading levels. The ever present lure of a "market with hundreds of millions of customers" seems to be just as strong today as it was in the nine-teenth century. China's sheer size and population magnetically attract traders who do not want to miss possible opportunities and do not want possible competitors to get there ahead of them. In making certain policy moves, therefore, trading countries may consider it opportune to take into account the possible reactions of the Chinese Communists. This statement would certainly apply to Japan and perhaps to a lesser extent to Canada, Australia, Britain, France, and some additional European countries. But in none of these cases is trade of such importance as to provide Communist China with enough political bargaining power to impose a sharp turn in the direction of foreign policy. . . .

COMMUNIST CHINA AS A DEVELOPMENT MODEL

To the extent that China does not rely upon force or the threat thereof—whether military or economic in nature—ideological appeal plays a significant role in its foreign-policy arsenal. An important ingredient of this ideological appeal is what may be termed the "development-model effect." Depending upon the actual course of economic development on the Mainland, the way this reality is handled in Chinese Communist propaganda, and the way it is perceived by the countries toward which the propaganda is directed, the effect may be either positive or negative. Here we are concerned only with the first aspect of this problem—namely, what this model effect might be in the absence of any propaganda effort based on it.

During the first decade of its existence, the Chinese Com-munist regime succeeded in creating an image of a vigorous, dynamic, and rapidly growing economy with some singular ac-complishments to its credit. First of all, the regime rapidly restored the war-devastated economy and brought the prolonged inflation and hyperinflation to a halt. Monetary and fiscal sta-bility was thus achieved despite the resource drain imposed by the Korean War. Moreover, a land redistribution program with significant appeal not only internally but externally was carried out during the same period.

This image was greatly reinforced by what at the time appeared to be a gradual and successful program of agrarian transformation based on an increasing degree of producer co-operation. As a result, strong sentiment in favor of learning from the Chinese experience and emulating at least some aspects of it began to develop in India in the mid-fifties. Two official Indian delegations visited China. One was concerned primarily with problems of agricultural production, and the other with problems of agricultural organization.

Rapid industrial growth coupled with the aforementioned agrarian transformation caused many to believe that the Chinese Communists had succeeded in adapting the Soviet growth model to the conditions of an underdeveloped, densely populated economy. Since 1958, however, this image seems to have been tarnished. The extreme regimentation of the communes and the mass labor mobilization projects of the Great Leap seem to have had a negative external impact. More importantly, the profound economic crisis of 1960–1962 dramatized the fact that the Chinese Communist regime had paid relatively little attention to agricultural development. At the same time, it again drove home the lesson that agricultural development is a necessary condition for economic development in densely populated, low-income countries.

The appeal of the Chinese Communist development model has no doubt been undermined by the economic setbacks on the mainland. Yet the force of the initial successes lingers on—partly because of an information lag, partly because of a statistical blackout since early 1960 which has helped to conceal the extent of the economic difficulties, and partly because of agricultural stagnation and difficulties of food supply in other underdeveloped countries (particularly India). . . .

IMPLICATIONS FOR U.S. TRADE POLICY

Since 1950, U.S. policy on trade with China has involved a virtually total embargo on all economic contacts between ourselves and the Mainland and the maintenance of as stringent controls as possible on trade between our allies and the Mainland. This policy was initiated as an emergency measure during the Korean War and was conceived within the context of economic warfare. It has been maintained since on the technical ground that the Korean War has never been formally terminated but ended only in an armistice.

To be more precise, U.S. policy and regulations concerning trade with China have remained unchanged since 1950, while those of our allies have gradually and progressively been liberalized, more or less to our displeasure and in a number of cases despite our resistance. As a result, essentially all that is left of the elaborate structure of COCOM controls constructed in the early fifties is a continuing ban on the shipment of arms, weapons, military matériel of all kinds, fissionable materials, and some other clearly strategic goods. In addition, there is an agreement to limit credits to a term of five years. . . .

U.S. policy toward China in effect is designed to isolate it and to contain it within its present boundaries, and trade controls are intended to support both these objectives. If adhered to by all major trading countries, such controls would, of course, limit intercourse with China and therefore isolate her not only commercially but politically as well. At the same time, they would deprive her of modern weapons and other defense materials and thus tend to weaken her militarily. Finally, to the extent that they could deny China the wherewithal for modern industrial development, they would at least retard the country's economic growth and postpone the day when it would acquire a large enough industrial base to support a strong and more or less modern military posture. U.S. trade policy, thus, is designed to reduce Communist China's military potential in both the short and the long run. . . .

IMPACT OF U.S. TRADE POLICY
ON COMMUNIST CHINA'S ECONOMY

Regardless of the merits of a policy designed to isolate China, are trade controls suitable and effective as one of the instruments for the implementation of this policy? As was shown above . . . a cutting off of all exports to China would undoubtedly have damaged her economy in several ways. It would have significantly reduced the country's economic growth, would have rendered difficult if not impossible the expansion of her heavy industry, and in the early 1960s would have greatly complicated her problem of food supply. The Chinese economy, however, did not suffer these consequences because (a) no other major trading nation followed the U.S. policy of total embargo and (b) up to 1960 China could obtain from other Communist countries virtually any commodities which allied trade controls denied her. During the period of intimate Sino-Soviet economic relations (1950–1960), therefore, the practical consequences of the U.S. embargo and allied trade controls were negligible. The Sino-Soviet trade relationships may possibly have increased the cost of China's imports, but the evidence on this matter is far from conclusive. Even if some costs did result, they were probably minimal.

The situation, however, changed after 1960. Sino-Soviet economic relations deteriorated markedly. As a result, China has had great difficulty in obtaining imports of armaments and military goods, and she has been unable to obtain long-term credits. For the first time, it could be argued, enforcement of the whole system of trade controls became theoretically possible. From the mid-1950s on, however, allied trade controls have gradually been eased. Therefore, Western countries were prepared and in a position to move into the breach left by the Soviets. While U.S. trade policy was formerly ineffective because China could obtain controlled and embargoed goods from the Communist countries, it is now ineffective because these same goods (except for military matériel) can be obtained from practically every country which exports them except the United States and, to some extent, the Soviet Union.

The only practical economic impediment to which China is still exposed under the controls lies in the field of credit. This fact raises two questions: how much damage do credit controls impose on the Chinese economy, and, conversely, to what extent could credits be used to induce modifications of Chinese Communist policies?

The Chinese Communists do not seem to have any difficulties in obtaining all the short- and medium-term credits they can use at present. Their international credit rating is good, and they have met their financial obligations without delay. In a practical sense, therefore, access to long-term credits would simply mean that China could either lighten her current annual debt burden by converting her present obligations or that she could service, at the current rate of yearly debt payment, a much larger credit.

Whether China could obtain sufficient economic benefits from this access to induce her to pay a political price for it is difficult to forecast. On the basis of experience, it would seem rather doubtful unless, perhaps, the economic gain to be derived were indeed of major proportions. The history of Sino-Soviet relations, for example, would suggest that the Chinese were not prepared to sacrifice what they considered to be vital political objectives even if they had to suffer the economic consequences of a break. In her relations with the West, therefore, China probably cannot be expected to give up or modify seriously any of her important foreign-policy objectives even though such decisions might benefit her economy. This judgment, however, does not necessarily mean that there may be no chance to obtain concessions in a mutual bargaining situation—at least concessions as to timing, relative priorities, and direction. For several years, for instance, the Chinese Communists maintained that they would not carry on trade with Japan unless the latter accorded them *de facto* recognition. Yet since 1962 trade relations, partly because of the Sino-Soviet split, have been reactivated and broadened essentially on Japanese terms.

POSSIBLE U.S. POLICY MOVES

As I have indicated, the U.S. embargo is practically of no economic significance, for China has been and is currently able to obtain virtually all the goods she needs from other countries at no significant additional cost. Therefore, the embargo has only a symbolic meaning. It stands as a symbol of our determination to isolate China, to treat her as an outlaw, and to refuse to have any dealings with her.

The embargo also serves, however, to maintain the illusion at home that we are somehow inflicting serious damage upon the Chinese Communists through it. Moreover, the embargo and our general policy on trade with China have three other consequences. They separate us from our allies, who do not see the point of our policy on either theoretical or practical grounds. They contribute to frictions between ourselves and our allies whenever we attempt to press our allies to bring their policies into line with ours. Finally, they deprive our businessmen of their potential share, however modest, of the China trade now carried on by other countries.

This analysis really indicates that a trade control policy inflicts costs not only on China but on other countries as well. The more important trade with China may be to the country concerned, the greater these costs tend to be. Actually, as we have noted earlier, the costs imposed are likely to be minimal in most cases, just as the costs imposed on China appear to be small. Nevertheless, to the extent that embargoes and controls reduce the gains in international trade it is far from clear which side incurs greater losses, Communist China or its potential trading partners.

Should the time arrive when a détente with China becomes a feasible policy alternative, removal of the embargo may be peculiarly well suited to serve as the first step on the road to normalization between the United States and China. It can be initiated unilaterally without resort to negotiation, and it can be implemented without any economic cost. If the move is made, it should be carried out as a low-key measure and as a signal that other overtures might possibly follow if the Chinese respond to it.

Just as the embargo now stands as a symbol of our determination to isolate Communist China, its removal could symbolize a new policy posture on the part of the United States. At the maximum, such a move, possibly coupled with other similar measures, might widen our channels of communication with China and maybe even improve the general atmosphere of U.S.-China relations. At the minimum, a complete rebuff to our overtures would place the onus for implacable hostility at the door of Communist China.

In the same general vein, it may be worth considering some experimentation in the field of credit policy. A rigid policy of credit limitation ties the hands of our allies and deprives them of any bargaining power. On the other hand, a policy which would leave credit terms vague and unpublished would make it much easier to obtain a *quid pro quo* not only in economic terms but perhaps in political terms as well.

Ultimately the crux of the problem is: What should be the

over-all character of our policy toward China? Should we assume a new posture and take new initiatives, or should we permit ourselves to remain preoccupied with the difficulties of change rather than with the penalties attendant upon holding a fixed position. These problems, of course, range well beyond the economic realm and carry us well beyond the scope of this study; they encompass the totality of our policy in Asia. In this realm, economic considerations and economic instruments can and should play only a subsidiary and supporting role.

☏ Life in the New Society

WHAT IS ordinary life like in China? To outsiders who have never set foot on the soil of the People's Republic, that is an almost impossible question to answer. And even if one could go and live there, how could one grasp something as elusive as the quality of life except by long and intimate contact with the people? Though we Americans cannot go there, many others have. More than two thousand foreign tourists visited China in 1965, and, barring war, the number is expected to increase. Thousands of Chinese go back and forth across the borders of the People's Republic, and are more than willing to discuss their experiences with the foreigner, particularly if he speaks Chinese. Bit by bit, by talking to people who have been there, by reading newspapers and listening to radio broadcasts, and by studying the many books that have been written on China today, one can construct an image of life in China.

Material conditions are best for those living in the big cities. The peasants are poor, but poverty appears to be greatest in the least developed inland areas. There is a cult of austerity and equality. Except for the quasi-pariah bourgeois who are allowed some luxury, most of the population, including leading cadres, live modestly. In the mid-1950s, city life improved, but hunger existed in many inland areas. In the late 1950s economic catastrophe struck China, and living standards dropped sharply. Food was scarce everywhere, though instances of starvation were rare. The Communists did their best to distribute available food, and Peking quietly began to buy foreign grain to feed its seaboard cities. By the mid-1960s living conditions have improved considerably. Tourists all report that food is plentiful, restaurants and hotels are good, and that the people appear satisfied.

The achievement of decent living conditions for the general population is a major step forward for a country so cursed with poverty as China. But what of the spiritual side of life? Tourists can say little about that because of their limited contacts with the Chinese population. Foreigners who have lived for extended periods in China have written of their impressions. Mainland Chinese in Hong Kong speak volubly of their life in China. The following selections present a picture of the material and spiritual quality of life in China today from different viewpoints. We leave it to the reader to construct his own image of how people live in China.

The first selection, on the differences between the old and new Shanghai, was written by Edgar Snow after his visit to China in 1960, not a good year in China. Yet Snow, like so many other "old China-hands" who have gone back, cannot but reflect on the great differences. Pre-1949 Shanghai belonged to a different era, a different world.

Sven Lindqvist is a young Swede who spent almost two years in Peking as a student of Chinese and later as cultural attaché to the Swedish Embassy. Lindqvist, who was in Peking during economic crisis and who left when conditions had greatly improved, states that his "experiences have not reconciled me to the Chinese social order, but they have made me realize the tragic necessity of much that is happening in China." Despite the terrible problems facing the new system, the leaders avoided Stalin's violent methods: "the leaders are prepared to build their country with sweat and tears, but not with blood."

Ordinary life in China today is marked by perpetual work and study. Chinese formerly drew a sharp dividing line between public and private life. They worked hard outside, but at home they intensely enjoyed family, friends, food, and gossip. Today the Communists teach all for the public and nothing for the private (ta-kung wu-ssu). People are taught that work is the core of man's identity, and that consciousness must pervade every moment of living; thus, time normally given over to private life must be spent in study, and throughout China people take part in after-hours study, averaging many hours a week. Private life and enjoyment have not disappeared, as recent visitors note, but the pressure is always there to give as much time as possible to self-cultivation.

The Communists today proclaim a new human ideal. Chinese formerly strove to become scholars, men of education, wealth, and official position who raised large families and spent their life in ease, in short the amateur ideal (see Volume I). Today's different human ideal is a Lei Feng. Lei Feng was a poor peasant orphan, oppressed in childhood by reactionaries and saved by the Communist Party. He became a model Communist, working hard, helping others, and studying all the time. He died young in a trivial accident. One can find the same pattern in the life stories of dozens of other Lei Fengs: born into suffering, salvation by the Party, and meaningful sacrifice, even death, in the service of people and country. If we remember that traditional life hopes were expressed in the phrase *fu-lu-shou*—happiness, high salary, and long life—then the Lei Feng ideal, with its values of nobility, poverty, and sacrifice, is its dialectical opposite.

The fourth selection, from a 1964 newspaper article, describes the emigration of city youth to distant rural areas. For several years the Communist authorities have urged young people to go to the countryside to take part in the great "socialist education movement." China has more middle- and higher-school graduates than it can use in the cities, so they have been given the task of serving the masses in the rural areas where they are needed. The "socialist education movement," of course, aims at political indoctrination, but it also is a means of educating the peasantry. China's leaders believe that the spiritual transformation of the peasantry is as necessary as the technological transformation of agriculture. That the city intellectuals are often not happy about this radical change in their living habits is clear from the selection.

The next selection, from a 1960 newspaper article, describes the new Communist view toward marriage and love. That "common political understanding" should be a reliable foundation for love strikes most Americans as amusing at best and Orwellian at worst. Nevertheless, we would do well to remember that the struggle for equality between the sexes has been one of the key elements in China's family revolution—

and the family has been one of the chief bulwarks of the conservative pre-modern tradition.

The final selection describes the experiences of ordinary people—peasants, workers, and clerks—who fled to Hong Kong and were interviewed by Stanley Karnow, an American foreign correspondent of long residence in Hong Kong. After noting the growing apathy in the country, a phenomenon changed after the intensification of war in Vietnam, Karnow concludes, ". . . the average Chinese appears at present to be seeking a personal rather than a political solution to his problems—to receive a remittance from abroad, to connive for extra rations, to market his produce or finally, if feasible, to escape to Hong Kong."

The Chinese leaders are well aware of the ordinary citizen's desire to devote himself to private life. The purpose of revolutionary study is to convince him that China's internal and external situation is still too precarious to allow deviance from service to people, cause, and country.

EDGAR SNOW *
Shanghai

Gone the glitter and glamour; gone the pompous wealth beside naked starvation; gone the strange excitement of a polyglot and many-sided city; gone the island of Western civilization flourishing in the vast slum that was Shanghai.

Good-bye to all that: the well-dressed Chinese in their chauffeured cars behind bulletproof glass; the gangsters, the shakedowns, the kidnappers; the exclusive foreign clubs, the men in white dinner jackets, their women beautifully gowned; the white-coated Chinese "boys" obsequiously waiting to be tipped; Jimmy's Kitchen with its good American coffee, hamburgers, chili, and sirloin steaks. Good-bye to all the night life: the gilded singing girl in her enameled hairdo, her stage makeup,

* Edgar Snow, *The Other Side of The River, op. cit.,* pp. 529–534.

her tight-fitting gown with its slit skirt breaking at the silk-clad
hip, and her polished ebony and silver-trimmed rickshaw with
its crown of lights; the hundred dance halls and the thousands
of taxi dolls; the opium dens and gambling halls; the flashing
lights of the great restaurants, the clatter of mah-jongg pieces,
the yells of Chinese feasting and playing the finger game for
bottoms-up drinking; the sailors in their smelly bars and friendly
brothels on Szechwan Road; the myriad short-time whores and
pimps busily darting in and out of the alleyways; the display
signs of foreign business, the innumerable shops spilling with
silks, jades, embroideries, porcelains, and all the wares of the
East; the generations of foreign families who called Shanghai
home and lived quiet conservative lives in their tiny vacuum
untouched by China; the beggars on every downtown block and
the scabby infants urinating or defecating on the curb while
mendicant mothers absently scratched for lice; the "honey carts"
hauling the night soil through the streets; the blocks-long fu-
nerals, the white-clad professional mourners weeping false tears,
the tiers of paper palaces and paper money burned on the rich
man's tomb; the jungle free-for-all struggle for gold or survival
and the day's toll of unwanted infants and suicides floating in
the canals; the knotted rickshaws with their owners fighting each
other for customers and arguing fares; the peddlers and their
plaintive cries; the armored white ships on the Whangpoo, "protecting foreign lives and property"; the Japanese conquerors and
their American and Kuomintang successors; gone the wickedest
and most colorful city of the old Orient: good-bye to all that.

Some of it has been carried by refugees to Hong Kong
today and some of it, with strip-tease added, you may find in
Tokyo. Shanghai still holds more people than either city, if
suburbs are included; in 1961 its population was 10,400,000.
Foreigners still say it is the "one place in China that really looks
like a great city." The tall buildings are there, but the International Settlement and the French Concession, which used to
be the heart of a modern megalopolis, are strangely like a village
now, and downtown after dark is as quiet as Wall Street on
Sunday.

There is plenty of heavy traffic in the new industrial suburbs, but many downtown office buildings of the Settlement
have been turned into schools, dwellings, and workers' clubs.

Here bicycles, pedicabs (not many), and trams move leisurely between shops selling necessities and a few luxuries to customers who give the impression of being village tourists taking in the city where the wicked imperialists used to rule. The once crowded Bund is a recreation center. Into it, each morning and afternoon, the former office buildings debouch swarms of little children to play and exercise in well-kept gardens along the river. Elderly folk also gather there to read, drowse, or play Chinese chess; one of them told me he remembered a time when Chinese (and dogs) were not admitted. So did I.

The Shanghai Club, once very exclusively for British gentlemen, used to boast the world's longest bar. It is now run by the Party as an international seamen's club, where sailors may play games or read books or see movies, but find no bedtime companions. Nearby, the ponderous old Hong Kong and Shanghai Bank Building (the paws of its huge bronze lions still shining from many hands that touched them for good luck) is now a government bureau. The old American Club building has been put to the same use as the National City Bank in Peking; both house police headquarters.

I stayed at the Cathay Hotel, which stands at Nanking Road and the Bund and was once Asia's finest hostelry. It is now called the Peace Hotel and is exceedingly so: quiet, orderly, the restaurant little used and subdued compared to its former aggressive gaiety, its famous bar and night club extinct, its lobby shops closed at dusk, and few lights on after ten. One got the impression here, as at certain large and empty provincial hotels, that the Chinese had not yet quite decided how to utilize these rooms since the Russians left. But the Cathay is still a fine place to live, furnished much as it was when owned by Sir Victor Sassoon: the simulated Chinese décor a bit tarnished now but the plumbing super, cuisine ditto, and more new American cars for hire outside its doors than anywhere in China.

I was offered my choice of Sir Victor's suite, usually reserved for VIPs, or an ordinary double room about the dimensions of the *Mayflower*. A single would do me nicely, I said, but I asked to see the suite. It was in the tower, high above the river, pseudo-Tudor, handsomely paneled and filled with light from wide leaded windows. The bedroom was sumptuously furnished with king-sized twin beds adjoining two large tiled bathrooms; there was a dressing room the size of a small flat, a private entrance foyer, servants' quarters, a bar, a kitchen and pantry, a private dining room with a fireplace, and a spacious living room with another fireplace.

"How much?" I asked the China Intourist agent.

"Thirty-five yuan a day."

"That's less than fifteen dollars. At the Waldorf it would cost me a hundred. Betraying incurable bourgeois romanticism," I said, "I'd like to wake up in the morning knowing how Victor Sassoon felt when he owned Shanghai. I'll take it for a night."

I did not rest comfortably. For a long time, as I looked down at the river life, I was filled with remembrance of things past in this city where I had invested or misspent some years of my youth, fallen in love and into a brief but eventful marriage, seen two wars and many men destroyed in futile combat, until, engulfed by China, I had turned abroad—to more wars. Returning to my present magnificence, I tried the first bed but could not sleep. Then I tried the other, soft and blissful, but had no better luck. I ended on the living room couch and woke up at dawn. If that was the way Sir Victor had felt when he owned Shanghai I did not envy him. Perhaps he had had better company than my thoughts.

At seven o'clock I went down to walk in the Bund gardens, which were already well populated. Eager young and middle-aged people were doing their *t'ai chi ch'üan* steps and some students wearing athletes' red sweatshirts and slacks were practicing sword dancing. Under a tree some small children were being led in song by their teacher. Everyone was much in earnest. I watched a family in a sampan eating a breakfast of rice and greens, waved to them, and they waved back, smiling. Encouraged, I sat down on a bench beside an elderly gentleman who looked my way. I spoke to him in Chinese.

"You are up early," I said.

"At my age you don't need much sleep."

"Your age? You don't look over fifty, Elder Born," I lied.

"Courtesy talk! I'm more than sixty. What does a man my age do in Russia, sir?"

"You take me for a Russian? No. I'm an American."

"American?" That's a dirty word in China now but they still use the old flattering term for it: *Mei-kuo,* the "beautiful country." He repeated it and I nodded. Now he began to speak in stilted but animated English. "You are certainly the first American I have seen for many years."

"I don't doubt that. How long is it since you spoke English?"

"Quite some years. I am forgetting it. You have been a long time in China? You speak Chinese."

I told him that I was a newspaperman and had once worked for the *China Weekly Review* in Shanghai. He remembered it; he had read it, he said. He had learned some English in his youth and had used it in business. Now he was retired.

"I take it you are not a Communist?" I said.

"Oh, no!" He grinned and showed half a dozen large teeth. "I'm a capitalist! That's what they tell me." He plucked at the sleeve of his dark-blue padded jacket of worn silk. "I used to own a silk store."

"How do you live?"

"I get my interest-dividends like other merchants."

"But how is it compared to the past? Before *chieh-fang* [liberation]?"

"We eat better than most. We live in our old house, my wife and I, sharing now with some others. That's all right. Good people. Hard-working people. We don't need the rooms. My children are married and live away. What is your thinking of China?"

"Officials show me something, then always ask me that. They want criticisms. Now I'll ask you, what are your criticisms?" I repeated the word in Chinese.

"Oh, I know." He looked at me shrewdly. "Americans think we have a bad time, maybe? I can say the truth, I have lived much better. But poor people have lived much worse. Everything is for the people. We used to think America was for the people too but it not look so now, eh? Is America only friend of Chiang Kai-shek? How is this?"

"Suppose I oppose that. Can you criticize your government?"

"Oh, I know. It makes bad mistakes. Who is ever right? I could tell you stories of people who have a bad time. Myself too, but not much. China is a socialist country now. Property rights are not the same, you know. One thing: this is an honest government. Hard, but honest. It has made China one great country again. Chinese can hold up their heads in the world. We are not foreign slaves any more." He drew back proudly. "What do you think about that, sir? Maybe the government is too strong, sometimes too young to listen to others. But—it does good things for China and does not steal. We forget much against that. Nobody wants Chiang Kai-shek back again, no!"

"Your son? What does he do?"

"Two sons. One is a teacher, all right. The other is in Hong Kong. He wants to come back but he should stay there. We are the old generations. We lost something. My grandchildren, they are the new life. They wear it. They like it. Things in China were too bad in old days. Well, they have ended the worst. I won't cry."

"Many people in jail—prison—arrested?"

"Very few I know. They convince you and convince. I see the point. All for China. You know old Shanghai? Everybody robbing, cheating. Crimes, gangs, bad men. Tu Yueh-sheng? You know him? Bad man. Now you see the *hsiao hai-tzu* [children] telling us older ones not even to spit, to use the spit bucket. Not to throw dirty things on the streets, that's good. Everybody working, everybody reading. No more starving people dying. How is that? Better. Building, building, building more —but nobody getting rich. Why? All for China family. I see the point."

"Maybe you aren't telling me everything. Maybe you're afraid I'll tell the government?" I smiled but he did not.

"Ha! I say the truth. Why should—"

An acquaintance of his stopped and he stood up to exchange greetings. They strolled off together, but before the capitalist left he turned and bowed to me and said, "So much building. You must see."

I took scores of pictures at random of all kinds of people in the Bund gardens and along the waterfront and in various Shanghai streets. Like the pictures I took everywhere else in China, they showed people poorly dressed, none of them fat. They were all dying but apparently only at about the same rate people are dying everywhere; among them were no diseased beggars, no mangy infants, no policemen beating up anybody, no rice riots. These pictures got the same reception abroad that others taken by foreign visitors have gotten. Editors thought they looked too "posed." They wanted to see "the real China." A few months after I left, the Swiss journalist Fernand Gigon photographed some summer-naked infants playing around a pile of coal balls. *Time* bought that, called it "scavenging children," and its readers got a full page of "the real China" at last. From the same source, NBC picked up some movie film, spliced it in to freshen ancient shots of pre-revolutionary China, and presented it under the title "White Paper on China." Included in it was a remarkable scene of street executions by Kuomintang gendarmes in Shanghai—presented in a context which left the audience with the misapprehension that it had witnessed Communists shooting down the people.

SVEN LINDQVIST *
Inside China

It was a stifling hot evening in June. The students' quarters at Peking University were being fumigated against vermin. Thousands of students were sitting in groups on the sandy field, waiting for a breath of wind to blow away the vile smell of the poison. Darkness had fallen and the air was absolutely still.

"I can respect your opinions," I said to one of the Chinese students, "except on one point. You know as well as I do that the Chinese press deliberately falsifies its image of the world. I can't understand why you defend it. I can't understand how a reasonable human being can choose to see the world in terms of simple black and white."

"You can't quote a single false report that has appeared in our newspapers."

"Even if every single item that your newspapers carry

* Sven Lindqvist, *China in Crisis* (New York: Thomas Y. Crowell, 1963), pp. 97–105.

about the West were accurate, the stories have been selected to
distort the truth. You tell me just one piece of good news your
papers have reported from the West."

We walked to and fro in the darkness. "You know yourself
that there aren't many success stories to report from China at
the moment," I said, "because the country is in the middle of a
serious crisis. But if someone were to write about the crisis
without mentioning all you are doing to try to solve it, without
the slightest sympathy for your struggle against enormous difficulties, wouldn't that be dishonest? And isn't it equally dishonest when your papers report only strikes, disasters, crimes,
and suicides in the West, without the slightest attempt to understand our efforts to solve these problems?"

We walked to and fro in the darkness and heat. "All that
you in the West believe in are mere superficialities," he said.
"The basic truth about your country is that the capitalists exploit the people, and your life is therefore bound to be unhappy.
You may have your own cars, you may be able to travel and
enjoy yourselves, but at a deeper level your unhappiness is the
true reality, and it's right that our newspapers should select the
facts that correspond with the essential truth. But when your
journalists describe China—they write what amounts to a libel,
even when their reports are based on facts. These unhappy facts
do not correspond with the essential truth about us. Our real
inner happiness lies in the knowledge that we are not exploited."

"That is why I defend our journalism," he went on. "It is
a weapon in the class struggle. Only the things that serve the
Party cause in the class struggle are right and true. There is no
other truth. You think that you can emerge from class consciousness and find objective truth. You think that you can report
what you have seen and heard without considering which class
is going to gain or lose by it. That's a delusion. Unless we consciously will ourselves to be the instruments of socialism, we
unconsciously become the puppets of imperialism."

The breeze did not come. I went back to my room in the
dormitory, my lungs full of the hot, dark poisonous air, sweating,
exhausted. Understanding demands constant practice. It is hard
to express your experiences accurately. Your vision is obscured
by prejudice; you are tempted out of loyalty to take a biased view
of things. Inevitably a certain amount of falsification occurs. But

the Chinese have to learn to be partisan and prejudiced as a deliberate policy, they must consciously put loyalty before objectivity and deny their own impulse toward truth. My whole spirit revolted against their teaching that respect for facts and respect for other people's opinions must be exterminated from man's soul like vermin.

Our own Swedish image of China contains no central, intentional distortion. It shows instead a confusing ambivalence; it is a puzzle picture with abrupt changes between good and bad, success and defeat.

One traveler comes back from China, stimulated, rejuvenated, enthusiastic, as if he had just had a good sail in a stiff breeze. The next one comes back critical, worried, frightened. Someone else has gone from one factory to another and has seen production increasing by leaps and bounds. He reports that China will soon reach the industrial level of the United States and Soviet Russia and has the resources to overtake them both. He has met cheerful people, ready to make sacrifices. Another visitor describes the people as indifferent, says their loyalty is forced. He has seen great slag heaps of scrap iron piled up outside abandoned factories. He describes the deathly stillness of the industrial battlefield and says that China is summoning her last resources in order to survive.

Anyone who has not been to China must ask: Are the contradictory accounts due to subjective differences between the observers, to varying degrees of comprehension? Were the visitors blinded by prejudice, or did they see no further than China's shop window? It seems improbable. Yet what actual changes can have caused such large discrepancies in their reports?

China has an enormous population and an economy working on a very small margin. A few grains of rice per person can make all the difference. If they are lacking, a shortage is caused which no country in the world can possibly overcome. If they are available, they form a surplus which allows industrialization to go ahead at exceptional speed. Every grain above the subsistence level can be—and at certain times has been—staked on the future. That is why it is possible that within our lifetime China will become the world's third great power. If the level falls by a few grains, however, this has a direct effect on the health and working ability of the people. That is why China is balanced on a razor's edge between victory and defeat.

A country like this changes rapidly. Someone who visited China in 1960 could report quite truthfully that the people in the towns were at the mercy of the street committees, that private enterprise was prohibited, that cooking pots had been turned into steel and people ate in communal feeding centers, that research and education were completely controlled by the cadres. But someone who visited China in 1962 would dismiss this description as sheer nonsense. By then the street committees had not even the power to prevent open trespassing on other people's property; people were eating at home, apart from exceptional cases; in most schools and institutions administrative power was divided between cadres and specialists. Private enterprise is now allowed in professions ranging from doctors to barbers, actors to shoemakers, and black-market prices for important commodities such as meat and cereals have been legalized in the free market.

You cannot make your personal snapshot of China three-dimensional unless you stay there long enough to observe the gradual change from one stage to another. You need to have seen how the dirty old black cycle rickshaws were cleaned and painted up when their owners were once again able to make a profit. You need to have seen how the hillsides which were left untilled under the commune system became a patchwork of ploughed fields once individual households were free to work on their own initiative. Unless you can make comparisons like this, it is impossible to judge between permanent and transitory phenomena.

Unless a visitor can speak Chinese, he is entirely dependent on his hosts. He cannot travel alone, still less make his own contacts. He cannot read the newspapers, let alone understand the background to the news. If an interpreter or an official accompanies him, the Chinese are on their guard, and most conversations become dreary, conventional, and conformist. You have to be able to go into a house where there is a public telephone and spend the afternoon chatting with the housewife in charge of it. You need to understand what people are saying to one another in a bus, what they are shouting to each other in a street brawl. You have to be able to fix a meeting with a new-found friend in the Western Hills, to have a drink one night with an old pedicab driver, to find a teacher of calligraphy by reading the notices on the telegraph poles. It is particularly revealing to talk to a Chinese first when other people are present and then to meet him alone. The picture suddenly comes to life; it acquires nuances, details, is shaded by admissions and objections and filled with hopes and misgivings.

Faced with two completely different reports on China the discerning reader should inquire whether both writers were in China simultaneously, for the same length of time, and whether they understood Chinese. Considerations like these will account for most of the discrepancies in their reports.

The January sun shone down on the honey-colored roof of the palace when I arrived in Peking, yet I felt as if I were living inside a thundercloud. Several months passed before I was able to understand what was happening around me and could explain that feeling. I lived with my wife in a little concrete cell in one of the dormitories of Peking University. Gradually I learned how I should behave toward these polite, courteously uncompromising people. I began to follow their intrigues, to sort out which of them were police informers, which of them could eat with the elite and had preferential treatment at the hospital, which of them had real power in the long chain of command, winding up from the "working friends"—caretakers—to the Party leadership of the faculty.

Several of the people with whom I had daily contact lived —"in accordance with the demands of their work"—separated from their families. Apart from consultations about their work, people avoided one another; old friends and neighbors kept themselves to themselves. What could they offer if anyone dropped in? Hot water. What could they talk about? The boils under the plaster on their neck, the hunger swellings on their legs, their son of twelve months, unable to sit up. A silent, icy suspicion divided people from each other. I have never experienced more total isolation.

I remember seeing the face of a woman in front of me in the bus. Protruding teeth, bad-tempered mouth. Eyes narrowed in a malicious stare. Black poker-straight hair with a parting curving up like a white scar. For some diseases of the eye they scrape the cornea. This face looked scraped; it was quite without feeling, imagination or compassion. It was merciless.

It was the happiest day of my stay in China when I eventually won the confidence of those fierce eyes and we were able to talk to each other freely. It is not particularly difficult to meet discontented Chinese intellectuals with a bias toward the West. But they themselves do not feel they are Chinese in the proper sense of the word. You have to pierce through the ideological armor of a loyal and genuinely convinced Communist to find a human being who can give reasons and accept arguments, who dares to doubt, who admits the existence of the informer system, the fear and the use of force, and can explain why he still believes in Communism.

After a breakthrough of this kind a freer relationship can be established with the Chinese. It is said that you can tell just by looking at a girl whether she is still a virgin. It is obvious that the Chinese look at a foreigner to see whether he is a man who *knows*. What does he know? The value they give to the words they use, how much is mere quotation, what hidden reservations they make, what motives lie behind what they say. Nobody knows this in a sociological sense, but when natural human curiosity about these questions has been satisfied, tension is relaxed and confidence grows. Suddenly in casual conversation questions are answered which earlier were asked in vain.

These experiences have not reconciled me to the Chinese social order, but they have made me realize the tragic necessity of much that is happening in China. Unnecessary evils are now in many cases being remedied. In two years I have seen a drastic change in the policy of the Chinese Communist Party. Without any apparent split the leaders have engineered this transformation in the middle of the gravest crisis at home and abroad in the history of the Party. Despite the Stalinist tendencies within the Party, they have avoided Stalin's violent methods. The leaders are prepared to build their country with sweat and tears, but not with blood. They were wise enough to know when they had lost the people's confidence, and now they have turned back in order—if possible—to win it again.

True, there is not much left now of the spontaneous enthusiasm witnessed by earlier observers, but there is instead more perception and awareness. Life in China is still harsh and demanding, but it has its idyllic moments. One evening in September I went for a walk with a young writer in the northwestern district of Peking. For the first time he had had one of his stories accepted without having to bring in a Party secretary as *deus ex machina*. We walked under the trees; people were dressed in summer clothes, there was a little outdoor café with lights and music, and some girls were sitting on a bench in the park, singing with pure, strong voices. We stopped at the railway barriers. The level crossing looked gay, with hollyhocks blooming on either side of the track and the signal box almost buried in greenery. A heavy engine, decorated with a red flag, passed by.

"Don't you think," he said, "that before the leaders came to power they sometimes sat and daydreamed about Peking? 'We shall have double rows of trees along all the streets,' said one, 'and there shall be benches in all the parks, where young girls can sit and sing with pure, strong voices.' 'You forget,' said another, 'that we shall have railways and a red flag on every engine. Hollyhocks shall bloom at the level crossings and the signal boxes will be almost buried in greenery.' "

During my time in China, Chinese society became more humane, more tolerant and more reasonable. It was a pleasure to follow this development day by day. Nobody knows how long these trends will continue. In a totalitarian society there is no guarantee of their permanence, but I believe that the present policy of the Chinese Communist Party is the best possible one for China.

With one important exception. The image of itself that China presents to the world and the image of the world that is presented to China are as doctrinaire and one-sided as ever. Every Chinese newspaper gives a deliberately and venomously false picture of the world. Certain trusted Party members have access to facts through two daily bulletins, both in varying degrees confidential. But the public is given a specially arranged selection of the news, containing some grotesque distortions of the truth.

The Chinese leaders have traveled outside their country only in exceptional circumstances. They seem to look on the rest of the world as a larger, not yet liberated China, where

hollyhocks have yet to bloom. They see modern western capitalism in terms of Chinese capitalism as it appeared to them in
their youth; they judge the economic and military strength of
the West on the basis of their own experiences in the Civil
War. They suppress all facts about the importance of the trade
union and workers' movements in the West, all facts about the
function of the balance of power as a means of preserving
freedom in a multicentered society. They create a hate-inspired
apocalyptic vision of a part of the world doomed to destruction.
Behind this vision you can sense a long-suppressed need for
vindication and a feeling of humiliation which has never been
erased. It is possible to understand how the vision has come to
be created, but that does not make it any less dangerous and
detestable.

We must guard against making the same mistake. We must
not regard China as a larger, more backward Sweden, which
has not yet learned to enjoy the blessings of democracy. We
must not judge the potential of Chinese Communism by the
behavior of our own Communists over here. We must use our
freedom to look at the facts without preconceived notions about
the truth. That is the spirit in which I have tried to describe
the Chinese crisis. I think I have seen something of the best
and the worst it involves. I believe that the years of crisis have
created a situation which, in spite of everything, is more hopeful
than that of the successful years. The earlier victories led toward defeat, but this defeat can be the basis of lasting progress.
Perhaps only progress of this kind, won by a realistic approach
and limited ambitions, can gradually change the tense, relentless
face that China now turns toward the world.

CHEN TUNG-LEI *
Lei Feng

A DOWNTRODDEN CHILDHOOD

Lei Feng was born on December 30, 1939, in a peasant family in Anching township, Wangcheng county, Hunan province. When he was a small child, his father was killed by Kuomintang bandit troops and Japanese invaders, leaving behind his wife and three children. Lei Feng's elder brother, who was hardly twelve years old, was driven by necessity to work as a child laborer at a factory. Toiling like a beast of burden, he fell a victim to consumption, whereupon he was dismissed by his boss. Poor and helpless, he finally died in his mother's arms. Soon starvation and disease took the life of Lei Feng's younger brother. The ill-fated mother, eager to preserve the only one that remained of her children, went out to work as a servant for a landlord, enduring every hardship that came her way. But who would have thought that she would be raped by the dissolute landlord! Filled with bitter resentment, she hanged herself one night after saying to Lei Feng, "Heaven bless you, my child! May you grow up to be a man and revenge our whole family!"

Thus Lei Feng became an orphan, who had to struggle hard for a living with the help of his poor relatives. One day, when cutting firewood in a hill occupied by a landlord, he was caught by the landlord's wife, who wrested the axe from him and struck him on the hand with its back.

Young Lei Feng had experienced all the miseries imposed on the laboring people by the old society under the rule of imperialism and Kuomintang reaction. A spark of hatred kindled in his heart, he waded through the tribulations of life that lasted for almost two years.

* Chen Tung-lei, "Lei Feng, A Fine Example of Chinese Youth," *Evergreen* (Peking), No. 2, April 1963.

FROM BITTER TO SWEET

In August 1949 the native place of Lei Feng was liberated. He was found by Peng Teh-mou, chairman of the peasants' association and later the head of the Township People's Government, who stroked the boy's head and said, "We all owe our liberation to Chairman Mao, the Communist Party, and the People's Liberation Army. Poor boy, you'd have been no more if Chairman Mao had not led our people to make a revolution."

And so, the bitter days had come to an end and Lei Feng began to taste the sweetness of the new life. However, his hatred for the oppressors and exploiters remained as bitter as ever. At the age of ten, a red-tasseled spear in hand, he plunged into the struggle against feudalism. When the landlords were brought to justice before a mass rally, Lei Feng appeared with his scarred hand, and seizing hold of the landlord's wife, poured out his long pent-up fury on her. This was the first time he was educated in class struggle.

Lei Feng went to school with the help of the people's government and the peasants' association. Among the first characters he learned were: Long live Chairman Mao! "Mamma," he thought aloud, "it's not Heaven but Chairman Mao and the Communist Party who have saved me!" Lei Feng was a good pupil, being diligent, keen on labor and eager to help his schoolmates, and was among the first group of children in his school to be admitted to the Young Pioneers. He got good marks for all the courses he studied, and graduated from the primary school with honors in 1956. . . .

In 1956, when the movement for cooperative farming rose to a high tide in his native district, sixteen-year-old Lei Feng joyfully left school for the agricultural front. Soon after, he worked in the office of the Wangcheng County Committee of the Communist Party. There he was very well looked after by the Party secretary, who often told him stories about revolutionary martyrs. Lei Feng was deeply moved by the heroism of many Communists who had refused to yield even when cruelly tortured by the enemy. Pledging to follow their example, he made very rapid progress under the guidance of the Party, and became a member of the Communist Youth League in 1957. When the Party committee decided to set up a farm at Tuanshanhu, Lei Feng did not hesitate to take up a new occupation —to learn to be a tractor driver—and soon became well qualified for the job. Then, in the autumn of 1958, the news came that Anshan, the iron and steel base in northeast China, was in need of more hands for the development of production. Lei Feng, eager to do more for the socialist construction of the motherland, was among the first to apply for a vacancy. Thus he became a bulldozer operator in Anshan. The bulldozer he handled was of enormous size, and fearing that the boy might overstrain himself a veteran worker suggested that he take a smaller one. But Lei Feng said in reply, "Don't worry, I can manage it all right!" . . .

A PEOPLE'S FIGHTER

Coming from a poor peasant family, Lei Feng had now schooled himself in the ranks of the working class and had become a man of broad vision, with a strong sense of revolutionary responsibility. Early on the morning of December 4, 1959, the day after he had heard a report on conscription, he went to the recruiting station to join up. But after a checkup, both his height and weight proved short of the mark. When the doctor saw the scars on Lei Feng's body and asked how he had got them, tears immediately welled up in the young man's eyes. He told the doctor all about his miserable childhood and said, "My hatred of the past evils makes me determined to join the army." Moved by Lei Feng's story, the doctor advised him to talk things over with the Bureau of Military Service. Lei Feng took the advice and called on a battalion commander at the Bureau. Taking the commander by the hand he said, "When I think of the past and the fact that our country is still faced with U.S. imperialist aggression, I feel an irrepressible urge to take up arms to defend our motherland. . . ." He spoke with such passion that tears began to trickle down his cheeks. Seeing his unfeigned eagerness, the battalion commander consented to enlist him.

The day Lei Feng entered the army, he wrote about his

fcclings and aspirations in his new diary: "My long cherished dream of joining the Chinese People's Liberation Army has now come true. . . . My mind is in a tumult; I can hardly calm myself. A downtrodden orphan in the old society, I have now become a fighter for national defense. I must live up to the Party's teachings and expectations. I must overcome any difficulty I may come across and carry on the fine revolutionary traditions of the elder generation. I would rather sacrifice my blood and lose my life than surrender to the enemy. I must learn to be a good soldier of Mao Tse-tung and devote all the golden time of my youth to the most splendid cause of the motherland."

Happy though Lei Feng was, he never forgot the oppression he had suffered in the past, and he regarded it a cherished task to safeguard the fruits of revolution. He also showed great concern for the revolutionary struggle of the oppressed people throughout the world.

Lei Feng showed remarkable grit in military training. At the beginning he was not even able to throw a grenade over the required distance, though he tried over and over again until his arm became swollen. The commander showed him an article on how to combat difficulties and told him not to lose heart. "Go on training hard and you will get there," he said encouragingly. That night, though a northerly wind was blowing and everybody had gone to bed, Lei Feng quietly went out to the drill ground and practiced his exercises by himself with all his might. At daybreak the following day, he went out as usual with the others to do morning exercise. In this way he improved daily until finally he was able to throw the grenades strongly and accurately.

Under the guidance of the Communist Party, Lei Feng continued to make rapid progress. On November 8, 1960, or ten months after his enlistment, he was admitted to the glorious Communist Party of China.

FOR A BETTER FUTURE OF THE MOTHERLAND

In working for a better future of the motherland and for the great cause of socialism, Lei Feng was brimming over with energy. Apart from his own assignments, he busied himself with all kinds of social activity. In his company's club he was responsible for organizing studies, and he enthusiastically helped others to learn Chairman Mao's works. In the drive to acquire general knowledge, he offered to teach and correct exercises for his comrades in his spare time. He was also the head of the technical study group and one of the leading spirits in the chorus of his company, as well as a Young Pioneer instructor at a primary school in the neighborhood.

One Sunday, on his way back from a clinic where he had his aching stomach examined, he passed a construction site. There the stirring scene of labor attracted his attention and made him forget his pain. Rolling up his sleeves, he set about carting bricks with a wheelbarrow. "It'd be a good thing even if I could add a brick to the edifice of socialism!" Thinking thus he pushed on at a dashing speed till large beads of sweat stood out on his forehead. The enthusiasm of this stranger made an immediate impact on the whole construction site. Soon a voice came through the loudspeaker, "Let's emulate our comrade from the People's Liberation Army!" When at last the workers found out he was ill, they were all deeply moved. Later, they wrote out their praises on a large sheet of paper and sent it to his unit. . . .

HE LIVES THAT OTHERS MAY LIVE BETTER

It was a habit with Lei Feng to help others and render wholehearted service to the people. . . .

One day, while Lei Feng was cleaning his truck near his barracks, dark clouds suddenly gathered in the sky and it began to rain very heavily. At this moment, a woman with a baby in her arm and two knapsacks across her shoulder and leading a child of five or six by the hand, was seen trudging down the road with great difficulty. Lei Feng jumped down from his truck, went up to her and asked where she was going. When he learned that she still had a long way to go, he took off his raincoat and threw it over her, took over her baby and offered to see them home. As the rain was accompanied by a strong wind, Lei Feng took off his coat and wrapped the baby in it for fear that the little thing might catch cold. After almost two hours they finally arrived at their destination. The woman felt much indebted to him and said, "Brother, I'll never forget your help!" But the reply was: "Don't mention it. We army men and the people belong to the same family."

In his diary Lei Feng wrote the following maxim: "A man's life is limited, but service to the people knows no bounds. I must devote my limited life to the boundless service for the people."

AN INEXHAUSTIBLE SOURCE

As a young tree grows with vitality in the sunshine of spring, so the noble revolutionary qualities of Lei Feng shone ever more brilliantly as a result of his earnest study of the teachings of Mao Tse-tung. Lei Feng had a satchel filled with Chairman Mao's works. This he kept as a treasure, an inseparable companion wherever he went—as a driver in the army he had to travel a lot. Whenever he had a few moments to spare, he would pore over the books and find great satisfaction even if he could have time enough to go through just one page or one paragraph. He said, "As food is to a man, weapons to a soldier or the steering wheel to a truck, so are Chairman Mao's works to us. A man cannot live without food, a soldier cannot fight without weapons, a truck cannot work without the steering wheel, and a revolutionary cannot do without learning Chairman Mao's works." He wrote in his diary, "The most important result I have got from studying the *Selected Works of Mao Tse-tung* is that they have taught me how to live as a man and for whom I should live." Lei Feng left behind him the four volumes of the *Selected Works,* the pages of which are full of lines and dots penciled by the careful reader, as well as a diary of more than two hundred thousand words. These are records of his serious study of Mao Tse-tung's works and his actual practice of Mao Tse-tung's thought. Mao Tse-tung's thought was the inexhaustible source of his heroic deeds and noble qualities. It was in the course of arming himself with Mao Tse-tung's thoughts that Lei Feng, a downtrodden child born in the old society, made rapid progress and finally became a great immortal fighter. Lei Feng will live in the hearts of the people for ever and ever. His image will serve as a splendid example for the Chinese youth and inspire them to march forward.

CHINA YOUTH DAILY *
Educated Youths Who Go to Rural and Mountainous Areas Have a Great Future

Recently, large numbers of educated youths in many cities have rushed to the countryside, forming a new revolutionary current. This is an indication of prosperity of our nation, and a symbol of unceasing development in education in our country. Going to rural and mountainous areas, urban educated youths have embarked upon a glorious revolutionary road—a road on which they can join the masses of workers and peasants.

Some urban educated youths may ask: What can we do in rural and mountainous areas? Is there a bright future in plowing the soil? Our reply is: Educated youths will have an endless, bright and great future in rural and mountainous areas.

Why do we say so?

In the eyes of a proletarian, the future of a revolutionary is always closely linked with the future of the revolutionary cause. Our country's agriculture has extensive prospects, and our country's five hundred million peasants have a great future. . . .

Educated youths in some cities say: "Rural life is hard!" Yes, this is true. Though agricultural construction is now much better than that before the liberation, the laboring conditions are still poorer and life is harder in the countryside than in urban areas. Going suddenly to the countryside, we may not be accustomed to the environment physically and technically and in everyday life. Only if we make up our minds to temper our-

* Translations nos. 34, 345, and 10,046 (Washington, D.C.: U.S. Joint Publications Research Service).

selves, shall we be able, after a certain period of time, to get accustomed to the rural environment. If we think that what slight hardships we suffer today are for the sake of building a new, socialist countryside, creating happiness for the younger generation, and rendering greater support to the revolutionary struggles undertaken by peoples of the world, we shall find happiness in rural life and shall not feel any suffering. It is good for youths to suffer some hardships during their time of growth. A revolutionary youth fears no hardships, does not wish to pass his days in quietness and comfort, but wishes to lead a life of fierce struggle. He is willing to create the world with his hands, instead of waiting to enjoy other people's achievements. The harder the conditions are, the more can he temper his revolutionary character and perseverance and learn the skills of overcoming difficulties. Many educated youths who have gone to the countryside have realized that it is impossible to carry out revolution and change the backward aspects of the countryside without first suffering some hardships and shedding blood and sweat. When they had just started to labor, blisters were formed on their hands, and their shoulders swelled as a result of carrying heavy loads. However, they were not scared by these difficulties. They said: "If we do not suffer hardships, we can never temper ourselves." "Suffering of hardships helps us get rid of arrogance and establish a revolutionary will." Imposing demands on themselves in this spirit, they will fear no hardships or tiring work, and can overcome all sorts of difficulties.

It can be easily understood that youths show concern for their future. The Party and the state also hope that the youths will have a beautiful and bright future. The purpose of carrying out the revolution and national reconstruction is to enable the people of the whole country and the younger generation to have a beautiful and bright future. Since we go to rural and mountainous areas for the purpose of carrying out revolution, we must, while considering problems concerning our future, combine our individual prospects with the great socialist cause. We must dedicate our wisdom and strength to the service of the motherland and the people and, by the effort of this generation, build a socialist new countryside. Educated-youth comrades, go bravely to the agricultural front, and let us press ahead bravely on the road of revolutionization! . . .

Views on Marriage

August 1960

Marriage is a matter of intimate concern for both men and women; it is also a social problem—a problem of human relationship.

Class consciousness plays an important role in forming one's viewpoint about marriage. The landlord class has its viewpoint about marriage; so has the bourgeois class. Both of them are formed on the basis of selfishness and exploitation. The working class has its own concept on marriage, too, but it is formed in accordance with the moral principle of Communism.

Living in the age of Socialism and Communism, young workers must follow the moral principle of Communism in dealing with their matrimonial problems.

With the advent of socialist society, a new economic, political, and legal concept has been introduced, enabling the young people to arrange their own matrimonial life happily according to the moral principle of Communism. As a matter of fact, this new concept of marriage has already been firmly established and its root goes deep into the heart of people everywhere. Many young men and young women have applied this concept in building their happy homes. Nevertheless, the old concept and system of marriage set up by the exploiting class throughout the last few thousand years still, more or less, have had influence on people, even on our young comrades. Some of them, while confronted by matrimonial problems, find their regular work and learning seriously affected and their political thinking stifled. They not only become a nuisance to other people, but also do terrible harms to themselves. For this reason, it is most important that the working class has to form a strong and correct viewpoint concerning marriage and family life, and to do away with the old concept which belongs to the exploiting bourgeois class.

ESTABLISH A CORRECT VIEWPOINT
TOWARD MARRIAGE

Now then, what is our viewpoint? Is it different from that of the exploiting bourgeois class?

For one thing, our basic concept on marriage is and must be that we build our happiness upon the premise that happiness should be shared by all. We advocate equal rights for man and woman, equal rights for husband and wife. We oppose the idea that man is superior to woman or that the husband has special prerogatives over his wife. We also oppose any discrimination against or ill treatment of the wife.

We believe that marriage should be based solely upon mutual consent. We oppose the so-called arranged marriage, or the use of any deceitful or compulsory method by one of the parties in this matter. We uphold the system of monogamy. Husband and wife ought to have true and exclusive love toward each other, and concubinage is not permitted.

We believe that the very basic foundations for love between man and woman are common political understanding, comradeship in work, mutual help, and mutual respect. Money, position, or the so-called prettiness should not be taken into consideration for a right marriage, because they are not reliable foundations for love.

We also believe that solemnity and fidelity are important elements for a correct relationship between husband and wife, and for a happy family life. To abandon one's partner by any improper means is to be opposed. In our society, those who intend to pursue their happiness at the expense of others run contradictory to the moral principle of Communism and will never be happy.

For the exploiting class, the concept about marriage is just the opposite. The landlord class believes in pursuing happiness by making other people suffer. They subscribe to such biased viewpoints as "man is superior to woman," "man is more important than woman," "man should dominate woman," etc. Under this type of ideology, women are merely slaves and properties of men and marriage is nothing but a process of buying and selling with compulsion. In the bourgeois society the whole matrimonial relationship is built upon money, and becomes simply a "monetary relationship." In economic relationship, women belong to men. Love is nothing but a merchandise; women trade their flesh for men's money. This concept about marriage is indeed reactionary and it shall meet with our firm opposition.

Among our young worker comrades there are still a few whose thinking is still under the influence of the exploiting class. They cannot do away with the thinking that man is superior to woman; they look down upon their own wives, especially those who have lower education and those who come from rural areas. When they look for lovers, what concerns the man most is whether the woman is pretty or not; what concerns the woman most is whether the man is earning high wages and has a high position. They disregard all the other elements for a good match.

Some of them even use deception to steal love or to force the other party to marry them. Their attitude toward love and marriage is most revolting. They love the new ones and forsake the old, get themselves involved in multi-angle romance, or even seek excuses as grounds for divorce. All this sort of thinking and behavior are certainly contradictory to the moral quality of the working class and Communism, and contradictory to the socialist concept and system of marriage. Therefore those who have formed such a wrong concept about marriage ought to adopt a correct one in accordance with the moral principle of Communism. Only then will there be possibility for true love and happy family life.

STANLEY KARNOW *
Why They Fled: Refugee Accounts

THE CHANCE TO LEAVE

It was a surprise to discover that so many people within the past year have been permitted to leave Communist China legally. Several of these were Overseas Chinese from Hong Kong and Southeast Asia who, out of patriotism, had gone to Mainland China, only to be disillusioned by what they found. But an unusual number of native Mainlanders were also allowed to emigrate from their country.

It has now been well established that the great exodus of refugees into Hong Kong in the spring of 1962 was due almost entirely to a relaxation of controls. Either through a misinterpretation of orders or perhaps on direct instructions from Peking, officials in Kwangtung province encouraged the flight of more than a hundred thousand Chinese across the border into the British colony. Significantly, there is no record of political cadres or military men of any importance among those who escaped.

The much-publicized riot that occurred at the Canton railway station in June 1962 also evolved from the Communists' loosening of regulations. As two eyewitnesses told me the story, hundreds of people armed with exit permits arrived at the station to take the train to Hong Kong. The train was not functioning. The crowd milled around, impatience warming into anger. There was shoving and shouting until police were called out to arrest about a hundred of the noisier demonstrators. "The police were remarkably well disciplined," observed one of the witnesses. "Had one of them even accidentally fired a shot, we would have had real violence in Canton that day."

Along with the easing of controls, elements of corruption seem to have crept into the granting of exit permits. Though no-

---

* Stanley Karnow, "Why They Fled: Refugee Accounts," *Current Scene, Developments in Mainland China*, II, 22, October 15, 1963.

body admitted to having participated in bribery, several people I questioned claimed that they had heard of Communist officials who would issue departure documents for a price. The price was enormous—seven hundred yuan, or roughly ten months' salary for a skilled worker (1 yuan = U.S. $0.42 or £0 2s. 9d.).

Sometimes visas were issued without any discernible rhyme or reason. A distinguished, Western-educated ex-banker from Shanghai was mystified by his being accorded an exit visa. He had made the mistake of not leaving China in 1949 ("I thought this Communist thing would blow over") and in the years since he had repeatedly applied for permission to emigrate to Hong Kong, where one of his sons lived. His requests were ignored until one day last September, when quite suddenly he was given papers to leave the country. The permit was accompanied by a short speech. "You see that there is no iron curtain that forces people to remain in China," said the Communist official blandly.

The flood of refugees out of China last year, I found, did not coincide with the worst period of food shortages. In fact, conditions inside China were actually improving somewhat at the time of the exodus. People fled because of an accumulation of past disasters and, because with controls relaxed, the opportunity appeared.

The nadir of living conditions, everyone agreed, was the winter of 1960–1961. The Great Leap Forward had, by 1959, left the country in chaos, which was aggravated the following year by bad weather. By late 1960, there was no meat, no fish, scarcely any vegetables, and reduced portions of rice. People spoke of having eaten wild herbs, of using a rancid rice-bran oil. A girl who had lived in Hupeh province at the time said that peasants ate cakes made from cotton seeds, a form of nourishment normally reserved for pigs. A young man from Canton described how raw rice was steamed twice so that the additional water would increase its weight and make the ration go further.

Nobody who came under my questioning had seen or heard of people starving, and a few of our refugees volunteered the comment that the Chinese Communists did a "fair and equitable" job of rationing in the face of shortages. (From highly reliable sources I did learn, however, that during the severe 1960–1961 winter, as many as seventy thousand people died of starvation in arid Kansu province, a marginal region in the best of times. The First Secretary of the Provincial Communist Party Committee, Chang Chung-liang, was reportedly purged for allowing this catastrophe to happen. He was charged with concealing the truth from Peking in order to create a good impression. Whether he was executed, sentenced to "labor reform," or merely demoted is unknown.)

IN SEARCH OF FOOD

During that 1960–1961 winter, peasants streamed into the cities in search of food. Several witnesses testified to seeing beggars in the streets of Canton. A man from Nanking described how bewildered, hungry country folk wandered into the city's few "free" restaurants—patronized by army officers, Party officials, and highly paid technicians—to steal leftover scraps from the tables. "The police would drive them out of town," he recalled, "but they drifted back."

Though generally eradicated by the Communists, prostitution seems to have made a reappearance during the period of food scarcities at prices ranging fom three or four ounces of rice to three-catty rice-ration coupons (1 catty = 1.1 lbs. or ½ kilo.).

According to the refugees I talked to, the 1960–1961 winter was also a time of widespread malnutrition and sickness. The diseases most frequently mentioned were hepatitis, tuberculosis, and edema, and testimony on the extent of these illnesses varies considerably. One peasant claimed that 95 per cent of the residents in his village suffered from swollen limbs, while a medical student from a nearby village estimated that not more than 3 or 4 per cent of its inhabitants were affected by edema. A doctor in Hong Kong later explained that the two observations were not necessarily in contradiction. "There are degrees of edema," he said. "The layman can truthfully state that 95 per cent of his villagers showed swelling, but the specialist examining the same people might consider that only 3 or 4 per cent of the cases are serious enough to merit a medical term."

Just as they were in accord on the worst period of food shortage, so my informants unanimously agreed that conditions had improved noticeably within the past year.

Rations in the cities had been increased. In Shanghai during 1961, for example, an office employee received thirty catties of rice per month but insufficient vegetables and no meat; now he would get twenty-four catties of grain, eight ounces per month of pork, one catty of fish, and adequate supplies of vegetables. The meat ration in Peking was recently raised from two to ten ounces per month, and cabbages have become such a glut on the market that with every twenty-kilogram purchase, the buyer is given an extra ration of flour.

A good deal of the flour being distributed in the coastal cities has been manufactured from Canadian and Australian wheat, on which Peking has so far spent some 357 million pounds sterling. Judging from these interviews, very few Chinese know that wheat is being imported. A man from Shanghai said that the foreign flour is mixed with domestic flour of inferior quality and distributed to ration-coupon holders. Another claimed that pure white bread made from imported flour is available only in "free" restaurants, at six yuan per pound—about two days' labor for a skilled worker.

Rural conditions have always lagged behind city conditions and still do. The Kwangtung province diets described to me have improved over the past couple of years, but they are still slim. One peasant explained that in 1961 he received about five ounces of rice per meal, and never any meat. Last year his rice ration was increased by two ounces per meal, with some allocations of meat for the New Year Festival and the Ch'ing Ming Festival. Though his allotment of rice has not increased appreciably, the peasant is now able to grow his own vegetables and buy some meat on "free markets." His meals are more palatable even if his caloric consumption has not risen appreciably.

Extracting information from frightened, puzzled, inarticulate peasants is extremely difficult. Generally, they are simple, rugged people with gnarled hands and leathery faces, who answer questions with shy hesitation, possibly thinking that they are undergoing some sort of official interrogation. I posed the most elementary questions and received elementary answers. Their responses indicated that their recent harvests have been better. One group of peasants who had sailed with their wives and children down the Kwangtung coast and out of Communist

China in a stolen junk told a fairly typical story. The 1961 crop, brushed by a typhoon, had been so poor that their "production team"—a labor unit of about two hundred people—had been obliged to borrow thirty thousand catties of rice from a state granary to eat. The 1962 harvest had been better, but the team had to repay its loan, and there was no prospect of an improved rice ration.

NO MORE MARCHING

All the peasants concurred that the military-style marches to and from the fields of the "people's communes" no longer exist. One man from a village near Swatow explained that peasants now learned of their collective duties from a bulletin board in the local square. A minor official was posted at the board to read the assignments for those who were illiterate. "In our village," said a Kwangtung peasant, "the brigade leader blows an ox horn to wake everyone up, and then he goes from house to house giving assignments for the day. People go to the fields individually, and when they finish their tasks they work on their private plots."

The small gardens distributed to peasants within the past year have contributed significantly toward improving the food situation. Peasants are now able to raise vegetables for themselves or for sale at government-sponsored "free markets." In remote rural areas, peasants barter their produce with state agents for manufactured goods like towels, toothbrushes, combs, or soap. Peasants living near cities are luckier. They can carry their meat, fowl, and vegetables into town and sell them for cash.

This creeping capitalism is marred by a serious shortage of consumer goods. The peasant with a bit of money to spend has very little to buy. This has provoked a small boom in the second-hand business. Used wristwatches, old sweaters, or slightly dented pots and pans are in heavy demand, and other articles command outlandish prices. A non-rationed pack of cigarettes sells for four or five yuan (the week's wage of an unskilled worker). A stout coffin—the dream of every Chinese—costs three hundred yuan (more than three months' salary for a skilled worker).

Paradoxically, many villagers splurge their market earnings on fancy meals in expensive city restaurants instead of taking the money home. "Ostentation in your own village," explained a Canton doctor, "may irritate the local Party official, and you may be branded 'bourgeois.' It can also irk your less fortunate neighbors. And perhaps a big dinner in a city restaurant gives them a feeling of wealth."

The Communists are clearly concerned by these "spontaneous tendencies toward capitalism," as Peking propaganda calls them. Though there is no indication of a radical return to political dogmatism, Peking has begun a gradual crackdown on the program of *Tzu-fa,* or "self-prosperity," during the past year.

Various efforts are being made to regulate the amount of time peasants spend cultivating their own gardens. In some cases, this is done directly and crudely by Party officials issuing orders to peasants to work more on collective land. More generally, however, the state is trying to discourage private enterprise by exerting stricter controls over free market activities. At several rural markets, "supervisors" have appeared to enforce fixed prices, and railroad police now limit the amount of produce peasants may carry into cities. Though peasants may still raise pigs in their spare time, they are, in many instances, required to sell them to state purchasing agents and are also being hit with sales taxes.

It seems clear that the Communists do not want to abolish the incentives that have contributed to increased food production. It is equally plain, however, that the "small freedoms" have met with such popularity that Peking may feel the Communist system itself is threatened. How to keep peasants under control yet offer them encouragement to work is a problem the Chinese Communists must somehow solve.

INDUSTRIAL SLOWDOWN

The city people interviewed were unanimous in describing a general industrial slowdown. I heard of steel mills in Nanking and Canton being merged or closed, either for lack of raw materials or because workers had been sent to the countryside as farm laborers.

An engineer from a sewing machine factory in Shanghai said that his plant, which normally employed some four thousand workers, had not operated to capacity since 1960. As materials and spare parts grew scarcer and workers were shipped out to farms, factory production gradually declined until now, he estimated, the plant was functioning half time. For lack of raw cotton, Shanghai's textile mills were also running half time; of the city's four or five cigarette factories, he knew of only one currently in operation. "On the other hand," he said, "little repair shops are doing well, mending shoes, pots and pans, farm tools, and so forth. It's cheaper to fix what you have than to buy something new."

Two refugees cited cases of managerial corruption in state companies. The Shanghai sewing machine engineer recounted how a much-decorated Korean War veteran, made financial director in his factory, was arrested for embezzling company funds. The swindler might never have been caught had he not been noticed one day buying a package of black market Lucky Strikes for four yuan, the equivalent of his daily wage. Suspicion led to his arrest. He was sent to "labor reform."

During a severe period of food and fuel shortages, said an acountant from Nanking, it was common for managers of different state enterprises to barter commodities for their own well-being. The director of a coal supply company, for example, would slyly send a shipment of coal to the director of a meat distribution outfit and be given food in exchange. There was allegedly trading in clothing, lumber, wristwatches and, as our accountant explained it, "these luxuries were divided up among the top managers and political cadres, and nobody was ever caught."

Within the past year or so a lively black market has burgeoned, especially in Kwangtung province, where the proximity of Hong Kong means availability of merchandise. Because of a widespread sugar shortage, a popular and maneuverable item is saccharine. A Hong Kong resident puts saccharine tablets into letters he sends to his relatives in Canton. They pass it off to an agent for a handsome price, and he in turn doubles his money by selling it to operatives from North China. Among higher officials and technicians, the cigarette lighter is a status symbol. This has sparked a similar demand for lighter flints, which are easily mailed and marketed, their price compounding geometrically as they travel north.

A genuine luxury, such as a bicycle, is a major black-market moneymaker. Imported by an Overseas Chinese, who enjoys special privileges, an English-made Raleigh is worth in Canton eight times its Hong Kong price—one thousand yuan or, in labor value, a factory manager's salary for about ten months. Such is the awareness of brand names on the Canton black market that a Hercules bicycle, less renowned than the Raleigh, brings only seven hundred yuan.

My very knowledgeable source on these shadowy dealings was a modest young schoolteacher from the suburbs of Canton. Once he warmed to his subject, he could quote black-market prices for everything from hundredweights of rice to old artillery shells. He was most bullish on Hong Kong currency. An estimated 25 per cent of the Hong Kong dollars in circulation are believed to be hoarded in South China, he said. High-paid technicians, recipients of remittances from abroad, Chinese returned from overseas, former property-owners receiving state indemnities, smugglers and others referred to in Communist propaganda as "bourgeois elements" will pay ten times the legal exchange rate to get them.

In an effort to regulate the sale of manufactured merchandise in the cities, Peking recently initiated a wage-ration system; citizens are awarded coupons on the strength of what they earn rather than what they spend. One coupon is issued for every ten yuan of salary. Thus an engineer earning one hundred yuan per month receives ten coupons. With fourteen coupons (plus half of his monthly wage) he can buy a fairly durable pair of shoes.

Having discarded the Marxist slogan "to each according to his needs," the Chinese Communists now seem to have adopted "to each according to his income." This control mechanism has added still another dram of confusion to daily life in China. A Shanghai mechanic commented dryly: "One day I put my hand into my pocket and pulled out twenty-three different kinds of ration coupons."

"WHAT KIND OF BIG BROTHER?"

Some of the refugees provided small insights into political moods inside Communist China. The former Shanghai banker, for instance, had discerned a slight but nonetheless significant easing of political pressures in 1962. It had previously required real courage to tune into foreign radio broadcasts, he said, recalling cases of children accusing their fathers of listening to anti-communist propaganda. Now it was no longer dangerous to tune in to BBC or the Voice of America, whose programs, he observed, were greatly appreciated.

Several urban refugees spoke of the growing propaganda campaign against Khrushchev. At neighborhood political meetings, Khrushchev is commonly depicted as the worst sort of villain. "Though the people of China and Russia are still brothers," said the chairman of a recent indoctrination session in Shanghai, "Khrushchev betrays the work of Stalin, the will of Lenin, follows the path of Tito and even betrays his own people." An eyewitness to the meeting added: "At that, we all banged the tables and booed. But I'll wager that half the people in the room didn't understand what was going on, and the rest didn't care."

In Nanking, explained a refugee from that city, free tickets to Soviet movies are no longer distributed as part of the "political study" curriculum. Long-standing Chinese Communist complaints against Moscow are being revived. "During the Korean War," said a Party official at a meeting not long ago, "Chinese soldiers shed their blood while the Soviet Union merely lent us weapons for which they are demanding repayment. What kind of Big Brother is that?"

ADVENTURES OF LING

Among the people I encountered was a man named Ling Shao-lu. Partly through passive resistance, partly through sheer ineptitude, Ling largely eluded the rigors of Communism. Ling Shao-lu was born forty years ago in Taiwan, when the island was controlled by Japan. He received a Japanese education and served in the Japanese Army. But he considers himself "pure Taiwanese." He emigrated to Japan in 1950, settled in Osaka as a hospital bookkeeper and married a Japanese girl. Ling had no serious political convictions. His most avid interest was folk music. He is a frail man with a large head who still carries a crumpled card attesting to his membership in the Osaka Folk Music Academy.

In 1955, Ling recounted, he succumbed to Communist blandishments to emigrate to China. "We were told that the Nationalists discriminated against us on Taiwan," he explained, "but that New China loved the Taiwanese and treated them well. We left Japan so quickly that I didn't even bother to get any kind of passport or identity papers."

Along with about a hundred other Chinese from Taiwan, they disembarked at Tientsin, where for two months life was as delightful as advertised. They were given free room and board at a comfortable hotel, toured by bus around the vicinity and visited factories, historic sites, and other tourist attractions. The only disagreeable interlude during this period was a two-week political seminar in which they were lectured on the theories of Marx, Lenin, and Mao Tse-tung. "I didn't understand a thing," Ling recalled. "The words passed into my ears and disappeared. I could read the characters in the books they gave us, like *Dictatorship of the New Democratic System,* but I had no idea what they meant. They gave my wife Japanese translations of the same books, but she didn't even open them. She preferred the novels she had brought along."

When the political course ended, Party officials interrogated the new immigrants and assigned them to jobs in different cities. Because he could use an abacus, Ling was made a clerk. Despite his request for a warm climate, he was dispatched to Nanking. "I explained that I doubted if the weather would suit me," he said, "but they told me that Nanking had been the Nationalist capital and was the best city in China. That impressed me, so we accepted Nanking."

At their destination, Ling and his wife were greeted with modest fanfare by local officials and taken on tours of the city. Finally, after a fortnight of settling in, they were escorted in pedicabs to a State enterprise called the Coal and Building Ma-

terials Company, where Ling was to work. It was an organization that distributed fuel, cement, bricks, and lumber to lesser
state companies and factories throughout the province. As Ling
remembers his arrival,

> We were led to a conference room, and when we en-
> tered, about fifty or sixty people rose and applauded. The
> manager and secretary shook my hand, and the manager
> made a short speech. "You have returned to the bosom of
> the motherland," he said. "Please say a few words to us."
> I didn't know what to say. It was all so new to me.
> I explained that I was all mixed up and couldn't make a
> speech. But then, as I looked at them, I couldn't resist ask-
> ing one question. "Why is it," I asked, "that all the people
> in China dress the same, like mah-jongg tiles of the same
> suit?"
> Everyone laughed and I got flustered. Nobody ever
> answered the question.

A few days later, Ling was given a desk and an abacus,
and instructed to prepare a financial statement from a ledger.
The department chief solicitously told him to take his time—
take a day if necessary. But it was only a matter of adding up
some figures, and Ling finished in an hour.

> So they gave me newspapers to read, and for the next six
> months I really suffered. I completed every job in a fraction
> of the time they expected me to take, and when I asked for
> more work, they pressed newspapers on me. You'd think
> reading newspapers was more important than working. I
> complained so much that they finally gave me other tasks.
> But I really think they would have preferred me to sit
> there and read newspapers.

For the first year or so, life was not bad. But gradually
Ling began to be irritated by small things. Going to the office
on Sunday, for example. "It was not compulsory, but you had to
go to be considered a 'constructive worker,' " Ling said. "So
instead of taking my wife and new baby to the park, I went to
the office and read newspapers."

OUT OF THE CAGE

Soon Ling started to feel pangs of regret for having come to
Communist China. A few Chinese he met chided him for his
foolishness, and one of them said to him: "We're hoping so
hard to be able to fly out of the cage, and you fly in."

Ling's first real trouble developed from his penchant for
good food. He and his wife considered themselves gourmets,
and at least twice a week they treated themselves to extravagant
dinners at a local restaurant. In fact, explained Ling proudly,
they spent almost half their monthly income in restaurants.

> The political cadres at my company didn't like this.
> One day I went to the office to find wall posters reading:
> "Ling has strong tastes for the capitalist-bourgeois way of
> life." I retaliated by putting up a poster which said: "What
> good is the Revolution if one cannot live comfortably?"
>
> This led to a special political meeting, attended by the
> twenty employees of our accounting department. I was
> criticized for "outright bourgeois living" and advised to
> admit that this criticism was accurate. The only person who
> defended me was the deputy chief of our department, who
> said: "Ling has just arrived from overseas and cannot live
> the way we do yet. Give him time to get adjusted."
>
> For the sake of this man, I confessed that I had done
> wrong, and the issue was dropped. Anyway, the cadres
> were busy preparing a big "anti-rightist" campaign at the
> time, and I probably wasn't important enough to be in-
> cluded in that.

When the Great Leap Forward was launched in 1958,
Ling recalled, everything in his company went askew. Railway
schedules were all confused. Shipments of coal and timber arrived when not needed, or failed to arrive when desperately
needed. Valuable coke and iron ore were diverted to "backyard
furnaces" to make "native steel" with everyone being exhorted
to work "harder and harder, faster, and better." Ling's reaction
was unorthodox.

I decided to stop working altogether. Without telling anybody, I took my wife, who was then pregnant, and my little daughter, and went by train to Canton. I intended to go from there to Hong Kong. But when we reached Canton, my wife's time was approaching. I took her to a hotel and delivered the child myself, our second daughter. After all, I had worked in a hospital in Japan. Somebody at the hotel must have informed on us, because the police soon paid us a visit. I told them that I was an Overseas Chinese looking for a job in Canton. The policeman laughed and said: "Don't you know what kind of society this is? You must belong to a unit. When you want a job, one unit must recommend you to another unit. Who do you think you are?"

I feigned ignorance. They took me to the police station and discussed my case. Then a policeman said: "Considering that you're a Taiwanese educated in Japan, you're excused this time. Go back to your unit."

A fortnight later, when his wife could travel, Ling returned to Nanking. There the political cadres at his company met him with astonishment, and a "self-criticism" session was hastily assembled.

I was told to write a report confessing to the thoughts that made me run away. I wrote a confession stating honestly that the weather in Nanking was too cold and also that I didn't like wearing cotton-quilt trousers. This confession was rejected on the grounds that my excuse was not adequate. I wrote a second confession declaring that my wife was Japanese and could not adapt to local conditions. This confession was also rejected. I wrote five more confessions and they were all rejected.

Finally, one of the political cadres helped me to write that I had "capitalist tendencies" and would henceforth obey Party instructions. I also pledged to study the works of Chairman Mao for two hours every day.

Throughout the following years, Ling and his wife resisted every rule they could. They refused to eat at mess halls ("so crowded you couldn't enjoy your meal") and Ling declined to work hard ("I deserved better treatment"). They sold the last of their Japanese clothes and what little jewelry they had left ("to the wives of rich cadres and army officers"), and purchased food on the black market. Conditions began to improve early last year but, said Ling, "I had had enough of China. My only thought was to return to Japan."

Last fall he applied for exit permits for his wife and himself, and at last, after five months of filling out forms and waiting, the papers were delivered. "When you go back to the *old* society," warned the official who signed the departure documents, "be careful what you say and to whom you speak."

THE TEMPER IS APATHY

The mosaic of refugee interviews left the impression that a number of China's Communist officials—perhaps because of their investment in the system—are still dedicated and hard-working. Some of the women cadres who feel they have been truly "emancipated" appear to be tougher than male officials. Several sound like Pasionarias. "Our block leader was a woman in her mid-fifties whose two sons were killed in the Korean War," reported a man from Shanghai. "She doesn't stop from morning until night, organizing, talking, snooping, absolutely indefatigable."

Despite the drive of such cadres, it would appear that the temper of Communist China today is apathy. The revolutionary momentum built up through 1957 was accelerated during the Great Leap Forward to a speed that the ancient machinery of China would not tolerate. The pieces are now being picked up amid a general reluctance to try going that fast again.

Certainly these refugee reports indicate that morale in Mainland China has declined steadily since the Leap Forward days of 1958. The urban intelligentsia of doctors, engineers, and professors who originally welcomed the Communists have, according to these accounts, now "lost confidence" in the Party. In the countryside, many peasants have adopted a rather cynical attitude toward the proliferation of slogans forced upon them over recent years. The sight of someone working diligently on collective land may evoke the crack: "Behold him! He expects ten thousand years of happiness in the future." A commonly sarcastic response to a complaint is: "Keep quiet, you're in paradise."

Despite the cynicism, the weariness, the boredom, despite reports of scattered food riots, widespread illness and tales of daring anti-Communist escapades, the average Chinese appears at present to be seeking a personal rather than a political solution to his problem—to receive a remittance from abroad, to connive for extra rations, to market his produce or finally, if feasible, to escape to Hong Kong.

❧ Science and Technology

LESS THAN two decades ago the belief was still widespread in Western countries that the Eastern peoples were incapable of mastering modern science and technology. When Russia exploded her first atomic bomb, many Americans darkly suspected that it had been the work of German scientists abetted by espionage. When Sputnik soared into the air in 1957, the myth of Russian inferiority, once so assiduously propagated by the Nazis, vanished. With the astonishing success of Japan, the development of theoretical sciences in countries like India, and the frequent sight of brilliant Chinese scientists in American universities and research laboratories, the myth of Eastern inferiority has gone. Unfortunately, what threatens to replace it is a Frankenstein image once applied to Germany, then to Russia, and which may now slowly be applied to China.

China has undergone a scientific revolution, which C. H. G. Oldham, a geophysicist with the University of Sussex in England, describes in the following selection. This does not only mean that China has an elite stratum of top scientists, but that the scientific mode of thinking has been spread far and wide among the Chinese people. As Oldham notes, "the Chinese . . . are making a great effort to replace the superstitions of old China with science and rational thought."

China's scientific and technological programs, like her economic development during the first half of the 1960s, appears to be pragmatic rather than ideological. As Oldham notes, "In a few branches of the physical sciences the Chinese work is probably on a par with the best in the world. In the majority of their work, however, the Chinese are still laying the foundations, but they appear to be doing this in a systematic and sensible way." Defense research is obviously being stressed, as is evident from their nuclear programs, but civilian research is not being neglected, given "the present emphasis of research . . . in agriculture." The Chinese have recently entered into scientific exchanges with the advanced countries of the world. Indeed, with the withdrawal of Chinese scientists and students from the Soviet Union, exchange of visits and information with non-Communist countries has become increasingly important. How this will be affected by the "great proletarian cultural revolution" remains to be seen.

The general impression of foreign scientists who have visited China is that they are advanced in the physical sciences and less so in the life sciences, that their research equipment and libraries are excellent, and that good scientific work is going on in many places of the country. China's advance toward world-level scientific and technological status is slow, but she will undoubtedly get there. However, her present leaders appear determined that scientific and technological development be marked not only by outstanding achievements in a few select fields, but by practical application throughout the society for the attainment of social and economic goals.

C. H. G. OLDHAM
Science in China*

ITS ORGANIZATION AND DEVELOPMENT

One of the important developments of the past decade has been the widespread recognition—particularly on the part of governments—given to the role of science in society. It is now accepted that science plays an important part in such diverse fields as defense, economic growth, social development, and foreign affairs. It is no longer possible to leave this complex interaction to

* C. H. G. Oldham, "Science and Education in China," *Bulletin of the Atomic Scientists,* June 1966, pp. 46–50.

chance ad hoc measures; governments must make rational choices from among many alternatives.

This means that a science policy is required, and many countries are still experimenting to find the best ways in which to formulate and then implement such policies.

The role of science in China is particularly fascinating and complex. China is a poor, economically underdeveloped country committed ideologically to the use of science for practical ends, and committed politically to developing her own indigenous science in order to help her become a major world power in the shortest possible time. China's problems of scientific choice are in many ways even more crucial and difficult than those of the richer countries.

A number of recent publications in Western languages have done much to illuminate some of these problems. The extent of our knowledge, however, on most of them is still very meager. The subject is enormous and complex. I shall limit my discussion to four of the many possible topics which could be included under the rubric "science in China."

China has a rich tradition of scientific and technological development, the extent of which has only recently been revealed by Joseph Needham of Cambridge University, and his collaborators. Although modern science never really developed in China until the twentieth century, technological innovations have a long history of practical application. The significance of this history and tradition for contemporary China is a subject which requires further study.

The current successes of Chinese science in some ways are a measure of efficacy of the science education established in China early in this century. It is the men who received their education in China and abroad long before the communist victory, who are in many instances so brilliantly leading China's scientific and technological renaissance, although only under the present government was it possible to provide the material resources with which they could use their skill.

The early years of communist rule brought a transformation from a science and education system modeled on essentially American lines to one modeled on Soviet lines. The Soviets also provided much help in drawing up the twelve-year science plan in 1956. More recently, the emphasis has been on finding a purely Chinese solution to organizational problems.

Throughout these sixteen years it seems to have been a problem for the Chinese leaders to determine the proper role for the Communist Party in the organization of science. At the present time it is in strong control at all levels, and this has led to some major difficulties, probably because few Chinese political leaders have scientific or technological training, and there is much they do not understand about the organization and nature of science. Although this is not a problem unique to China, it perhaps has more serious consequences here. In China a directive from the central government can quickly be implemented throughout the country. If the directive is good, the country quickly benefits; similarly, if the directive is not good, the mistakes can be very costly.

Things came to a head during the Great Leap Forward when, in science as in education, quantity and politics seem to have been emphasized at the cost of quality. Since 1961 more rational policies have been implemented, and although the Communist Party is still in tight control, many of its members have shown a willingness to learn from their mistakes. Western visitors, well qualified to judge, comment on the sensible approach to science now prevailing.

THE PYRAMID

At the top of the science pyramid is the State Science and Technological Commission. This group is responsible for the planning of science and supervising the implementation of these plans. The chairman and vice-chairman of the Commission are all members of the Communist Party. There are branches of the Commission in the provinces.

Under the Commission is the foremost scientific body in China—the Academia Sinica. This organization operates 112 research institutes, which concentrate mainly on oriented basic research, *i.e.,* basic research with specific economic objectives in mind. It is usual for each Academy institute to have a scientist as director, and a member of the Communist Party, often a nonscientist, as vice-director or secretary. The Academy also has branch institutes in each province.

In addition to the Academia Sinica, two other academies, one for agriculture and the other for medicine, operate research institutes. Altogether, in 1963, there were 315 research institutes attached to the three academies.

Applied research is mainly carried on by institutes attached to various ministries, and by the end of 1963 the government was operating 345 research institutes.

In all there are about 800 research institutes in China, of which 305 are in life sciences, 205 in physical sciences, and 271 in engineering. Since the Great Leap Forward the greatest increase in effort, as judged by new institutes established, has been in the life sciences, presumably as a result of the current economic emphasis on agriculture.

In 1960, when the last statistics were published, China spent 1,081 million yuan ($441 million) on science. This represented 1.54 per cent of the national budget. In 1952 only .07 per cent of the national budget was spent on science.

In 1962 there were 40 scientific societies of national status with a membership of more than 100,000, and 53 scientific journals with nationwide coverage were published. In addition, there are more than 170 fortnightly and monthly journals which provide abstracts in Chinese of foreign scientific papers.

RESEARCH INSTITUTES OF THE ACADEMY

Over the past few years an increasing number of British, French, Canadian, and other Western scientists have visited research institutes of the three Chinese academies. From their reports it is possible to piece together the following summary of impressions about some of the research institutes of the Academia Sinica.

1. The library facilities are generally excellent, with up-to-date collections of journals from throughout the world.

2. The equipment and instrumentation are variable in quality, although mostly good. At some institutes it was first class, and one Fellow of the Royal Society commented on the fact that when it was sufficiently important, the Chinese appeared

to have selected and purchased the best piece of equipment available in the world, America excepted. Visitors noted a growing tendency for the Chinese to develop their own equipment, and most institutes had good workshops for instrument repair and manufacture.

3. Chinese research in the physical sciences is generally more advanced than that in the life sciences.

4. Most visitors noted the relative scarcity of senior scientists, although many were impressed by the high caliber of the few there were. Also scarce are project leaders—men with more than ten years of research experience who should form the backbone of any country's research effort. By contrast, the large number of young scientists is especially noticeable. It is the consensus of the visiting scientists that the majority of these young scientists were bright and eager, and showed an excellent grasp of their research problems.

As would be expected under these circumstances, the research effort is usually concentrated on relatively few problems, which, although in basic research, have a definite relation to practical needs. In a few branches of the physical sciences the Chinese work is probably on a par with the best in the world. In the majority of their work, however, the Chinese are still laying the foundations, but they appear to be doing this in a systematic and sensible way.

5. Each institute has its own objectives and is expected to work within these limits. The funds allocated to each institute seem to be determined by the relative importance of the subject area to state development plans, although details about the allocation of research funds are not known. The individual scientists at the institutes help to determine the research program which is submitted to the Academy for approval.

6. Political cadres were always present at my interviews and visits, and although the scientists would usually give the introductory talk and answer scientific questions, any question with a political bias was given to the cadre to answer. Also, during the introductory talks mention would always be made of the importance of politics in scientific work. I found it completely impossible, however, to assess the impact of ideology on the quality of scientific work. The Pedology Institute in Nanking was both the most political—in the content of the

introductory speech and the fact that many scientists had copies of Mao Tse-tung's books on their desks—and at the same time one of the most impressive research institutes I have visited in Asia.

7. One visitor commented on the fact that the Chinese did not argue when he presented one side of a scientifically controversial issue, which would have immediately provoked an intense debate in both the West and the Soviet Union. He knew that the Chinese were familiar with the literature on the subject and therefore must have been aware of the controversy. He believed that the explanation may have been traditional Chinese politeness to a foreign guest.

INTERNATIONAL SCIENTIFIC RELATIONS

China will not adhere to any international organization— scientific or other—of which Taiwan is a member. This has meant that China has effectively cut herself off from most international scientific intercourse. For example, China is not a member of the International Council of Scientific Unions, although she does belong to the International Union of the History and Philosophy of Science.

However, China is a member of the World Federation of Scientific Workers and, in August 1964, under the partial sponsorship of this organization, held a scientific symposium in Peking. Delegates came from forty-three countries, and a good deal of genuine science was discussed. The meeting also had its political objectives: only delegates from Africa, Asia, Latin America, and Oceania were invited. A continuing committee was set up and other symposia are to be arranged.

It was claimed in the Chinese press that the symposium demonstrated that the monopoly of modern science by scientists from the developed world had once and for all been shattered. There seems little doubt from the available evidence that this was part of the Chinese effort to set up international organizations, with membership limited to the "emerging countries," which would rival the more truly international organizations already in existence.

Bilaterally, China has had scientific exchange agreements

with a number of countries. Closest ties were those once maintained with Soviet scientists. In fact, as already noted, much of the organizational framework of Chinese science is modeled after the pattern of science in the Soviet Union. The Soviet Union also provided many experts (perhaps as many as eleven thousand) in both science and engineering, but, as is well known, these were all withdrawn in 1960.

Despite the fact that one of the most common slogans on the walls of China today is "Rely on our own efforts," the Chinese always freely admit that they have much to learn from the advanced countries of the world. English has now become the most popular foreign language, and scientific exchanges are being increasingly developed with Western countries.

For example, a delegation from the Royal Society visited China in October 1964. They discussed with representatives of the Academia Sinica the exchange of British and Chinese scientists. It was proposed that both groups would continue the ad hoc exchanges of senior scientists, either individually or as delegations, for short visits. At a senior-to-medium level, there would be exchanges of longer duration. The Academia Sinica representatives suggested that the fields of most immediate interest for Chinese scientists to study in Britain were meteorology, geology (especially radioactive dating), and biophysics. Second in priority were high-energy physics, molecular biology, and heart and cardiovascular surgery. Senior-to-medium-level British scientists would visit China for a period of a few months to give lectures, with priority given the fields of paleomagnetism and biophysics. At the junior scientist level, China would send a number of postgraduate research workers to Britain, beginning in 1965, while junior British scientists might begin visiting China in 1966 or later, probably to work in mathematics and physiology.

Scientific exchanges are also beginning between China and France. A recent cultural exchange agreement between these two countries made provision for more than a hundred and fifty Chinese students to study in France on Chinese fellowships and thirty more on French fellowships. In addition, ten Chinese will come to France for research purposes. At the same time, thirty French students and ten research workers will go to China.

THE POPULARIZATION OF SCIENCE AND TECHNOLOGY

Popularization of science in China serves a double purpose. First, it helps to increase agricultural and industrial production. Second, it is helping to transform an old traditional society into a new modern one.

This process of social change is little understood, and the role of science in the transformation is not clear. But there is sufficient evidence to suggest that science may be an important catalyst in this change. The Chinese clearly believe this is the case and are making a great effort to replace the superstitions of old China with science and rational thought.

The comment of a commune director in Peking was symbolic. He said, "Fifteen years ago the people in this commune believed it was the Dragon King who controlled the rain—now we understand the scientific reasons." Elsewhere, I was told that in the old days the peasants regarded a diseased crop as a visitation from the gods and did nothing about it. Now every production team in the commune I was visiting had its own member trained to recognize the most common insect pests and types of plant disease, and to know what remedial steps to take if he found them.

Everywhere in China the people are being taught that laws of nature not only can be understood by man, but that man can often use this knowledge for his own ends. The significance of this realization on a mass scale may yet prove to be one of the most important accomplishments of the Chinese Communists.

At least six of the eight communes I visited had experimental fields where work with new seeds, new techniques of planting, and new types of fertilizer was in progress. Some of the communes which encompassed different natural regions and soil types had several experimental fields in different parts of the commune. There was no question of a single technique or seed being given universal application over the whole commune. Two of the communes had their own research institutes. These were very crude and the experiments very simple. But the important point is that the peasants were beginning to realize that by doing scientific experiments they could improve production. In fact, science has quite literally become one of the three revolutionary movements in China. One of the most common slogans is: "Support the three great revolutionary movements—the class struggle, the struggle for production, and scientific experiment."

This rational experimental approach has not always been the vogue in Communist China. On the contrary, many observers note that it was the wholesale application of technical innovations quite unsuited to local conditions, such as deep plowing and close planting, that led to failures in the Great Leap Forward. These actions dictated by the central government apparently even led to an "anti-science" attitude on the part of some peasants. Also, one must be careful not to conclude that because experimental fields exist in six communes, they are necessarily general in the rest of the seventy-four thousand communes in China. All that can be said is that these six probably represent what the Chinese are striving for.

Another interesting, and often misunderstood, aspect of the introduction of scientific innovations in the countryside has been the use of peasant scientists. These are men with little or no formal education who have demonstrated an ability to experiment and empirically to find ways to increase production. One such case was Chen Yung-kang, a peasant who was working at Kiangsi headquarters of the Agricultural Academy of Science, which I visited in Nanking. He had been provided with a plot of land at the institute and invited to grow rice according to his own technique, which had consistently produced double the yield of his neighbors. A team of experts from the Agricultural Academy in Peking and the Soil Science Research Institute in Nanking had then studied the technique to understand the reasons for his success. They made some modifications and Chen was then provided with a large demonstration field near Soochow and asked to grow rice according to his technique. In 1963 ninety thousand peasants were brought in to see the demonstration.

What is particularly significant about this example is the way the peasant scientist was used as an intermediary between the professional scientists and the peasants. He was given all the credit and publicity. The peasants would be much more likely to adopt a new technique which was accredited to a fellow peasant than one promulgated by a government scientist. Also, other peasants might be encouraged to experiment as a result of the prestige and honor of being called a "peasant scientist."

There are similarities between this use of peasant scientists to popularize agricultural innovations in China, and the county agent system, adopted by the U.S. Department of Agriculture in the early 1900s to popularize agricultural innovations in the United States.

Again, it should be noted that not all peasant scientists have been used so sensibly. There are several recorded instances of irrational use of peasant scientists which were quite common during the Great Leap Forward.

TECHNOLOGICAL INNOVATION IN INDUSTRY

I tried very hard when in China to get to see an industrial research institute. I never succeeded. Instead, I was always told that it was the workers who were responsible for the technical innovations in this or that particular factory. Judging by the Heath Robinson (I think in America it's Rube Goldberg) appearance of some of the equipment, I could believe it! The workers were all supposed to have accomplished these feats of innovation by reading the *Works* of Chairman Mao.

Other visitors tell the same story. The London *Times* correspondent reports that at one factory two thousand suggestions for innovation had been received from the workers in one year and eight hundred had been put into operation. And all are ascribed to Mao. In fact, it is impossible to visit China without coming away with a collection of "Maoisms." All begin, "After reading the *Works* of Chairman Mao I found how to" and go on to such statements as "increase the speed of rotation of my cotton spinning machine from 9,000 revolutions per minute to 13,000 revolutions per minute" or "cure the children at our school of shortsightedness" or "become world table tennis champion." It became a favorite ploy when told such stories to ask for chapter and verse and to be taken step by step from Mao's political statement to the specific technical innovation.

But, in fact, this use of political indoctrination to stimulate innovation cannot be summarily dismissed as nonsense, as I had been prone to do before visiting China. The explanation of the factory manager at the No. 17 textile factory in Shanghai is revealing. I had asked him how Chairman Mao had helped increase the speed of rotation of the spinning machines. He said:

> It's like this. At the time of Liberation we were an old factory, the equipment was old, and the workers relatively old. In fact, we called ourselves "the three olds." In China's condition it was impossible to discard the factory and equipment, but the big problem was the attitude of the workers. . . . It never occurred to them that the machine or process could be improved—let alone that they themselves could do it.
>
> It would have taken too long to give them a full technical education. . . . Political indoctrination was the answer. The workers studied the *Works* of Chairman Mao and gradually their political awareness improved. They said, "We must build a new country."
>
> Before, they did not think it was possible to improve their lot. . . . Now Chairman Mao has liberated their thoughts. With this new spirit they look to see how they can improve their work and knowledge. Their thirst for knowledge is met by the spare-time schools and universities—so bit by bit their technical competence also improves. Once they believed it was possible to innovate they found many places in the factory where simple innovations improved quality and productivity. One worker studied the problem of the spinning machines and found a way to increase the speed from 9,000 to 13,000 revolutions per minute.

At this level, politics obviously can help to generate enthusiasm. If this enthusiasm is directed into scientific and technical channels, and opportunities and incentives are provided—and they are—then useful innovations are possible.

Problems occur when the spirit of research and the craze for technological change go too far without the appropriate technological training to back them up. It would seem likely that when this first flush of worker-initiated innovations has passed, Chinese industry will have to turn more to science-based innovations for continued growth.

SCIENCE AND SOCIETY—PRESENT AND FUTURE

Our knowledge of Chinese science and its interrelation with the rest of society is extremely limited. About all that can be said at the moment is that a solid foundation has been laid for future development of advanced science and that a sincere effort is being made to bring the fruits of science to the people. The present emphasis of research is in agriculture, but judging by the successful detonation of two atomic bombs, national defense research is also stressed.

The Chinese are the first to admit that they are a long way behind advanced world levels in many branches of science. What is impressive to the foreign visitor is the fantastic determination to catch up, primarily by their own efforts. It will be a pity, however, if in these efforts the Chinese stress "fashionable" areas of scientific research which have little relevance to the economic needs of their own country.

It is a favorite guessing game to try to estimate when the Chinese will catch up on a broad front. My own guess is about twenty years. The first reason for thinking this is that in 1960 China spent 1.54 per cent of her national budget on science, but this was still only the equivalent of about $450 million. It is difficult to make direct comparisons with other countries, but we may note that the Soviet Union spent almost ten times this amount on her science budget in 1961. Scientific research work cannot expand too rapidly, largely because of the long time it takes to train research workers. For this reason it is likely to be some time before the money spent on scientific research can be significantly and, at the same time effectively increased.

The problem of the numbers of research workers, and highly trained experts generally, seems to be the biggest constraint on China's rapid scientific growth. There are only 12 students at higher education institutes per 10,000 of population, compared with 72 in Japan and 186 in the United States. The number of research scientists with the equivalent of the M.A. or the Ph.D. degree is probably not more than fifteen or sixteen

thousand and relatively few of these have the necessary experience to direct projects. It will not be until the younger
scientists reach scientific maturity that China herself can make
many significant contributions to basic science.

There is another unpredictable factor which can affect the
rate of growth of Chinese science. The Communist Party may
decide to de-emphasize the effort to catch up with the advanced
countries in basic science and instead concentrate its scientific
resources on economic and social goals.

CHINESE DEVELOPMENT AND WORLD PEACE

I subscribe to the view that the sooner the living standards of
China's millions are improved, the better will be the prospects
for world peace. I further believe that science and technology
can play a big part in improving this standard of living. For
this reason, I welcome the cooperative science agreements between the Academia Sinica and the Royal Society, and between
China and France. Such exchanges not only promote mutual
understanding and are of benefit for science, but also contribute
to China's development. They should be encouraged and expanded. The State Department's relaxation of travel restrictions
to China for American scientists is a step in the right direction.

Not everyone will agree with this attitude. American
congressmen have already criticized the Royal Society exchange,
suggesting that this will help China's capability to wage war.
To a certain limited extent they are correct, but I believe that
the long-term dangers of war are lessened by such exchanges.
Also, when talking of war it becomes very important to be
quite clear about Chinese objectives.

It is true that the Chinese leaders are committed to communism and believe in the inevitability of a communist world.
But I think it wrong to view all of China's apparent belligerence
in terms of power politics and a quest for world domination.
The Chinese leaders believe that two thirds of the world's
population live in societies where the majority exist in abject
poverty and the few in great riches. They believe this situation
is socially unjust and should be changed. Here, they are right.
The majority of people do live under deplorable conditions, and

this should be changed. The question is how. The Chinese argue that such a condition can be changed only by armed revolution and have shown their willingness to support such revolutions wherever they occur in the world.

The implications for the rest of the world are clear. We must show the Chinese and the millions of undernourished, sick, and illiterate people of the world that there is a way to better their condition than by armed revolution, a way which is both more peaceful and quicker.

To bring about this change will mean both technological and social upheavals; we are woefully ignorant of how best to proceed. Some of us believe that each developing country will have to experience its own scientific revolution, developing an indigenous science which will help to bring about the required technological and social changes. How to create such scientific revolutions is not clear. This is why it is so important to learn the lessons of China's scientific revolution. It is why the problem of science and the developing countries is one of the greatest challenges facing both governments and the scientific community today.

3. FOREIGN DEVELOPMENTS
𝕰 The Worsening
of the Sino-Soviet Dispute

AS OF the spring of 1966 the Sino-Soviet dispute was still raging. In the last few years, however, a number of new elements have entered into it. The signing of the Test-Ban Treaty in the summer of 1963 and the first Chinese atomic explosion in the autumn of 1964 pushed the Soviets and the Chinese even farther apart. The Test-Ban Treaty appeared to inaugurate a new period of Soviet-American cooperation. The Chinese not only refused to sign the treaty but intensified their efforts to build up an independent nuclear weapons system. The Chinese accused the United States of following a "two-handed policy," extending a hand of friendship to the Soviet Union but a menacing fist to China. They not only attacked the Soviets for agreeing to this policy, but began to speak of signs of a "capitalist restoration" in the Soviet Union and, finally, of a Soviet-American plot to rule the world.

By 1964 it was evident that a part of the Sino-Soviet dispute consisted in a personal feud between Mao Tse-tung and Khrushchev, understandable if one remembers that friendship betrayed is one of the cardinal sins in the Chinese conception of human relations. The ouster of Khrushchev on almost the same day as the first Chinese atomic explosion failed to lead to any dramatic improvement in Sino-Soviet relations (although the Chinese press was evidently pleased with the turn of events in the Soviet Union). Since then, however, the Soviets have clearly modified their public polemics against the Chinese, and have extended several offers intended to heal the split. The Chinese have rejected the offers and continued their violent polemics against the new Soviet leadership, although refraining from personally attacking Brezhnev and Kosygin as they did Khrushchev.

The escalated war in Vietnam is one of the current major factors in the dispute. Of the three great powers involved directly or indirectly, the Soviets have been most eager to see it ended. In the summer of 1964 and again early in 1965 the Soviets proposed reconvening a Geneva Conference to discuss "Indochina." Though the Chinese supported these efforts as late as the summer of 1964, their position hardened perceptibly after the Tonkin Bay incident of August 1964. The Chinese, convinced that the United States was intent on extending the Vietnamese war, during the past year have accused the United States of aiming ultimately to extend hostilities to China herself. Mao's writings have suggested two general tactics toward an enemy: do not fight unless victory is certain, and only strength will finally force your opponent to back down. The Chinese have followed both admonitions. While taking a very cautious approach in their actual participation in the hostilities, they have maintained an uncompromising attitude toward all talk of peace negotiations. In turn, they have accused the Soviets of plotting with the United States to help the latter find a face-saving way out of the Vietnamese imbroglio.

A favorite Chinese term for describing an opponent's foreign policies is "two-handed policies," *i.e.,* simultaneously pursuing two contradictory policies. Thus they accuse the United States of ostensibly seeking negotiations in the Vietnam conflict while escalating the war. In particular, they have accused the Soviets of following such a line, specifically of maintaining their collaborative relations with the United States while seeking "joint action" of the entire socialist camp, including China, to help North Vietnam and the National Liberation Front in their struggle with the United States.

In February 1966, following their practice of playing down the dispute, the Soviets invited the Chinese Communist Party to send a delegation to the Twenty-third Party Congress, which was to begin on March 29, 1966. The Chinese refused to attend, offering as an excuse a letter critical of the Chinese which the Soviets had distributed to other Communist Parties. A copy of that letter reached the West and was published in the West

German magazine *Die Welt*. We present excerpts from the Soviet letter and from the Chinese open letter of refusal to attend. The letters are of considerable interest in that they pinpoint the major areas of dispute between the two countries.

The Soviets accuse the Chinese of having rejected all offers of "joint action" to support North Vietnam, and of hindering the transport of Soviet military aid to that country. They claim that the Chinese are trying to instigate a war between the Soviet Union and the United States. They describe Chinese strategy vis-à-vis Vietnam as needing "a lengthy Vietnam war to maintain international tensions, to represent China as a 'besieged fortress.'" The Soviet letter notes that the Chinese press has ceased speaking of the fundamental division in the world between capitalism and socialism, and that Chinese foreign policy appears to be directed more against the socialist than the imperialist states. It alleges that, in fact, the Chinese "show extraordinary caution in their own practical deeds, as well as extreme patience toward imperialist powers and their policy, including the policy that is aimed against China itself." On the other hand, the Chinese have been provocative regarding the Sino-Soviet borders and have continually attacked the Soviet Union within their own country. The Soviet letter accuses the Chinese of not seeing that the international revolutionary movement can move over many different paths.

The Chinese letter, brief and emotional, claims that the Soviets have shown no sign of deviating from Khrushchev's external and internal policies. It repeats the allegation of Soviet-United States collaboration to end the Vietnamese war, and adds the now current accusation that the Soviet Union and the United States are intent on encircling China with a ring of hostile countries. It ends, however, by promising full Chinese assistance to the Soviet Union in the event that it should be attacked, with the unspoken implication that the Soviet Union might not do the same if China were attacked.

Leaving aside such issues in the dispute as its emotionalism, Chinese efforts to combat "revisionism" at home, and disagreement over different revolutionary strategies, we may ask what the major foreign policy differences are that divide the two countries. The Soviets appear to be seeking bloc solidarity to face the United States with a position of strength from which the war can be ended with maximal advantage to the Communist side. The Chinese appear to be arguing that a long, drawn-out war in Vietnam will best serve their own national interests. We would suggest two lines of reasoning that may lie behind the Chinese approach: on the one hand, such a protracted war would probably in the long run rekindle the Cold War, forcing the Soviets into an even harder direction and thus into greater dependence on China; on the other hand, it might force the United States ultimately to seek an accommodation with China, in which case the Chinese could demand concessions regarding their paramount foreign-policy goal, the acquisition of Taiwan. Thus, in their own way, the Chinese too are playing at "two-handed policies."

THE CENTRAL COMMITTEE OF THE COMMUNIST PARTY OF THE SOVIET UNION *
Moscow Letter

The Central Committee of the Communist Party of the Soviet Union deems it necessary to inform you of our position on the new steps taken by the Chinese Communist Party that are aimed at strengthening the divisive line in the Socialist community and in the Communist world movement, as well as of the conclusion we draw from these facts. . . .

Our efforts, however, both failed to meet with understanding and met with obstinate resistance from the Chinese leaders. The CCP Central Committee completely ignored the proposal on a bilateral meeting on the highest level. The CCP leadership failed to accede to an expansion of economic, technical, and cultural cooperation and even took additional steps to further curtail such cooperation. In April 1965 the CPR government officially renounced cooperation with the USSR in

* *The New York Times*, March 24, 1966.

constructing a number of industrial projects stipulated in the Chinese-Soviet 1961 agreement. . . .

The Chinese people are made to believe that the Soviet Union is one of their chief enemies. Meetings are being conducted at Chinese offices and enterprises at which every participant is obliged to come up with some criticism of the Soviet Union. The organizing of anti-Soviet rallies has become a system. On March 6, 1965, an anti-Soviet demonstration was even organized in front of the USSR Embassy. . . .

The CPR leadership propagates ever more obstinately the thesis of potential military clashes between China and the Soviet Union. On Sept. 29, 1965, Ch'en Yi, a member of the Politburo of the CCP Central Committee, Deputy Premier and Foreign Minister of the CPR, at a press conference in Peking, spoke utterly falsely of a possible "coordination" of Soviet actions in the North of China with the aggressive war of the United States against the CPR.

The attitude of the CPR leadership toward the struggle of the DRV and all Vietnamese people against the United States aggression is currently causing great damage to the joint cause of the countries of socialism and the worldwide liberation movement.

The Soviet Union delivers large amounts of weapons to the DRV, including rocket installations, anti-aircraft artillery, airplanes, tanks, coastal guns, warships, and other items. In 1965 alone, weapons and other war matériel worth about 500 million rubles [$550 million] were placed at the disposal of the DRV. The DRV is receiving support in the training of pilots, rocket personnel, tank drivers, artillerymen, and so on. Our military aid is being rendered to the extent the Vietnamese leadership itself thinks necessary. The Soviet Union grants extensive military and material support to the N.F.L.S.V. (National Liberation Front of South Vietnam).

The CPSU has proposed to the Chinese leaders more than once that joint actions [of all Socialist countries] to support Vietnam be organized. But the Chinese leadership opposed such action by the Socialist states. In connection with the expansion of the United States aggression against the DRV, our Party has proposed twice that the representatives of the three Parties—the Vietnam Workers Party, the CPSU, and the

CCP—meet at the highest level to achieve agreement on co-ordinated action for aid for the DRV. These proposals, which were received by the Politburo of the Central Committee of the Vietnam Workers Party with approval, were not accepted by the Chinese leaders.

At the same time, the CCP leadership hindered the implementation of the agreement of the government of the USSR with the government of the DRV on an immediate increase in military aid for the DRV. The CCP leaders did not permit Soviet transport planes with weapons to fly over CPR territory.

Then, Chinese personalities also placed obstacles in the way of the transportation of war matériel to Vietnam by rail. Thus, at their request, an additional shipment of military equipment, including anti-aircraft artillery, which is needed so urgently to protect the Vietnamese cities and villages against the United States air pirates, was recently delivered to the Vietnamese comrades. The Chinese authorities refused for a long time to relay the freight, under the pretense that the papers for its transit had not yet been filled out and that they did not know "whether Vietnam needs this war matériel."

By stating openly that they do not desire joint action with the USSR and the other Socialist countries, by emphasizing their differences of views with the Soviet Union, and by hindering its aid to the DRV, the Chinese leaders basically encourage the United States aggressors in their war acts against Vietnam.

From all this it becomes clear that the Chinese leaders need a lengthy Vietnam war to maintain international tensions, to represent China as a "besieged fortress." There is every reason to assert that it is one of the goals of the policy of the Chinese leadership in the Vietnam question to originate a military conflict between the USSR and the United States. They want a clash of the USSR with the United States so that they may, as they say themselves, "sit on the mountain and watch the fight of the tigers."

New facts constantly prove the readiness of the Chinese leaders to sacrifice the interests of the National Liberation Movement to their chauvinist big-power plans. For example, their attitude toward the conference of countries of Asia and Africa, the Second Bandung Conference, is evidence of it. The Chinese leadership has not subordinated the entire question of the conference to the interests of the struggle against imperialism, but to their special plans to try to enforce China's hegemony at this forum.

The nationalist big-power policy of the Chinese leaders has led to the fact that the CPR recently has suffered a number of serious setbacks on the international scene. The actions of the CCP leaders have led to a spreading of mistrust of the CPR, even in countries which until very recently were regarded as its friends. This became especially clear on the African continent and in a number of Asian countries.

The facts show that the CCP leaders today are directing their foreign-political activity not so much against the imperialist states but against the Soviet Union and the Socialist world system as a whole. The subdivision of the world into two contrasting systems, the Socialist and the capitalist, has disappeared from the materials of the Chinese press.

Now the role of the ideological-theoretical platform of the Chinese leadership is quite plain. Its exclusive purpose is to serve the nationalistic big-power policy of the Chinese leadership. In this lies the most important feature of the evolution through which the position of the CCP leaders on the main issues of the present has passed in the last few years.

The meaning of their ideas on questions concerning war, peace, and revolution has become completely clear. The course toward Socialist revolution, which the working class, rallying the people's masses around itself, accomplishes, has been replaced with a course toward a world war. These ideas were most completely explained in the recent article by Lin Piao, Deputy Chairman of the CCP, published in September 1965, under the heading "Long Live the Victory of the People's War!"

Referring to Mao Tse-tung, Lin Piao contends that world revolution is nothing but a "people's war" of the countries of Asia, Africa, and Latin America—of the "world village"—against the states of North America and Western Europe—the "world city."

"In a certain sense it is possible to characterize the present situation in the world revolution as an encirclement of the city by the village," it is stressed in Lin Piao's article. The concept of revolution as the struggle of the world village against the world city is tantamount to the rejection of the leading role of the working class and constitutes a complete revision of the Marxist-Leninist doctrine of the world-historical mission of the working class.

The CPSU, under whose leadership the October Socialist Revolution was carried out, has always recognized armed as well as peaceful forms of struggle of the working class for power. . . .

The Chinese leaders, in contrast, derive from the whole arsenal of forms of struggle only one—armed revolt, war. They claim that the thesis of Mao Tse-tung concerning "conquest through arms, that is, solution of the problem through war" is the "general" revolutionary principle correct everywhere and at all times. . . .

Our people, who have taken up arms more than once to defend the achievements of revolution, are not afraid of threats from imperialism. We are, however, definitely against adventures, against urging people toward thermonuclear world war.

The character of the present ideological-political platform of the CCP leaders consists of militant great-power chauvinism and hegemony. Ultrarevolutionary phrasemongering and petty-bourgeois revolutionary activities are being used as an instrument to implement the chauvinist, hegemonic course.

In connection with the above, we believe that the hegemonic activities of the Chinese leaders are aimed at subordinating the policy of Socialist countries, the international Communist and workers' movement, and the National Liberation Movement to their great-power interests while simultaneously protecting the interests of the CCP and the CPR against particular dangers.

It is not without intention that the Chinese leaders, while criticizing the other fraternal parties and Socialist countries because of their alleged insufficient revolutionary spirit, because of undecisiveness in the fight against imperialism, show extraordinary caution in their own practical deeds, as well as extreme patience toward imperialist powers and their policy, including the policy that is aimed against China itself.

The emphasis on armed struggle as the only way of revolution, moreover, is tantamount to denying the historical significance of the building of socialism and communism, its role in the development of the worldwide revolutionary process.

The efforts of the CCP leaders to force all parties of the non-Socialist countries to accept the goal of an immediate revolution independent of actual conditions in effect means to try to force upon the Communist movement putschist, conspiratory tactics. These tactics, however, offer the imperialist bourgeoisie the opportunity to bleed the revolutionary Communist and workers' movement, to expose the leadership and the activists of a number of Communist Parties to destruction.

The CCP leadership completely ignores the extremely great diversity of the conditions in the countries of Asia, Africa, and Latin America. It addresses all nations of these countries with the appeal for armed revolt. Just as formerly, the Chinese leaders ignore the fact that in a number of former colonies and semi-colonial countries, patriotic and revolutionary-democratic forces are in power. It is natural that the Chinese appeals for armed actions against these governments spark protests by the democratic forces.

More and more persistently the Chinese leaders emphasize the ideal that international tension is favorable for revolution by force, that it creates favorable prerequisites for their struggle. They come forth with statements that can hardly be assessed as anything but provocatory.

Thus Ch'en Yi declared in one of his latest interviews: "If the United States imperialists have decided to force a war of aggression upon us, then we would welcome it, if they can, even earlier. We would welcome it if they came as early as tomorrow." And what should one think, for example, of the statement of the same Ch'en Yi: "With the help of the atom bomb one may destroy one or two generations of people. But the third generation will rise to offer resistance. And peace will be restored."

Such a disparaging approach to the life of millions of people, to the fate of entire nations, can only compromise the ideology and goals of Communists.

THE CENTRAL COMMITTEE OF
THE CHINESE COMMUNIST PARTY *
Peking Letter

The Communist Party of China has received the letter of the Central Committee of the Communist Party of the Soviet Union dated February 24, 1966, inviting us to send a delegation to attend your Twenty-third Congress as guests.

In normal circumstances, it would be considered an indication of friendship for one Party to invite another fraternal Party to send a delegation to its congress. But around the time you sent this invitation, you distributed an anti-Chinese document in the Soviet Union, both inside and outside the Party, and organized a whole series of anti-Chinese reports from top to bottom, right down to the basic units, whipping up hysteria against China.

Moreover, you sent an anti-Chinese letter to other parties, instigating them to join you in opposing China. You wantonly vilified the Chinese Communist Party as being "bellicose" and "pseudo-revolutionary," as "refusing to oppose imperialism" and "encouraging United States imperialist aggression," and as being guilty of "adventurism," "splitism," "Trotskyism," "nationalism," "great power chauvinism," "dogmatism," and so on and so forth.

You have also been spreading rumors alleging that China "is obstructing aid to Vietnam" and that "China has been encroaching on Soviet territory." You have gone so far as to state that "China is not a Socialist country." These anti-Chinese activities all go to show that your present invitation is merely a gesture and is sent with ulterior motives. In these circumstances, how can the Chinese Communist Party, which you look upon as an enemy, be expected to attend your congress?

* *Ibid.*

The Chinese Communist Party has attended many of the congresses of the CPSU. Also, we sent delegations to your Twentieth, Twenty-first, and Twenty-second Congresses, after the Khrushchev revisionist group usurped the leadership of the CPSU. But at the Twentieth Congress of the CPSU you suddenly lashed out at Stalin. Stalin was a great Marxist-Leninist.

In attacking Stalin, you were attacking Marxism-Leninism, the Soviet Union, Communist Parties, China, the people, and all the Marxist-Leninists of the world. At the Twenty-second Congress, you adopted an out-and-out revisionist program, made a wild public attack on Albania and reproached the Chinese Communist Party, so that the head of our delegation had to leave for home while the congress was only halfway through.

Russia is the native land of Leninism and used to be the center of the international working-class movement. After Stalin's death, the leaders of the CPSU headed by Khrushchev gradually revealed their true features as betrayers of Lenin and Leninism and embarked on the old path of the German Social Democrats Bernstein and Kautsky, who betrayed Marx and Engels and Marxism. As a result, the leadership of the CPSU has become the center of modern revisionism.

Over the last ten years, we have made a series of efforts in the hope that you would return to the path of Marxism-Leninism. Since Khrushchev's downfall, we have advised the new leaders of the CPSU on a number of occasions to make a fresh start. We have done everything we could, but you have not shown the slightest repentance. . . .

Far from publicly retracting the anti-Chinese open letter of July 1963 and the anti-Chinese report and resolution of February 1964, you have intensified your activities against China by more insidious tactics. Despite the tricks you have been playing to deceive people, you are pursuing United States-Soviet collaboration for the domination of the world with your whole heart and soul. In mouthing a few words against United States imperialism and in making a show of supporting anti-imperialist struggles, you are conducting only minor attacks on United States imperialism while rendering it major help.

In following this tactic you very well know what you are up to, and so does United States imperialism. Your clamor for "united action," especially on the Vietnam question, is nothing but a trap for the purpose of deceiving the Soviet people and the revolutionary people of the world. You have all along been acting in coordination with the United States in its plot for peace talks, vainly attempting to sell out the struggle of the Vietnamese people against United States aggression and for national salvation and to drag the Vietnam question into the orbit of Soviet-United States collaboration.

You have worked hand in glove with the United States in a whole series of dirty deals inside and outside the United Nations. In close coordination with the counter-revolutionary "global strategy" of United States imperialism, you are now actively trying to build a ring of encirclement around socialist China. Not only have you excluded yourselves from the international united front of all the peoples against United States imperialism and its lackeys, you have even aligned yourselves with United States imperialism, the main enemy of the people of the world, and established a holy alliance against China, against the movement and against the Marxist-Leninists. . . .

We would like to inform you explicitly that since you have gone so far, the Chinese Communist Party, as a serious Marxist-Leninist Party, cannot send its delegation to attend this congress of yours.

We are confident that in all parts of the world, including the Soviet Union, the masses of the people, who constitute more than 90 per cent of the population, are for revolution and against imperialism and its lackeys. In the ranks of the international Communist movement, including the Communist Party of the Soviet Union, more than 90 per cent of the Communists and cadres will eventually march along the path of Marxism-Leninism.

The revolutionary peoples of the world, the great international Communist movement, the great Socialist camp, and the great peoples of China and the Soviet Union will eventually sweep away all obstacles and unite on the basis of Marxism-Leninism and proletarian internationalism. The Soviet people may rest assured that once the Soviet Union meets with imperialist aggression and puts up resolute resistance, China will definitely stand side by side with the Soviet Union and fight against the common enemy.

𝕰 The State of the Sino-American Confrontation

FROM THE time of the Hilsman speech in December 1963 to the spring of 1966, there was little change in American policy toward China, and China's attitude toward the United States remained as firm and hostile as ever. Even though the official attitudes did not change, however, the Vietnam war introduced a new and dangerous factor into Sino-American relations. The Chinese, as we point out in the selections on Vietnam, began to talk of an eventual clash between China and the United States arising from a continued escalation of the Vietnam war, while the Americans claimed that Chinese expansionism was the root cause of that war. Thus, instead of one overriding specific issue between the United States and China—Taiwan—there is now another one of equal gravity—Vietnam. A decade and a half ago Korea played the role in Sino-American relations now played by Vietnam. That war was settled without any change in the status of Taiwan, implying that the two issues were not inextricably linked, and there is no evidence at present that either China or America wishes to link the two issues. America has so far rejected any participation by the Chinese Nationalists in the Vietnam war, and China has never stated that settlement of the Vietnam war was tied in with a more general settlement of Far Eastern problems.

The resumption of the bombing of North Vietnam by the United States early in 1966 increased the danger of a collision between the two countries, and led to China's becoming a major issue of national debate in the United States. At this time the State Department liberalized travel restrictions on American nationals wishing to travel to China and indicated a willingness to allow Chinese nationals to come here from the Mainland. On

March 16, 1966, Dean Rusk delivered a statement on China policy to the Far Eastern subcommittee of the House Foreign Affairs Committee, excerpts of which we present here.

Leaving aside his detailed review of the development of United States policy toward China, his outline of the "elements of future policy" are, of course, of greatest interest. He sets forth ten major points of policy: America must remain firm in resisting aggression; she must continue to support and help set up non-Communist governments in Asia; her commitment to Taiwan must remain firm and the Chinese must renounce the use of force in the area of Taiwan; the United States must continue to oppose Communist China's membership in the United Nations; America does not intend to attack China (although "there are, of course, risks of war with China"); China may yet change; unofficial contacts should be encouraged; the Warsaw meetings should be continued; Peking is invited to take part in international conferences on disarmament; the gathering of up-to-date knowledge on China should be continued.

In this policy review only one small change can be detected: the United States finally agreed to the 1956 Chinese proposal for cultural contacts. Unfortunately, this came at a time when the Chinese had long since dropped their offer. The willingness to allow Chinese participation in international conferences on disarmament must be seen in the light of firm Chinese refusal to attend such conferences. There is no reference to the desirability of bilateral talks above the ambassadorial level, something proposed by Chou En-lai in the past. There is no reference to Vietnam as an issue between China and America, except in Rusk's review of "Mao's doctrine of world revolution," and a brief allusion to the possibility of a Sino-American war over Vietnam.

The Chinese selection, "Old Tune, New Plot," was signed by "Observer," indicating high-level official approval of the line stated. The article reiterates that America has been continuously hostile to China for the past sixteen years:

> It pursues this policy in a more brazen and truculent manner. It publicly declares that China is the "principal enemy" of the United States. It has switched the emphasis of its global strategy to Asia, speeded up its military disposi-

tions to encircle China, and is feverishly planning to carry the war of aggression from Vietnam to China.

The article claims that "the United States will not depart a whit from its fundamental China policy," specifically because it refuses to make any concessions on Taiwan and on China's entry into the United Nations. The article ridicules State Department concessions on travel to China as "dual counter-revolutionary tactics," designed only to fool people. "Observer" sees United States "flexible policy" only as "pretenses for intensifying the 'containment' of China." He vows continuing resistance to American threats, but notes "the profound friendship between the Chinese and the American peoples" which exists despite the "schemes of the U.S. reactionaries" (the U.S. government).

Premier Chou En-lai's four-point statement on China's Policy toward the U.S. was made on April 10, 1966. Chou's opening remark—"China will not take the initiative to provoke a war with the United States"—indicates that the growing possibility of a war between China and the United States was uppermost in his mind. He reiterates the Chinese position regarding Taiwan, and warns that if China should be attacked from the air, she will fight back on the ground; in other words, China would send her troops to fight in Vietnam. For a further elaboration of the current Chinese position on Vietnam, we refer the reader to Anna Louise Strong's letter from Peking (pp. 596–603).

It is clear from Chou En-lai's remarks that there can be no talk about China policy except in relation to the war in Vietnam. Along with Taiwan, Vietnam has emerged as a great issue standing between the United States and China. The two issues are, of course, related, for China sees both the war in Vietnam and the existence of Taiwan as a threat to her national security. Given the conditions prevailing in Eastern Asia in the spring of 1966, one can only conclude that the gap between China and the United States is as wide as ever.

DEAN RUSK *
United States Policy Toward Communist China

During the last month and a half, this distinguished committee and its corresponding members in the other House have heard testimony on Communist China from a number of prominent scholars and distinguished experts on Asia.

I welcome these hearings. For Communist China's policies and intentions, in all these aspects, need to be examined and re-examined continually. . . .

First, the Chinese Communist leaders seek to bring China on the world stage as a great power. They hold that China's history, size, and geographic position entitle it to great power status. They seek to overcome the humiliation of a hundred and fifty years of economic, cultural, and political domination by outside powers.

Our concern is with the way they are pursuing their quest for power and influence in the world. And it is not only our concern but that of many other countries, including in recent years the Soviet Union.

Peking is aware that it still lacks many of the attributes of great-power status, and it chafes bitterly under this realization.

The Chinese Communists are determined to rectify this situation. They already have one of the largest armies in the world. They are now developing nuclear weapons and missile delivery systems. They are pouring a disproportionately large proportion of their industrial and scientific effort into military and military-related fields. . . .

But such weapons need not serve a defensive role. They

* Dean Rusk, Statement before the House Subcommittee on Far Eastern Affairs on United States Policy Toward Communist China (*The New York Times*, April 17, 1966).

can be used directly by Peking to try to intimidate its neighbors, or in efforts to blackmail Asian countries into breaking defense alliances with the United States, or in an attempt to create a nuclear "balance" in Asia in which Peking's potentially almost unlimited conventional forces might be used with increased effect.

These weapons can ultimately be employed to attack Peking's Asian neighbors and, in time, even the United States or the Soviet Union. This would be mad and suicidal, as Peking must know, despite cavalier statements that Mainland China can survive nuclear war. Nevertheless, a potential nuclear capability, on top of enormous conventional forces, represents a new factor in the equilibrium of power in Asia that this country and its friends and allies cannot ignore.

Peking's use of power is closely related to what I believe are its second and third objectives: dominance within Asia and leadership of the Communist world revolution, employing Maoist tactics. Peking is striving to restore traditional Chinese influence or dominance in South, Southeast, and East Asia. . . .

. . . We have told them both publicly and privately, and I believe have demonstrated in our actions in times of crisis and even under grave provocation, that we want no war with Communist China. The President restated this only last month in New York. We do not seek the overthrow by force of the Peking regime; we do object to its attempt to overthrow other regimes by force.

How much Peking's "fear" of the United States is genuine and how much of it is artificially induced for domestic political purposes only the Chinese Communist leaders themselves know. I am convinced, however, that their desire to expel our influence and activity from the Western Pacific and Southeast Asia is not motivated by fears that we are threatening them.

I wish I could believe that Communist China seeks merely a guarantee of friendly states around its borders, as some commentators have suggested. If it were as simple as this, they would have only to abandon their policies which cause their neighbors to seek help from the United States.

The trouble is that Peking's leaders want neighboring countries to accept subordination to Chinese power. They want them to become political and economic dependencies of Peking. If the

United States can be driven from Asia this goal will be in their grasp. The "influence," therefore, that Peking's present leaders seek in Asia is indeed far-reaching. . . .

We can see that the Communist Chinese have set vast goals for themselves, both internally and externally. The disastrous results of the so-called Great Leap Forward have forced them to acknowledge that it will take them generations to achieve their goals.

They have wrought considerable changes on the mainland of China. Perhaps their greatest feat has been to establish their complete political authority throughout the country. They have made some progress in industrialization, education, and public health, although at the expense of human freedom, originality, and creativity. But their efforts to improve agriculture and to mold the Chinese people into a uniform Marxist pattern have been far less successful.

The economic, political, and social problems still confronting the Chinese Communist leaders today are staggering. . . .

I do not predict any quick changes in China. Nor are there simple solutions. Peking's present state of mind is a combination of aggressive arrogance and obsessions of its own making. There are doubtless many reasons, cultural, historical, political, for this state of mind. Psychologists have struggled for years in an effort to characterize what is a normal personality. The definition of what a normal-state personality might be is beyond my abilities. I would be inclined, however, to advance the view that a country whose behavior is as violent, irascible, unyielding, and hostile as that of Communist China is led by leaders whose view of the world and of life itself is unreal. It is said that we have isolated them. But to me they have isolated themselves—both in the non-Communist and Communist world.

We have little hope of changing the outlook of these leaders. They are products of their entire lives. They seem to be immune to agreement or persuasion by anyone, including their own allies.

It is of no help in formulating policy to describe Peking's behavior as neurotic. Its present policies pose grave and immediate problems for the United States and other countries. These must be dealt with now. The weapons and advisers that Peking exports to promote and assist insurrections in other countries cannot be met by psychoanalysis. At the present time there is a need for a counterweight of real power to Chinese Communist pressures. This has had to be supplied primarily by the United States and our allies. . . .

We should be under no illusion that by yielding to Peking's bellicose demands today we would in some way ease the path toward peace in Asia. If Peking reaps success from its current policies, not only its present leaders, but those who follow, will be emboldened to continue them. This is the path to increased tension, and even greater dangers to world peace in the years ahead.

We expect China to become some day a great world power. Communist China is a major Asian power today. In the ordinary course of events, a peaceful China would be expected to have close relations—political, cultural, and economic—with the countries around its borders and with the United States.

It is not part of the policy of the United States to block the peaceful attainment of these objectives.

More than any other Western people, we have had close and warm ties with the Chinese people. We opposed the staking out of spheres of influence in China. We used our share of the Boxer indemnity to establish scholarships for Chinese students in the United States. We welcomed the Revolution of Sun Yat-sen. We took the lead in relinquishing Western extraterritorial privileges in China. We refused to recognize the puppet regime established by Japan in Manchuria. And it was our refusal to accept or endorse, even by implication, Japan's Imperial conquests and further designs in China that made it impossible for us to achieve a *modus vivendi* with Japan in 1940–1941.

We look forward hopefully—and confidently—to a time in the future when the government of Mainland China will permit the restoration of the historic ties of friendship between the people of Mainland China and ourselves. . . .

Peking has not refrained from the use of force to pursue its objectives. Following Korea, there were Tibet and the attacks on the offshore islands in the Taiwan Straits. There have been the attacks on India. It is true that, since Korea, Peking has moved only against weaker foes and has carefully avoided situations which might bring it face to face with the United States. It has probed for weaknesses around its frontier but drawn back when the possibility of a wider conflict loomed.

While the massive and direct use of Chinese Communists troops in overt aggression cannot be ruled out, Peking's behavior up to now suggests it would approach any such decision with caution.

If the costs and risks of a greater use of force were reduced by, for example, our unilateral withdrawal from the region, Peking might well feel freer to use its power to intimidate or overwhelm a recalcitrant opponent or to aid directly insurgent forces.

As I have said, the Chinese Communist leaders are dedicated to a fanatical and bellicose Marxist-Leninist-Maoist doctrine of world revolution. Last fall, Lin Piao, the Chinese Communist Minister of Defense, recapitulated in a long article Peking's strategy of violence for achieving Communist domination of the world.

This strategy involves the mobilization of the underdeveloped areas of the world—which the Chinese Communists compare to the "rural" areas—against the industrialized or "urban" areas. It involves the relentless prosecution of what they call "people's wars." The final stage of all this violence is to be what they frankly describe as "wars of annihilation."

It is true that this doctrine calls for revolution by the "natives" of each country. In that sense it may be considered a "do-it-yourself kit."

But Peking is prepared to train and indoctrinate the leaders of these revolutions and to support them with funds, arms, and propaganda, as well as politically. It is even prepared to manufacture these revolutionary movements out of whole cloth.

Peking has encouraged and assisted, with arms and other means, the aggressions of the North Vietnamese Communists in Laos and against South Vietnam. It has publicly declared its support for so-called National Liberation forces in Thailand, and there are already terrorist attacks in the remote rural areas of Northeast Thailand.

There is talk in Peking that Malaysia is next on the list. The basic tactics of these "wars of liberation" have been set forth by Mao and his disciples, including General [Vo Nguyen] Giap, the North Vietnamese Communist Minister of Defense. They progress from the undermining of independent governments and economic and social fabrics of society by terror and assassination, through guerrilla warfare, to large-scale military action.

Peking has sought to promote Communist coups and "wars of liberation" against independent governments in Africa and Latin America as well as Asia. . . .

Some say we should ignore what the Chinese Communist leaders say and judge them only by what they do. It is true that they have been more cautious in action than in words—more cautious in what they do themselves than in what they have urged the Soviet Union to do. Undoubtedly, they recognize that their power is limited. They have shown, in many ways, that they have a healthy respect for the power of the United States.

But it does not follow that we should disregard the intentions and plans for the future which they have proclaimed. To do so would be to repeat the catastrophic miscalculation that so many people made about the ambitions of Hitler and that many have made at various times in appraising the intentions of the Soviet leaders.

I have noted criticism of the so-called analogy between Hitler and Mao Tse-tung. I am perfectly aware of the important differences between these two and the countries in which they have exercised power. The seizure of Manchuria by Japanese militarists, of Ethiopia by Mussolini, and of the Rhineland, Austria, and Czechoslovakia by Hitler were laboratory experiments in the anatomy and physiology of aggression. How to deal with the phenomenon of aggression was the principal problem faced in drafting the United Nations Charter, and the answer was collective action. We do ourselves no service by insisting that each source of aggression or each instance of aggression is unique. My own view is that we have learned a good deal about this phenomenon and its potentiality for leading into catastrophe if the problem is not met in a timely fashion.

What should be the main elements in our policy toward Communist China?

We must take care to do nothing which encourages Peking —or anyone else—to believe that it can reap gains from its aggressive actions and designs. It is just as essential to "contain" Communist aggression in Asia as it was, and is, to "contain" Communist aggression in Europe.

At the same time, we must continue to make it plain that, if Peking abandons its belief that force is the best way to resolve disputes and gives up its violent strategy of world revolution, we would welcome an era of good relations.

More specifically, I believe, there should be ten elements in our policy.

First, we must remain firm in our determination to help those allied nations which seek our help to resist the direct or indirect use of threat or force against their territory by Peking.

Second, we must continue to assist the countries of Asia in building broadly based effective governments, devoted to progressive economic and social policies, which can better withstand Asian Communist pressures and maintain the security of their people.

Third, we must honor our commitments to the Republic of China and to the people on Taiwan who do not want to live under Communism. We will continue to assist in their defense and to try to persuade the Chinese Communists to join with us in renouncing the use of force in the area of Taiwan.

Fourth, we will continue our efforts to prevent the expulsion of the Republic of China from the United Nations or its agencies. So long as Peking follows its present course it is extremely difficult for us to see how it can be held to fulfill the requirements set forth in the Charter for membership, and the United States opposes its membership. It is worth recalling that the Chinese Communists have set forth some interesting conditions which must be fulfilled before they are even willing to consider membership:

The United Nations resolution of 1950 condemning Chinese Communist aggression in Korea must be rescinded;

There must be a new United Nations resolution condemning U.S. "aggression";

The United Nations must be reorganized;

The Republic of China must be expelled;

All other "imperialist puppets" must be expelled. One can only ask whether the Chinese Communists seriously want membership or whether they mean to destroy the United Nations. We believe the United Nations must approach this issue with the utmost caution and deliberation.

Fifth, we should continue our efforts to reassure Peking

that the United States does not intend to attack Mainland China. There are, of course, risks of war with China. This was true in 1950. It was true in the Taiwan Straits crises of 1955 and 1956. It was true in the Chinese Communist drive into Indian territory in 1962. It is true today in Vietnam. But we do not want war. We do not intend to provoke war. There is no fatal inevitability of war with Communist China. The Chinese Communists have, as I have already said, acted with caution when they foresaw a collision with the United States. We have acted with restraint and care in the past and we are doing so today. I hope that they will realize this and guide their actions accordingly.

Sixth, we must keep firmly in our minds that there is nothing eternal about the policies and attitudes of Communist China. We must avoid assuming the existence of an unending and inevitable state of hostility between ourselves and the rulers of Mainland China.

Seventh, when it can be done without jeopardizing other U.S. interests, we should continue to enlarge the possibilities for unofficial contacts between Communist China and ourselves— contacts which may gradually assist in altering Peking's picture of the United States.

In this connection, we have gradually expanded the categories of American citizens who may travel to Communist China. American libraries may freely purchase Chinese Communist publications. American citizens may send and receive mail from the Mainland. We have in the past indicated that if the Chinese themselves were interested in purchasing grain we would consider such sales. We have indicated our willingness to allow Chinese Communist newspapermen to come to the United States. We are prepared to permit American universities to invite Chinese Communist scientists to visit their institutions.

We do not expect that for the time being the Chinese Communists will seize upon these avenues of contact or exchange. All the evidence suggests Peking wishes to remain isolated from the United States. But we believe it is in our interests that such channels be opened and kept open. We believe contact and communications are not incompatible with a firm policy of containment.

Eighth, we should keep open our direct diplomatic contacts with Peking in Warsaw. While these meetings frequently provide merely an opportunity for a reiteration of known positions, they play a role in enabling each side to communicate information and attitude in times of crisis. It is our hope that they might at some time become the channel for a more fruitful dialogue.

Ninth, we are prepared to sit down with Peking and other countries to discuss the critical problems of disarmament and nonproliferation of nuclear weapons. Peking has rejected all suggestions and invitations to join in such talks. It has attacked the Test-Ban Treaty. It has advocated the further spread of nuclear weapons to non-nuclear countries. It is an urgent task of all countries to persuade Peking to change its stand.

Tenth, we must continue to explore and analyze all available information on Communist China and keep our own policies up to date. We hope that Peking's policies may one day take account of the desire of the people of Asia and her own people for peace and security. We have said, in successive administrations, that when Peking abandons the aggressive use of force and shows that it is not irrevocably hostile to the United States, then expanded contacts and improved relations may become possible. This continues to be our position.

These, I believe, are the essential ingredients of a sound policy in regard to Communist China.

I believe that they serve the interests not only of the United States and of the free world as a whole—but of the Chinese people. We have always known of the pragmatic genius of the Chinese people, and we can see evidence of it even today. The practices and doctrines of the present Peking regime are yielding poor returns to the Chinese people. I believe that the Chinese people, no less than their neighbors and the American people, crave the opportunity to move toward the enduring goals of mankind: a better life, safety, freedom, human dignity, and peace.

OBSERVER *
Old Tune, New Plot

Recently, Johnson and some U.S government officials under him suddenly struck up the old tune of "improving relations with China." The United States, so they say, "stands ready to take up a more flexible position" with regard to China; it does not wish to "isolate [China] from the rest of the international community"; "the United States is holding the door open for peaceful relations with China"; it is "very anxious to try to have more contact with her and more exchange with her"; and "must take every opportunity to show our friendship for the Chinese people"; and so on and so forth. In a word, it sounds as if the U.S. ruling circles are really thinking of making a fresh start in their policy toward China and living amicably with the Chinese people. These blasts of "good will," set off by Washington at a time when U.S. imperialism is working more energetically than ever to direct the spearhead of its aggression at China, are quite absurd and ridiculous.

WASHINGTON'S WORDS AND DEEDS—POLES APART

For sixteen years U.S. imperialism has consistently followed a policy of hostility toward China, and throughout these years it has never stopped its aggression and threats against this country. It has been occupying Chinese territory, Taiwan province, by force and has used the Chiang Kai-shek gang to usurp China's seat in the United Nations. It has imposed an embargo against this country and built a string of military bases around it. It has unceasingly sent secret agents to carry out subversive ac-

* Observer, "Old Tune, New Plot," *Peking Review*, No. 14, April 1, 1966, pp. 13–15.

tivities and sabotage against China. Its warships have violated China's territorial waters and its aircraft have intruded into China's air space on countless occasions for military provocations. What U.S. imperialism has done clearly shows that it is the sworn enemy of the Chinese people. The policy of the U.S. government toward China has remained the same from Truman and Eisenhower down to Kennedy and Johnson. The present Johnson Administration has not, in the least, changed the U.S. policy of hostility, aggression, and "containment" in relation to China. In fact, it pursues this policy in a more brazen and truculent manner. It publicly declares that China is the "principal enemy" of the United States. It has switched the emphasis of its global strategy to Asia, speeded up its military dispositions to encircle China and is feverishly planning to carry the war of aggression from Vietnam to China. Top U.S. military and civilian officials even openly talk about a trial of strength with China. What the Johnson Administration is earnestly doing and what it is now prattling are poles apart.

U.S. Secretary of State Rusk kept a straight face when he stated that the United States is going to follow a "flexible policy" with regard to China. If, by this, he means that the U.S. government is now resolved to redeem its past wrongs, that would be a different matter. But it may be recalled that, a little over two years ago, the then Assistant Secretary of State for Far Eastern Affairs Hilsman also spoke volubly of the "flexibility" of United States China policy and indicated that the United States would "open the door" to China. However, events in the past two years have proved that the basic U.S. policy of hostility toward China remained unchanged. Hilsman's "flexibility" was no more than a smokescreen. Now Rusk is harping on the same old theme, but it is of no earthly use.

TRUE MEANING OF "FLEXIBLE POLICY"

As a matter of fact, Rusk himself added an enlightening footnote to his "flexible policy." He said: One: the United States is "not prepared to surrender" Taiwan. Two: the United States will not change its attitude toward the restoration to China of its legitimate seat in the United Nations. This means that the United

States will go on occupying China's territory and that it will cling to its position of hostility toward China. In short, the United States will not depart a whit from its fundamental China policy. The "flexible policy" is only for the purpose of making the Chinese people abandon their just stand in face of the U.S. policy of aggression and "containment." Rusk stated explicitly that peaceful relations can be established only if China changes its attitude. This lets the cat out of the bag and shows what the U.S. "flexible policy" really means.

But, according to U.S. Vice-President Humphrey and others, Washington's China policy is nevertheless about to undergo a major change and this change is said to be one from "containment through isolation" in the past to "containment without isolation." Listen, Chinese people! The American gentlemen have kindly decided not to "isolate" us any longer. Should not this move us to tears of gratitude?

WHY THE PRESENT DIN?

The United States has been "isolating" China for sixteen years. U.S. ruling circles have never veered from their belief that China must and can only be "contained through isolation." According to Johnson and company, China has become the principal enemy of the United States. Does it not then follow that there is all the more need for the United States to "isolate" China? Again, according to Johnson and company, China now suffers "setbacks" everywhere and is plagued by misfortune. Does it not then follow that there is still greater possibility for the United States to "isolate" China? But why should Washington choose this particular moment to din into people's ears that it does not intend to "isolate" China any longer? The China experts testifying in the U.S. Senate have given the answer. They have grudgingly admitted that "the seventeen-year-old American policy of 'containment plus isolation' has not worked." So an effort is made to gloss over the failure of their policy of "isolating China."

Are the U.S. ruling circles really abandoning their policy of "containment plus isolation," after all? It is common knowledge that, in addition to whipping up a campaign against China in all parts of the world, the United States is redoubling its efforts to form an anti-China front in Asia with the Soviet revisionists, Japanese militarists, and Indian reactionaries as its core. This indicates that U.S. imperialism intends to carry on its policy of "containment plus isolation" with still greater vigor, something which Johnson and company cannot cover up with all their talk about "flexibility."

To demonstrate their "sincere desire" to "improve" Sino-American relations, the U.S. government has, not long ago, kicked up a rumpus over the interflow of people between the two countries. It has proposed more than once that Chinese and American correspondents visit each other's country. In addition, departing from its customary practice, it has indicated that it would permit some American physicians, scientists, and other scholars to visit China. The American propaganda machine pitched in and played this up as if the United States honestly wanted to ease its relations with China.

THE SOURCE OF SINO-AMERICAN TENSION

Everybody knows that the cause of the continued strained relations between China and the United States has nothing to do with the fact that no American doctors have come to China to study its medical and health conditions, nor with the fact that no Chinese correspondents have gone to the United States to report on the American way of life. The source of all the tension springs from the extremely hostile policy that the U.S. government persistently pursues toward China, and primarily because the United States is forcefully occupying China's province of Taiwan. So long as the U.S. government does not change its hostile policy toward China and refuses to pull its armed forces out of Taiwan and the Taiwan Straits, the normalization of Sino-American relations is entirely out of the question and so is the solution of such concrete questions as exchange of visits between people of the two countries. But what is the attitude of the Johnson Administration to this? Dean Rusk stated bluntly not long ago that the answer to the demand for U.S. evacuation of Taiwan is "No, we are not prepared to do so." This reveals that the steps the

U.S. government proposes for an "improvement" of Sino-American relations are just so many petty actions announced with much fanfare to fool the public.

FEIGNING RETREAT FOR ANOTHER ONSLAUGHT

It must be pointed out that, in feigning eagerness to "improve" Sino-American relations, the U.S. ruling circles are merely maneuvering a "retreat" for another onslaught. Determined to widen the war in Vietnam, the Johnson Administration is rushing up the path of "escalation" and preparing to expand its aggressive war to all parts of Indochina, and even to China. This adventurous policy has caused grave anxiety and widespread censure at home and abroad. Johnson and his like have therefore come out with this new gesture to ease public opinion at home and abroad, and lay the blame of what they call "Sino-American confrontation" at the door of the Chinese people. They fondly hope that, in this way, they will be able to distract public attention from the stepped-up U.S. deployments for aggression against China. Surely nobody will allow himself to be fooled by such dual counter-revolutionary tactics used by the Johnson Administration. Could it be that the eastward shift of the focus of the U.S. global strategy and the U.S. military buildup around China are not for aggression against China, but for the "improvement" of Sino-American relations? Could it be that while working feverishly to escalate its aggressive war in Vietnam one step after another, the United States is not preparing for a trial of strength with the Chinese people, but for the "improvement" of its relations with China? Could it be that the United States recently concluded the so-called "agreement on military status in China" with the Chiang Kai-shek gang not for the purpose of taking further steps to turn China's Taiwan province into its colony and military base, but for the "improvement" of its relations with China? Judging their words by their deeds, one can easily see that in the mouths of Johnson and his kind, all such expressions as "a flexible policy," "without isolation," and "more contact" are only pretenses for intensifying the U.S. "containment" of China.

FAR-REACHING AIMS

This is not all. The Washington authorities have far-reaching aims behind their pose of "relaxation." They do not even bother to conceal the fact that they are still dreaming of an eventual "peaceful evolution" in China and that they are still placing their hopes on its "younger generation." They are vainly hoping to bring about such "evolution" through certain measures of "relaxation" and "flexibility." Their mouthpiece, the *New York Times,* has clearly revealed this design when it said in an editorial: "The day when that group comes to power might very well be hastened by an American policy that offers an 'open door' to contact and accommodation." The U.S. imperialists think that by making some "contact" and "visits," they can weaken the revolutionary will of the great Chinese people and shake their firm stand of combating U.S. imperialism and supporting the revolutionary struggle of all peoples. This is sheer daydreaming. The American rulers have spent so many dollars to gather intelligence about China, but their knowledge about China is nil. What a pity!

The Chinese people have clearly seen through the aggressive nature of U.S. imperialism. It will never lay down its butcher's knife and will never become a Buddha. Nor is it ever possible for U.S. imperialism to abandon its policy of hostility toward the Chinese people particularly today when it regards the Chinese people, who hold aloft the revolutionary banner of opposing U.S. imperialism, as the main obstacle to its counter-revolutionary global strategy for the domination of the world. The Chinese people are sober-minded. They will never be frightened by U.S. imperialism's threats, nor will they believe in its "fine words." The Johnson Administration had better keep all its tricks to itself!

The Chinese people have always drawn a distinction between U.S. imperialism and the American people. Chairman Mao Tse-tung has said: "The Chinese people know that United States imperialism has done many bad things to China and to the whole world as well; they understand that only the United States ruling group is bad, while the people of the United States are very good." There is a profound friendship between the Chinese and American peoples. We Chinese people understand full well the American people's desire for resuming contact with us. But, we will not, and we cannot, allow the U.S. ruling group to exploit this justified desire of the American people for its own sinister ends. We are convinced that some day the Chinese and American peoples will smash the schemes of the U.S. reactionaries, sweep away all obstacles, and truly establish close contact so as to bring about a tremendous growth of the friendship between our two peoples.

CHOU EN-LAI *
China's Policy Toward the United States

(1) China will not take the initiative to provoke a war with the United States. China has not sent any troops to Hawaii; it is the United States that has occupied China's territory of Taiwan province. Nevertheless, China has been making efforts in demanding, through negotiations, that the United States withdraw all its armed forces from Taiwan province and the Taiwan Straits, and she has held talks with the United States for more than ten years, first in Geneva and then in Warsaw, on this question of principle, which admits of no concession whatsoever. All this serves as a very good proof.

(2) The Chinese mean what they say. In other words, if any country in Asia, Africa, or elsewhere meets with aggression by the imperialists headed by the United States, the Chinese government and people definitely will give it support and help. Should such just action bring on U.S. aggression against China, we will unhesitatingly rise in resistance and fight to the end.

(3) China is prepared. Should the United States impose a war on China, it can be said with certainty that, once in China,

*Chou En-lai, "Four-Point Statement on China's Policy Toward the United States," *Peking Review,* May 13, 1966.

the United States will not be able to pull out, however many men it may send over and whatever weapons it may use, nuclear weapons included. Since the fourteen million people of Southern Vietnam can cope with over two hundred thousand U.S. troops, the six hundred fifty million people of China can undoubtedly cope with ten million of them. No matter how many U.S. aggressor troops may come, they will certainly be annihilated in China.

(4) Once the war breaks out, it will have no boundaries. Some U.S. strategists want to bombard China by relying on their air and naval superiority and avoid a ground war. This is wishful thinking. Once the war gets started with air or sea action, it will not be for the United States alone to decide how the war will continue. If you can come from the sky, why can't we fight back on the ground? That is why we say the war will have no boundaries once it breaks out.

✸ The China Hearings

THE FIRST great China debate in the United States began while the Chinese Civil War was still in progress (see Volume II). Generally speaking, American liberals at that time favored a withdrawal of American aid to the collapsing Chiang government, whereas conservatives wanted an all-out effort to prevent China from going Communist. The debate was still reasoned and dealt with policy alternatives, but after the Communist victory in 1949 the China debate became part of that national phenomenon known as McCarthyism. McCarthy's key accusation was that Communists and Communist sympathizers at the highest levels of American government had betrayed American national interests to the Communists. Yalta was seen as the first great betrayal to the Soviet Union, and the cutting-off of aid to Chiang Kai-shek as the first great betrayal to the Chinese Communists, making their victory possible. The chief sufferer from these attacks was the State Department: its carefully built corps of China experts was decimated. But the attacks reached farther out into the academic world: leading scholars on China were accused of pro-Communism, not only by McCarthy and his followers, but by other scholars as well.

American policy toward China, already hardened early in 1950, reached a freezing point with Korea, thus ending the first great China debate. What followed was a witch-hunt, with the liberals moving increasingly to the defensive and finally into silence. McCarthyism had a destructive impact on China scholarship: for years, little serious study of Communist China was pursued in American universities, and when it began again in the mid-1950s, scholars were careful to avoid sensitive issues. The attitude of the American public, as revealed in opinion polls and Congressional speeches, remained adamantly hostile to China.

By the 1960s, however, scholarship on China was in full swing: every major university and many smaller schools had China programs; no country in the world, with the possible exception of Japan, was doing as much research on China as the United States. Not surprisingly, a large part of the work dealt with problems of direct interest to the government: leadership, economic development, foreign policy, and so on. Whereas McCarthyism had brought about a break between universities and government, the growing liberalization of attitudes on the part of official America during the latter years of the Eisenhower Administration and the three years of the Kennedy Administration reversed the trend. Through consultantships, conferences, seminars, and through agencies like the Council on Foreign Relations, American China scholars once again came into close relationship with government.

The advent of the Johnson Administration and, in particular, the escalation of the Vietnam war weakened the university-government bonds that had grown up. The universities became the forum in which sharp criticisms were voiced against the government's Far Eastern policy. The China issue soon became a major part of the debates. However, just as Taiwan and Vietnam are not ostensibly linked in the picture of Sino-American relations, so the China and the Vietnam issues were not always brought together in these debates. Thus, some scholars who supported Administration policy on Vietnam urged Washington to pursue a more moderate policy toward China. Among the China scholars there appeared to be far broader agreement that U.S. China policy had to be changed than that America had to make some radical changes in her Vietnam policy. Many scholars, while privately critical of Vietnam policy, refused to speak out on grounds that they knew little about Vietnam. And, indeed, despite the historical ties between China and Vietnam, the two countries are very different.

Congress, however, was worried about China precisely because of the increasingly grave Vietnam situation. Early in 1966 a House Subcommittee on Far Eastern Affairs, under the chairmanship of Representative Clement J. Zablocki of Wisconsin, held hearings on China, at which leading members of the Sinological community were invited to testify. Shortly thereafter the Senate Foreign Relations Committee, under the chairmanship of Senator J. William Fulbright of Arkansas, held its celebrated China hearings, launched by testimony from two of America's leading scholars on contemporary China, A. Doak Barnett of Columbia and John King Fairbank of Harvard. In universities and other public forums throughout the country, China once again became an issue of discussion.

Although one could find strands from the earlier China debate, the immediate issues were different. The earlier debate went through three stages: debate about whether or not to try and save Chiang Kai-shek, about whether or not to recognize the Peking government, and about who was to blame for the loss of China. Now the overriding question was: Was the United States on a collision course with China? Two conflicting views prevailed in official Washington: one argued that despite all their talk, the Chinese were cautious and would not intervene in Vietnam; the other view cited the Korean War as a precedent to indicate the Chinese would intervene if they felt their national interests threatened. The hearings were held not so much to elicit estimations from scholars on the probability of a Sino-American war, but to learn their images and conceptions of China and their recommendations for future policy. The key issue was: Are or are not the Chinese expansionist?

The following selections reflect two divergent academic views on the subject. The first consists of excerpts from the testimony of John King Fairbank, and the second of excerpts from the testimony of George E. Taylor, Director of the Far Eastern and Russian Institute at the University of Washington and a scholar of long experience in China.

In their respective testimony we find the same argument over what Communist China really is as we found in the 1949 debate over recognition. Fairbank argues that the Chinese Communists are basically Chinese and, as such, remain in their age-old Imperial tradition. Taylor, arguing that they are basically Communist, denies their nationalism. Fairbank, in stressing China's ethnocentrism, implicitly plays down any basic relationship to world Communism. Taylor answers that "I do not think . . . that the evidence supports the fashionable view that the Communist world is falling apart."

Fairbank implies that the issue of expansionism is not really an issue: ". . . this biggest, most isolated and distinctive, most long-continued culture and society developed a strong tendency to look inward." He suggests that "we should not get too excited over Peking's vast blueprints for the onward course of the Maoist revolution." Taylor takes the opposite view: "In my view [the Lin Piao statement] should be taken seriously as a general indication of the objectives and strategy of the Peking wing of the movement."

The policy recommendations of each follow from their basic images of China. Fairbank advocates "a better balance between destruction and construction in our own efforts in Vietnam," and "getting China into greater contact with the outside world." Taylor answers: "I am strongly in favor of containing Chinese Communist aggression."

In general, Taylor's policy recommendations are little different from those now pursued by Washington. He even hints that in time "the international status of the two parts of China must correspond to the facts of power," in other words, a "two China solution." Fairbank, in effect, expresses moderate agreement with current American policy and actions: "Military containment on the Korean border, in the Formosa Strait, and somehow in Vietnam cannot soon be abandoned." However, while suggesting nothing new on the Taiwan question, Fairbank argues for a de-escalation in the Vietnam war, but without going into specific detail.

Perhaps the most important thrust of Fairbank's testimony, and that of other witnesses, was that official America had to change its image, in short to change its ideological conception of China. He was arguing for an abandonment of new myths and a return to old realities, namely, to give up the idea that China is basically Communist and see her in the ancient Imperial tradition. Taylor argues strongly for the retention of the current official conception, and by denying the depth of the Sino-Soviet split, goes even further.

The debate must thus be seen as part of the discussion on the fundamental premises of American foreign policy, something strongly advocated by Senator Fulbright. How far it will go and what influence it will have is unclear. Dean Rusk indicated in his own testimony before the Senate Foreign Relations Com-

mittee that the current United States conception of the world
has its roots in the immediate postwar period. Such conceptions
take a long time to change. Obviously, if the collision course
with China should materialize, the question as to what the correct image of China is will become academic.

JOHN KING FAIRBANK *

[*Testimony before the Senate Foreign
Relations Committee*]

Motivate Chinese Behavior
According to China's Needs

. . . I think we need more perspective on the Chinese style of
political behavior. What did the world [in the past] look like
from Peking? How was power held there down to 1912, within
the lifetime of many of us? How did Peking handle her foreign
relations, and what kind of heritage is operating today in Peking's
motives and methods toward the outside world?

I imagine we would all agree on a first point—China's remarkable feeling of superiority. Here was a very big, ancient,
isolated, unified, and self-sufficient empire, stretching from the
latitude of Hudson's Bay to Cuba or from the Baltic Sea to the
Sahara Desert, with a great deal of domestic commerce to meet
its needs, cut off from West Asia by the high mountains and
deserts of Central Asia and thus isolated throughout most of its
history, preserving a continuity of development in the same area
over some three or four thousand years, during most of which
time the Chinese state has been a unified entity.

As we might expect, this biggest, most isolated and distinctive, most long-continued culture and society developed a strong
tendency to look inward, an attitude of ethnocentrism or Sino-
centrism, China being the center of the known world and of

* Abridged from *The Christian Science Monitor.*

civilization, the non-Chinese being peripheral and inferior, China being superior to all foreign regions. . . .

A second point is that the old Peking rulers were the custodians and propagators of a true teaching, the Confucian classical doctrines of social order, an orthodoxy which told every man how to behave in his proper place and kept the social pyramid intact with the Emperor on top. . . .

We need not labor the point that China today still has a ruling class selected for their abilities who propagate a true teaching under a sage ruler and strive to keep the various social classes in order. . . .

Ancient China never developed these [Western] concepts of supremacy of law and natural rights or civil liberties. Instead it spread the Confucian faith as to proper conduct in all relationships and so reinforced the ruler's claim that he ruled by his virtuous example.

In their foreign relations the Chinese rulers down to 1912 extended their domestic doctrines across their frontiers and applied the national myth of rule by virtue to their foreign relations. Foreign rulers could have contact with the Peking monarch only by sending tribute to him and having their envoys perform the three kneelings and nine prostrations of the kowtow ritual. . . .

It became well established that all foreign relations must be tributary relations, reinforcing the myth of Chinese supremacy and particularly the myth that foreign rulers were attracted by the Emperor's virtue and "turned toward him" to offer their submission to the center of civilization. . . .

Applying all this background to the present moment, I suggest we should not get too excited over Peking's vast blueprints for the onward course of the Maoist Revolution. Some American commentators who really ought to know better have overreacted to the visionary blueprint of world revolution put out by Lin Piao last September in Peking (about the strangling of the world's advanced countries or "cities" from the underdeveloped countries or "countryside"). This was, I think, a reassertion of faith that the Chinese Communists' own parochial example of rural-based revolution is the model for the rest of the underdeveloped world to emulate. . . .

The disaster that hit China in the nineteenth century is one of the most comprehensive any people ever experienced. . . .

The Opium War and the unequal treaties in the 1840s gave our merchants and missionaries a privileged status as agents of Westernization in the Chinese treaty ports. Throughout the next century, Western influence gradually disintegrated the old Chinese civilization. . . . The prestige of the Confucian classics evaporated. The Confucian type of a family structure began to crack. China's superiority vanished even culturally. . . .

So complete was the disaster that a new order had to be built from the ground up. Western doctrines of all kinds were tried out. The thing that proved effective was the Leninist type of Party dictatorship, an elite recruited under discipline according to a new orthodoxy, organized something like an old Chinese secret society, united in the effort to seize power and re-create a strong state. . . .

It would not be naïve to agree that China's early sense of superiority had some justification, and that her modern sense of victimization also has some justification. To have been so advanced and superior and then to find herself so backward and weak was a shattering experience. . . .

As Americans we can only begin to imagine how the Chinese have suffered from being on the receiving end of modernization rather than the giving end. It has been hard for them to take, because under their traditional code there should be reciprocity between people, one should not accept gifts without paying them back. . . .

We Americans, being on the giving end of modernization, got a great deal more fun out of Sino-American relations. In the privileged status thrust upon them by the treaty system, most Americans enjoyed their contact with China, the chance to be an upper-class foreigner riding in a rickshaw while still remaining an egalitarian grass-roots democrat in one's own conscience. . . .

The American people built up a genuine, though sometimes patronizing, fondness for China. Unfortunately, this now turns out to have been an unrealistic and rather naïve attitude for two reasons.

In the first place, the Americans were conscious of their own good intentions and less conscious of the humiliation that their superior circumstances often inflicted upon their Chinese friends.

In the second place, the Americans were able in the nineteenth century to share all the special privileges of foreigners in China under the unequal treaties without fighting for them. The British and others fought the colonial wars and the Americans enjoyed the fruits of such aggression without the moral responsibility. . . .

Today we find ourselves in an onerous situation trying to maintain the power balance in East Asia. It is reminiscent in some ways of the colonial wars of the nineteenth century, a type of situation that we generally succeeded in avoiding in that era. . . .

My conclusion is that the alternative to war with Peking, over Vietnam or elsewhere, lies along two lines of effort—one is to achieve a better balance between destruction and construction in our own efforts in Vietnam, so that the non-Communist model of nation-building there can compete more effectively with the Chinese Communist model of nation-building.

The other line of effort is to defuse or dampen Peking's militancy by getting China into greater contact with the outside world, more connected with the international scene, and more interested in participating in it like other countries. . . .

American policy should work toward a gradual shift from trying to isolate Peking, which only worsens our problem, to a less exposed position where we can acquiesce in the growth of contact between Peking and other countries and let *them* suffer the impact of Peking's abrasiveness.

In gradually manipulating Peking into an acceptance of the international world, as an alternative to trying to subvert it, we must motivate Chinese behavior according to China's needs:

> 1. One of these is the craving for greater prestige in the world to redress the balance of the last century's humiliations. . . .
> 2. We can also use the Peking government's need for prestige to maintain itself domestically. . . .
> 3. In addition, the Chinese people positively need certain kinds of aid through exchanges of technology or of goods, like all developing countries.
> 4. Peking may also be motivated by the opportunity to manipulate foreigners against one another. This tradi-

tional way of dealing with outsiders can be attempted in any conclave like the United Nations. But any number can play this game, and, in fact, it is the essence of diplomacy.

As these types of motives come into play, we may expect the Peking regime to be involved in bilateral relationships and be influenced by others whose desire is for peace rather than violence. In the end all this may make coexistence more attractive and feasible.

Opening the door for China's participation in the world scene is only one part of an American policy. The other part is to hold the line. The Chinese are no more amenable to pure sweetness and light than other revolutionaries. Encouraging them to participate in the UN and other parts of the international scene has to be combined with a cognate attitude of firmness backed by force.

Military containment on the Korean border, in the Formosa Strait, and somehow in Vietnam cannot soon be abandoned and may have to be maintained for some time. But containment alone is a blind alley unless we add policies of constructive competition and of international contact.

In short, my reading of history is that Peking's rulers shout aggressively, out of manifold frustration, that isolation intensifies their ailment and makes it self-perpetuating, and that we need to encourage international contact with China on many fronts.

GEORGE E. TAYLOR *

[*Testimony before the Senate Foreign Relations Committee*]

Why Help Peking . . . ?

. . . The United States is better informed about Communist China today than is any other country in the free world. . . .

* *Ibid.*

I wish to mention this point . . . because there are those who feel that we would be much better informed if we recognized Communist China and could send our scholars and journalists to that country. Unless there were a radical change in the attitude of the Communist regime, the evidence does not suggest, considering the price we would have to pay, either that access to the Mainland would make that much difference or that access depends upon recognition. . . .

Much is made of the assumption that we have stabilized our relations with the Soviet Union and that the same can be done with Communist China. . . . But in my view the present stability is brittle in the extreme and is based mainly on the superior military power of the United States and its allies and on a common interest in avoiding one kind of war . . . nuclear conflict between the United States and the USSR. . . .

. . . There are those who think that present Soviet behavior arises from the fact that we followed a policy of containment combined with recognition and membership in the UN. The same formula applied to China should produce the same results. . . .

This is a doubtful analogy on which to base action. Nor is there any real parallel between Communist China and the USSR or surety that the same techniques will bring the same results. . . .

In my view it is safer to proceed on the premise that there is no world community, as the phrase goes, into which we can induce the Chinese to enter. Unfortunately we live in a world in which there are at least two violently opposed concepts of international relations, of political and social organization, and of world order. . . .

Further to clarify my premises, I do not think . . . that the evidence supports the fashionable view that the Communist world is falling apart. . . . The social and political content of nationalism is determined by the institutional power configuration, and this is what is new and lasting about Communism. It is because it is the nature of power that determines foreign policy . . . that I feel so little hope of any changes in Chinese Communist policies that are not forced on her. . . .

In my view the Communists represent a complete break

with the past. Their world view is not conditioned by the Imperial past, although they are willing to exploit it. . . .

There is nothing about Chinese nationalism that calls for the hate campaign of the Chinese Communists against the United States, for the militarization of a quarter of the people of the earth, for the racial invective that pervades so much of their propaganda, even in Hong Kong, or for the support of revolutionary movements in Southeast Asia, Africa, and Latin America—spelled out in the Central Committee decisions of 1963. . . .

A true nationalism would call for attention to domestic problems and would certainly avoid a quarrel with a powerful neighbor.

Like most of the witnesses, I am strongly in favor of containing Chinese Communist aggression. . . . But one gets the impression that some witnesses think that there is almost nothing to contain. Most have referred to the most recent statement of Chinese Communist political goals, the Lin Piao position paper of September 1965, but it is variously interpreted. . . .

In my view it should be taken seriously as a general indication of the objectives and strategy of the Peking wing of the movement. It is not impossible that this strategy could be made to work.

It is based on the assumption that the revolution is not going to occur in the great industrial states, that the Achilles heel of the West is the "third world"—that the promotion of wars of national liberation in Africa, Latin America, and Southeast Asia will distract and waste the energies of the Western powers, confuse their peoples, and demoralize their leaders. . . .

How do we contain this sort of threat . . . ?

The answer is clearly to assist in building up viable states in the many parts of the world that might come under Communist pressure, Chinese or Soviet. To do this is going to require not force backed by a political program, but a political program backed by force. . . .

How far should containment go? Clearly far enough to prevent the exploitation of wars of national liberation. . . .

But the real problem is the future of the National Government of the Republic of China. . . . One of the Chinas has a permanent seat on the Security Council and the other China has, in effect, been at war with the UN since 1950. . . .

Some day, some time, the international status of the two parts of China must correspond to the facts of power, but there is no hurry. At the present time there is no advantage to the United States in talking about recognition or admission to the UN. . . . Why help the Peking regime when it is in trouble? What conceivable interest do we have in assisting this regime to become a great power? . . .

❦ One Aspect of the Sino-American Relationship

IN THE COSMIC STRUGGLE between "American imperialism" and "Chinese expansionism," one aspect of it has deeply puzzled the Chinese: Why should the United States government be so afraid of things from Red China entering the country? The Taiwan government strictly bans any Communist written material from entering, but is reported to be unconcerned about rhinoceros horn and dried shrimp. The United States government takes just the opposite approach: Americans can read Communist Chinese publications but must not consume their products. The Chinese can only conclude from this that the United States government regards contamination through the stomach as far more dangerous than contamination through the mind. We present a short poem which expresses the Chinese puzzlement on this aspect of the Sino-American relationship.

YUAN SHUI-PO *
Soy Sauce and Prawns

News item: May 1959: The United States has prohibited the transhipment of a cargo of Chinese canned prawns and soy sauce destined for Canada.

* Yuan Shui-po, *Soy Sauce and Prawns* (Peking: Foreign Languages Press, 1963), p. 29.

Neither canned prawns nor soy sauce
May America's borders cross;
Canadians, amazed, confused,
Are irritated and amused.

Soy sauce endangers security,
The reason's there for all to see,
So deeply red it's purple nearly
—Criminal nature proven clearly.

And as to Chinese big prawns canned,
They obviously must be banned;
In armor cased from tail to head,
When boiled they turn a fiery red.

An Iron Curtain America blinds,
Hysteria grips the White House minds;
"Strategic goods"—what if they're edible?
Such idiocy is scarcely credible.

🥠 China's Foreign Relations
with Other Countries

OUR OTHER selections on foreign policy have focused mainly on the triangle of relations between China, America, and the Soviet Union. Needless to say, China has had a whole range of other worldwide involvements. American policy to isolate China had some effect in the first half of the 1950s, when for a long time China's contacts were almost exclusively with the Communist world. But after the Bandung Conference in April 1955 China began to move out into the world. In the spring of 1966 China had formal diplomatic relations with forty-eight countries, and semi-official contacts with many more; she is a world diplomatic power, and the trend is toward greater involvement. Thousands of foreign diplomats have traveled to Peking, and Chinese emissaries have been to most parts of the globe. Life for the diplomat stationed in Peking is not easy; the Chinese abroad still keep largely to themselves.

We present excerpts from a press conference given on September 29, 1965, by Foreign Minister Ch'en Yi to a large number of Chinese and foreign correspondents. Ch'en Yi briefly stated China's position on several issues of international significance.

In 1965 and 1966 Peking suffered a series of reverses whose effect on China's foreign policy is still not clear. The destruction of the Indonesian Communist Party and the worsening of Sino-Indonesian relations were perhaps the worst blows. Elsewhere in Asia, Outer Mongolia clearly sided with the Soviets in the Sino-Soviet dispute, and North Korea and North Vietnam moved closer to the Soviet position. Soviet initiative in the Tashkent peacemaking conference between India and Pakistan was not welcomed by China. The reverses in Africa came one after another: several African states expelled Chinese diplomats for interfering in their internal affairs. The overthrow of Kwame Nkrumah of Ghana deprived China of one of her best friends in Black Africa. Fidel Castro's denunciation of China, following a heated dispute over rice exports to Cuba, came as a bitter blow, in view of Fidel's great prestige in China. In the international Communist movement the strength of the pro-Peking parties and splinter movements weakened, and even the pro-Peking Japanese Communist Party having made efforts to heal the rift between Moscow and Peking, drifted closer to Moscow.

Paradoxically, while China's relations with the socialist world and with the underdeveloped countries worsened, her relations with the advanced "bourgeois" countries improved. Despite Premier Eisaku Sato's pro-American policy, trade between China and Japan grew. The purchase by China of a complete $150-million steel plant in early 1966 from Western Germany points to an anomaly of long-standing in Sino-German relations. German businessmen have for years been active in China, but as Walter Ulbricht faithfully followed the Soviet line, Chinese business contracts have increasingly gone to the West Germans. Relations with France are cordial. Despite the close ties Canada and Australia have with America, China does a brisk trade with both nations, particularly in food grains.

The conclusion appears inescapable that where the Chinese mixed ideology with diplomacy they did not do well. But where relations were purely businesslike, they did much better.

China has concluded border agreements with Outer Mongolia, Afghanistan, Pakistan, Nepal, and Burma. Two border areas remain in dispute: the Sino-Soviet border and the Sino-Indian border. Although on several occasions the Soviets have accused the Chinese of covetous designs on the Soviet Far East and the Chinese have raised the question of "unequal treaties" by which Russia acquired her Far Eastern lands, no one knows what Chinese aims in this region really are. It is noteworthy, however, that Ch'en Yi flatly accepted the independence of the Mongolian People's Republic, a land traditionally within the Chinese Empire (comments omitted in our selection).

The Sino-Indian border dispute has its roots in the Tibetan problem, and is bound up with ideological considerations on both sides. China's growing friendship with Pakistan, a member of both CENTO and SEATO, which was marked by a state visit in spring 1966 to that country by Liu Shao-ch'i, obviously derives from common hostility to India.

Ch'en Yi's comments on trade relations between China and West Germany are interesting. While stating that China can have no official relations with West Germany as long as the latter has designs on East Germany, Ch'en Yi reiterated that he hoped the "traditional friendship between the people, the workers, peasants, scientists, and intellectuals of West Germany and the Chinese people" would develop. That friendship, one might note, has taken the form of a very healthy two-way trade. Perhaps what the Chinese mean by the "traditional friendship between the Chinese and American peoples" is a similar sort of relationship, assuming certain problems (namely Taiwan) can be settled.

On sharing nuclear knowledge, Ch'en Yi indicated that China was not going to help any other nation manufacture an atomic bomb (comments omitted in our selection).

The failure of the second Afro-Asian conference to meet in Algiers (because of the overthrow of Ahmed Ben Bella) was a major setback for the Chinese, who had hoped to become the leader of a bloc of third-world nations, thus bolstering the Chinese position against the Soviet Union and the United States. Afro-Asian unity was more a dream than a reality, however, and a rightward drift among several Afro-Asian nations made the formation of an Afro-Asian anti-imperialist bloc even more unlikely. The failure of the conference to meet marked the beginning of a series of reverses in China's ideological foreign policy. Ch'en Yi clearly indicated that there would be little prospect of reconvening the conference, and by the summer of 1966 nothing more has been heard of it.

In regard to the United Nations, Ch'en Yi posed a set of conditions that made it all but impossible for Peking to be admitted in place of Taipei. China has recently shown decreasing interest in the United Nations, which it regards as "a place where the two big powers, the United States and the Soviet Union, conduct political transactions." One might add that the role of the United Nations in world affairs has been steadily declining, a factor making the Chinese less anxious to join.

On Taiwan, Ch'en Yi extended an invitation, made many times previously, to China's brethren on that island to rejoin the Mainland. What did he mean when he said: "to break away from U.S. imperialist control and be loyal to the motherland. There are no other conditions"? Presumably, if Taiwan accepted Peking as the legitimate government of China, the "local authorities" (as the Chinese Communists refer to the Chiang regime) could remain in charge.

On atomic weapons, Ch'en Yi implied that China still had a way to go: "atomic technology and delivery technology are, of course, rather complicated, but Chinese, Asians, and Africans certainly can all master them, if efforts are made."

Finally, Ch'en Yi spoke at length and with evident anger about Hong Kong. Ostensibly he was angry because American troops in Vietnam had been using Hong Kong for rest and recreation purposes. The real reason for his anger actually came from Soviet accusations that while the Chinese urged other nations to oppose imperialism, they quietly tolerated Hong Kong and Macao on their doorsteps. The explanation is not very difficult: Hong Kong is China's biggest foreign-exchange earner. A lesser explanation is that it serves as a kind of "Miami" for unhappy citizens who want to leave China.

Even more significant was Ch'en Yi's warning to the United States on Vietnam: "It is up to the U.S. President and the Pentagon to decide whether the United States wants a big war with China today." Putting the warning under the Hong Kong rather than the Vietnam rubric (comments omitted in our selection) indicated that the Chinese still wanted to keep the issue of Vietnam out of the framework of Sino-American relations. However, what Ch'en Yi meant by the warning is clear: if the war escalates further, China will intervene.

All in all, Ch'en Yi took the attitude that no matter with whom China has relations, her own national interests come first. One need hardly note that such would be the attitude of any foreign minister.

CH'EN YI *
Remarks at a Press Conference

September 29, 1965

ON THE SINO-INDIAN BOUNDARY QUESTION

Answering a question about the Sino-Indian border issue raised by the editor of the Voice of Revolution *of the Congo (Brazzaville), Vice-Premier Ch'en Yi said:*

In its note of September 16, the Chinese government demanded that India dismantle the fifty-six aggressive military works she had built within Chinese territory on the China-Sikkim border and withdraw the intruding Indian troops. The China-Sikkim boundary is the boundary between China and Sikkim and does not fall within the scope of the Sino-Indian boundary. It has long been delimited. India not only regards Sikkim as her protectorate, but has gone to the length of intruding into Chinese territory across the China-Sikkim boundary. It was her right as a sovereign state and entirely reasonable for China to lodge the protest and raise the demands in her note to the Indian government. We had shown forbearance for several years. Knowing that it was in the wrong, the Indian government withdrew all the intruding Indian troops and demolished a part of the aggressive military works upon receiving our notification. That was a good thing, and it was wise of them to do so. If India had failed to do so, the Chinese government would have been entitled to act in self-defense, drive out the intruders, and destroy the aggressive military works.

Along the Sino-Indian boundary of several thousand kilometers, Indian troops have crossed the line of actual control at many other places and carried out harassing raids. India is

---

* Ch'en Yi, *Important Remarks at a Press Conference attended by Chinese and Foreign Correspondents* (Peking: Foreign Languages Press, 1966), pp. 1–26 [abridged].

still occupying over ninety-two thousand square kilometers of Chinese territory in the eastern, western, and middle sectors of the Sino-Indian border. The Indian government should understand that there is a limit to our forbearance, that it must cease its intrusions and harassments and that the question of Chinese territory occupied by it will have to be thoroughly settled.

ON THE INDIAN-PAKISTAN CONFLICT

A correspondent of the London Daily Express *asked what assistance the Chinese government would give Pakistan with the resumption of the conflict between India and Pakistan. Vice-Premier Ch'en Yi said:*

The fact is that Pakistan is the victim of aggression and India the aggressor. Recently Indian troops have continued to launch attacks in the Lahore area. We do not wish to see the aggravation of the situation, and we hope that the Indian side knows how to restrain itself. If the situation is aggravated, it is certain that the Chinese government and people will give moral and material support to Pakistan. Relying on the support of the United States, the Soviet Union, and Britain, the Indian government wants to do whatever it pleases, but that can frighten nobody. We hope that it will come to its senses.

India's aggression against Pakistan is not in the interest of the Indian people. I believe that the great Indian people of more than four hundred million wish to live in peace with the other Afro-Asian peoples and unite with them in opposing imperialism and old and new colonialism. It is regrettable that the Indian leaders have failed to reflect this wish, but instead have perpetrated aggression by relying on foreign forces, and particularly on U.S. imperialism. Such an adventurist policy is bound to fail, and indeed it has already failed. If it is not altered, it will continue to meet with failure.

ON TRADE RELATIONS BETWEEN
CHINA AND WEST GERMANY

A West German D.P.A. correspondent asked on what conditions China would enter into official trade relations with West Germany. Vice-Premier Ch'en Yi said:

At present, China already has trade relations with West Germany. But conditions are not ripe for the establishment of official trade relations. In close collaboration with the United States, West Germany is restoring militarism and posing a threat to the security of Europe. West Germany has not given up her plan of annexing the German Democratic Republic. In these circumstances, China cannot enter into any official trade relations with West Germany.

There exists a traditional friendship between the people, the workers, peasants, scientists, and intellectuals, of West Germany and the Chinese people. We hope that this friendship will develop.

ON THE SECOND AFRICAN-ASIAN CONFERENCE

Vice-Premier Ch'en Yi said:

The African-Asian Conference is a meeting of the heads of state or government of the more than sixty African and Asian countries which have won independence. If this conference can develop the Bandung spirit and discuss the questions of fighting imperialism and colonialism and of the national liberation movement of the world, I believe it will be of great significance in international life. The conference should support the people of Vietnam, Laos, the Congo (Leopoldville), the Dominican Republic, Angola, Mozambique, Portuguese Guinea, South Africa, the Arab people of Palestine, and the people of South Yemen, Malaya, Singapore, and North Kalimantan in their struggles against the aggression of the imperialists, colonialists, and neo-colonialists headed by the United States. The Chinese government has always stood for holding the conference along these lines and making it a success.

U.S. imperialism dislikes this conference very much and is trying to sabotage it by every means. It is anticipated that the first item on the agenda after the opening session will be the condemnation of U.S. imperialism for its aggressions throughout the world. If this is done, the Bandung spirit will be raised to a new level. If it fails to make an open denunciation of U.S. imperialism but only opposes imperialism and colonialism in general terms, then it will not have much significance.

Recently, a cabinet minister of a certain country told me that some newly independent countries could not openly denounce U.S. imperialism at the African-Asian Conference because of their need for U.S. aid to solve the bread question. On the other hand, some other Afro-Asian countries hold that the first and foremost task of the African-Asian Conference is to denounce U.S. imperialism, otherwise there will be no sense in convening the conference. These two tendencies are now engaged in a struggle. China firmly sides with those that stand for condemnation of U.S. imperialism. This position of China's will never change. For without adopting resolutions condemning U.S. imperialism, the African-Asian Conference will disappoint the people of Asia, Africa, and Latin America. To hold such a conference would be a waste. As for the bread question, it is my view that if one relies on U.S. aid, one will get less and less bread, while by relying on one's own efforts one will get more and more. So far as certain countries are concerned, the more they denounce U.S. imperialism, the more bread they will probably get from it, otherwise they will not get any. Such is the character of U.S. imperialism—bullying the weak-kneed and fearing the strong.

I have told the leaders of some Afro-Asian countries: since many Afro-Asian countries are receiving aid and loans from the United States and other countries, thus incurring ever increasing burdens, it may be advisable to adopt a resolution at the African-Asian Conference declaring the cancellation of all debts which Afro-Asian countries owe to the United States. If this can be done, the debts owed to China may also be canceled. They said this was a very good idea and could be considered.

In order to sabotage the African-Asian Conference, the imperialists are trying to hook it up with the United Nations. The Bandung Conference has enjoyed high prestige among the people of the world precisely because, having nothing to do with the United Nations, it was free from UN influence and contributed to the anti-imperialist and anti-colonialist cause of the people of the world independently and outside the United Nations. If the conference is to be linked with the United Nations, it will be tantamount to discarding the Bandung spirit. The Chinese government is firmly against this.

To invite a representative of the United Nations or anyone from it to the African-Asian Conference would mean, in effect, to bring the United States into the conference. Is it not ludicrous to invite agents of U.S. imperialism to an anti-imperialist conference?

The Chinese government is resolutely against the participation of U Thant, Secretary-General of the United Nations, in the African-Asian Conference. Everybody is clear about the role U Thant is playing. He is not the head of the United Nations; the head of the United Nations is the United States. Not being the head of any Afro-Asian state, what qualifications has he to participate in the African-Asian Conference?

The United Nations has excluded China for sixteen years. China cannot sit together with its representative. The Chinese government does not force other countries to boycott UN meetings, nor should others force us to sit together with a representative of the United Nations. Otherwise, it would be running counter to the Bandung spirit. Joint struggle against imperialism is possible only when no one imposes his will on others. The invitation for U Thant to attend the African-Asian Conference was issued before Ben Bella's fall. I am thankful to President Houari Boumédienne because he showed sympathy with China's stand and said he would try to find a solution to this problem.

The Chinese government categorically states that no representative of the United Nations should be admitted to the African-Asian Conference.

As for inviting the Soviet Union to the African-Asian Conference, the Chinese government is firmly opposed to it. Whether historically or politically, the Soviet Union is by tradition a European country, and there is no reason for its participation in the African-Asian Conference. The Soviet Union did not ask for participation in the First Asian-African Conference. At that time, Prime Minister Nehru openly declared that the Soviet

Union, a European country, was not to be invited. Last year, India demanded Soviet participation, but the twenty-two countries failed to reach agreement, which means in effect the rejection of the demand for Soviet participation in the African-Asian Conference. Khrushchev stated last year that the Soviet Union would not put forward its request, if its participation would not conduce to Afro-Asian solidarity.

This question was already closed and should no longer exist. It was only recently, after the new leaders of the Soviet Union received the support and encouragement of the United States, India, Tito, and some other countries that they raised this question anew.

The question now is whether we should uphold the Bandung spirit and have the heads of the independent Afro-Asian countries meet and proclaim independent political views to promote the further progress of the anti-imperialist and anti-colonialist struggle in Asia and Africa, or whether we should submit to the unreasonable demand of a big power to gatecrash into the African-Asian Conference. The Chinese government is firmly opposed to Soviet participation in the African-Asian Conference.

Some U.S. and other Western newspapers declare outright that injection of the Soviet Union into the African-Asian Conference is the only way to offset the influence of China. The real implication of these words is that injection of the Soviet Union is the only way to water down the influence of the African-Asian Conference in opposing U.S. imperialism, colonialism, and neo-colonialism. This is a major issue of principle, on which there can be no compromise or concession.

China is not afraid of an all-round debate with the Soviet Union. The injection of the Soviet Union into the African-Asian Conference will mean nothing more than the opening of a new battlefront in the struggle against modern revisionism.

. . . Algeria is the host country of the Second African-Asian Conference. Some people hesitate to go to Algiers for the conference because they have reservations about the new Algerian government. We hold that the change of leadership in Algeria is her internal affair in which no foreign state should interfere. One should not link the convening of the African-

Asian Conference in Algeria with her internal affairs. To do so would be running counter to the Bandung spirit.

. . . Another important question which the African-Asian Conference should discuss is how the Afro-Asian countries are to free themselves from imperialist control and develop their national economy independently.

The more foreign aid with conditions attached a country receives, the more difficult will it be for her to stand up. This is like drinking poison to quench one's thirst.

Before liberation, China was wholly controlled by the United States, and it was with political, economic, and military aid from the United States that Chiang Kai-shek collapsed. And the situation in New China has become still better after she thoroughly embarked on a path of self-reliance upon the stoppage of all aid by Khrushchev. A country's economy will gain vigor in a few years' time, if she makes up her mind to stop relying on foreign aid, carries on construction with her own efforts and resources and turns out the products she needs. So long as this path is followed with determination, all Afro-Asian countries can solve their own economic problems, because they have all got a certain foundation for economic development.

Of course, on the above basis, Afro-Asian countries need to help supply each other's wants and aid each other on the principle of equality and mutual benefit. Such aid is not harmful but helpful. However, it is only of secondary importance. The point of primary importance is to rely on one's own efforts in national construction instead of being dependent on others. The Second African-Asian Conference will have more far-reaching significance than the first one if it can adopt a resolution for the building of independent national economies by the Afro-Asian countries through self-reliance and for their mutual economic cooperation on terms of equality and mutual benefit.

In brief, we should make a success of the conference. Otherwise, it would be better for the conference to be postponed until conditions are ripe than to drag everybody together to make a hodgepodge. The African-Asian Conference is a matter for all the Afro-Asian countries, and not for China alone. China has nothing to ask from the African-Asian Conference, and it is not that she cannot do without it. China stresses that the conference should support the anti-imperialist struggles of all peoples, but this is her wish and does not mean that she wants to gain anything from the conference.

The African-Asian Conference must be made a success. If there are assurances that it will be a success, the Chinese government is for its convocation. Without such assurances, the Chinese government is in favor of waiting till the conditions are ripe.

ON THE RESTORATION OF CHINA'S
LEGITIMATE RIGHTS IN THE UNITED NATIONS

Concerning the question of restoring to China her legitimate rights in the United Nations, which was raised by the Japanese correspondents, Vice-Premier Ch'en Yi said:

The United Nations has long been controlled by the United States and has today become a place where two big powers, the United States and the Soviet Union, conduct political transactions. This state of affairs has not changed although dozens of Afro-Asian and peace-loving countries have made no small amount of efforts in the United Nations. China need not take part in such a United Nations.

During the U.S. war of aggression against Korea, the United Nations adopted a resolution naming China as an aggressor. How can China be expected to take part in an international organization which calls her an aggressor? Calling China an aggressor and then asking the aggressor to join, would not the United Nations be slapping its own face?

The question now is how to reform the United Nations in accordance with the purposes and principles of its Charter and to free it from the control of the United States and other big powers. If the task of reforming the United Nations cannot be accomplished, conditions will no doubt gradually ripen for the establishment of a revolutionary United Nations.

Will the present UN General Assembly adopt a resolution expelling the elements of the Chiang Kai-shek clique and restoring China's legitimate rights? I think this is impossible as the United Nations is now controlled by the United States. If things really turn out that way, the question would still remain unsolved.

The United Nations must rectify its mistakes and undergo a thorough reorganization and reform. It must admit and correct all its past mistakes. Among other things, it should cancel its resolution condemning China and the Democratic People's Republic of Korea as aggressors and adopt a resolution condemning the United States as the aggressor; the UN Charter must be reviewed and revised jointly by all countries, big and small; all independent states should be included in the United Nations; and all imperialist puppets should be expelled.

For more than ten years, many countries have in the United Nations firmly demanded the expulsion of the representatives of the Chiang Kai-shek clique and the restoration of China's legitimate rights. China is always grateful for this just and friendly action.

ON KUOMINTANG-COMMUNIST COOPERATION

The Japanese correspondents asked about the possibility of cooperation between the Kuomintang and the Chinese Communist Party. Vice-Premier Ch'en Yi said:

At present there are Revolutionary Committees of the Kuomintang in the provinces and municipalities as well as in Peking, which are cooperating very well with the Communist Party. New China is a country in which eight democratic parties cooperate with the Communist Party and are led by it. We welcome Mr. Li Tsung-jen's participation in this cooperation. Chiang Kai-shek and Chiang Ching-kuo are also welcome to join in this cooperation as Mr. Li Tsung-jen has done. Taiwan province and any individual or group in Taiwan are welcome to come back to the embrace of the motherland and join in this cooperation. Only one condition is required: to break away from U.S. imperialist control and be loyal to the motherland. There are no other conditions. In my view, the possibility of Kuomintang-Communist cooperation is great and is moreover increasing.

ON SINO-JAPANESE RELATIONS

The Japanese correspondents asked about the prospects of Sino-Japanese relations. Vice-Premier Ch'en Yi replied:

A lot has been said on this question by leaders of our country, so I will only give a brief answer here. If the present Japanese government stops tailing after the United States, pursues an independent policy, and renounces its anti-Chinese policy, possibilities will increase for the normalization of Sino-Japanese relations. At present the Sato Cabinet is politically following the U.S. anti-Chinese policy, while economically it wants to reap gains from Sino-Japanese trade. Such a policy is self-contradictory and cannot help normalize Sino-Japanese relations. It is up to Japan to remove this obstacle. Out of consideration for the traditional friendship between the great nations and peoples of China and Japan, the Chinese government is willing to carry on trade between the two countries on the present level, but it is impossible to expand it.

The Japanese nation is full of promise, and the Japanese people love peace. They demand the liquidation of U.S. imperialist control and the dismantling of U.S. bases in Japan. We have deep sympathy with their demands.

ON CHINA'S DEVELOPMENT
OF NUCLEAR WEAPONS

The Japanese correspondents asked about the development of nuclear weapons in China. Vice-Premier Ch'en Yi said:

China has exploded two atom bombs. I know this and so do you. A third atom bomb may be exploded. As to the time of its explosion, please wait for our communiqué. Atomic technology and delivery technology are, of course, rather complicated, but Chinese, Asians, and Africans certainly can all master them, if efforts are made.

China does not decide her foreign policies according to whether or not she has got atom bombs. We are ready to enter into friendly cooperation with still more countries in order to oppose imperialism and colonialism, isolate U.S. imperialism, and safeguard world peace.

We reaffirm that all countries, big and small, should come together and agree on the destruction of atom bombs and on the prohibition of the use, manufacture, stockpiling, and testing of nuclear weapons. China is manufacturing atom bombs in order to liquidate them and for the purpose of self-defense. China has pledged never to be the first to use atom bombs. Our nuclear weapons will only be used for defense.

ON THE U.S. USE OF HONG KONG AS A BASE FOR ITS AGGRESSIVE WAR IN VIETNAM

Answering questions put by the correspondents of the Hong Kong Cheng Wu Pao, The Hong Kong Evening News, *and* The Global Digest *about the use of Hong Kong by the United States in its war of aggression against Vietnam, Vice-Premier Ch'en Yi said:*

The fact that Britain and the Hong Kong authorities allow the United States to use Hong Kong as a base for aggression against Vietnam has caused the anxiety of the local inhabitants. The Chinese government considers the question not only one of using Hong Kong as a base for aggression against Vietnam but also of preparing to use it in future as a base for aggression against China. The Chinese government is firmly opposed to this. This action of the British Government is most stupid. We hope that it will choose a wiser course in its own interests. Otherwise, China will take measures when necessary. . . .

The heroic struggle of the Vietnamese people is not merely their own affair, but a contribution to the worldwide struggle against imperialism and colonialism. If war should spread to China, she will put up staunch resistance and will be determined to defeat U.S. imperialism.

China sees not just the question of Taiwan, the question of Hong Kong, and the question of Macao, each on its own; what we see is the global strategy of U.S. imperialism. One must be prepared to wage a worldwide struggle before U.S. imperialism can be defeated. Will the imperialists allow the socialist countries in Eastern Europe and the Soviet Union to live in security?

The Khrushchev revisionists place implicit trust in what U.S. imperialism says, and they will sooner or later come to grief for it.

Khrushchev said that instead of liberating Hong Kong and Macao herself, China was making other Asians and Africans fight imperialism and colonialism and pull chestnuts out of the fire for China. This is a malicious provocation. Khrushchev wanted to dictate China's policy. Our reply is: China's policy must be decided by China herself and not by the Khrushchev revisionists.

The Chinese people are ready to make all necessary sacrifices in the fight against imperialism. It is up to the U.S. President and the Pentagon to decide whether the United States wants a big war with China today. We cherish no illusions about U.S. imperialism. We are fully prepared against U.S. aggression. If the U.S. imperialists are determined to launch a war of aggression against us, they are welcome to come sooner, to come as early as tomorrow. Let the Indian reactionaries, the British imperialists, and the Japanese militarists come along with them! Let the modern revisionists act in coordination with them from the North! We will still win in the end. The great Soviet people and the Communist Party of the Soviet Union will not allow their leaders to take such a criminal decision. Who will meet with destruction—the U.S. imperialists or the people of the world? It can be said with certainty that the U.S. imperialists will perish, while the people of the whole world will win liberation. As a Chinese saying goes, good will be rewarded with good, and evil with evil; if the reward is not forthcoming, it is because the time has not arrived; and when the time arrives, one will get all the reward he deserves!

In the struggle against U.S. imperialism, constant vacillation without a final determination will only lead to defeat and not to victory.

In the Korean war, the United States had a trial of strength with the peoples of Korea and China, and now it is having a trial of strength with the heroic Vietnamese people. The United States admits that such trials of strength are very much to its disadvantage. To us and to the people of the whole world, such trials of strength have great advantages; they have united the entire Vietnamese people and the entire Chinese people, and pushed the world anti-imperialist and anti-colonialist struggle to a new stage.

For sixteen years we have been waiting for the U.S. imperialists to come in and attack us. My hair has turned gray in waiting. Perhaps I will not have the luck to see the U.S. imperialist invasion of China, but my children may see it, and they will resolutely carry on the fight. Let no correspondent think that I am bellicose. It is the U.S. imperialists who are brutal and vicious and who bully others too much. They are bullying the Chinese, the Koreans, the Vietnamese, the Khmers, the Laotians, the Indonesians, the Congolese, and the Dominicans. Even their ally France is being bullied by them. Those who are bullied by them have risen against them and become friends of China. This is of the United States' own making.

Should the U.S. imperialists invade China's mainland, we will take all necessary measures to defeat them. By then, the war will have no boundaries. It is the United States, and not China, that will have broken down the boundaries. We are willing to respect boundaries, but the United States wilfully violates boundaries and drives in wherever it likes. With the defeat of U.S. imperialism, the time will come when imperialism and colonialism will be really liquidated throughout the world. The ideal is bound to come true with the world truly becoming a community of nations with different social systems coexisting peacefully. China is ready to make all the necessary sacrifices for this noble ideal. She will never take the modern revisionist position of betraying Marxism-Leninism and proletarian internationalism.

The choice now is either to reimpose colonial shackles on the people of various countries in accordance with the global strategy of U.S. imperialism so as to subject them to enslavement and plunder, or to wage resolute struggles to defeat U.S. imperialism and put an end to the colonial system according to the will of the people, who dare to fight and dare to oppose imperialism, so that countries with different social systems can truly coexist peacefully throughout the world. One has to choose either of the two alternatives. The modern revisionist way of seeking ease and comfort at the expense of principles is a blind alley. China is ready to make her contribution to the struggle against U.S. imperialism and old and new colonialism.

𝕽 Minorities and Borders

THOUGH THE overwhelming majority of China's population is Han, *i.e.,* ethnic Chinese, there are a large number and variety of minorities. Manchuria has a sizable Korean population, Chinese Muslims (Hui) can be found in many parts of the country, and the mountainous regions of Southern China are inhabited by peoples related to those of neighboring Southeast Asian countries. Though Inner Mongolia is largely Han, it contains the bulk of China's Mongol minority. The two most significant minority regions, however, are Sinkiang and Tibet, which are also the regions that have given Peking the most trouble.

Sinkiang resembles Central Asia more than it does China proper. Its northern part consists of great mountain plains inhabited by Kazakh and Mongol herdsmen; its southern part consists of deserts and oases inhabited by Uighurs, ethnically close to the Uzbeks of the Soviet Union. Until its conquest by the K'ang-hsi Emperor in the seventeenth century, Sinkiang was ruled by a number of small sheikhdoms, but China's political presence in Sinkiang was not new. As early as the Han Dynasty the Chinese had extended control over large areas of what is now Sinkiang. Some of the most ancient relics of Chinese civilization have been unearthed in Sinkiang, notably at Khotan and Turfan. In the latter part of the nineteenth century a great rebellion led by the Moslem Ya'qub Beg broke out, which was finally suppressed by Manchu arms.

As Russia moved into Central Asia, her influence began to spread into Sinkiang, where Russian colonies arose, largely made up of "Old Believers" (also called "Old Ritualists," from the Russian *Raskolniki, i.e.,* "dissenters," they were members of a rigoristic schismatic sect which originated in seventeenth-century Russia to protest the Patriarch Nikon's liturgical reforms and the Czars' Europeanizing policy; they subsequently split into several small sects). Further immigration of Russians took place after the October Revolution, notably of Tatars and Uzbeks who were opposed to the Revolution and its secularizing tendencies. The former, in particular, have played a notable role in the political life of Sinkiang. During the 1930s Soviet influence was strong as a result of collaboration with the then warlord of Sinkiang, Sheng Shih-ts'ai. During the war an independent Communist movement developed in the northern Ili region. The Chinese Communists occupied the region with difficulty. Though they reached agreement with the Ili insurgents, other groups, notably the Kazakhs, continued resistance. Many fled to Pakistan.

The Chinese Communists have generally followed Soviet nationality policy: national cultures have been encouraged, minority individuals have been recruited into political positions, special developmental programs for minorities have been instituted. Friction, however, continued in Sinkiang. From the time of the occupation the People's Liberation Army maintained large garrisons in Sinkiang, and many of the huge state farms which arose in Sinkiang were operated by the PLA. Nevertheless, by the mid-1950s calm appeared to prevail, and the Chinese authorities allowed some foreigners to visit the region.

Despite periodic attacks on "local nationalism," the most serious trouble began as a result of the Sino-Soviet dispute. In April and May 1962 thousands of Sinkiang citizens, notably Kazakhs, fled across the border into the Soviet Union. The cause of the flight is still unclear. The Chinese accused the Soviets of having stirred up trouble, and the latter retorted by claiming that the Chinese were trying to suppress the minorities. Whether there was some relationship between the Kazakhs' flight to the Soviet Union and a similar and almost simultaneous exodus of people to Hong Kong is also not known. Undoubtedly, one of the underlying causes was the rapidly growing immigration to Sinkiang of Chinese from China proper. Sinkiang has something of a "California" quality: it is a rich frontier land which, if adequately irrigated, could support a much larger population than it does now. It has some of China's richest oil deposits and has become a major center of her atomic energy program. The local population has always feared that someday they might be outnumbered by the Chinese. Just as New York City has provided California with many of its immigrants, so today Shanghai sends a steady stream of young people into distant Sinkiang.

Tibet, though comparable in size to Sinkiang, is of a different order. It is still of little economic value to China, since most of it consists of uninhabited wastelands, where aggressive nomadic tribes, like the Ngoloks and Khampas, wander. The settled part of the country is to the south, bordering on India. Just as Islam characterizes Sinkiang, Lamaist Buddhism characterizes Tibet. The Chinese assumed suzerainty over Tibet in the seventeenth century, but were largely content to control from afar; the land was governed by a theocracy centered on the Dalai Lama in Lhasa. Though Tibet was traditionally oriented toward India (its script is of Indian origin), no Indian state made any attempt to extend its control onto the Tibetan highlands. The establishment of British rule in India, however, led to a gradual penetration of British political and Indian economic influence into Tibet. Sikkim and Bhutan, small Lamaist principalities, became British protectorates. The so-called McMahon Line, drawn at the Simla Conference in 1913–1914, set up a delimited border between Tibet and India, though no Chinese government ever formally accepted that delimitation.

Tibet remained quiet until Chinese Communist armies approached its borders in 1949. Alarmed, the Lhasa authorities prepared to send diplomatic missions to the United States, Britain, India, and Nepal to seek support. The Tibetans also entered into negotiations with the Chinese Communists. In October 1950, almost simultaneously with their entry into the Korean War, the Chinese invaded and occupied Tibet. Even after Communist occupation, however, Tibet enjoyed a special status. The Dalai Lama remained as ruler (though sharing his power with the more pro-Chinese Panchen Lama), and the basic structure of Tibetan society continued more or less intact. Sino-Indian relations over Tibet were good. In 1954 India signed a treaty with China which accepted Chinese claims to Tibet and withdrew all previous Indian rights to maintain military forces in Tibet. In the mid-1950s, when the Chinese built a third road to Tibet, leading from Western Sinkiang through the disputed Aksai-Chin region, India did not protest openly.

In March 1959 a great rebellion, whose cause is unclear, broke out in Tibet, and the Dalai Lama fled to India. The Tibetans had always been suspicious of Chinese intentions, and their worries were increased by the intensity of the Great Leap Forward. Moreover, the Chinese were having increasing trouble with tribal guerrillas, notably Khampas, who were attacking Chinese supply convoys, allegedly with arms dropped by foreign planes. The flight of the Dalai Lama to India with thousands of other Tibetans aroused much sympathy in India, and there can be little doubt that the Tibetan Rebellion was the factor that sparked the deterioration of Sino-Indian relations. By the summer of 1959 there were border incidents.

The border conflict, in words and deeds, continued over the next years. Despite pleas on both sides to settle the dispute, neither the Chinese nor the Indians would move from their basic positions: each claimed the disputed territory for itself. In October 1962 the Chinese launched a sudden but limited attack on India in the Ladakh and the Northeast Frontier Agency areas (NEFA). The Indians were routed, while the Chinese suffered minimal losses. With that attack Sino-Indian relations reached a nadir from which they have not recovered to this day.

In both Sinkiang and Tibet the minority and the border problems are related, with ideology an apparent third factor complicating the situation. The Sino-Soviet ideological dispute is well known, but less known is the fact that the Chinese have also waged an ideological conflict with India. India has been taunted for her neutralism, and in particular for her economic dependence on the United States. As Western nations have regarded India as the counter-model to China, the Chinese have portrayed India as the wrong model for underdeveloped countries to follow. Although the Sino-Indian border conflict arose from concrete issues between the two countries, it is likely that ideological factors bound up with India's relations and China's quarrel with the Soviet Union played a part.

In recent years the Chinese have strengthened their position in Sinkiang and in Tibet; the political system prevailing in China proper has been fully introduced into both areas. In Tibet the rebellion was followed by a full-scale land reform which appears to have broken the power of the traditional monastic theocracy. The Chinese are obviously not happy about the world image created by minority resistance within China. Thus, in past years, they have made great efforts to assuage discontent and once again bring about stability.

&Taiwan

TAIWAN is a province of China, a point on which Peking and Taipei have been in consistent accord. Traditionally under Chinese rule, Taiwan (called Formosa, the beautiful isle, by the Portuguese) was ceded to Japan in 1895, and restored to China in 1945 in accordance with the Cairo Conference agreements of 1943. In 1949 it became the location of the Nationalist government, which still bears the name Republic of China. Since both the Peking and the Taipei governments claim jurisdiction over all of China, there is no dispute between them on Taiwan's legal status.

An island about half the size of Ireland with a population of thirteen million, Taiwan enjoys natural advantages which helped economic progress during the period of Japanese rule and now help under Nationalist rule. The American-aided land reform played a major role in Taiwan's remarkable agricultural development. In recent years, industry has made considerable progress, turning Taiwan into one of Asia's more prosperous regions. As Robert Scalapino, Professor of Political Science at the University of California, points out however, "this rich island would have a fairly bright economic future if it did not face a population explosion on the one hand, and unrealistic military-political ambitions on the other." The huge military establishment Taipei supports puts an immense burden on its own economic resources and those supplied from the United States.

Despite its good economic prospects, Taiwan poses major political problems. Its part in the relationship between the United States and Communist China is discussed in the section on Sino-American relations (see pp. 295–302). Taiwan's main internal political problems, as Joyce K. Kallgren, Professor of Political Science at the University of California (Davis), notes, lie in the regime's return-to-the-Mainland ideology: "either we exist to return to the Mainland or we have no existence worth mentioning." With the exception of the Taiwanese nationalists, every major political group in Taiwan is committed to this ideology. Now, with the waning of the former, the voices of Taiwanese separatism have become weaker than ever before.

There is no doubt that the majority of the Mainlanders, who still keep their distance from the native Taiwanese, live for the day when they can return to their Mainland homes, an end to which Taipei maintains an immense military establishment with which year after year it proclaims its intention to recover the Mainland. Yet aside from a few commando raids and periodic shelling from the offshore islands, the Nationalists have been militarily inactive since their coming to Taiwan. Even with strong American military support, the chances of the Nationalists to mount an invasion of the China coast are almost zero.

A war between China and the United States would obviously alter the Nationalists' military prospects. From the moment of their arrival on Taiwan, the Nationalists expressed the hope for World War III as their best chance for getting back. Yet despite Chinese intervention in the Korean War, the United States, disregarding the urgings of certain conservative American military leaders, refused to invite Nationalist participation. When the Republican Administration of Dwight D. Eisenhower "unleashed" Chiang Kai-shek, nothing happened. The Nationalists still hold the offshore islands of Quemoy and Matsu which they have fortified into almost impregnable bastions, but they can hardly serve as springboards for an invasion. A curious truce now prevails in the Taiwan Straits. Shelling still goes on, but with leaflets rather than shells as ammunition. Communist and Nationalist fishing boats do not interfere with each other. Occasionally something dramatic happens, as when, in 1965, the Communists shot down a Nationalist plane carrying three Communist defectors to Taiwan. But things are generally quiet.

Vietnam appeared to change the situation: "the Vietnam crisis offered renewed hope to those seeking to invigorate the Mainland-return philosophy." If a war between China and America should break out over Vietnam, the chances for the

Nationalists to become active allies of the United States are good. Yet the Taiwan government is not directly involved in the Vietnam war. The United States has solicited South Korean troops to fight in South Vietnam, but it has invited none from Taiwan. The South Vietnamese government remains cautious in its relations with Taipei. Apparently, the United States does not now wish to complicate the South Vietnamese situation by the presence of Nationalist troops.

Like Peking, Taipei is also facing a succession crisis. Chiang Kai-shek is even older than Mao Tse-tung, and like his mortal enemy, he has been giving much thought to the problem of succession. Chiang too has managed to act as a bridge between contending factions, and his disappearance could lead to a struggle for power.

Since there is little sympathy for the so-called "two China" policy anywhere in Taiwan, it would appear that the future of Taiwan will remain closely linked to the course of Sino-American relations and to internal changes both on the Mainland and on Taiwan.

Since many in America argue as to what "we can do about Taiwan," it would be well to note the words of a group of Chinese intellectuals on Taiwan in an open letter to Americans:

> We also want to make clear that we Chinese can set-
> tle our domestic affairs . . . and we are confident no one
> can succeed in ultimately selling us out. And we solemnly
> declare that we have no wish to see the United States go
> to war with the Chinese Communists (*Central Daily,* May
> 25, 1966).

Whatever Taiwan's international role in the Sino-American relationship, one must remember that although Peking and Taipei are still in a state of civil war, bloodshed is not the only possible relationship between the two.

ROBERT A. SCALAPINO *
Communist China and Taiwan

Prior to a discussion of our China policy, it would be well to examine current trends in Taiwan, which is under the control of the National Government.

(a) Taiwan remains heavily dependent upon American aid. The huge sums given in the last decade have helped to produce substantial improvements in the Taiwan economy as in its military defenses. Certain difficult economic problems, however, remain and cannot be solved under present conditions. Since 1948, the United States has extended over one billion dollars to the National Government. On a per capita basis, few countries in the world have received so much American aid.

Taiwan did not enter the postwar era without advantages. Progress under Japan had been extensive. Prior to World War II, the Taiwanese had a standard of living second only to that of Japan itself in Asia. The people had acquired many industrial and agrarian skills. The years immediately after 1945, however, were years of chaos. Wartime damage and disorganization produced near-collapse. The early Nationalist era complicated rather than solved economic and political problems. Not until the end of 1952 did Taiwan reach prewar levels of production in industry.

Both industrial and agrarian gains have been substantial in the last seven years. Industrial production has risen about 80 per cent since 1952. The emphasis has been chiefly upon those light industries suitable to island resources such as processing industries and textiles. Major increases have also been registered in electric power, chemicals, and metal products. This stress

* Robert A. Scalapino, "Communist China and Taiwan," in *United States Foreign Policy—Asia* (Submitted to the Senate Committee on Foreign Relations by Conlon Associates, January 19, 1960), pp. 14–17.

upon mining and industrial production must continue in Taiwan. There is no other feasible approach to the economic problems of the island. Unless remedial measures are taken, the population density of Taiwan may become one of the highest in the world; it is already greater than that of Japan. Ten and one half million people live on less than fourteen thousand square miles, with more than two thirds of the island being mountainous and unsuited for cultivation. All available land is being used intensively. And the population is increasing at a rate of 3.5 per cent annually—one of the highest rates in Asia. The growing labor force must be accommodated through industrialization.

The gross national product of Taiwan increased substantially between 1950 and 1956, and is probably rising at a rate of at least 4 to 5 per cent annually at present. While industrial gains account for much of this expansion, agrarian output still contributes over one and a half times as much as industry to the national product. Production in agriculture has also improved as a result of better seeds, more effective irrigation, extensive use of fertilizer, and new cultivation methods. Some rural mechanization is beginning. Socioeconomic conditions in the rural areas have greatly improved, aided by the 1953 land-reform program and the excellent work of the Sino-American Joint Commission on Rural Reconstruction. Taiwan and Japan are notable examples of what can be accomplished by land reform in non-Communist Asia. Nearly 75 per cent of the Taiwanese rural families were affected by land redistribution or rental reduction. Tenant-cultivated land was reduced from 41 to 16 per cent of the total land under cultivation. Today approximately 80 per cent of rural families own all or part of their land, while 20 per cent are tenants or hired hands. The Joint Commission has supplemented this basic change through an effective program of technical assistance and social services in the rural areas.

Rural living standards in Taiwan are undoubtedly high and in the cities also economic conditions for the common man are generally improved over earlier periods. However, this should not obscure certain basic problems that have social and political as well as economic implications:

1. Taiwan supports a huge army in proportion to the size of its population. Despite the fact that military pay is extremely

low, the total costs constitute a heavy drain, and will continue
to do so unless and until the military force is reduced in size.

2. In addition to its military forces, the National Government maintains a sizable bureaucracy. This is partly to take
care of the mainland refugees. Most of the two million refugees
presently in Taiwan must be supported directly or indirectly by
the government. The heads of family are either attached to the
civil government, to the military services, or to such occupations
as university teaching. Some hold straight sinecures or pensions.
The socioeconomic problems herein contained are grave. On the
one hand, most of the refugees are deeply unhappy with their
present economic lot. Official salaries and wages in all of the
above fields are woefully inadequate. Indeed, Taiwan has witnessed a great leveling process, whereby the common man,
particularly the farmer, has been brought up in standards while
most of the elite, transplanted from the mainland, have come
down. One can hear bitter complaints from the latter that they
have lost everything and that most of the wealth belongs to the
Taiwanese. This has affected morale, efficiency, and even honesty
in government circles. Many of the children from these groups,
moreover, seeing few opportunities ahead, are desperately anxious to emigrate to the West. On the other hand, not a few
Taiwanese feel that they have to support a large number of "un-
productive" people, and at the same time are denied access to
official positions, and thus to the social and political status some
of them desire.

3. Under these general conditions, serious inflation is always a threat, and the government, remembering the economic
debacle on the Mainland, does worry about this problem. The
price index continues to rise rather steadily, however, and it is
difficult under the circumstances to keep inflation moderate.

4. For political and cultural reasons, the government is
quite unwilling to support any program of birth control, and
thus this problem is becoming ever more critical. Unless economic development can move much more rapidly than in the
past, underemployment and unemployment will advance. There
is a special problem with respect to the intellectual elite. High-
school and college graduates are not finding sufficient outlet at
present for their training and talents. A dissatisfied, displaced
young intellectual class is developing.

5. Foreign investment has increased and can be of assistance. However, overbureaucratization, limited markets, and political uncertainties combine to discourage it. Changes have been proposed which may ameliorate the former difficulty, but the latter one will remain.

Most of the serious economic problems of Taiwan have a close connection with politics. This rich island would have a fairly bright economic future if it did not face a population explosion on the one hand, and unrealistic military-political ambitions on the other. If the population problem were tackled seriously, and if the military forces were reduced to dimensions fitting the defense needs of Taiwan, there could be optimism concerning the economic prospects. Otherwise, the future is cloudy notwithstanding the impressive gains of the recent past and the prospects of continuing American aid.

(b) The political situation in Taiwan has mixed elements of stability and instability. The elements of instability are sufficient to make a serious crisis at some unexpected point conceivable. On balance, however, the elements of stability seem to predominate, and politics on Taiwan will probably undergo an evolutionary development, barring international conflict. The following factors deserve close attention:

1. The Kuomintang remains an elitist party with limited public appeal and with serious factional problems. After its Mainland defeat, the Kuomintang conducted its own "self-criticism" and "rectification" campaigns. Grave shortcomings were admitted and a call to Spartanism was issued. The experience of total defeat was not without some benefits to the Party; many opportunists and unsavory elements disappeared along with good men. Among the leaders remaining, a sizable number are dedicated, sincere, and able. In the last decade, they have lived modestly, worked to the extent possible, and sought to vindicate a movement that once burned brightly.

While their efforts have borne some fruit, various problems remain. The Party still tends to fall between two stools. It does not allow the range of political freedom and competition associated with political democracy on the one hand, and it does not possess the ruthlessness, dynamism, and efficiency of Communist totalitarianism on the other. Power seems held at the moment by rather tired hands.

Essentially, the Kuomintang continues to follow the Communist organizational model which it acquired shortly after World War I. It has made some progress in establishing cell organizations throughout the island and channeling political action through them. There is little indication, however, that the party has really appealed to the Taiwanese, or that it has genuine mass support. Meanwhile, factionalism within the Party continues to be very strong. The internal struggle for position and power can probably be contained as long as Chiang Kai-shek remains active, but the question of succession looms increasingly large.

A deepening power struggle within the Kuomintang could produce various possibilities: further flights to the West by unhappy or discouraged elements; defections to the Communists; the use of the army for internal political purposes; a broader appeal on the part of some faction or factions to the Taiwanese people for support. These possibilities are not mutually exclusive. Flights to the West by prominent Party men have taken place in the past and, indeed, irrespective of political conditions, a growing number of Mainland refugees will seek opportunities for emigration as hope of returning home recedes.

The Communists have made a definite bid for a bloodless victory on Taiwan. Their message has been "Come home and all will be forgiven." Lavish promises of pardons and positions have been made to any who will forsake American imperialism and return to the motherland. The strategy is obvious: to exploit Party cleavages, refugee fears of being absorbed by the Taiwanese, and the declining morale of people who must face the increasing probability that they cannot go back to China under Nationalist banners. It is also a clever method of trying to undercut any possible change in American policy. But there is no evidence that it is likely to achieve its objectives. Some defection to the Communists is conceivable, but only a few refugees will ever become so desperate or so angry as to take this kind of chance.

It is much more probable that a Party struggle at some point will involve the greater utilization of the Taiwanese. Even the use of the army internally, or the use of such groups as the Youth Corps would represent a trend in this direction. But there may also be an appeal issued in broader political terms, a turning outward on the part of some Party elements to the public, in the hope of getting the support necessary to sustain their position. Thus increasing democratization could occur under the Kuomintang, but if it does, it is likely to produce new political crises. Some of these will almost certainly reflect the unresolved differences between the Taiwanese and the Mainlanders.

2. Personal relations between the Mainland refugees and Taiwanese have probably improved in recent years. Various channels of communication have been established, and cultural links have been forged. Strong elements of differences and distrust still exist, however, and the largest gap between these two groups can be spelled out in one word: commitment. The Taiwanese are committed to Taiwan; the great majority of the refugees are still committed to returning home, or this failing, to emigrating elsewhere.

Refugee-Taiwanese relations constitute a troubled and complex aspect of politics in Taiwan. There are two million Mainland refugees and eight and a half million Taiwanese. Of the same race and general culture, these two groups have differences not easy to bridge. In the last fifteen years, their relations have been marked by both revolution and evolution; which will prevail in the future? Today, Taiwanese revolutionary activities are mainly centered abroad, in Peiping, Tokyo, and the United States. The Peiping operation is naturally Communist and seems to have little, if any, support. The organizations in Japan and the United States are devoted to Taiwanese independence. They are manned by a small band of intellectuals, mainly overseas students very reminiscent of the Chinese Nationalist movement itself fifty years ago. These groups claim wide underground support in Taiwan, an assertion difficult to prove under present conditions.

In all probability most Taiwanese would regard "independence" in some form as their ideal. Pro-Communist sentiment at present is negligible; Nationalist support fairly limited; and nostalgia for the Japanese era rather more widespread but perhaps strongest among the older groups, and fading. As has been noted, the issue of commitment is a prominent one separating Taiwanese from refugees. For example, are "the local people" really interested in fighting to "return" to a place where they have never been? Then there are the deeply felt grievances held by upper-class Taiwanese over their lack of social and political recognition. The refugees are a dispossessed elite, and they cannot avoid thinking of themselves as an elite; moreover, they must have some means of sustenance, and their profession has generally been officeholding.

Still, there are fairly good chances that this general problem will be solved by evolution. As long as economic conditions remain reasonably firm and some social mobility is possible, there will be no mass revolt. Meanwhile, a dual process of acculturation and assimilation is taking place. The acculturation affects mainly the Taiwanese. In place of the Japanese past, a modernized Chinese culture is being implanted via the new educational system and other forms of cultural interaction. The refugees are not unaffected by this process, however, for the borrowings both from Japan and the West are substantial. And at the same time, assimilation is beginning, a process whereby the dominant Taiwanese population is starting to absorb the refugee minority through intermarriage and a variety of other ways.

These developments provide the socioeconomic basis for an evolutionary change in politics on Taiwan. In the case of serious economic reversals, military overcommitment, or continued political rigidity, the Kuomintang will suffer further slippage, and Taiwanese resistance might take revolutionary forms. Under present trends, however, gradualism will prevail, with increased pressures for local autonomy and expanded social and political rights. One prediction is fairly safe: either Taiwan will be joined with Mainland China or the process of Taiwanization will continue. In the concrete terms of the present, if Taiwan does not go to the Communists, it will go increasingly to the Taiwanese.

(c) The Nationalist military force today remains largely an unknown quantity. Increasingly, it is manned by Taiwanese personnel. It has not been tested in large-scale combat and opinions on its capacities and morale differ. It is safe to say, however, that it is much more than adequate to defend Taiwan at present, and much less than adequate to engage the Communists on the continent. Already, Taiwanese recruits constitute a substantial bloc in the Nationalist Army. Their numbers can only rise. There is a small, well-trained air force, and it is possibly the most effective of the three services. All units are equipped with modern American weapons.

Taiwan could be defended adequately at present with a substantially smaller force. Until recently, however, the Nationalists had nearly one third of their active forces on the islands of Quemoy-Matsu where they are much more vulnerable. Over the next decade, it must be assumed that the military balance with respect to Taiwan will shift. The Chinese Communists will certainly seek weapons and strength attuned to their ambitions. If Taiwan has to be defended militarily, the ultimate burden will surely fall upon the United States in company with the Taiwanese. . . .

JOYCE K. KALLGREN *

Vietnam and Politics in Taiwan

The developments relative to Taiwan in 1965 contain one element of supreme irony. In a year when the "two China" alternative was clearly a specter in United Nations debate and when there was considerable evidence of maturation in a Nationalist commitment to the future of the island, the Vietnam crisis offered renewed hope to those seeking to invigorate the Mainland-return philosophy. In recent years, the Nationalists have been realistic in emphasizing that their opportunity will come within the context of a larger international confrontation. Could the Vietnam crisis be such a confrontation? Last year, the United States, the People's Republic of China, and the South Vietnamese government were cautious in their relations with Taiwan

* Joyce K. Kallgren, "Vietnam and Politics in Taiwan," *Asian Survey,* VI, 1, January 1966, pp. 28–33.

and thus kept Nationalist China a relative observer to the struggle. The Vietnam crisis, however, will serve to reinforce those factions on Taiwan who oppose the mounting costs of an ongoing modernization program on the island, and in the future may lead the Nationalists to a more direct participation in the Southeast Asian crisis.

A resolution of the status of Taiwan is among the most difficult problems in international affairs. The "two China" alternative has been seen largely at the level of state-to-state relations where both Chinas have precluded its adoption. In 1965 the policy assumed importance in the United Nations General Assembly debate. Through political negotiations, plus the intransigence of the People's Republic of China, the Nationalists retained the Chinese seat in an extraordinarily close vote. The Kuomintang analyze their future as intimately related to the African states' vote and recognize the difficulties that beset their cause, especially by virtue of the increased political prestige of the Communist Chinese resulting from nuclear developments. For the present, the Nationalists continue to restate their claims, expand emphasis upon the technical-aid program in Africa, and begin to downgrade the importance of United Nations membership in preparation for possible ejection or withdrawal. Whether or not the General Assembly will ultimately opt for some form of a "two China" policy is not clear, nor should the response of the Nationalist government if confronted with a United Nations decision be assumed, since there is ample evidence that the government is not a total prisoner of its philosophy. The final decision will take into account the importance of UN membership, the relative positions of the Nationalists and the Communists, and the domestic situation on Taiwan.

For the present, the important dangers posed by the publicly maintained Nationalist position on "two Chinas" are these: first, there are the potential consequences to specific military programs that the government routinely supports; secondly, there are potential repercussions in those internal policies derived from the commitment to return to the Mainland. With regard to military activities, the Nationalist government supervises an ongoing program of guerrilla operations on the Mainland designed to foment unrest and sabotage. It also gives continual support for remnant Chinese forces in Burma (more for their symbolic than for their military value). The Nationalists routinely headline any military encounters with the People's Republic of China and continue a program of Mainland overflights. They encourage defection from Communist military units and occasionally report success. All of these activities are designed to give substance to their ultimate goal of a return.

Obvious difficulties preclude more aggressive and more effective actions. In addition to the overwhelming Communist military strength specifically deployed in the provinces facing Taiwan, there is the presence of the American Seventh Fleet patrolling the Taiwan Straits and the United States-Republic of China agreements which provide military assistance for defensive purposes only and require mutual consultation prior to any alterations in the agreement. Thus the Nationalists consistently maintain that their guerrilla operations are not financed through Mutual Assistance funds (though the recent India-Pakistan clashes illustrate the difficulties of placing effective restrictions upon the uses of military equipment). The American policy of limiting aid to military items essentially defensive in nature is a more effective restraint. The Chinese Air Force therefore received F-105 fighter planes in 1965 to replace the older F-86s but their bombers and transports remain antiquated.

Against this background of military preparedness, the Nationalist government is at once circumspect about the necessity for an American participation in Nationalists plans yet vigorously aggressive in interpreting international events. For example, Chiang Ching-kuo, Defense Minister, specifically disclaimed the Nationalist intention to start a large-scale war or to involve American troops. At the same time, a continuing thread in Nationalist statements, specifically in those of Madame Chiang Kai-shek, is the necessity to meet the challenge in Vietnam, and the potentially dangerous consequences of Communist Chinese domination of Southeast Asia. Other Chinese statements indicated support for an air strike on Mainland China's nuclear installations. A public tie between Nationalist power and Vietnam was rather clearly implied by a proposal of Senator Dirksen, who called for an increase of one hundred millions dollars in the foreign-aid bill to modernize the Nationalist military establishment. The proposal was withdrawn when State and Defense representatives assured him that if Nationalist forces were used in Vietnam they would be suitably equipped. As the Vietnam struggle mounts, the connection between Vietnam and the Nationalist military may well be tempting.

The Vietnam struggle had other implications for Nationalist Chinese foreign policy in 1965: Nationalist leaders engaged in discussion with South Vietnamese Premier Nguyen Cao Ky about the types of aid that Taiwan might provide. No military participation was involved but the Nationalists committed themselves to the provision of technical assistance and the South Vietnamese military have indicated an interest in the psychological warfare programs developed on Taiwan. Throughout the year, the Kuomintang pursued its goal of establishing an effective anti-Communist alliance, specifically involving the South Koreans, the Philippines, Taiwan, and South Vietnam. The need for American participation is obvious and apparently has yet to be obtained. In 1965, an additional reason for seeking international support and commitment from Asian neighbors may well have been to hedge against the possibility of an unfavorable decision within the United Nations.

The Kuomintang has always recognized that an independent Formosa movement is a threat both to the political hegemony of the Mainlanders and to the validity of Nationalist claims to represent China. Last year they achieved a notable victory that weakened any such claim. For some years, two Formosan exile groups, operating in Japan, have tried to keep alive a Formosan independence movement and a shadow government. The older of these groups was headed by Thomas Liao (Liao Wen-i). In 1965, after extensive negotiations, the Nationalists induced Liao to return to Taiwan, eschew all separatist programs, and call for unity against the Mainland. His subsequent statements from Taiwan and the propaganda uses made of his "change of heart" have done much to weaken the Formosan case.

Undoubtedly, Liao's return is not solely explained by the wish to see his aged mother nor his desire to recover extensive land holdings confiscated by the government. Certainly his defection surprised his remaining supporters and left the group leaderless. Shortly after Liao's return, Mr. Richard Koo, newly elected President of the Formosan Association, the second émigré organization, visited the United States and apparently received little support. Internally the Nationalists exact a heavy penalty from those convicted of supporting independence activities. In April it was announced that Professor P'eng Ming-min of National Taiwan University had received an eight-year prison sentence for his alleged activities in support of Formosan independence. Though the sentence is obviously severe for Professor P'eng, it is modest if treason were really the issue. Here, as in a number of other cases, the trial and sentence are designed to underscore the government's determination to curtail any activities that cast doubt upon the Nationalist legitimacy more as a matter of politics than as punishment for betrayal.

An important byproduct of the Nationalist claim of representation is the preservation of Kuomintang hegemony in what is effectively a one-party state. Given the age of the top leaders of the government and the Party, the Nationalists (as well as their Mainland opponents) have the problem of political succession. In Taiwan there is infinitely less discussion of the topic although perhaps no less concern. In view of the rigidity of the governmental and Party structure, cues as to change in political strength are elusive and difficult to quantify, but in 1965 there was one major and definitive change.

Underneath the omnipresence of Chiang Kai-shek there have long been power groups emerging whose influence could be expected to grow as Chiang aged and receded further from effective political control. The two major forces were those of the General's eldest son, Chiang Ching-kuo, and the Generalissimo's long-time colleague, Ch'en Ch'eng. In recent years the balance, despite outward appearances, has been moving in Chiang Ching-kuo's direction. The contest ended last March with the death of Ch'en Ch'eng, though his virtual elimination from real power had been signaled in the January 13th appointment of Chiang Ching-kuo as Minister of Defense (aging Yü Ta-wei remains in the Cabinet as Minister without Portfolio). Other new appointments announced simultaneously with that of Chiang, namely the appointment of well-regarded K. T. Li as Minister of Economic Affairs and that of Yen Chen-hsing as Minister of Education, reinforced Chiang's strength.

Since Chiang [Ching-kuo] is comparatively unknown in the United States, and has certainly been the center of controversy in the past, it was not surprising that he should visit the United States. In September [1965] he arrived for a series of meetings that included discussion with military and intelligence officials in Washington as well as an appointment with President Johnson. The official Taiwanese press thought the trip had served to dispel the image of Chiang Ching-kuo as a stranger and to reinforce the feeling of identity of interest between China and the United States. Despite the rise of Ching-kuo it seems unlikely that he will be elected Vice-President in next year's election. His father is already being urged to run again for office, but the most likely decision in connection with the Vice-Presidency is the selection of an older political figure. Such a decision would be an interim one, leaving open the question of reconciling the political situation upon the death of Chiang himself.

The realism of Nationalist interest and planning for the future of Taiwan was clearly demonstrated throughout the past year. The overt explanation for such a program is to demonstrate the skill that would be devoted to Chinese Mainland reconstruction after a successful campaign. In fact, Taiwanese developments do suggest considerable Nationalist ability and progress. Their application to the Mainland is another matter.

The Kuomintang modernization efforts started with two important advantages, specifically, a large pool of technical talent often in short supply in a developing country and the willingness of a foreign power to invest major amounts of aid. On June 30, 1965, the formal aid program ended. Though the Nationalist government may not be as sanguine as its American counterpart about the future problems of the island, Taiwan has moved with considerable success along a number of fronts, specifically agricultural production and ownership, effective industrialization, and the creation of a climate favorable to foreign investors. On the last point, much of Taiwan's future will depend. In 1965, the Nationalists sought foreign loans and expanded trade, for example in the Sino-Japanese agreement of September 23rd, and the Australian-Republic of China of $5.5-million contract for trade. The government also implemented a long overdue program to encourage and develop technical skills on the island through the creation of academic centers in the field of physics, chemistry, biology, mathematics, and engineering research. The Nationalists revealed extensive planning for Taiwan's economic future that took cognizance of the changed circumstances resulting from the end of American economic aid. Both the National Nine Point Economic Program of May and the Taiwan Ten Year Program of August call for increased productivity, and a vigorous economic program to continue Taiwan's growth.

As industrialization has proceeded, the government has been deficient in planning and financing for welfare needs. Though the industrial hazards for individuals and families have grown, the Kuomintang has used financial limitations as an explanation for its modest programs. In March of last year, the government started large-scale planning for a number of social problems such as housing, employment, and welfare services. Later in the year, the provincial government announced an impressive program in industrial safety. In addition, the government decided to supplement very low government pay levels through the provision of extra bonuses. But such programs are very susceptible to the "guns and butter" dilemma.

The practicality that has characterized much of Taiwan's economic development in recent years would suggest that the government is prepared to carry through its planning on a realistic basis. Other indicators in 1965 reinforce the impression that the government is carefully balancing current demands with its long-range hopes. Exit and entrance visa procedures have been simplified to aid Taiwan's tourist trade. The press is finally editorializing about the desirability of scholarly research dealing with the Mainland (such study has been under way for some years). Much of the economic planning on Taiwan has been done without fear of compromising the political position that "return" is inevitable. The rising standard of income on Taiwan, second only to Japan, is testimony to growth. In 1966, as the tasks of financing social welfare become clear, the government will face another turning point.

Many of the events of 1965 would augur for reasonableness and moderation and hence an optimistic appraisal of the New Year. But the current of leadership statements about Vietnam and nuclear development may well reflect the expectation that the Vietnam crisis offers the last opportunity for the Mainlanders now in exile. If such an expectation is translated into policy, domestic achievements may be jeopardized or curtailed precisely at the moment when progress on Taiwan would give a more positive impression within the United Nations. It would be a tragedy for Taiwan if the illusion of a Mainland return compromised the potential of the island.

🦋 Vietnam and the
Sino-American Confrontation

UNTIL RECENTLY, the United States and China were not directly involved over Vietnam. In the Geneva negotiations over Vietnam in 1954 and in the Geneva Conference of 1961–1962 on Laos, the Soviet Union acted as the leader of the Communist bloc, with the Chinese supporting the Soviet positions. However, after the bombing of North Vietnam began, China refused all support for initiatives seeking negotiations, in particular any Soviet-directed effort to convene a new Geneva Conference. Ever since the beginning of escalation, the Chinese accused the United States of gradually moving toward armed conflict with China. On the other side, the United States increasingly used the terms "Chinese expansionism" and "Chinese aggression" to designate the root cause of the Vietnamese war; it accused China of using Vietnam as a "testing ground" for wars of national liberation, support of which the Chinese proclaimed as a cardinal principle of Communist foreign policy. Thus, whether as testing ground for "American imperialism" or "Chinese expansionism," Vietnam brought the United States and China closer to the brink of war than at any time since the Quemoy crisis of 1958.

In the following selections, we present material from early 1966: Dean Rusk's analysis and defense of American policy in Vietnam; former Assistant Secretary of State for Far Eastern Affairs Roger Hilsman's critique of that policy; Chou En-lai's estimations of the future course of the Vietnam war; and Anna Louise Strong's analysis of the Vietnam war from the Chinese point of view.

Dean Rusk's statement, which James Reston called "the Rusk Doctrine," sets forth in direct terms the rationale for American involvement in Vietnam. Rusk notes that World War II "ripped apart a structure of power that had existed for a hundred years," followed by efforts of the Communist nations to exploit "the turmoil of a time of transition in an effort to extend Communist control into other areas of the world." Rusk then states the cardinal principle of American foreign policy: "that the Communist world should not be permitted to expand by overrunning one after another of the arrangements built during and since the war to mark the outer limits of Communist expansion by force." In sum, lines have been drawn throughout the world between the Communist and non-Communist world (the Iron Curtain in Europe, the Soviet boundaries in Asia, the 38th Parallel, the Formosa Straits, and of course the 17th Parallel dividing North from South Vietnam). Since, as Rusk sees it, the war in South Vietnam is an instance of aggression from the North, American attempts to defeat it are in accord with the stated cardinal principle of American foreign policy.

Rusk notes that the Sino-Soviet split is "one of the major political facts of our time," but whereas Moscow "has recognized that the Western Alliance cannot permit it to extend its dominion by force," "Peking . . . must learn that they cannot redraw the boundaries of the world by force." Thus, while not saying so directly, Rusk, in effect, identifies "Chinese expansionism" as the underlying cause of the Vietnamese war.

Hilsman appears to agree with Rusk on the matter of Chinese expansionism: ". . . no matter how wise and restrained the United States makes its policies, Chinese Communist ambitions may be so great that they will insist on a showdown." What is of gravest concern to Hilsman, however, is that "today, Communist China and the United States are on a collision course. The outcome can only be war." The theme of a "collision course" between China and America has been widely repeated in the United States. Hilsman notes that while the Russians are afraid of the holocaust of war, the Chinese appear to be unafraid, even of a nuclear confrontation with the United States.

To avoid the oncoming collision, Hilsman advocates a de-escalation of the war, notably through the termination of the bombing of North Vietnam, and initial moves to bring the Chinese closer into the international family of nations, resting his hopes for an eventual accommodation with China on the appearance of a "second echelon" of Chinese leaders who might take a more moderate approach to world problems.

Whereas both Rusk and Hilsman seem to agree on Chinese aggression as the main underlying cause of the Vietnamese war, they differ in the priorities assigned to American foreign-policy goals. Rusk argues that keeping South Vietnam out of Communist hands is the major goal of American policy in Southeast Asia. Hilsman implies that avoiding war with Communist China should have first priority, and recommends closer ties with the nationalist movements of Southeast Asia as a way of maintaining American influence in that part of the world.

Chou En-lai's speech, given in December 1965, begins with a prediction as to the future course of the war, in effect, a two-stage escalation. First, the United States would extend the war in and around the existing areas of conflict. But then, if this were to fail, "it is possible that in accordance with the objective laws governing the development of aggressive wars, U.S. imperialism will go a step further and extend its war of aggression to the whole of Indo-China and to China." What Chou implies is that the Vietnam war might be extended to China. He then states what China thinks correct policy toward the Vietnamese war should be on the part of the Communist countries: first, full-scale aid to North Vietnam and the National Liberation Front; second, ceasing of all efforts to bring about peace negotiations. Chou labeled Johnson's peace offensive a trick serving "only as a prelude and smokescreen in expanding its war"—another instance of "dual tactics," or "the two-handed policy."

It is clear that a wide chasm separates the positions of Rusk and Chou En-lai. Rusk argues flatly that the United States would not tolerate a Communist government in South Vietnam, while Chou argues that only complete American withdrawal with almost certain victory for the National Liberation Front is an acceptable condition for negotiations. These conditions seem to indicate no room for compromise, at least not between China and the United States. Thus, the key question, as both Hilsman and Chou En-lai indicate, is whether the war would finally turn into a Sino-American conflict. Again, Hilsman and Chou En-lai agree that it might well.

In late 1965 and early 1966 both the Chinese and the

American press spoke widely of the dangers of a collision course leading to war between the two countries. The Chinese challenged the Americans to attack, and the American press printed statements by leading American political figures about the probability of such a collision course in the event of a further escalation of the Vietnam war.

In her letter of April 1966 Anna Louise Strong, an American journalist who has lived in China for many years, elaborated on the then current Chinese position concerning the Vietnam war. By recapitulating the reasons for China's entry into the Korean War, she indicated under what conditions China would enter the Vietnam war. First, North Korea was overrun and requested Chinese intervention; second, China's own borders were threatened; third, MacArthur had indicated his intent to drive into Manchuria. In the context of the Vietnam war, Miss Strong appears to indicate that three circumstances would again provoke Chinese intervention: a direct threat to the existence and security of North Vietnam, an attack on China itself, and a conviction that American policies were leading directly to a planned armed confrontation with China.

Writing in the summer of 1966, we cannot know what the situation will be at the time of publication. Anna Louise Strong's statement—"even now it is hard to tell whether the U.S. ruling class really want the long war which the experts say it will take to subdue South Vietnam, or whether they are on a tiger and cannot dismount"—revealed something significant about the Chinese view of American actions in South Vietnam. Three not entirely incompatible options appeared to be available to the Americans in the summer of 1966: escalation of the war beyond South Vietnam, intensification of the war in South Vietnam, and the seeking of negotiations. The Chinese clearly did not believe that the United States had any serious intentions of seeking a negotiated solution, yet they were not at all sure which of the first two options the Americans would take up. The Chinese appeared to be saying: if you escalate the war, at some point we shall intervene; if you want to fight it out in South Vietnam, then you will have a protracted war of national liberation on your hands which in the end you will lose.

DEAN RUSK *

[*Testimony before the Senate Foreign
Relations Committee, February 18, 1966*]

Since World War II, which projected the United States into the role of major world power, we Americans have had to face a series of difficult tasks and trials. On the whole, we have faced them very well. Today we are facing another ordeal in Southeast Asia, which again is costing us both lives and treasure.

South Vietnam is a long way from the United States, and the issues posed may seem remote from our daily experience and our immediate interests. It is essential, therefore, that we clearly understand—and so far as possible agree on—our mission and purpose in that faraway land.

Why are we in Vietnam? Certainly we are not there merely because we have power and like to use it. We do not regard ourselves as the policeman of the universe. We do not go around the world looking for quarrels in which we can intervene.

Quite the contrary. We have recognized that, just as we are not gendarmes of the universe, neither are we the magistrate of the universe. If other governments, other institutions, or other regional organizations can find solutions to the quarrels which disturb the present scene, we are anxious to have this occur. But we are in Vietnam because the issues posed there are deeply intertwined with our own security and because the outcome of the struggle can profoundly affect the nature of the world in which we and our children will live.

The situation we face in Southeast Asia is obviously complex, but, in my view, the underlying issues are relatively simple and are utterly fundamental. I am confident that Americans, who have a deep and mature understanding of world responsibility, are fully capable of cutting through the underbrush of complex-

* Abridged from *U.S. News & World Report,* February 28, 1966.

ity and finding the simple issues which involve our largest interests and deepest purposes. I regard it, therefore, as a privilege to be able to discuss these problems with the Committee this morning—to consult with you and at the same time to try to clarify for the American people the issues we must squarely face.

I do not approach this task on the assumption that anyone, anywhere, has all the answers, or that all wisdom belongs to the Executive branch of the government, or even to the government itself. The questions at issue affect the well-being of all Americans, and I am confident that all Americans will make up their own minds in the tradition of a free and independent people. Yet those of us who have special responsibilities for the conduct of our foreign policy have had to think hard and deeply about these problems for a very long time. The President, his Cabinet colleagues, and the Congress, who share the weightiest responsibilities under our constitutional system, have come to certain conclusions that form the basis for the policies we are now pursuing.

Perhaps it is worth pointing out that those who are officially responsible for the conduct of our public affairs must make decisions—and must make decisions among existing alternatives. None of us in the Executive or the Legislative branch has fulfilled our responsibilities merely by formulating an opinion. We are required to decide what this nation shall do and shall not do, and are required to accept the consequences of our determinations.

What are our world security interests involved in the struggle in Vietnam? They cannot be seen clearly in terms of Southeast Asia only, or merely in terms of the events of the past few months. We must view the problem in perspective. We must recognize that what we are seeking to achieve in South Vietnam is part of a process that has continued for a long time—a process of preventing the expansion and extension of Communist domination by the use of force against the weaker nations on the perimeter of Communist power.

This is the problem as it looks to us. Nor do the Communists themselves see the problem in isolation. They see the struggle in South Vietnam as part of a larger design for the steady extension of Communist power through force and threat.

I have observed in the course of your hearings that some

objection has been raised to the use of the term "Communist aggression." It seems to me that we should not confuse ourselves or our people by turning our eyes away from what that phrase means. The underlying crisis of this postwar period turns about a major struggle over the very nature of the political structure of the world.

Before the guns were silent in World War II, many governments sat down and thought long and hard about the structure of international life, the kind of world which we ought to try to build, and wrote those ideas into the United Nations Charter. That Charter establishes an international society of independent states, large and small, entitled to their own national existence, entitled to be free from aggression, cooperating freely across national frontiers in their common interests, and resolving their disputes by peaceful means. But the Communist world has returned to its demand for what it calls a "world revolution," a world of coercion in direct contradiction to the Charter of the United Nations. There may be differences within the Communist world about methods and techniques and leadership within the Communist world itself, but they share a common attachment to their "world revolution" and to its support through what they call "wars of liberation."

So what we face in Vietnam is what we have faced on many occasions before—the need to check the extension of Communist power in order to maintain a reasonable stability in a precarious world. That stability was achieved in the years after the war by the valor of free nations in defending the integrity of postwar territorial arrangements. And we have achieved a certain stability for the last decade and a half. It must not be overthrown now.

Like so many of our problems today, the struggle in South Vietnam stems from the disruption of two world wars. The second World War completed a process begun by the first. It ripped apart a structure of power that had existed for a hundred years. It set in train new forces and energies that have remade the map of the world. Not only did it weaken the nations actively engaged in the fighting, but it had far-reaching secondary effects. It undermined the foundations of the colonial structures through which a handful of powers controlled one third of the world's population. And the winds of change and progress that have blown fiercely during the last twenty years have toppled those structures almost completely.

Meanwhile, the Communist nations have exploited the turmoil of a time of transition in an effort to extend Communist control into other areas of the world.

The United States first faced the menace of Communist ambition in Europe when one after another of the nations on the boundaries of the Soviet Union fell under the dominion of Moscow through the presence of the Red Army.

To check this tidal wave, the United States provided the Marshall Plan to strengthen the nations of Western Europe and then moved to organize with those nations a collective-security system through the North Atlantic Treaty Organization. As a result, the advance of Soviet Communist power was stopped, and the Soviet Union gradually adjusted its policies to this situation.

But within a year after the establishment of NATO, the Communists took over China. This posed a new and serious threat, particularly to those weak new nations of the Far East that had been formed out of colonial empires. The problems in Asia were, of course, different from those in Europe. But the result was much the same—instability, uncertainty, and vulnerability to both the bully and the aggressor. Western Europe, with its established governmental and traditional social institutions, recovered quickly. But certain of the new nations of Asia—particularly those that had not known self-government for a century or more—continued to face a far more formidable problem, which they still face.

The first test in Asia came in Korea when the United Nations forces—predominantly American—stopped the drive of Communist North Korea supported by material aid from the Soviet Union. It stopped the Chinese Army that followed. It brought to a halt the Communist effort to push out the line that had been drawn, and to establish Communist control over the Korean Peninsula.

We fought the Korean War—which, like the struggle in Vietnam, occurred in a remote area thousands of miles away— to sustain a principle vital to the freedom and security of America: the principle that the Communist world should not be permitted to expand by overrunning one after another of the arrangements built during and since the war to mark the outer limits of Communist expansion by force. . . .

In order to give support to the nations of Southeast Asia, the United States took the lead in the creation of an alliance embodied in a treaty and reinforced by a collective-security system known as SEATO—the Southeast Asia Treaty Organization. In this alliance, the United States joined with Great Britain, France, Australia, New Zealand, Thailand, Pakistan, and the Philippines to guarantee the security not only of the member nations, but also to come to the aid of certain protocol states and territories if they so requested.

South Vietnam was included in this protocol. The United States had not been a party to the agreements made in Geneva in 1954, which France had concluded with the Communist Vietnamese forces known as the Viet Minh. But the Under Secretary of State, Walter Bedell Smith, stated under instructions that the United States would not disturb the agreements and "would view any renewal of the aggression in violation of the . . . agreements with grave concern, and as seriously threatening international peace and security."

Under Secretary Smith's statement was only a unilateral declaration, but in joining SEATO the United States took a solemn treaty engagement of far-reaching effect. Article IV, paragraph 1, provides that "each party recognizes that aggression by means of armed attack . . . would endanger its own peace and safety, and agrees that it will in that event act to meet the common danger in accordance with its constitutional processes."

It is this fundamental SEATO obligation that has from the outset guided our actions in South Vietnam.

The language of this treaty is worth careful attention. The obligation it imposes is not only joint but several. The finding that an armed attack has occurred does not have to be made by a collective determination before the obligation of each member becomes operative. Nor does the treaty require a collective decision on actions to be taken to meet the common danger. If the United States determines that an armed attack has occurred against any nation to whom the protection of the treaty applies, then it is obligated "to act to meet the common danger" without regard to the views or actions of any other treaty member. . . .

These then are the commitments we have taken to protect South Vietnam as a part of protecting our own "peace and security." We have sent American forces to fight in the jungles of that beleaguered country because South Vietnam has, under the language of the SEATO Treaty, been the victim of "aggression by means of armed attack."

There can be no serious question as to the existence and nature of this aggression. The war is clearly an "armed attack," cynically and systematically mounted by the Hanoi regime against the people of South Vietnam.

The North Vietnamese regime has sought deliberately to confuse the issue by seeking to make its aggression appear as an indigenous revolt. But we should not be deceived by this subterfuge. It is a familiar Communist practice. Impeded in their efforts to extend their power by the use of classical forms of force, such as the invasion of Korea, the Communists have, over many years, developed an elaborate doctrine for so-called "wars of national liberation" to cloak their aggressions in ambiguity.

A "war of national liberation," in the Communist lexicon, depends on the tactics of terror and sabotage, of stealth and subversion. It has a particular utility for them, since it gives an advantage to a disciplined and ruthless minority, particularly in countries where the physical terrain makes clandestine infiltration relatively easy.

At the same time, the Communists have a more subtle reason for favoring this type of aggression. It creates in any situation a sense of ambiguity that they can exploit to their own advantage. . . .

Beginning over a year ago, the Communists apparently exhausted their reservoir of Southerners who had gone North. Since then the greater number of men infiltrated into the South have been native-born North Vietnamese. Most recently, Hanoi has begun to infiltrate elements of the North Vietnamese Army in increasingly larger numbers. Today, there is evidence that nine regiments of regular North Vietnamese forces are fighting in organized units in the South.

I have reviewed these facts—which are familiar enough to most of you—because, it seems to me, they demonstrate beyond question that the war in Vietnam is as much an act of outside aggression as though the Hanoi regime had sent an army across the 17th Parallel rather than infiltrating armed forces by stealth.

This point is important, since it goes to the heart of our own involvement. Much of the confusion about the struggle in South Vietnam has arisen over a failure to understand the nature of the conflict.

For if the war in South Vietnam were—as the Communists try to make it appear—merely an indigenous revolt, then the United States would not have its own combat troops in South Vietnam. But the evidence is overwhelming that it is, in fact, something quite different—a systematic aggression by Hanoi against the people of South Vietnam. It is one further effort by a Communist regime in one half of a divided country to take over the people of the other half at the point of a gun and against their will. . . .

I conclude, therefore, with certain simple points which are at the heart of the problem and at the heart of United States policy in South Vietnam:

(1) The elementary fact is that there is an aggression in the form of an armed attack by North Vietnam against South Vietnam.

(2) The United States has commitments to assist South Vietnam to repel this aggression.

(3) Our commitments to South Vietnam were not taken in isolation, but are a part of a systematic effort in the postwar period to assure a stable peace.

(4) The issue in Southeast Asia becomes worldwide because we must make clear that the United States keeps its word wherever it is pledged.

(5) No nation is more interested in peace in Southeast Asia or elsewhere than is the United States. If the armed attack against South Vietnam is brought to an end, peace can come very quickly. Every channel or forum for contact, discussion, or negotiation will remain active in order that no possibility for peace will be overlooked.

ROGER HILSMAN *

[*Testimony before the House Foreign
Affairs Committee, February 1, 1966*]

. . . Our fate and the fate of much of the world may well turn
on events in Asia, and our policy is now at a crossroads as momentous as any in our history.

The issue is both political and strategic, and it concerns a
long and ominous shadow cast over the whole of the great arc
of Asia from Japan and Korea in the North to the subcontinent
of India and Pakistan in the South—a shadow cast by Communist China, a nation of seven hundred million people and continental size whose energies and resources are directed by a
ruthless, ambitious leadership.

Today, Communist China and the United States are on a
collision course. The outcome can only be war.

Indeed, in the present situation the questions are only when
the war will come and under what circumstances—whether it
will come in ten or fifteen years and be fought with nuclear
weapons; whether it will be fought in the next year or two in the
limited arena of Southeast Asia as a bloody, hand-to-hand struggle against the awesome mass of Chinese manpower; or whether
it will be fought in the next year or two in a wider arena and on
a larger scale, in which case the question will turn on the use of
"battlefield" nuclear weapons and the role of the Soviet Union.
And what makes the whole issue so foreboding is that no matter
how wise and restrained the United States makes its policies,
Chinese Communist ambitions may be so great that they will insist on a showdown.

What should our policy toward Communist China be? In
1957, Secretary Dulles enunciated a policy toward Communist
China based on the assumption that Communism on the Main-

* Abridged from *ADA World Magazine*, n.d.

land was a "passing phase." The policy that flowed from that assumption was to do everything possible short of war to quicken its passing—rigid opposition in every way. "We owe it to ourselves, our allies, and the Chinese people," Mr. Dulles said, "to contribute to that passing."

In 1963, it was my great privilege to be the spokesman for a different United States policy, enunciated in a speech at San Francisco. This policy was based on what we had learned about the Chinese Communist regime in the six years following Mr. Dulles's speech—which was that, unfortunate though it may be, the Chinese Communist regime is not a "passing phase." Reviewing the history of failure of the Great Leap Forward and the commune program, the speech noted that the Mainland economy collapsed, but that the regime did not. "Nor was its authority," the speech continued, "effectively challenged." And the basic assumption was inescapable—that "we have no reason to believe that there is a present likelihood that the Communist regime will be overthrown."

From this analysis a different policy inevitably flows, a policy of firmness, flexibility, and dispassion. By firmness we mean firmness in our determination to maintain our strength in Asia; to stand by our commitments to our allies, including our friends on Taiwan; and to deter and meet Chinese Communist aggression. By flexibility, we mean a willingness to negotiate, to talk, to maintain, in the words of the speech, an "open door" to a lessening of hostility. And by dispassion we mean a capacity to look at China policy coolly, with the interests of our nation and of humanity in mind and without the blinding emotion that has clouded our analysis of the problem of dealing with China in the past.

I think certain concrete steps can be taken to implement this policy, as I outlined in another speech in California in November 1964 and before this Subcommittee last March. If we took these steps—arranging to have the Chinese invited to the arms control talks in Geneva, lifting U.S. travel restrictions, re-examining some of our trade policies, and proceeding to the recognition of Outer Mongolia—there would be no dramatic results, but these steps would at least begin to put political pressure on the Chinese Communists, to get the United States off the hook it is now on, and to help persuade the peoples and nations of Asia that it is not we who are isolating the Chinese Communists, but the Chinese Communists themselves through their pariah policies and attitudes.

In addition, these steps might also lay the groundwork with the second echelon of Chinese Communist leaders, those who will replace the Long March veterans who are coming to the end of their years, so that they understand that the only hope for the Chinese—and for mankind—is in the long run some form of accommodation.

President Johnson recently has moved in these directions —by lifting the travel restrictions on medical scientists and by agreeing to an invitation to the Chinese Communists to participate in the Geneva arms control talks—both of which are a wise beginning to a very long journey.

The goal, then, is Southeast Asia for the Southeast Asians. This will mean a neutralized buffer zone including Laos, Cambodia, and South Vietnam, and it will require not only a willingness to negotiate but an over-all strategy that puts military measures into a political context.

Let me say first of all that I believe the United States should *stay* in South Vietnam, that we should continue to support the South Vietnamese. A few weeks ago, the United States suffered two hundred and forty casualties in one week in South Vietnam. What some of the critics ought to remember is that there are three times as many South Vietnamese fighting there than Americans and that the Vietnamese have been suffering between two hundred and five hundred casualties a week, week after week for some years. Thus in spite of what the critics say, there are quite a lot of Vietnamese who want to fight the Communists and have done so gallantly. The United States should not—and cannot—desert them. To do so would be to turn our backs on everything our country stands for. And what my liberal friends sometimes forget is that to desert our friends would bring about the most fundamental realignment of the power balance of the world. Many of the countries that are willing to rely on the United States to hold the balance of nuclear power in the world, for example, would immediately begin to look to their own nuclear defenses—and the shape of the world in which we live would change radically, and overnight.

I am, therefore, heartily in favor of the decision to send United States ground forces to Vietnam, and of giving the Vietnamese military and economic support to the extent of our capability.

But beyond that decision, I have grave doubts. I said that I thought we needed an over-all strategy that put military measures into a political context. By this, I mean first of all that the South Vietnamese must themselves be able to take whatever credit there is for defeating the guerrilla terrorism they face. If we over-Americanize the struggle in Vietnam, if we get out in front and make of it an American war, then no matter how thoroughly we pulverize the Viet Cong, the struggle itself will have been lost in a political sense, which is the only permanent form of either victory or defeat in such a situation. Our ground forces should be used to hold the ports and bases, and to serve as a reserve if the Vietnamese forces are in an emergency. As General [James M.] Gavin has said, they should be used to *deter* the Communist side from escalation, from upping the ante, but they should not take over from the Vietnamese themselves.

In its international political aspects, a strategy that puts military measures into a political context should maintain a posture of responsibility and disciplined restraint, avoiding any escalation or violation of existing agreements except those that are absolutely essential and then only as we at the same time press continuously for negotiations and a return to the Geneva Agreements as a basis for settlement.

Judged by these standards, the bombing of North Vietnam, for example, was a mistake. It was further escalation and violation of the Geneva Accords at a time when the United States should have held to a posture of restraint and of preserving as much of the Geneva Agreements as possible. In international terms it was bad politics, raising questions in the minds of the in-between world and doubts among our allies, thus increasing the pressure on us for unacceptable concessions toward negotiations. The one surely predictable consequence of bombing the North was that the pressures on the United States for negotiations would become unbearable. And has anyone asked what would have happened if Hanoi had not been stupid, and accepted the Baltimore offer of negotiations before American ground forces were introduced into South Vietnam?

The bombing of North Vietnam, furthermore, put an obstacle in the way of steps furthering the détente with the Soviet Union and thus strengthened the hand of the Chinese in their dispute with the Soviets and added credibility to the Chinese argument for more belligerent Communist policies. It made it impossible for the Soviet Union to pursue its own national interests, which was to damp down the possibility of war in Southeast Asia, and thus made it impossible for the Soviets to put pressure on Hanoi for negotiations.

If we escalate our bombing of the North, the most probable Communist response would be to introduce the three hundred thousand North Vietnamese regular troops into the fighting—for the North Vietnamese would then have nothing left to lose.

What then? There would be nothing left to bomb in the North and no counter-measure open to the United States except introducing three hundred thousand additional Americans.

Again, the most probable Communist response would be to introduce Chinese "People's Army Volunteers" in very, very large numbers.

The debate would then be the same as now, but with the word "Peking" substituted for the word "Hanoi" and the word "Moscow" substituted for "Peking." Should we bomb Peking to force the Communists to desist in Vietnam, and if we did, what would Moscow do?

CHOU EN-LAI *
China Is Ready To Take Up U.S. Challenge

At present, U.S. imperialism is deeply bogged down in its war of aggression against Vietnam. . . . The more extended the war, the heavier the defeats of U.S. imperialism and the greater the internal and external difficulties of the Johnson Administra-

* Chou En-lai, excerpts from a speech given in Peking, December 20, 1965 (*Peking Review,* December 24, 1965, pp. 5–6).

tion. However, U.S. imperialism will not reconcile itself to its defeat. It will continue to put up a desperate struggle, to pursue its reckless course and to try to seek a way out by war blackmail.

Recently, the U.S. Defense Secretary McNamara visited Southern Vietnam for the seventh time, and U.S. military and government bigwigs are busy conferring and rushing here and there to plot new schemes for expanding the war. First in South Vietnam itself, the United States is continuing to send in reinforcements, building large military harbors and airfields and increasing its armed strength on the sea. Meanwhile, outside of Southern Vietnam, too, the United States is preparing to take further actions.

These actions include: extensively bombing Northern Vietnam including Haiphong and Hanoi in an attempt to sap the fighting will of the North Vietnamese people to defend their fatherland and support and assist the South; harassing and blockading the Bac Bo Gulf in the hope of cutting the sea communications of the Democratic Republic of Vietnam; bombing the central and southern parts of Laos liberated by the Neo Lao Haksat and preparing to dispatch U.S. and Thai troops to occupy this area together with the troops of the Laotian rightists in an attempt to link it with Thailand and South Vietnam; bombing and attacking the Xieng Khouang area of Laos in an attempt to block the main highways linking the Democratic Republic of Vietnam and Laos; and instigating the puppet cliques of Thailand and South Vietnam to intensify attacks and disruptive activities against Cambodia in the hope of sealing off the borders between Cambodia and South Vietnam.

Obviously, **the aim of the United States is to enforce a watertight blockade on South Vietnam and render the South Vietnamese people isolated and bereft of help in their just struggle against U.S. aggression and for national salvation, thus saving itself from defeat in South Vietnam. If it still fails to achieve this aim—and it certainly will fail—it is possible that in accordance with the objective laws governing the development of aggressive wars, U.S. imperialism will go a step further and extend its war of aggression to the whole of Indo-China and to China. And indeed U.S. imperialism is now making preparations for this eventuality.**

In order to cover up the truth of its expansion of the war

of aggression and gain time for making arrangements according to its wild military plans, U.S. imperialism is at the moment again chanting "peace talks." . . . The Johnson Administration proclaims that the United States "is ready to talk, unconditionally, anywhere"; it is preparing to play once again the trick of the "temporary suspension of bombing," saying that it is "not excluding the possibility of another halt in the bombing as a step toward peace." Following the clamor by the Johnson Administration, some people who are keen on helping U.S. imperialism have become more active in running errands for it, trying to make people believe that the Johnson Administration has changed its nature and that on the question of Vietnam it is really willing to lay down its butcher's knife and give up aggression.

But people have had experience of this trick of the Johnson Administration several times. . . . Since the beginning of this year, it has been playing the trick of "peace talks"; it did so every time it brought reinforcements to South Vietnam and took a step to escalate its war of aggression in Vietnam. There are actually conditions in its so-called "unconditional negotiations"; in other words, the South Vietnamese people are asked to lay down their arms and stop their resistance and the North Vietnamese people are asked to desist from supporting and assisting their compatriots in the South.

The "temporary suspension of bombing" in May this year has long been proved a clumsy act of war blackmail. **People know full well that while playing the trick of dual tactics, the Johnson Administration has only one objective in mind, namely, to occupy Southern Vietnam, perpetuate the division of Vietnam, and turn Southern Vietnam into its colony and base for aggression.** It is for this objective that U.S. imperialism has unleashed and expanded its aggressive war, and it is likewise for this objective that U.S. imperialism clamors about "unconditional negotiations" and is even preparing to stage once again the farce of "temporary suspension of bombing." **This objective remains the same despite all the changes. U.S. imperialism will not give up this arrogant attempt until its thorough defeat. Before that, the outcries of the Johnson Administration about "unconditional negotiations" and "temporary suspension of bomb-**

ing" serve only as a prelude and smokescreen in expanding its war.

The facts are very clear. The Vietnamese people have not committed any aggression against the United States. It is the United States that has committed aggression against Vietnam. The war of aggression in Vietnam has been launched against the Vietnamese people entirely by U.S. imperialism. Therefore, the liberation of South Vietnam and then the achievement of peaceful reunification of Vietnam must never be based on the terms laid down by the aggressors, but must be based on the four-point proposition put forward by the government of the Democratic Republic of Vietnam on April 8 and the five-part statement made by the South Vietnam National Liberation Front on March 22, to the effect that U.S. imperialism must stop its aggression against Vietnam, withdraw all U.S. troops and war matériel from South Vietnam, and leave the Vietnamese people to settle their own problems. **In a word, the aggressors must withdraw from Vietnam and there can be no other alternative.**

Instead of accepting the above reasonable propositions of the Vietnamese people, U.S. imperialism is now "escalating" its war of aggression in Vietnam. In these circumstances, the only choice for the Vietnamese people is to carry on the fight resolutely and vigorously until the U.S. aggressors are driven out of Vietnam. The only thing for all peace-loving countries and peoples to do is to give resolute support to the Vietnamese people in thoroughly defeating the U.S. aggressors.

It is all the more the bounden international duty of every socialist country to give all-out support to the fraternal Vietnamese people. Therefore, whether or not a socialist country firmly supports the Democratic Republic of Vietnam and the South Vietnam National Liberation Front in their just stand against U.S. aggression and for national salvation, whether or not it constantly exposes and combats the peace talk scheme of U.S. imperialism, and whether or not it genuinely gives the Vietnamese people effective and practical material aid in good time constitute an important criterion for judging whether its anti-imperialism is real or sham and whether its help to the Vietnamese people is real or sham.

If a person covertly conspires with U.S. imperialism while giving some superficial aid to the Vietnamese people, if he actually serves the U.S. imperialist plot of peace talks while shouting a few slogans against U.S. imperialist aggression in Vietnam, and if he actually sows discord in an attempt to undermine the Vietnamese people's unity against U.S. aggression and the unity of the Vietnamese and Chinese peoples against U.S. imperialism while professing that the socialist countries should unite to fight imperialism, then he is definitely not helping the Vietnamese people but is capitalizing on the revolutionary cause of the Vietnamese people for a dirty deal with the United States and hoping to attain his ulterior motive through such "aid." This is an impermissible betrayal not only of the Vietnamese people, but of the people of all the socialist countries and the people of the whole world as well. . . .

. . . The Chinese people have long been prepared. Should U.S. imperialism insist on going further along the road of war expansion and having another trial of strength with the Chinese people, the Chinese people will resolutely take up the challenge and fight to the end. Come what may, the Chinese people will unswervingly side with the fraternal Vietnamese people and contribute all our efforts to the defeat of U.S. imperialism until final victory.

ANNA LOUISE STRONG *
When and How Will China Go to War?

Peking, April 1966

The subject most debated just now by a guessing-game of Washington's "experts" is **"When and how will China go to war."** This has been answered many times by China's leaders but the experts misinterpret or refuse to believe. A campaign is on by part of the U.S. administration to assure the American people

* Anna Louise Strong, "When and How Will China Go to War?" (Supplement to *Letter from China*, 38, April 25, 1966, pp. 1–4).

that China "never will come in." Other campaigns contradict this by claiming that China is "bellicose."

General Matthew B. Ridgway, who commanded the U.S. forces in the Korean War, warns that the U.S. must limit the Vietnam War "or risk an upward-spiraling course that may approach annihilation" and adds that "easy conquest through airpower" is a delusion. **Senator J. William Fulbright says the danger of war between the U.S. and China is "real" and blames it on China's "abnormal and agitated state of mind."** His solution goes only as far as the "two China policy" which the U.S. State Department favored long ago. And when some claim that a "shift of U.S. policy" may induce "later generations of leaders in Peking . . . to turn away from conquest" (*Christian Science Monitor,* March 16, 1966) this seems the ultimate in insolent ignorance. "Conquest"? It is Washington, not Peking, that sends troops to all continents to invade and dominate other lands.

As seen from Peking, China does not intend to go to war but expects that war may come to China. China has not a single soldier outside her borders and has never attacked another nation despite the Western myths of her "aggression" in Korea, Tibet, and India. She is, however, prepared to defend her country and its socialist achievements if attacked. She also supports the Vietnamese people "in their heroic and just struggle against U.S. aggression." The U.S., now escalating war in Vietnam, is thus on a collision course with China. If China's support of the Vietnamese people's resistance leads to a U.S. attack on China, the Chinese are prepared to make this a war that the U.S cannot win. . . .

It is instructive to consider the Korean War which the West commonly cites as one of China's "aggressions." China had no part in this war until four months after the U.S. troops had invaded North Korea; **China did not enter until the U.S. troops reached China's own border, dropped bombs on Manchurian cities, and threatened to march into China.** Peking sent warning to President Truman through the Indian Ambassador as to the point at which China would be forced to enter the war. The big scandal of U.S. intelligence in that war was General MacArthur's assurance to Truman that China's warnings were only bluff. Greater disaster may now attend disregard of China's warnings about Vietnam.

Note that China had three reasons for entering the Korean war and that all these were widely discussed in China: (a) a friendly neighbor, overrun by aggressors, asked aid; (b) China's own border was threatened and some areas in China had been bombed; (c) MacArthur's obvious intent was to drive as far as he could through Manchuria, against both the USSR and the new Chinese government in Peking, which would have threatened a third world war. China's unofficial volunteers caused no such peril. They helped drive the U.S. troops back to the Parallel and brought the war to an end. Both China's actions and the method she chose were successful in keeping the war from spreading. Yet the United Nations, under U.S. pressure, declared China an aggressor, a fact which has disqualified the UN in Chinese eyes ever since. China's volunteers, after helping the Koreans repair the devastation made by the U.S.A., returned home in 1958, while U.S. armed forces made a permanent base in South Korea. Who is the aggressor in all this?

The U.S. automatically repeating that China is "bellicose," takes as proof a much publicized press conference by Foreign Minister Ch'en Yi last September in which he said: "For sixteen years we have been waiting for U.S. imperialism to attack us. My hair has turned gray in waiting." "If the U.S. imperialists are determined to launch a war of aggression against us . . . they are welcome to come [as early as] tomorrow."

Note that Ch'en Yi never said: "I have waited sixteen years to attack the U.S.A." **His expectation of attack by the U.S. is quite rational and not, as Senator Fulbright thinks, an indication of China's "agitated and abnormal state of mind." For twenty years the U.S. has been attacking the Chinese Communists** in many ways. When I visited Yenan in 1946, Washington had already spent billions to help Chiang Kai-shek fight the Chinese Communists, even though General Joseph Stilwell, chief of the U.S. Military Mission, reported that the Communists, not Chiang, had been the main Chinese force in defeating Japan. Stilwell was recalled; the U.S. kept on helping Chiang after he lost China [see Volume II]. Washington thus put class lines higher than national interests.

Washington not only waged the Korean War to reverse China's Revolution but used it as excuse to seize Taiwan (which had been restored to China by agreement) and financed French action in Indo-China. When none of this halted the new China's progress, Washington put embargo on China's trade and encouraged the bombing of Shanghai with many civilian casualties and the seizing of offshore islands to block the ports of Amoy and Foochow. China today trades with more than a hundred nations but **her coastal navigation is still harassed by the U.S. Seventh Fleet and Chiang's protected gunboats. Recently U.S. planes have directly bombed and strafed Chinese fishing boats on the high seas.**

China has sent some four hundred "serious warnings" of violations of China's air and waters in recent years by the U.S. Seventh Fleet. Washington ignores them but China puts them down for the record. What would the U.S. have done if any nation had similarly violated her air and waters four hundred times in seven years? Unlike the U.S., China is patient. Mao's strategy is to let the aggressor reveal himself to the world by many aggressions so that, if war comes, world opinion will know where to fix the blame.

Washington announces that an aim of the present Vietnam war is "to contain China." But it is Washington, not China, that sends soldiers to make war in Southeast Asia and all over the world. . . .

All this provocation is sound reason for China's belief that the U.S. intends war. In a sense the U.S. has waged against China for twenty years, a cold war and at times a shooting war in which Washington never made peace. But when the West speaks of war, it means big war, possibly nuclear war. Will such a big war develop? The answer is that if the U.S. keeps on its present collision course, it probably will.

China's leaders have given their position, both in general terms and concrete terms with respect to Vietnam for more than a year. Support to the Vietnamese people in their resistance to U.S. aggression has been repeatedly stated: in the *People's Daily* March 23, 1965; by Foreign Minister Ch'en Yi March 28; by Premier Chou En-lai March 29, and on April 20, 1965, by the resolution of the National People's Congress, the body which, like the U.S. Congress, has power to declare peace or war.

This response to an appeal on April 10 by the National Assembly of the D.R.V. in Hanoi to the "parliamentary bodies of the world," declared that as signatory to the 1954 Geneva Agreements, and also as a member of the socialist camp of which the D.R.V. is also a member, China solemnly states that "aggression by the U.S. against the D.R.V. means aggression against China," that "the Chinese people have done and will continue to do their utmost to assist the Vietnamese people to defeat the U.S. aggressors completely."

The resolution then calls on the Chinese people to do two things: to join with the peoples throughout the world in a "mighty mass movement to compel the U.S. aggressors to get out of Vietnam," and specifically in China **"to make full preparation to send our own people to fight together with the Vietnamese people and drive out the U.S. aggressors in the event that U.S. imperialism continues to escalate its war of aggression and the Vietnamese people need them."** These two things were deliberately confused in the Western press. Secretary Rusk said "more threats"; sensation writers said "mobilization for war." What Rusk called "more threats" will be seen by history as a clear promise of utmost support to the Vietnamese people and a warning to Washington.

For reasons of mutual security China does not publicize what help she gives to Vietnam or how much. Premier Pham Van Dong thanked China a year ago on April 25 for "the most powerful, most resolute, most effective assistance." The Vietnamese leader whom I interviewed last November for the *Guardian* said: "China gives us all that we ask and considers us as her own front."

None of this help makes China a belligerent as yet. To those Western experts who one day say "China won't fight" and the next day China "is bellicose" and the third day that "Ho Chi Minh doesn't want Chinese troops anyway," one replies: "No nation wants its allies' troops on its territory unless it needs them to repel its enemies." Both North and South Vietnam have effective armed forces for present needs. If the U.S. continues to pour in troops until the Vietnamese feel a need, the Chinese will be there. China's guarantee thus makes the Vietnam war what the West called "open-ended," *i.e.,* the Vietnamese resistance will continue to be able to match the U.S. aggression.

The further the U.S. escalates the more it will be entangled. Even now it is hard to tell whether the U.S. ruling class really wants the long war which the experts say it will take to subdue South Vietnam, or whether they are on a tiger and cannot dismount. This past month they have greatly increased the bombing in Laos and the threats against Cambodia and settled deep into Thailand. They have moved troops and weapons and ships from Europe to Southeast Asia. Hence one must face the fact that a big war with China is possible, either as gradual escalation or by sudden attack. Opinion on this is confused in America. A prevalent view is that such a war can be won by bombing, without the entanglement of a big land war. This delusion is promoted to calm the American people, already disturbed by the casualties and defeats in South Vietnam with its fourteen million people and unwilling to take on China, whose seven hundred million people equal fifty South Vietnams!

The American people's instinct in this is very sound. The dream of winning a war by bombing is a myth. Conventional bombs were found powerless in World War II to win final victories; they are failing now against North Vietnam. Some people think nuclear bombs might wreck China with little damage to the U.S.A. Chinese are aware of what American scientists also begin to admit, that **nuclear bombing sufficient to wreck China would also wreck by fallout several nearby countries, Japan, Korea, Southeast Asia, and the Philippines, as well as nearby areas of the USSR.** The ten thousand-megaton bombardment, estimated in *Life* magazine, May 28, 1965, as adequate to kill half of China's population, would raise the radioactivity of the world's atmosphere by twenty times, making a world health hazard even in the United States. It is delusion to think the U.S.A. can thus ruin China without danger to itself.

Chinese know from experience, as Hanoi knows, that they can survive and win without cities, railroads, or bridges. They did it once and can do it again. When I saw the people's communes in 1958 I said at once: "This is the country that can best survive even nuclear war." Every commune, which is a township, is a local unit combining state power, economic resources, and home defense. It produces food and often textiles. The great steel drive of 1958, at which the West laughed, taught sixty million Chinese people how to make steel in their own backyards, and also where the nearest iron ore and coal was found. **If China was split into its seventy-five thousand communes, each of them would be able to raise food, make clothing and housing, and even tools and ammunition from homemade steel.** The county level would be even more self-sufficient than the township, and the provinces more self-sufficient still. Even the splitting of China by wide zones of radioactive waste would not prevent the Chinese people in all these isolated areas from organizing life and defense in a fairly efficient manner, communicating by radio as in Yenan days.

At some stage in the bombing the U.S. would realize that nothing had been won except the scorn and hatred of an outraged world. . . .

On the background of these comments, the official statements by Chinese leaders on the subject may be better understood. One of the earliest was that by Lo Jui-ch'ing, Chief of Staff of the People's Liberation Army, published in *Peking Review,* May 14, 1965, celebrating the anniversary of the anti-Nazi victory over Hitler. "Our principle is: **We will not attack unless we are attacked; if we are attacked, we will certainly counterattack. On whatever scale the U.S. attacks us, we shall reply on that scale.**" The author sees no contradiction in stating in the same article: "We are prepared to send our men to fight together with the Vietnamese people when they need us."

A longer statement was that by Lin Piao, Minister of Defense, in his famous pamphlet on "People's War." "Chinese people definitely have ways of their own for coping with the U.S. imperialist war of aggression . . . **the most important is still the mobilization of the people, reliance on the people, making everyone a soldier and waging a people's war.** We want to tell the U.S. imperialists that the vast ocean of several hundred million Chinese people in arms will be more than enough to submerge your few million aggressor troops. If you dare to impose war on us, we shall gain freedom of action. It will then not be up to you to decide how the war shall be fought. . . .

The naval and air superiority you boast cannot intimidate us and neither can the atom bomb you brandish. We have the courage to shoulder the heavy burden of combating U.S. imperialism and to contribute our share in the struggle for final victory over the most ferocious enemy of the people of the world."

Vice-Premier Ch'en Yi said in that press conference last September: **"Should the U.S. imperialists invade China's mainland, we will take all necessary measures to defeat them. By then, the war will have no boundaries. . . .** With the defeat of U.S. imperialism, the time will come when imperialism and colonialism will be really liquidated throughout the world. . . . China is ready to make all the necessary sacrifices for this noble ideal."

Mao Tse-tung said it in essence nearly ten years ago in a speech on "The Correct Handling of Contradictions Among the People," February 27, 1957, "People all over the world are discussing whether a third world war will break out. . . . **We stand firmly for peace and against war. But if the imperialists insist on unleashing another war, we should not be afraid of it. . . . Our attitude is: First, we are against it; second, we are not afraid of it."** He goes on to state that in such a war **"the whole structure of imperialism"** might collapse.

Epilogue

[*When we completed the three volumes of* The China Reader *in June 1966, the "Great Proletarian Cultural Revolution" had just begun. When we received the first galleys early in October, we decided to add a section on what undoubtedly is one of the most important events in the history of the People's Republic of China. Whether the picture we present through our introductory analysis and the selections will still be valid from a future perspective remains to be seen. Many of our sections in this volume end with unresolved questions, and so it is fitting that this one does too.*]

THE "GREAT PROLETARIAN CULTURAL REVOLUTION"

In the summer of 1966 a volcanic mass movement swept over China, the like of which that country had never experienced. What appeared to have begun as another in the long series of ideological rectifications became a student-led mass movement which violently attacked "academic power cliques," was succeeded by the fall from power of one after another of China's great leaders, and culminated, in August, in the Red Defense Guard movement. An unexpected frenzy came over the country. As late as the spring the Chinese government was encouraging foreign tourists to come to China. Those who wrote about their experiences reported a calm, disciplined country, and were generally surprised at the ease with which foreigners could travel. Food was abundant, hotels were good, and guide services were said to be superior to those found in other socialist countries. The number of refugees coming out to Hong Kong and Macao had diminished as the conditions of life within China improved. Obviously there was growing tension over the possibility that the Vietnam war would escalate in the direction of China, but that tension was more visible in the Chinese press than in actuality. Despite some measures taken to prepare the population against possible air raids from abroad, the general atmosphere was calm.

But then, early in May, the volcano began to erupt. Article after article appeared in the leading newspapers attacking "anti-Party, anti-socialist elements" in an ever growing crescendo. In the universities "left-wing" students began to form bands which publicly attacked leading university officials, old-fashioned professors, and bourgeois students. When Lu P'ing, President of Peking University fell in June, one after another of his colleagues in other major universities also fell.

The universities became so turbulent that new student admissions for the fall semester were canceled; foreign reporters were prohibited from entering the university campuses. Subsequently the Chinese government requested that all foreign governments temporarily withdraw their students from China. In July the movement appeared to have abated somewhat, and from August 1 to 12 the Central Committee of the Chinese Communist Party met in its eleventh plenary session (the first since September 1962). The relatively short communiqué issued reaffirmed all policies apparently in force, without giving special attention to the "great proletarian cultural revolution." On August 18 a rally was held in Peking, attended by hundreds of thousands of high school and university students from the entire country. Mao Tse-tung, Lin Piao, and Chou En-lai were the three prominent leaders who appeared before the masses; Lin Piao and Chou En-lai were the main speakers. Suddenly bands of teen-agers and young adults, called the Red Defense Guards, sprouted up in Peking and then in other parts of the country. The Red Defense Guard armband was pinned symbolically on Mao Tse-tung, making him the personal leader of these new formations. "Defend Mao Tse-tung" was the rallying cry of the Red Defense Guards, implying that Mao's power had been threatened by conspiratorial forces within the highest levels of Party, government, and army. And so it seemed, for the line-up of political leaders who appeared with the great trio showed so radical a rearrangement of power positions that foreign observers were stunned. The onetime heir apparent, Liu Shao-ch'i, slipped to eighth place. P'eng Chen, Mayor of Peking, second in command of the Party Secretariat, after Teng Hsiao-p'ing, was absent (his fall from power was already evident early in June), Lo Jui-ch'ing, chief of staff of People's Liberation Army, had been purged. Other prominent military names were missing from the line-up. Lu Ting-i, once the Party's chief propagandist, was gone. Lesser names, earlier associated with P'eng Chen, Lo Jui-ch'ing, and Lu Ting-i, also were gone. Communist China had experienced the most profound shake-up in its leadership since the founding of the People's Republic.

From mid-August on the Red Defense Guards leaped into action. In most of China's major cities they attacked anything old, bourgeois, or foreign. Cultural objects from the past (Buddhist statues and ancient books) were burned. China's national capitalists who had hitherto earned "fixed interest" from their nationalized enterprises were paraded through the streets with dunce caps on their heads. Though few foreigners as such were molested, Overseas Chinese with their Hong Kong suits and Western appearance were reviled. Western observers saw all this as a massive attempt to cut China off once and for all from her past history. However, the Soviet view was different. For the first time since the Sino-Soviet split, Soviet newspapers carried extensive reports about China. The dominant Soviet theme was that the Red Defense Guards were attacking the organizational structure of the Communist Party itself. *Pravda* reported on September 23, 1966, that in Harbin the Red Defense Guards cried "open fire" against the city and province Party committees and paraded local Party leaders around the city in trucks. It was evident that the Red Defense Guards, mainly students, were the instruments of a shake-up that went from the highest to the lowest levels of the Party's organizational structure. Behind the Red Defense Guards stood military units, Lin Piao's men, ready to back them if necessary or to restrain them if they got out of hand. The army did not intervene openly in the attacks on Party cadres.

The communiqué of the Central Committee plenum said that "an unprecedented great proletarian cultural revolution has just arisen in our country," and so it may be that what has already transpired (until September 1966) is but the first chapter in a history yet to be made. When did the history of the "great proletarian cultural revolution" begin? The July 1966 issue of *Red Flag* made clear that it began with an attack on Wu Han, leading writer and historian and first Deputy Mayor of Peking: "the criticism of Wu Han's play *Hai-Jui Dismissed From Office,* initiated by the Shanghai City Committee of the Chinese Communist Party under the direct leadership of Chairman Mao and the Party Center, sounded the trumpet call of the Great Proletarian Cultural Revolution." The date was November 10, 1965. From what transpired since then, namely the ouster of P'eng Chen and the purge of the entire Peking City Party Committee, we know that the attack on Wu Han marked the beginning of a major attack on the entire Peking Party structure. The use of Shanghai as a springboard for the attack suggested that Mao was making use of the provincial Party apparatus to dislodge his opponents in the central Party apparatus. The use of regional power to fight central power is not unprecedented in the history of Communist Parties. In May 1957, when Nikita Khrushchev found himself outvoted in the Politburo by his Stalinist opponents, he mobilized the regional Party leaders, hastily summoned a Central Committee meeting, and emerged on top; thereupon he quickly eliminated his opponents from their power positions. The momentary rise to prominence of Teng Hsiao-p'ing in May 1966 suggested that as the leader of the nationwide Party network, he was called on to use his power against P'eng Chen, whose power resided in Peking and in the immense apparatus of the Chinese central government.

Since the term "power struggles" has been so commonly used to describe political fights in Communist countries, we might consider what it actually means. Power struggles occur when different groups of men compete to gain command of policymaking positions and crucial organizational networks. This means not only gaining top-level executive power, but putting one's own men into leadership and administrative positions from top to bottom in the organizational hierarchy. In short, it is a question of cadre training and staffing. Power struggles do not take place in a vacuum, however. It is usually major disagreement over policy issues which leads to conflict. Thus whichever group wins can then implement the policies it advocates.

What were the great conflicts over organizational control which went on in China as the "great proletarian cultural revolution" began? During the economic crisis of the years 1960–1962 the Party underwent a rectification campaign during which middle- and lower-echelon cadres were severely criticized. This necessitated a rebuilding of the Party which continued during the entire period of recovery of the early 1960s. At the same time the internal role of the army had greatly increased. The army kept order during the terrible years. Subsequently it began to play an increasingly important role in the economic administration of the country. For example, general political departments were established in many important economic sectors which exerted control and direction over economic activity. Personnel training and staffing policies changed during the early 1960s. Instead of the one-sided emphasis on "redness" characteristic of the Great Leap Forward, the need for "expertise" was increasingly stressed. This, of course, made the country's higher schools an important training ground for the new cadres. The army, on the other hand, apparently followed the lines advocated by Lin Piao late in 1960: stress on political education, implementation of the mass line, and preferential recruitment of soldiers and officers from poor workers and peasants. With the army moving into domestic leadership and administrative positions, conflict over personnel training and staffing developed. Thus the perennial "red and expert" problem took a new turn, with the army increasingly representing the "red" approach, and significant segments of the Party, particularly those associated with cadre-training programs in the higher schools, advocating the "expert" approach.

If the known shake-ups in the universities and in the cultural organizations and the presumed shake-up in the military point to power struggles within those organizational sectors, there are only the most veiled indications as to the issues. Was the main issue the "successor" to Mao Tse-tung? Obviously yes, for the men who gained control of the country's leading organizational sectors would be those with the best chances of emerging on top after Mao Tse-tung has passed from the scene. Yet one may ask whether other momentous issues were involved. It may be significant that on November 11, 1965, the *People's Daily* published one of the most important documents on the Sino-Soviet dispute in relation to the Vietnam war. In the editorial, which ran to almost three pages, "Reject the So-called 'United Action' of the New Soviet Leadership," the *People's Daily* accused the Soviet Union of collusion with the United States to end the Vietnam war. Since the *People's Daily* was clearly under attack in the late spring of 1966 (as evident in the bitter criticisms of Teng T'o, its former editor), one may conclude that it was under the control of P'eng Chen's Peking Party apparatus and was expressing its policy views. In our discussions of Chinese foreign policy (see pp. 231–236) we have pointed out that relations with the Soviet Union and the United

States have always been issues of preponderant concern to the Chinese. In the latter part of 1965 both issues coalesced in the Vietnam problem. Whatever policies Peking decided to pursue regarding Vietnam would decisively affect its relations with both of the superpowers.

During 1965, the Vietnam war had been steadily escalating, though interspersed with periodic peace efforts (again becoming prominent in November and December). Alarums of war spreading over Vietnam's boundaries into China were sounded with increasing frequency from Peking (see pp. 592–596). As in the past, three options appeared to be open to Peking: (1) prepare for war through military mobilization and eventual entry into the fighting (as happened in Korea); (2) do nothing to provoke the United States but dig in and await a possible attack, relying on ideological and organizational mobilization and a strategy of protracted war for eventual survival and victory; (3) seek reconciliation with the Soviet Union and, by agreeing to "united action," reacquire the protection of the Soviet nuclear shield.

Since almost all of the top leaders who subsequently fell from power were openly and actively concerned with foreign policy, we can presume that they were involved in the agonized debate over Vietnam. Since Mao Tse-tung and Lin Piao are now loudly identified as the strategists of "people's war" (that is, protracted revolutionary war), one may presume that those who fell advocated the other policy approaches.

In the months following November 1965 only small signs of the struggle appeared openly. On January 25, 1966, Hsiao Hua, head of the general political department of the People's Liberation Army, made a speech which implied dissension over major issues in the army and called for a sharing of army command with the provincial Party committees. China's Third Five Year Plan formally began on January 1966, but little was heard about it; presumably if basic policy issues had not been decided, final plan allocations of men and resources could not be made. In the middle of April editorials from the *Liberation Army Daily,* on the subject of the importance of the Thought of Mao Tse-tung, of political work in the army, and finally on the cultural revolution, began to be reprinted in the *People's Daily.* Early in May, the storm broke with violent attacks on "anti-

Party, anti-socialist monsters." By June, it became clear that P'eng Chen had fallen from power, soon followed by Lu Ting-i and Chou Yang, chief Party propagandists and the men in control of the country's "cultural" organizations (that is, the mass media, so important in China and in a Communist country in general). A short while later it became evident that Lo Jui-ch'ing, chief of staff of the People's Liberation Army and former head of the public security forces (secret police), who had not been seen publicly since November 1965, had also fallen from power. At the time of the great August 18 demonstrations in Peking's T'ien An Men Square, it appeared that Liu Shao-ch'i, one of Mao's closest associates and, until then, heir apparent, had fallen far down in the hierarchy of power. The conclusion seemed inescapable that a group of leaders (Liu Shao-ch'i, P'eng Chen, Lo Jui-ch'ing, Lu Ting-i) and organizational sectors they controlled constituted a political force which sought decisively to expand their power and control and implement policies which they advocated in opposition to others, notably Mao Tse-tung himself.

The attacks on Wu Han and Teng T'o (a cover for the real targets, P'eng Chen and Lu Ting-i) led to a major cleaning out of personnel in the country's mass media, as is implied in the selection by Kao Chü presented below (and in the furious attacks mounted against Chou Yang, Lu Ting-i's closest collaborator). During the summer the *People's Daily* changed radically (even its masthead was altered). Almost nothing but fulsome praise of Mao and accounts of the "cultural revolution" were published, virtually displacing all other news. New men were obviously being brought into the cultural sector.

The attacks on Lu P'ing, President of Peking University, coincided with a major restructuring of the higher school system. In the selection from the June 18 issue of the *People's Daily* on transforming the educational system we might note the emphasis given enrollment. Peking had announced that all enrollment for the fall 1966 semester would be canceled until new policies could be worked out. As had happened in Russia in the early 1930s the children of poor workers, peasants, and soldiers were to be brought into the schools, and the power of bourgeois authorities and scholar-tyrants broken.

In the serious conflict over personnel training and staffing the advocates of "redness" scored a victory over the "experts." With the emergence of Lin Piao as the second man after Mao himself, the army can be said to have gained the decisive voice in determining who the country's civilian cadres should be.

The *Liberation Army Daily* editorial of August 1, 1966, from which we present excerpts, makes it clear that a struggle over military policy was a major issue in the "great proletarian cultural revolution": "exposed in this struggle were representatives of the bourgeoisie who had usurped important posts in the army and were important members of the counter-revolutionary anti-Party, anti-socialist clique recently uncovered by our Party." Obviously Peking was not going to say what these issues were, for they involved the most sensitive areas of politics, namely, the country's national security. Let us recall that those purged had for years spoken out prominently on foreign policy. Lu Ting-i wrote one of the first open attacks on the Soviet Union in April 1960, and was closely associated since then with the campaign against "modern revisionism." P'eng Chen continued the attack on the Soviet Union in the summer of 1960, and had for the later years been closely identified with China's revolutionary politics in the "third world." In December 1965, at the time when the fifth anniversary of the South Vietnamese National Liberation Front was celebrated in Peking, he gave the keynote address, calling for absolute withdrawal of American forces from South Vietnam. He was also closely associated with Peking's policy toward Indonesia, which failed so dramatically with the Indonesian events of October 1965. Lo Jui-ch'ing gave two major speeches on the military situation in Vietnam (May and September 1965). The first, in particular, came close to threatening preventive action (*e.g.* "in order not to take up arms, we must take up arms").

Judging from their past words, those purged could hardly be considered moderates. Regarding the three options in foreign policy mentioned above, we have already noted that Mao Tse-tung and Lin Piao favored strategies of protracted war. Since Lo Jui-ch'ing had spoken out strongly in favor of a policy of "active defense," one may wonder whether the whole group centered around Liu Shao-ch'i may have advocated a similar policy.

The selection on the great demonstrations of August 18

describes the beginnings of the Red Guard movement, and the selection from *Pravda* indicates the Soviet reaction.

As of the writing of this introduction (November 1966), the Red Guard movement continues. China is undergoing an intensive campaign of organizational restructuring and ideological mobilization. Though the situation in Vietnam remains as dangerous as ever, there is no public sign of military mobilization in China. As the world wonders whether it faces a future of peace or greater war, China is going through the throes of her cultural revolution. The eventual outcome of that struggle will deeply affect not only China's internal constitution but her role in the world. As we have said in our discussion of foreign policy, there is a triangular relationship between Peking, Washington, and Moscow: what one does will directly affect what the others do. Thus, China's coming history will be determined by the course of her cultural revolution and by the direction the Vietnam war takes, for it is in Vietnam that the Chinese-Russian-American triangle is centered.

KAO CHÜ *
Open Fire Against the Anti-Party Anti-Socialist Black Line

Chairman Mao has always warned us: even after the enemy who carries a gun has been destroyed, there remains the enemy who does not carry a gun; they will absolutely carry on a mortal struggle against us; we cannot disregard this kind of enemies. The struggle between the two roads of socialism and capitalism runs through all stages of socialism. In order to assure the construction of socialism and prevent the restoration of capitalism, we must carry the socialist revolution to its completion, on the political front, the economic front, on the ideological and the

* Translated by Franz Schurmann from *People's Daily*, May 9, 1966; originally published in the *Liberation Army Daily*, May 8, 1966.

cultural fronts. We must always remember Chairman Mao's instructions never to disregard the enemy in the area of consciousness, never to forget the class struggle.

Teng T'o's "Evening Talks on Swallow Hill" and "Account of Three-Family Village" (written under pseudonyms by Wu Han, Teng T'o, and Liao Mo-sha) make quite clear to us that in our society the class struggle is still very sharp, complex, and fierce. Our class enemies, not only from without but from within, desperately smash at and attack us. Against whom is the spear of all these anti-Party anti-socialist elements directed when they attack? Our Party and our socialist system.

Teng T'o is the shopkeeper of this "Three-Family Village" black shop which he opened up with Wu Han and Liao Mo-sha; he is a ringleader of this small handful of anti-Party anti-socialist elements. They made use of the publications *Front* [of the Central Committee of the Peking City Party organization], the *People's Daily,* and the Peking *Evening News* as their tools for shooting poisoned arrows and violently attacking the Party and socialism.

The anti-Party anti-socialist activities of Teng T'o and this small handful of people is by no means an accidental and isolated phenomenon. In 1958 our people, under the glorious brilliance of the Thought of Mao Tse-tung and under the guidance of the general line of our Party, striking out and soaring upward, carried out our all-sided Great Leap Forward. On the political, economic, ideological, and cultural fronts, with the force of ten thousand thunderbolts, we resolutely smashed the remnant forces of capitalism and feudalism. As the socialist revolution went deeper and deeper, the right-leaning elements within the Party, heeding the demands of imperialism, modern revisionism, and our own internal landlord, rich peasant, counter-revolutionary, and corrupt elements, unleashed a wild attack against the Party in its Lushan Plenum of August 1959. Under the brilliant leadership of the Party Central Committee and of Chairman Mao, we gave these right-leaning elements a resolute response, snatched away their "weapons," kicked them out of office, and decisively cracked their anti-Party plots. Afterward, during the period between 1959 and 1962, as a result of our having suffered several successive years of natural disasters and the blows of modern revisionism, we encountered some temporary difficulties. At that time, our class enemies inside and out, gleeful over our troubles, came crawling out; the right-leaning elements in the Party made league with them and unleashed a new attack against the Party. Teng T'o and his crowd, given these conditions, could hardly wait "to crack open the door and come out."

Beginning in 1961 Teng T'o and his crowd, who harbored bone-deep hatred for the Party, spewed forth their "Evening Talks on Swallow Hill" and "Account of Three-Family Village." They talked about history, spread knowledge, told stories, recited jokes, but only as a cover. They used the old to satirize the new, pointed at one tree but cursed the other, spewed out malice at others, aimed dirty blows—they carried out an all-sided poisonous attack against our great Party. They maligned the "fanaticism" of our Party, its "raising a high fever," said we talked "big empty words," and accused us of amnesia. Poisonously they attacked our general line, said our Great Leap Forward was "just a lot of boasting," "wild imagination," that we used "illusions to replace reality," that we took the "few possessions" we had and "entirely destroyed them," that face to face with reality we "cracked our heads bloody." With all their powers they went around whining and crying about injustice done to those right-leaning elements which we had kicked out of office, boasted of their anti-Party "real nature" and "subversive character," and encouraged them to come forth again. They slandered our dictatorship of the proletariat; they did everything they could to inflame dissatisfaction against our socialist system; they propagandized the rotten and discredited feudal morality and capitalistic ideology; they opened the road for a capitalist restoration. Teng T'o went so far as wildly to call upon our Party to step down and "take a rest" quickly. We should keep our mouths shut, stop doing anything. We should listen to their "guidance" and let them take over our government.

I ask you comrades to reflect for a moment. Didn't the Khrushchev revisionists curse us for our "big talk," our "boasting," that our Great Leap Forward was "adventurism"? Didn't they praise the right-leaning elements within our Party for having "so much courage"? What is the difference between Teng T'o's anti-Party outcries and the insults and attacks of the Khrushchev revisionists against us?

Teng T'o's "Evening Talks on Swallow Hill" are thorough-going anti-Party anti-socialist slander. We must grab it, crack it open, spear it down, tear off its mask, let this stinking face of Teng T'o and his handful of anti-Party anti-socialist fellows be completely exposed to the full light of day. Debts must be paid back. If Teng T'o thinks he can get away with this, then he is mistaken. Not only is Teng T'o not going to slip away, but neither will his crowd. Not only the two stories mentioned have to be eradicated, but the poisonous weeds in many others as well. Anything that is anti-Party anti-socialist has to be eradicated piece by piece, without exception. . . .

As long as we have classes, there will be class struggle. This is a law of necessity. To pull out from our midst a small handful of these anti-Party anti-socialist elements is not a bad thing. That's good. It is the triumph of the Thought of Mao Tse-tung. The insults and attacks of a small handful of anti-Party anti-socialist elements are just the buzzings of a couple of flies. They cannot do any harm to the great glory of our Party. We have got to tell these anti-Party anti-socialist elements: it is you who first opened fire on the Party. "You can't just give and not get back." We are not going to let you get away with this. We are absolutely not going to let you demons get off. We are going to open fire against this anti-Party anti-socialist black shop. We shall carry the great socialist cultural revolution to its end. We'll not withdraw our troops before we have finally won!

PEOPLE'S DAILY *

Carry Out the Cultural Revolution Thoroughly
and Transform the Educational System Completely

On June 13 the Central Committee of the Chinese Communist Party and the State Council issued a notice announcing the decision to transform the existing entrance examination method of enrolling students in institutes of higher learning and to post-pone the 1966 enrollment in these institutes for half a year. This decision is an important measure for carrying out thoroughly the great cultural revolution in the field of education and completely transforming China's educational system.

Today the vast numbers of revolutionary students, administrative and other staff, and teachers in many universities, colleges, and middle schools in Peking and other places are holding aloft the great red banner of Mao Tse-tung's Thought, breaking through all the obstacles and restraints imposed by the bourgeois royalists, and directing a fierce barrage of fire at the black anti-Party and anti-socialist line in the field of education. However, the struggle has only just begun and there are still many stubborn bourgeois strongholds which have not yet been breached. If the entrance examination of enrolling new students went ahead as usual just now, this would undoubtedly bring the great proletarian cultural revolution in the field of education to a stop halfway, cripple the revolutionary enthusiasm of the Left students, and encourage the counter-revolutionary arrogance of the bourgeois Right. This decision of the Central Committee of the Chinese Communist Party and the State Council is an enormous support to the development of the great proletarian cultural revolution, a tremendous encourage-

* *Peking Review,* June 24, 1966, pp. 15–17 (translated from *People's Daily,* June 18, 1966).

ment to the Left students and a heavy blow for the bourgeois Right.

For a long time now the broad masses of workers, peasants, and soldiers, and revolutionary students and teachers have made it clear that they are very angry about the old entrance examination system of enrolling students, and have been urgently demanding that it should be scrapped once for all. . . .

The Central Committee of the Chinese Communist Party and the State Council took the decision to abolish the existing entrance examination method of enrolling students in institutes of higher learning in accordance with Chairman Mao's instructions and the demands of the masses. Beginning this year, a new method of enrollment, a combination of recommendation and selection, in which proletarian politics are put first and the mass line is followed, will go into effect; the best students will be admitted, selected from among those recommended for their outstanding moral, intellectual, and physical qualities. The same method will be used in enrolling students of senior middle schools.

Again and again the Central Committee of the Party and Chairman Mao have pointed out that the old bourgeois educational system, including the enrolling of students by examination, must be thoroughly transformed. This old examination system of enrolling students is most dangerous and harmful to our socialist cause. It places not proletarian but bourgeois politics in command, it places school marks in command. This system is a serious violation of the Party's class line, shuts out many outstanding children of workers, poor and lower-middle peasants, revolutionary cadres, revolutionary army men, and revolutionary martyrs, and opens the gates wide to the bourgeoisie to cultivate its own successors. This system is a great obstacle to the revolutionizing of young people's minds and encourages them to become bourgeois specialists by the bourgeois method of "making one's own way" and achieving individual fame, wealth, and position. . . .

It is through schools that the proletariat trains and cultivates its successors for the proletarian cause and through schools, too, the bourgeoisie trains its successors for purposes of a capitalist comeback. There is sharp class struggle here, between the proletariat and the bourgeoisie, to win over the younger generation. The Party's Central Committee and Chairman Mao Tse-tung have always placed great weight on proletarian education and on revolutionizing the educational system. Chairman Mao has put forward the policy that education must serve proletarian politics and must be combined with productive labor; he has pointed out that "our educational policy must enable everyone who gets an education, to develop morally, intellectually, and physically and become a cultured, socialist-minded worker." The series of instructions given by Chairman Mao on proletarian education light the way in China's socialist and communist cause like a great beacon. . . .

The transformation of the present entrance examination system represents a true breakthrough in the struggle to apply Chairman Mao Tse-tung's educational line consistently and eliminate the bourgeois educational line thoroughly. That will be the beginning of a complete revolution in the whole of the old educational system. It is not only the system of enrollment that requires transforming, all the arrangements for schooling, for testing, for going up or not going up to the higher class, and so on must be transformed, and so must the content of education. Further studies must be made as to how to implement the policy of combining education with productive labor. We must relegate to the morgue all the old teaching material that goes against Mao Tse-tung's Thought, that seriously departs from the three great revolutionary movements of class struggle, the struggle for production, and scientific experiment, or that inculcates an exploiting class world outlook. New teaching material must be compiled under the guidance of Mao Tse-tung's Thought and the principle of putting proletarian politics first. The junior classes in primary schools can study some extracts from Chairman Mao's works and the senior classes can study more of them and also some of the articles including "Serve the People," "In Memory of Norman Bethune," and "The Foolish Old Man Who Removed the Mountains." Middle-school students can study *Selected Readings from Mao Tse-tung's Works* and articles related to these readings. College students can study *Selected Works of Mao Tse-tung*. The study of Chairman Mao's works should be listed as a required course in all schools, whether primary or intermediate or institutions of higher learning. . . .

We must warn those anti-Party and anti-socialist bourgeois "authorities" who are entrenched in the educational world: the food you eat is provided by the working people, the clothes you wear are provided by the working people, and yet under the signboard of "serving the people" you are doing evil against the people and the Revolution. You have taken the offspring of the reactionary classes to your bosoms and in a hundred and one ways have thwarted, spurned, and attacked the children of the working people. You have collaborated with and encouraged the anti-Party and anti-socialist bourgeois "specialists" and "professors" to spread widely bourgeois and revisionist poison. With so much wickedness to your account, with such a debt you owe the people, can we possibly allow you to continue your misdeeds without exposing you, without criticizing you, without fighting you? Don't imagine that you will remain on your "thrones" just because you have established a group of royalists, don't dream that you will be able to carry on and get by. Don't harbor any illusion that after a time you will revert to your former state and resurrect your reactionary class "hereditary treasures." This is absolutely out of the question. Responding to the fighting call of the Central Committee of the Chinese Communist Party and Chairman Mao, the masses of the workers, peasants, and soldiers and of the revolutionary cadres and revolutionary intellectuals have made up their minds to expose all you monsters, to uproot you, to rid you of all your "imposing airs" and smash your bourgeois "hereditary treasures" to pieces.

The transformation of the educational system is a complicated and difficult task. So long as we, in firm accordance with Chairman Mao's instructions, have full confidence in the masses, rely on them, mobilize them fully, and energetically develop the mass movements, we shall certainly be able to destroy the stubborn strongholds of the bourgeoisie and win complete victory for the revolution of the educational system.

Let the great red banner of Mao Tse-tung's Thought fly high over our proletarian educational front! Let it fly forever.

LIBERATION ARMY DAILY *
Make Our Army a Great School of Mao Tse-tung's Thought

IN COMMEMORATION OF THE 39TH ANNIVERSARY
OF THE FOUNDING OF OUR ARMY

Chairman Mao wants us to run our army as a great school. Working mainly as a fighting force, it concurrently studies, engages in agriculture, runs factories, and does mass work; it carries on and further develops the fine traditions of our Party and our army, and trains and tempers millions of successors to the proletarian revolutionary cause, so that our people's army of several million can play a still greater role in the cause of socialist revolution and socialist construction. It is a great school for the study, implementation, dissemination, and safeguarding of Mao Tse-tung's Thought.

It is now thirty-nine years since Chairman Mao himself created this army of ours. It is a worker and peasant army under the absolute leadership of the Chinese Communist Party and built in accordance with the principles of Marxism-Leninism, a people's army of a totally new type, completely different from the feudal warlord of bourgeois armies.

At an early stage in the creation of our army, Chairman Mao clearly pointed out that it should certainly not confine itself to fighting, but should be an armed body for carrying out the political tasks of the revolution. In the famous resolution at the Kutien Congress, Chairman Mao wrote: "The Red Army fights not merely for the sake of fighting but in order to conduct propaganda among the masses, organize them, arm them, and help them to establish revolutionary political power. Without

* *Peking Review*, August 5, 1966 (translated from *Liberation Army Daily*, August 1, 1966).

these objectives, fighting loses its meaning and the Red Army loses the reason for its existence."

Chairman Mao set our army three great tasks, namely, fighting, mass work, and production. He pointed out that our army was always a fighting force, and at the same time it was a working force and a production force.

On the eve of nationwide victory, Chairman Mao said: "The army is a school." And "we must look upon the field armies with their 2,100,000 men as a gigantic school for cadres."

In the past decades, our army has done precisely what Chairman Mao has taught us to.

The directive recently given by Chairman Mao constitutes the most recent summing up of our army's experience in previous decades and represents a development of Chairman Mao's consistent thinking on army building in the new historical conditions. This directive is of great historic and strategic significance for enabling our army to preserve forever its distinctive character as a people's army, for consolidating the dictatorship of the proletariat, for pushing forward China's socialist revolution and socialist construction, strengthening national defense, bringing the mighty force of people's war into full play, and countering possible attacks by U.S. imperialism and its accomplices.

Chairman Mao's thinking on army building constitutes the most thorough, correct, and comprehensive body of proletarian ideas on army building.

Chairman Mao's thinking on army building is diametrically opposed to the purely military viewpoint in which consideration is given solely to military affairs in complete disregard of politics, reducing the army's task merely to fighting; it is diametrically opposed to all bourgeois military ideas.

Throughout the thirty-nine-year history of our army, the struggle between Chairman Mao's thinking and line on army building and bourgeois military ideas of various kinds has never ceased. This was true of the entire period of the democratic revolution, and is equally true of the period of the socialist revolution.

In the sixteen years since the founding of the People's Republic of China, we have waged three big struggles against representatives of the bourgeois military line who wormed their way into the Party and the army.

The first big struggle started after the conclusion of the war to resist U.S. aggression and aid Korea. Under the pretext of "regularization" and "modernization," a handful of representatives of the bourgeois military line, making a complete carbon copy of foreign practice, vainly attempted to negate our army's historical experience and fine traditions and to lead our army on to the road followed by bourgeois armies. The bourgeois military dogmatism which they tried to push through was strongly resisted and opposed by the broad masses of cadres and fighters in our army. Responding to Chairman Mao's call of "Down with the slave mentality! Bury dogmatism!" the 1958 Enlarged Session of the Military Commission of the Central Committee of the Chinese Communist Party smashed their frantic attack and defended Chairman Mao's thinking and line on army building.

The second big struggle took place at the same time as our Party's struggle against the Right opportunist anti-Party clique in 1959. Taking advantage of the important posts they had usurped in the army, the principal members of the anti-Party clique—who were exposed at the Party's Lushan Conference—made a great effort to do away with the Party's absolute leadership over the army, to abrogate political work, to reject the army's tasks of participating in socialist construction and doing mass work, and to abolish the local armed forces and the militia; in this way, they tried to completely negate Chairman Mao's thinking on the people's army and people's war. They vainly hoped to refashion our army according to the bourgeois, revisionist miltary line so that it would become an instrument for their usurping leadership of the Party and the government, and for realizing their personal ambitions. The Enlarged Session of the Military Commission held after the Party's Lushan Conference thoroughly settled accounts with them in regard to their crimes and dismissed them from office. This was a great victory for Mao Tse-tung's Thought!

Since he took charge of the work of the Military Commission of the Party's Central Committee, Comrade Lin Piao has most resolutely and thoroughly implemented Chairman Mao's thinking and line concerning army building. In 1960, with the attention and guidance of the Party's Central Committee and Chairman Mao, the Enlarged Session of the Military Commission presided over by Comrade Lin Piao went further in eradicating the influence of the bourgeois military line, corrected the orientation in political work, adopted the "Resolution Concerning the Strengthening of Political and Ideological Work in the Armed Forces," and carried on and developed the spirit of the Kutien Congress, and thus established a new milestone in our army's road of advance. In the last few years, under the leadership of the Military Commission of the Party's Central Committee and Comrade Lin Piao, the whole army has held high the great red banner of Mao Tse-tung's Thought and creatively studied and applied Chairman Mao's works, given prominence to politics, upheld the "four firsts," vigorously fostered the "three-eight" working style, given full scope to democracy in the three main fields of work, launched the "four-good" companies campaign, and taken part in the socialist education movement and the great proletarian cultural revolution, took part in and supported socialist construction, so that an excellent, flourishing situation has emerged in the revolutionization of our army and in all other fields of work.

The third big struggle took place not long ago. Exposed in this struggle were representatives of the bourgeoisie who had usurped important posts in the army and were important members of counter-revolutionary anti-Party, anti-socialist clique recently uncovered by our Party. They had opposed the Party's Central Committee and Mao Tse-tung's Thought, had overtly agreed to but covertly opposed Comrade Lin Piao's directives on giving prominence to politics, had talked about putting politics in command but in practice had put military affairs first, technique first, and work first. They had waved "red flags" to oppose the red flag and vigorously spread eclecticism, *i.e.*, opportunism, in the vain attempt to substitute a bourgeois military line for Chairman Mao Tse-tung's proletarian military line. Our Party's thorough exposure and repudiation of the handful of anti-Party careerists is a great new victory for Mao Tse-tung's Thought!

The representatives of the bourgeoisie, who were exposed in these big struggles of our army since the founding of the

People's Republic of China, opposed Chairman Mao's principle of building our army into a powerful revolutionary army of the proletariat, opposed absolute leadership by the Party over the army, opposed political work, and opposed the mass line. What they wanted was bourgeois regularization and not proletarian revolutionization. They discarded our army's glorious traditions, reduced its three great tasks to the single task of training in combat skill in peacetime and fighting in times of war. In short, everything they did was the diametrical opposite of Chairman Mao's thinking on army building and on turning our army into a great school. Their criminal aim was to turn our army into a bourgeois army serving a few careerists, an army divorced from Mao Tse-tung's Thought, from proletarian politics, from the masses of the people and from productive labor. . . .

The history of our army over the decades has proved to the hilt that Chairman Mao's thinking and line on army building represent irrefutable truth and are our army's lifeline. At no time and in no circumstances is it permissible for us to depart in the slightest from the orbit of Chairman Mao's thinking and line on army building. . . .

We shall resolutely adhere to Chairman Mao's directive that the army should concurrently study, engage in agriculture, run factories and do mass work. Everyone should take part in productive labor and forever maintain the distinctive character of working people. Everyone should do mass work, abide by the three main rules of discipline and the eight points for attention, so that the army will always be at one with the masses. Militia work should be done well and the idea of people's war should be implanted among the masses of the people. We must enthusiastically take part and help in socialist construction, actively help with local work, learn modestly from the local districts, and strengthen the unity between the army and the local district. . . .

Let us march forward valiantly under the great banner of Mao Tse-tung's Thought!

PEOPLE'S DAILY *
Chairman Mao Celebrates the Great Cultural
Revolution with Millions of the Masses

New China News Agency
August 18, 1966

Today our glorious leader, our glorious commander, our glorious helmsman Chairman Mao, together with a million revolutionary masses from Peking and the entire country, in the capital of our glorious motherland, on the heroic T'ien An Men Square, convened a great rally in celebration of the great proletarian cultural revolution.

Today at five o'clock, at dawn, when the sun had just barely burst brightly forth from the East, Chairman Mao arrived at T'ien An Men Square, where the masses were like an ocean and the red banners like a forest. One could see that revolutionary masses had begun to gather from all over very early in the morning. Chairman Mao wore a grass-green military tunic; the red star on his military cap shone brightly. Chairman Mao walked across Golden River Bridge in front of T'ien An Men straight into the ranks of the masses, and shook hands firmly with a few of the people who encircled him on all sides. He then raised his hands in greeting to the revolutionary masses out in the square. Just then an uproar arose in the vast square. Everyone threw his arms in the air and strained forward toward Chairman Mao, cheering and clapping. Many people clapped their hands until they were sore. Many people shed tears of emotion. They cried happily: "Chairman Mao has come, Chairman Mao has come into our midst." Out on the vast square thousands shouted, "Long live Chairman Mao! May he live ten thousand years—ten and ten thousand years." Each wave of the din rose above the last, rending the sky above the capital.

Today our glorious leader, Chairman Mao, spent a full six

* Translated by Orville Schell from *People's Daily*, August 18, 1966.

hours with the millions of revolutionary masses. While reviewing the mass parade of the great proletarian cultural revolution,
Chairman Mao and Comrade Lin Piao stood shoulder to shoulder on T'ien An Men, watching the vast rank and file of the
paraders. Chairman Mao said happily to Comrade Lin Piao,
"The scale of this movement is large. It is certain to stir up the
masses and have great significance in the ideological revolutionization of the entire people."

Tens of thousands of Red Defense Guards, wearing red
armbands, heroic and eager as real dragons and tigers, were
the focus of attention at today's rally. The Red Defense Guards
are a revolutionary proletarian organization of university and
middle-school students from Peking which arose from the proletarian cultural revolutionary movement. They showed that they
were willing to spend their whole lives protecting Chairman
Mao, the Chinese Communist Party, and the red vanguard of
the motherland. Representatives of the Red Defense Guards
stood on the ramparts of T'ien An Men and on the reviewing
stands at both sides of the ramparts. On the ramparts of T'ien
An Men, on the T'ien An Men Square, on the streets at both
sides of the square, everywhere, the heroic Red Defense Guards
today maintained public order.

As the meeting got under way a Red Defense Guard from
the women's middle school of the Teachers' College mounted
the T'ien An Men ramparts and pinned a Red Defense Guard
armband on Chairman Mao, who warmly clasped her hand.
The Red Defense Guards above and below the ramparts
were delighted beyond measure; some leaped up and very
excitedly cried, "Chairman Mao is our commander-in-chief, we
are his soldiers!" Others cried, "By joining our Red Defense
Guard, Chairman Mao has given us strong backing and encouragement. With Chairman Mao's support, we are afraid of
nothing."

Fifteen hundred student representatives mounted the T'ien
An Men ramparts to join the rally with leaders from the Party
and government. Chairman Mao and Lin Piao, Chou En Lai,
Chiang Ch'ing [Mao's wife], and other comrades individually
greeted them, chatted with them, and posed for photographs
together with them. When it was time for them to meet Chairman Mao, the students excitedly crowded around their beloved

Chairman Mao, and ceaselessly cried, "Long live Chairman Mao!"

The rally began at seven in the morning. Chairman Mao, Lin Piao, and other comrades appeared on the T'ien An Men ramparts to the strains of the tune "The East Is Red." At this point the masses throughout the square rose with great clamor. Countless hands only holding red copies of *The Sayings of Mao Tse-tung* stretched up toward the T'ien An Men ramparts. A million fiery hearts flew out to Chairman Mao. A million eyes gleaming with revolutionary pride gazed up at Chairman Mao. When everyone saw that their beloved Chairman Mao wore a plain and simple military tunic, they became all the more moved. They said: "By wearing a military tunic, Chairman Mao makes us feel even closer to him. Chairman Mao will struggle on with us forever." Others said: "We feel unbounded happiness to have Chairman Mao as our supreme commander!" "We wish to be Chairman Mao's soldiers for life and with Chairman Mao carry out a lifetime of revolutionary struggle!". . .

While Comrade Lin Piao and Comrade Chou En-lai were speaking, the vast square was rent time and time again by the cries of millions of the masses: "Long live the glorious proletarian cultural revolution!" "Long live the glorious Chinese Communist Party!" "Long live the glorious Thought of Mao Tse-tung!" "Long live our glorious leader Chairman Mao! May he live ten thousand years. May he live ten and ten thousand years!"

The representative of Peking University, Nieh Yüan-tzu, university and middle-school students from Peking, Harbin, Changsha, and Nanking spoke successively. They were filled with unbounded affection, with unbounded sincere feelings for the glorious leader Chairman Mao. They were filled with the iron determination of the millions of revolutionary teachers and students in our country to carry through decisively the great proletarian cultural revolution. They resolved to accept and hand down the Thought of Mao Tse-tung, guaranteeing that our iron-clad socialist land will never change its color. They said:

Our nation is now undergoing an unprecedented great proletarian cultural revolution under the leadership of our glorious leader, Chairman Mao. This is a revolution of worldwide significance. We shall smash the old world, create a new world, and decisively carry out the great proletarian cultural revolution.

When sailing on the high seas, one relies on the helmsman; all living things depend on the sun for growth. For making revolution, one relies on the thought of Mao Tsetung. We deeply pray for the unlimited long life of our most beloved glorious leader, Chairman Mao. We shall heed the words of Chairman Mao. We shall follow the guidance of Chairman Mao. We are his most reliable revolutionary successors as we carry out the cause of proletarian revolution, encountering wind and rain midst the storms and the waves and facing the world.

Chairman Mao is the reddest of all suns in our hearts. The Chinese people's revolution was never like a gentle breeze or the calm sea. We must always remember Chairman Mao's advice, that when in storms and on waves, we must temper and test ourselves. We swear to protect the Central Committee of the Party. We swear to protect Chairman Mao. Before us lie jagged peaks and turbulent seas, but we also have the blazing lighthouse of Chairman Mao's Thought before us. Under the guidance of Mao Tsetung's Thought we are certain of victory.

Chairman Mao stands together with us. This is the most important and the most happy moment in our lives. We shall study the works of Chairman Mao for our whole lifetime, pay heed to his words, and act according to his directives. We shall be the good students of Chairman Mao.

Filled with these stirring revolutionary words, revolutionary students from all over the country broke forth in a long and thunderous applause.

After the rally had ended, a great army of the proletarian cultural revolution made up of millions of people swarmed over T'ien An Men Square and passed in review before Chairman Mao. Revolutionary professors and students from the capital and throughout the country, workers from Peking, farmers, representatives from the People's Liberation Army, and government cadres left T'ien An Men Square, their fighting will aroused, their determination raised, and their spirits lifted. They showed Chairman Mao and the Central Committee that they would resolutely uphold the decisions of the Central Committee on the great proletarian cultural revolution, that they would uphold the communiqué of the Eleventh Plenum of the Eighth Central Committee, that they would be the shock troops of the great proletarian cultural revolution, that they would carry the great proletarian cultural revolution to the end, that they would carry the socialist revolution to the end.

Chairman Mao and Lin Piao, Comrade Chou En-lai, and other comrades stood on top of T'ien An Men and reviewed the rank and file as they passed by and waved continuously to the millions of revolutionary masses. While the parade was in process, Chairman Mao and Comrade Lin Piao and other comrades on top of T'ien An Men repeatedly applauded the millions of revolutionary masses out on the square. The masses cried time and time again, "When sailing on the high seas, one relies on the helmsman." Over and over they joyously cried, "Long live Chairman Mao!" "May he live ten thousand years! May he live ten and ten thousand years."

LIST OF DIGNITARIES ATTENDING
ACCORDING TO ORDER IN *JMJP:*

Mao Tse-tung	Chu Teh
Lin Piao	Li Fu-ch'un
Chou En-lai	Ch'en Yün
T'ao Chu	Tung Pi-wu
Teng Hsiao P'ing	Ch'en Yi
K'ang Sheng	Ho Lung
Liu Shao-ch'i	Li Hsien-nien

and many others

PRAVDA *
The Hung-wei-ping *In Action*

Aside from the numerous pamphlets and proclamations with which the walls of houses, fences, and the showcases of stores are plastered, the streets of Peking now have huge bright-red slogans which glorify "the great teacher, the great commander, the great helmsman Mao Tse-tung" and his Thought.

A special order of the Tung-Ch'eng section of the headquarters of the patrol squads, which was distributed throughout the city, is a reminder of the approach of the October 1 national holiday. The order notes that "international friends" will be arriving in Peking. Considering that the "social situation in the city is relatively complex," the *ta-tzu-pao* posters of a critical nature might "create unfavorable international impressions." Therefore it was ordered that all *ta-tzu-pao* be divided into "internal" and "external" types. It was strictly forbidden to post the former type in the streets.

In another pre-holiday order, it was stated that "Chairman Mao is a red sun in the hearts of revolutionary people throughout the world," and that Peking is "the center of the world proletarian revolution." The *Hung-wei-ping* [Red Defense Guards] have undertaken "to use . . . the visits of overseas friends, conversations, and particular meetings with them to carry out broad propaganda for the ideas of Mao Tse-tung."

One proclamation written in the name of the workers and employees of the first Peking Textile Factory discussed the events which happened in that enterprise during the night of September 11 and 12. A band from the "headquarters of the *Hung-wei-ping*," headed by a certain Fan I-p'eng, tried "to steal important documents of the former Party committee." A number of workers and employees, learning of this, resolved to obstruct these attempts of the *Hung-wei-ping*. Clashes occurred

* Translated by Franz Schurmann from *Pravda*, September 23, 1966.

which began in the evening and continued to the following morning. The *Hung-wei-ping* beat up more than forty people, among whom ten received serious injuries. One was so badly hit on the head that he had not regained consciousness three days later.

In Chungking local *Hung-wei-ping* accused the city Party committee of "subversion" and "revisionism," and demanded its "reorganization along the lines of the Peking committee." The city Party committee was forced to appeal to all workers and employees of the city "to protect the city committee, the district committee, and all local Party organizations." In this appeal, the *Hung-wei-ping* were accused of having provoked bloody incidents.

Students and teachers from the Hofei pedagogical institute reported "criminal actions on the part of a group of *Hung-wei-ping*—"Mao Tse-tung'ists," who committed all kinds of trouble-making, hooliganism, and beating of people. On September 9, one pamphlet noted, "Hung-wei-ping and Mao Tse-tung'ists" beat up some workers whom they thereupon cursed as monarchists. The "red watch" also called for "opening fire against the Anhwei provincial committee and the Hofei city committee," and smashed a car in which Li Jen-chih, member of the secretariat of the provincial committee, was on his way to the pedagogical institute.

Under the title "Extraordinary Event," the teachers and students of the electro-energy school of the city of Yangchow in the province of Kiangsu described the activities of the *Hung-wei-ping*, which consisted of so-called "squads of revolutionary unity" coming from Peking and other cities:

> Hardly had these people left the train when they raised the cry: "Open fire against the city Party committee." "We must fight with weapons and not with words." Everywhere they created trouble, demanding that the radio stations be turned over to them, tearing up local radio network lines, and beating people. Victims of the *Hung-wei-ping* included three old women, who were brought to the hospital in serious condition. One old worker beaten by them said, as was stated in their report: "Before the Liberation, the capitalists beat me, and now you beat me."

Those in command of the *Hung-wei-ping,* according to materials posted around the city, are now trying to restrain their "extreme" actions which have aroused discontent among the people and created an "unfavorable international impression." The beatings and killings of workers, party cadres, and the attacks on foreigners are now said to have been the result of "provocations by bad people," although the press has repeatedly called the activity of the *Hung-wei-ping* "completely legal" and "revolutionary."

Recently the "revolutionary participants" and the *Hung-wei-ping* were called upon to "solidarize themselves" with workers and peasants, to set up contacts with revolutionary committees in the enterprises (Party committees in many enterprises were dissolved because they were supposedly "subversive"). Attention has been called to the fact that there has been close contact between the *Hung-wei-ping* and the organs of public security. The *Hung-wei-ping* are seriously urged "to learn from the army, to master its tactical methods." One of these methods, as is well known, is called "beat the enemy by bits."

Now, for example, the sending of *Hung-wei-ping* from Peking to other regions "for the support of the cultural revolution in various areas" is to be carried out in a centralized manner. This, according to the leaders of the *Hung-wei-ping,* will make it possible "to concentrate the blows" and avoid the occurrence of "erroneous" actions, "such as those which happened in Harbin."

What were the "erroneous" actions in Harbin? A squad of Peking *Hung-wei-ping,* headed by the middle-school student Li Chin-piao, went there from Peking with the special mission of evaluating the activities of the Harbin city committee and the Heilungkiang provincial committee of the Party. The Peking headquarters of the *Hung-wei-ping* did not accept their evaluation, and indicated that the Harbin and Heilungkiang committees were "an obstacle on the road of the cultural revolution." The headquarters stressed the need for the creation of a "new and beautiful city of Harbin, a new and beautiful province of Heilungkiang." Judging from reports from Harbin, these appeals of the Peking headquarters of the *Hung-wei-ping* are being realized: "Open fire against the city and province committees!" A number of Party leaders from the city and province committees, with their wives, were paraded around Harbin in trucks, bound together and covered with dirt.

In the latest issue of the theoretical journal of the Central Committee, *Hung-ch'i,* an article was published entitled "Praise the *Hung-wei-ping*." It said that the *Hung-wei-ping* are the "red fighters of Mao Tse-tung" who are carrying out a "heroic and stubborn struggle" against "those who have enjoyed power and who are in the Party." *Hung-ch'i* said that now in the streets of China's cities "millions of *Hung-wei-ping* are streaming," who are the "attack squads" in the "cultural revolution." The article noted that they had carried out "unforgettable feats" and "received the warmest approval from Chairman Mao Tse-tung."

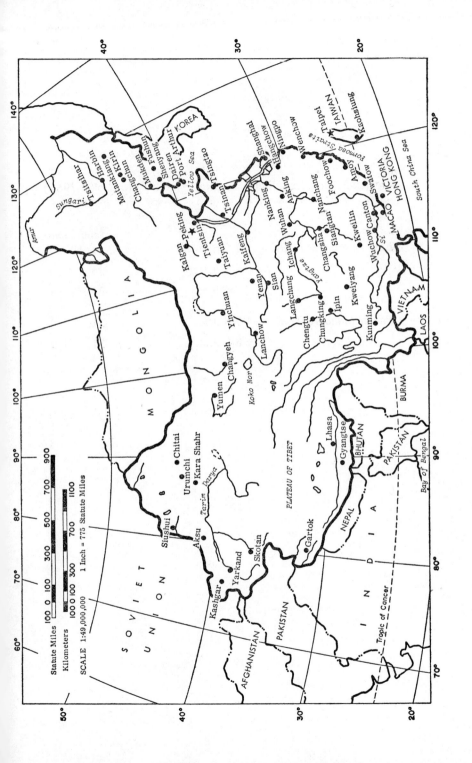

Radio Peking's English-Language Broadcasts to North America

(schedule, courtesy Radio Peking, effective April 20, 1966)

		Meter Bands
Eastern Standard Time	7-8 P.M.	19, 16
	8-9 P.M.	25, 19, 16
	9-10 P.M.	25, 19, 16
Pacific Standard Time	7-8 P.M.	31, 25, 19
	8-9 P.M.	31, 25, 19

Chronology

1949: Communists occupy all of Mainland China and set up People's Republic of China with capital at Peking; U.S. publishes White Paper and indicates abandonment of support for Nationalists; friction between Communist authorities and American diplomats begins; Mao Tse-tung goes to Moscow; Nationalists establish government on Taiwan

1950: *February:* Sino-Soviet Pact of Friendship and Alliance, and trade agreement concluded

April: New liberal marriage law promulgated

June: Land-reform law adopted; Korean War begins; Truman orders Seventh Fleet into Taiwan Straits

October: China enters Korean War; Chinese armies enter Tibet

1951: *May:* Thought reform movement launched among writers

July: Korean armistice negotiations begin

October: Publication of Mao Tse-tung's *Selected Works* begins

November: Three-Anti and Five-Anti movements begin against political and economic corruption, lasting into the following year

1952: *October:* Land reform completed

November: State Planning Commission established under leadership of Kao Kang

December: Democratic reform and nationalization of private business completed; Soviets return Central Manchurian Railway to China

1953: *January:* Inauguration of the First Five Year Plan

February: Resolution on formation of mutual aid teams adopted

June: Population census taken

July: Korean armistice concluded

December: Resolution on formation of Agricultural Producers Cooperatives adopted

1954: *February:* Struggle against Separatist Kao Kang movement in Manchuria begins

June: "Large Administrative Region" (notably Manchuria) abolished, country becomes politically unified; Chou En-lai and Nehru issue their "Five Principles" (*Panch Shila*) as guides for peaceful relations between states

May: Geneva Conference begins on Indochina, China participates

September: First National People's Congress convenes; Constitution proclaimed; Mao Tse-tung and Khrushchev confer in Peking with display of Sino-Soviet amity; first bombardment of Quemoy

December: Defense pact signed by Taiwan and United States

1955: *March:* Kao Kang expelled from Party; Party recruitment expanded in rural areas

April: Bandung Conference, Chou En-lai proposes coexistence and easing of relations with United States

July: First Five Year Plan officially adopted; drive launched to fulfill production targets; Mao gives speech on rural cooperativization

August: Sino-American ambassadorial talks begin in Geneva; China frees U.S. war prisoners

October: Cooperativization drive begins

1956: *January:* China rejects U.S. formula for renouncing use of force to settle problems of Taiwan

February: Khrushchev denounces Stalin at the Twentieth Party Congress

April: China slows down her economic program

May: "Hundred Flowers" period of criticism and free expression begins (in the West the "Hundred Flowers" movement is often inaccurately considered only the May 1957 period)

September: Eighth Party Congress convenes in Peking

October: China proposes cultural exchanges with the U.S. at Geneva talks; U.S. rejects proposals; Gomulka comes to power in Poland; Hungarian revolt; Chinese support Soviet intervention in Hungary

1957: *January:* Chou En-lai goes to Moscow, praises Soviet leadership

April: Rectification movement launched in China

May: "Blooming and Contending" period of open criticism at Peking University; U.S. sends missiles to Taiwan; anti-U.S. riots in Taipei

June: Anti-rightist movement begins in China against government critics

August: Soviets achieve breakthrough in ICBM field; movement to send intellectuals to villages and factories begins; forty-one American youths defy State Department travel ban and leave for China; U.S. allows twenty-four newsmen to go to China, China balks because U.S. refuses to make the agreement reciprocal

October: Central Committee plenum adopts Mao's program for mass social mobilization; Sputnik launched; Sino-Soviet nuclear sharing agreement signed

November: Mao visits Moscow to attend international meeting of Communist Parties and states his "east wind prevails over the west wind" thesis, indicating belief that balance of world forces had changed

December: Purge of rightist critics begins; Sino-American Ambassadorial talks suspended in Geneva

1958: *January:* Great Leap Forward begins

April: Transfer of industries to local control begins as part of decentralization plan

May: Second Session of the Eighth Party Congress convenes; Liu Shao-ch'i explains strategy of Great Leap; selection of a Politburo and Central Committee

July: First communes formed; conflict in Taiwan Straits begins; Quemoy shelled, U.S. convoys Nationalist ships to offshore islands

September: People's Militia established; Eisenhower asks

Khrushchev to restrain the Chinese; U.S. opens talks with the Chinese in Warsaw over Taiwan

October: Chiang Kai-shek renounces the use of force to reconquer the Mainland

1959: *March:* Tibetan Revolt

April: Dalai Lama flees to India; Liu Shao-ch'i named President of Communist China to succeed Mao (Mao remains Party head)

June: Soviets reportedly abrogate nuclear sharing agreement guaranteeing protection of China

August: Nehru accuses China of provoking border incidents; Central Committee plenum liberalizes commune policy

September: Camp David meeting between Eisenhower and Khrushchev (the turning point in Sino-Soviet relations); Khrushchev goes to Moscow via Peking; Defense Minister P'eng Te-huai dismissed for anti-Party activity

1960: *January:* Sino-Burman boundary treaty signed

April: "Long Live Leninism" editorial signals first open polemic in the Sino-Soviet dispute; Chou En-lai holds talks with Nehru

June: Bucharest Conference, P'eng Chen represents China; Khrushchev attacks Mao

July: Cuba agrees to sell Peking half a million tons of sugar annually for five years

August: Soviet technicians withdraw from China

September: Castro establishes diplomatic relations with Peking; Great Leap production drive intensifies

October: Publication of Volume IV of Mao's *Selected Works* (On the Civil War)

November: Further decentralization of the communes; Moscow meeting of eighty-one Communist Parties attended by Liu Shao-ch'i; Sino-Soviet dispute worsens

December: China in deep economic crisis

1961: *January:* Reversal of the Great Leap policy; liberalization of economic policy

March: U.S. sends Special Forces to Laos

May: International Conference on Laos opens in Geneva

October: Chou En-lai arrives in Moscow for Twenty-second Party Congress

November: Twenty-second Party Congress begins, Khrushchev bitterly denounces Albania, Chou defends Albania; Sino-Soviet conflict worsens

1962: *March:* Supreme State Conference presided over by Liu Shao-ch'i

April: Rumors of Nationalist plans to attack the Mainland; U.S. reassures China via Warsaw that Chiang lacks U.S. support

May: Kennedy orders troops to Thailand against possible Communist thrust from Laos; China halts flow of seventy thousand refugees to Hong Kong

June: Laotian coalition government formed

September: Central Committee plenum attacks Russian "modern revisionism" and calls for strengthening of the Party

October: Cuba crisis and attack on India by Chinese forces almost coincide

November: Chinese order cease-fire in border war with India

1963: *February:* Public exchange of hostile letters between China and the Soviet Union begins

March: New financial procedures adopted in China

April: Directive on political work circulates in PLA, pointing up problem of Party control of Army

May: The Soviet Union and China agree to meet and discuss their ideological differences

June: The Soviet Union demands the recall of three Chinese Embassy officials who had allegedly distributed a letter critical of the Soviet Union

July: Sino-Soviet bilateral talks in Moscow end without resolution; test-ban treaty talks begin

August: Test-ban treaty concluded; China refuses to sign

November: Ngo Dinh Diem's regime overthrown; Kennedy assassinated

1964: *January:* France recognizes Peking

February: France provokes Taiwan into breaking diplomatic relations; Chou En-lai returns from seven-week trip to Africa

May: Peking rejects Soviet call for early world conference of Communist parties to settle ideological disputes

June: National Congress of Chinese Communist Youth League meets; campaign to train "revoluntionary successor generation" begins

August: First air attacks on North Vietnam after Gulf of Tonkin incident; China supports proposal for a Geneva Conference for settlement of Vietnam conflict

October: Khrushchev falls; China explodes first atomic bomb

November: Chou En-lai goes to Moscow to confer on Sino-Soviet split

December: National People's Congress meets; Roger Hilsman delivers speech on China policy in which he intimates need for changes in America's China policy

1965: *February:* Escalation of the war in Vietnam; Kosygin visits Peking on way home from Hanoi

March: Chinese and Vietnamese students demonstrate in Moscow against the war in Vietnam; Johnson says there is no possibility of negotiating an end to the war until North Vietnam ends aggression

May: China explodes second nuclear test bomb; U.S. orders lull in raids against North Vietnam for six days

June: All Chinese Army ranks abolished; Ben Bella overthrown; Afro-Asian Conference in Algeria called off despite Chinese protestations

July: Johnson orders fifty thousand more troops into Vietnam and doubles the U.S. draft

September: Lin Piao's article "Long Live the Victory of the People's War" is published; Ch'en Yi clarifies China's foreign policy at a large press conference

October: Palace guard coup in Indonesia fails; Indonesian Communist Party is destroyed; Red China agrees to buy $403 million worth of Canadian wheat over a three-year period

December: U.S. announces temporary cessation in North Vietnam air strikes

1966: *January:* Third Five Year Plan officially begins; military reorganization with indications of command decentralization;

U.S. resumes bombing of North Vietnam; Castro denounces China

March: China debates in Senate Foreign Relations Committee hearings begin; China refuses to attend the Twenty-third Party Congress in Moscow; Nkrumah ousted by Ghana coup while in Peking

April: Liu Shao-ch'i visits Pakistan, Afghanistan, and Burma; U.S. State Department partially lifts travel restrictions to China

May: Attacks against "anti-party" elements gain momentum; China explodes her third nuclear bomb; Chiang Kai-shek inaugurated as President of Republic of China for fourth time

June: Peking Mayor P'eng Chen ousted, leadership struggle takes shape; Chou En-lai visits Rumania and Albania; "Great Proletarian Cultural Revolution" erupts in the universities; United States bombs the outskirts of Hanoi and Haiphong

July: Liu Shao-ch'i announces China no longer regards the Geneva Agreements as valid and China henceforth will be the "rear force base" for North Vietnam; Mao dramatically reappears in public by swimming the Yangtze River; "Great Proletarian Cultural Revolution" gains in intensity

August: Central Committee meets in Eleventh Plenary session; Red Guards formed at great mass meeting in Peking on August 18, presided over by Mao Tse-tung, Lin Piao, and Chou En-lai; rank order of leaders at demonstration indicates major shifts in leadership positions (particularly in regard to Liu Shao-ch'i); Red Guards carry out the "cultural revolution" in all major cities

September: Mass demonstrations continue; Red Guards openly criticize top Party leaders

October: Chinese students expelled from Soviet Union; China explodes intermediate ballistics missile with nuclear warhead; Manila Conference of six nations fighting in Vietnam

Vote in the UN over Admitting Red China*

Year	For Peking	Against	Abstentions
1950	16	32	10
1951	11	37	4
1952	7	42	11
1953	10	44	2
1954	11	43	6
1955	12	42	6
1956	24	47	8
1957	27	48	6
1958	28	44	9
1959	29	44	9
1960	34	42	22
1961	34	61	7
1962	42	56	12
1963	41	57	12
1964†			
1965	47	47	20
1966	46	57	17

* It is important to note that the wording of the resolutions before the UN has varied somewhat from year to year.
† In 1964 there was no vote.

Bibliography*

Barnett, A. Doak, *Communist China: The Early Years, 1949–55* (New York, 1964); *Communist China in Perspective* (New York, 1965).

Bowie, Robert R., and Fairbank, John K., *Communist China 1955–59, Policy Documents with Analysis* (Cambridge, 1962).

Cheng, Chu-yuan, *Communist China's Economy 1949–62, Structural Changes and Crisis* (New Jersey, 1963).

Cowan, C. D., *The Economic Development of China and Japan* (New York, 1964).

Greene, Felix, *Awakened China* (New York, 1961); *China: The Country Americans Are Not Allowed to Know* (New York, 1965).

Halpern, A. M., *Policies Toward China; Views from Six Continents* (New York, 1966).

Hobbs, Lisa, *I Saw China* (New York, 1966).

Hsieh, Alice Langley, *Communist China's Strategy in the Nuclear Era* (Englewood Cliffs, 1962).

Hudson, G. F., Lowenthal, Richard, and MacFarquhar, Roderick, *The Sino-Soviet Dispute* (London, 1961).

Kerr, George, *Formosa Betrayed* (Boston, 1966).

Levi, Werner, *Modern China's Foreign Policy* (Minneapolis, 1953).

Lewis, John Wilson, *Leadership in Communist China* (Ithaca, 1963).

Li, Choh-ming, *The Statistical System of Communist China* (Berkeley, 1962).

Lifton, Robert J., *Thought Reform and the Psychology of Totalism* (London, 1960).

MacFarquhar, Roderick, *The Hundred Flowers Campaign and the Chinese Intellectuals* (New York, 1960).

Mu, Fu-sheng, *The Wilting of the Hundred Flowers: The Chinese Intelligentsia Under Mao* (New York, 1963).

* This bibliography does not include works cited in the text or in Volumes I and II.

Myrdal, Jan, *Report From a Chinese Village* (New York, 1965).

Perkins, Dwight H., *Market Control and Planning in Communist China* (Cambridge, 1966).

Rostow, W. W., *The Prospects for Communist China* (New York, 1954).

Steele, A. T., *The American People and China* (New York, 1966).

Tang, Peter S. H., *Domestic and Foreign Policies,* Vol. I of *Communist China Today* (Washington, 1961).

Whiting, Allen S., *China Crosses the Yalu: The Decision to Enter the Korean War* (New York, 1960).

Wu, Yuan-li, *The Economy of Communist China* (New York, 1965).

Zagoria, Donald S., *The Sino-Soviet Conflict, 1951–1961* (Princeton, 1962).

The following periodicals provide information on current developments in China:

Asian Survey (Berkeley)

China Mainland Press (U.S. Consulate General, Hong Kong)

China News Analysis (Hong Kong)

China Pictorial (Peking)

China Quarterly (London)

China Reconstructs (Peking)

China Youth (Peking)

Current Background (U.S. Consulate General, Hong Kong)

Current Scene (Hong Kong)

Evergreen, Magazine of Chinese Youth and Students (Peking)

Extracts from China Mainland Magazines (U.S. Consulate General, Hong Kong

Far Eastern Economic Review (Hong Kong)

Letter From Peking—Anna Louise Strong (Peking)

Pacific Affairs (Vancouver)

Peking Review (Peking)

Problems of Communism (Washington, D.C.)

It may also interest the reader to know that the Peking Foreign Languages Press publishes an abundance of materials—including information on current events, fiction, history, etc.—in a variety of languages, available in American bookstores.

𝕊 Index

᪇ FRANZ SCHURMANN is Director of the Center for Chinese Studies at the University of California at Berkeley. Born in New York City, he received his Bachelor's degree from Trinity College and his Doctorate from Harvard University; he served in the United States Army during World War II. He is the author of *The Ideology and Organization of Communist China*, and co-author of *The Politics of Escalation in Vietnam*. Professor Schurmann writes frequently on Chinese History and Southeast Asian current affairs for both scholarly and popular periodicals. He makes his home in Oakland, California.

᪇ ORVILLE SCHELL was also born in New York City. He has been educated at Harvard, Stanford, and Taiwan National Universities. He is presently a graduate assistant in Chinese Studies at the University of California at Berkeley. Mr. Schell has worked for the Ford Foundation Overseas Development Office in Indonesia and has been a newspaper correspondent in Southeast Asia.